Advancing Socio-grammatical Variation and Change

Throughout her long and illustrious career, Jenny Cheshire has shaped the field of sociolinguistics. Her contributions span a broad spectrum, ranging from the development of multiethnic varieties and the ways in which linguists can influence educational policy to the impact of gender and adolescent networks on linguistic innovation and language change more generally. Most particularly, however, her name is associated with sociolinguistic research above the level of phonology: the analysis of variation in syntax, discourse, and pragmatics. To date, the sociolinguistic exploration of grammatical variation and change, which Cheshire has so relentlessly championed throughout her career, continues to be underexplored within the sociolinguistic enterprise. This volume pays tribute to and builds on Cheshire's influential work in the area of quantitative analysis of socio-grammatical variation and change, revealing the breadth of research currently being done in this increasingly dynamic field. This collection showcases cutting-edge research from leading researchers in the field, with particular focus on syntactic, morphosyntactic and discourse-pragmatic variation and change. The contributors to the volume run the gamut of contemporary socio-grammatical analysis, from exploring new empirical methods for the collection and analysis of morphosyntactic and discourse-pragmatic variation and change to addressing the theoretical implications underpinning heterogeneity at these levels of linguistic structure. Overall, this volume provides a go-to collection of socio-grammatical variation, advancing our understanding of language variation and change as a holistic process.

Karen V. Beaman is a doctoral candidate at Queen Mary University of London and guest doctoral candidate at Eberhard Karls Universität Tübingen, Germany.

Isabelle Buchstaller is professor at the University of Duisburg-Essen, Germany.

Sue Fox is senior lecturer at the University of Bern, Switzerland.

James A. Walker is professor at La Trobe University in Melbourne.

Routledge Studies in Sociolinguistics

Re-positioning Accent Attitude in the Global Englishes Paradigm
A Critical Phenomenological Case Study in the Chinese Context
Fan (Gabriel) Fang

Revivals, Nationalism, and Linguistic Discrimination
Threatening Languages
Kara Fleming and Umberto Ansaldo

Crosslinguistic Influence in Singapore English
Linguistic and Social Aspects
Ming Chew Teo

Ageing Identities and Women's Everyday Talk in a Hair Salon
Rachel Heinrichsmeier

How we really say 'no': Linguistic mitigation in English and Spanish
Nydia Flores-Ferrán

Linguistic Variation and Social Practices of Normative Masculinity
Authority and Multifunctional Humour in a Dublin Sports Club
Fergus O'Dwyer

A Sociolinguistic View of a Japanese Ethnic Church Community
Tyler Barrett

Advancing Socio-grammatical Variation and Change
In Honour of Jenny Cheshire
Edited by Karen V. Beaman, Isabelle Buchstaller, Sue Fox and James A. Walker

For more information about this series, please visit https://www.routledge.com/Routledge-Studies-in-Sociolinguistics/book-series/RSSL

Advancing Socio-grammatical Variation and Change
In Honour of Jenny Cheshire

Edited by
Karen V. Beaman, Isabelle Buchstaller,
Sue Fox and James A. Walker

NEW YORK AND LONDON

First published 2021
by Routledge
52 Vanderbilt Avenue, New York, NY 10017

and by Routledge
2 Park Square, Milton Park, Abingdon, Oxon, OX14 4RN

Routledge is an imprint of the Taylor & Francis Group, an informa business

© 2021 Taylor & Francis

The right of Karen V. Beaman, Isabelle Buchstaller, Sue Fox and James A. Walker to be identified as the authors of the editorial material, and of the authors for their individual chapters, has been asserted in accordance with sections 77 and 78 of the Copyright, Designs and Patents Act 1988.

All rights reserved. No part of this book may be reprinted or reproduced or utilised in any form or by any electronic, mechanical, or other means, now known or hereafter invented, including photocopying and recording, or in any information storage or retrieval system, without permission in writing from the publishers.

Trademark notice: Product or corporate names may be trademarks or registered trademarks, and are used only for identification and explanation without intent to infringe.

Library of Congress Cataloging-in-Publication Data
A catalog record for this title has been requested

ISBN: 978-0-367-24479-8 (hbk)
ISBN: 978-0-429-28272-0 (ebk)

Typeset in Sabon
by codeMantra

For Jenny, who inspired us to embrace both the social and the grammatical in language variation and change.

Contents

List of Figures	xi
List of Tables	xv
List of Contributors	xix
Foreword by Peter Trudgill	xxiii
Acknowledgements	xxvii

**Introduction: Advancing Socio-grammatical Variation
and Change: Theoretical and Methodological Implications**   1
KAREN V. BEAMAN, ISABELLE BUCHSTALLER, SUE FOX,
AND JAMES A. WALKER

SECTION 1
Conceptualising Social Meaning   13

**1.1 Historical and Ideological Dimensions of
Grammatical Variation and Change**   15
LESLEY MILROY

**1.2 Towards an Integrated Model of Perception:
Linguistic Architecture and the Dynamics of
Sociolinguistic Cognition**   32
EREZ LEVON, ISABELLE BUCHSTALLER,
AND ADAM MEARNS

**1.3 Prestige Factors in Contact-Induced
Grammatical Change**   55
DEVYANI SHARMA

viii *Contents*

1.4 The Role of Syntax in the Study of Sociolinguistic Meaning: Evidence from an Analysis of Right Dislocation 73
EMMA MOORE

SECTION 2
Combining the Social and the Grammatical 91

2.1 What Happened to Those Relatives from East Anglia? A Multilocality Analysis of Dialect Levelling in the Relative Marker System 93
DAVID BRITAIN

2.2 Restrictions on Relative Clauses in Auckland, New Zealand 115
MIRIAM MEYERHOFF, ALEXANDRA BIRCHFIELD, ELAINE BALLARD, CATHERINE WATSON, AND HELEN CHARTERS

2.3 Swabian Relatives: Variation in the Use of the *wo*-relativiser 134
KAREN V. BEAMAN

2.4 Modelling Socio-grammatical Variation: Plural Existentials in Toronto English 165
JAMES A. WALKER

SECTION 3
Formal Approaches to Syntactic Variation 185

3.1 A Socio-grammatical Analysis of Linguistic Gaps and Transitional Forms 187
SJEF BARBIERS

3.2 Variation and Change in the Particle Verb Alternation across English Dialects 205
BILL HADDICAN, DANIEL EZRA JOHNSON, JOEL WALLENBERG, AND ANDERS HOLMBERG

3.3 Explaining Variability in Negative Concord: A Socio-Syntactic Analysis 229
DAVID ADGER AND JENNIFER SMITH

Contents ix

SECTION 4
Language Contact and Multiethnolects 247

4.1 Tracing the Origins of an Urban Youth Vernacular:
Founder Effects, Frequency, and Culture in the
Emergence of Multicultural London English 249
PAUL KERSWILL AND EIVIND TORGERSEN

4.2 Bare Nouns in Prepositional Phrases in *Cité Duits*,
a Moribund Miners' Multiethnolect (and Other
Varieties of Dutch and German) 277
PETER AUER AND LEONIE CORNIPS

4.3 When Contact Does Not Matter: The Robust
Nature of Vernacular Universals 303
DANIEL SCHREIER

4.4 From Killycomain to Melbourne: Historical
Contact and the Feature Pool 319
KAREN P. CORRIGAN

SECTION 5
Discourse and Pragmatic Variation 341

5.1 *That* Beyond Convention: The Interface of Syntax,
Social Structure, and Discourse 343
SALI A. TAGLIAMONTE AND ALEXANDRA D'ARCY

5.2 Sociolinguistic Variation in the Marking of New
Information: The Case of Indefinite *this* 360
STEPHEN LEVEY, CARMEN KLEIN, AND YASMINE ABOU TAHA

5.3 Tagging Monologic Narratives of Personal Experience:
Utterance-Final Tags and the Construction of
Adolescent Masculinity 377
HEIKE PICHLER

Index 399

Figures

1.2.1	Aligning linguistic features with change-points	38
1.2.2	Listener evaluations of vernacular realisations of Hyper-s - ING - FACE in the woman's speech	40
1.2.3a	Listener evaluations of vernacular realisations of FACE - Hyper-s - Hyper-s - FACE in the man's speech	42
1.2.3b	Listener evaluations of vernacular realisations of FACE - Hyper-s - Hyper-s -FACE in the woman's speech	43
1.2.4	Listener evaluations of vernacular realisations of 4 tokens of FACE in the woman's speech	44
1.2.5a	Listener evaluations of vernacular realisations of FACE and ING in the woman's speech	45
1.2.5b	Listener evaluations of vernacular realisations of FACE and ING in the man's speech	46
1.2.6	Listener evaluations of a *zero* subject relative in the woman's speech	50
1.3.1	Percentage use of non-standard *was/were* forms across British Asian generations and relevant comparison groups	61
1.3.2	Percentage use of non-standard *was* by subject type	62
1.3.3	Absence of indefinite article allomorphy across British Asian generations and relevant comparison groups	64
1.3.4	Absence of definite article allomorphy across British Asian men, women, and relevant comparison groups	65
1.3.5	Quotative use among older Gen 2 BAE speakers and comparison IndE and Cockney groups	68
1.3.6	Quotative use among younger Gen 2 BAE speakers and comparison MLE group	68
1.4.1	Frequency of RD per 1000 words according to social class	78
1.4.2	Frequency of RD per 1000 words according to community of practice	79
1.4.3	RD by type of right-dislocated tag, according to community of practice membership	79
1.4.4	RD tags by personal-pronoun type, according to community of practice membership	80

xii *Figures*

1.4.5 Verb processes and evaluative stances which co-occur with instances of Right Dislocation, according to personal pronoun tag and community of practice membership   83

2.1.1 The maximal extent of relative marker *as* in data from the Survey of English Dialects   97

2.1.2 The maximal extent of relative marker *what* in data from the Survey of English Dialects   98

2.1.3 Location of localities examined in this chapter   101

2.1.4 The use of *what* across apparent-time, subject and object relatives combined, in the six East Anglian localities   108

2.1.5 The use of *zero* subject relatives across apparent-time in the six East Anglian localities   109

2.1.6 The use of *that* as a relative marker across apparent-time in the six East Anglian localities   109

2.2.1 Distribution of *that*, *wh-* and *zero* relativisers in many varieties of English, including Auckland English   115

2.2.2 Syntactic structure underlying *several people who/ that/Ø she kissed* (Birchfield 2019: 9)   118

2.3.1 Frequency of *wo*-relatives and *d*-relatives in Swabian by community and recording year   148

2.3.2 Frequency of *wo*-relatives and *d*-relatives in Swabian by case, community and recording year   150

2.3.3 Google Books Ngram Viewer for German *dem*   156

2.4.1 Overall rates of *there*-existentials per speaker by number of tokens per speaker   173

2.4.2 Conditional inference trees for variants of *there*-existentials with plural reference for older speakers of Toronto English   175

2.4.3 Conditional inference tree for *there*-existentials with plural reference for younger speakers of Toronto English   176

2.4.4 Variable importance of factors for *there*-existentials with plural reference for younger speakers of Toronto English   177

3.1.1 A lexical gap explained by a syntactic principle   189

3.1.2 The geographic distribution of strong reflexive forms in the Dutch language area (from Barbiers et al. 2005)   191

3.1.3 Attestations of the form *zich eigen* SIG OWN in the Dutch language area (based on van der Feest 2007)   193

3.1.4 The geographic distribution of word orders in three-verb clusters containing two modals in the Dutch language area (from Barbiers et al. 2008)   196

3.1.5 Uniform hierarchical structure of three-verb clusters in Dutch   198

3.1.6	Dialects of Dutch that have at least one 3-2-1 order and dialects that have at least one 1-2-3 order from BBD (2018)	198
3.1.7	Geographic distribution of verb cluster interruption (Barbiers et al. 2008)	199
3.1.8	Geographic distribution of 1-3-2 with 3 = participle (Barbiers et al. 2008)	200
3.2.1	Mean normalised ratings for VPO and VOP orders by country	210
3.2.2	Mean normalised ratings for VPO and VOP orders by object type	211
3.2.3	Mean normalised ratings for VPO and VOP orders by object weight	211
3.2.4	Correlation between object weight effects for VOP and VPO orders	212
3.2.5	Twitter corpus catchment for US dialects	213
3.2.6	Twitter corpus catchment for UK dialects	214
3.2.7	Proportional use of VPO and VOP orders by region	215
3.2.8	Proportion of VOP use by year *(Penn/Helsinki/York Corpora)*	216
3.2.9	Proportion of VOP use by year (Brown Corpora)	218
3.2.10	VOP order in the Corpus of Historical American English 1850–2009	219
4.1.1	Dates of entry of West Indian, Indian and Pakistani people to Great Britain (Owen 1995:4, Figure 4)	260
4.1.2	Ethnic groups in Hackney (percent), 2001	265
4.1.3	Percentage of population in Hackney which is not White British, by ward (Census 2001)	266
4.1.4	Population density of four different ethnic groups in Hackney (Census 2001)	267
4.2.1	Percentage of bare nouns, clitic and determiner NPs in *Cité Duits*, the Stuttgart multiethnolect, the Duisburg miners' vernacular of miners and the Dutch (multi)ethnolect	291
4.2.2	Percentage of bare nouns, preposition/determiner contraction (cliticisation) and full NPs in PNCs of weak versus strong referentiality in the Stuttgart multiethnolect, *Cité Duits*, the Dutch (multi)ethnolect in Gouda and the Duisburg miners' corpus	293
4.3.1	Past *be* regularisation rates by individual speaker	310
4.4.1	Digitised copy of the 1836 Census of Port Phillip District (Melbourne)	326
5.1.1	Frequency of the null complementiser, from Late Middle English and Early Modern English	

xiv *Figures*

	(Rissanen 1991; Warner 1982) to Present Day English (Tagliamonte and Smith 2005; Torres Cacoullos and Walker 2009)	348
5.1.2	Cross-tabulation of age and occupation: *that*	352
5.1.3	Constraint ranking of all predictors selected as significant, as reflected by range: *that*	353
5.2.1	Distribution of indefinite *this* and *a(n)* in Ottawa English by syntactic position	369

Tables

1.2.1	Variables under investigation	34
1.4.1	Verb process types used in the analysis according to Halliday (1985)	77
1.4.2	Evaluative stances expressed in the context of RD use	77
2.1.1	Gravity model calculations of the hypothetical influence London has on each of the six East Anglian localities under investigation	102
2.1.2	Structure of the East Anglian corpus used for this analysis	102
2.1.3a	Overall Subject Relatives (middle-aged only for Colchester)	104
2.1.3b	Overall Object Relatives (middle-aged only for Colchester)	104
2.1.4	East Anglian relative markers across apparent-time: *wh*-forms, versus *that* and *zero*	104
2.1.5	East Anglian relative markers across apparent-time for all localities	105
2.2.1	Distribution of relative complementisers across varieties of spoken English	119
2.2.2	Profiles of the three communities in the Auckland Voices project	124
2.2.3	Two independent multiple regression analyses of the contribution of factors to the occurrence of relativisers other than *that*, in non-subject and subject relative clauses, in the Auckland Voices corpus	126
2.3.1	Corpus of 20 Swabian panel speakers, in Stuttgart and Schwäbisch Gmünd, recorded in 1982 and in 2017	139
2.3.2	Multivariate analysis relative pronoun usage in 20 Swabian panel speakers across two points in time (1982 and 2017)	151
2.3.3	Summary of predictors influencing the use of *wo*-relatives	152
2.4.1	Distribution of speakers included in the study by ethnicity, generation and sex	167
2.4.2	Overall distribution of variants of *there*-existentials with plural reference in Toronto English by *social* factors	171

xvi *Tables*

2.4.3	Overall distribution of variants of *there*-existentials with plural reference in Toronto English by *linguistic* factors	172
3.2.1	Coefficients (logits), standard errors, *z*-values and *p*-values for fixed effects in the combined model	217
3.3.1	Distribution of sentential negation in Buckie	232
3.3.2	Distribution of sentential negation by verb type in Buckie	233
4.1.1	Possible sources of MLE features	253
4.1.2	Realisation of FLEECE and GOOSE vowels in London (Cockney), London Jamaican and Multicultural London English	256
4.1.3	Total arrivals in the UK from the Caribbean (West Indies), 1948–1961	259
4.1.4	London: Country of birth 1971 (1971 census)	261
4.1.5	London: Country of birth 1981 (1981 census)	261
4.1.6	London: Country of birth and size of New Commonwealth ethnic groups 1991 (1991 census)	261
4.2.1	N-based PPs with and without definite determiner in four speakers *of Cité Duits*	284
4.2.2	PNCs with a bare or definite noun in *Cité Duits*, weak/strong referentiality, and pragmatic/semantic definiteness	289
4.2.3	PNCs with a bare or definite nouns in the Stuttgart multiethnolect, weak/strong referentiality and semantic/pragmatic definiteness	292
4.2.4	Frequency distribution and percentages of presence and absence of (definite and indefinite) determiners per syntactic position in a Dutch (multi)ethnolect	294
4.2.5	PNCs with a bare or definite noun expressing weak/strong referentiality or semantic definiteness in the Dutch (multi)ethnolect	295
4.2.6	PNCs with a bare or definite noun expressing weak/strong referentiality or semantic definiteness in Ruhr German	296
4.3.1	St Helena's socio-demographics in 1815	307
4.3.2	GoldVarb analysis of past *be* levelling (age group, internal constraints, speaker sex; default application value: *was*)	311
4.3.3	Past *be* levelling in StHE: Regional variation	312
4.3.4	Past *be* levelling rates in English varieties around the world (adapted from Schreier 2002: 85)	313
4.4.1	Places of birth and affiliations of the inhabitants of the Municipality of Melbourne, according to the 1854 Census	327

Tables xvii

4.4.2	Places of birth, affiliations and spatial distributions of the inhabitants of the Municipality of Melbourne and its environs, according to the 1854 Census	332
5.1.1	Sample for complementiser variation drawn from *Toronto English Archive* (Tagliamonte 2003–2006)	345
5.1.2	Frequency of the null complementiser with *I think*, *I mean*, *I guess* and *you know*	349
5.1.3	Fixed effects logistic regression of linguistic predictors conditioning the use of *that*	350
5.1.4	Fixed effects logistic regression of social predictors conditioning the use of *that*	351
5.2.1	Stratification of informants by sex and age group	364
5.2.2	Overall distribution of indefinite *a(n)* and *this* by speaker sex and age group	368
5.2.3	Multivariate analysis of the contribution of social and linguistic factors to the probability that indefinite *this* will be selected in subject and non-subject positions	370
5.2.4	Multivariate analysis of the contribution of linguistic factors to the probability that indefinite *this* will be selected in non-subject position	372
5.3.1	Distribution of UFT variants in the adolescent narratives	381
5.3.2	Numbers of (tagged) narratives and proportion of tagged declaratives across individuals and social groups	382
5.3.3	Proportion of tagged declaratives across narrative components in the female and male adolescent narratives, with an indication of the number of narratives containing each component and the average length (in declaratives) of each component	386
5.3.4	Story worlds created in males' and females' tagged and non-tagged narratives	390

Contributors

David Adger, professor at Queen Mary University of London, researches syntactic theory and how syntax connects to other aspects of language, including semantics, pragmatics, prosody, morphology, and sociolinguistics.

Peter Auer, professor at Albert-Ludwigs-Universität, Freiburg, Germany, is devoted to a wide range of fields of linguistics, including bilingualism, social dialectology, phonology, syntax of spoken language, conversation analysis, patholinguistics, and sociolinguistics.

Elaine Ballard, senior lecturer at the University of Auckland, New Zealand, investigates speech and vocabulary development in bilingual paediatric populations and how language and culture impact identity in bilingual populations.

Sjef Barbiers, professor at Leiden University, specialises in syntactic microvariation, combining theoretical and dialectological perspectives, and investigating what the geographic distribution of syntactic variables tells us about human language as a cognitive system.

Karen V. Beaman, doctoral candidate at Queen Mary University of London and guest doctoral candidate at Eberhard Karls Universität Tübingen, Germany, is currently completing her dissertation on sociolinguistic variation and change in the German dialect of Swabian.

Alexandra Birchfield, master's student at Victoria University of Wellington, researches relative clauses in Auckland English as well as issues in language and gender, historical sociolinguistics, and language contact.

David Britain, professor at the University of Bern, Switzerland, researches language variation and change, dialect contact, attrition, and ideology, and the dialectology-human geography interface with respect to space/place, urban/rural, and the role of mobilities.

Isabelle Buchstaller, professor at the University of Duisburg-Essen, Germany, researches language variation and change in morphosyntax and discourse, focussing in particular on the range and the determinants of linguistic malleability across the lifespan of the individual.

xx *Contributors*

Helen Charters, independent scholar, works on the relationship between syntax and information structure, as influenced by interactive discourse, in the area of the acquisition of second language syntax by adults, with a particular focus on Mandarin.

Leonie Cornips, senior researcher at the Humanities Cluster (KNAW) and professor of language culture in Limburg at Maastricht University, investigates regional identity construction through multilingual practices, bidialectal child acquisition, and animal language.

Karen P. Corrigan, professor at Newcastle University, UK, has published on language contact, variation, and change in Antipodean, British, North American, and Irish English dialects, and the acquisition of discourse-pragmatic, morphosyntactic, and phonetic variation and change.

Alexandra D'Arcy, professor at University of Victoria, Canada, specialises in language variation and change in varieties of English, and has published widely on discourse-pragmatic and morphosyntactic variables in both a synchronic and a diachronic perspective.

Sue Fox, senior lecturer at the University of Bern, Switzerland, is interested in language variation and change; dialect contact; the impact of immigration on language change; and the language of adolescents, especially in urban, multicultural contexts.

Bill Haddican, associate at City University of New York, Queens College, uses production data and controlled judgment data to investigate formal syntactic problems and issues in language change, principally in dialects of Basque and English.

Anders Holmberg, professor at Newcastle University, UK, works on verb second; object shift; stylistic fronting in Scandinavian; word order and topic-focus syntax in Finnish; and syntax of answers to yes-no questions in a cross-linguistic, comparative perspective.

Daniel Ezra Johnson, formerly a lecturer at Lancaster University and developer of the Rbrul statistical software tool for mixed-effects linguistic analysis, is interested in the sociolinguistic quantitative analysis of language change, with a focus on statistical modelling.

Paul Kerswill, professor at the University of York, researches dialect contact following migration and development of Multicultural London English (MLE), and most recently has been involved in several interdisciplinary projects on development in Ghana.

Carmen Klein, master's student at the University of Bonn, Germany, is interested in intercultural communication, variational pragmatics, and sociolinguistics, with a focus on Canadian English.

Stephen Levey, associate professor at the University of Ottawa, focusses on grammatical variation and change in varieties of English, language contact between French and English, and sociolinguistic approaches to the acquisition of English as a first and second language.

Erez Levon, professor at Queen Mary University of London, uses quantitative, qualitative, and experimental methods to examine patterns of socially meaningful variation, in particular, how linguistic forms come to be associated with different categories of speakers.

Adam Mearns, lecturer at Newcastle University, UK, is interested in language variation and change in the North East of England; corpus linguistic methods; and the history of English, especially the lexical semantics of Old and Middle English.

Miriam Meyerhoff, professor at Victoria University of Wellington, studies language variation and change, particularly creole languages and languages of urban migrants, focussed on syntactic, discourse, and social factors, especially social perceptions of gender.

Lesley Milroy, professor emerita at the University of Michigan, visiting professor at the University of York, and honorary fellow of the Royal College of Speech and Language Therapy, researches language variation and change, social networks, and language ideology.

Emma Moore, professor at the University of Sheffield and a British Academy Mid-Career Fellow (2019–2020), explores sociolinguistic variation and how individuals and communities use language to construct social styles and identities.

Heike Pichler, senior lecturer at Newcastle University, UK, studies discourse-pragmatic and morphosyntactic variation and change, language contact, language variation in mental health consultations, and old-age language variation and change.

Daniel Schreier, professor at the University of Zurich, Switzerland, works on language variation and change; historical and contemporary sociolinguistics; dialectology; and contact linguistics, including pidgins, creoles, and varieties of better- and lesser-known English.

Devyani Sharma, professor at Queen Mary University of London, examines dialect variation and change in postcolonial and diaspora situations, language contact, typology, and bilingualism, with particular focus on the Indian diaspora.

Jennifer Smith, professor at the University of Glasgow, works on language variation and change, focussing on the morphosyntactic forms of dialects and studying the acquisition of variation in preschool children and how sociolinguistic norms develop in later life.

xxii *Contributors*

Sali A. Tagliamonte, professor at the University of Toronto, works on British, Irish, and Canadian dialects, teen language, and social media varieties, focussing on cross-community and apparent-time comparisons to explore linguistic variation and change.

Yasmine Abou Taha, post-graduate student in linguistics at the University of Ottawa, studies phonological and syntactic variation in Levantine Arabic, with a special focus on the Lebanese dialect and the dialect spoken by Palestinian refugees in Lebanon.

Eivind Torgersen, professor at the Norwegian University in Trondheim, Norway, works on language variation and change in Multicultural London English, modelling phonological change, segmental and suprasegmental variation, vowels, and speech rhythm.

Peter Trudgill, emeritus professor at Fribourg University and honorary professor at the University of East Anglia, Norwich, is a theoretical dialectologist with a focus on dialect formation, socio- and historical linguistics, and social determinants of linguistic complexity.

James A. Walker, professor at La Trobe University in Melbourne, focusses on language contact, bilingualism, and ethnicity in varieties of English and English-based creoles as well as Sango (Central African Republic), Swedish, Brazilian Portuguese, and other languages.

Joel Wallenberg, lecturer at Newcastle University, is interested in how quantitative and sociolinguistic studies of variation and change bear on issues of linguistic theory, with particular focus on morphosyntax, language acquisition, and neuroscientific implications.

Catherine Watson, associate professor at the University of Auckland, specialises in speech processing in machines and humans, using both signal processing and acoustic phonetic techniques, with a particular focus on New Zealand English and Māori.

Foreword

Peter Trudgill

One of the best things that ever happened to me in my academic life was when I was asked by our enormously respected and very well-loved head of department, the late Frank Palmer, to accept Jenny Cheshire as a PhD student. Her project sounded very exciting and innovative to me, and it seemed rather likely to open up much wider sociolinguistic horizons than those which I myself had been working within for the previous few years. I quickly and enthusiastically accepted the role as Jenny's official "supervisor" in the Department of Linguistic Science at the University of Reading. And that was the happy beginning of what is now not too far short of fifty years – and counting – of the most enjoyable and profitable partnership of equals as well as of academic cooperation and personal friendship.

I have used the inverted commas a round the word *supervisor* in the previous paragraph in order to indicate that supervision as such was not really needed. I was only 29 at the time, and Jenny was just two or three years younger than that, so I was barely senior to her in any real way, even if I had completed my own PhD a couple of years before. As her supervisor, I learned more from Jenny than she ever did from me, and the sessions when we met to discuss her work consisted mostly of her telling me what she had done and what she was going to do – and of me then approving and admiring this. These meetings in my office were always memorable. Sometimes Jenny arrived from her home outside Reading on a rather large motorbike, and sometimes she arrived with her baby son in a carry-cot – I think I am right in saying that he was never actually transported on the motorbike to my office. The baby, having inherited the equable temperament of his mother, always slept peacefully in a corner.

By the way, I am not just mentioning Jenny's motorbike as an irrelevant detail. Jenny has a background and a personality which made her a superb field-worker for carrying out research with all kinds of informants, but especially perhaps with the local Reading dialect-speaking, working-class adolescents who she mostly worked with for her PhD. In a positive review of the book which eventually emerged from Jenny's research (see below), Suzanne Romaine astutely and correctly wrote that xxiv *Peter Trudgill*

Jenny was to be commended for her enterprise in gaining entry to the culture of the playgrounds where she did most of her research. Jenny carried out long-term participant-observation with boys and girls aged 9 to 17 at two adventure playgrounds in working-class areas of Reading, patiently getting to know the young people and winning their confidence; she succeeded in recording examples of speech from these pre-adolescent and adolescent boys and girls which were of an extraordinary naturalness and vernacular quality.

Indeed, the degree to which she was successful in overcoming the Observer's Paradox – to the extent that it is in fact possible to overcome it – of wanting to "observe how people speak when they are not being observed" can be judged from the content as well as the form of the language that Jenny was able to record. I remember being particularly struck by one passage of dialogue in which, when asked why he wanted to become a slaughterman when he left school, one of the boys memorably replied, "I wants to kill animals". And when you have obtained samples of speech containing sentences such as "I knows how to stick in the boot", you know that you have been successful in following Labov's advice that, when it comes to the study of dialects at their most vernacular, the best informants are those who adhere least closely to official mainstream societal values and norms.

I do not necessarily want to say that Jenny made a point of seeking out juvenile delinquents, but her motorbike did give her a certain amount of what we might now call *street cred* (a term first recorded by the Oxford English Dictionary from 1979), and the result is that we now have a brilliant and unparalleled record of the systematicity of the grammatical structures as employed by non-standard dialect speakers from that area of England at their most non-standard. As Labov wrote in his justly famous paper "The linguistic consequences of being a lame", the goal of this type of work is to capture "the vernacular of every-day life in which the minimum amount of attention is paid to speech [because] this is the most systematic level of linguistic behavior and of greatest interest to the linguist who wants to explain the structure and evolution of language" (Labov 1973:82). Also, importantly, "we usually find that the most consistent vernacular is spoken by those between the ages of 9 and 18".

Jenny's thesis was entitled *Grammatical Variation in the English spoken in Reading, Berkshire*. It was a brilliantly innovative project, focussing on casual, vernacular, working-class speech, just as Labov advocated. Particularly pioneering, however, was her concentration on the morphology and syntax as opposed to the phonology which had hitherto typically been the focus of sociolinguistic work in Britain. Also, her investigation of the linguistic, rather than social, constraints on the usage of particular grammatical variants was an especially important innovation.

Foreword xxv

Jenny was awarded her PhD degree for this work in 1979. It was one of my earliest academic moments of pride, and it is one which I have remained proud of ever since. The thesis was published in 1982, by Cambridge University Press, under the title *Variation in an English Dialect: A Sociolinguistic Study*, and the book received good recognition and favourable reviews: Sandra Clarke wrote in the *Journal of Language and Social Psychology* that it represented an "exciting new application of sociolinguistic methodology". When the volume was reissued in 2010, this was an obvious testament to the continuing impact of her book.

Before *Variation in an English Dialect* came out, Jenny published two ground-breaking papers. The first was "Present tense verbs in Reading English" which appeared, I am pleased to say, in a book edited by me – in honour of William Labov's seminal book *Sociolinguistic Patterns* – which was called *Sociolinguistic Patterns in British English* (1978). The second was her 1981 article "Variation in the use of *ain't* in an urban British dialect", which appeared in volume 10 of the by then already highly prestigious journal *Language in Society*; entirely appropriately, she became the editor-in-chief of this journal more than thirty years later. These two papers, as their titles suggest, were based on data and analyses from her research on the Reading dialect, and they were perfect illustrations of the sort of work which was going to become the trademark of Jenny's research and publications throughout her career; since 1981, she has produced very many careful and insightful analyses of real-life linguistic data, as produced by real-life speakers. It is not an accident that her co-authored paper "Urban British dialect grammar: the question of dialect levelling", which appeared originally in the journal *English World-wide*, was reprinted in 1993 in James and Lesley Milroy's edited volume *Real English*. But Jenny has also always proffered many important and original theoretical conclusions, clearly drawn and cogently presented: the title of her 1987 paper "Syntactic variation, the linguistic variable and sociolinguistic theory", which appeared in the major journal *Linguistics*, tells some of this story of the importance of theoretical issues in her thinking and in her writing.

Jenny's important and complex research has always had an unmistakably human face. Her interest in speakers as human beings rather than simply as suppliers of linguistic data comes across very clearly, for instance, in her work on narratives as well as her studies involving everyday discourse and natural conversation. Jenny's 2000 paper in the *Journal of Sociolinguistics*, "The telling or the tale? Narratives and gender in adolescent friendship networks", shows this side of her work very nicely, as does "Discourse variation, grammaticalisation and stuff like that" (*Journal of Sociolinguistics*, 2006).

These aspects of Jenny's work, together with her many contributions to the wider study of varieties of English (witness her book *English around*

xxvi *Peter Trudgill*

the World: *Sociolinguistic Perspectives*, 1991), to dialect levelling (e.g., "Urban British dialect grammar: the question of dialect levelling", 1989), and multiethnolects (e.g., "Contact, the feature pool and the speech community: the emergence of Multicultural London English", 2011) are all represented within the covers of this splendid book of articles written in her honour by this group of highly distinguished scholars. The volume is a very fitting and extremely well-deserved tribute to Jenny's academic achievements so far, and it is a great honour, for me as well to have been allowed to have a presence in these pages alongside everyone else. Those "not too far short of fifty years" have really been something rather special.

Acknowledgements

When we first embarked on this journey to create an edited volume honouring Jenny Cheshire, we could have never fathomed such an outpouring of interest and commitment to this effort. Beyond the 20 contributors to this volume, many others have offered their support in many different ways. It has been inspiring and heart-warming to experience this level of professional and personal support for Jenny and her work. As co-editors of this volume, we would like to extend a special thanks to the contributing authors for the considerable time and effort they took to follow the trail that Jenny has blazed and for producing an incredible testimony to the role she has played in fostering research on socio-grammatical variation in its many shapes and forms. We would also like to thank the many peer reviewers whose work behind the scenes has made this volume possible. We are immensely grateful to our wonderfully supportive editors at Routledge for coaching us throughout this process. And, of course, it goes without saying, we thank Jenny for inspiring us all in the relentless pursuit to embrace both the social and the grammatical in language variation and change.

Advancing Socio-grammatical Variation and Change
Theoretical and Methodological Implications

Karen V. Beaman, Isabelle Buchstaller, Sue Fox, and James A. Walker

Introduction

The study of sociolinguistic variation and change, which began with William Labov's work on English phonetic variables in Massachusetts and New York in the 1960s (Labov 1963, 1966), was quickly taken up by researchers in other locales working on English and other languages (Sankoff and Cedergren 1972; Trudgill 1972) and constitutes its own branch of linguistic inquiry today. However, the extension of this research paradigm to the study of grammatical variation (Labov et al. 1968; Weiner and Labov 1983) was not without controversy (Labov 1978; Lavandera 1978). At issue is the question of whether or to what extent grammatical variants can be considered 'different ways of saying the same thing' (the crucial definition of a linguistic variable), a question that the study of socio-grammatical variation has continued to wrestle with. Nevertheless, research on socio-grammatical variation has continued to grow, and its relevance to linguistics more widely has begun to be recognised.

This volume pays tribute to and builds on Jenny Cheshire's influential body of research in the quantitative analysis of socio-grammatical variation, which began with her doctoral research in Reading in the 1970s (Cheshire 1979, 1981). To this aim, we have brought together cutting-edge research from key players in the field, with a particular focus on syntactic, morphosyntactic and discourse-pragmatic variation and change. The contributors to the volume run the gamut of contemporary socio-grammatical analysis, from exploring new empirical methods for the collection and analysis of morphosyntactic and discourse-pragmatic variation and change to addressing the theoretical models underpinning heterogeneity at these levels of linguistic structure. By demonstrating the critical role of socio-grammatical variation in our understanding of language change as a holistic process, this volume fills a significant gap in sociolinguistic research while showcasing the breadth of work currently being done in this increasingly dynamic field of linguistic inquiry.

Background

Jenny Cheshire has shaped the field of sociolinguistic inquiry throughout her long and illustrious career, ranging from the development of multi-ethnic varieties (Cheshire et al. 2005) and the ways in which linguists can influence educational policy (Cheshire et al. 1989) to the impact of gender and adolescent networks on linguistic innovation and on language change (Cheshire 2000, 2005b). Most particularly, however, her name is associated with the sociolinguistic exploration of grammatical variation and change, specifically, the analysis of variation in syntax, discourse, and pragmatics (Cheshire 1979, 1981, 1985, 1987, 1989, 1999, 2005a). While Cheshire has been instrumental in fostering this vibrant and productive research environment, championing many of the scholars that are represented in this volume, socio-grammatical research continues to be relatively underexplored (as compared with other major fields of linguistic inquiry such as sociophonetic research or formal syntax). Some of the reasons for the relative dearth of socio-grammatical research are:

1. **Diachronic precedence and dominance of sociophonetic/phonological research:** Variationist sociolinguistics was launched with the analysis of variation in phonetics/phonology, and the extension of the variationist paradigm "above and beyond" phonology (Sankoff 1973) was not without controversy (Cheshire 1987, 2005a; Lavandera 1978; Romaine 1984; Winford 1984). Although studies of grammatical variation abound, sociophonetics continues (at least quantitatively) to dominate variationist conferences and journals. Cheshire's tireless championing of socio-grammatical research throughout her career has played a crucial role in strengthening the theoretical basis of this line of research, developing epistemological precedent and establishing it as a prominent strand of variationist research. This volume aims to give exposure to some of the most exciting work that is currently being conducted in the field of socio-grammatical variationist analysis.
2. **Dominance of formal linguistics:** Mainstream linguistics is dominated by formal (usually generative) paradigms that have historically relegated variation to the domain of 'performance', with little interest in its potential contribution to linguistic theory (e.g., Chomsky 1957, 1965; Pollard and Sag 1994). While some recent collaborative research has begun to transcend these disciplinary boundaries (see Adger and Smith 2010; Cornips and Corrigan 2005; *inter alia*), cross-pollination between the study of language variation and change and linguistic theory remains relatively limited. This volume aims to showcase some of the most leading-edge work currently conducted at the interface between formal linguistics and sociolinguistics.

3. **Low frequency of occurrence:** The relative infrequency of grammatical variables in natural discourse (compared to phonetic variables) necessitates collecting much larger amounts of data to establish statistically significant results (Cheshire 1999). In addition, the focus of sociolinguistic research on urban middle-class speakers, whose language features much less grammatical variation, creates challenges for the analysis of stylistic factors and the investigation of ongoing language change (Cheshire 1999; Meyerhoff and Walker 2013; Winford 1996). Studies of grammatical variation have developed innovative methods to transcend these problems. Some of the contributors to this volume showcase state-of-the-art solutions to procure and explore data of different kinds to examine the patterning of socio-grammatical variables.

4. **Sharp social stratification:** In contrast to the gradient stratification of phonetic and phonological variation, grammatical variation tends to be characterised by 'sharp' social delineation (Sankoff and Laberge 1978), mainly because "variation involving grammatical inflections tends to have been consistently codified, with the result that some non-standard variants are rarely, if ever, used by the educated middle-class sections of society" (Cheshire 1987:272; see also Torres Cacoullos 2001). The present volume questions this dichotomy by calling attention to the intricate ways in which (some) grammatical variables have eschewed prescriptive attention and the complex processes through which variability at higher levels is noticed and processed.

5. **Challenges of functional equivalence:** According to Labov (1972:271), "social and stylistic variation presuppose the option of saying 'the same thing' in several different ways: that is, the variants are identical in reference or truth value, but opposed in their social and/or stylistic significance". The field has seen a contentious debate regarding the problem of determining functional equivalence among different syntactic forms (Campbell-Kibler 2011; Cheshire 1987; Lavandera 1978; Romaine 1984; Sankoff 1988; Winford 1996). To date, the study of non-phonological variation suffers from a "lack of an articulated theory of meaning" (Romaine 1984:171) which is complicated by processes of grammaticalisation and semantic reduction and bleaching (Torres Cacoullos 2001:446). The studies reported here support Cheshire's contention that "syntactic variation [is] always motivated by pragmatic factors" (Cheshire 2005a:86), drawing attention to a wealth of interactional and interpersonal factors that definitions of socio-grammatical variables need to take into consideration.

6. **Distinction between social variation and spoken grammar:** We do not know enough about the "norms of grammar in speech" since research on grammatical variability tends to focus on the same salient

4 Beaman, Buchstaller, Fox and Walker

features that result from the process of standardisation (McCarthy 1991). Only once we have information across the spectrum of socio-grammatical variability will sociolinguists be able to assess Labov's "sociolinguistic monitor" claim that grammatical variation is less sensitive to social factors due to the different ways that linguistic information is organised and stored (Labov et al. 2011; Levon and Buchstaller 2015; Levon and Fox 2014; Meyerhoff and Walker 2013). The authors in this volume explore grammatical variables as varied as the Northern subject rule, relativisers, reflexives, word order variation in multi-verb clusters, right dislocation, sentence-final tags, inflectional patterns of the verb *to be*, quotation, negative concord, bare nouns, particle alternation, definite articles, demonstratives, complementisers, existentials and a wealth of other variable features above and beyond the phonological. By following Cheshire and her co-authors' call to explore "the extent to which linguistic variation in different components of language patterns in similar ways" (Cheshire et al. 2005:135), the chapters in this volume jointly advance our understanding of the wealth of factors that condition linguistic heterogeneity at higher levels of linguistic architecture.

Despite these outstanding controversies, and spearheaded by Jenny Cheshire's trailblazing research trajectory, the analysis of grammatical variation has become an increasingly vibrant field of linguistic inquiry. This work is crucial because the analysis of "the social distribution of a variable syntactic construction can throw light on the nature of its ... function, and sometimes help us to discover more about the social aspects of language use" (Cheshire 1999:59).

Overview of the Volume

This volume is organised into five sections that bring to light innovative research that is currently being conducted within the area of socio-grammatical variation. In what follows, we briefly describe the contribution of each chapter to the focus of the respective section.

Section 1: Conceptualising Social Meaning

The role of linguistic variation in constructing and expressing social meaning is central to Cheshire's research but, as she argues "we must consider [grammatical] functions within the local contexts in which they occur, to take account of their interaction with other linguistic forms" (Cheshire 2007:155). In other words, sociolinguists need to account for aspects of grammatical variation that often go unheeded, such as the competing pressures of variants and the construction of social meaning at the local level. The differences between phonological and grammatical variation may result from considerations of speaker interaction (social and conversational) and external forces of standardisation, which more readily apply to grammar than to phonology, rather than from inherent properties of the linguistic system.

The chapters collected in this section showcase variationist work that carefully conceptualises the social meaning of grammatical variation, drawing on a wealth of different methods and sources of data to do so. **Milroy** considers variables that are relevant to grammar and language contact but are difficult to analyse in terms of a clear vernacular/standard continuum. Showing that highly educated Belfast and Newcastle speakers use clearly non-standard grammatical variants, she raises ideological questions of how the spoken standard is understood away from the southern areas of the UK. **Levon, Buchstaller, and Mearns'** chapter tests the assumption that grammatical variation does not attract sociolinguistic meaning in the same way as phonetic variability. Exploring moment-by-moment listener reactions to situated variability at different levels of linguistic structure reveals that listeners attend to different types of features in fundamentally contingent ways, which underlines the complex nature of sociolinguistic cognition. In **Sharma's** exploration of dialect shift involving the selection of features from competing sources of prestige, British Asian English speakers combine standard British English features with a few higher-prestige Indian features to signal an upwardly mobile, ethnically Asian style, supporting the view that dialect shift does not simply reflect frequency of input but is sensitive to competing prestige values and non-local influences. Finally, **Moore's** analysis of right dislocation (e.g., *They're horrible, them*) in four communities of practice (CofP) of female adolescents in north-western England reveals that each CofP uses different strategies that are influenced by interpersonal stance. Her study demonstrates that syntactic variation can carry nuanced social meanings that can be used strategically to construct and express style, stance, and positionality.

Section 2: Combining the Social and the Grammatical

Due to the early primacy of sociophonetic inquiry into language variation, the systematic study of variation at higher levels of linguistic structure has taken much longer to produce consolidated findings of the form collected for phonology (Guy 2007; Hazen 2007). Cheshire's work has been instrumental in pushing forward a research agenda that answers questions relevant to syntactic theory and social structure (Cheshire 1998, 1982, 2005b). She maintains that social factors surrounding socio-grammatical variation are merely "different" from those influencing phonological variation: "syntactic variation can be intricately involved in the construction of social meaning, but ... the involvement is of a different kind from that of phonological and morphosyntactic variation" (Cheshire 2003:246). Her work on topic-marking *who* (Cheshire 2013) and the interactional perspective of *that* (Cheshire 1996) demonstrates how different aspects of social structure impact linguistic structure.

The chapters in this section further Cheshire's efforts by examining the interaction between social and linguistic factors that condition syntactic variation in different linguistic varieties. In the first chapter of this section, **Britain's** exploration of changes in the use of relative markers across six localities in East Anglia finds a process of *counter*urbanisation, with larger urban areas conserving traditional dialect forms and smaller rural areas taking up the innovative variants. This finding points to an account of koinéisation based on mobility and contact. **Meyerhoff, Birchfield, Ballard, Watson, and Charters'** analysis of relativiser use across three ethnically diverse Auckland communities provides little evidence of social constraints, corroborating Cheshire's (1998) claim that their infrequency and characteristically semantic and discourse functions lend relatives to being primarily linguistically constrained. In the same vein, **Beaman** also finds strong linguistic constraints on relativiser choice in Swabian German, although these constraints interact with two social factors (education and the rural/urban divide), reflecting influences of prescriptivism and supralocalisation. Modelling socio-grammatical variation with plural *there*-existentials in Toronto English, **Walker** finds that linguistic and social factors are interwoven in conditioning the variation, with ethnicity exerting the most significant effect. He makes a powerful argument for expanding statistical methods to help solve some of the issues raised by socio-grammatical variation.

Section 3: Formal Approaches to Syntactic Variation

Research on language structure has explored the origins of syntactic variation through principles of formal (usually generative) syntactic theory. Very little of this work, however, has considered the social situatedness of grammatical variation (see, however, Barbiers 2005, Henry 1995; *inter alia*). On the other side of the coin, variationist sociolinguistic research, while investigating some of the intralinguistic factors that constrain variability, has tended not to reflect upon the formal implications of such findings and their influence on the refinement of structural linguistic theory. There is thus ample scope for socio-syntactic research exploring the extent to which the integration of these two paradigms can elucidate questions that have hitherto been broached from within disciplinary silos, either from a purely formal syntactic or a variationist linguistic perspective. Following Cheshire's call for an interdisciplinary framework, which she concedes in 1987 has "yet to be constructed" (Cheshire 1987:275), the three chapters in this section showcase critical research that bridges paradigms in their attempt to explain the

Socio-Grammatical Variation and Change   7

systematicity of observed grammatical variation. **Barbiers** heeds Cheshire's appeal through an integration of variationist and generative methods and analyses, illustrated by an explanation of the complex yet systematic patterns observed in dialect-contact zones while delimiting the universal structural constraints placed on variation. The next two chapters are written by teams of authors that represent researchers from both research traditions, demonstrating the added effect of integrating different epistemologies for the exploration of syntactic variation. **Haddican, Johnson, Wallenberg, and Holmberg** draw on various data sources to explain regional grammatical effects on the English particle verb alternation. Considering information-structural constraints on particle placement, the authors describe the observed variation as arising from competing grammars that govern word-order alternation across English dialects. **Smith and Adger** combine minimalist and variationist analyses to propose an account of negative concord in Buckie Scots. They argue that speakers have an abstract set of grammatical rules governing variation (including interactions of categorical and variable phenomena), with implications for the universal occurrence of negative concord while accounting for individual grammatical differences.

Section 4: Language Contact and Multiethnic Varieties

The amount and diversity of immigration across the globe in the last 50 years or so has led to new ways of speaking and to the creation of new forms of language in multilingual cities across Europe and elsewhere. Building on Cheshire et al.'s (2011) work on *Multicultural London English (MLE)*, the chapters in this section report on contexts where multiethnic contact plays a significant role. In attempting to trace the origins of MLE, **Kerswill and Torgersen** consider the relevance of both Mufwene's (1996) *founder effect* and Trudgill's (2004) *determinism model*. They conclude that although African Caribbeans, as the first major post-war immigrant group, exerted their influence on youth language in the 1950s and 1960s, it is likely that MLE arose later, in the 1980s, when the proportions of non-speakers of the local London vernacular started to significantly increase. They argue for social, cultural, and historical factors to be considered when searching for an understanding of the emergence of multiethnolects. **Auer and Cornips** focus on syntactic variation in *Cité Duits* (a multiethnolectal variety of Limburg Dutch) in comparison with non-standard German and urban (multi-)ethnolectal German and Dutch. They find differences among varieties on the basis of semantic and pragmatic grounds (Dutch) and as a result of competition between forms on a structural basis (German). **Schreier's** study of past *be* regularisation in St Helenian English addresses the question of how internal constraints develop in situations of extensive contact. Examining local contact demographics, historical interaction patterns and

8 Beaman, Buchstaller, Fox and Walker

regional feature pools, the author shows how internal constraints have changed across the course of the twentieth century. **Corrigan** focusses on the consequences of immigratory trends on the language ecology of Melbourne from the 1830s to the 1850s. Exploring the processes of competition and selection among discourse-pragmatic, morphosyntactic and phonological features which contributed to Melbourne's emerging multiethnolect, the author explores the putative Irish-English influence on the ways in which diverse ethnic groups forged contemporary multicultural Australian English.

Section 5: Discourse and Pragmatic Variation

Cheshire (2016, 2012, 2007, 2000) has spearheaded a strand of variationist research that aims for a fuller integration of discourse-pragmatic features into variationist sociolinguistic research using an empirically accountable framework of analysis (see also D'Arcy 2017; Levey 2012; Pichler 2016). Each chapter in this section takes as its point of departure Cheshire's seminal contributions to the topic, judiciously combining qualitative and quantitative approaches to bring new findings to bear on discourse-pragmatic variation. **Tagliamonte and D'Arcy**'s analysis of *that*-complementisation in Toronto English reveals that linguistic factors are overshadowed by social and discursive pressures. The role of complements in signalling clausal boundaries in complex structures to help interlocutors navigate interaction underlines Cheshire's (1996) call for more attention to interactional pressures on linguistic variation. Investigating the alternation of *a(n)* with indefinite *this* as markers of discourse-new referents in Canadian English, **Levey, Klein, and Taha** relate the social and linguistic constraints conditioning the variation to cross-linguistic phenomena of argument marking, which not only provides insights into the conditioning of variant selection but also shows how a discourse-pragmatic variable can reflect cataphoric properties of indefinite NPs found in other languages. **Pichler** explains the strategic use of utterance-final tags (UFTs) by adolescents to stimulate listener involvement and guide interpretation of tagged and non-tagged story materials. She proposes that male adolescents strategically select variants to assert their rights to be heard and to signal their desire to be viewed as possessing an urban working-class adolescent masculinity.

Closing Remarks

Overall, this volume constitutes a go-to collection showcasing cutting-edge research on syntactic, morphosyntactic and discourse-pragmatic variation and change. By addressing the theoretical implications underpinning research on these levels of linguistic structure, the research in this collection advance our understanding of language variation and

Socio-Grammatical Variation and Change   9

change at higher levels of linguistic architecture, contributing jointly to the underlying objective of Cheshire's research: to understand linguistic heterogeneity as a holistic process.

References

Adger, David and Jennifer Smith. 2010. "Variation in agreement: A lexical feature-based approach". *Lingua* 120(5):1109–1134.

Barbiers, Sjef. 2005. "Word order variation in three-verb clusters and the division of labour between generative linguistics and sociolinguistics". In *Syntax and Variation: Reconciling the Biological and the Social*, L. Cornips and K.P. Corrigan (eds.). Amsterdam: John Benjamins Publishing Company. 233–264.

Campbell-Kibler, Kathryn. 2011. "The sociolinguistic variant as a carrier of social meaning". *Language Variation and Change* 22(3):423–441.

Cheshire, Jenny. 1979. Grammatical variation in the English spoken in reading. Berkshire. Ph.D. dissertation, University of Reading, UK.

Cheshire, Jenny. 1981. "Variation in the use of *Ain't* in an urban British dialect". *Language in Society* 10:365–388.

Cheshire, Jenny. 1982. *Variation in an English Dialect*. Cambridge: Cambridge University Press.

Cheshire, Jenny. 1985. "English *Never* and the problem of where grammars stop". *Polyglot* 6.

Cheshire, Jenny. 1987. "Syntactic variation, the linguistic variable and sociolinguistic theory". *Linguistics* 25(2):257–282.

Cheshire, Jenny. 1989. "Addressee-oriented features in spoken discourse". *York Papers in Linguistics* 3:49–63.

Cheshire, Jenny. 1996. "That Jacksprat: An interactional perspective on English *That*". *Journal of Pragmatics* 25(3):369–393.

Cheshire, Jenny. 1997. "Involvement in 'Standard' and 'Non-Standard' English". In *Taming the Vernacular: From Dialect to Written Standard Language*, J. Cheshire and D. Stein (eds.). Harlow: Longman. 68–82.

Cheshire, Jenny. 1998. "English negation from an interactional perspective". In *Negation in the history of English*, I. Tieken-Boon van Ostade, G. Tottie and W. Van de Wurff (eds.). Berlin: Mouton de Gruyter. 29–53.

Cheshire, Jenny. 1999. "Taming the vernacular: Some repercussions for the study of syntactic variation and spoken grammar". *Cuadernos de Filología Inglesa* 8:59–80.

Cheshire, Jenny. 2000. "The telling or the tale? Narratives and gender in adolescent friendship networks". *Journal of Sociolinguistics* 4(2):234–262.

Cheshire, Jenny. 2002. "Sex and gender in variationist research". In *The Handbook of Language Variation and Change*, J.K. Chambers, P. Trudgill and N. Schilling-Estes (eds.). Oxford: Blackwell Publishing. 423–43.

Cheshire, Jenny. 2003. "Social dimensions of syntactic variation: The case of *when* clauses". In *Social Dialectology: In Honour of Peter Trudgill*, D. Britain and J. Cheshire (eds.). Amsterdam: John Benjamins Publishing Company. 245–261.

Cheshire, Jenny. 2005a. "Syntactic variation and spoken language". In *Syntax and Variation: Reconciling the Biological and the Social*, L. Cornips and K.P. Corrigan (eds.). Amsterdam: John Benjamins. 81–106.

10 Beaman, Buchstaller, Fox and Walker

Cheshire, Jenny. 2005b. "Syntactic variation and beyond: Gender and social class variation in the use of discourse-new markers". *Journal of Sociolinguistics* 9:479–507.

Cheshire, Jenny. 2007. "Discourse variation, grammaticalisation and stuff like that". *Journal of Sociolinguistics* 11(2):155–193.

Cheshire, Jenny. 2012. "What was it like before *like?* Discourse-pragmatic variation and discourse style". In *First Discourse-Pragmatic Variation & Change Conference (DipVaC1)*. Salford: University of Salford.

Cheshire, Jenny. 2013. "Grammaticalisation in social context: The emergence of a new English pronoun". *Journal of Sociolingusitics* 17(5):608–633.

Cheshire, Jenny. 2016. "The future of discourse-pragmatic variation and change research". In *Discourse-Pragmatic Variation and Change in English: New Methods and Insights*, H. Pichler (ed.). Cambridge: Cambridge University Press. 252–266.

Cheshire, Jenny, Viv Edwards and Paul Whittle. 1989. "Urban British dialect grammar: The question of dialect levelling". *English World Wide* 10:185–225.

Cheshire, Jenny, Viv Edwards, Henk Münstermann and Bert Weltens (eds.). 1989. *Dialect and Education: Some European Perspectives*. Clevedon: Multilingual Matters.

Cheshire, Jenny and Sue Fox. 2009. *Was/Were* "Variation: A Perspective from London". *Language Variation and Change.* 21(1):1–38.

Cheshire, Jenny, Sue Fox and David Britain. 2007a. "Relatives from the South". In UK Language Variation and Change (UKLVC) 6. *Lancaster, September 2007.*

Cheshire, Jenny, Sue Fox, Paul Kerswill and Eivind Torgersen. 2007b. *Linguistic Innovators: The English of Adolescents in London*. Full Research Report submitted to Economic and Social Research Council. RES-000-23-0680, Swindon: ESRC.

Cheshire, Jenny, Sue Fox, Paul Kerswill and Eivind Torgersen. 2008. "Ethnicity, friendship network and social practices as the motor of dialect change: Linguistic innovation in London". *Sociolinguistica* 1–23.

Cheshire, Jenny, Paul Kerswill, Sue Fox and Eivind Torgersen. 2011. "Contact, the feature pool and the speech community: The emergence of multicultural London English". *Journal of Sociolinguistics* 15(2):151–196.

Cheshire, Jenny, Paul Kerswill and Ann Williams. 2005. "Phonology, grammar, and discourse in dialect convergence". In *Dialect Change: Convergence and Divergence in European Languages*, P. Auer, F. Hinskens and P. Kerswill (eds.). Cambridge: Cambridge University Press. 135–168.

Cheshire, Jenny and Sue Ziebland. 2005. "Narrative as a resource in accounts of the experience of illness". In *The Sociolinguistics of Narrative*, J. Thornborrow and J. Coates (eds.). Amsterdam: John Benjamins Publishing Company. 17–40.

Chomsky, Noam. 1957. *Syntactic Structures*. The Hague/Paris: Mouton de Gruyter.

Chomsky, Noam. 1965. *Aspects of the Theory of Syntax*. Cambridge: MIT Press.

Cornips, Leonie and Karen Corrigan. 2005. "Convergence and divergence in grammar". In *Dialect Change: Convergence and Divergence in European Languages*, P. Auer, F. Hinskens and P. Kerswill (eds.). Cambridge: Cambridge University Press. 96–134.

D'Arcy, Alexandra. 2017. *Discourse-Pragmatic Variation in Context – Eight Hundred Years of LIKE.* Amsterdam: John Benjamins Publishing Company.

Guy, Gregory R. 2007. "Variation and phonological theory". In *Sociolinguistic Variation: Theories, Methods, and Analysis*, R. Bayley and C. Lucas (eds.). Cambridge: Cambridge University Press. 5–23.

Hazen, Kirk. 2007. "The study of variation in historical perspective". In *Sociolinguistic Variation: Theories, Methods, and Analysis*, R. Bayley and C. Lucas (eds.). Cambridge: Cambridge University Press. 70–89.

Henry, Alison. 1995. *Belfast English and Standard English: Dialect Variation and Parameter Setting.* New York: Oxford University Press.

Labov, William. 1963. "The social motivation of a sound change". *Word* 19(3):273–309.

Labov, William. 1966. *The Social Stratification of English in New York City.* Washington, D.C.: Center for Applied Linguistics.

Labov, William, Philip Cohen, Clarence Robins and John Lewis. 1968. *A Study of the Non-standard English of Negro and Puerto Rican Speakers in New York City.* Co-operative Research Report 3288, Vol. I. Philadelphia: U.S. Regional Survey.

Labov, William. 1972. *Sociolinguistic Patterns.* Philadelphia: University of Pennsylvania.

Labov, William. 1978. Where does the linguistic variable stop? A response to Beatriz Lavandera. *Working Papers in Sociolinguistics.* Austin, Texas: Southwest Educational Development Laboratory.

Labov, William, Sharon Ash, Maya Ravindranath, Tracey Weldon, Maciej Baranowski and Naomi Nagy. 2011. "Properties of the sociolinguistic monitor". *Journal of Sociolinguistics* 15(4):431–463.

Lavandera, Beatriz R. 1978. "Where does the sociolinguistic variable stop?" *Language in Society* 7(2):171–182.

Levey, Stephen. 2012. "General extenders and grammaticalization: Insights from London preadolescents". *Applied Linguistics* 33(3):257–281.

Levon, Erez and Isabelle Buchstaller. 2015. "Perception, cognition, and linguistic structure: The effect of linguistic modularity and cognitive style on sociolinguistic processing". *Language Variation and Change* 27(3):319–348.

Levon, Erez and Sue Fox. 2014. "Social salience and the sociolinguistic monitor: A case study of ING and TH-fronting in Britain". *Journal of English Linguistics* 42(3):185–217.

McCarthy, Michael. 1991. *Discourse Analysis for Language Teachers.* Cambridge: Cambridge University Press.

Meyerhoff, Miriam and James A. Walker. 2013. "An existential problem: The sociolinguistic monitor and variation in existential constructions on Bequia (St. Vincent and the Grenadines)". *Language in Society* 42(4):407–428.

Mufwene, Salikoko S. 1996. "The founder principle in creole genesis". *Diachronica* 13(1):83–134.

Pichler, Heike (ed.). 2016. *Discourse-Pragmatic Variation and Change in English.* Cambridge: Cambridge University Press.

Pollard, Carl and Ivan A. Sag. 1994. *Head-Driven Phrase Structure Grammar.* Chicago: Chicago University Press.

Romaine, Suzanne. 1984. "On the problem of syntactic variation and pragmatic meaning in sociolinguistic theory". *Folia Linguistica* 18(3–4):409–438.

12 Beaman, Buchstaller, Fox and Walker

Sankoff, Gillian. 1973. "Above and beyond phonology in variable rules". In *New Ways of Analyzing Variation in English*, Charles-James N. Bailey and Roger W. Shuy (eds.). Washington, D.C.: Georgetown University Press. 44–61.

Sankoff, David. 1988. "Sociolinguistics and syntactic variation". In *Linguistics: The Cambridge Survey: Volume 4, Language: The Socio-Cultural Context*, F.J. Newmeyer (ed.). Cambridge: Cambridge University Press. 140–161.

Sankoff, David and Suzanne Laberge. 1978. "The linguistic market and the statistical explanation of variability". In *Linguistic Variation: Models and Methods*, D. Sankoff (ed.). New York: Academic Press. 239–250.

Sankoff, Gillian and Henrietta Cedergren. 1972. "Sociolinguistic research on French in Montréal". *Language in Society* 1(1):173–174.

Torres Cacoullos, Rena. 2001. "From lexical to grammatical to social meaning". *Language in Society* 30(3):443–478.

Trudgill, Peter. 1972. "Sex, covert prestige and linguistic change in the Urban British English of Norwich". *Language in Society* 1(2):179–195.

Trudgill, Peter. 2004. "The dialect of East Anglia: Morphology and syntax". In *A Handbook of Varieties of English: Morphology and Syntax*, B. Kortmann, K. Burridge, R. Mesthrie, E. Schneider and C. Upton (eds.). Berlin: Mouton de Gruyter. 142–153.

Weiner, E. Judith and William Labov. 1983. "Constraints on the agentless passive". *Journal of Linguistics* 19(1):28–58.

Winford, Donald. 1984. "The linguistic variable and syntactic variation in Creole Continua". *Lingua* 62(4):267–288.

Winford, Donald. 1996. "The problem of syntactic variation". In *Sociolinguistic Variation: Data, Theory and Analysis. Selected Papers from NWAV 23*, J. Arnold (ed.). Stanford: CSLI Publications.

Section 1

Conceptualising Social Meaning

1.1 Historical and Ideological Dimensions of Grammatical Variation and Change

Lesley Milroy

1.1.1 Introduction

The goal of this chapter is to examine recurrent themes emerging from quantitative research on grammatical variation and change. These range from methodological considerations to more abstract issues such as the identification of a particular community's linguistic standard. I refer both to historical sociolinguistic investigations and to research in contemporary communities. In subsequent sections, I look first at historical sociolinguistic research, moving on to analyses in contemporary communities of a specific variable: subject-verb agreement. Finally, we come to the standard language question, which has regularly emerged as interesting and problematic but has seldom been systematically addressed.

For a variety of reasons widely discussed in the sociolinguistic literature, some morphological variables are viewed as relatively amenable to quantitative analysis. Cheshire (1999) has observed that this same set of apparently simple variables has tended to get analysed repeatedly, i.e., various non-standard verb forms, subject-verb agreement, multiple negatives and non-standard negative forms such as *ain't*. She also notes that the saliency of such non-standard forms to laypersons and linguists alike makes them a target for prescriptive comment. The analytic procedure is generally to relate speakers' choices to social variation with a view to inferring patterns of change. However, the extension of these basic quantitative methods to high-level grammatical variation raises methodological questions which regularly impinge on broader theoretical concerns. For this reason, sociolinguists have often argued that the concept of the variable can be usefully applied only to low-level morphological variation (see further Milroy and Gordon 2003:169–172).

One intrinsic difference between phonological and grammatical systems has far-reaching implications for quantitative analysis. Since speakers make use of a sharply limited and therefore frequently recurring, inventory of phonological contrasts, realisations of any given variable are likely to show up frequently in even a short sample of speech. This is not the case for grammatical variables, since a sufficient quantity of tokens of a given type of construction cannot usually be guaranteed to

16   *Lesley Milroy*

appear in a piece of spontaneous discourse. This difficulty is partly a consequence of the non-finite or "leaky" nature of syntactic systems, which in turn is associated with the susceptibility of syntactic choices to pragmatic and semantic constraints. Speakers can exercise considerable choice in the way they use grammatical resources to encode meanings since there is no isomorphic relationship between function and form. For example, questions are not always realised syntactically as interrogatives, and interrogative forms may realise many different functions (Coveney 1996:123).

These more "difficult" types of variable often present interesting issues of analysis and interpretation. Conversely, apparently low-level morphological variation is not always as simple as it seems, and analyses of grammatical variables have often focussed on internal linguistic constraints rather than on relationships between linguistic and social variation. Indeed, grammatical variation has regularly been found to benefit from the insights of formal syntactic analysis (see further Milroy and Gordon 2003:190ff). The social distribution of a grammatical variable on a vernacular/standard continuum is often far from straightforward; contrary to what we might expect from reports in the variationist literature, clearly non-standard grammatical variants are used by high-status local speakers in some communities, as noted by Beal (1993) in Tyneside and by J. Milroy (1981) and Harris (1984) in Belfast. This pattern of use raises ideological issues of how a spoken standard English is imagined in dialect areas distant from the central and southern regions of the UK. Generally speaking, the problems summarised above are less relevant to historical sociolinguists than to those who work in contemporary communities. Accordingly, we look now at some particularly illuminating historical analyses of two frequently studied morphological variables.

1.1.2 Historical Sociolinguistics

Sociolinguists have regularly followed Labov's (1972:275) excellent advice to "obtain at least one measurement at some contrasting point in real time". Thus, for example, our understanding of the direction of change around 1980 of the complex (a) variable in Belfast was greatly enhanced by evidence provided by the elocutionist David Patterson in 1860. But variationist work on earlier stages of the language has gone far beyond the methodologically motivated search for a linguistic anchor in real-time; investigators have regularly used older written texts to add historical depth to their analyses. Sankoff and Vincent (1980) report that stylistically stratified patterns of variable deletion of the French negative particle *ne* have hardly changed since the sixteenth century, when deletion was associated with informal styles. They note that *ne* now appears only rarely in conversational contexts but is favoured in certain formal (particularly written) styles. Romaine (1982) reports a similar stability over time of the relative pronouns system of Middle Scots, where the ranking of stylistic and syntactic constraints on choice of relative pronoun variant appears to have changed little in 450 years; *zero* marking in subject position was preferred in written Scots in less formal styles and continues to be a characteristic of the contemporary dialect. Trudgill (1996) provides details of a language contact situation in sixteenth-century Norwich to account for a contemporary pattern of alternation between *zero* and *–s* present-tense, third-person singular verb forms in contemporary Norwich vernacular.

Thus, the relationship between sociolinguistics and historical linguistics has always been close, but the influence has not all been in one direction. Historical linguistics in general has been quite extensively influenced by the methods and theories of variationist sociolinguistics, giving rise to a fruitful two-way exchange of findings and ideas. Twenty years ago, Pratt and Denison (2000) noted that sociolinguistic models were attracting increasing interest among historians of language who have previously concentrated on language internal accounts of change. More recently, Auer and Voeste's (2012) review of the methods and findings of historical sociolinguistic work on grammatical variables reveals the development of a subfield employing variationist methods to investigate trajectories of changes which have often been completed at early stages of the language.

Historical linguists work with the uniformitarian principle, which holds that patterns of variation in the past are similar to those observed in contemporary speech communities (see Lass 1997:26ff), but the methodological challenges encountered in applying this principle have led Labov (1994:11) to describe historical linguistics generally as "the art of making the best use of bad data". The "bad-data" problem has several dimensions: data are often patchy as a consequence of the random preservation of some texts and the equally random loss of others; the relationship between data derived from various kinds of written source and the data of spoken interaction which forms the basis of much contemporary sociolinguistic work is unclear; reconstructing the social information needed to interpret patterns of variation in written texts is not always straightforward. Given, however, the difficulties of obtaining sufficient tokens of grammatical variables in contemporary speech communities, the bad data problem is surely of limited relevance to accounts which draw on substantial computerised corpora. Historical researchers also have some benefit of hindsight in assessing the social significance of particular changes. In a number of publications (e.g., Nevalainen and Raumolin-Brunberg 1996, 2017; Nevalainen 2000a, 2000b; Nevalainen et al. 2011) Nevalainen and her colleagues report on a series of analyses which draw on the University of Helsinki's Corpus of Early English Correspondence (CEEC). This extensive corpus spans the years 1410–1681 and includes the letters of 778 writers. The researchers show that earlier

18   *Lesley Milroy*

social worlds can be reconstructed from the detailed findings of social historians, some of which are of considerable sociolinguistic relevance (see, for example, Keene 2000). Nevalainen and Raumolin-Brunberg (2012:32) suggest that

> personal correspondence provides the 'next best thing' to authentic spoken language, and even with its obvious limitations makes it possible to extend the variationist paradigm into the more distant past. It enables the researcher to combine macro- and micro-level approaches and place individuals within their language communities.

Researchers are able to present well-motivated accounts of the social trajectories of particular grammatical changes associated with the sixteenth and seventeenth century, a period of particularly rapid social change (Nevalainen 2000b). Beal (2020) similarly shows that the personal letters of the naturalist Thomas Bewick, along with other "ego-documents" such as notes and diaries, are akin to spoken language, showing a clear contrast with Bewick's professional published work (see comments in Section 1.1.3 below).

The Helsinki group has examined a wide range of grammatical variables, and I comment here on just two of them. The first is the change from the older third-person present singular verb form *-eth* as opposed to the innovatory northern dialect form *-(e)s* in the sixteenth century. These variants were in competition for over 200 years before *-es*, which had emerged as an alternating variant in the fifteenth century, took over from *-eth*, becoming the norm by about 1600 in all but "high registers" (Lass 1999:162–165). The following example (dated 1585) shows Queen Elizabeth I of England using both variants in a single letter:

> He *knoweth* not the pryse of my bloude, wiche shuld be spilt by the bloudy hande of a murtherar......I am assured he *knowes* and therefor I hope he wil not dare deny you a truthe.
>
> (Nevalainen 2000a:48)

This extract gives a flavour of the very rich data collected in CEEC, and in fact Nevalainen and Raumolin-Brunberg (2012:35) report that by the late sixteenth century the *-es* variant was already fashionable in Elizabeth's court. Interestingly, however, the social trajectory of this change in the work of male writers somewhat earlier – between 1540 and 1559 – shows that the incoming form *-es* is overwhelmingly preferred by men of lower social rank. Five social ranks are examined: gentry, social aspirers, professionals, merchants and non-gentry. The lowest social rank (non-gentry) use *-es* 80% of the time, while all other categories record a use of less than 20%, overwhelmingly preferring the conservative form *-eth* (Nevalainen 1999:519).

Historical and Ideological Dimensions   19

The social embedding of a second variable – the decline of multiple negation in the period 1520–1681 – is quite different. Nevalainen (1999:523) sets out the variable patterns of male and female writers of three ranks: upper (royalty, nobility, gentry), middle (professionals, merchants, social aspirers), and lower (other ranks below the gentry). This, of course, is one of the relatively simple morphological variables identified by Cheshire (1999) as subject to frequent analysis by sociolinguists, and indeed the pattern which emerges is familiar in the contemporary English-speaking world. The effect of rank on choice of variant is quite different from that described above for the decline of the *-eth* variant, which, in Labov's terms, might reasonably be described as change from below. It is also attributable to contact between southern English dialect speakers and numerous northern migrants to London during the sixteenth and seventeenth centuries. In contrast, the decline of multiple negation is symmetrically graded according to rank, being most marked in the writing of the highest social ranks, with persons of low rank being most resistant to change. Middle ranks occupy a position between the two. Interestingly, women lag behind men in promoting this change, which, unlike the change to *-es* discussed above, is oriented towards emergent prescriptive norms. While it is possible that low levels of female literacy are relevant to this pattern, Nevalainen points out that men also lead changes to incoming prestige forms with respect to other variables, even when there is ample evidence that educated women can read and write (1999:526). Thus, while these findings show a strong similarity to the familiar contemporary patterns of double negation (see Cheshire 1999:61), they confirm the need for caution in offering global interpretations of the effect of locally embedded social variables such as status and gender.

Importantly, however, the Helsinki group's focus on low level and relatively easily quantifiable morphological variables shows very clearly how the classic methods of Labovian sociolinguistics illuminate the contrasting social trajectories of two well-documented historical changes. We turn now to a different morphological variable which turns out to be of considerable sociohistorical and theoretical interest but somewhat resistant to quantitative analysis in a contemporary speech community.

1.1.3 Singular Concord in Belfast

In the corpus of Belfast vernacular speech recorded in the 1970s and 1980s (Milroy J. and Milroy L. 1977; J. Milroy et al. 1981), we encountered alternation between standard and non-standard number agreement, such that a plural subject could occur with a singular verb as in (1) and (2) below:

(1) Her sons was in the Orange Order
(2) Them eggs is cracked/so they are

20   *Lesley Milroy*

Our initial impression was that such utterances, alternating with their standard counterparts, occurred quite regularly, and so we assumed that a quantitative analysis of the type pioneered by Cheshire (1982) was feasible. However, Policansky (1982) reports that in around 100 hours of the spontaneous speech of 48 inner-city Belfast speakers it was possible to extract only 560 utterance tokens: an average of less than 12 per speaker. Cheshire (1982:73) reports the same problem quite generally with morphological variables, often arising from internal linguistic constraints on the distribution of variants.

In fact, non-standard concord in Belfast, turned out to be in no sense a simple, low-level variable and to be sensitive to a range of grammatical constraints. Observing that such constraints amount to structural divergences underlying differences between varieties intuitively thought to be "dialects of the same language", Wilson and Henry (1998) point out the relevance to variationists of the generative notion of *parameters*. Developed specifically to deal with variability between languages, the idea is potentially applicable to variability between dialects. In an extended analysis within the framework of a Principles and Parameters theory, Henry (1995) examines the relationship between standard and non-standard grammars with reference to five features of the Belfast dialect of English, one of which is non-standard concord. While my focus here is on a description of the linguistic constraints on social, regional and historical dimensions of the Belfast non-standard concord variable, Henry's work further demonstrates its complexity.

The most important internal constraint is the nature of the subject itself. Generally speaking, the non-standard form occurs freely with noun phrase subjects, as in (1) and (2), but hardly ever where the subject is a personal pronoun – we found only a single example in the corpus. Thus *They is cracked* or *They was in the Orange Order* appear to be ungrammatical in Belfast vernacular English. Nor were any examples found of *we* or *you* co-occurring with singular forms; the different effects of full NP versus pronoun subjects are illustrated in (2) above. This subject-type constraint distinguishes the dialect of Belfast from other varieties of non-standard English where forms such as *we was, you was* regularly occur:

(3) We was living in the other house then

Interestingly, Cheshire et al. (1993:72) report that this more widely distributed non-standard concord pattern is common in southern and central England, but much rarer in northern English urban centres and even rarer in Glasgow. The subject-type constraint affects demonstrative pronouns also. No instances of *these* (in either pronoun or determiner function) or of the related form *theseuns* were found as subjects of singular verbs in the Belfast corpus. However, the syntactically equivalent item *them* (in both pronoun and determiner functions), along with the related form *themuns*, co-occurs freely with singular verbs:

(4) Them two fellows was hit
(5) Them's the words he used to me
(6) Themuns is thieves

Two further grammatical contexts favouring the application of the Belfast concord rule are noted by Harris (1993:155–156). The first is a preceding relative pronoun, as in (7) and (8); the second is VS questions, as in (9):

(7) Some of them that was released are all right
(8) You get wee ones that screws things
(9) Is my hands clean?

A considerable amount of research has been carried out on subject/verb agreement of this type, often called The Northern Subject Rule. It extends much further than Belfast, being found in areas settled by Scottish and Ulster migrants to the United States, as well as in early African American English. Within the British Isles it appears to be characteristic also of Scottish and Northumbrian dialects, which of course are historically related to each other, as well as to Ulster English. Beal (1993) notes that in Tyneside non-standard utterances like the following occur only with a full NP subject:

(10) Her sisters was quite near
(11) Things has changed

Further north, in Buckie, a village in North-East Scotland, Tagliamonte (2013:14) reports a dramatic pattern. Speakers use non-standard *was* in 81% of utterances with full NP third-person plural subjects, but *were* is categorical where the subject is a third-person plural pronoun.

  The Northern Subject Rule has a long history, going back to the thirteenth century. James Milroy notes that it occurs in "...Middle Scots (and before) where it is found in the politer sort of literary texts. In Middle Scots the same rule applied: i.e., [it] was not allowed after plural personal pronouns" (1981:13). Tagliamonte and Smith (2000:153) cite Murray's formulation:

> When the subject is a noun, adjective or relative pronoun or when the verb and subject are separated by a clause, the verb takes the termination –*s* in all persons.
>
> (Murray 1873:211)

22 *Lesley Milroy*

This rule produces such sentences as (2), (7) and (8), which Murray is at pains to stress "are not vulgar corruptions but strictly grammatical in the northern dialect" (1873:211). It also predicts that *They was in the Orange Order* will not occur. The two constraints identified by Murray (i.e., type of subject and adjacency of subject and verb) are widely reported in the United States in much more recent accounts (see, for example, Wolfram et al. (1999) and Montgomery (1996)). Joan Beal (pers. com) finds clear examples of the rule closer to home in a personal letter written in 1826 by Thomas Bewick to his friend John Dovaston, lamenting the inadequate response of the London stationers with whom he had placed an order for paper. The subject-type constraint is clearly evident, confirming Murray's judgement half a century later of its strict grammaticality 'in the northern dialect'. The italics are mine:

> ...*our letters was returned repeated applications to our stationers was taken the least notice of* there till last week when *we were given to understand* the paper had been to make.....I had long known that the generality of Cockney's knew nothing of geography – and that the *precincts of London was sufficient* for them ......*we were done* with Mr Edmonston.
>
> (Williams 1968:78)

Beal (2020) provides more detail on the "ego documents" of Thomas Bewick, following the Helsinki group in arguing that they offer a basis for understanding his informal spoken language patterns (see comments in Section 1.1.2).

It is plain, then, that far from being a simple, low-level morphological variable as the Belfast researchers originally assumed, the Northern Subject Rule is complex on several dimensions: linguistic, social and historical. The question of how we might define the standard end of a vernacular/standard continuum is raised by Murray's insistence that it should not be viewed as a 'vulgar corruption'. This ideological issue is the focus of the following section.

1.1.4 Ideological Dimensions of Variation and Change

In her account of freestanding subordinate clauses in the discourse of adolescents, Cheshire (2003:245) again notes a tendency of research on grammatical variation and change to be centred mainly on language internal constraints, social dimensions being much less frequently examined. This comment holds true a quarter of a century later, when the most successful work on social dimensions of grammatical variation and change is arguably found in historical sociolinguistic work, such as that of the Helsinki researchers. More specifically, Cheshire notes a failure

Historical and Ideological Dimensions 23

in work on grammatical variation in contemporary communities to address the "question of what is 'standard' in spoken English apart from what is prescriptively defined as such" (2003:253). Indeed, prescriptivists have nothing at all to say about many features of spoken English, including adverbial clauses which are not attached to a main clause – the focus of Cheshire's (2003) interest.

A few years earlier, however, Cheshire (1999) had commented on comparable problems with frequently analysed and apparently simple morphological variables. She noted that the envelope of variation was usually specified to reflect prescriptively identified patterns, in that the variants selected for study were non-standard forms alternating with the prescribed standard form (as in the example of multiple negation). Cheshire suggests that such a focus on the alternations derived from prescriptive ideologies rather than on the structure of spoken grammars might lead not only to a neglect of important features of spoken language but also to misidentification of variants. This point is illustrated with reference to existential *there* constructions where a plural noun phrase complements some form of *be* (see Walker in this volume for a detailed analysis of existential *there*). Although absence of agreement between *be* and the following noun phrase is generally treated as non-standard, social distributions reported by several researchers suggest that speakers do not treat existential constructions like (12) in the same way as other non-standard concord variants like (13) and (14):

(12) There was no roads
(13) You was only away a bit
(14) All their belongings was taken to the cattle market

For example, Tagliamonte and Hudson (1999) report that young women use non-standard *was* in non-existential constructions like (13) and (14) less than females in any other age group, while on the other hand non-standard existential constructions like (12) are used much more frequently. Schilling-Estes and Wolfram (1994:285) also point out that singular forms appear almost categorically in existential constructions, suggesting that *there was* effectively functions as a lexical unit in both singular and plural contexts (285). Cheshire (1999) similarly reports the same pattern in an analysis of the distribution of multiple negation variants in the speech of 32 adolescents in Milton Keynes. Thus, instead of the sharp pattern of stratification by social class and gender evident in other linguistic contexts, invariant existential *there* constructions are used by male and female speakers in both social groups almost categorically. Noting the existence of similar invariant structures in French and German (*il y a* and *es gibt*), Cheshire concludes that constructions like (12) should be excluded from the set of non-standard variants in

24 *Lesley Milroy*

accounts of subject-verb agreement. She further suggests that existentials are more appropriately treated as one of a set of similarly invariant constructions all of which function to introduce topics in informal spoken English (Cheshire 1999:72). This discussion raises important issues about the way in which grammatical variation in spoken English should be addressed, particularly what constitutes "non-standardness" apart from forms which are prescriptively defined as such.

Cheshire has identified these problems with particular reference to properly conceptualised accounts of *grammatical* variation, but in fact difficulties in identifying the envelope of variation and in specifying a spoken standard can also affect analyses of *phonological* variation and change. In the UK, these difficulties are particularly evident to analysts working in places distant from the metropolitan centre and have been reported in Northern Ireland, Northumberland and Scotland. Labov's landmark 1966 work in New York City provided a model for relating social stratification to phonological variation and change. Since then, variationist work has very often used the standard language as a pivotal reference point. Yet, as Cheshire's comments suggest, the concept of the standard is surprisingly underspecified and undertheorised; particularly, it is both misleading and unhelpful to treat Standard English as a cross-culturally comparable and sociolinguistically unproblematic entity.

In early work by Labov, Trudgill and others, the standard is treated *ad hoc* as the norm to which speakers shift in careful speech, this norm being generally identified with a prescriptive standard. For example, Labov (1972:64–65) notes that the spoken standard to which speakers shift in careful styles is oriented to the norm prescribed by the New York school system and adopted by radio networks in the 1940s. Prior to that, the prestige accent in New York City and along the Eastern seaboard was non-rhotic. For Trudgill, however, the codified British elite accent, Received Pronunciation (RP), provides the standard reference point. Even such a limited comparison between what Labov and Trudgill mean by "Standard English" reveals the quite different sociologies underlying British and American images of the standard; Mencken (1948:28) characterises general American (i.e., the variety spoken west of the Eastern seaboard) as "mainstream" and as an ideal candidate for the standard, while it would be hard to describe RP as "mainstream". Bonfiglio (2002) offers a convincing account of the social and cultural changes triggering the valorisation of (r) and the emergence of this new "mainstream" American standard. L. Milroy (2004) suggests that standard languages are best treated as localised constructs emerging from the particulars of a nation's history and social structure. This being so, we would not expect "Standard English" to be a comparable sociolinguistic entity in different English-speaking countries. Nevertheless, it is important to acknowledge that Norwich speakers appeared to orient to RP norms in a way which made it possible for Trudgill in the early seventies to adapt Labov's (1966) framework without much difficulty.

Scotland and Ireland are, however, a different story. Both have long histories of independence from and opposition to the English metropolis. Similar conditions apply to Northumberland – recall the evident perception of "otherness" in Thomas Bewick's comments on Londoners. Sociolinguists who attempt to employ Labov's framework in these geopolitical contexts report significant difficulties in specifying the norms to which individuals shift in careful speech. Consider for example the behaviour of Belfast working-class speakers who modified vernacular norms in careful spontaneous speech, but not when reading word lists (Milroy 1987). Furthermore, in both Edinburgh (Romaine 1978) and Belfast, a range of different middle-class/educated accents could be heard; unlike the situation reported in New York City or Norwich, more than one high-status linguistic model was available.

As noted by Harris (1991) and Gunn (1990), ethnicity in Belfast is indexed by a speaker's choice of norm in careful or rhetorical speech more overtly than in the vernacular varieties described by Milroy (1987). This situation was not envisioned in earlier research, which assumed a relatively unitary and focussed set of standard norms. These norms were associated unproblematically both with social class and stylistic variability, represented on intersecting continua from most to least standard. It is clear also that the target phonological system(s) of careful speakers in Glasgow, Edinburgh and Belfast rarely orient to RP. Indeed, the phonologies of dialects cannot be mapped directly on to RP, as is shown by the example of the low vowel /a/ in both Glasgow and Belfast (Macaulay 1977; Milroy 1987). Comparable difficulties emerge in Northumberland for historical, cultural and geographical reasons (Beal 1993; Watt 2002).

I turn now to the notion of levelling, a concept drawn from the dialect contact framework introduced and more recently greatly elaborated by Trudgill (1986, 2011). Britain (2018) describes levelling as a linguistic process which has the effect of eradicating socially or locally marked variants in conditions of social or geographical mobility, both within and across language systems. An understanding of the linguistic effects of levelling is helpful in conceptualising the varieties traditionally described as regional standards, such as the distinctive varieties used by educated speakers in the American south (Preston 1996; Hartley and Preston 1999), in Northern Ireland, or in the Tyneside area of England. Watt (2002) discusses the convergence of Tyneside speakers on socially unmarked supralocal variants (o) and (e) (as in *goat* and *gate*) in these terms, arguing that regional standards originate not as modified versions of exonorms, such as British Received Pronunciation, but as supralocal levelled varieties (see also Watt and Milroy 1999). Consider also the case of the Belfast low front vowel /a/ (as in *pat, pass*). As in Tyneside, higher

26   *Lesley Milroy*

status Belfast speakers do not usually orient to RP where back and front low vowels are phonologically contrastive (as in *psalm: Sam*). Rather, they reduce the number of linguistically conditioned allophones of /a/ by eliminating the extreme back and front variants characteristic of the vernacular system, often converging on a narrow area of vowel space around the centre of the vernacular range (Milroy 2004:165). James Milroy (1982) describes this process as "normalisation", a phenomenon which he takes care to distinguish from standardisation, where institutional intervention is implicated.

At the time this research was carried out in Belfast (1975–1980), no model was easily available for describing the dynamics of this contrast between high- and low-status speakers; following Labov (1966) most researchers operated with a single dimension, such as relative vowel height or relative backness, which was linearly correlated with status. However, a dialect contact framework treats speakers' variable realisations of /a/ in Belfast (and indeed of other vowels) as a straightforward instance of levelling, whereby socially marked or stigmatised elements are eliminated from the pool of variants. Grammatical variants are subject to the same process. Thus, for example, in Belfast the non-standard variants *them/themuns* in both pronoun and determiner function (see examples 4–6 above) are socially stigmatised along with a wide range of other local and supralocal non-standard items such as multiple negative or non-standard past tense forms (Milroy 1981:11–15). Like the extreme back and front variants of /a/ they are eliminated from the pool of variants acceptable to high-status speakers. But as Harris (1993) and Milroy (1981) show, many distinctively local grammatical patterns are socially unmarked and have not been eliminated in this way. They might therefore reasonably be viewed as standard. For example, Harris (1993:1960–1962) describes a range of forms expressing various perfect tense/aspect distinctions which are used regularly by both high- and low-status speakers; *I was after coming down the stairs / We're living here 17 years* correspond to 'I had just come down the stairs' / 'We've been living here for seventeen years.'

It seems then that levelled norms can function socially as standards; this is what appears to have happened in the United States, where, as in Belfast or Newcastle (see again Beal 1993), it is much easier to define the standard negatively, in terms of the socially marked phonological, grammatical or discourse variants which speakers avoid, than positively, in terms of the (unmarked) characteristics of any putative standard target variety (Wolfram and Schilling-Estes 1998:12). Preston's work on language attitudes in the United States suggests that this kind of levelled norm coincides with native speaker judgements of standardness and correctness (2013:172ff.). The distinction between an institutionally legitimised exonorm, such as RP, and a levelled norm, which develops in a structurally regular fashion independently of an identifiable exonorm, is important. Certainly, it can help us deconstruct the socially and culturally variable notion of a standard. Thus, we can address the question highlighted by Cheshire of what is meant by a standard, independently of a prescriptive definition.

1.1.5 Conclusion

I began this chapter by noting the distinction sometimes drawn by researchers between 'simple' and apparently easily quantifiable morphological variables, and more complex grammatical and discourse variables. The latter type is commonly approached with reference to internal linguistic constraints, and analyses of their social distribution are relatively uncommon. However, with particular reference to the Northern Subject Rule, I have suggested that the apparently simple morphological variable of subject-verb agreement is in fact complex on several dimensions. It is subject to a number of internal constraints, and variants are difficult to analyse straightforwardly with reference to their position on a vernacular-standard continuum. This discussion addresses the question of what is meant by the term "standard" in different national and cultural contexts.

I have also suggested that particularly successful work on variation and change with respect to apparently simple morphological variables may be found in historical sociolinguistic research, such as that of the Helsinki group. It is clear that Nevalainen and her colleagues can avoid many of the problems encountered by researchers in contemporary communities. Perhaps most importantly, historical sociolinguists can specify the earlier and later points of morphological changes, such as the emergence of the -es third-person singular form of *be*, in terms of 'conservative' versus 'innovative' variants, rather than as 'standard' versus 'non-standard'. The same terminology can be applied to changes such as the decline of multiple negation, where the older form is still used, while in the contemporary social world the old 'innovative' variant has become prescriptively defined as standard. Such an avoidance of the ideological problems discussed in this chapter is a happy consequence of the historical linguist's ability to focus on changes which can be tracked over several centuries in extensive computerised corpora.

References

Auer, A. and Voeste, A. 2012. "Grammatical variables". In *The Handbook of Historical Sociolinguistics*, Hernandez-Campoy, Juan Manuel and Juan Camilo Conde-Silvestre (eds.). Chichester: Wiley Blackwell. 253–270.

28   Lesley Milroy

Beal, J. 1993. "The grammar of Tyneside and Northumbrian English". In *Real English; The grammar of English Dialects in the British Isles*, J. Milroy and L. Milroy (eds.). London: Longman. 187–213.

Beal, J. 2020. "Dialect and the construction of identity in the ego-documents of Thomas Bewick". In *Dialect Writing and the North of England*, P. Honeybone and W. Maguire (eds.). Edinburgh: Edinburgh University Press. 45–60.

Bonfiglio, T. P. 2002. *Race and the Rise of Standard American*. Berlin and New York: Mouton de Gruyter.

Britain, D. 2018. "Dialect contact and new dialect formation". In *The Handbook of Dialectology*, C. Boberg, J. Nerbonne and D. Watts (eds.). Chichester: Wiley Blackwell. 143–158.

Cheshire, J. 1982. *Variation in an English Dialect: A Sociolinguistic Study*. Cambridge: Cambridge University Press.

Cheshire, J. 1999. "Taming the vernacular: Some repercussions for variation and spoken grammar". *Cuadernos de Filologia Inglesa*, 8, Departamento de Filologia Inglesa de la Universidad de Murcia. 59–80.

Cheshire, J. 2003. "Social dimensions of syntactic variation: The case of *when* clauses". In *Social Dialectology: In Honour of Peter Trudgill*, D. Britain and J. Cheshire (eds.). Amsterdam: John Benjamins. 245–261.

Cheshire, J., Edwards, V. and Whittle, P. 1993. "Non-standard English and dialect leveling". In *Real English; The Grammar of English Dialects in the British Isles*, J. Milroy and L. Milroy (eds.). London: Longman. 53–96.

Coveney, A. 1996. *Variability in Spoken French: A Sociolinguistic Study of Interrogation and Negation*. Exeter, England: Elm Bank Publications. Arnold. 47–71.

Gunn, B. 1990. *The Politic Word*. Unpublished doctoral dissertation, University of Ulster at Jordanstown.

Harris, J. 1984. "Syntactic variation and dialect divergence". *Journal of Linguistics* 20(2):303–327. Reprinted in R. Singh (ed.) *Towards a Critical Sociolinguistics*. Amsterdam and Philadelphia: Benjamins. 31–58.

Harris, J. 1991. "Ireland". In *English around the World: Sociolinguistic Perspectives*, J. Cheshire (ed.). Cambridge: Cambridge University Press. 37–50.

Harris, J. 1993. "The grammar of Irish English". In *Real English: The Grammar of English Dialects in the British Isles*, J. Milroy and L. Milroy (eds.). London: Longman. 139–186.

Hartley, L. C. and Preston, D. R. 1999. "The names of US English: Valley girl, cowboy, yankee, normal, nasal and ignorant". In *Standard English: The Widening Debate*, T. Bex and R. Watts (eds.). London: Routledge. 207–238.

Henry, A. 1995. *Belfast English and Standard English: Dialect Variation and Parameter Setting*. Oxford: Oxford University Press.

Keene, D. 2000. "Metropolitan values: Migration, mobility and cultural norms, London 1100–1700". In *The Development of Standard English, 1300–1800*, L. Wright (ed.). Cambridge: Cambridge University Press. 93–114.

Labov, W. 1966. *The Social Stratification of English in New York City*. Washington, DC: Center for Applied Linguistics.

Labov, W. 1972. *Sociolinguistic Patterns*. Philadelphia: Pennsylvania University Press.

Labov, W. 1994. *Principles of Linguistic Change, Volume 1: Internal Factors.* Oxford: Blackwell.

Lass, R. 1997. *Historical Linguistics and Language Change.* Cambridge: Cambridge University Press.

Lass, R. 1999. "Phonology and morphology". In *The Cambridge History of the English Language*, R. Lass (ed.). Vol. III, 1476–1776. Cambridge: Cambridge University Press. 56–186.

Macaulay, R. K. S. 1977. *Language, Social Class, and Education.* Edinburgh: Edinburgh University Press.

Mencken, H. L. 1948. *The American Language: An Inquiry into the Development of English in the United States. Supplement II.* New York: Alfred A. Knopf.

Milroy, J. 1981. *Regional Accents of English: Belfast.* Belfast: Blackstaff.

Milroy, J. 1982. "Probing under the tip of the ice-berg: phonological normalization and the shape of speech communities". *In Sociolinguistic variation in speech communities*, S. Romaine (ed). London: Arnold, 35–47.

Milroy, J. and Milroy, L. 1977. *Speech Community and Language Variety in Belfast.* Report to the Social Science Research Council (UK). Grant no. HR3771.

Milroy, J., Milroy, L., Harris, J., Policansky, L., Gunn, B. and Pitts, A. 1981. *Sociolinguistic Variation and Linguistic Change in Belfast.* Report to the Social Science Research Council (UK). Grant no. HR5777.

Milroy, L. 1987. *Language and Social Networks* (2nd edition). Oxford: Blackwell.

Milroy, L. 2004. "Language ideologies and linguistic change". In *Sociolinguistic Variation: Critical Reflections*, C. Fought (ed.). Oxford: Oxford University Press. 161–177.

Milroy, L. and Gordon, M. 2003. *Sociolinguistics: Method and Interpretation.* Oxford: Blackwell.

Montgomery, M. 1996. "Was colonial American a koine?" In *Speech Past and Present. Studies in English Dialectology in Memory of Ossi Ihalainen*, J. Klemola, M. Kyto, and M. Rissanen (eds.). New York: P. Lang. 213–235.

Murray, J. A. H. 1873. *The Dialect of the Southern Counties of Scotland: Its Pronunciation, Grammar and Historical Relations.* London: Philological Society.

Nevalainen, T. 1999. "Making the best use of "bad" data: Evidence for sociolinguistic variation in early modern English". *Neophilologische Mitteilungen* 4(C):499–533.

Nevalainen, T. 2000a. "Gender differences in the evolution of Standard English". *Journal of English Linguistics* 28(1):38–59.

Nevalainen, T. 2000b. "Mobility, social networks and language change in early modern England". *European Journal of English Studies* 4(3):253–264.

Nevalainen, T. and Raumolin-Brunberg, H. 1996. *Sociolinguistics and Language History.* Amsterdam and Atlanta: Rodopi.

Nevalainen, T. and Raumolin-Brunberg, H. 2012. "Historical sociolinguistics: Origins, motivations and paradigms". In *The Handbook of Historical Sociolinguistics*, J. M. Hernandez-Campoy and J. C. Conde-Silvestre (eds.). Chichester: Wiley Blackwell. 22–40.

30 Lesley Milroy

Nevalainen, T. and Raumolin-Brunberg, H. 2017. *Historical Sociolinguistics* (2nd edition). London: Longman.

Nevalainen, T., Raumolin-Brunberg, H. and Mannila, H. 2011. "The diffusion of language change in real time: Progressive and conservative individuals and the time depth of change". *Language Variation and Change* 23:1–43.

Patterson, D. 1860. *Provincialisms of Belfast*. Belfast: Mayne Boyd.

Policansky, L. 1982. "Grammatical variation in Belfast English". *Belfast Working Papers in Language and Linguistics* 6:37–66.

Pratt, L. and Denison, D. 2000. "The language of the Southey-Coleridge circle". *Language Sciences* 22:401–402.

Preston, D. 1996. "Where the worst English is spoken". In *Focus on the USA*, E. W. Schneider (ed.). Amsterdam: Benjamins. 297–361.

Preston, D. 2013. "Language with an attitude". In *Handbook of Variation and Change*, J. K. Chambers and N. Schilling (eds.). (2nd edition). Oxford: Blackwell. 157–182.

Romaine, S. 1978. "Problems in the investigation of linguistic attitudes in *Work in Progress*. 11–29, Department of Linguistics, University of Edinburgh.

Romaine, S. (ed.) 1982. *Socio-Historical Linguistics: Its Status and Methodology*. Cambridge: Cambridge University Press.

Sankoff, G. and Vincent, D. 1980. "The productive use of *ne* in spoken Montreal French". In *The Social Life of Language*, G. Sankoff (ed.). Philadelphia: University of Pennsylvania Press. 295–310.

Schilling-Estes, N. and Wolfram, W. 1994. "Convergent explanation and alternative regularization patterns: Were/weren't leveling in a vernacular variety". *Language Variation and Change* 6:273–302.

Tagliamonte, S. 2013. "Comparative sociolinguistics". In *Handbook of Variation and Change*, J. K. Chambers and N. Schilling (eds.). (2nd edition). Oxford: Blackwell. 128–156.

Tagliamonte, S. and Hudson, R. 1999. "*be like* et al. beyond America: The quotative system in British and Canadian youth". *Journal of Sociolinguistics* 3(2):147–172.

Tagliamonte, S. and Smith, J. 2000. "Old *was*, new ecology: Viewing English through the sociolinguistic filter". In *The English History of African American English*, S. Poplack (ed.). Oxford: Blackwell. 141–171.

Trudgill, P. 1986. *Dialects in Contact*. Oxford: Blackwell.

Trudgill, P. 1996. "Language contact and inherent variability: The absence of hypercorrection in East Anglian present tense forms". In *Speech Past and Present: Studies in English Dialectology in Memory of Ossi Ihalainen*, J. Klemola, M. Kyto and M. Rissanen (eds.). Frankfurt: Peter Lang. 412–445.

Trudgill, P. 2011. *Sociolinguistic Typology: Social Determinants of Linguistic Complexity*. Oxford: Oxford University Press.

Watt, D. J. L. 2002. "I don't speak with a Geordie accent, I speak like, the Northern accent". *Journal of Sociolinguistics* 6:44–63.

Watt, D. J. L. and Milroy, L. 1999. "Patterns of variation and change in three Tyneside vowels: Is this dialect levelling?" In *Urban Voices*, P. Foulkes and G. J. Docherty (eds.). London: Arnold. 25–46.

Williams, G. (ed.) 1968. *Bewick to Dovaston. Letters 1824–1828*. London: Nattali and Maurice.

Wilson, J. and Henry, A. 1998. "Parameter setting within a socially realistic linguistics". *Language in Society* 27(1):1–21.

Wolfram, W. and Schilling-Estes, N. 1998. *American English*. Oxford: Blackwell.

Wolfram, W., Hazan, K. and Schilling-Estes, N. 1999. *Dialect Change and Maintenance on the Outer Banks*. Publication of the American Dialect Society. Tuscaloosa and London: University of Alabama Press.

1.2 Towards an Integrated Model of Perception

Linguistic Architecture and the Dynamics of Sociolinguistic Cognition

Erez Levon, Isabelle Buchstaller, and Adam Mearns

1.2.1 Introduction

Speech perception research has accumulated much evidence on how different linguistic features are perceived and evaluated (see, e.g., Campbell-Kibler (2009) and Hay et al. (2018) for reviews). These studies have highlighted the contingent nature of language evaluation, demonstrating how it can vary both from listener to listener and within the same listener depending on the socio-indexical context in which a linguistic feature is heard. One trajectory of research on intra-listener variation has examined how perceptual evaluations of a given variable are constrained by the frequency distributions of a feature across a speech sample. Studies of the "sociolinguistic monitor" (Labov et al. 2011) have shown that altering the variable distribution of a particular feature can have a significant influence on listener judgments of the speaker (Levon and Fox 2014; Wagner and Hesson 2014; Levon and Buchstaller 2015). This finding suggests that evaluative reactions to linguistic variability are dynamic and constantly updated as listeners process the ongoing speech stream (Watson and Clark 2013). Research has thus begun to trace the moment-by-moment formation of evaluative reactions and to model the online process of real-time perception (Hesson and Shellgren 2015; Montgomery and Moore 2018).

Most studies in this area to date have examined the perception of single phonetic variables. Such monodimensional approaches do not capture the sociolinguistic axiom that speakers combine available linguistic features to imbue these resources with new and emergent meanings. Any given style can thus be characterised by the co-occurrence of a certain set of features, and the way in which these features are combined may not be the same from one speaker and context to the next (Pharao et al. 2014). Only recently have perceptual studies started to explore the perceptual impact of clusters of phonetic features and, in particular, how evaluations of a variable can change across different linguistic contexts (e.g., Campbell-Kibler 2011; Levon 2014; Pharao et al. 2014; Pharao and Maegaard 2017). These studies have suggested that the perception of features is fundamentally context-dependent, such that certain features can be more or less prominent when arising alongside or embedded within other features. For example, Pharao and Maegaard (2017) reported that effects for specific segmental features can be attenuated by the presence of other socially salient features. Campbell-Kibler (2011) found that listener assumptions about a speaker's social background can affect how some features are perceived vis-à-vis intelligence or femininity. Overall, these findings suggest that the socio-indexical meanings of specific variants vary as a function of social, interactional and linguistic context.

Combined with the studies of real-time perception outlined above, these studies have laid the foundation for a theory of perception as a *cumulative* phenomenon, one that is sensitive to both the surrounding linguistic context and the unfolding and sequential nature of speech. Nonetheless, important questions remain in relation to the perception of speakers and the linguistic features they use (e.g. Drager and Kirtley 2016). On the one hand, this is a methodological issue: current methods are not very good at tracking what hearers notice and how they interpret and classify what they encounter in everyday talk. Furthermore, we still know very little about how variables at levels "above and beyond the phonology" (Sankoff 1973) participate in this process, mainly because previous research has tended to focus almost uniquely on clusters of phonetic variation (see Cheshire 1987, 2005).

The present study aims to contribute to the analysis of real-time processing of linguistic variation by exploring the cumulative effect of linguistic features at different levels of linguistic architecture in the formation of perceptual evaluations. More specifically, we aim to document the dynamic and contingent nature of sociolinguistic perception by probing listener evaluations of singular and clustered occurrences of vernacular forms at different levels of language structure in a moment-by-moment experimental set-up (cf. Levon and Buchstaller 2015).

1.2.2 Data and Method

Our discussion is based on the results of a speaker evaluation experiment. We recruited two speakers, one man and one woman, who at the time of recording were both students in their early 20s at Newcastle University and who had lived their entire lives in the North-East of England. The speakers were recorded reading 16 short passages that cumulatively mimic an advertisement for Newcastle University in which students describe different aspects of student life at the university in their own vernacular variety. We did not alter the recordings in any way (other than to scale intensity to 70 dB).

34 *Erez Levon et al.*

Due to the socio-indexical richness of the speech stimulus, every moment of speech contains multiple linguistic items that might trigger evaluative reactions. Given this, it has been difficult to understand which specific features in a speech signal cause particular reactions, except in very short and experimentally controlled stimuli (cf. Campbell-Kibler 2008). Perception researchers have therefore developed novel approaches to capture listener reactions online as they process indexically rich talk-in-interaction. Watson and Clark (2013, 2015) took a significant step forward by developing a slider tool which allowed listeners to manipulate their ratings along a scale in real-time as they heard a speech stimulus. Montgomery and Moore's (2018) study provided time-aligned reactions to a wealth of phonetic features in the variety of English spoken on the Isles of Scilly. These real-time methods are able to capture reactions to features considered to be regional at exactly the point in the stimulus at which listeners notice them.

In the present research, we aim to broaden the real-time perceptual approach to capture moment-by-moment reactions to variables at different linguistic levels occurring in naturalistic settings of indexically rich stimuli. We focus on listener reactions to two phonetic and three morphosyntactic phenomena, as shown in Table 1.2.1.

Since the experiment aimed to collect listener reactions to both singular and cumulative occurrences of linguistic variables, both in isolation and in combination, each of the 16 stimulus passages was designed to

Table 1.2.1 Variables under investigation

Variable	Envelope of variation
ING	standard [ɪŋ] versus non-standard [ɪn] in the present progressive -*ing* suffix, as in *talking* versus *talkin'* (e.g., Campbell-Kibler 2007, Levon and Fox 2014)
FACE	standard closing diphthong [eɪ], supralocal monophthong [e:] or local centralised diphthong [ɪə] in a word like *face* (e.g., Haddican et al. 2013, Buchstaller et al. 2017)
Hyper-s	non-standard use of the -*s* suffix on present-tense verbs when the subject noun-phrase is not third-person singular in function, as in *They really like[s] ice cream* (e.g., McCafferty 2003, 2004; de Haas 2011; Buchstaller et al. 2013; Childs 2013; Levon and Buchstaller 2015)
zero subject defining relatives	relative pronouns in subject defining relative clauses as in standard *who* or as with the non-standard *zero* form, as in *The facilities are open to students who/ø come to university* (e.g., Beal et al. 2012, Buchstaller and Corrigan 2015)
Stative possessives	standard *has/has got* versus non-standard *got* in stative possessive constructions, as in *He has/has got/got a cat* (e.g., Tagliamonte et al. 2010, Buchstaller 2016)

vary the number and combination of tokens they contained. The passages were roughly matched for length, and each described different aspects of Newcastle University ranging across sport, housing, university experience and entertainment. Consider, for example, the extract in (1), which contains four tokens of the FACE variable (bolded and underlined):

(1) [4 FACE] It's been r<u>a</u>ted as one of the top twenty for student experience in the U<u>K</u> and it's loc<u>a</u>ted in the heart of one of Britain's f<u>a</u>vourite cities.

Due to space restrictions, in the current chapter we present detailed results from only five experimental stimuli. In addition to the text in (1), the other four stimuli considered in this analysis are listed in (2) through (5):

(2) [FACE – ING – ING – FACE] But at the <u>same</u> time they're constantly build<u>ing</u> and there's all sorts of new halls go<u>ing</u> up so it feels like it's up to <u>date</u> as well.
(3) [hyper-s – ING – FACE] What I also really <u>likes</u> is that the sports centre is nearby. I can go swimm<u>ing</u> there during <u>breaks</u>.
(4) [*zero*-relative – hyper-s] The facilities are open to all students [<u>ø</u>] come to campus. They are accessible all days and they usually <u>opens</u> during the weekends too.
(5) [FACE – hyper-s – hyper-s – FACE] <u>Ba</u>sically when you're finished with lectures then you can just wander off. <u>There's</u> so many bars and cafes and there <u>is</u> loads of music <u>pla</u>ces as well.

The target phonetic and morphosyntactic features are highlighted in (1) through (5). Given the naturalness of the speech samples, these target features were never presented in isolation but rather co-occurred with a wealth of other non-standard variables that we would expect in sequences of spontaneous, naturally occurring speech in the region. These other variables, all typical for Newcastle, include *t*-glottaling (Buchstaller et al. 2017), GOOSE-fronting (Watt and Milroy 1999) and GOAT-monophthongisation (Watt and Milroy 1999), among others.

Stimuli were presented online to 115 listeners aged between 16 and 55 (mean age = 24.9) from the North-East and the North-West of England and from Scotland.[1] All listeners identified as "White" or "White British", with 76% identifying as women and 24% as men. Listeners heard all 16 stimuli in the same order in which they were spoken, 8 read by the woman and 8 read by the man, with speaker gender counter-balanced across listeners (i.e., half of the listeners heard the woman read stimuli 1–8 and the man read stimuli 9–16, the other half heard the man read 1–8 and the woman 9–16, always in the same order). Listeners were told that the speakers had applied for a job with the Newcastle University student radio station and were asked to rate the speakers based on how 'professional' they sounded (cf. Labov et al. 2011).

36 *Erez Levon et al.*

Our empirical tool builds on Watson and Clark's (2013) novel evaluation tool, which allows listeners to manipulate their ratings along a scale in real-time as they heard a speech stimulus. We relied on the Information Technology Services at Queen Mary University of London to adapt this graphical sliding tool to capture real-time evaluations, embedding it in an experiment built with the Experigen experimental platform (Becker and Levine 2013) which facilitated online access. The Experigen interface allowed us to present stimuli to listeners in an interactive fashion: while listening to stimuli, participants were instructed to move the sliding scale on the computer screen in order to provide in-the-moment evaluations of the speaker's perceived level of professionalism.

Analysis of real-time evaluations was conducted using Change-Point Analysis (CPA), a statistical method for estimating the point at which a sequence of observations significantly changes (using the changepoint package Killick et al. 2012; Killick and Eckley 2014; see also Watson and Clark 2015) in R version 3.5.2 (R Core Team 2019). This statistical method uses a Pruned Exact Linear Time (PELT) algorithm to detect changes in mean ratings across a time-series (in our case, data sampled at one-second intervals). By scanning the slider movement and checking for changes in evaluations, CPA detects the best change-points by selecting the time points at which the group of respondents shows consistent and significant changes in their perceptual reactions (based on significance tests determined via an adaptation of a maximum likelihood statistic; see Eckley et al. 2011 for further details). Once a change-point is detected, the data are partitioned and the algorithm is applied to each partition independently. Once no further change-points are detected, calculation stops. Thus, CPA provides us with an indication of the zones of evaluative stability and intervals of evaluative change. As a second interpretive step, we then correlate the change-points with linguistic features contained in the stimulus, to the extent possible.

Before turning to our results and their implications for an integrated theory of sociolinguistic perception, we briefly illustrate our method for capturing real-time reactions to singular and cumulative occurrences of vernacular features in real-time speech via CPA. The plot in the top half of Figure 1.2.1 illustrates the moment-by-moment results of the change-point analysis for stimulus 1 spoken by the woman. The response curve shown represents an average for all listeners, with higher numbers on the y-axis corresponding to higher ratings of the speaker (scored on a scale of 0–100, where 50 represents a "neutral" evaluation) as sounding "professional" (as evidenced by listeners' slider movements to the right). Periods of stability in evaluation (i.e., when mean ratings are not changing) are represented as solid bold horizontal lines. The space between these periods of stability are the change-points (i.e., the intervals during which the listeners are shifting their evaluative responses to the stimuli).

To uncover whether a change-point might correspond to a particular linguistic feature (see Watson and Clark 2013), we imported the change-point solutions into the transcription software ELAN and aligned them with the audio file and transcription (see the third tier (CP) in the bottom half of Figure 1.2.1). The second tier (NS) shows intervals where target non-standard variables occur (in Figure 1.2.1, these are instances of the FACE vowel). When attempting to align change-points with specific variables, we allowed for 1.5 seconds after the realisation of an individual feature for respondents to listen to the auditory information, process it on the basis of their socio-cognitive background knowledge and express their evaluative reaction via slider movement.

We demarcated a reaction time window starting 1.5 seconds before an actual change-point (as exemplified by the dashed box around the tiers in Figure 1.2.1).[2] On the basis of these calculations, we hypothesise that if a change-point and a vernacular linguistic feature occur within the same reaction time window, the perceptual reaction might be due to the occurrence of the linguistic feature. In Figure 1.2.1, for example, the second and third instances of the FACE vowel (in the _UK_ and _located_) occur within the reaction time window of the first change-point, and the fourth FACE vowel (in _favourite_) occurs within the reaction-time window of the second change-point. Of course we cannot rule out with absolute certainty that other vernacular features might have triggered the observed change-point effect. But since the guises (including the naturally occurring richness of the stimuli) are the same for all listeners and since we were unable to detect any other conspicuous vernacular realisations in this temporal region that might have triggered this reaction, we feel relatively confident in interpreting the consistent reaction across listeners as an indication that the tokens of FACE did indeed trigger the change-points. We therefore take these findings to mean that the occurrence of the FACE vowel resulted in a consistent and measurable perceptual reaction amongst our respondents. In the following sections, we apply this method in exploring respondents' real-time perceptual sensitivity to phonetic and morphosyntactic variability in the stimuli.

1.2.3 Towards an Integrated Model of Real-Time Social Perception

Prior to examining listener reactions to the different stimuli in detail, it is important to note that our experiment was successful in capturing real-time reactions to sociolinguistic processing: inspection of change-points suggests that our respondents react to many of the vernacular features we were testing. Moreover, while the patterns of evaluative reactions differ between individual guises and speakers, the general trend throughout all but one passage tested is a decrease in perceived professionalism across a given stimulus. This trend appears to indicate that

38 *Erez Levon et al.*

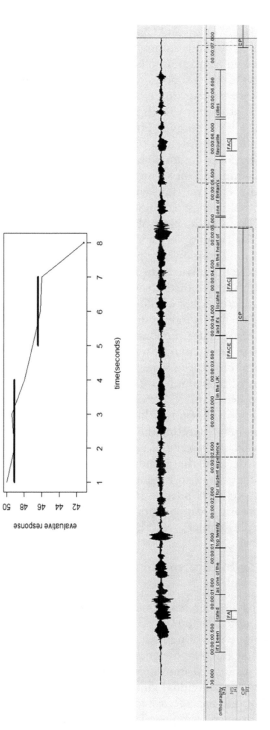

Figure 1.2.1 Aligning linguistic features with change-points.

there is a general cumulative effect of vernacular language features on listener evaluations: as the speakers continue to produce language features typical for North-East varieties of English across the course of a stimulus, they are judged as sounding progressively "less professional" by listeners (i.e., while listening to the stimulus, the listeners increasingly moved the slider towards the left-hand, "unprofessional", side).[3]

Analyses reveal that evaluations of both the woman and the man are broadly comparable. In the interest of space, we therefore illustrate our findings with reference to only one of the speakers, though the findings can be understood as applying to both, unless otherwise noted. We begin with evaluations of the utterance in (3) above, reproduced in (6):

(6) [hyper-s - ING - FACE] What I also really **likes** is that the sports centre is nearby. I can go swimm**ing** there during **breaks**.

Figure 1.2.2 presents the results of the change-point analysis for the woman's realisation of this utterance. We see that listeners are sensitive to both morphosyntactic and phonetic variants in the woman's speech: The occurrence of an instance of hyper-s (the first feature demarcated on the NS tier in Figure 1.2.2) lies well within the 1.5-second buffer zone prior to the change-point (dashed box in Figure 1.2.2). Similarly, the occurrence of vernacular [ɪn] in *swimming* (the second feature demarcated on the NS tier in Figure 1.2.2) appears to have triggered a perceptual reaction from listeners. These results thus lead us to suggest that real-time sociolinguistic processing is sensitive to both the hyper-s (a morphosyntactic feature) and alveolar (ING) (a phonetic one). Note that the presence of a monophthongal FACE vowel at the end of the utterance does not have an apparent effect on listener reactions as measured by the Change-Point Analysis algorithm. There are two possible interpretations of this result. First, listeners might have already formed an opinion of the speaker on the basis of the previous features, so that this last instance of FACE does not change their rating. However, changes in ratings might also not be registered due to the feature's proximity to the end of the stimulus passage (however, we point out that in other instances features at the end of a passage are attended to and evaluated).

The result presented in Figure 1.2.2 thus illustrates the general pattern that we find for morphosyntactic features in our data: respondents appear to be sensitive to even the first occurrence of a phenomenon like hyper-s. Figure 1.2.3 provides further evidence for this pattern, first noted in Levon and Buchstaller (2015). In Figure 1.2.3a, we illustrate the results with respect to the man's realisation of the utterance in (5) above, with two instances of hyper-s occurring between two tokens of monophthongal FACE. Figure 1.2.3b illustrates evaluations of the woman's realisation of the same utterance. We see that in both Figures 1.2.3a and 1.2.3b, the first instance of the hyper-s corresponds to the occurrence

40 *Erez Levon et al.*

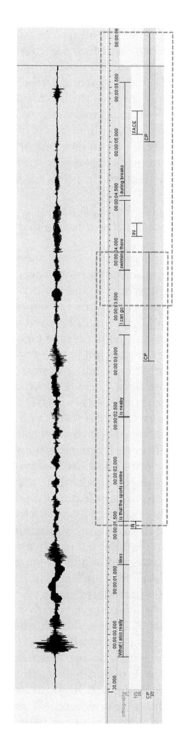

Figure 1.2.2 Listener evaluations of vernacular realisations of Hyper-s - ING - FACE in the woman's speech.

of a change-point within the 1.5 second window. For the man (Figure 1.2.3a), the second instance of hyper-*s* does as well, although for the woman (Figure 1.2.3b) it does not. For the FACE vowel, in contrast, there is no evidence of evaluative change in response to the first vernacular realisation in either the woman's or the man's speech. After the second occurrence of the vowel (in *places*, at the end of the utterance), a significant change-point does occur. The results of Figures (1.2.3a) and (1.2.3b), therefore, seem to suggest a pattern whereby informants are sensitive to the first occurrence of a morphosyntactic feature, and in some cases also to subsequent occurrences of the same variant. This contrasts with what we find for the phonetic feature (FACE), which – as we illustrate in more detail below – listeners only appear to react to after having encountered it multiple times.

Consider, for example, the results in Figure 1.2.4. There, we see listeners' evaluations of the woman's realisation of the utterance in (1) above, in which four monophthongal tokens of FACE occur in succession. A change-point only occurs in response to the second of these monophthongal tokens, with another change-point occurring after the fourth token. Though not illustrated, evaluations of the man's speech are even more extreme in this regard, with a change-point only appearing after all four tokens of monophthongal FACE have occurred. Thus, the pattern evident in Figure 1.2.4 resonates with what appears in Figure 1.2.3, where it seems that multiple tokens of a FACE monophthongal variant must occur before listener evaluations show evidence of significant change. The next paragraphs explore to what extent this finding can be extended to other vernacular phonological features.

As can be seen in Figure 1.2.5, a very similar result to the one discussed above is illustrated with respect to the evaluations of the utterance in (2), which contains a combination of FACE and (ING). Once again, initial instances of a vernacular phonological feature do not result in any measurable differences in evaluation. For the woman (Figure 1.2.5a), alveolar (ING) does not seem to be perceptually salient at all and only the second instance of FACE results in a systematic response. For the man, in contrast, consistent perceptual reactions occur after the second occurrences of both alveolar (ING) and monophthongal FACE.

The finding that phonetic variables seem to need more than one vernacular token to trigger consistent evaluative responses is interesting given that Labov et al.'s (2011) classic sociolinguistic-monitor experiment found a logarithmic pattern of evaluation, whereby the first token of a vernacular phonetic variant triggered a substantial evaluative response while subsequent occurrences of the same token resulted in consistent but attenuated reactions (though cf., e.g., Levon and Fox 2014, who were unable to replicate this pattern). While our informants seem to be sensitive to the first (and potentially subsequent) instances of morphosyntactic features, we find no evidence for the type of logarithmic evaluative pattern in the

42 *Erez Levon et al.*

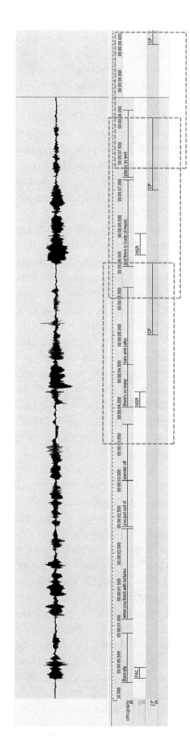

Figure 1.2.3a Listener evaluations of vernacular realisations of FACE - Hyper-s - Hyper-s - FACE in the man's speech.

Towards an Integrated Model of Perception 43

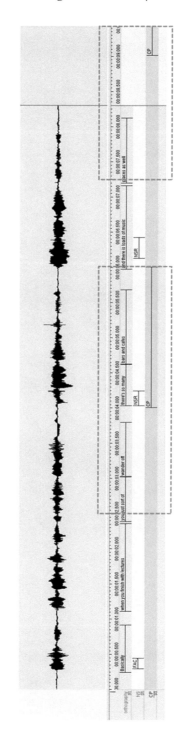

Figure 1.2.3b Listener evaluations of vernacular realisations of FACE - Hyper-s - Hyper-s -FACE in the woman's speech.

44 *Erez Levon et al.*

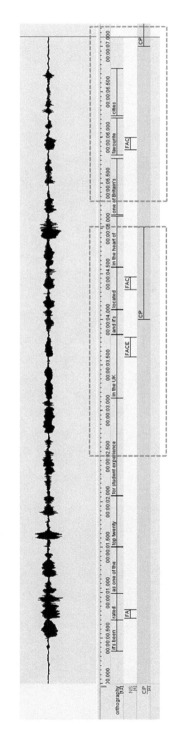

Figure 1.2.4 Listener evaluations of vernacular realisations of 4 tokens of FACE in the woman's speech.

Towards an Integrated Model of Perception 45

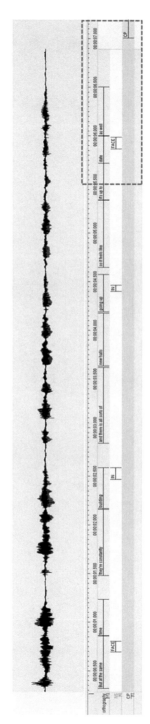

Figure 1.2.5a Listener evaluations of vernacular realisations of FACE and ING in the woman's speech.

46 *Erez Levon et al.*

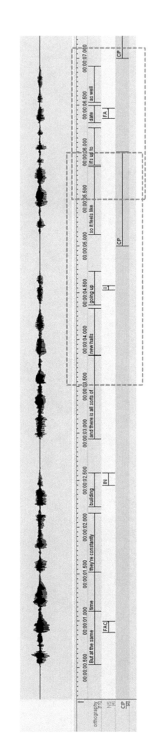

Figure 1.2.5b Listener evaluations of vernacular realisations of FACE and ING in the man's speech.

perception of phonetic features that Labov et al. (2006, 2011) discuss. Rather, our listeners appear to require multiple tokens of phonetic variants in order to arrive at a consolidated evaluative reaction. It is important to note that our experiment differs from the classic sociolinguistic monitor studies (e.g., Labov et al. 2011; Levon and Fox 2014; Levon and Buchstaller 2015) in that our stimuli are embedded in naturally occurring vernacular speech rather than in the prestige standard. We therefore hypothesise that when occurring in a lectally focussed stretch of talk, containing ample socio-indexical material (cf. Sharma 2011), listeners require multiple occurrences of phonetic variation before they arrive at a clear and consistent evaluative judgment (cf. Montgomery and Moore 2018).

The difference in perceptual reactions to phonetic versus morphosyntactic features could also be due to the multitude of overt prescriptive norms associated with variation at different levels of grammar and, consequently, with the types of processing involved in evaluating phonetic versus morphosyntactic forms. During processes of standardisation, many English syntactic and morphosyntactic features are codified (i.e., enshrined in prescriptive canon) and thus function as linguistic shibboleths, sharply stratifying social groups (Cheshire et al. 2005; Buchstaller 2009). On the other hand, phonological variation is typically more gradient, with frequencies generally varying in proportion to a speaker's position in relation to a social class hierarchy (Trudgill 1974; Walker, this volume). Given the stark social stratification of grammatical forms (Cheshire 1999; Cheshire et al. 2005), and especially in the context of the social meaning tested in this experiment (namely ratings on a "professionalism" scale), it might not be surprising that one vernacular token of a morphosyntactic variable is sufficient to trigger consistent and measurable responses amongst our respondents. In contrast, listeners may not be prepared to rate a speaker on the basis of a single occurrence of a vernacular phonetic feature, instead waiting for cumulative instances of the feature, allowing them to form a perception based on broader probabilistic patterns.[4] Overall, we interpret the results from Figures 1.2.2 to 1.2.5 as preliminary evidence that in naturally-occurring vernacular speech, listeners may need to encounter multiple occurrences of non-standard phonetic variation in order to arrive at an evaluative profile of a speaker, whereas, for non-standard morphosyntactic variables, this process seems to happen more quickly and on the basis of a single token. We acknowledge that our argument is at a very preliminary stage and requires further empirical investigation. Nevertheless, we believe that the patterns exhibited above could be indicative of the social meanings these variables index as well as the role that different levels of linguistic architecture may play in structuring listeners' perceptual responses to socially meaningful patterns of variation.

Finally, while all of the vernacular features discussed above were shown to reduce the perceived professionalism of the speakers, there is one exception in our data: the occurrence of a *zero* subject relative

48   *Erez Levon et al.*

increased listeners' evaluations of the speaker's professionalism (see Figure 1.2.6). While *zero* forms in object position, as in (8), are acceptable in standard varieties of British English, speakers of North-Eastern varieties also regularly use *zero* forms in subject position, as in (7) (see Buchstaller and Corrigan 2015):

(7) The facilities are open to students ø come to university.
(8) The students ø we've recruited were very good.

Figure 1.2.6 reveals that our respondents react to the occurrence of a vernacular *zero* form like the one in (7) by rating the woman as sounding more professional (note the steep positive and significant increment of the ratings curve for the speaker at around three seconds, which is well within the 1.5 seconds margin we are using). The occurrence of a glottal stop in the word *university* just after the *zero* relative form appears to counteract the positive effect on evaluations, as evident in the flattening of the ratings curve (though we acknowledge that the change-point analysis is not fine-grained enough to capture this change).

We propose that the apparent positive evaluative effect for the *zero* subject relative is due to the moment-by-moment nature of speech processing. Real-time perceptions are formed on the fly, based on continuous real-time audio stimuli. Given the frequent occurrence of standard *zero* object relatives in written and other prototypically formal genres, our respondents might have formed a general association between *zero* relatives and formal registers of speech (Ball 1996; Beal and Corrigan 2007). If correct, this analysis would indicate that listeners perceive the *zero* relative as a signal of formality, ignoring the specific syntactic context in which it occurs (and the prescriptive language ideologies associated with subject versus object relatives).[5] In other words, this could be a sort of "perceptual hyper-correction", where a given form (in this case, *zero* relative marking) is treated as indexical of formal speech even when it occurs in a non-standard syntactic position. We could further argue that this interpretation is supported by the final upwards trend in the ratings curve, which sees a marked rise in listeners' overall evaluations. In all other stimuli, evaluations tended to decrease over the course of the utterance, as non-standard features accumulated. Here, however, the occurrence of a form that is (falsely) associated with formal speech could leave a lasting and measurable evaluative impression. While this positive evaluative response might have been counterbalanced temporarily by the occurrence of a glottal stop, it may also have a lasting longer-term effect that persists even in the presence of clearly vernacular forms such as Hyper-s and alveolar realisations of ING. While we concede that this argument is highly speculative, we nevertheless contend that such a finding lends further support to the notion that morphosyntactic features, in particular those that have undergone standardisation and thus carry potent indexical weight, can serve as important perceptual diagnostics of a speaker's social status. More generally, we would also argue that the evaluative pattern in Figure 1.2.6 indicates that even relatively complex linguistic features, such as those that require the resolution of gapping in relative clauses, can trigger perceptual reactions.

In making these arguments, it is important for us to note that the analyses we provide here are exploratory in nature. Change-point analyses are not correlational and make no predictions whatsoever about what may be driving patterns of evaluative change. Rather, CPA is a quantitative data-mining procedure, the results of which must then be qualitatively interpreted in relation to the speech signal. Thus, while CPA solutions are distinct from the results of more traditional variationist analyses, we believe they provide useful information about average patterns of evaluation among listeners and, in particular, help us to pinpoint specific features of interest for future study. Once such features have been identified, the findings reported here can be implemented in different types of regression modelling procedures and/or in matched-guise experiments in order to obtain more robust correlational evidence regarding the ways in which variables influence perceptual evaluations, and how such evaluative patterning may differ across social groups. We have begun experimenting with using generalised additive models (GAMs) as a way of doing this and will report on the results of our GAM modelling in future research.

1.2.4 Conclusion

One of the principal goals of sociolinguistic cognition research is to develop an ecologically valid model of sociolinguistic perception that provides an integrated view of the different factors (social, linguistic and cognitive) influencing how listeners ascribe social meaning to variation. To date, empirical studies have struggled to document the dynamic and contingent nature of sociolinguistic perception in real-time (Watson and Clark 2015; Montgomery and Moore 2018). To a large extent, this challenge is due to the difficulty of using current methods to track what hearers notice and how they interpret the socio-indexical information they encounter in everyday talk. In this chapter, we reported on our initial research on the sociolinguistic processing of cumulative instances of vernacular features at different levels of linguistic architecture in speech from the North-East of England. The findings derived from this work suggest that while respondents are sensitive to phonetic and morphosyntactic features in real-time, the two types of features differ in their characteristic response patterns. Indeed, while our results are preliminary, they suggest that when it comes to how professional a speaker sounds, morphosyntactic features may trigger perceptual reactions very quickly (after a single occurrence), while phonetic features, in contrast, appear to require cumulative occurrences before eliciting significant evaluative contrasts. We hypothesise that the difference between the two types of variable may be due to overt prescriptive norms associated with different levels of

50   *Erez Levon et al.*

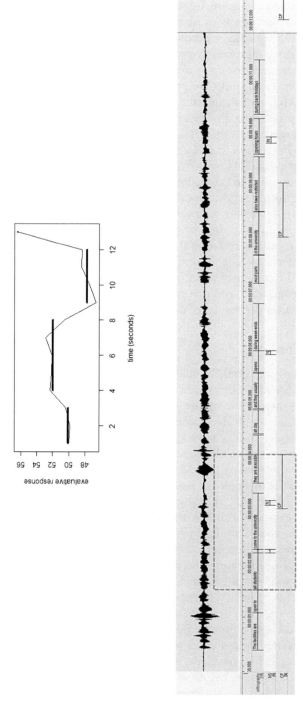

Figure 1.2.6 Listener evaluations of a *zero* subject relative in the woman's speech.

Towards an Integrated Model of Perception 51

variation, as well as to the cognitive processing required to evaluate phonetic versus morphosyntactic variables in context. Thus, while this line of research is in its earliest stages, we nevertheless hope to have demonstrated the importance of adopting a real-time approach to the study of sociolinguistic cognition and to have further highlighted that both phonetic and morphosyntactic variables are able to carry socio-indexical meaning (Cheshire 1982, 1999, 2009), although the meanings of these variables (at least in terms of professionalism) appear to be perceived and cognitively processed in systematically different ways. Finally, while this method resulted only in monodimensional data (e.g., movements up and down a single scale of professionalism), in future research we aim to explore the ways in which listeners incrementally update perceptual interpretations of features based on a number of evaluative dimensions.

Notes

1 We did not collect information about respondent level of education or other possible indicators of socioeconomic background. While we concede that some of the features we examine (particularly the non-standard morphosyntactic forms) may be evaluated differently as a function of listener social class, our primary goal in this chapter is to provide an initial exploration of methods for identifying which combinations of features are identified by listeners. Future work will examine social and psychological parameters that may further constrain these response patterns.

2 We experimented with the length of the time window. Given our relatively short stimuli (7–15 seconds), we found that 1.5 seconds was the most appropriate window for our experimental set up (compared to the 2 seconds used by Watson and Clark 2015). This meant that some of the possible reactions to the pre-selected linguistic cues fall outside of this time bracket and we would encourage future research investigating how to determine such windows in a more principled fashion. Note, too, that we did not calibrate our analyses for global reaction time differences among listeners. This is another dimension that could be profitably included in future research (see also Montgomery and Moore 2018).

3 Recall that listeners were from the North-East and North-West of England and from Scotland. It is entirely possible (and even likely) that listeners from different regions would react to these features differently (see, e.g., Bailey 2018 on differences in perceptual evaluations among listeners from the North of England). Future research will explore differences due to listener provenance. For the current discussion, however, we focus on global reactions to phonetic versus morphosyntactic variables.

4 While there is some evidence that one vernacular token of a phonetic variable is enough to trigger retrospective reactions (see e.g., Mendes 2016), our findings suggest that in the context of the North-East, speakers are not immediately reacting to sociophonetic variables, as shown at different axes of indexicality: (ING) is a supralocally available variable indexing the educated standard, while the complex FACE variable contains three variants that index local [ɪə], generally northern [eː] and southern-standard [eɪ] identities. Hence, while the consistency of the CPA results allow us to state with some confidence that our listeners do not display immediate and consistent reactions to the occurrence of the first tokens of these variables, the time lag involved in retrospective testing might allow such reactions to emerge.

52 *Erez Levon et al.*

5 It would be very interesting to test whether the same voice would be perceived as professional-sounding with an overt relative pronoun and with(out) the glottal stop in *university*, though we leave this for a future study.

References

Bailey, George. 2018. *Variation and Change in Northern English Velar Nasals: Production and Perception.* Unpublished Ph.D. thesis, University of Manchester.

Ball, Catherine. 1996. "A diachronic study of relative markers in spoken and written English". *Language Variation and Change* 8(2):227–258.

Beal, Joan and Karen Corrigan. 2007. "'Time and Tyne': A corpus-based study of variation and change in relativization strategies in Tyneside English". In *Germanic Language Histories 'from Below' (1700–2000)*, S. Elspaß, N. Langer, J. Scharloth and W. Vandenbussche (eds.). Berlin: Walter de Gruyter. 99–114.

Beal, Joan, Burbano-Elizondo, Lourdes and Carmen Llamas. 2012. *Urban North-Eastern English: Tyneside to Teesside.* Edinburgh: Edinburgh University Press.

Becker, Michael and Jonathan Levine. 2013. *Experigen: An Online Experiment Platform.* Available at http://becker.phonologist.org/experigen.

Buchstaller, Isabelle. 2016. Investigating the Effect of Socio-Cognitive Salience and Speaker-Based Factors in Morpho-Syntactic Life-Span Change". *Journal of English Linguistics* 44(2): 199–229.

Buchstaller, Isabelle. 2009. "The quantitative analysis of morphosyntactic variation: Constructing and quantifying the denominator". *Language and Linguistics Compass* 3(4):1010–1033 (doi:10.1111/j.1749-818X.2009.00142.x).

Buchstaller, Isabelle and Karen Corrigan. 2015. Morphosyntactic features of Northern English. In Hickey, Raymond (ed.) *Researching Northern English*, 71–98. Amsterdam: John Benjamins.

Buchstaller, Isabelle, Anne Lerche, and Adam Mearns. 2017. "Down to a (t): Exploring the complex conditioning effects on t-glottaling across the life-span". In Paper presented at *International Conference on Language Variation in Europe (ICLaVE)*, University of Malaga.

Buchstaller, Isabelle, Anne Krause, Anja Auer and Stefanie Otte. 2017. Levelling across the life-span? Tracing the FACE vowel in panel data from the North East of England. *Journal of Sociolinguistics* 21(1): 3–33.

Buchstaller, Isabelle, Karen Corrigan, Anders Holmberg, Patrick Honeybone, and Warren Maguire. 2013. T-to-R and the Northern Subject Rule: questionnaire-based spatial, social and structural linguistics. *Journal of English Linguistics* 17(1): 85–128.

Campbell-Kibler, Kathryn. 2007. "Accent, (ing), and the social logic of listener perceptions". *American Speech* 82(1):32–64.

Campbell-Kibler, Kathryn. 2008. "I'll be the judge of that: Diversity in social perceptions of (ING)". *Language in Society* 37(5):637–659.

Campbell-Kibler, Kathryn. 2009. "The nature of sociolinguistic perception". *Language Variation and Change* 21(1):135–156.

Campbell-Kibler, Kathryn. 2011. "Intersecting variables and perceived sexual orientation in men". *American Speech* 86(1):52–68.

Cheshire, Jenny. 1982. *Variation in an English Dialect: A Sociolinguistic Study.* Cambridge: Cambridge University Press.

Cheshire, Jenny. 1987. "Syntactic variation, the linguistic variable and sociolinguistic theory". *Linguistics* 25:257–282.

Cheshire, Jenny. 1999. "Spoken standard English". In *Standard English: The Widening Debate*, T. Bex and R. J. Watts (eds.). London: Routledge. 129–148.

Cheshire, Jenny. 2005. "Syntactic variation and beyond: Gender and social class variation in the use of discourse-new markers". *Journal of Sociolinguistics* 9(4):479–509.

Cheshire, Jenny. 2009. "Syntactic variation and beyond". In *The New Sociolinguistics Reader*, N. Coupland and A. Jaworski (eds.). Basingstoke: Palgrave Macmillan. 119–135.

Cheshire, Jenny, Paul Kerswill and Ann Williams. 2005. "Phonology, grammar and discourse in dialect convergence". In *Dialect Change: Convergence and Divergence of Dialects in Contemporary Societies*, P. Auer, F. Hinskens and P. Kerswill (eds.). Cambridge, UK: Cambridge University Press. 135–167.

Childs, Claire. 2013. Verbal –s and the Northern Subject Rule: Spatial variation in linguistic and sociolinguistic constraints. In: Ernestina Carrilho, Catarina Magro & Xosé Alvarez (eds.), *Current approaches to limits and areas in dialectology*, 311–344. Newcastle upon Tyne: Cambridge Scholars.

Drager, Katie and M. Joelle Kirtley. 2016. "Awareness, salience, and stereotypes in exemplar-based models of speech production and perception". In *Awareness and Control in Sociolinguistic Research*, M. Babel (ed.). Cambridge: Cambridge University Press. 1–24.

de Haas, Nynke K. 2011. *Morphosyntactic variation in Northern English: The Northern Subject Rule, its origins and early history.* Utrecht: LOT Publications.

Eckley, Idris A., Paul Fearnhead and Rebecca Killick. 2011. "Analysis of change-point models". In *Bayesian Time Series Models*, D. Barber, A. Cemgil and S. Chiappa (eds.). Cambridge: Cambridge University Press. 205–224.

Haddican, Bill, Paul Foulkes, Vincent Hughes and Hazel Richards. 2013. Interaction of social and linguistic constraints on two vowel changes in Northern England. *Language Variation and Change* 25:371–403.

Hay, Jennifer, Katie Drager and Andy Gibson. 2018. "Hearing r-sandhi: The role of past experience". *Language* 94(2):360–404.

Hesson, Ashley and Madeline Shellgren. 2015. "Discourse marker *like* in real time: Characterizing the time-course of sociolinguistic impression formation". *American Speech* 90(2):154–186.

Killick, Rebecca, Paul Fearnhead and Idris Eckley. 2012. "Optimal detection of changepoints with a linear computational cost". *Journal of the American Statistical Association* 107(500):1590–1598.

Killick, Rebecca and Idris A. Eckley. 2014. "Changepoint: An R package for changepoint analysis". *Journal of Statistical Software* 58(3). (doi:10.18637/jss.v058.i03).

Labov, William, Sharon Ash, Maya Ravindranath, Tracey Weldon, Maciej Baranowski and Naomi Nagy. 2006. "Listeners' sensitivity to the frequency of sociolinguistic variables". *University of Pennsylvania Working Papers in Linguistics* 12(2):105–129.

Labov, William, Sharon Ash, Maya Ravindranath, Tracey Weldon and Naomi Nagy. 2011. "Properties of the sociolinguistic monitor". *Journal of Sociolinguistics* 15(4):431–463.

Levon, Erez. 2014. "Categories, stereotypes and the linguistic perception of sexuality". *Language in Society* 43(5):539–566.

Levon, Erez and Isabelle Buchstaller. 2015. "Perception, cognition and linguistic structure: The effect of linguistic modularity and cognitive style on sociolinguistic processing". *Language Variation and Change* 27:319–348.

Levon, Erez and Sue Fox. 2014. "Salience and the sociolinguistic monitor: A case study of ING and TH-fronting in Britain". *Journal of English Linguistics* 42(3):185–217.

McCafferty, Kevin. 2003. The Northern Subject Rule in Ulster: How Scots, how English? *Language Variation and Change* 15, 105–39.

McCafferty, Kevin. 2004. '[T]hunder storms is verry dangese in this countrey they come in less than a minnits notice . . . ': The Northern Subject Rule in Southern Irish English. *English World-Wide* 25, 51–79.

Mendes, Ronald Beline. 2016. "Non-standard plural Noun Phrase agreement as an index of masculinity". In *Language, Sexuality and Power: Studies in Intersectional Sociolinguistics*, E. Levon and R. Beline Mendes (eds.). Oxford: Oxford University Press. 105–129.

Montgomery, Chris and Emma Moore. 2018. "Evaluating S(c)Illy voices: The effects of salience, stereotypes, and co-present language variables on real-time reactions to regional speech". *Language* 94(3):629–661.

Pharao, Nicolai and Marie Maegaard. 2017. "On the influence of coronal sibilants and stops on the perception of social meanings in Copenhagen Danish". *Linguistics* 55(5):1141–1167.

Pharao, Nicolai, Marie Maegaard, Janus Møller and Tore Kristiansen. 2014. "Indexical meanings of [s+] among Copenhagen youth: Social perception of a phonetic variant in different prosodic contexts". *Language in Society* 43(1):1–31.

R Core Team. 2019. *R: A Language and Environment for Statistical Computing*. Vienna: R Foundation for Statistical Computing.

Sankoff, Gillian. 1973. "Above and beyond phonology in variable rules". In *New Ways of Analyzing Variation in English*, C.-J. Bailey and R. Shuy (eds.). Washington, DC: Georgetown University Press. 44–62.

Sharma, Devyani. 2011. "Style repertoire and social change in British Asian English". *Journal of Sociolinguistics* 15(4):464–492.

Tagliamonte, Sali A., Alexandra D'Arcy & Bridget Jankowski. 2010. "Social work and linguistic systems: Marking possession in Canadian English". *Language Variation and Change* 22(1): 1–25.

Trudgill, Peter. 1974. *The Social Differentiation of English in Norwich*. Cambridge: Cambridge University Press.

Wagner, Suzanne Evans and Ashley Hesson. 2014. "Individual sensitivity to the frequency of socially meaningful linguistic cues affects language attitudes". *Journal of Language and Social Psychology* 33(6):651–666.

Watson, Kevin and Lynn Clark. 2013. "How salient is the NURSE~SQUARE merger?" *English Language and Linguistics* 17(2):297–323.

Watson, Kevin and Lynn Clark. 2015. "Exploring listeners' real-time reactions to regional accents". *Language Awareness* 24(1):38–59.

Watt, Dominic and Lesley Milroy. 1999. "Patterns of variation and change in three Newcastle vowels: Is this dialect levelling?" In *Urban Voices: Accent Studies in the British Isles*, P. Foulkes and D. Watt (eds.). London: Arnold. 25–46.

1.3 Prestige Factors in Contact-Induced Grammatical Change

Devyani Sharma

1.3.1 Introduction

A number of new speech varieties have emerged in London through in-migration and contact in recent decades. Multicultural London English (MLE; Cheshire et al. 2011) is a major new dialect that has arisen out of multiethnic contact in working-class parts of East London. In other parts of London, particularly West London, a more monoethnic variety of British Asian English (BAE) has developed, with particularly distinctive phonetic features (Sharma 2011; Sharma and Sankaran 2011). Comparing these two contemporaneous developments in the city, Fox and Sharma (2017) found that, even in two Asian-dominant neighbourhoods, marginally different socioeconomic conditions or 'micro-ecologies' have led to very different linguistic feature pools, and types and rates of change. In particular, different patterns of housing and schooling, which can arise from even slight income differences, lead to radically different dialect outcomes. MLE emerged and diffused rapidly in East London. It has shown a tendency to innovate rather than replicate parent dialects and exhibit these innovative traits at all linguistic levels. By contrast, the more ethnically homogeneous lower-middle-class BAE in West London has developed more gradually with less radical change, incorporating Indian English elements more directly from the parent generation (Sharma and Sankaran 2011).

To date, these comparisons have been limited to phonetic features. This study extends the comparison between MLE and BAE to morpho-syntax, focussing on three questions:

1. Grammatical system: Does morphosyntax across generations of British Asians in West London resemble that of Standard Southern British English (SSBE), Indian English (IndE), traditional London vernacular (Cockney)[1] or MLE?
2. Sources of change: How do we account for observed morphosyntactic patterns? Is the primary influence from British peers (Cockney among older British Asians, MLE among younger), family (IndE), prestige (SSBE), or linguistic factors (e.g., frequency in input,

56   Devyani Sharma

typological predictions)? What is the balance of structural and social factors in observed change?

3. Do morphosyntactic and phonetic change seem to follow similar trajectories over generations? If not, why not?

Using data from first-generation (Gen 1) and from older and younger second-generation (Gen 2) Punjabi-heritage British Asians in West London, the study analyses four morphosyntactic features: *was/were* levelling, *a* allomorphy, *the* allomorphy, and the quotative system. In the case of the two features that are more stigmatised (when in contact with prescriptive norms, Chambers 2004; Gabrielatos et al. 2010) – *was/were* levelling and *a* allomorphy – we find an abrupt shift to SSBE-like usage among older and younger Gen 2 speakers, with no usage that resembles IndE, MLE, or Cockney, despite the robust presence of these features in the environment of Gen 2 individuals. By contrast, for the two less stigmatised features – quotative use and *the* allomorphy – we see slightly more influence of London vernacular and IndE on BAE speakers. A comparison between these findings and previous findings for many phonetic features of BAE suggests that phonetic divergence is more robust than morphosyntactic divergence in BAE.

The findings show that lower-middle-class British Asians in London avoid the two more 'risky' morphosyntactic features, moving away from parent and peer forms that have either strong working-class or learner indexicalities. By adopting a combination of high prestige SSBE and elite IndE forms, they create an ethnically marked but upwardly mobile grammatical style. In this way, prestige accounts for the findings for all four grammatical variables more consistently than frequency in parent speech, frequency in British counterparts' speech, or structural level of the variant in question.

MLE morphosyntactic features are not found to be prevalent in the speech of lower-middle-class British Asians, supporting the view that multiethnolects emerge under very specific micro-ecological conditions within the city (Cheshire et al. 2011; Fox and Sharma 2017). Only a couple of individuals in the BAE dataset have isolated instances of MLE morphosyntax and phonology, and these are exclusively the youngest and most working-class in the entire dataset, suggesting that MLE use in West London is recent and restricted to working-class networks.

The findings strongly suggest that dialect shift is not entirely mechanistic: it involves selectivity based on competing prestige valuations, often overriding frequency in input and accommodating non-local, transnational influences.

1.3.2 Background and Data

At 7.5% of the total population (Census 2001), South Asians are the largest non-White ethnic group in the UK, with 35.9% of British South Asians living in London. In the post-war period, the UK faced severe labour shortages and encouraged labour migration from former colonies through the British Nationality Act of 1948. This initially permitted unrestricted entry to the UK from the Commonwealth. The Asian population in the UK grew substantially until 1971, before a series of immigration acts began to limit numbers, but migration has continued to the present day.

The British Asian data used in this study were collected in Southall, a suburb within the West London borough of Ealing. Since the mid-twenty-first century, Southall has attracted Punjabi speakers from across South Asia and East Africa. It is considered the historic heart of the British Punjabi community, encompassing large numbers of Sikh, Hindu, and Muslim Punjabis. Demographic estimates vary (Census 2011; DMAG 2006; Ealing JSNA 2010), but it is reasonable to estimate that the Asian population is well over 60% and that the overall ethnic minority population exceeds 80%.

The population of Southall includes both foreign-born (first generation, or Gen 1) and British-born (Gen 2 and Gen 3) residents. Members of the Gen 1 group were born in South Asia and migrated to the UK in adulthood; this group is continually renewed through ongoing migration. Due to their continuous arrival, the Gen 2 group – born in London to migrant parents – has a very diverse age range. The earliest British-born are now in their 50s, even 60s, but children being born now to recent India-born migrants are also technically Gen 2 individuals. In past work I have shown that the recent history of Southall is crucial to understanding ethnicity and language variation in the area. In particular, it points to two broad phases, which led to starkly different life experiences for Gen 2 individuals of different ages and different accent repertoires according to age (Sharma 2011; Sharma and Sankaran 2011).

Fieldwork was conducted over nine months by two fieldworkers. Data of three broad types were collected: sociolinguistic interviews and social background questionnaires (on network, language use, and cultural practices) with 75 individuals and self-recordings with ten individuals. Sociolinguistic interview data from a representative sample of 24 individuals across three generations (Gen 1, Gen 2 older, Gen 2 younger; 4 men and 4 women per group) are the basis of the present analysis.

1.3.3 Predictions for Grammatical Change

In considering which morphosyntactic variables to examine in BAE, we can look at two broad sources of grammatical structure in contact situations: retentions from the exogenous variety of (often L2) English spoken by the Gen 1 parent generation, and adoption of forms specific to the local varieties of English spoken in London. To examine the latter category of local London influences, it is necessary to consider both class and ethnic complexity. In the class dimension, 'London' may refer to

58 *Devyani Sharma*

the variety of higher-class strata (SSBE) or lower strata (MLE; Estuary English; Cockney English). In the ethnic dimension within lower-class strata, 'London' speech can refer to traditional Anglo (autochthonous White) speech, such as Cockney or other Cockney styles, particularly as a peer variety that was prevalent in the environment of older British Asians growing up in the 1970s and 1980s. Or it can refer to MLE, a more recent and more multiethnic variety, more prevalent in the wider London context for younger British Asians growing up in the 1990s.

The study therefore makes four broad comparisons of BAE (as spoken by older and younger Gen 2, or British-born, individuals), to IndE, SSBE, Cockney, and MLE. These are associated with three broad hypotheses for sources of change in contact:

Hypothesis 1 (IndE) – orientation to parent norms

If IndE syntactic patterns are retained in some form among Gen 2 individuals, we can conclude that 'vertical' parent/generational influence is significant and that being local-born does not necessitate an abrupt shift away from the exogenous system. Chambers (2002) proposes that an exogenous parent variety should not exert such an effect. For phonetic features of BAE across older and younger Gen 2, Sharma and Sankaran (2011) found only partial support for Chambers's prediction: they did find an abrupt shift in the system of glottal replacement of /t/, reflecting an effect of being local-born, but gradual reallocation and bidialectalism in the use of IndE retroflex /t/ over two generations (cf. Trudgill 2004), mirroring changes in social demographics and race relations rather than native speaker status.

There are in fact two versions of Hypothesis 1 – superficial retention of elements of parent traits by Gen 2 but not the full system (as in Hoffman and Walker 2010) and deep retention of Gen 1 grammars with bidialectal ability in the first Gen 2 generation, which was shown for phonetic features for this sample of speakers (Sharma 2011; Sharma and Sankaran 2011). The comparison data for IndE will come from Gen 1 speakers, all of whom migrated as adults from South Asia and have not significantly restructured their grammars.

Hypothesis 2 (SSBE) – orientation to local overt prestige norms

If SSBE is prevalent in Gen 2, we can conclude that Gen 2 is discounting both parent speech and vernacular British peer speech in favour of a high prestige variety (cf. Drummond 2013).

Hypothesis 3 (MLE/Cockney) – orientation to local peer norms

If varieties of London vernacular are prevalent, we can conclude that Gen 2 is showing an abrupt shift towards local native peer group norms, as widely predicted in sociolinguistic theory (Chambers 2009:171). For the older Gen 2, Cockney would be the relevant British peer norm (older Gen 2 men can adopt a Cockney phonetic style and some older speakers have Cockney phonetic features in their routine speech, see Sharma and

Prestige Factors in Grammatical Change 59

Rampton 2015). For the younger Gen 2, features of MLE may be the relevant peer norm.

The comparison data will therefore come from two different groups reported on in recent studies of MLE (e.g., Cheshire et al. 2011): white working-class (age 65+) Havering speakers and young multiethnic (age 16–19) Hackney speakers. I examine four morphosyntactic features that differ across the four varieties in contact with BAE: *was/were* levelling, indefinite article allomorphy, definite article allomorphy, and the quotative system. Of these, the first two are more stigmatised, for example being more subject to corrective input in educational and other prescriptive contexts (Chambers 2004; Gabrielatos et al. 2010).

Variable patterns of levelling of *was/wasn't* and *were/weren't* have been reported for London (Cheshire 1999; Cheshire and Fox 2009), in some ways mirroring wider patterns of levelling (Tagliamonte 1998; Anderwald 2001; Britain 2002; Schreier 2002; Chambers 2004). Crucial for the present discussion is the difference between what has been described as 'Pattern 1', namely levelling to *was* across person and number in the affirmative and to *wasn't* in the negative, as opposed to 'Pattern 2', which also sees levelling to *was* in the affirmative but retention of markedness of negation with a distinct form, *weren't*, for negative contexts (Cheshire et al. 2011). Pattern 1 is more common, arising around the world in situations of contact, acquisition, and dialects where the standard variety has limited influence, and described as a 'vernacular universal' (Chambers 2004). Pattern 2 is widespread across the UK in large urban areas and is associated with indigenous, Anglo-British communities (Britain 2002; Cheshire and Fox 2009). The study compares 615 *was/were* tokens across the three Asian generations to secondary data from Cheshire and Fox (2009) of older Havering and young Hackney usage.

Indefinite article allomorphy is a morphophonological alternation in SSBE, such that the indefinite article takes the form of *an* when preceding a vowel, in order to resolve vowel-vowel hiatus. SSBE speakers very rarely violate this rule: Raymond et al. (2002) found that only 3.4% of responses violated the standard rule, with some influence of stress placement and spelling. However, there has been a documented reduction in the use of *a~an* allomorphy in new varieties of English in London, particularly MLE and other high-contact East London speech (Fox 2007; Gabrielatos et al. 2010). Indefinite article allomorphy is also variable in IndE and tends to be higher among non-native or less dominant users of English. The study examines 1159 tokens of *a/an* across the three Asian generations and in corresponding British comparison groups.

Definite article allomorphy is a parallel morphophonological alternation in SSBE, whereby *the* takes on the form [ði] when preceding a vowel, again to resolve vowel-vowel hiatus. This system has also seen

60   *Devyani Sharma*

a reduction in use among high-contact East London English speakers in recent years (Fox 2007; Britain and Fox 2009). Absence of definite article allomorphy is the norm in IndE, but unlike indefinite article allomorphy this is not limited to L2 speakers. It is a feature of the speech of native and dominant English speakers in South Asia too, and may be on the rise globally (cf. Meyerhoff et al. 2018). As with indefinite article allomorphy, we can ask whether West London Asian speakers have mirrored this recent development in their grammatical system. The study examines 1,500 tokens of *the* across the three Asian generations and in corresponding British comparison groups.

Finally, the quotative system of English has been studied extensively (e.g., Tagliamonte and Hudson 1999; Buchstaller 2014). Once again, the focus in the present comparative study is specifically on the degree of resemblance between British Asian speakers' usage and that of their same-age British cohorts and that of Gen 1 IndE speakers. Seven hundred twenty-four tokens of quotative verbs are examined alongside these comparison groups.

Multivariate analysis is not used in the present study for two reasons: first, we see sharp declines in most non-standard forms over time, and so most variables have very low instantiations of non-standard variants, and second, this study is a brief, exploratory comparison of a range of variables rather than a complete analysis of a single variable.

1.3.4 Results

1.3.4.1 *Was/Were* **Variation**

The four ambient dialect systems mentioned for the three hypotheses above make different predictions for what we might expect to see in BAE usage of past tense forms of *be*:

Hypothesis 1 (IndE): High rates of non-standardness as found in L2 speakers, particularly default levelling to *was/wasn't*, found in many global vernaculars (Chambers 2004).

Hypothesis 2 (SSBE): Little variation except with existential subjects (Walker 2007).

Hypothesis 3a for older group (Cockney): Levelling to *was* in the affirmative and *weren't* negative clauses (a traditional urban British system, 'Pattern 2' in Britain 2002; Chambers 2004; Cheshire et al. 2011).

Hypothesis 3b for younger group (MLE): Levelling to *was/wasn't* (newer system found in high-contact urban British English and global vernaculars; 'Pattern 1' in Britain 2002; Chambers 2004; Cheshire et al. 2011).

Prestige Factors in Grammatical Change 61

Figure 1.3.1 reports on the usage of *was/were* variation found among older and younger Gen 2 BAE speakers. The relevant comparison groups are also included: Gen 1 for Hypothesis 1 (IndE), Havering speakers for Hypothesis 3a (Cockney), and young Hackney speakers for Hypothesis 3b (MLE), details drawn from Cheshire and Fox (2009). The SSBE system for Hypothesis 2 predicts low values for all three categories and is not represented explicitly by a comparison group.

Figure 1.3.1 shows an early shift away from IndE usage. We see a sharp drop off in the use of non-standard *wasn't* in the Older Gen 2 BAE speakers, a feature that is common in the primarily L2 speech of Gen 1. The comparison to Cockney and MLE cohorts shows that BAE speakers are more standard than their British counterparts with regard to this feature, and so are also not tracking London vernacular usage. We see no instances of the traditional British non-standard *weren't* levelling, and we also see low-level use of *was* with plural subjects. Figure 1.3.2 shows that the use of *was* with plural subjects by BAE speakers is almost exclusively in existential constructions (e.g., *There was kids who just didn't want to learn*). The slight increase between older and younger

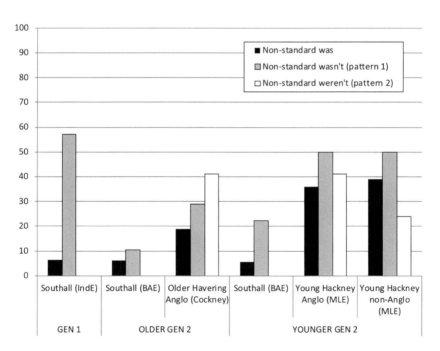

Figure 1.3.1 Percentage use of non-standard *was/were* forms across British Asian generations and relevant comparison groups (n: Gen 1 = 101, older Gen 2 = 214; younger Gen 2 = 187).

BAE speakers is also in this domain (e.g., *There wasn't computers*). This parallels a general increase in the use of levelled *was/wasn't* with existentials (Tagliamonte 1998), and so only indicates that BAE speakers are tracking changes in the standard system, not increasing their vernacular style for this variable.

These low BAE rates mirror the standard system (SSBE), confirming Hypothesis 2. SSBE is of course widely present in the social networks of British-born lower-middle-class Asians and so certainly diffuses to this group via networks. However, non-standard vernacular and parent variants are also present in this feature pool. As *was/were* levelling is a stigmatised feature, we can provisionally interpret this as a reluctance to adopt non-standard variants of this variable.

Gender and class skewing in the data support this. Three of the four non-standard *wasn't* forms used by Gen 2 BAE speakers were produced by men (e.g., *There wasn't any Christians*), and while non-standard *was* forms are balanced across gender in the older group, in the younger Gen 2 group they are mainly accounted for by one more working-class man (1.1% for women, e.g., *There was like animals grazing everywhere*, note a potential effect of proximity to the verb here (see Tagliamonte 1998:173) versus 10% for men, e.g., *Intoxicants was a big thing*).

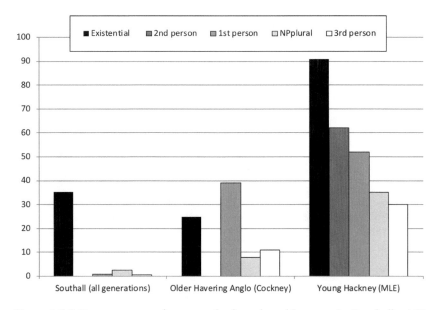

Figure 1.3.2 Percentage use of non-standard *was* by subject type (n: Southall = 467, Havering = 122, Hackney = 699).

Prestige Factors in Grammatical Change 63

Figures 1.3.1 and 1.3.2 show a clear difference between levels of use of non-standard *was/were* forms among West London South Asians as compared to young working-class speakers in East London. However, these figures mask an important similarity, namely that within the MLE data, the only South Asian subgroup (of Bangladeshi heritage) had the lowest use of non-standard *was/wasn't* and had no use of non-standard *weren't*. Cheshire and Fox (2009:18–19, 30) speculate that this may be due to social insularity and L2 speaker status early in life, with young Bangladeshi British children being more reliant on school English when their English use increases. Even though their friendship networks expand later, this early acquisitional context may affect their grammar. This is quite distinct from the early linguistic socialisation of Anglo and Afro-Caribbean MLE speakers but is comparable to that of other South Asians elsewhere in London.

Thus, although BAE speakers resemble SSBE for this feature, there is a subtle parallel to Bangladeshi-heritage MLE speakers too. This may arise out of a similar lack of network ties outside the community in early childhood in both South Asian groups, as suggested for Bangladeshi-heritage MLE speakers. It is worth noting, however, that the phonetic systems of the two groups are very finely tuned to their respective peer groups (Sharma and Sankaran 2011; Fox 2015) and do not reflect such social isolation. This may be something that develops through later peer group ties. The comparison to other morphosyntactic features below will point to the possibility of an additional influence, namely the greater social risk associated with non-standard grammatical (as opposed to phonetic) forms, which can be seen as more direct signals of low competence or learner status. BAE speakers' phonetic choices – a mix of SSBE and elite IndE – are discussed later and support this interpretation. It is also possible that literacy plays a part in the absence of such variants among these lower middle-class BAE speakers.

It is worth commenting briefly on a few further trends in Figures 1.3.1 and 1.3.2 that relate not to the social basis of variation but to the universal syntactic and semantic effects noted in the literature. First, across these very disparate contact and heritage groups, we can see a sustained preference for levelling in negation, in line with universal typological predictions of levelling in contexts of negative polarity to mark this marked context (Payne 1985). The results are also clearly in line with a more English-specific generalisation that greater levelling of agreement will be found in existential constructions. Chambers (2004:140) attributes this to the different 'look-forward' basis for agreement with the predicate in such constructions. By contrast, the wider prediction made in Chambers (2004) and related work (Tagliamonte 1998; Schreier 2002) for the ordering of non-standardness by subject type, although perfectly instantiated in the MLE ordering, is not reflected in the other two data sets in Figure 1.3.2.

64 *Devyani Sharma*

1.3.4.2 Indefinite Article Allomorphy

We see a similar sharp drop in BAE use of another stigmatised feature that is prevalent in both IndE and MLE: namely the absence of allomorphy in the use of the indefinite article. In the case of this variable, we can predict the following competing influences on BAE speakers:

Hypothesis 1 (IndE): Absence of indefinite article allomorphy, characteristic of IndE
Hypothesis 2 (SSBE): Standard use of *an* before vowels
Hypothesis 3a for older group (Cockney): Standard use of *an* before vowels
Hypothesis 3b for younger group (MLE): Absence of indefinite article allomorphy (Gabrielatos et al. 2010; Fox 2015)

Figure 1.3.3 shows that both older and younger BAE speakers have very SSBE-like use of the indefinite article, with almost no instances of the use of *a* rather than *an* before a following vowel. Once again, we see an early and sustained shift away from a Gen 1 feature and avoidance of any tracking of contemporary vernacular MLE usage. Again, this is a feature that is associated with learner English and so may risk being heard as having limited competence, a concern that is heightened for recently 'nativised' speakers (Sharma 2005). This compromises its availability for identity work. Usage is also likely to be reduced by higher

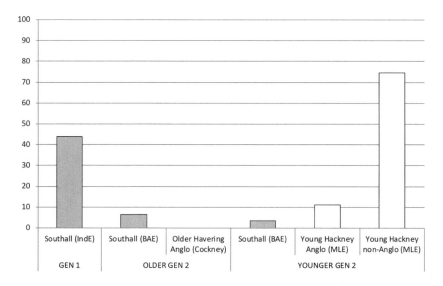

Figure 1.3.3 Absence of indefinite article allomorphy across British Asian generations (grey bars) and relevant comparison groups (white bars) (n: Gen 1 = 25, older Gen 2 = 79; younger Gen 2 = 116).

levels of literacy due to its visible spelling contrast. (Many morphosyntactic changes in the history of English have been impervious to the presence of explicit contrasts in the written form, but literacy can play a part when explicit proscription is present). It is interesting to note that these lower-middle-class British Asian speakers are quite different from more working-class Bangladeshi British young people, who were found by Fox (2015) to have the highest levels of absence of indefinite article allomorphy. Social class – whether active class affiliation or simply access to variants – plays an important role here. Once again, we see confirmation of Hypothesis 2, with an orientation to SSBE (and implicitly also Cockney, though that is not likely the indexical target) rather than IndE or MLE.

1.3.4.3 Definite Article Allomorphy

In the case of definite article allomorphy, we predict the following competing influences on BAE speakers:

Hypothesis 1 (IndE): Absence of definite article allomorphy, characteristic of IndE

Hypothesis 2 (SSBE): Standard usage of [ði] before vowels

Hypothesis 3a for older group (Cockney): Standard usage of [ði] before vowels

Hypothesis 3b for younger group (MLE): Absence of definite article allomorphy (Britain and Fox 2009; Fox 2015)

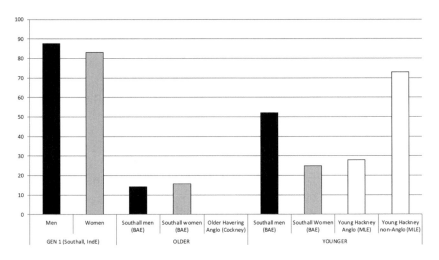

Figure 1.3.4 Absence of definite article allomorphy across British Asian men (black bars), women (grey bars), and relevant comparison groups (white bars) (n: Gen 1 = 136, older Gen 2 = 169; younger Gen 2 = 166).

66   *Devyani Sharma*

Figure 1.3.4 shows a distribution that is quite different from what was observed earlier for *was/were* variation and for indefinite article allomorphy. Whereas Gen 1 migrants had some use of indefinite article allomorphy – perhaps for reasons of literacy and salience – their English shows a near-total absence of definite article allomorphy. In the two Gen 2 groups, we see a non-linear distribution. Older Gen 2 BAE speakers show a sharp drop in rates of use of this feature as compared to Gen 1 IndE speakers. In contrast to both of the previous variables examined, however, this decline in use is not maintained among the younger Gen 2 group. This group shows a significant increase in absence of definite article allomorphy (χ^2 (1) = 24.59, p < .001) – a so-called 'boomerang' effect over generations. The younger group's usage also shows a new gendering in usage in Figure 1.3.4, with significantly higher use (χ^2 (1) = 12.43, p < .001) by young men. Their usage (52.3%) approaches the level of use found among non-Anglo MLE speakers, but only for this feature.

This feature shows clearly that frequency in Gen 1 parents' IndE usage is not a determinant of later use in Gen 2 groups. The high frequency of use does not lead to higher rates among the older Gen 2, nor does it show a continued, incremental decline in the younger Gen 2. Why do we see this resurgent use among younger individuals for this feature but not the two earlier features? The main contrast to the previous two morpho-syntactic features is that definite article allomorphy is much less stigmatised, less salient, not visible in the written form, and present at low rates among speakers of standard varieties (Raymond et al. 2002; Meyerhoff et al. 2018). This might mean less risk in the use of this pattern, and less attention paid to eliminating it. However, this explanation should predict a continually declining distribution over BAE generations. It does not account for the dramatic drop in use in the oldest British-born group and the significant increase in the younger group. The older group appears to conform to British norms for this feature, also observable in their levels of glottal stop use and other indicators of needing to show conformity in an adverse social setting (Sharma and Sankaran 2011). The younger BAE group, who have encountered less hostility as community numbers grew, have developed a more fused British Asian identity, combining an upwardly mobile orientation to SSBE with a few phonetic features from educated IndE (not their parents' variety). They explicitly align with this variety of IndE, seeing it as an ethnically Asian speech variety associated with increasing global prestige. For example, a 19-year-old British Asian man remarked: "I think I've got quite a posh accent maybe ... [now] I want to have a bit of Indian tone to my voice, to show cultural heritage". Lack of definite article allomorphy fits well with this idealised combination of Asian ethnic indexicality and upwardly mobility SSBE. The low stigmatisation of this form also makes it a good choice for developing a vernacular style range, in line with MLE speakers for instance, without adopting their more socially salient syntactic forms. In short, we see potential support for a version of Hypothesis

1 (IndE) and Hypothesis 3b (MLE) in the use of definite article allomorphy. This is in contrast to the support for Hypothesis 2 (SSBE) that was found the two more stigmatised features.

Moving briefly again from social to linguistic factors, the one linguistic factor briefly examined was the stress placement of the following word. Healy and Sherrod (1994, cited in Raymond et al. 2002) found a significant non-first syllable effect in experiments with Standard American English speakers, though with very low overall rates of non-use. This constraint emerged in the younger BAE speakers (16% versus 57.1% absence of [ði] in first versus second or later syllables). Again, as with the predicted effects of negation or existential clause type in *was/ were* variation, we see here a persistence and independence of linguistic constraints from social constraints.

1.3.4.4 *Quotatives*

A full examination of quotatives is beyond the scope of this chapter, but I offer a broad comparison of BAE speakers to the four main parallel cohorts – IndE, SSBE, Cockney, and MLE – to explore correspondences among these systems. Like definite article allomorphy, many dimensions of this grammatical system are not stigmatised. The *be like* construction has become globally prevalent and is not nearly as marked as it once was. There is a very marked MLE quotative, *this is me*, but this is not attested at all in the BAE recordings.

Figures 1.3.5 and 1.3.6 show a very close tracking of same-age British cohorts by older and younger Gen 2 BAE speakers. In Figure 1.3.5, we see that the older BAE group closely parallels Cockney rates, such as high use of *say* and low use of *be like* and *think* (shown in with a dotted line), while the younger speakers in Figure 1.3.6 parallel their equivalent MLE cohort in significantly reducing their rates of *say* and expanding their use of *think* and *be like*. It is worth noting that the British comparison groups' quotative systems do not reflect generic settings for quotatives, such that most English speakers resemble these rates. MLE, and possibly young inner-city London speech more generally, has notably low rates of use of *be like* compared to many other young English speakers, who often exhibit rates of 50% or higher (Buchstaller 2014). So we can be confident that these distributions specifically track British cohorts' grammatical systems.

This is further supported by the non-replication of various finer details from Gen 1 IndE usage in Figure 1.3.5, e.g., the almost complete lack of use of *go*, lower rates of use of *say*, and higher rates of *zero* use (the latter includes non-standard constructions such as *tell that* and *tell OBJ that* for introducing quoted speech, a tendency that shows some traces of continued use among Gen 2 BAE speakers). It may be the case that patterns of use of quotatives are more acquirable across peers due to their high pragmatic load in interaction, lack of complex grammatical condition (unlike,

68 *Devyani Sharma*

e.g., *weren't* levelling), and low stigma. Here again, as with definite article allomorphy, we see support for a version of Hypothesis 1 (IndE) and Hypothesis 3 (Cockney, MLE), in contrast to the shift to SSBE (confirming Hypothesis 2) for the two more stigmatised features.

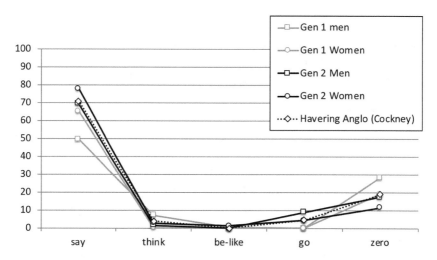

Figure 1.3.5 Quotative use among older Gen 2 BAE speakers and comparison IndE and Cockney groups (n: Gen 1 = 247, older Gen 2 = 189).

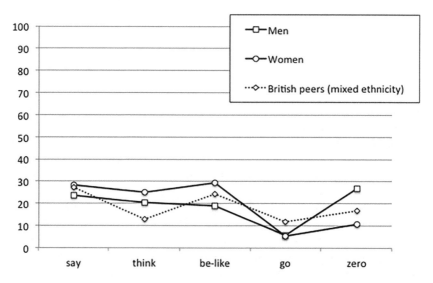

Figure 1.3.6 Quotative use among younger Gen 2 BAE speakers and comparison MLE group (younger Gen 2, n = 288).

1.3.5 Discussion and Conclusions

Two of the four features examined – *was/were* levelling and lack of indefinite article allomorphy – are more associated with strictly non-standard status, and are therefore stigmatised in terms of overt prestige in London. These are the two forms that lower-middle-class Gen 2 British Asians move away from very abruptly, despite their presence in their parents' speech. These features risk being heard not just as vernacular but as learner errors that mark low English competence. This may be why the community quickly distances itself from these forms.

In the case of the other two features – lack of definite article allomorphy and quotative use – stigmatisation is less clear and we do not see the same abrupt shift away from these forms. In the case of quotatives, we see close tracking of age-equivalent British groups (but no use of marked or non-standard MLE forms). In the case of definite article allomorphy, we actually see a marked increase in the use of this form among younger British Asian men. This last feature is associated with an educated/elite variety of IndE, one with increasing global presence and status; the other features, though present in their parents' variety of IndE, do not share this status. In short, the direction of grammatical change among younger Gen 2 British Asians constructs an upwardly mobile, globalised Asian identity, very different from the personae associated with MLE, and not clearly predicted by frequencies in parent or same-age cohorts.

A number of further IndE constructions crop up in the speech of Gen 2 individuals, shown in (1). However, these uses tend to be isolated, very low in frequency, and lexically restricted, and so are arguably not deep properties of the grammar.

(1)	a.	Article omission:	They think it's ø easy life.	(F 45, F 50)
	b.	Extended use of –*ing*:	I'm mostly watch<u>ing</u> TV.	(M 19)
	c.	Count-mass levelling:	They got their hair<u>s</u> in like ponytails and stuff.	(M 19)
	d.	Numerical approximation:	about <u>five-six</u> times after that	(M 19)
	e.	Reduplication:	<u>Slowly slowly</u> I will start getting into...; They got <u>different different</u> places.	(M 22, F 48, M 40)
	f.	Resumption:	I don't think <u>so</u> I can handle that.	(M 48)
	g.	Intensifiers:	People who were <u>so much</u> interested.	(M 42)

70   *Devyani Sharma*

Similarly, although we do not see any major mirroring of MLE grammatical systems, we do see isolated use of constructions common in MLE, but these are only found in the youngest and more working-class participants, e.g., *go cinema, go toilet, go prison, go school*. These are the same individuals in whom we find some presence of MLE phonetic forms too, suggesting only a recent and limited spread of MLE to West London via working-class networks.

How do these findings for morphosyntactic forms compare to what we see for phonetic forms? In the phonetic systems of these three generations of British Asians we observed gradual change and reallocation in several IndE features alongside abrupt (at the nativeness/local-born boundary) adoption of local forms such as glottal replacement of /t/ (Sharma and Sankaran 2011). Very few of these BAE speakers show a complete loss of IndE-derived phonetic forms, a notable contrast to their widespread loss of IndE-derived morphosyntax. The one type of phonetic feature that shows a similar rapid loss is associated with learner-like status, such as /v/~/w/ alternation. In the present study, BAE speakers' speech behaviour reflects this concern in a selective avoidance of syntactic forms associated with non-native or less educated status (cf. Sharma 2005), and generally greater use of accent for identity work. Further factors are also relevant: the continuous nature of many phonetic forms affords speakers a fine range of social indexicality (Podesva 2007; Eckert and Labov 2017), and, of course, the wholesale shift to the native acquisition of English among Gen 2 fundamentally transforms the extent and nature of variation in the system (Plag 2011).

MLE has been described in terms of group second language acquisition operating over a complex feature pool (Cheshire et al. 2011). The data presented here show that feature pools exist in socially structured space: both social structure (an individual's location in, and therefore exposure to, sociolinguistic space) and social ideology (evaluation of that sociolinguistic space).

Finally, several of the features supported predictions for internal constraints on variation, suggesting some independence of social and linguistic conditioning. And one feature illustrated the potential for boomerang effects in syntax, namely initial distancing from parent systems, possibly for reasons of social integration and survival, and a delayed expression of ethnic or vernacular affiliation, of 're-ethnicisation' (Silverstein 2003).

The stark contrast between how BAE and MLE have developed in West and East London simultaneously, just a subway ride apart, reminds us that we cannot treat London as a single speech community undergoing unified processes of change. Nor can we even speak of change within a single ethnic group within a city as a unified process, as seen here in the contrasts between South Asian Londoners who speak BAE and those who speak MLE.

Note

1 I use the term 'Cockney' here to aid readability throughout the article. The term is used here to refer to features of traditional London vernacular, all of which predate the emergence of MLE (Cheshire, Edwards, and Whittle 1989). Relevant overlaps and contrasts from MLE are clarified in the course of the chapter.

References

Anderwald, Liselotte. 2001. "Was/were variation in non-standard British English today". *English World-Wide* 22(1):1–21.

Britain, David. 2002. "Diffusion, levelling, simplification and reallocation in past tense BE in the English Fens". *Journal of Sociolinguistics* 6(1):16–43.

Britain, David and Sue Fox. 2009. "The regularisation of hiatus resolution in British English". In *Vernacular Universals and Language Contact*, M. Filppula, J. Klemola and H. Paulasto (eds.). New York: Routledge. 177–205.

Buchstaller, Isabelle. 2014. *Quotatives: New Trends and Sociolinguistic Implications*. Oxford: Wiley-Blackwell.

Census 2001. United Kingdom Office for National Statistics, accessed on 8 May 2020 from https://www.ons.gov.uk/census/2011census.

Chambers, J.K. 2002. "Dynamics of dialect convergence". *Journal of Sociolinguistics* 6(1):117–130.

Chambers, J.K. 2004. "Dynamic typology and vernacular universals". In *Dialectology Meets Typology: Dialect Grammar from a Cross-Linguistic Perspective*, Vol. 153. B. Kortmann (ed.). Berlin: de Gruyter. 127–145.

Chambers, Jack. 2009. *Sociolinguistic Theory*, revised edition. Oxford: Wiley-Blackwell.

Cheshire, Jenny. 1999. "Spoken standard English". In *Standard English: The Widening Debate*, T. Bex and R. Watts (eds.). London: Routledge. 129–148.

Cheshire, Jenny and Sue Fox. 2009. "*Was/were* variation: A perspective from London". *Language Variation and Change* 21:1–38.

Cheshire, Jenny, Viv Edwards and Pamela Whittle. 1989. "Urban British dialect grammar: The question of dialect levelling". *English World-Wide* 10(2):185–225.

Cheshire, Jenny, Paul Kerswill, Sue Fox and Eivind Torgersen. 2011. "Contact, the feature pool and the speech community: The emergence of multicultural London English". *Journal of Sociolinguistics* 15(2):151–196.

DMAG (Data Management and Analysis Group, Greater London Authority) Briefing, 2006. Accessed on 3 November 2010 from www.london.gov.uk.

Drummond, Rob. 2013. "The Manchester Polish STRUT: Dialect acquisition in a second language". *Journal of English Linguistics* 41(1):65–93.

Ealing JSNA (Joint Strategic Needs Assessment) report. 2010. Accessed on 3 November 2010 from: http://www.ealingpct.nhs.uk/Publications/needs-assessment.asp

Eckert, Penelope and William Labov. 2017. "Phonetics, phonology, and social meaning". *Journal of Sociolinguistics* 21(4):467–496.

Fox, Susan. 2007. The demise of Cockneys? Language change in London's 'traditional' East End. Ph.D. thesis, University of Essex.

Fox, Susan. 2015. The new Cockney: New ethnicities and adolescent speech in the traditional East End of London. Basingstoke: Palgrave Macmillan.

72 Devyani Sharma

Fox, Susan and Devyani Sharma. 2017. "The language of London and Londoners". In *Urban Sociolinguistics: The City as a Linguistic Process and Experience*. D. Smakman and P. Heinrich (eds.). London: Routledge. 115–129.

Gabrielatos, Costas, Eivind Torgersen, Sebastian Hoffman and Susan Fox. 2010. "A corpus-based sociolinguistic study of indefinite article forms in London English". *Journal of English Linguistics* 38(4):297–334.

Healy, Alice and Nancy Sherrod. 1994. "The/Thee pronunciation distinction: A local model of linguistic categories". In *Paper Presented at the 35th Annual Meeting of the Psychonomic Society*, St. Louis, MO.

Hoffman, Michol and James Walker. 2010. "Ethnolects and the city: Ethnic orientation and linguistic variation in Toronto English". *Language Variation and Change* 22:37–67.

Meyerhoff, Miriam, Elaine Ballard, Alexandra Birchfield, Helen Charters and Catherine Watson. 2018. "Definite change taking place: Determiner realization in multiethnic communities in New Zealand". In *Paper presented at NWAV 47, New York University*. October 20, 2018.

Payne, John R. 1985. "Negation". In *Language Typology and Syntactic Description*, Timothy Shopen (ed.). Cambridge: Cambridge University Press. 197–242.

Plag, Ingo. 2011. "Creolization and admixture: Typology, feature pools, and second language acquisition". *Journal of Pidgin and Creole Languages* 26(1):89–110.

Podesva, Robert J. 2007. "Phonation type as a stylistic variable: The use of falsetto in constructing a persona". *Journal of Sociolinguistics* 11(4):478–504.

Raymond, William, Julia Fisher, and Alice Healy. 2002. Linguistic knowledge and language performance in English article variant preference. Language and Cognitive Processes 17(6): 613–662.

Schreier, Daniel. 2002. "Past *be* in Tristan da Cunha: The rise and fall of categoricality in language change". *American Speech* 77:70–99.

Sharma, Devyani. 2005. Dialect stabilization and speaker awareness in nonnative varieties of English. *Journal of Sociolinguistics* 9:2: 194–225.

Sharma, Devyani. 2011. "Style repertoire and social change in British Asian English". *Journal of Sociolinguistics* 15(4):464–492.

Sharma, Devyani, and Ben Rampton. 2015. Lectal focusing in interaction: A new methodology for the study of style variation. *Journal of English Linguistics* 43(1):3–35.

Sharma, Devyani and Lavanya Sankaran. 2011. "Cognitive and social forces in dialect shift: Gradual change in London Asian speech". *Language Variation and Change* 23(3):55–76.

Silverstein, Michael. 2003. "The whens and wheres—as well as hows—of ethnolinguistic recognition". *Public Culture* 15(3):531–557.

Tagliamonte, S. 1998. "*Was/were* variation across the generations: View from the city of York". *Language Variation and Change* 10:153–192.

Tagliamonte, Sali, and Hudson, Rachel. 1999. *Be like* et al. beyond America: The quotative system in British and Canadian youth. *Journal of Sociolinguistics* 3: 147–172.

Trudgill, Peter. 2004. *New Dialect Formation: The Inevitability of Colonial Englishes*. Edinburgh: Edinburgh University Press.

Walker, James. 2007. "There's bears back there: Plural existentials and vernacular universals in (Quebec) English". *English World-Wide* 28(2):147–166.

1.4 The Role of Syntax in the Study of Sociolinguistic Meaning
Evidence from an Analysis of Right Dislocation

Emma Moore

1.4.1 Introduction

It has been argued that syntactic variables tend to have "quite fixed social meanings associated with external facts like class and particularly education" (Eckert 2018:190). However, as Cheshire has noted repeatedly (1987, 1999, 2005), the finding that syntactic variables are more sharply socially stratified than phonological variables is based on a limited analysis of a limited set of variables. Furthermore, the features typically studied tend to be at the morphological end of the morpho-syntactic continuum – most likely because they fit the definition of 'the linguistic variable' more easily (Romaine 1984; Winford 1996). Consequently, Cheshire (2005:87) notes that we simply do not know enough about syntactic variation in speech, given that the items selected for observation have tended to be those defined by their relationship with the codified written standard.

Nonetheless, recent interest in the socio-pragmatics of syntax (Acton and Potts 2014; Beltrama and Staum Casasanto 2017; forthcoming; Acton forthcoming; Glass 2015) is transforming what it means to talk about syntactic variation and its social meanings. These studies have shown how the pragmatic function of syntactic items may be exploited by speakers to make social meaning in interaction. For instance, Acton and Potts (2014) consider the context-dependent semantics of demonstratives, showing how they can be utilised to suggest a sense of shared perspective between interlocutors. This potential is then available to speakers to promote alignments with interlocutors, thus becoming a stylistic resource which may be used variably by individuals. Studies have also suggested that grammatical formulation itself is a resource for meaning-making. For instance, Beltrama and Staum Casasanto (forthcoming) explore how the grammatical properties of intensifiers contributes to their socio-indexical value – such that the intensifiers *totally* in US English and *–issimo* in Italian are perceived to more markedly index speaker qualities (such as friendliness or excitability) when they occur

74 *Emma Moore*

with predicates that cannot be scaled or graded (compare *the bus is totally full* with *she was totally born 25 ago*). Their work suggests that the social meaning of intensifiers is dependent upon the precise syntax of the phrase containing them.

As with more traditional variationist studies of morphosyntax, these emerging socio-pragmatic studies have tended to focus on linguistic features at the lexical end of the morphosyntactic spectrum; for instance, Acton and Potts (2014) focus on demonstratives, Beltrama and Staum Casasanto (2017, forthcoming) examine intensifiers, and Glass (2015) considers modal verbs. To add to this emerging field of research, this chapter will present a socio-pragmatic analysis of a more 'purely' syntactic phenomenon: right dislocation (RD).

RD refers to the occurrence of a clause followed by a noun phrase or pronoun tag which is co-referential with the preceding subject or object pronoun; for instance, *She's lovely, her mum* or *I've not got an accent, me*. RD (also known as 'postponed identification' and 'tails') is described as common in colloquial British English (Huddleston and Pullum 2002:1408; Shorrocks 1999:85; Wales 1996:43), but there are few empirical accounts of its social distribution. Moore and Snell (2011) suggest that it is found more frequently in data from Northern English speakers who are either categorised as working-class (a finding further explored in Snell (2018)) or are in communities of practice which orient towards working-class practice. Durham (2011), the only other variationist study available on RD, does not include class in the analysis but finds some ambiguous gender and age differences in how RD forms are distributed.

Whilst the data on the social distribution of RD is sparse, there exist several accounts of its discourse function (Aijmer 1989; Carter and McCarthy 1995; Guo 1999; Ziv 1994). In line with previous cross-linguistic work on the right periphery of the clause (Ashby 1988; Fretheim 1995; Lambrecht 2001), these studies suggest that RD has expressive, evaluative and/or affective functions. This suggests that RD is available for socio-pragmatic work. As mentioned above, Moore and Snell (2011) and Snell (2018) suggest that the types of meanings communicated by RD are exploited particularly effectively by speakers engaged in working-class social practice, suggesting an indexical link between the pragmatic function of RD tags and 'working-class'. Nonetheless, precisely how this indexical link is mediated by the grammatical formulation of RD tags themselves remains unclear.

In order to further explore the socio-pragmatic function of RD, this chapter considers how the social and grammatical distributions of RD interact to create social meaning. It does so by considering how different social groups of speakers combine subject type of the tag with verb processes – material, mental, relational, behavioural and verbal (Halliday 1985) – and evaluative stance. Notwithstanding critiques of

Halliday (see, e.g., Levin 1993 for a more comprehensive account of verb typology), Halliday's verb processes are considered because they offer a window on the semantics of the verb phrase, enabling (a somewhat imprecise, but nonetheless instructive) consideration of the types of 'experience' expressed through the use of RD (see Kirkham and Moore (2016) for a similar approach combining quantitative and qualitative analysis). Evaluative stance is considered in order to examine how speakers orient to the content of the token of RD (in line with other studies on the construction of social meaning in interactions, e.g., Kiesling 2009). The subject type of the main clause preceding the RD tag is considered to infer how the use of RD relates to the particular persons evaluated.

The findings reveal that the precise grammatical environment in which RD occurs may intensify or attenuate its pragmatic function, such that different social groups interact with this variable in socially meaningful and socially nuanced ways. By interrogating the intersection of pragmatic function, grammatical formulation, and social distribution, the analysis shows that syntactic variables can have quite nuanced and flexible social meanings, which only indirectly index abstract "external facts like class and ... education" (Eckert 2018:190). This has wider implications for how we think about the effects of linguistic environment on syntactic variation. In most variationist studies, linguistic environment (e.g., subject or verb type) is included in order to separate linguistic constraints from social ones, but these findings suggest that non-categorical linguistic constraints (i.e., linguistic factors which have a probabilistic effect on whether or not a variant occurs) and social meaning may be intertwined in complex ways. This possibility is suggested by Bender (2001) and further evidenced here.

1.4.2 Data and Methodology

This chapter analyses 354 tokens of RD collected during a two-year ethnography of 39 female adolescents at a high school (Midlan High) in the north-west of England. The ethnographic materials comprise over 50 hours of recordings, a 262,000-word corpus, and 196,400 words of fieldwork notes. The ethnography uncovered four distinct communities of practice (CofPs): the Eden Villagers, the Geeks, the Populars and the Townies. The CofPs were variably orientated along a pro-/anti-school continuum, with the Eden Villagers and Geeks considerably more pro-school than the Populars, and the Townies more anti-school than any other CofP. Previous analyses of other morphosyntactic variables used by this community have shown patterns associated with social class categories, but these patterns are not as robust as the correlations with CofP membership (Moore 2010). This reflects the actuality that an individual's CofP membership does not generally correlate with their social class category, with the exception of the Eden Village CofP (all members

76   *Emma Moore*

of which come from the highest social class groups and reside in the same village three miles from the school).

Instances of RD were extracted from recordings of peer interactions. These generally took the form of informal recordings sessions in which girls relayed information about their daily lives and activities. In the analysis presented here, instances of RD were initially sorted by tag type (for a fuller analysis of RD coding in this corpus see Moore (2003: Chapter 4)). At Midlan High, RD tags can be (1) full noun phrases (i.e., where a full noun form as opposed to a pronoun is used), (2) demonstrative pronouns, (3) personal pronouns, and (4) non-finite verb phrases or clauses, as shown below.

(1) *He's weird, my dad* (Kim, Popular)
(2) *That really did my head in, that* (Michelle, Geek)
(3) *He's on drugs, him* (Meg, Townie)
(4) *It's quite funny, coming to secondary school* (Alex, Eden Villager)

Aligning with Quirk et al. (1985:1310), who refer to RD as "postponed identification", Huddleston and Pullum (2002:1411–1412) suggest that noun phrase tags have a clarifying function. In example (1), the information in the tag, "my dad", provides additional detail that is not retrievable from the initial pronoun "he" alone. They note that speakers may use a pronoun in subject or object position, only realising that it is not clear what the pronoun refers to until after it has been uttered. The tag, then, is added as clause-final information to identify the preceding pronoun. Consequently, it is argued that RD tags occur as a consequence of delayed "utterance processing" (Huddleston and Pullum 2002:1411).

Whilst this may be true for noun phrase tags – and indeed, non-finite verb or clause tags, like that in (4) – this cannot be true for pronoun tags, which lack this explicit giving-of-information function. For instance, the tags in (2) and (3) simply reiterate the previous subject in an object form (the unmarked case for pronouns in the absence of case assigning information; cf. Denison (1998:109–110)), making the 'what' or 'who' of the subject no more explicit than the previous reference to it. This provides further support for RD having distinct pragmatic functions, such as being expressive, evaluative or affective, as noted above.

In order to investigate how pronoun tags function, tokens containing personal pronouns ($n = 101$) were also coded for the verbal processes of the verb contained in the preceding main clause. This was undertaken to obtain a sense of the states or actions articulated by the verb itself and to determine to whom these states or actions were assigned. The verb process types used in the analysis are given in Table 1.4.1.

The personal pronoun tags were also coded for the evaluative stance expressed towards the subject in the clause associated with the RD tag. The term "stance" has been defined in a number of ways in

Role of Syntax in Sociolinguistic Meaning 77

sociolinguistics (Jaffe 2009; Kockelman 2004), but most approaches use the term to refer to inferences that can be made about the speaker's alignment with the content of their talk or to their interlocutors. This analysis considers what can be inferred about a speaker's alignment with the person referenced by the main clause's subject. This was determined qualitatively by close listening to the data and consideration of the context in which the token was uttered. Evaluative stance was coded as positive, negative and neutral, and examples are given in Table 1.4.2. Note that the stance represents how the speaker orients to the subject of the main clause; in the example from Michelle, below, the clause is negated, but Michelle is expressing a positive evaluation of herself in this context (she is the 'good girl' who has never had a detention).

Table 1.4.1 Verb process types used in the analysis according to Halliday (1985)

Verb process	*Processes*	*Example from dataset*
Material	'doing'	*I'm going out, me* (Tanya, Geek)
Mental	'sensing'	*I'd hate to do that, me* (Cindy, Popular)
Relational	'being'	*He's a muppet, him* (Ellie, Townie)
Verbal	'saying'	*I talk dead high, me* (Georgia, Popular)
Behavioural	'sensing represented as external behaviour'	*He were knocking me sick, him* (Amanda, Townie)

Table 1.4.2 Evaluative stances expressed in the context of RD use

Evaluative stance to subject	*Example from dataset*	*Context*
Positive	*I've never had a detention, me* (Michelle, Geek)	Michelle is contrasting her own behaviour to a peer's, who is portrayed negatively for being expelled from school
Negative	*You're tight, you* (Meg, Townie)	Meg is criticising Kim (represented by 'you') for monopolising all of the sweets they are sharing
Neutral	*Oh, that's where she lives, her* (Georgia, Popular)	Georgia is telling Emma that Jennifer (also present, represented by 'she/her') lives on the same road as a friend of Emma's who has just moved house

78 Emma Moore

By considering the subject type of the tag, the process of the verb associated with the tag, and the evaluative stance towards the tag's co-referential subject in the main clause, it is possible to observe distinct patterns of socio-pragmatic variation which correlate with the differential behaviour of the CofPs compared in this analysis. These patterns are described in the next section.

1.4.3 Results

1.4.3.1 Frequency and Distribution of RD Tags

Figures 1.4.1 and 1.4.2 show how RD use correlates with social class and CofP at Midlan High. Each data point in the figures represents one person in the study; for instance, in Figure 1.4.2, each individual member of the Eden Village CofP is shown as a white circle. Social class was determined using an index that calculated scores based on parental education and occupation, and home address/house price (see Moore 2003:82).

Comparison of the two figures suggests a neater correlation with CofP than with social class. Whilst, generally, individuals categorised in the lowest social classes (3 and 4) have higher frequencies of RD (note in particular that the two highest users of RD are members of Class 4), there is a clearer correlation between RD use and CofP in Figure 1.4.2; generally speaking the Eden Villagers and the Geeks are found in the lower half of the dataset, and Populars and Townies are found in the upper half of the dataset.

The differences in how CofPs use RD is shown in more detail in Figure 1.4.3, which indicates how right-dislocated tags pattern by CofP

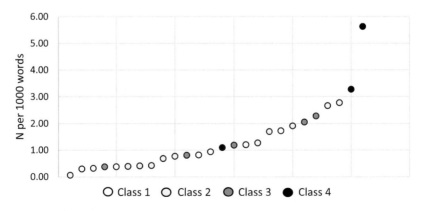

Figure 1.4.1 Frequency of RD per 1000 words according to social class (nb. Class 1 is the highest social class group and Class 4 is the lowest).

Role of Syntax in Sociolinguistic Meaning 79

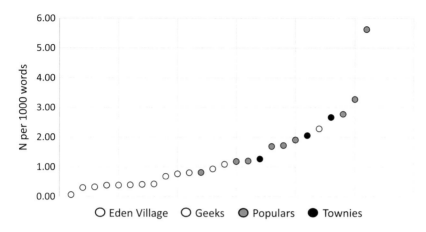

Figure 1.4.2 Frequency of RD per 1000 words according to community of practice.

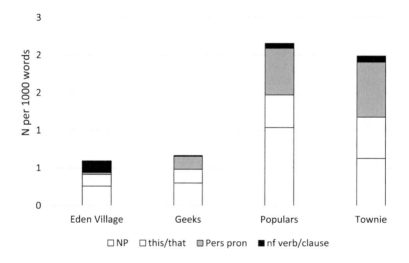

Figure 1.4.3 RD by type of right-dislocated tag, according to community of practice membership.

membership. In addition to showing that Populars and Townies use right-dislocated tags more than Eden Villagers and Geeks do, Figure 1.4.3 also shows differences in the type of tag each CofP tends to use. Whilst all groups use noun phrase, demonstrative pronoun, and non-finite verb phrase/clause tags, personal pronoun tags are more variably used. Eden Villagers scarcely use personal pronoun tags at all (there is only one personal pronoun tag in their entire dataset); Geeks use these less frequently than they use noun phrase tags (but at a similar frequency to demonstrative pronoun tags); Populars use personal pronoun tags less frequently than noun phrase tags but more frequently than demonstrative tags; and Townies use personal pronoun tags more frequently than any other type of tag.

In order to explore the distribution of pronoun tags, Figure 1.4.4 shows the type of personal pronoun tags used by each community of practice. Of the CofPs which show a range of personal pronoun types (note that the Eden Village group use only one personal pronoun tag – *He's a geek, him*; Ruth), the Geeks and the Populars use first-person pronoun tags at a greater frequency than any other type. Geeks never use second-person pronoun tags, and Populars only use one second-person pronoun tag (*You're a bitch, you*; Beverley). On the other hand, Townies make robust use of all types of personal pronoun tags, including second-person pronoun tags.

The data so far show the following notable patterns. First, there appears to be a more consistent correlation between CofP membership and RD use than there is between social class membership and RD use. The more anti-school CofPs use RD tags at more than twice the frequency of the more pro-school CofPs. Second, RD types are variably distributed across different CofPs. Noun phrases tags, demonstrative pronoun tags, and non-finite verb phrase/clause tags are robustly used by all CofPs.

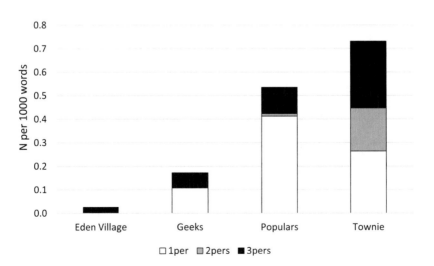

Figure 1.4.4 RD tags by personal-pronoun type, according to community of practice membership.

On the other hand, the distribution of personal pronoun tags seems to correlate with CofP membership. One of the most pro-school CofPs, the Eden Village group, use only one personal pronoun tag. The other pro-school group, the Geeks, use more first-person tags than third-person ones, and they do not use second-person tags at all. The anti-school groups (the Populars and the Townies) use all types of personal pronoun tags, although only the Townies (the most rebellious group), make robust use of second-person pronoun tags.

As noted earlier, noun phrase and non-finite verb phrase/clause tags may have information-giving functions which are not shared with pronoun tags. Another thing to note is that demonstrative pronoun tags, like examples (5) and (6), tend to reference events or artefacts. People are referenced in these constructions (e.g., the event in (5) refers to something another person did; the artefact discussed in (6) refers to an interpretation of another person's behaviour) but only indirectly. If the tag serves to emphasise an evaluation (as suggested in the discussion above), the evaluation is directed at the event or the artefact, rather than directly at a particular person. The same is not true where personal pronoun tags are used, as in (7–9). Here the referent is always a directly referenced person, although who is referenced depends upon the precise person of the pronoun. In (7) the referent is the speaker themself, in (8) it is someone else present in the interaction who is directly addressed, and in (9), it is another person who is typically (although not always) absent at the time of the interaction in which the tag occurs.

(5) *it really tickled me, that* (Michelle, Geek: about a friend who was singing the wrong song lyrics)
(6) *that's nasty, that* (Lindsey, Popular: about a piece of graffiti that claims a peer is sexually promiscuous)
(7) *I hate her nanna, me* (Tanya, Geek: about a peer's grandmother)
(8) *Aw, you well pissed me off, you* (Ellie, Townie: addressed to a friend)
(9) *He's fit, him* (Beverley, Popular: about the attractiveness of a male peer)

These differences in referent represent different levels of face-threat (Brown and Levinson 1987), with a most-to-least cline of second-person > third-person > first-person (given that evaluating someone directly to their face is potentially more offensive than evaluating someone who is – in most instances – absent, and that evaluating oneself has little to no impact on someone else's face). However, the degree of potential face-threat may be modulated by the degree to which the evaluation is negative and the precise nature of what it evaluated. In order to interpret these subtleties, the next section provides an analysis of how different social groups of speakers combine evaluative stances with personal

82 *Emma Moore*

pronoun tag type and verbal processes – material, mental, relational, behavioural and verbal (Halliday 1985).

1.4.3.2 Personal Pronoun Tags, Evaluative Stance and Verb Processes

In Figure 1.4.5, the top row shows the verb processes that co-occur with instances of right dislocation, and the bottom row shows the evaluative stances that co-occur with instances of right dislocation. The figure is arranged by personal pronoun type, with first-person pronouns on the left, second-person pronouns in the middle, and third-person pronouns on the right. The bars show patterns for each CofP where data are available.

Beginning with first-person pronouns, Figure 1.4.5 shows that, across CofPs, first-person pronoun tags are used in constructions which convey a wide range of verbal processes: material, mental, relational, behavioural, and verbal. For the most frequent users of these tags, the Populars and the Townies, mental processes are the most frequent. In practice, this means first-person pronoun tags most frequently occur in constructions that are likely to portray and evaluate the thoughts, perceptions, desires and affective states of the speakers themselves. However, the other verb process categories also occur robustly with first-person tags across CofPs. This suggests that first-person tags are also used in constructions that portray and evaluate speakers' actions ('material processes'), their attributes and identities ('relational processes'), their projection of internal states ('behavioural processes'), and their speech ('verbal processes').

Figure 1.4.5 also shows that first-person pronoun tags are used in constructions that articulate a range of evaluative stances across CofPs. For the most frequent users of these tags, the Populars and the Townies, first-person pronoun tags most frequently occur in statements where the subject is positively evaluated; however they also co-occur with negative and neutral evaluative stances.

Turning to second-person tags, Figure 1.4.5 shows that these tags are predominantly used in constructions that articulate relational processes. In practice, this suggests that they are predominantly used in statements that position and evaluate the attributes and identities of others. Figure 1.4.5 also shows that second-person pronoun tags most frequently occur in statements where the stance towards the subject of the main clause is negative.

Finally, like second-person pronoun tags, third-person pronoun tags are predominantly used to articulate relational processes. This means that they most frequently occur in statements that most likely position and evaluate the attributes and identities of others. Third-person pronoun tags are also predominantly used in constructions that articulate negative evaluative stances towards the subject of the main clause (but

Role of Syntax in Sociolinguistic Meaning 83

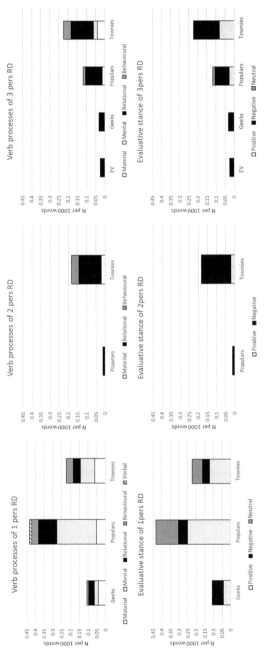

Figure 1.4.5 Verb processes and evaluative stances which co-occur with instances of Right Dislocation, according to personal pronoun tag and community of practice membership.

84 *Emma Moore*

note that there are proportionally more positive stances articulated with third-person tags than with second-person ones).

Given the patterns outlined above, we might surmise that first-person tags occur in constructions that dynamically present a wide range of speakers' evaluative stances towards their own thoughts, perceptions, desires, and experiences. The contexts in which second- and third-person tags occur is much narrower. They seem to predominantly occur in contexts that negatively evaluate someone else's identity or an attribute associated with an individual. In the case of second-person tags, the person evaluated is addressed directly, whereas the person evaluated is more typically absent from the current interaction in the case of third-person tags.

In the light of how personal pronoun types, verb processes and evaluative stances co-occur, we can reflect further on how personal pronoun types are distributed by CofP. Recall that, whilst all the CofPs who make robust use of personal pronoun tags (the Geeks, Populars and Townies) use first-person pronoun tags, the Populars and Townies make use of third-person pronoun tags much more frequently than the other groups, and only the Townies consistently use second-person pronoun tags (there is one token from a Popular speaker). Given what we know about the potential face-threat involved in the use of second- and third-person pronoun tags, and the typical Popular and Townies styles (anti-school, rebellious) this is not a surprising result. This is discussed further in the next section.

1.4.4 Discussion

This chapter began by considering how the syntactic configuration of RD determines its pragmatic function. As a constituent at the right of the clause periphery, RD has been identified as having intersubjective functions (Traugott 2012), such as attending to interpersonal relations or expressing evaluative stance. These functions have been identified in several previous studies on the discourse function of RD and are borne out by the data presented here.

By examining the precise grammatical environment in which RD occurs, it has been possible to show how pragmatic function interacts with the types of things people talk about and who they talk about. The intersubjective functions of RD mean that combining these constructions in particular ways results in varying levels of face-threat. So, whilst the frequency counts in Figures 1.4.1 and 1.4.2 demonstrate that all of the speakers studied are capable of producing RD tags, not all speakers fully exploit the range of grammatical environments in which RD can potentially occur. That certain subject types seem to be off-limits to certain groups implies a process where social and grammatical constraints interact. This suggests that the pragmatics of a syntactic construction are fundamental to its social distribution, such that the effect of the grammatical environment on the social value of a variant would follow from Gricean principles: if the speaker went out of his/her way to use a variant disfavoured by the environment, then s/he must be particularly interested in conveying the social value associated with that variant.

(Bender 2001:258)

That is to say, it is not necessarily the case that speakers avoid grammatical environments simply because of probabilistic variability in input/output, but also because certain syntactic configurations result in certain inferences.

The Townies' use of second-person pronoun tags is a case in point; here, grammatical environment intensifies the social meaning of a syntactic configuration. Like all forms of RD, second-person pronoun tags have the potential to be evaluative, but the subject of evaluation in these instances is another person who is typically present in the interaction. In this way, the function of RD creates a greater interactional risk when a second-person pronoun tag is used. That the Townies engage with this danger is evident from the co-occurring verb processes and stances. They not only directly evaluate an interlocutor, but they typically baldly express a negative evaluation of that person's identity or personal attributes. Compare this with the use of first-person pronoun tags. Here the risk is only to self; the full range of verb processes and stances are available because evaluating oneself carries few risks – indeed it can even be perceived positively as modesty or self-effacement. Consequently, this type of right dislocated tag is used by a wider range of individuals, irrespective of their persona type or style.

These findings suggest that the pragmatic function of RD itself directly influences the way in which speakers engage with it. It also reveals something about the way in which social meaning is constructed. We might think of social meaning as the set of inferences that can be drawn on the basis of how someone utters a proposition. For syntactic constructions, the core of this social meaning is rooted in the potential pragmatic functions enabled by the construction's grammatical configuration; for RD, this entails intersubjective functions, such as evaluation or expression of affect or alignment. Speakers may then make more or less use of a syntactic item by virtue of their exposure to it, the utility of its function in their discourse, and the ability to tailor its function to achieve communicative goals. As different types of people make more or less use of the RD, we may come to associate its use, not just with its pragmatic functions, but also with the interactional stances it conveys and/or the characteristics of the people who make the most use of it. In this way, the social meaning of RD may be associated with pragmatic function, stances, personae and social types. This is, of course, the process of indexicality as articulated by Ochs (1992), Silverstein (2003), and expanded elsewhere (Eckert 2008; Moore and Podesva 2009).

86   *Emma Moore*

How this meaning is ordered sequentially remains an open question and one which has not been fully resolved in the variationist literature on social meaning. For instance, it is not likely a coincidence (given Snell's 2018 findings) that the two girls with the most frequent use of RD at Midlan High are also in the lowest social classes. Opportunities to acquire and practice forms of RD may be more numerous in working-class communities than in middle-class ones. Furthermore, Moore and Snell (2011:106–107) suggest that the functions of RD index the transparent and candid forms of social interaction that typify intragroup working-class interactions. However, note too that, whilst the highest user of RD in the entire sample, Georgia, comes from the lowest social class group, 90% (18/20) of her personal pronoun tags are first-person ones. So, whilst her working-class status may have provided ample opportunities to acquire and practice RD, how she employs this form may be determined by more than her working-class status. By only exploiting a limited range of person types that co-occur with RD, Georgia may restrict the inferences drawn about her speech and, in doing so, she crafts a persona appropriate to her status as a Popular girl. Conversely, the highest Townie user of RD, Amanda, is in the second to highest social class grouping. Nonetheless, she is able to style her RD use to intensify her self-presentation as overtly evaluative, critical and candid. For Georgia and Amanda, the stylisation of linguistic practice is not a reflex of their social class status, but reflective and constructive of their social engagement and persona style.

This discussion exposes how the social meanings of RD are multifaceted and iteratively constructed. They may be rooted in pragmatic function, but they also reflect "what speakers choose to talk about" (Cheshire 2005:99) and how they choose to talk about them. As a syntactic construction, I would suggest that RD is not particularly notable in this regard. The implications of studying syntactic items like RD is considered further in the conclusion.

1.4.5 Conclusion

This chapter has proposed that the social meanings of syntactic variation are best accessed by considering the precise context of a feature's utterance. In considering context, it becomes possible to examine the inferences made about the speaker and the content of their talk. This type of research is essential if we are to fully appreciate how syntactic variables become socially meaningful. Despite early vigorous debate about the social meaning potentials of syntactic variation (Cheshire 1987; Dines 1980; Labov 1978; Lavandera 1978; Romaine 1984), variationist research on the social meaning of syntax continues to lag behind that on phonological variation. In part, this may be attributed to the narrow focus on how a limited set of morphosyntactic features correlate with broad demographic social categories (Cheshire 1987:257). Items selected for analysis (e.g., negative concord, adverbs, verbal agreement) tend to be highly codified, stigmatised features. However, there are many more purely syntactic constructions, like RD, which vary by pragmatic function and social use. These types of constructions have been the focus of recent work in the emerging field of syntactic micro-variation (a cross-linguistic approach to the analysis of syntactic structure that seeks to accounts for dialect variation, e.g., Brandner 2012). There is much potential for collaborations between sociolinguists and syntacticians to gain insight into the relationship between the semantics of syntactic structure and the social meanings constructed when these structures occur in social interaction (see, e.g., Burnett et al. 2018).

Although much of the current thinking on the social meanings of syntax – as laid out in this chapter – has been facilitated by advances in third wave variationist sociolinguistics (Eckert 2018), diverse ways of conceiving and investigating syntactic variation (i.e., going beyond the correlation of morphosyntactic variables and broad demographic categories) have been articulated by Cheshire in many of her publications across her career. In seeking to further develop our understanding of the role of syntactic variation in sociolinguistic meaning, Cheshire has highlighted issues discussed in this chapter, such as the need for sociolinguists to attend more closely to the unique properties of syntax (Cheshire 1987), our lack of insight into the syntactic variation (in its purest form) in speech (Cheshire 1999), the conflation of 'stigmatised' and 'non-standard' forms when assigning meaning to syntax (Cheshire 2005), and the role of syntactic variation in constructing interactional meaning (Cheshire et al. 2005). In proposing an analysis that considers the levels of social meaning communicated by a broader range of syntactic items, this chapter seeks to further our understanding of the issues so clearly and carefully outlined in Cheshire's seminal work.

References

Acton, Eric. forthcoming. "Pragmatics and the third wave". In *Social Meaning and Linguistic Variation: Theorizing the Third Wave*, L. Hall-Lew, E. Moore and R.J. Podesva (eds.). Cambridge: Cambridge University Press.

Acton, Eric K. and Christopher Potts. 2014. "That straight talk: Sarah Palin and the sociolinguistics of demonstratives". *Journal of Sociolinguistics* 18(1):3–31.

Aijmer, Karin. 1989. "Themes and tails: The discourse functions of dislocated elements". *Nordic Journal of Linguistics* 12:137–154.

Ashby, William. 1988. "The syntax, pragmatics, and sociolinguistics of left- and right-dislocation in French". *Lingua* 75:203–229.

Beltrama, Andrea and Laura Staum Casasanto. forthcoming. "The social meaning of semantic properties". In *Social Meaning and Linguistic Variation:*

88 *Emma Moore*

Theorizing the Third Wave, L. Hall-Lew, E. Moore and R. Podesva (eds.). Cambridge: Cambridge University Press.

Beltrama, Andrea and Laura Staum Casasanto. 2017. "Totally tall sounds totally younger: Intensification at the socio-semantics interface". *Journal of Sociolinguistics* 21(2):154–182.

Bender, Emily M. 2001. *Syntactic Variation and Linguistic Competence: The Case of AAVE Copula Absence.* California: Stanford University.

Brandner, Ellen. 2012. "Syntactic microvariation". *Language and Linguistics Compass* 6(2):113–130.

Brown, Penelope and Stephen C. Levinson. 1987. *Politeness: Some Universals in Language Usage.* Cambridge: Cambridge University Press.

Burnett, Heather, Hilda Koopman and Sali A. Tagliamonte. 2018. "Structural explanations in syntactic variation: The evolution of English negative and polarity indefinites". *Language Variation and Change* 30(1):83–107.

Carter, Ronald and Michael McCarthy. 1995. "Grammar and the spoken language". *Applied Linguistics* 16(2):141–158.

Cheshire, Jenny. 1987. "Syntactic variation, the linguistic variable, and sociolinguistic theory". *Linguistics* 25(2):257–282.

Cheshire, Jenny. 1999. "Taming the vernacular: Some repercussions for the study of syntactic variation and spoken grammar". *Cuadernos de Filologia Inglesa* 8:59–80.

Cheshire, Jenny. 2005. "Syntactic variation and spoken language". In *Syntax and Variation: Reconciling the Biological and the Social*, L. Cornips and Karen P. Corrigan (eds.). Amsterdam: John Benjamins. 81–106.

Cheshire, Jenny, Paul Kerswill and Ann Williams. 2005. "Phonology, grammar and discourse in dialect convergence". In *Dialect Change: The Convergence and Divergence of Dialects in Contemporary Societies*, P. Auer, F. Hinskens and P. Kerswill (eds.). Cambridge: Cambridge University Press. 135–167.

Denison, David. 1998. "Syntax". In *The Cambridge History of the English Language*, Vol. IV: 1776–1997, Suzanne Romaine (ed.). Cambridge: Cambridge University Press. 92–329.

Dines, Elizabeth R. 1980. "Variation in discourse – 'and stuff like that.'" *Language in Society* 9(1):13–31.

Durham, Mercedes. 2011. "Right dislocation in Northern England: Frequency and use – perception meets reality". *English World-Wide* 32(3):257–279.

Eckert, Penelope. 2008. "Variation and the indexical field". *Journal of Sociolinguistics* 12(4):453–476.

Eckert, Penelope. 2018. *Meaning and Linguistic Variation: The Third Wave in Sociolinguistics.* Cambridge; New York: Cambridge University Press.

Fretheim, T. 1995. "Why Norwegian right dislocated phrases are not afterthoughts". *Nordic Journal of Linguistics* 18(1):31–54.

Glass, Lelia. 2015. "Strong necessity modals: Four socio-pragmatic corpus studies". *Penn Working Papers in Linguistics* 21(2):77–88.

Guo, Jiansheng. 1999. "From information to emotion: The affective function of right-dislocation in Mandarin Chinese". *Journal of Pragmatics* 31(9):1103–1128.

Halliday, Michael A. K. 1985. *An Introduction to Functional Grammar.* London: Edward Arnold.

Huddleston, Rodney and Geoffrey K. Pullum. 2002. *The Cambridge Grammar of the English Language.* Cambridge: Cambridge University Press.

Jaffe, Alexandra (ed.). 2009. *Stance: Sociolinguistic Perspectives.* Oxford: Oxford University Press.

Kiesling, Scott F. 2009. "Style as stance". In *Stance: Sociolinguistic Perspectives*, Alexandra Jaffe (ed.). Oxford: Oxford University Press. 171–195.

Kirkham, Sam and Emma Moore. 2016. "Constructing social meaning in political discourse: Phonetic variation and verb processes in Ed Miliband's speeches". *Language in Society* 45(1):87–111.

Kockelman, Paul. 2004. "Stance and subjectivity". *Journal of Linguistic Anthropology* 14:127–150.

Labov, William. 1978. "Where does the sociolinguistic variable stop: A response to Beatriz R. Lavandera". *Working Papers in Sociolinguistics* 44.

Lambrecht, Knud. 2001. "Dislocation". In *Language Typology and Language Universals: An International Handbook*, volume 2, M. Haspelmath, E. Konig, W. Oesterreicher and W. Raible (eds.). Berlin: Walter de Gruyter. 1050–1078.

Lavandera, Beatriz R. 1978. "Where does the sociolinguistic variable stop?" *Language in Society* 7(2):171–182.

Levin, Beth. 1993. *English Verb Classes and Alternations: A Preliminary Investigation.* Chicago: University of Chicago Press.

Moore, Emma. 2003. *Learning Style and Identity: A Sociolinguistic Analysis of a Bolton High School.* Unpublished PhD dissertation. University of Manchester, ms.

Moore, Emma. 2010. "The interaction between social category and social practice: Explaining was/were variation". *Language Variation and Change* 22:347–371.

Moore, Emma and Robert Podesva. 2009. "Style, indexicality, and the social meaning of tag questions". *Language in Society* 38(4):447–485.

Moore, Emma and Julia Snell. 2011. "'Oh, they're top, them': Right dislocated tags and interactional stance". In *Language Variation – European Perspectives III*, F. Gregersen, J. K. Parrott and P. Quist (eds.). Amsterdam: John Benjamins. 97–110.

Ochs, Elinor. 1992. "Indexing Gender". In *Language as Interactive Phenomenon*, A. Duranti and C. Goodwin (eds.). Cambridge: Cambridge University Press. 335–358.

Quirk, Randolph, Sidney Greenbaum, Geoffrey Leech and Jan Svartvik. 1985. *A Comprehensive Grammar of the English Language.* London: Longman.

Romaine, Suzanne. 1984. "On the problem of syntactic variation and pragmatic meaning in sociolinguistic theory". *Folia Linguistica* 18(3–4):409–438.

Shorrocks, Graham. 1999. *A Grammar of the Dialect of the Bolton Area: Introduction, Phonology.* Frankfurt: Peter Lang.

Silverstein, Michael. 2003. "Indexical order and the dialectics of sociolinguistic life". *Language and Communication* 23:193–229.

Snell, Julia. 2018. "Solidarity, stance, and class identities". *Language in Society* 47(5):665–691.

Traugott, Elizabeth Closs. 2012. "Intersubjectification and clause periphery". *English Text Construction* 5:7–28.

Wales, Katie. 1996. *Personal Pronouns in Present-day English*. Cambridge: Cambridge University Press.

Winford, Donald. 1996. "The problem of syntactic variation". In *Sociolinguistic Variation: Data, Theory and Analysis. Selected Papers from NWAVE 23*, J. Arnold, R. Blake, B. Davidson, S. Schwenter and J. Solomon (eds.). Stanford University, USA: CSLI Publications. 177–192.

Ziv, Yael. 1994. "Left and right dislocations: Discourse functions and anaphora". *Journal of Pragmatics* 22(6):629–645.

Section 2

Combining the Social and the Grammatical

2.1 What Happened to Those Relatives from East Anglia? A Multilocality Analysis of Dialect Levelling in the Relative Marker System

David Britain

2.1.1 Dialect Contact, Dialect Levelling, and Uneven Mobilities

As a result of variationist and other dialectological investigations of language change over the last 30 years, evidence that England's traditional dialects have been undergoing attrition has been emerging thick and fast (Britain 2009). Much of the evidence we have for this comes from studies of phonological variation and change, which have, amongst other things, highlighted the levelling of localised or marked variants, the emergence of new variants from contact between old ones, the regional (re)invigoration of regional forms or the geographical and social spread of innovative and/or unmarked and/or majority forms (Trudgill 1986; Kerswill and Williams 2000; Britain 2005, 2018). Foulkes and Docherty's (1999) volume *Urban Voices*, for example, contains many case studies of such levelling across the British Isles and acted in many ways as a catalyst for others to track these changes in more places. It was generally agreed that one (if not the main) cause of these changes was mobility-induced dialect contact. One aim of some earlier work (Britain 2009, 2010) was to argue not just that such contact did indeed lead to levelling of traditional dialects, but that such mobility (bringing with it different ingredient language features into the local feature pool) was also the generator of new dialect forms and that mobility did not necessarily lead to an inevitable and unidirectional shrinking of dialect diversity but rather had the potential to increase such diversity as well. This has been best demonstrated in recent years by the large London English projects conducted by Jenny Cheshire, Paul Kerswill, Sue Fox, and Eivind Torgersen (e.g., Cheshire et al. 2011), projects which have critically reminded us of the importance of considering the contribution of migrant and immigrant communities when investigating the causes behind local linguistic change (see Kerswill and Torgersen, this volume).

Seemingly ever-increasing mobility over the past half century provided a valuable starting point for researchers wishing to understand why dialect change appeared to be so rapid and dialect levelling so widespread.

94   *David Britain*

But as Skeggs (2004:49) argued "mobility is a resource to which not everyone has an equal relationship", and so it has become increasingly important in contact dialectology to consider *who* is mobile, *where* is mobile, and how these potentially affect our understanding of change, rather than simply assuming that we are all being equally swept up in the same demographic whirlwind. In Britain (2013), I argue that many, though not all, of the mobilities that we have blamed for dialect levelling over the past 20 years are indeed both highly *classed* and *geographically uneven*. Many of the most vigorous mobilities of the last 50 years have been disproportionately engaged in by the middle classes – internal migration, commuting, university attendance, tertiary sector job mobility, private transport mobility, and so on. This huge demographic churn has been disproportionately churning wealthier, more educated, more white-collar employed people and their dialects. One of the most dramatic demographic shifts has been counterurbanisation, a shift away from the larger cities into the countryside.[2] This trend has not only been affecting middle-class urbanites proportionately more, but also their destinations have tended to be the most rural areas rather than smaller cities and towns (for a fuller discussion of these issues see Britain 2013). That these migrations appeared not to follow the predictions of the urban hierarchical model of geographical diffusion prompted the establishment of a multilocality project (Britain 2014) to investigate the implications for traditional dialect of this counterurbanisation-induced demographic churn, with East Anglia as its focus. East Anglia was chosen partly because it has been an especially popular destination for counterurbanisers and partly because it has a distinctive and well-described traditional dialect (e.g., Trudgill 2003, 2004). In this chapter, I report on one linguistic variable from that project, relative marker choice, but the results from all of the other variables that we examined, perhaps not unexpectedly, show that traditional dialect attrition is greatest in the sparsely populated rural areas that have been the most attractive to counterurbanisers, with the traditional dialect being best preserved in the larger urban areas that have not been a target for the predominantly more middle-class in-migrants. This finding, for both phonological (e.g., palatal glide deletion in words such as 'music' and 'few') and morphological variables (e.g., third person singular present tense *zero*, as in 'she smoke and he drink', see, for example, Kingston 2000; Potter 2018), runs counter to the urban hierarchy model predictions but makes absolute sense in terms of which localities have actually been most affected by demographic upheaval. Evidence so far suggests that simply examining the geographical destinations of the counterurbanisers is a much better predictor of language change than abstract paradigms, such as the urban hierarchy or contagion diffusion models. It is in this context that relative markers are examined in this chapter from a subset of the locations investigated in the larger project.

2.1.2 Non-standard Relative Markers in England

The marking system for restrictive relative clauses in English is notoriously variable. Even standard varieties of English, which by definition shun variability as much as possible (Milroy 2001), show a wide variety of legitimated markers, which, although sensitive to, for example, animacy and the syntactic position of the noun in the relative clause, nevertheless demonstrate optionality. These include: *who* as in (1), *which* as in (2), *that* as in (3), and *zero* as in (4). Very rarely in the spoken language, even in spoken Standard English, is *whom* found as in (5):[3]

(1) She's only worried about the people *who*'s got plenty of money
(2) With the new underfelt *which* he chose
(3) It's only that there river bank *that* saved us from being flooded
(4) There's all these hundreds of houses Ø are going up
(5) The applicants *whom* we interviewed were not especially impressive

In this chapter, I focus on the non-standard markers of restrictive relatives and the extent to which they have been able to survive given the socio-demographic upheaval of the last century that often has led to the levelling away of traditional dialect forms. There are three which are of relevance here: *what*, as in (6), *as* as in (7), and *zero* subject relatives as in (8).

(6) You know that thing *what* you can alter channels with
(7) Her and her neighbour *as* lived there then, they're here
(8) There in't such a thing as a thing Ø can't be repaired, is there?

While there are a number of studies which have noted the presence of different non-standard markers in different individual locations across England, there has been very little variationist investigation of their contemporary use or vitality. Cheshire's (1982) pioneering study of grammatical variation among adolescents in Reading, which included an analysis of relative markers such as *what*, set the scene for quantitative research on grammatical variation in England, but few have followed in her variationist footsteps with respect to tracking non-standard relatives. Piecing together the vernacular history of these non-standard forms from the existing literature is difficult, but doing so for the contemporary dialect landscape is even harder.

  We have two main sources which can provide some sense of the historical geographical distribution of non-standard relatives over the past couple of centuries: Alexander Ellis's 1889 survey of the Anglophone British Isles and Orton et al.'s (1962–1971) *Survey of English Dialects*. Ellis's survey, whilst a goldmine for those interested in nineteenth-century phonological variation, is less useful for the investigation of

96   *David Britain*

morphosyntax. First, he is clearly less interested in it, commenting on it in passing rather than systematically. Second, we are reliant on the longer of his two dialect translation tasks for our knowledge about relative markers. These translation tasks are two short stories, chunked up into individual sentences, which teachers and clergy, and others from individual villages are asked to translate into the local dialect. These were then checked by Ellis and his assistant Thomas Hallam: sometimes Hallam was sent out to confirm certain details, sometimes particular translations were queried with the translators themselves. In the longer of the two tasks, there are three sentences in which there is the potential for a relative marker:

Line 4: some of those folks *who* went through the whole thing
Line 8: when she found the drunken beast *that* she calls her husband
Line 15: it is a weak fool *that* prates without reason

There are none in the shorter translation task. This is problematic because the longer task was administered to fewer locations, so the coverage, especially in the South, is fairly patchy. Ellis finds, however, four widespread non-standard forms: *what, as,* and subject relative *zero* as noted above, but also [ət] in the far north of England. Subject relative *zero* is found across the country in his survey, and he provides ample examples of it in his text. *As* covers a wide area of the country, reaching from Hampshire in the South, up through Gloucestershire and Oxfordshire to the East and West Midlands, much of Southern and Mid Lancashire, and Lincolnshire. He finds no *as,* however, in the far north, in the South-West, in Kent, East Anglia, or in and around London. *What* is found in a relatively restricted area – Norfolk, Suffolk, Kent, West Somerset, and a few pockets in South Yorkshire and the Midlands.

The Survey of English Dialects (SED) investigates Non-Mobile Old Rural mostly Men (NORMs) born in the final third of the nineteenth century and so provides a countrywide snapshot of a generation or two on from Ellis's survey. Evidence of relative markers comes from two items in the SED questionnaire:

Book 3 (3) (7): If I didn't know what a cowman is, you would tell me: He is the man ____ looks after the cows.
Book 9 (9) (5): The woman next door says: The work in this garden is getting me down. You say: Well, get some help in. I know a man ____ will do it for you.

Figures 2.1.1 and 2.1.2, drawn on the basis of the evidence from these two questions, show the maximal regional distribution of *as* and *what,* respectively. Both *as* and *what* cover larger areas than can be seen in Ellis, but this is probably due to the patchiness of the data coverage in

Ellis rather than to an absence of these features. The SED shows, as did Ellis, that *what* is a predominantly Eastern feature found in East Anglia, the South-East (including those areas for which Ellis presented no data), Yorkshire, and the East Midlands but also stretching down into parts of the South-West. *As*, meanwhile, is more common in the west of the country, with only the far north, the eastern coast of Yorkshire and Lincolnshire, Norfolk, Suffolk, Essex, Kent, and the south coast where it is not present. *As* was also found in the far South-West, in Devon especially. Note, therefore, the considerable overlap between the *what* area and the *as* area. Subject *zero* relatives are found across England in the SED and [ət] again in the far north (not shown on the maps). A large number of individual locality studies, almost all in the traditional dialectological tradition of studying NORMs, have mentioned the existence of non-standard relative markers, and these largely confirm the maps shown in the SED data above (see Herrmann 2003 for an excellent overview of these, and her own investigation of NORMs from the *Freiburg English Dialect* (FRED) corpus).[4]

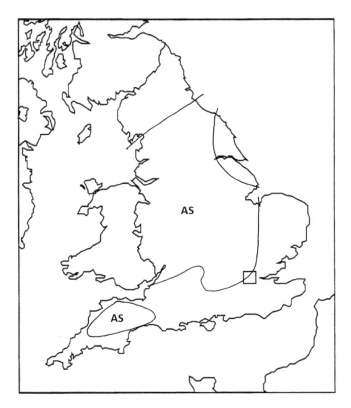

Figure 2.1.1 The maximal extent of relative marker *as* in data from the Survey of English Dialects.

98 *David Britain*

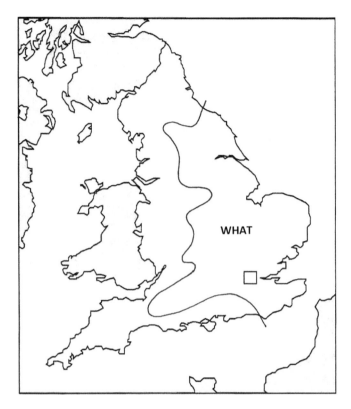

Figure 2.1.2 The maximal extent of relative marker *what* in data from the Survey of English Dialects.

There are relatively few studies, however, that have examined non-standard relative markers using contemporary data, based on non-NORM respondents, following quantitative variationist techniques. Cheshire's (1982) research in Reading is the first to tick all three of these boxes, conducting a quantitative analysis of young speakers in a contemporary dataset. She found that *what* was a robustly used marker, especially relativising non-personal nouns, and accounting for between 11% and 38% of all tokens, depending on the grammatical context. She also found that 14% of her personal subject tokens had *zero* marking (Cheshire 1982:73). Subsequent research suggests that time has not been kind to either *what* or *as*. In their study of inner and outer London, Cheshire, Adger, and Fox (2013:57) found that while their Inner London elderly speakers still used *what* 13% of the time, it was barely used by the outer London elderly (1.5%) or by either of the younger groups (inner London 2.1%, outer 1.6%). Levey's (2006) study of London pre-adolescents found that between 8% and 15% of all relative markers were *what*, depending on the syntactic position of the noun in the relative clause and personal versus non-personal animacy. Tagliamonte, Smith and Lawrence (2005:88) found just three tokens of *what* and three of *as* out of a total of 716 in the Northern English locality of Maryport and only 31 tokens of *what* and one of *as* in a larger corpus of 2,280 relatives that also included data from York, Somerset, and Devon (Tagliamonte 2002:153). Beal and Corrigan (2002:132) found just one token in their Tyneside analysis. Van den Eynden Morpeth (2002:182) showed that 7% of her tokens from NORMs in Dorset had *what*, and there were no tokens of *as*. She points to earlier studies of NORMs from nearby Somerset and Devon where *what* use was 16% and 9%, and *as* use 5% and 0%, respectively. Petyt (1983) showed that [ət] is still used relatively frequently in West Yorkshire (but *as* much less so), though his analysis does not permit estimates of its proportion of the total number of relative markers in his corpus. These variationist investigations nevertheless leave several parts of the country unexamined, and it is therefore hard to gauge the vitality of the overt non-standard markers in, say, the Midlands, and much of the north, especially Lancashire. Braber and Robinson (2018:85), reporting on the East Midlands, claim that "*what* appears to be nowadays more common throughout the region as a whole" and Beal (2004:133) states that *what* in Sheffield is 'common' (Beal and Corrigan later (2005:217) show it to account for 17% of relatives there). More detailed variationist investigations are needed to more precisely plot the apparent vitality of *what* in the Midlands and South Yorkshire, particularly in light of its apparent obsolescence in the South.

There have been a number of detailed investigations of relative markers in East Anglian English, some descriptive, some quantitative, but all have been interested solely in NORMs (and their female equivalent, NORFs). All have focussed to some extent on the prevalence of *what* in the region. Mentions of the use of *what* in East Anglian English date back to Forby (1830). It is found in the region both by Ellis (1889) and in the Survey of English Dialects, as shown above. Kökeritz (1932) recorded his Eastern Suffolk informants translating Ellis's longer reading passage, and his IPA transcriptions of those recordings show a number of instances of relative *what*. Poussa (1994) focussed on six NORMs and NORFs from rural North-East Norfolk and found that roughly 25% of her tokens were *what* (based on data in Poussa 1994:420) and 24% of all subject relatives had *zero* marking. Peitsara (2002) examined 19 NORMs and NORFs from Eastern Suffolk and found 18% *what* (2002:170), 23% of subject relatives were *zero* (2002:174), and five tokens of *as* (1.3% of the total) (2002:170). Ojanen (1982) (in Peitsara 2002:180), investigating NORMS and NORFs in Cambridgeshire, found: (a) very high levels of *what* (53%) and *zero* (38%) (though the figures do not distinguish between subject and object relatives); (b) very low levels of *that* (1.6%) and *who* (3.4%); and (c) a few examples of *as*.

100 David Britain

None of these studies have been able to comment on the trajectory of change, given the focus on older speakers only.

The question that arises from the apparent levelling of non-standard *what* and *as*, if this is indeed what is happening, is what is replacing them? The best candidate to take over, it has been suggested, is *that*, since it is the typologically more frequent means of marking relativisation, using an invariant form that is unmarked for case, number, gender or animacy (Cheshire et al. 2013:56). Tagliamonte's (2002) research on Northern and South-Western varieties in England found *that* to be dominant, and *wh-* forms to play only a small role in the system. On the other hand, some have argued that *wh-* forms are more common in the south (Nevalainen and Raumolin-Brunberg 2002), and others have suggested that the South-East, and especially East Anglia, seems to be rather 'that-less' (Poussa 1994; Tagliamonte 2002:155), leading Poussa (1994:424) to suggest that the relative absence of *that* to the east and its abundance to the west "could be a major syntactic marker of the east-west dialect division in southern dialects". This examination of several localities in East Anglia aims to address these questions about the direction of change in the aforementioned context of contemporary demographic churn.

2.1.3 Methods and Data

In order to investigate evidence for change in the relative marker system in East Anglia, a multilocality approach was adopted, which enabled us to assess the extent to which urban or rural locations were more affected by the change and whether distance and travelling time from London were also factors accounting for the speed of change (see above).[5] Small corpora from six localities, all within the traditional dialect area of East Anglia, were analysed for this study:

> Ipswich – a large town of 130,000 people in Eastern Suffolk, and the largest in the county. The town lies 106km as the crow flies, 110 minutes by car and 85 minutes by public transport from London with which it has dual carriageway road and mainline intercity rail connections.
>
> Colchester – a large town of 110,000 people in North-East Essex. The town lies 82km as the crow flies, 90 minutes by car and 60 minutes by public transport from London and has good road and rail connections to London, with a significant commuter population travelling into the capital for work.
>
> Wisbech – a town of 31,000 people in the Northern Cambridgeshire Fenland. It is 128km as the crow flies, 170 minutes by car, 130 minutes by public transport from London, with poor road connections south towards London because of the physical restrictions imposed by the marshland terrain, and the nearest direct rail

lines to London either 36km to the west in Peterborough or 20km to the east in Downham Market.

Holbrook - a village of just over 2,000 people in the extreme southeast of Suffolk, 103km as the crow flies from London, 120 minutes by car, 105 minutes by public transport, it is a 30-minute bus ride from the nearest railway stations at Ipswich or Manningtree.

Coggeshall – a village of 4,500 people in North Essex, 68km as the crow flies, 80 minutes by car and 110 minutes by public transport from London, 20 minutes by bus from Marks Tey where stopping trains to London can be caught.

Silver End – a settlement of around 4,000 people in North Essex, it was designed as a 'model village', in essence a small, planned, New Town, in the early 20th century. It lies 63km as the crow flies, 80 minutes by car and 90 minutes by public transport from London. Its nearest town is Braintree which has mostly indirect rail connections to London.

The locations of these settlements are shown in Figure 2.1.3.

Figure 2.1.3 Location of localities examined in this chapter.

102 David Britain

If we apply a simple, but often applied, gravity model formula[6] to examine the potential influence London has on these places, we get the results in Table 2.1.1.[7]

On any count of 'distance', if a gravity model accounts best for the patterns found, Colchester should show most similarity and influence from London, then Ipswich, with Wisbech showing more influence from London than the smaller Suffolk (Holbrook) and Essex (Silver End) villages. As noted above, however, earlier analyses of other variables across this corpus tended to suggest an 'anti-hierarchical' pattern, with the smaller locations affected more by linguistic influences from outside of East Anglia than the larger.

Each corpus consisted of recordings of informal conversations, sociolinguistic interviews without formal reading tasks, each around 45 minutes administered by young adults from those localities. In most of the localities, data were collected from speakers aged 18–28 and 60–70; however, in Colchester we additionally collected data from speakers aged 35–50. The final sample analysed here is presented in Table 2.1.2.

Table 2.1.1 Gravity model calculations of the hypothetical influence London has on each of the six East Anglian localities under investigation

			Gravity model scores		
London's influence on....	*Distance from London (in km)*	*Population in 000*	*As the crow flies distance*	*Time by car*	*Time by public transport*
Wisbech	128	31	17	10	17
Ipswich	106	130	104	97	162
Holbrook	103	2	2	1	2
Colchester	82	110	147	122	275
Coggeshall	68	4.5	9	6	3
Silver End	63	4	9	6	4

Table 2.1.2 Structure of the East Anglian corpus used for this analysis

	60–70 years		*35–50 years*		*18–28 years*	
	Female	*Male*	*Female*	*Male*	*Female*	*Male*
Wisbech	5	5			3	3
Ipswich	3	3			3	3
Holbrook	3	3			3	3
Colchester	3	3	3	3	3	3
Coggeshall	3	3			3	3
Silver End	3	3			3	3

Dialect Levelling in Relative Markers 103

The corpora were transcribed and all restrictive relative clauses extracted[8] and coded for relative marker choice and whether the relativised noun served a subject or non-subject (object or oblique) role in the relative clause. In total, 1177 tokens were extracted, 677 subject relatives as in (9), and 500 object/oblique relatives as in (10).

(9) You know these hair things *what* goes up and down your neck
(10) That's worth the 70 pound *what* they pay

In considering the results, I focus on the three questions related specifically to levelling presented earlier:

a) What is the fate of the non-standard forms: *what, as,* and subject *zero* relatives?
b) Is the system as a whole shifting towards being more dominated by *that*?
c) Is there continued evidence of a prevalence of *wh-* forms, given that all of these localities are southern?

I consider in the discussion the extent to which the directions of change in these East Anglian data suggest an orientation towards a London system, such as that presented in Cheshire et al. (2013).

2.1.4 Results

The overall results for the six locations combined are shown in Table 2.1.3a for subject relatives and Table 2.1.3b for object relatives.

Overall, the East Anglian data show:
a) an apparent-time decline in the use of *what*, accounting for over 20% of relatives among the older speakers across the region but fewer than 6% among the young;
b) *as* was clearly already obsolescent among the older speakers and has completely disappeared among the young; and,
c) subject relatives with *zero*, an apparently mostly male form, are also undergoing levelling to the same extent as *what*.

Non-standard forms, then, appear to be being levelled away in the data as a whole. Table 2.1.4 compares *wh-* forms as a whole, *that* and *zero* across apparent-time.[9] This table enables us to see more clearly that:
d) there is a significant increase in the use of *that*, across both subject and object relatives; and
e) there is a reduction in the use of *zero* relatives, both subject and object, over apparent-time.

104   *David Britain*

Table 2.1.3a Overall subject relatives (middle-aged only for Colchester)

| Marker | Old (60–70 years) | | | | Middle (35–50 years) | | | | Young (18–28 years) | | | |
| | Male | | Female | | Male | | Female | | Male | | Female | |
	n	%	n	%	n	%	n	%	n	%	n	%
who	44	27.7	41	25.1	1	3.6	9	33.3	39	26.4	59	38.8
which	7	4.4	2	1.2	3	10.7	1	3.7	14	9.5	9	5.9
that	35	22.0	56	34.4	24	85.7	17	63.0	72	48.6	78	51.3
zero	39	24.5	23	14.1	0	0.0	0	0.0	11	7.4	4	2.6
what	32	20.1	41	25.1	0	0.0	0	0.0	12	8.1	2	1.3
as	2	1.3	0	0.0	0	0.0	0	0.0	0	0.0	0	0.0
Total	159	100.0	163	100.0	28	100.0	27	100.0	148	100.0	152	100.0

Table 2.1.3b Overall object relatives (middle-aged only for Colchester)

| Marker | Old (60–70 years) | | | | Middle (35–50 years) | | | | Young (18–28 years) | | | |
| | Male | | Female | | Male | | Female | | Male | | Female | |
	n	%	n	%	n	%	n	%	n	%	n	%
who	6	6.1	6	4.3	0	0.0	1	6.7	4	2.7	10	6.6
which	2	2.0	3	2.1	0	0.0	3	20.0	5	3.4	4	2.6
that	14	14.3	37	26.2	4	36.4	8	53.3	56	37.8	49	32.2
zero	58	59.2	58	41.1	6	54.5	3	20.0	47	31.8	43	28.3
what	18	18.4	37	26.2	1	9.1	0	0.0	10	6.8	7	4.6
as	0	0.0	0	0.0	0	0.0	0	0.0	0	0.0	0	0.0
Total	98	100.0	141	100.0	11	100.0	15	100.0	122	100.0	113	100.0

Table 2.1.4 East Anglian relative markers across apparent-time: *wh-* forms, versus *that* and *zero*

| Marker | Old (60–70 years) | | Young (18–28 years) | |
	n	%	n	%
Subject relatives				
wh-	167	52.2	135	45.0
that	91	28.4	150	50.0
zero	62	19.4	15	5.0
Total	320	100.0	300	100.0
Object relatives				
wh-	72	30.1	40	17.0
that	51	21.3	105	44.7
zero	116	48.5	90	38.3
Total	239	100.0	235	100.0

We can shed more specific light on change in the relative marker system by considering each locality separately (see Table 2.1.5). Focussing initially on the non-standard markers, we see first, as expected given the historical evidence, the only examples of *as* are found in Wisbech; being further west, the town falls into the area in which, according to the SED, both *as* and *what* were found. Second, the results show not only that levels of *what* are by far the highest in Wisbech, but also that this non-standard form, despite some reduction across apparent-time, remains a notable and significant marker in this town. Figure 2.1.4 shows the use of *what* across apparent-time in the six locations, subject and objective relatives combined. *What* has clearly fared badly in the other locations – among older speakers it was a frequently used variant in both Ipswich and Coggeshall but is now only sporadically found at best among younger speakers, even in Colchester which bucks the apparent-time trend towards obsolescence.

Table 2.1.5 East Anglian relative markers across apparent-time for all localities

Wisbech

	Old		Young	
	n	%	*n*	%
Subject relatives:				
who	12	7.8	20	36.4
which	0	0.0	0	0.0
that	31	20.3	14	25.5
zero	46	30.1	8	14.5
what	62	40.5	13	23.6
as	2	1.3	0	0.0
Total	153	100.0	55	100.0
Object relatives:				
who	3	3.1	1	2.0
which	1	1.0	0	0.0
that	4	4.1	12	24.5
zero	49	50.0	22	44.9
what	41	41.8	14	28.6
as	0	0.0	0	0.0
Total	98	100.0	49	100.0

(*Continued*)

Ipswich

	Old		Young	
	n	%	*n*	%
who	5	27.8	8	17.4
which	3	16.7	9	19.6
that	7	38.9	29	63.0
zero	1	5.6	0	0.0
what	2	11.1	0	0.0
as	0	0.0	0	0.0
Total	18	100.0	46	100.0
who	1	3.4	0	0.0
which	2	6.9	4	16.7
that	5	17.2	10	41.7
zero	17	58.6	9	37.5
what	4	13.8	1	4.2
as	0	0.0	0	0.0
Total	29	100.0	24	100.0

Holbrook

	Old		Young	
	n	%	*n*	%
who	35	52.2	32	47.1
which	1	1.5	7	10.3
that	21	31.3	28	41.2
zero	5	7.5	1	1.5
what	5	7.5	0	0.0
as	0	0.0	0	0.0
Total	67	100.0	68	100.0
who	5	8.3	5	6.8
which	0	0.0	1	1.4
that	22	36.7	40	54.1
zero	32	53.3	28	37.8
what	1	1.7	0	0.0
as	0	0.0	0	0.0
Total	60	100.0	74	100.0

(*Continued*)

Colchester

	Old		Middle aged		Young	
	n	%	*n*	%	*n*	%
Subject relatives:						
who	13	86.7	10	18.2	9	52.9
which	0	0.0	4	7.3	2	11.8
that	2	13.3	41	74.5	5	29.4
zero	0	0.0	0	0.0	0	0.0
what	0	0.0	0	0.0	1	5.9
as	0	0.0	0	0.0	0	0.0
Total	15	100.0	55	100.0	17	100.0
Object relatives:						
who	2	13.3	1	3.8	3	12.5
which	1	6.7	3	11.5	3	12.5
that	3	20.0	12	46.1	4	16.7
zero	9	60.0	9	34.6	13	54.2
what	0	0.0	1	3.8	1	4.1
as	0	0.0	0	0.0	0	0.0
Total	15	100.0	26	100.0	24	100.0

Coggeshall

	Old		Young	
	n	%	*n*	%
who	15	28.9	15	22.4
which	5	9.6	1	1.5
that	19	36.5	45	67.2
zero	9	17.3	6	9.0
what	4	7.7	0	0.0
as	0	0.0	0	0.0
Total	52	100.0	67	100.0
who	1	3.7	3	7.5
which	1	3.7	0	0.0
that	11	40.7	30	75.0
zero	7	25.9	7	17.5
what	7	25.9	0	0.0
as	0	0.0	0	0.0
Total	27	100.0	40	100.0

(*Continued*)

108 *David Britain*

Silver End

	Old		Young	
	n	%	n	%
who	5	29.4	14	29.8
which	0	0.0	4	8.6
that	11	64.7	29	61.8
zero	1	5.9	0	0.0
what	0	0.0	0	0.0
as	0	0.0	0	0.0
Total	17	100.0	47	100.0
who	0	0.0	2	8.4
which	0	0.0	1	4.2
that	6	60.0	9	37.5
zero	2	20.0	11	45.8
what	2	20.0	1	4.2
as	0	0.0	0	0.0
Total	10	100.0	24	100.0

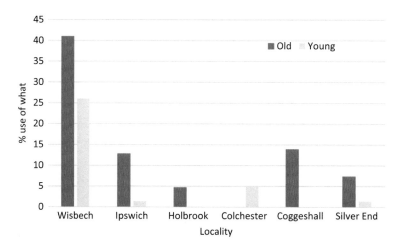

Figure 2.1.4 The use of *what* across apparent-time, subject and object relatives combined, in the six East Anglian localities.

Figure 2.1.5 shows the use of *zero* subject relatives across apparent-time. Again, levelling is the order of the day, with every community showing a shift away from the non-standard form and only Coggeshall, and especially, Wisbech, showing higher levels of *zero* and higher levels of retention among the young.

Dialect Levelling in Relative Markers 109

We saw earlier the contraction of *wh-* and *zero* forms in general across East Anglia. *That*, therefore, has been the beneficiary. An apparent-time presentation of the use of *that* in Figure 2.1.6 shows a rise in five localities and a slight drop in Silver End from an already very high level among the older speakers there. Although on the increase, *that* remains less frequent than *what* in Wisbech even among the young, a rather clear reminder of the conservatism of this Fenland location with respect to this variable.

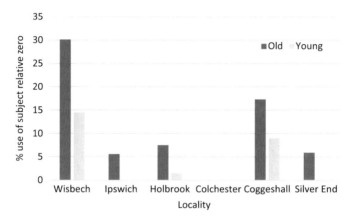

Figure 2.1.5 The use of *zero* subject relatives across apparent-time in the six East Anglian localities.

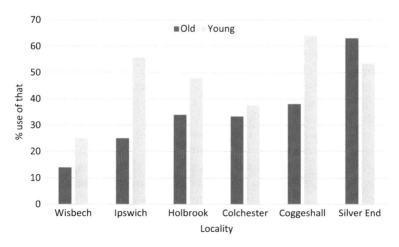

Figure 2.1.6 The use of *that* as a relative marker across apparent-time in the six East Anglian localities.

110 David Britain

2.1.5 Discussion

Having seen, on the one hand, a set of rather common trends across the region, yet, on the other hand, rather considerable variability in frequencies of different variants based on location, we can now turn to examine how these patterns of variation compare to those found in contemporary London. Such an analysis enables us to assess whether these varieties are heading in the direction of contemporary London English or elsewhere.

Cheshire et al. (2013:58) found that:

a) *that*, used around half the time by older speakers in both inner and outer London became even more dominant over apparent-time;
b) *zero* declined across apparent-time, especially in subject relatives;
c) *what* and *which* were at very low levels across the corpus; and
d) *who*, used far more in subject than object relatives, had remained quite stable and appeared in inner London to perform a special topic-marking function.

Findings a) and b) apply to the East Anglian data as well, but what is notable is that levels of *that* among the older age group are much lower than those in London, except in Silver End. Pattern c) in the London data suggests that the shift away from *what* occurred earlier in London than in most of East Anglia, but it is now a peripheral marker even there, except in Wisbech. The use of *who* across the East Anglian data sets is diverse: it dramatically increases across apparent-time in Wisbech, is relatively stable in Holbrook and Silver End, and falls in Colchester, Ipswich and Coggeshall. Everywhere it is more common in subject than object relatives, but it is used at very high levels indeed in both Holbrook and Colchester. Research to assess whether *who* has the same topic-marking function as in Cheshire et al.'s (2013) analysis of Hackney has yet to be conducted. Their hypothesis, that *who* as a topic-marker arises from the language and dialect contact of this highly multicultural part of the capital city, would suggest that we would *not* find such an effect in East Anglia.

Attempts to impose an urban hierarchy model on these localities fail. Wisbech is the most distant location from London, but, given its size, it should, in theory, be influenced by the capital more than the smaller locations in this study. It is not. As for many of the other linguistic variables analysed as part of this multilocality analysis of East Anglian English, Wisbech remains the most traditional dialect speaking of all those localities considered. Its levels of *what* and *zero* subject relatives are considerably higher than elsewhere, and its levels of *that* are much lower, typical of traditional East Anglia (cf. Poussa 1994). The urban hierarchy model would predict Colchester to be much more like London than elsewhere, yet its levels of *that* are exceeded by several other East

Anglian locations, it retains vestigial *what* like the other more southern locations, and its levels of *who* have decreased. Holbrook, the apparently least likely place to be influenced by London has a very un-East Anglian system with the lowest overall level of *what* and very high levels of *who*. The very high levels of *who* in Colchester and Holbrook (the locations that are most and least likely to be influenced by London respectively) could also potentially be explained by sheer exposure to standard Englishes through contact with middle-class speech: Holbrook is a typical destination village for counterurbanisers, who, as we saw earlier, are disproportionately mobile, educated, and middle class; Colchester has long had a very active and highly mobile tertiary sector economy and an increasingly large university, factors that have only recently also become applicable to Ipswich. A high level of *who* is noted in the few studies that have examined spoken Standard English (e.g., Quirk 1957:106).

Among young speakers, there is indeed little to distinguish any location, apart from Wisbech: low *what*, low subject *zero* and lowering levels of *zero* generally, significant levels of *who*, and very high *that*, suggesting a mobility and contact-induced pan-South(-East)ern koineised system that has levelled away minority and marked *what*, *as* and subject *zero*, and is orienting increasingly towards generalised typologically unmarked *that*, with *who* reserved for some personal (especially subject) relatives. The East (and South-East) appears to be losing its 'that-lessness', especially among the young, suggesting that Poussa's (1994) east-west dialect boundary mentioned earlier may be breaking down. Furthermore, *wh-* forms appear to be gradually losing ground as well, though from relatively high levels, especially in subject relatives. Wisbech shows some of the same tendencies as London and other East Anglian locations – *what* is decreasing, *as* has gone, *who* and *that* are increasing, *zero* decreasing – but nowhere near to the same extent as the more southerly localities. Further research into other South-Eastern localities will be needed to ascertain the scope of regional levelling in the relative marker system, but significant change is clearly afoot.

Notes

1 Many thanks indeed to Jenny Cheshire, for encouraging me to think about relative pronouns – this led me to investigate the Fenland data from Wisbech first, and then, later, data from the other East Anglian sites. It also led to our collaboration with Sue Fox on this topic (Cheshire, Fox, and Britain 2007), who I would also like to thank here.
2 Between 1981 and 2005, around 2,250,000 more people moved from large metropolitan cities to the countryside than from the countryside to the cities (based on Champion 2009: 163).
3 Possessive relative markers, such as *whose*, will not be examined in this article.
4 See www2.anglistik.uni-freiburg.de/institut/lskortmann/FRED/

112   *David Britain*

5 Many thanks go to Billie Watkins, Makayla Braddy, Matt Wesley, Juliette Spurling, Sarah Grossenbacher, Mayra Macpherson and Selina Von Allmen for their assistance with this research.

6 I have used here the model adopted by Trudgill (1983:74). The influence of London on place X is the population of London (divided by 1000) multiplied by the population of X (divided by 1000), divided by the square of the distance between the two.

7 London is assumed to have a population of 9,000,000. Distances are from locality to London Liverpool Street Railway Station (the London hub for East Anglia) (a) in kilometres as the crow flies, (b) in minutes driven by car according to Google Maps, (c) in minutes by public transport. Populations are calculated in thousands.

8 In cases where it was difficult to distinguish between restrictive and nonrestrictive, these tokens were not considered in the analysis. Possessive relatives were also not considered.

9 Tokens of *as* were not included in this table. Because of rounding, not all % totals add to 100.

References

Beal, Joan. 2004. "English dialects in the North of England: morphology and syntax". In *A Handbook of Varieties of English: Morphology and Syntax*, B. Kortmann, K. Burridge, R. Mesthrie, E. Schneider and C. Upton (eds.). Berlin: Mouton de Gruyter. 114–141.

Beal, Joan and Karen P. Corrigan. 2002. "Relatives in Tyneside and Northumbrian English". In *Relativisation on the North Sea Littoral*, P. Poussa (ed.). Munich: Lincom Europa. 125–134.

Beal, Joan and Karen P. Corrigan. 2005. "A tale of two dialects: relativization in Newcastle and Sheffield". In *Dialects across Borders*, M. Filppula, J. Klemola, M. Palander and E. Penttilä (eds.). Amsterdam: Benjamins. 211–229.

Braber, Natalie and Jonnie Robinson. 2018. *East Midlands English*. Berlin: De Gruyter.

Britain, David. 2005. "Innovation diffusion, 'Estuary English' and local dialect differentiation: the survival of Fenland Englishes". *Linguistics* 43(5): 995–1022.

Britain, David. 2009. "One foot in the grave?: Dialect death, dialect contact and dialect birth in England". *International Journal of the Sociology of Language* 196/197:121–155.

Britain, David. 2010. "Contact and dialectology". In *Handbook of Language Contact*, R. Hickey (ed.). Oxford: Blackwell. 208–229.

Britain, David. 2013. "The role of mundane mobility and contact in dialect death and dialect birth". In *English as a Contact Language*, D. Schreier and M. Hundt (eds.). Cambridge: Cambridge University Press. 165–181.

Britain, David. 2014. "Linguistic diffusion and the social heterogeneity of space and mobility". In *3rd International Society for the Linguistics of English Conference*, Universität Zürich.

Britain, David. 2018. "Dialect contact and new dialect formation". In *Handbook of Dialectology*, C. Boberg, J. Nerbonne and D. Watt (eds.). Oxford: Wiley Blackwell. 143–158.

Champion, Tony. 2009. "Urban-Rural differences in commuting in England: a challenge to the rural sustainability agenda?" *Planning, Practice and Research* 24:161–183.

Cheshire, Jenny. 1982. *Variation in an English Dialect: A Sociolinguistic Study.* Cambridge: Cambridge University Press.

Cheshire, Jenny, Sue Fox and David Britain. 2007. *Relatives from the South.* Paper presented at UKLVC6, Lancaster, September 2007.

Cheshire, Jenny, Paul Kerswill, Sue Fox and Eivind Torgersen. 2011. "Contact, the feature pool and the speech community: The emergence of multicultural London English". *Journal of Sociolinguistics* 15:151–196.

Cheshire, Jenny, David Adger and Sue Fox. 2013. "Relative *who* and the actuation problem". *Lingua* 126:51–77.

Ellis, Alexander. 1889. *On Early English Pronunciation (Volume 5).* London: Truebner and Co.

Forby, Robert. 1830. *The Vocabulary of East-Anglia: An Attempt to Record the Vulgar Tongue of the Twin Sister Counties Norfolk and Suffolk, as it Existed in the Last Twenty Years.* London: J. B. Nichols and Son.

Foulkes, Paul and Gerry Docherty. 1999. *Urban Voices: Accent Studies in the British Isles.* London: Routledge.

Herrmann, Tanja. 2003. *Relative Clauses in Dialects of English: A Typological Approach.* Unpublished PhD dissertation. Freiburg: Albert-Ludwigs-Universität Freiburg.

Kerswill, Paul and Ann Williams. 2000. "Creating a new town koine". *Language in Society* 29:65–115.

Kingston, Michelle. 2000. *Dialects in Danger: Dialect Attrition in the East Anglian County of Suffolk.* Unpublished MA dissertation. Colchester: University of Essex.

Kökeritz, Helge. 1932. *The Phonology of the Suffolk Dialect.* Uppsala: Aktibolag.

Levey, Stephen. 2006. "Visiting London relatives". *English World-Wide* 27:45–70.

Milroy, James. 2001. "Language ideologies and the consequences of standardization". *Journal of Sociolinguistics* 5:530–555.

Nevalainen, Terttu and Helena Raumolin-Brunberg. 2002. "The rise of the relative *who* in early modern English". In *Relativisation on the North Sea Littoral*, P. Poussa (ed.). Munich: Lincom Europa. 109–121.

Ojanen, Anna-Liisa. 1982. *A Syntax of the Cambridgeshire Dialect.* Unpublished Licentiate dissertation. Helsinki: University of Helsinki.

Orton, Harold. et al. 1962–1971. *Survey of English Dialects: Basic Materials: Introduction and 4 Volumes (Each in 3 Parts).* Leeds: E. J. Arnold & Son.

Peitsara, Kirsti. 2002. "Relativizers in the Suffolk dialect". In *Relativisation on the North Sea Littoral*, P. Poussa (ed.). Munich: Lincom Europa. 167–180.

Petyt, K. M. 1983. *Dialect and Accent in Industrial West Yorkshire.* Amsterdam: John Benjamins.

Potter, Robert. 2018. *A Variationist Multilocality Study of Unstressed Vowels and Verbal –s Marking in the Peripheral Dialect of East Suffolk.* Unpublished PhD dissertation. Colchester: University of Essex.

Poussa, Patricia. 1994. "Norfolk relatives (Broadland)". In *Regionalsprachliche Variation, Umgangs- und Standardsprachen: Verhandlungen des*

114 David Britain

Internationalen Dialektologenkongresses: Band 3, W. Viereck (ed.). Stuttgart: Franz Steiner Verlag. 418–426.

Quirk, Randolph. 1957. "Relative clauses in educated spoken English". *English Studies* 38:97–109.

Skeggs, Beverley. 2004. *Class, Self, Culture*. London: Routledge.

Tagliamonte, Sali. 2002. "Variation and change in the British relative marker system". In *Relativisation on the North Sea Littoral*, P. Poussa (ed.). Munich: Lincom Europa. 147–165.

Tagliamonte, Sali, Jennifer Smith and Helen Lawrence. 2005. "No taming the vernacular!: Insights from the relatives in northern Britain". *Language Variation and Change* 17:75–112.

Trudgill, Peter. 1983. *On Dialect*. New York: New York University Press.

Trudgill, Peter. 1986. *Dialects in Contact*. Oxford: Blackwell.

Trudgill, Peter. 2003. *The Norfolk Dialect*. Cromer: Poppyland.

Trudgill, Peter. 2004. "The dialect of East Anglia: morphology and syntax". In *A Handbook of Varieties of English: Morphology and Syntax*, B. Kortmann, K. Burridge, R. Mesthrie, E. Schneider and C. Upton (eds.). Berlin: Mouton de Gruyter. 142–153.

Van den Eynden Morpeth, Nadine. 2002. "Relativisers in the South West of England". In *Relativisation on the North Sea Littoral*, P. Poussa (ed.). Munich: Lincom Europa. 181–194.

2.2 Restrictions on Relative Clauses in Auckland, New Zealand

Miriam Meyerhoff, Alexandra Birchfield, Elaine Ballard, Catherine Watson, and Helen Charters

2.2.1 Introduction[1]

English relative clauses are historically and synchronically complex syntactic structures, with variation in the relativiser (the item that introduces the relative clause) one of the most obvious surface-level manifestations of this complexity. The most common relativiser, *that*, alternates with a *wh-* form or *zero*, but *wh-*relativisers only seem to be fully productive in non-restrictive relative clauses. In restrictive relative clauses, only *who* is used with any great frequency. The use of a phonetically null or *zero* relativiser in most varieties of spoken English is proscribed for subject relative clauses. Thus, there is a semantic preference for the selection of *wh-* relativisers and a syntactic preference for the selection of *zero* relativisers, as illustrated in Figure 2.2.1.

Relative clauses are canonically partitioned into two types, restrictive (providing specificational information on the head noun) and non-restrictive (providing additional, parenthetical information on the head noun or sometimes the entire proposition), a distinction that some researchers claim can be reliably made in terms of semantics, syntax, and intonation (Tagliamonte et al. 2005). While we agree that there is often

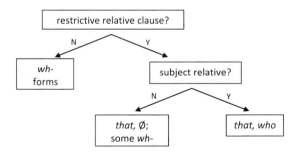

Figure 2.2.1 Distribution of *that*, *wh-* and *zero* relativisers in many varieties of English, including Auckland English.

116 *Miriam Meyerhoff et al.*

native-speaker agreement about whether a relative clause is restrictive or non-restrictive, there are also ambiguous cases. Sigley (1997) suggested (we think, rightly) that it is probably more accurate to think of the restrictive/non-restrictive distinction as a semantic cline.

The idea that the distinction between the two types of relative clauses might be fuzzy is supported by the historical record. Gisborne and Truswell (2017) showed that *wh-* relativisers originated in non-restrictive relatives (where a *wh-* pronoun is semantically compatible with the non-specifying nature of non-restrictive relatives), with restrictive *wh-*relativisers emerging later as an extension of the non-restrictive forms. This historical trajectory, and the principle of persistence in grammaticalisation (Hopper 1991), account for the higher frequency with which *wh-* forms are used in non-restrictive relatives, even today.

Within the class of restrictive relative clauses, there is again a two-way choice of relativiser. In clauses where the extracted argument is the subject of the subordinate clause, the choice is largely between *that* (1) and *wh-* forms (2). Outside of dialectal British English, subject relatives seldom occur with a *zero* relativiser (3) (*n* = 8 in our corpus) and the *wh-* form that most commonly occurs is *who*. There are, of course, other dialectal differences, such as dialects that use *what* as an alternative even for animate referents (cf. Cheshire 1982; Cheshire et al. 2013; Kortmann and Lunkenheimer 2013). Outside of England, the *what* relativiser is predominantly restricted to Atlantic English creoles or what Kortmann and Lunkenheimer (2013) called "high-contact L1 varieties" of English.[2]

In non-subject relatives, the alternation is principally between *that* (4) and *zero* (5), with *wh-* forms (6) used much less often with non-subject relatives.

Subject relative clauses

(1) a) She does have a few friends [**that** ____ are there]. (Mary, MR, older)[3]

b) There are also places in New Zealand [**that** I do feel like maybe have more sort of personality]". (Caitlyn, TR, younger)

(2) a) "But this time", he said, "We haven't got anyone [**who** ____ can do the job]". (Chub, MR, older)

b) I have a friend who went to Roskill [**who** ___ was in my year]. (Noor, MR, younger)

c) I'll have my own room up the far end [**which** ____ is my room now], I'll just go up there. (June, SA, older)

(3) He has to sign the work off, but these are guys [Ø ___ wouldn't know what way was up]. (June, SA, older)

Non-subject relative clauses

(4) a) People have done tattoos [**that** they regret ___]. Charlotte (TR, older)

    b) I guess the goal of cooking is to make something [**that** people would enjoy ___]. (Max Power, TR, younger)

(5) a) That was like literally the first thing [Ø I did ___]. (Eoin, MR, younger)

    b) That's not something [Ø you inherit ___]. (Luke, MR, older)

(6) a) Now everyone in our class has their own device [**which** they use a lot for writing]. (Bindi, TR, younger)

    b) People are like 'oh your internet friends [**who** you've never met ___]'. (Caitlyn, TR, younger)

As noted, the *wh-* forms emerged as options for English dependent relatives much later than *that* and *zero*. Gisborne and Truswell (2017) documented the options for introducing relative clauses at different stages in English, as shown in (7) (see also Romaine 1984):

(7) Old English: *se* demonstratives, *þe* and Ø
    Middle English: *se* demonstratives (lost early), *wh* forms, *þe/þat* and Ø
    Modern English: *wh-* forms, *that* and Ø.

In Modern English, *wh-* relativisers and *that* are widely agreed to occupy different syntactic positions, as shown in Figure 2.2.2, where the *wh-* relativiser occurs in the specifier position of the complementiser phrase (CP) and *that* occurs in its head.

Diachronic evidence supports an analysis in which *that* and *wh-* forms occur in complementary positions. While it is no longer grammatical to use both to introduce a relative clause (**the person who that you saw*; **the house which that we bought*), such combinations were attested through the fourteenth and fifteenth centuries, the period when *wh-* forms consolidated their foothold in English grammar (Gisborne and Truswell 2017).

The proper analysis of *zero* relatives (as in (5)) is less self-evident, since they are of course phonetically null. In Figure 2.2.2, we follow the general consensus that a null operator is base-generated in the subordinate clause (to satisfy the 'theta criterion'; Chomsky 1981) and moved into [Spec, CP] (Kayne 1994; De Vries 2002; Carnie 2013). If we differentiate relativisers according to their hypothesised underlying positions, we can (following Gisborne and Truswell 2017:27) refer to *that* as a 'relative complementiser' and *wh-* (and *zero*) forms as 'relative specifiers'. In most generative accounts, the movement of the null operator is stipulative or

118 *Miriam Meyerhoff et al.*

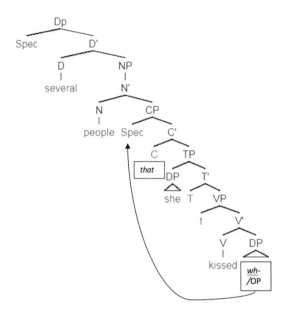

Figure 2.2.2 Syntaectic structure underlying *several people who/that/Ø she kissed* (Birchfield 2019:9).

motivated on theory-internal grounds. We believe that our data on the distribution of *zero* and *wh-* relativisers provide independent, empirical evidence in support of an analysis of *zero* relativisers as formally equivalent to *wh*-specifiers.

Our observations and analysis are congruent with Cheshire's (1998) observation that the infrequency of syntactic variables and their role in expressing pragmatic information make them much less likely to acquire social indexicality than phonetic variables. In our data, the selection of relativiser is primarily a *linguistic* phenomenon. Our analysis attempts to provide a principled account not only for the selection of the less frequent forms (*zero* and *who*) but also for the selection of *that*, which has largely been ignored or treated as an 'elsewhere' variant (Hinrichs et al. 2015).

We start by presenting a historical overview of the emergence of English relativisers, drawing on more recent research than previous variationist analyses have had access to and providing a more nuanced reading of some of the classic historical works on this variable. Contrary to Romaine (1984) and D'Arcy and Tagliamonte (2010), we conclude that it is not at all clear that *wh-* relativisers were introduced through language contact as prestige or formal variants. We then briefly present

Restrictions on Relative Clauses 119

our corpus and our results on the selection of relativisers in Auckland English. Finally, we probe the implications of the only consistent constraint favouring selection of *zero* or *wh-* relativisers in our corpus, confirming Cheshire's claim that "both the analysis of syntactic variation and the structure of spoken syntax" (1998:13) are enhanced by close examination of how language is used within a speech community.

2.2.2 The Historical Emergence of *wh-* relativisers

The emergence of English *wh-* relativisers is something of a mystery: as Gisborne and Truswell (2017:35) pithily put it, they were (and are) fundamentally "quite useless", given the other options already available (as shown in (6)). This superfluity perhaps explains their low frequency over time: in spoken English, *wh-* relativisers seem to hover at rates between 15% and 30% of all relative clauses, regardless of variety. Table 2.2.1 shows the distribution of relativisers in five studies of spoken (adult) English and in our corpus (we limit the studies to *spoken* English to enable cross-study comparison). Dekeyser's (1984) analysis of Early Modern English showed that in dramatic works (the most informal and speechlike genres in his corpus) the proportion of *wh-* relatives was 30%. A plausible interpretation of the historical and synchronic record is that the frequency of *wh-* relatives in *spoken* English has held rather steady for as much as 400 years.

Table 2.2.1 Distribution of relative complementisers across varieties of spoken English

	United Kingdom						Canada				New Zealand	
	London (Cheshire et al. 2013)		Reading (Cheshire 1982)		Northern (Tagliamonte et al. 2005)		Toronto (D'Arcy & Tagliamonte 2010)		Ottawa, adults (Levey 2014)		Auckland (Birchfield 2019)	
	%	*n*	%	*n*	%	*n*	%	*n*	%	*n*	%	*n*
that	56	1157	22	18[a]	64	1230	56	1790	56	409	61	1373
Ø	15	220	22	18	28	528	27	859	24	175	21	466
who	22	399	30	25	7[b]	131	17	554	20	143	14	309
which	3	33	5	4	1	19	0	1 4	0	1	5	113

a This is based on a reconstruction of the actual number of relative clauses involved, Table 33 in Cheshire (1982:73) shows percentages. Reading also falls within the *what* relativisation zone, and 17 relative clauses are introduced with *what* as the relative specifier, hence the rather low percentage for *that*.

b We break down this average in the discussion that follows.

120   *Miriam Meyerhoff et al.*

Two previously reported studies might appear to contradict the 30% ceiling for *wh-* relativisers. Tagliamonte et al. (2005) reported a rate of 57% for *who* in Cheshire (1982). However, on closer examination, this rate only applies to utterances with a [+human] subject antecedent; with object antecedents, the rate is much lower. Hence, the correct rate for *who* in Cheshire's spoken English data is 30% (Cheshire 1982:73), as shown in Table 2.2.1, within our suggested typical historical range of 15%–30% (cf. Peitsara 2002, cited in Tagliamonte et al. 2005). The second apparent counterexample is the extraordinarily high frequency of *wh-* subject relatives (91%) reported for the British National Corpus (Tottie 1997, cited in Tagliamonte et al. 2005). However, it is well-known that when only average percentage frequencies are reported, and if appropriate statistical tests have not been used, it is easy for individual speakers to skew results (Brezina and Meyerhoff 2014).[4]

Note that the overall (aggregated) frequency of *wh-* forms in spoken northern Englishes reported in Tagliamonte et al. (2005) and in Table 2.2.1 masks important differences between communities. We have had to reconstruct the raw numbers from several tables in Tagliamonte et al. (2005) because of discrepancies in their original Tables 3–5. Based on our reanalysis, we can say that the use of *wh-* forms is extremely low in Lowland Scotland (7%) and Northern Ireland (5%), while the community in north-west England uses *wh-* specifiers 14% of the time with subject relative clauses. That is, there seems to be a fundamental difference between English English and British English in the Celtic periphery (see also Romaine 1982 on Scots).

In this chapter, we extend the view of relative clause formation in English to one of the youngest diaspora varieties, New Zealand English. We present evidence suggesting that recent variationist analyses of English relative clauses, in which relativiser selection is framed as fundamentally social, do not hold in our data.

2.2.3 The Status of Relative Specifiers and Complementisers in the History of English

The use of *wh-* forms to introduce relative clauses is typologically unusual, with languages that make use of this strategy over-represented in the Indo-European family. Gisborne and Truswell (2017) argued that the historical data indicates that this property was not inherited from Proto-Indo-European but rather is a shared parallel innovation.

In English, *wh-*forms began to emerge as a means of introducing dependent relative clauses as early as the twelfth century, spreading their way up the NP *accessibility hierarchy* (AH) (Keenan and Comrie 1977); that is, from examples like (8), where the relative involves raising of an argument very low in the AH, it took several hundred years before they were used with any regularity with core arguments, as in (9).

Restrictions on Relative Clauses 121

(8) *ungewædera [[for hwan] eorðwestmas wurdon __ swiðe*
    bad.weather for which earth.fruits were very
    amyrde]
    damaged

'bad weather, which seriously damaged the crops' (early 12th century; Gisborne and Truswell 2017: 30, their example 16)

(9) a) *our Lord, [þe which makeþ sauf þe ryʒtful*
       our lord the which makes saved the pious
       of heret]
       of heart

'our lord, who saves the pious of heart' (mid-fourteenth century, Gisborne and Truswell 2017: 38, their example 26a)

   b) *seke euery man vpon his feblest and wekest/ [who otherwyse wylle now haunte and vse the world]* (late fifteenth century, Gisborne and Truswell 2017:38, their example 28)

Gisborne and Truswell (2017) argued that the spread from (8) to (9) was not a manifestation of *wh*-forms climbing the AH, but rather reflected the gradual spread of the capacity to introduce dependent relatives from *wh*-lexeme to *wh*-lexeme. For instance, (9a) and (9b) show that subject relatives were introduced with the now obsolete *wh*-form *(the) which* more than a 100 years before *who* was used to introduce subject relatives: that is, *which* was used to introduce subject relatives (the highest NP position on the AH) well before *who* was used in this position. Gisborne and Truswell (2017, 2018) noted that English began to generalise the use of *wh*- interrogatives as relativisers very early, first to introduce clause-final, free relatives. This was followed, they concluded (tentatively, given some critical gaps in the historical record) by the gradual reanalysis and spread of *wh*- to restrictive relatives (2017:41). Not only did this change in the use of interrogative pronouns happen when there were already two other relativisers in play (*se (þe)*, the – now lost – inflecting forms of the demonstrative pronouns and the uninflected relative complementiser *þe*, from which we get modern *that*), but it is also notable that the demonstrative relatives "disappear last where *wh*- relatives appear first, and vice versa" (2017:40).

Previous work has suggested that the generalisation of *wh*- pronouns as relativisers occurred as a consequence of language contact (a transfer from French in Early Modern English; Romaine 1984; Tagliamonte et al. 2005; D'Arcy and Tagliamonte 2010, 2015). However, as (8) and (9) show, the innovation started in English much earlier. In addition, it is not clear that the historical record provides good evidence in favour of transfer from French. Sakalauskaitė (2016), who undertook a careful comparison of the distribution and syntax of *the which*-type relative clauses in Northern and Southern varieties of English with the distribution and syntax of the purported French source *lequel*, showed that *the which* was initially more frequent

122 *Miriam Meyerhoff et al.*

in the North than in the South and appears to have been an endogenous innovation that then spread south. If these forms resulted from language contact, this would imply greater influence of French in northern England than in the South, contrary to the facts. Additionally, as Rob Truswell (personal communication) observes, the language contact hypothesis fails to account for (a) the fact that *qu-* relativisers seldom occurred in Norman French (the best potential source given the timing of examples like (8)) and (b) why only *some* French models for relativisation were borrowed (English produced nothing equivalent to French *dont*, for instance). Sakalauskaitė concluded that the syntax of the English *the which* relatives "is substantially different from the French" (2016:33). The data presented in Gisborne and Truswell (2017) and Sakalauskaitė (2016) should make us cautious about assuming that the *wh-* relatives were borrowings from French and that they have always had connotations of prestige.

Although *wh-* forms may be more frequent today in educated, careful, and monitored speech and writing in general, we are not warranted to assume that this reflects how and where they emerged in English. Instead, we are more sympathetic to Meier (1967:281), who observed that other (obvious) *wh-* calques did not survive, leaving it to the researcher to account for why these particular forms, with these particular functions, at this particular time did (Bickel 2007; Gisborne and Truswell 2018). Meier argued that "foreign elements are never received into a given language simply intralingual as such, unless some intralingual foundations for their reception have been laid" (1967:279–280; Jakobson [1938] and King [2000] make similar assertions). In Meier's opinion, the alternation between *wh-* relatives and other relativisers might well have been, from the outset, partly "elegant variation" (1967:283), but it was certainly also linguistic, reflecting a difference in information structure. As we will see, our corpus suggests that semantics and pragmatics remain relevant to speakers in their selection of relativisers even today.

In short, while it is perfectly possible that overt *wh-* relative specifiers might have become an index of prestige or carefulness in speech once they were introduced as variants, sociolinguists should be critical of claims that their current indexicality is a direct legacy of the circumstances under which they arose.[5] Recent historical syntax research provides clear evidence that: (a) they entered English several hundred years earlier than was previously thought; (b) their expansion was the result of language-internal (not contact-induced) change; and, (c) the replacement of demonstrative relative specifiers by *wh-* relative specifiers was accelerated or aided by prestige, education or social standing. What makes *wh-* relativisers, on the face of it, "quite useless" (Gisborne and Truswell 2017:35) is that at the time they emerged in the history of English, there was already a series of relative specifiers.

The significance of these observations for our Auckland Voices data will become apparent: as we will show, the use of *that, wh-* and *zero* relative specifiers seems to be constrained much more by linguistic constraints than by social ones. In addition, the principal linguistic constraint in the Auckland Voices data suggests that *that* complementisers are not simply the default (synchronic and historical) option, but rather that *that* carries semantic and pragmatic meaning.

2.2.4 Auckland Voices

Auckland's very heterogeneous population comprises roughly one-third of that of New Zealand.[6] In 2013,[7] 27% of Aucklanders were born overseas (compared to 19% nationally), and many Aucklanders are migrants from other parts of New Zealand. Migration is, of course, not a new phenomenon to New Zealand – the islands were populated through successive migration waves beginning around 1300 CE, and very large numbers of Europeans arrived beginning in the mid-1800s. After the Second World War, there was quite substantial immigration to Auckland from neighbouring Pacific Islands (the Pacific Islander population grew from 3,600 in 1951 to over 50,000 in 1972; Phillips 2015). While Pacific migration continues today, it slowed substantially after the oil shocks and economic recession in the 1970s. A large proportion of the Pacific migrants who arrived in the late twentieth century settled in Auckland, laying the ground for its claim to be the largest Polynesian city in the world (Fraenkel 2012). Since the 1990s, most migration to Auckland has consisted of people identified by the Census as Asian, largely from Mainland China, Hong Kong, India, Sri Lanka, and the Philippines (Phillips 2015). This migration has diversified traditionally white (Pakeha) suburbs in Auckland, to the point where in some Auckland Census tracts there is no longer any single ethnic majority.

Research in ethnolinguistically diverse areas of London (Cheshire et al. 2011, 2013, 2015; Cheshire 2013) indicated that such areas can be febrile areas of linguistic innovation and change, which has generated some sociolinguistically surprising results. Instead of the expected pattern of young women leading change from below (Labov 1994, 2001), the London data showed changes being led by young men, specifically, young men who are not from the traditional Anglo speech community. It is not clear whether these unexpected patterns are a peculiarity of Inner London or characteristic of highly mixed communities in general, the harbinger of new principles to be applied in sociolinguistics in an era of increasing and rapid urbanisation worldwide (Smakman and Heinrich 2017). Our project was, therefore, designed to elucidate some of these matters as well as to provide a baseline documenting the way Aucklanders speak. Although Aucklanders have always made up between a fifth and a third of the total New Zealand population (and seem likely to continue to increase as a proportion of the total population of New Zealand), there has been no systematic study of how they talk.[8]

124 *Miriam Meyerhoff et al.*

Interviews were conducted with 64 people who live in and grew up in Auckland, divided into two age-groups (25 and under, 40 and over), affording apparent-time data to allow inferences about possible changes in progress. While all are native speakers of New Zealand English, some (especially younger speakers) grew up with another language or languages in the home. Interviews, which lasted between one and three hours, were conducted by a single interviewer or an interviewer with a friend, who were generally also local to the area. Interviews were recorded in three areas of Auckland selected to capture the changing demographics of the city. All three areas had experienced average growth between 2006 and 2013, but they have experienced very different patterns of migration. Some of the key properties of the three communities are summarised in Table 2.2.2. The recorded interviews were transcribed in ELAN (Sloetjes and Wittenberg 2008) and proof-read twice. Transcriptions were used to identify all subject and non-subject restrictive relative clauses (two coders conferred on problematic cases),[9] resulting in a dataset of 1,373 relative clauses.

The competition between relativisers is, on the face of it, a likely point of linguistic levelling in multiethnic and ethnolinguistically diverse communities (older and younger speakers in South Auckland, and younger speakers in Mount Roskill). All relative clauses were coded for a range of social (community, age group, gender) and linguistic factors: the definiteness, grammatical role, and animacy of the antecedent, and

Table 2.2.2 Profiles of the three communities in the Auckland Voices project

Community	Demographic profile (2013)[a]	Demographic change since 2001	Born overseas (2013)	Median household income (2013 rounded)
Titirangi (West Auckland)	• 74% Pakeha • 10% Maori • 10% Pacific • 9% Asian	• Little • Small increases in Pacific and Asian population	28%	$80,000
Papatoetoe-Manurewa-Otara (South Auckland)	• 26% Pakeha • 19% Maori • 36% Pacific • 23% Asian	• 15% decrease in Pakeha proportion • 11% increase in Asian proportion	43%	$50,000
Mount Roskill (Central)	• 36% Pakeha • 5% Maori • 15% Pacific • 42% Asian	• No longer Pakeha majority • All increase in the internally- diverse Asian group	51%	$58,000

a Small percentages of Middle Eastern, Latin American and African respondents and people choosing to identify as 'New Zealander' omitted.

Restrictions on Relative Clauses 125

the length and syntactic complexity of the relative clause. Details of the coding and discussion of the similarities and differences between communities are documented in Birchfield (2019). Here we focus on the single linguistic constraint that emerges as significant across areas of Auckland, and we consider its implications for our understanding of the syntax of spoken English.

2.2.5 Selection of Relativiser in the Auckland Voices Corpus

As Table 2.2.1 showed, the proportion of relativisers in Auckland is comparable to the proportions documented for other varieties of English: *that* is most frequent (61%), followed by *zero* (21%) and *wh-* forms (19%). As in most other varieties of English, we are effectively dealing with two variables: (i) subject relatives, which principally involve an alternation between *that* and *wh-* (with a strong animacy constraint, such that the most frequently used form *who* (14%) only occurs with [+human] antecedents), and (ii) non-subject relatives, which mainly occur with *that* or the *zero* relative specifier (there are 16 *who* tokens and 26 *which* tokens introducing non-subject relative clauses).

Unlike in Toronto (D'Arcy and Tagliamonte 2010), there is no evidence that the choice of relativiser in Auckland is determined on the basis of social facts. While *wh-* forms are most frequent in Titirangi (the more wealthy white community), the only significant inter-community difference is between South Auckland and *both* Mount Roskill and Titirangi. This result suggests that social class or prestige is not a strong factor driving the choice of relativiser in our corpus. Among South Auckland speakers, *that* is the preferred relativiser, and the other social factors (age group and gender) are not significant. There is a very weak ($p < 0.05$) gender effect (men favour *zero* in non-subject relative clauses), but this effect is localised to Mount Roskill and not in Titirangi, as we might expect if this were a stable, prestige-laden variable.

Only one constraint is significant for both subject and non-subject relative clauses, the semantics of the antecedent. Indeed, for subject relatives, it is the *only* significant constraint. In other words, the selection of relativiser in Auckland is fundamentally a *linguistic* variable. The manifestation of this constraint suggests that New Zealand speakers have creatively reanalysed the long-standing variation in English relativisers so that there are linguistically principled grounds for the use of all three options: *zero, who,* and *that.*[10]

2.2.6 Indefinite Pronouns and the Selection of Relativiser

In both subject and non-subject relative clauses, the strongest predictor of whether a relative clause will be introduced by *that* or a relative specifier is the semantics of the antecedent. In non-subject relatives (where

126   *Miriam Meyerhoff et al.*

the alternation is between *that* and *zero*), the *zero* relativiser is favoured when the antecedent noun is an indefinite pronoun (e.g., *someone, anybody, anyone, nobody*). Likewise, in subject relatives (where the alternation is between *that* and *wh-*), a *wh-* relativiser is favoured when the antecedent is an indefinite pronoun. This pattern appears to be a local and possibly recent innovation as it is not consistent with previous findings with respect to indefinite pronoun antecedents (Ball 1996).

A multiple regression analysis of the data modelling speaker as a random effect in Rbrul (Johnson 2009) found that *only* the semantics of the antecedent is significant for subject relatives and that semantics of the antecedent is the most significant predictor for non-subject relatives. Table 2.2.3 shows the results for both non-subject and subject relative clauses.

Examples of indefinite pronoun antecedents are shown in (10)–(14).

Table 2.2.3 Two independent multiple regression analyses of the contribution of factors to the occurrence of relativisers other than *that*, in non-subject and subject relative clauses, in the Auckland Voices corpus. Individual speaker modelled as a random effect

	Factor weight (probability)	% *non-*that	*n*
Non-subject relatives (zero relative specifier) (r^2 = 0.253)			
Antecedent			
Indefinite pronoun	.67	62	104
Definite NP	.46	46	556
Indefinite NP	.36	32	404
Speaker sex			
Male	.58	49	420
Female	.42	38	644
Length of relative clause			
Short (< 3 words)	.54	48	512
Long	.46	37	552
Subject relatives (wh- relative specifier) (r^2 = 0.105)			
Antecedent			
Indefinite pronoun	.65	57	42
Indefinite NP	.49	47	365
Definite NP	.36	35	261

Factor groups not selected as significant: Grammatical role of antecedent in the matrix clause, syntactic complexity of relative clause, animacy of antecedent, community, age group.

Restrictions on Relative Clauses   127

Indefinite pronouns with (subject) **who** *relatives*

(10) a) Somebody ***who*** thought they were smarter than they are. (Freya, MR, younger)

      b) It's not respectful to like argue with someone ***who***'s older than you. (Siale, MR, younger)

      c) He said, "We haven't got anyone ***who*** can do the job". (Annie, MR, older)

Indefinite pronouns with (non-subject) **zero** *relatives*

(11) a) It was just somewhere Ø you worked, but it's a lovely old home. (June, SA, older)

      b) That's maybe something Ø we impose on our kids. (Mishti, MR, younger)

      c) I can't really think of anything Ø I don't like. Freya (MR, younger)

      d) Just because they give you everything Ø you want doesn't necessarily equate to love. Kristin (MR, younger)

      e) Absolutely nothing Ø we could do. Annie (MR, older)

Indefinite pronouns with **that** *relatives*

(12) a) For babysitting it's [important] to find somebody ***that*** you feel comfortable with. June (MR, older)

      b) Is that something ***that*** happened or like did we misremember? Caitlyn (TR, younger)

      c) really interested in anything ***that*** was going to help them do a better job. Jim (TR, older)

      d) There's nowhere in New Zealand **that** you can't see hills. Luke (MR, older)

Examining the results by community, the antecedent effect in non-subject relatives remains significant in Titirangi and Mount Roskill but not in South Auckland, where none of the linguistic or social predictors are significant. Birchfield (2019) suggests this is a measure of the levelling that has perhaps occurred as a consequence of a longer history as a highly diverse community (including substantial numbers of L2 users of English). The numbers of subject relatives are rather small when we break down the analysis of *that* and *wh-* for each of the three communities (Titirangi, n = 168; Mount Roskill, n = 248; South Auckland, n = 251), and in only Titirangi do any of our predictors emerge as significant constraints on the use of *wh*-forms. These are all linguistic: the semantics of the antecedent, syntactic role of the antecedent, and syntactic complexity of the relative clause. The absence of any gender effect

128 *Miriam Meyerhoff et al.*

strengthens our conviction that this variable is not associated indexically with prestige in the Auckland Voices corpus.

The preference for the relative specifiers *wh-* and *zero* with indefinite pronoun antecedents suggests that our Auckland speakers are using semantic and syntactic features to scaffold and make sense of variation which has been present in English for centuries. In order to unpack what this sense might be, we have to consider the internal syntax of the relative clause and how this might articulate with the semantic features associated with an indefinite pronoun antecedent.

As Figure 2.2.2 showed, in the widely-accepted syntactic analysis of relative clauses, the relativiser is raised to [Spec, CP], where it is realised as either a *wh-* or null operator coindexed with a gap/trace in the subordinate clause. Among our Auckland speakers, a semantically indefinite antecedent noun favours the selection of one of the operator variants (*wh-* or *zero*) to introduce a relative clause. But crucially, it is not just any indefinite antecedent. As Table 2.2.3 shows, indefinite NPs such as *a friend* (1a, 2b), *some places* (1b) do not favour the occurrence of *wh-* and *zero* relative specifiers. Like definite antecedents, indefinite NPs favour *that* complementisers. It is only indefinite pronouns as the antecedent that favour the *wh-* and *zero* relative specifiers. In other words, relative clauses as in (10) and (11) are favoured more than relative clauses as in (12).

An explanation for this pattern may lie in the semantics of the antecedent and the relativiser. An indefinite pronoun, such as *somebody, nobody, anyone*, opens a possible set of referents that is underspecified in the extreme. When an indefinite pronoun antecedent in the matrix clause is coindexed with a *zero* or a *wh-* operator, this reinforces a reading of non-specific reference. The preference for an operator following an indefinite pronoun antecedent might be construed as a type of feature agreement that links all the coindexed constituents in the main and the subordinate clause.

This analytic conjecture is supported by the intuitions of some speakers of New Zealand English, who report that (for them) there is an interpretive distinction between *anyone **who** can do the job* (cf. 10c) and *anybody **that** can do the job* or between *something Ø we impose on our kids* (cf. 11b) and *something **that** we impose on our kids*. For these speakers, a *that* relative clause presupposes the existence of a specific referent, while the *wh-* and *zero* variants carry no such presupposition; the reference is non-specific and, indeed, there may not exist any such referent or state of affairs. If this intuition proves to be generalisable (not yet tested), then the preference for an indefinite pronoun and the operator variants makes considerable semantic sense.

By extension, if the speaker wishes to implicate specific reference with an indefinite pronoun antecedent, then the *that* complementiser is well-suited to the task. While complementiser *that* is largely bleached of its historical sense as a deictic or demonstrative, it would appear that the specificity associated with a demonstrative remains accessible to speakers and can be used to provide a systematic linguistic basis for the variation in relative clauses. As Labov (1984) showed, diachronic change may leave formerly productive syntactic distinctions fossils in the present-day grammar. But long-lost distinctions may perdure for centuries in patterns of synchronic variation – a kind of variationist analogue of Hopper's (1991) notion of persistence in grammaticalisation.

Much about this account is conjectural, but it seems to us to warrant further investigation. It reframes the variation in English relative clauses as considerably more linguistically interesting than hitherto suspected and suggests that synchronic variation has direct links to the historical derivation of English relativisers.

2.2.7 Conclusion

The alternation between *that, wh-* and *zero* relativisers attracted the attention of some of the earliest, founding mothers of variationist sociolinguistics (Cheshire 1982; Romaine 1982). While the recent orthodoxy appears to favouring a social explanation for the use of, in particular, the *wh-* specifiers, this chapter provides evidence that, where linguists can resist the prescriptive temptation to try and "tame the vernacular" (Cheshire 1998), we still have much to learn by embracing the variation inherent in spoken English syntax.

In this chapter, we have examined the distribution of different relativisers in the spoken English of New Zealand's most ethnolinguistically diverse city, Auckland. We have shown that the syntax of spoken English in Auckland favours the use of *wh-* and *zero* relative specifiers only after an indefinite pronoun antecedent. In presenting data from a variety of English where the principal constraints on relativiser selection do not appear to be social, we offer an alternative view to the deterministic picture of *wh-* selection that has been forwarded in some recent studies of English relativisation. Moreover, by drawing on recent research in historical syntax and the history of language contact in English, we have problematised the notion that the alternation between *that* and *wh-* was historically predetermined to express differences in the prestige or formality of the *wh-* variants over *that* and *zero*. Instead, we present an account of the selection of relativisers that is semantically grounded, with the advantages of (i) not only accounting for the distribution of *wh-*, but also of *that*, (ii) providing an empirical basis for postulating the *zero* variant as structurally equivalent to the *wh-* operator, and (iii) linking the synchronic distribution of relativisers to the semantically driven generalisation of *wh-* relativisers in the history of English.

Notes

1 It is our great pleasure to offer the analysis in this chapter to Jenny Cheshire, who has been a steadfast supporter of New Zealand sociolinguistics and a strong advocate for Aotearoa New Zealand linguists in general. Jenny's foresight and originality in identifying multicultural enclaves as a site for challenging sociolinguistic preconceptions was the primary motivation for undertaking the Auckland Voices project. Her rigorous study of syntactic and pragmatic variation in English has inspired many of us. *He wahine toa nei. Arohanui e Jenny.*

2 The electronic World Atlas of Varieties of English (eWAVE) showed *what* as a relativiser as pervasive in seven varieties and "neither pervasive nor rare" in an additional 13 (out of a total of 76). ewave-atlas.org.

3 Example sentences are reproduced verbatim from speaker interviews and are identified by pseudonym, location (MR = Mount Roskill, TR = Titirangi, SA = South Auckland) and age-group.

4 Ball (1996) also shows a very high frequency of *wh-* relatives in the Watergate recordings (61%), for which we have no explanation. However, we note that (profanities notwithstanding) it was clear that these recordings were a matter of record within the Nixon White House, so whether they reflect *unmonitored* spoken English norms of the time is an open question.

5 As Ball (1996) astutely pointed out, continuity between Middle Scots and modern spoken English syntax is unproven. We have already noted that there seem to be profound differences between the Celtic periphery varieties of English in Britain and other varieties.

6 Research was supported by a grant from the Royal Society of New Zealand Te Apārangi Marsden Fund (PIs Meyerhoff, Watson; AIs: Ballard, Charters) and by University of Auckland support for a Summer Scholar, Ruby Papali'i-Curtin, supervised by Helen Charters. See Meyerhoff et al. (in prep.) We acknowledge our interviewers and the 'Auckland Angels' who helped find people to take part in the study: Anusha Malavalli, Ruchika Rajkumar, Victoria Marchant, Ingrid Dubbelt, Ruby Papali'i-Curtin, Fa'alei Pailegutu, Miriam Meyerhoff, Brooke Ross; Andrew Beach, Innes Clarke, Fiona Larsen, Judy Tuilaga McFall-McCaffery, Sam Meyerhoff, Suzanne Purdy, Michael Wood.

7 The 2018 Census in New Zealand was administered online only. It has become clear that this has resulted in serious under-counting (Manch 2019). Since this may disproportionately affect some of the groups of residents we are particularly interested in, we prefer to continue to cite the 2013 data.

8 Recordings by Allan Bell and Donna Starks in the 1990s focussed only on Aucklanders of Pacific descent.

9 Coding was done by Alexandra Birchfield and Helen Charters.

10 Our analysis has benefitted from discussions with Nik Gisborne and Rob Truswell. The insight that our analysis of *wh-* and zero also suggests a principled reason for the use of *that* is Gisborne's. Any lack of lucidity in the presentation of these arguments is our responsibility alone.

References

Ball, Catherine N. 1996. "A diachronic study of relative markers in spoken and written English". *Language Variation and Change* 8:227–258.

Bickel, Balthasar. 2007. "Typology in the 21st century: major current developments". *Linguistic Typology* 11:239–251.

Restrictions on Relative Clauses 131

Birchfield, Alexandra. 2019. "'All the people who live in Auckland': A study of subject and non-subject relative clauses in Auckland English". Unpublished MA thesis, Victoria University of Wellington.

Brezina, Vaclav and Miriam Meyerhoff. 2014. "Significant or random? A critical review of statistical analyses in corpus-based sociolinguistic studies". *International Journal of Corpus Linguistics* 19(1):1–28.

Carnie, Andrew. 2013. *Syntax: A Generative Introduction*. 3rd edition. Oxford: Wiley-Blackwell.

Cheshire, Jenny. 1982. *Variation in an English Dialect*. Oxford: Oxford University Press.

Cheshire, Jenny. 1998. "Taming the vernacular: some repercussions for the study of syntactic variation and spoken grammar". *Te Reo* 41:6–27.

Cheshire, Jenny. 2013. "Grammaticalisation in social context: the emergence of a new English pronoun". *Journal of Sociolinguistics* 17:608–633.

Cheshire, Jenny, Paul Kerswill, Sue Fox and Eivind Torgersen. 2011. "Contact, the feature pool and the speech community: The emergence of multicultural London English". *Journal of Sociolinguistics* 15:151–196.

Cheshire, Jenny, David Adger and Sue Fox. 2013. "Relative *Who* and the actuation problem". *Lingua* 126:51–77.

Cheshire, Jenny, Jacomine Nortier and David Adger. 2015. "Emerging multiethnolects in Europe". *Queen Mary's Occasional Papers Advancing Linguistics* 33:1–27.

Chomsky, Noam. 1981. *Lectures on Government and Binding*. Dordrecht: Foris Publications.

D'Arcy, Alexandra and Sali A. Tagliamonte. 2010. "Prestige, accommodation, and the legacy of relative *Who*". *Language in Society* 39:383–410.

D'Arcy, Alexandra and Sali A. Tagliamonte. 2015. "Not always variable: Probing the vernacular grammar". *Language Variation and Change* 27:255–285.

Dekeyser, Xavier. 1984. "Relativicers [sic.] in early modern English: A dynamic quantitative study". In *Historical Syntax*, J. Fisiak (ed.). Berlin: Mouton de Gruyter. 61–87.

De Vries, Mark. 2002. *The Syntax of Relativization*. Utrecht: LOT Publications.

Fraenkel, Jon. 2012. "Pacific Islands and New Zealand". *Te Ara - The Encyclopedia of New Zealand*. www.TeAra.govt.nz/en/pacific-islands-and-new-zealand (accessed 20 March 2019).

Gisborne, Nikolas and Robert Truswell. 2017. "Where do relative specifiers come from?" In *Micro-Change and Macro-Change in Diachronic Syntax*, E. Mathieu and R. Truswell (eds.). Oxford: Oxford University Press. 25–42.

Gisborne, Nikolas and Robert Truswell. 2018. "Parallel evolution of relative clauses in Indo-European". In *Paper delivered to the Philological Society Annual General Meeting*, Oxford.

Hinrichs, Lars, Benedikt Szmrecsanyi and Axel Bohmann. 2015. "Whichhunting and the standard English relative clause". *Language* 91(4):806–836.

Hopper, Paul J. 1991. "On some principles of grammaticalization". In *Approaches to Grammaticalization, Volume I*, E.C. Traugott and B. Heine (eds.). Amsterdam: John Benjamins. 17–36.

132   Miriam Meyerhoff et al.

Jakobson, Roman. 1938. "Sur la Théorie des Affinités Phonologiques des Langues". *Actes du 4e congrès des linguistes*. Copenhagen: Einar Munksgaard. 48–59.

Johnson, Daniel, E. 2009. "Getting off the GoldVarb standard: Introducing Rbrul for mixed-effects variable rule analysis". *Language and Linguistics Compass* 3(1):359–383.

Kayne, Richard. 1994. *The Antisymmetry of Syntax*. Cambridge, MA: The MIT Press.

Keenan, Edward L. and Bernard Comrie. 1977. "Noun phrase accessibility and universal grammar". *Linguistic Inquiry* 8(1):63–99.

King, Ruth. 2000. *The Lexical Basis of Grammatical Borrowing*. Amsterdam/Philadelphia: John Benjamins.

Kortmann, Bernd and Kerstin Lunkenheimer (eds.). 2013. *The Electronic World Atlas of Varieties of English*. Leipzig: Max Planck Institute for Evolutionary Anthropology. http://ewave-atlas.org (Accessed on 2019-07-21).

Labov, William. 1984. Field methods of the project Linguistic Change and Variation. In *Language in Use: Readings in sociolinguistics*, John Baugh and Joel Scherzer (eds.). Englewood Cliffs: Prentice-Hall. 28–53.

Labov, William. 1994. *Principles of Linguistic Change, Volume 1: Internal Factors*. Oxford: Blackwell.

Labov, William. 2001. *Principles of Linguistic Change, Volume 2: Social Factors*. Oxford: Blackwell.

Levey, Stephen. 2014. "A comparative variationist perspective on relative clauses in child and adult speech". In *Linguistic Variation: Confronting Fact and Theory*, R. Torres Cacoullos, N. Dion and A. Lapierre (eds.). New York: Routledge. 22–37.

Manch, Thomas. 2019. "Census 2018: Stats NZ says full results to be released mid-2020". *Stuff*. www.stuff.co.nz/national/112309580/census-2018-stats-nz-to-release-data-in-september (Accessed 4 July 2019).

Meier, Hans Heinrich. 1967. "The lag of relative *Who* in the nominative". *Neophilologus* 51:277–286.

Meyerhoff, Miriam, Elaine Ballard, Helen Charters, Alexandra Birchfield and Catherine Watson. Forthcoming. The Auckland Voices Project: Language change in a changing city. In *Varieties of English in the Indo-Pacific*, K. Burridge and P. Peters (eds.). Cambridge: Cambridge University Press.

Peitsara, Kirsti. 2002. "Relativizers in the Suffolk dialect". In *Relativization on the North Sea Littoral*, P. Poussa and M. Lundberg (eds.). Munich: Lincom. 167–180.

Phillips, Jock. 2015. "History of immigration - the end of a 'White New Zealand' policy". *Te Ara - The Encyclopedia of New Zealand*. www.TeAra.govt.nz/en/history-of-immigration/page-15 (Accessed 20 March 2019).

Romaine, Suzanne. 1982. *Socio-Historical Linguistics: Its Status and Methodology*. Cambridge: Cambridge University Press.

Romaine, Suzanne. 1984. "Towards a typology of relative clause formation strategies in Germanic". In *Historical Syntax*, J. Fisiak (ed.). Berlin: Mouton de Gruyter. 437–470.

Sakalauskaitė, Julija. 2016. "Endogenous and exogenous influence on the which". Unpublished MSc in English Language thesis, University of Edinburgh.

Sigley, Robert J. 1997. "Choosing your relatives: Relative clauses in New Zealand English". Unpublished PhD thesis, Victoria University of Wellington.

Sloetjes, Han and Peter Wittenburg. 2008. "Annotation by category – ELAN and ISO DCR". In *Proceedings of the 6th International Conference on Language Resources and Evaluation* (LREC 2008).

Smakman, Dirk and Patrick Heinrich (eds.). 2017. *Urban Sociolinguistics: The City as a Linguistic Process and Experience*. London: Routledge.

Tagliamonte, Sali A., Jennifer Smith and Helen Lawrence. 2005. "No taming the vernacular! Insights from the relatives in Northern Britain". *Language Variation and Change* 17(1):74–112.

Tottie, Gunnel. 1997. "Relatively speaking: Relative markers usage in the British National Corpus". In *To Explain the Present: Studies in the Changing English Language in Honour of Matti Rissanen*, T. Nevalainen and L. Kahlas-Tarkka (eds.). Helsinki: Société Néophilologique. 465–481.

2.3 Swabian Relatives
Variation in the Use of the *wo*-relativiser

Karen V. Beaman

2.3.1 Introduction

Numerous studies have found that grammatical variables are not as socially stratified as phonological ones, causing some sociolinguists to theorise that they lie outside the range of the sociolinguistic monitor (Labov 1993; see Levon, Buchstaller and Mearns 2020; Labov et al. 2011; Lavandera 1978; Scherre and Naro 1992; Walker 2020). Cheshire (2003:245) contends, however, that morphosyntactic variation is merely "different" from phonological variation and, indeed, is often "intricately involved in the construction of social meaning" (see Moore and Carter 2015; Moore, this volume) or in the conveyance of semantic and pragmatic information (see Cheshire, Adger, and Fox 2013; Meyerhoff et al. 2020).[1]

To investigate these claims, this chapter aims to explore one type of grammatical variation common in several southern German varieties: variation between traditional relative pronoun usage prescribed in standard German (e.g., *der, die, das, dem, den, dessen, deren*) (henceforth referred to as *d*-relatives) and the use of *wo* 'where' as a relativiser common in the spoken language. Some linguists have proposed that *wo*-relatives spread from referring to notions of place to a broader set of linguistic environments (Brandner and Bräuning 2013). Many have argued that pronouns originally used as interrogatives are logical candidates for relativisers due to their close relationship with indirect questions: both involve phrases with declarative illocutionary force and exhibit a high level of referentiality (Keenan and Hull 1973; Matos and Brito 2013; Sankoff and Brown 1976). There is also considerable evidence that locative adverbs have evolved into generalised relative markers from other languages (e.g., Brook 2011; Katis and Nikiforidou 2010; Krapova 2010). To date, no sociolinguistic variation analysis has been conducted on the use of *wo*-relatives in German dialects. Thus, this chapter aims to answer three questions: (1) what are the internal and external factors influencing the use of *wo* as a relative marker in Swabian German, (2) is the usage of the *wo*-relativiser stable or changing and, if changing, (3) what are the drivers and/or inhibitors of the change?

2.3.2 Theoretical Background

2.3.2.1 English Relatives

The system of relativisation has been extensively researched in many varieties of English by both sociolinguists and formal syntacticians (e.g., Cheshire 1996; Cheshire, Adger, and Fox 2013; Tagliamonte, Smith, and Lawrence 2005; Meyerhoff et al. 2020), from a socio-historical perspective (e.g., Ball 1996; Hendery 2012; Romaine 1982, 1992), in spoken and written genres (e.g., Guy and Bayley 1995; Hinrichs, Szmrecsanyi, and Bohmann 2015; Jankowski 2009, 2013), and in vernacular speech (e.g., Cheshire et al. 2013; D'Arcy and Tagliamonte 2010; Jankowski 2009, 2013; Levey 2006, 2014; Tagliamonte et al. 2005).

Much early sociolinguistic work has suggested that relative pronoun usage is a 'covert variable' not readily available for social evaluation (Tottie and Rey 1997:245). However, researchers in the 1980s and 1990s working within the variationist framework began to find that variation in relative pronoun usage was not only constrained by linguistic conditioning and syntactic position but was also correlated with various social factors, such as genre, style, education, and socio-economic status. Romaine (1982) observed that *wh-* pronouns are generally restricted to written texts and to specific groups of speakers, that is, educated individuals with middle-class aspirations. Quirk (1957), and later Tottie (1995), found that *zero* relatives are strongly favoured with personal pronouns that are the subject of the relative clause, while *wh*-relatives are correlated with speakers' educational level. Guy and Bayley (1995) established that the channel of communication (spoken or written), the animacy of the antecedent, the syntactic position of the relativiser, and the distance between the antecedent and the relativiser all have significant effects on speakers' choice of relative pronouns. Cheshire's (1996) investigation of the lexical item *that* revealed that relative pronouns can serve as a linguistic 'sign-post' in communication, reflecting "general social principles of cooperative activity between individuals" (Cheshire 1996:392).

Recently, research on relative pronoun usage has focussed on the differences between changes imposed from above (such as social status, education, prescriptivism, and language ideologies) and those that arise from within (such as grammatical and structural constraints). Investigating relative pronoun usage in three varieties of English, Tagliamonte, Smith, and Lawrence (2005) uncovered both universal constraints (e.g., clause length, clause complexity, level of education and local involvement) as well as dialect-specific factors. D'Arcy and Tagliamonte (2010:384) argued that speakers' use of relative pronouns "evince their social position within the community and indicate accommodation to their interlocutors") (see, however, Meyerhoff et al. 2020). Cheshire, Adger, and Fox (2013)

136 *Karen V. Beaman*

observed that the emergence of relative *who* has developed into a 'topic-marking strategy' in Hackney London English linked to the multiethnicity of the friendship network. Investigating lexical density and information status, Jankowski (2013) uncovered "changing stylistic notions" in relative usage brought on by prescriptivist conventions and literacy ('change from above'). Hinrichs, Szmrecsanyi and Bohmann (2015) adopted a machine-learning-based method to automatically retrieve *zero* relative clauses and evaluate 22 language-internal, language-external, stylistic, and prescriptivism-related predictors. Their multivariate analysis exposed a complex set of factors driving relativiser choice, principal among them genre and prescriptivism. Notably, a dominant standard language ideology is prevalent in varieties of English, suggesting that "prescriptive norms and ideologies of standard speech are determinants of variation among relative pronoun choice" (D'Arcy and Tagliamonte 2010:384). These works and many others have firmly established that both intra- and extra-linguistic factors play significant roles in speakers' choice of grammatical variables, such as relative pronouns.

2.3.2.2 *German Relatives*

The wealth of research on relatives in various English varieties leads to the question: which of these factors and findings are relevant for varieties of German? We start first with a description of the German system of relativisation. Modern standard German provides three[2] primary ways to introduce a relative clause (Duden 2016:1045–1055): (a) inflected *d*-pronouns (e.g., *der, die, das, den, dem, deren, dessen*), (b) inflected *w*-pronouns (e.g., *welcher, welche, welches, welchen, welchem*), and (c) non-inflected complementisers (e.g., *wo* 'where'; *wie* 'how'; 'as'; *was* 'what'; *wer* 'who'; and *als* 'as', 'than', 'when', 'while') which are common in many southern German varieties. The inflected *w*-pronouns are generally restricted to written language or to highly stylised spoken varieties; hence, the primary variation in relative pronoun usage in south-western Germany is between the case-marked *d*-relative pronouns and the invariant complementiser, *wo*, as demonstrated in example (1):

(1) <u>Angela-1982</u>:[3]
> *es gibt erfolgreiche Mensche __wo__ Karriere gmacht hen*
> 'there are successful people __who__ have made their careers'

> *und jetzt en Haufe Geld verdienet*
> 'and now earn a ton of money'

> *es gibt au andere __die__ vielleicht gar net so viel Geld hen*
> 'there are also others __who__ perhaps don't have nearly so much money'

Pittner (2004) provides a functional typology for the particle *wo*. First, and most common, *wo* is used as an interrogative adverb, as in (2):

(2) Herbert-1982
__wo__ warn mr dabei?
'__where__ were we in the process?'

Second, *wo* is commonly used as a locative adverb, as in (3):

(3) Angela-2017
Schwââbe bleibet gern dâ __wo__ se gebore sin
'Swabians like to stay there __where__ they are born'

Less commonly, and only in spoken language Pittner says, *wo* can be used as a temporal adverb, as in (4):

(4) Jurgen-1982
am Āfang __wo__ se sich kenneglernt
'in the beginning __where/when__ they met'

Pittner considers (4) to be non-standard usage; in standard German, the conjunction *als* 'as' or 'when' would typically be used.

Also considered non-standard, Pittner states that invariant *wo* can be used as a relative pronoun, as in (5):

(5) Angela-1982
ds beschte Daitsch __wo__ s gib
'the best German __where/that__ there is'

The standard German equivalent for example (5) requires the nominative neuter pronoun, *das,* as is: *das beste Deutsch, __das__ es gibt.* Duden (2016:1050–1052) clearly declares examples (1), (4) and (5), in which *wo* refers to a person or thing, to be *landschaftlich salopp* 'country slang' (Duden Online 2018) and *nicht standardsprachlich* 'not standard language' (Duden 2016:1052).

Previous analyses of relative pronouns in German have focussed solely on formal, linguistic constraints (i.e., syntactic structure, semantic content, prosodic realisation, and functional role) (Bayer 1984; Bidese, Padovan, and Tomaselli 2012; Brandner and Bräuning 2013; Fleischer 2006, 2004, 2005; Pittner 1995, 2004; van Riemsdijk 1989; Salzmann and Seiler 2010; Schaffranietz 1999; Schubö et al. 2015; de Vries 2002; Weise 1916). Salzmann and Seiler's (2010) analysis of variation in relative clauses in Swiss German showed that, while the use of resumptive pronouns is obligatory for obliques and impossible for subjects and direct object clauses, it is optional with datives, influenced by the morphosyntactic environment, in particular, case matching and the semantics of the head noun (Salzmann and Seiler 2010:79–80). Günthner (2002) investigated the polyfunctional use of *wo* (temporal, causal, and conjunctive) in spontaneous conversations

138　*Karen V. Beaman*

across several middle and southern Germany varieties. She opined that the *wo*-construction is "ambiguous", interpretable solely from the pragmatics of the situation (i.e., context and performance):

> *Die jeweilige Interpretation scheint also nicht am Konnektor ,wo' selbst fest-machbar zu sein, vielmehr markiert ,wo' einen Zusammenhang zwischen zwei Syntagmen, wobei das eine dem anderen untergeordnet ist und die im syntaktisch untergeordneten Teilsatz präsentierte Information zugleich als evident und nicht weiter fraglich gilt (Günthner 2002:25).*

> The particular interpretation thus does not seem to be fixed on the 'wo' connector itself, rather 'wo' marks a relationship between two syntagmas, in which one is subordinate to the other, and the information in the syntactically subordinate clause is simultaneously presented as evident and no longer questionable (my translation).

Despite the considerable descriptive and pragmatic investigations of *wo*-relatives, no studies have conferred any consideration to extra-linguistic factors, such as speaker age, sex, education, occupation, community, orientation/identity. Hence, the dire need for the current socio-grammatical investigation.

2.3.3 Data and Methods

The current investigation follows the quantitative variationist sociolinguistic framework (Labov 1963, 1966, 1972, 1984) in analysing the use of *wo*-relatives in Central Swabian, a high Alemannic dialect spoken in south-western Germany by around 820,000 people or 1% of the German population. This section describes the speech communities, the study participants, the data collection methods, the linguistic variable, and the internal and external predictors evaluated.

2.3.3.1 The Speech Communities

Two communities were selected for this research: the large international city of Stuttgart and its surrounding suburbs and the mid-sized town of Schwäbisch Gmünd and its surrounding rural villages. Stuttgart is the heart of Swabia. It is a large urban centre with over one million inhabitants and is home to many well-known global firms, such as Daimler-Mercedes-Benz, Porsche, Bosch, and Siemens. Schwäbisch Gmünd lies 100 kilometres east of Stuttgart. With 60,000 inhabitants, it is a typical mid-sized, semi-rural town, surrounded by small villages with 77% of the land dedicated to woodland and agriculture.

2.3.3.2 The Study Participants

The data were drawn from a real-time panel study of 20 native Swabian speakers, who were recorded in 1982 and again in 2017 (see Table 2.3.1).

Variation in Swabian wo-*Relatives* 139

Table 2.3.1 Corpus of 20 Swabian panel speakers, in Stuttgart and
Schwäbisch Gmünd, recorded in 1982 and 2017

		Schwäbisch Gmünd		*Stuttgart*		*Total*
		Hi Edu	*Lo Ed*	*Hi Ed*	*Lo Ed*	
1982	Men	0	1	0	0	1
31–60 years	Women	0	2	0	1	3
1982	Men	6	0	4	0	10
18–30 years	Women	3	1	1	1	6
2017	Men	0	1	0	0	1
61–90 years	Women	0	2	0	1	3
2017	Men	6	0	4	0	10
31–60 years	Women	3	1	1	1	6
Totals		18	8	10	4	
		26		14		40

Sixteen of the 20 speakers are of the same age group (i.e., 18–25 in
1982 and 53–60 in 2017), and 14 have post-secondary education (i.e.,
completed the *Abitur* 'German college preparatory exam') and are of
similar socio-economic status (i.e., middle class). The participants are
balanced for two sexes (as self-reported in the demographic questionnaire completed at the end of the interview). The speakers come from
two different social networks: 13 from the semi-rural township of
Schwäbisch Gmünd and seven from the large urban centre of Stuttgart.
In 1982 all participants were family members and close friends of the
interviewers with 'strong ties' in closed, tight-knit communities (Milroy
1987). By 2017, many speakers had moved away and grown apart, and
both communities had evolved into more open and dispersed social networks with 'weak ties' (Milroy 1987). This diversified sample provides
the opportunity to investigate real-time change in relative pronoun usage in different communities (urban versus semi-rural), speaker sexes
(men versus women), and levels of education (high versus low) across a
35-year timespan (1982 versus 2017).

2.3.3.3 *The Interviews*

The data were collected via Labovian-style sociolinguistic interviews
(Labov 1984), covering topics about the speakers' childhood games,
hobbies, neighbourhood, friends and family, and attitudes towards the
Swabian language and culture. In order to increase compatibility across
years, the same survey instrument was used in both years. All interviews were conducted by native Swabian speakers matched for key social

140   *Karen V. Beaman*

characteristics (e.g., same age, gender, education level), with the principal investigator in attendance in the role of a friend-of-a-friend (Milroy and Milroy 1985). Interviews were conducted in the speakers' homes, typically over coffee and cake, with goal of replicating the two recording periods as closely as possible. Transcriptions were completed by native German speakers, university students at the University of Tübingen, using ELAN (Nagy and Meyerhoff 2015; Wittenburg et al. 2006) following a structured orthography developed specifically for Swabian. The 40 interviews comprise 42.1 hours: 17.9 hours (1075 minutes) from 1982 and 24.2 hours (1451 minutes) from 2017.

2.3.3.4 *The Linguistic Variable*

In defining syntactic variables, Cheshire (1987:269) points out several methodological challenges, chief among them is finding a method to determine whether different variants constitute different ways of saying 'the same thing' (Cheshire 2016:264). Although some linguists propose identifying relative clauses semantically (including any type of clause that modifies a nominal phrase (e.g., Keenan and Comrie 1977:63; Lehman 1984:47), the current analysis is based on a strict syntactic definition of (grammatical) functional equivalency (Fleischer 2004; de Vries 2002). This avoids the issue of 'semantic equivalence', which is subjective and likely a function of differing discourse strategies than to the specific syntactic choice of a relative pronoun. Hence, this investigation follows de Vries (2002:14–15) who offers two 'defining' properties and one 'essential' property for identifying relative clauses in German. Consequently, a relative clause is one that is:

1. conveniently disambiguated in German by a finite verb-final syntactic structure;
2. connected to the matrix clause by a 'semantically shared' pivot constituent or relative clause introducer, i.e., either a *d*-relative or a *wo*-relative;
3. independent from the matrix clause in its semantic and syntactic roles.

Thus, it follows that other relative-like structures such as the following, all of which are quite rare in spoken German, have been excluded from the analysis:

a. participial constructions, e.g., *der in seinem Büro arbeitende Mann* 'who in his office working man' (Keenan and Comrie 1977:64);
b. pronominalisation, in which a personal pronoun is used as an anaphoric marker in place of a relative pronoun, e.g., *she teaches young people, they [who] have not finished school yet;*

c. reduced relatives and appositive structures, e.g., *the man, he [who]
    drove a blue car;*
d. unmarked relative clauses, in which only prosodic cues designate the
    presence of a relative.

2.3.3.5 The Corpus

Relative clauses are not very common in speech: less than 5% of all
clauses in the current corpus are relatives. Following the criteria outlined above, relative clauses were manually extracted, hand-coded, and
loaded into R for analysis (R Core Team 2014). This resulted in a total of
1446 relative clauses: 691 from 1982 and 755 from 2017. Overall relative
usage shows 53% (n = 767) for *d*-relatives and 47% (n = 679) for *wo*-
relatives, with the use of *wo* significantly more frequent in Schwäbisch
Gmünd (41%, n = 456) than in Stuttgart (30%, n = 223) (p = 0.0004).
Further detail on the numbers and types of relatives is provided in the
ensuing analysis and results section.

2.3.3.5.1 Restrictiveness

When analysing relatives in English varieties, most researchers have typically excluded non-restrictive relative clauses because they tend to have
different semantic and discourse functions, as well as different prosodic
cues (Tagliamonte, Smith, and Lawrence 2005:85). In addition, non-
restrictive relative clauses in English are "supposedly" categorically introduced by the pronoun *which* (Bohmann and Schultz 2011; Pullum
2009; Quirk 1957). However, in English, this distinction can be "fuzzy"
(see Meyerhoff et al. 2020) and, in German, it is definitely questionable.
For example, in a relative clause extraposition production experiment,
Poschmann and Wagner (2016:36) ascertained that both restrictive and
appositive clauses were "equally natural", when distance, temporal, and
anaphoric elements were controlled for. However, to ensure that there is
indeed no discernible or noteworthy restrictiveness difference with Swabian relatives, all relatives in the dataset were included in the analysis.

2.3.3.5.2 Locatives and Temporals

As previously discussed, a typical use of *wo* is when the antecedent noun
is a physical place (locative) or a notion time (temporal), and indeed
these clauses are a 'knock-out' condition in the Swabian corpus, showing
100% (n = 242) usage of *wo* as the relativiser. Hence, following standard
variationist convention, these clauses were eliminated from the dataset,
leaving a total of 1204 relative clauses for further analysis.

142 *Karen V. Beaman*

2.3.3.5.3 *Resumptives*

Before delving deeper into the analysis, it is important to point out that Swabian also has a resumptive relative, the doubly-filled complementiser: *der wo* 'he who' or *da wo* 'there that', for example,

(6) Ema-1982:
    *des seid die Faule-Weiber-Spätzle, **die wo** durch Press dorchdricket*
    'they are the lazy-wife-noodles, **those that** they put through the press'

(7) Louise-2017:
    *wie alt war dn der, **der wo** Pfarrer worre isch*
    'how old was he then, **he who** became [a] preacher'

This variant is considered characteristic of Swabian *von der Alb* 'from the countryside', reflective of rural and uneducated speech (cf. Labov (1972) 'sociolinguistic stereotype') and is highly stigmatised. Likely due to this stigmatisation and to increasing levels of education ('change from above'), this variant is in stark decline across both communities, from 9% and 11% of all relatives in 1982 to 2% and 3% in 2017. There were only 13 tokens in all 20 interviews in 2017, and those occurred exclusively with the older or less educated speakers.

2.3.3.6 *The Predictors*

Cheshire (1998:65) points out that "in variationist analyses we are limited in what we discover by what we set out to look for". Hence, since no sociolinguistic investigation has previously been conducted on *wo*-relatives, it is important to cast our net wide with the goal of uncovering the critical constraints influencing the choice of *wo* or *d*-relativisers in Swabian.

2.3.3.6.1 *Internal Linguistic Predictors*

Drawn from findings from other research on relative constructions, 16 previously attested internal constraints were selected for exploratory analysis in Swabian. In the following, each predictor is described, references to other relevant studies are cited, and the hypotheses of the current study are stated.

1. Restrictiveness: relative clauses with defining, essential, specifying, and/or propositional information were coded as 'restrictive', whereas those with non-essential, amplifying, supplementary, and/or parenthetical information were coded as 'non-restrictive' (Cheshire et al. 2013; Quirk 1957; Tagliamonte 2002).

- Hypothesis: based on findings from previous studies of German relatives, there will be no significant difference between restrictive and non-restrictive relatives in Swabian.

2. Place: antecedents were coded for referring to a specific physical place or location, to an abstract notion of place (e.g., "in a situation"), or not to any notion of place (Brandner and Bräuning 2013; Pittner 2004).

   - Hypothesis: since physical notions of place favour *wo* usage, abstract notions of place will also favour the use of *wo*.

3. Time: antecedents were coded for referring to a specific date or time, to an abstract notion of time (e.g., "before", "later", "at that moment"), or no reference to any notion of time (Pittner 2004).

   - Hypothesis: since specific notions of time favour *wo* usage, abstract notions of time will also favour the use of *wo*.

4. Antecedent Category: antecedents were coded for different grammatical categories, e.g., noun, pronoun, adverbial, etc. (Fleischer 2006; Hinrichs et al. 2015).

   - Hypothesis: due to their non-specificity with respect to grammatical gender, *wo*-relatives will more likely be favoured with adverbial antecedents.

5. Antecedent Case: antecedents were coded for case, i.e., nominative, accusative, dative, or genitive (Fleischer 2006; Hinrichs et al. 2015).

   - Hypothesis: following the *Accessibility Hierarchy* (Keenan and Comrie 1977), less explicit *wo*-relatives will be more common with antecedents in the more accessible positions, e.g., first nominatives, then accusatives, then datives.

6. Relative Case: relative pronouns were coded for case, i.e., nominative, accusative, dative, or genitive (Cheshire et al. 2013; Fleischer 2006; Hinrichs et al. 2015; Levey 2001; Rohdenburg 1996; Salzmann and Seiler 2010; Tottie and Rey 1997).

   - Hypothesis: following the *Accessibility Hierarchy* (Keenan and Comrie 1977), less explicit *wo*-relatives will be more common with relativisers in the more accessible positions, e.g., first nominatives, then accusatives, then datives.

7. Case Matching: relative pronouns were coded for whether the case between the antecedent and the relativiser were the 'same' or 'not' (Fleischer 2006; Salzmann and Seiler 2010).

   - Hypothesis: because *wo*-relatives are less explicit, they will more likely be favoured when the cases between the relativiser and antecedent head do not match.

8. <u>Resumptive</u>: relative clauses were coded for the presence or absence of the double complementiser, i.e., *der wo* 'that where' (Pittner 2004; Salzmann and Seiler 2010).

   - <u>Hypothesis</u>: due to their more explicit and direct nature, resumptive relatives will more likely be favoured with definite and human antecedents.

9. <u>Animacy</u>: antecedents were coded for 'animate', i.e., living, ambulatory things such as humans, animals, robots, or 'inanimate', i.e., non-living, immobile things, such as plants and concepts[4] (Cheshire et al. 2013; D'Arcy and Tagliamonte 2010; Levey 2006; Quirk 1957; Zaenen et al. 2004).

   - <u>Hypothesis</u>: as *wo* retains some of its original semantics, inanimate antecedents will more likely favour *wo*-relatives.

10. <u>Definiteness</u>: antecedents were coded for 'definite', i.e., containing a definite article, demonstrative or possessive pronoun, numeral, proper name or 'indefinite' (Hinrichs et al. 2015; Levey 2006; Tagliamonte et al. 2005; Meyerhoff et al. 2020).

    - <u>Hypothesis</u>: as indefinite antecedents are less explicit, they will more likely favour less explicit *wo*-relatives.

11. <u>Topic Persistence</u>: relative clauses were coded for whether the 'same' or a 'different' topic is talked about over consecutive clauses – without intervening material – up to a maximum of ten clauses (Cheshire et al. 2013; Wright and Givón 1987).

    - <u>Hypothesis</u>: as topics that persist over a greater number of clauses are non-marked, they will more likely favour less explicit *wo*-relatives.

12. <u>Structural Persistence</u>: relative clauses were coded for the 'same' or 'different' relativiser used previously to the current one (Hinrichs et al. 2015).

    - <u>Hypothesis</u>: for reasons of parallelism, consistency, and priming, the same relativiser will more likely be used as the previous one (up to a maximum of ten intervening clauses).

13. <u>Structural Count</u>: relative clauses were coded for the number of non-relative clauses occurring in between relativisers (up to a maximum of 10 intervening clauses).

    - <u>Hypothesis</u>: due to limitations on cognitive processing, succeeding relativisers will more likely be the same when they occur relatively close to one another (i.e., three or fewer intervening clauses).

14. <u>Relative Clause Length:</u> a continuous measure of the number of words in the relative clause, including the relativiser and its antecedent (Hinrichs et al. 2015; Quirk 1957; Tagliamonte et al. 2005).

Variation in Swabian wo-Relatives 145

- Hypothesis: following the *Complexity Principle* (Rohdenburg 1996), more cognitively complex noun phrases (i.e., longer antecedents) will likely favour more explicit *d*-relative pronouns.

15. Antecedent Length: a continuous measure of the number of words in the antecedent, excluding the relativiser itself (Guy and Bayley 1995; Hinrichs et al. 2015; Rohdenburg 1996).

  - Hypothesis: following the *Complexity Principle*, longer antecedents are more complex and hence will more likely favour an explicit *d*-relative pronoun.

16. Antecedent Distance: also called adjacency, a continuous measure of the number of words between the antecedent head and the relativiser (Guy and Bayley 1995; Hinrichs et al. 2015; Lopes Câmara 2018; Poschmann and Wagner 2016; Rohdenburg 1996; Tagliamonte et al. 2005).

  - Hypothesis: following the *Complexity Principle*, more distant antecedents will more likely favour the more explicit *d*-relative pronouns to help in clarifying ambiguities.

2.3.3.6.2 External Social Predictors

Eight external social predictors were evaluated:

1. Recording year: relative clauses were coded for which recording year they were used, i.e., 1982 or 2017.

  - Hypothesis: as a result of increasing education, standard language convergence, and pervasive prescriptivism, overall use of *wo*-relatives is decreasing and will, therefore, be less frequent in 2017 than in 1982.

2. Speech community: relative clauses were coded for community, i.e., Stuttgart or Schwäbisch Gmünd.

  - Hypothesis: *wo*-relatives will likely be more frequent in the semi-rural town of Schwäbisch Gmünd, where more dialect features are typically used, versus the urban centre of Stuttgart, where a more standardised, supralocalised variety is spoken (i.e., 'change from above' (Labov 1966)).

3. Speaker education: speakers were coded for whether they have a university degree or not.

  - Hypothesis: *wo*-relatives will be favoured by the less educated who have not been as heavily influenced by prescriptivism in the schools (i.e., 'change from above').

4. Speaker occupation: speakers were coded for whether they are currently in a managerial or a non-managerial role.

146　*Karen V. Beaman*

- Hypothesis: as with education, *wo*-relatives will be favoured by speakers in non-managerial roles who have been less influenced by education and prescriptivism (i.e., 'change from above').

5. Speaker age: speakers' age was coded as a continuous variable from 18 to 88.

   - Hypothesis: assuming age is an indicator of change, younger speakers will likely use fewer *wo*-relatives than older speakers.

6. Speaker sex: speakers' sex was coded as 'male' or 'female' as self-reported in the demographic survey.

   - Hypothesis: as many studies have shown that men use more dialect features than women, the men in this study will be more likely to use more *wo*-relatives.

7. Sex of speaker and interviewer: relative clauses were coded for whether the speaker and the interviewer were of the 'same' or 'different' sex.

   - Hypothesis: based on prior studies that show more informal speech styles are typical when the speaker and interviewer are of the same sex, 'same' sex will favour *wo*-relatives.

8. Swabian orientation: speakers were coded for their level of "Swabianness", a continuous variable from 1 to 5 based on an evaluation of 16 questions asked during the interview covering topics such as the speakers' knowledge of Swabian culture and icons, their affinity with and perceptions of the Swabian language, and their self-reported use of Swabian with friends and family (Beaman 2018).

   - Hypothesis: based on prior studies that show high levels of local orientation correlate with greater dialect density, speakers with high Swabian orientation scores will likely use more *wo*-relatives.

2.3.4 Analysis and Results

This section presents the analysis and results of the investigation into Swabian *wo*-relatives. First, a summary of the predictors that turned out to be significant and not significant in the multivariate modelling are listed; second, an overall analysis of *wo* and *d*-relatives by speech community and recording year is described; third, a frequency analysis of *wo* versus *d*-relatives with respect to case is provided; and fourth, a multivariate analysis showing the significant predictors and interaction effects is presented.

2.3.4.1 Analysis of Predictors

Concerning the 16 internal linguistic predictors discussed in Section 2.3.3.6, as previously mentioned, place and time were eliminated as knock-out constraints. As a result of the multivariate modelling (see Section 2.3.4.4), ten other internal predictors showed no significant effects on the choice of relativiser, either singly or in interaction with other predictors, and hence have been eliminated from further discussion:

1. Restrictiveness
4. Antecedent Category
5. Antecedent Case
7. Case Matching
8. Resumptive
11. Topic Persistence
12. Structural Persistence
13. Structural Count
14. Relative Clause Length
15. Antecedent Length

Through multivariate modelling (see Section 2.3.4.4 for full details), four internal predictors showed significant results and will be discussed further in the subsequent sections:

6. Relative Case
9. Animacy
10. Definiteness
16. Antecedent Distance

In addition, four of the eight social predictors from Section 2.3.3.6 proved to be significant and will also be discussed in the following sections:

1. Recording year
2. Speech Community
3. Speaker Education
4. Speaker Occupation[5]

Contrary to expectations, Swabian orientation showed no significant effect on speakers' choice of relative pronouns. Although prior research on Swabian has shown that dialect features index Swabian identity (Beaman 2018), surprisingly *wo*-relatives do not appear to be one of them. Similarly, speaker sex, a strong predictor of linguistic variation in many highly stratified environments, shows no significant effect on the use of *wo* versus a *d*-relative pronoun (cf. Meyerhoff et al. 2020). Finegan and Biber (2001:3145) claim that

> most linguistic features do *not* achieve sufficient salience to index either speaker or situation identity…. For example, the frequency of relative clause types and other particular aspects of relative clauses have been shown to

correlate with social groups, but that frequency is not sufficiently salient for relative clauses to index social identity.

As we will see, the Swabian panel speakers support this claim, exposing education to be a much stronger predictor of relative pronoun usage than other aspects of social identity.

2.3.4.2 Community Change

One of the strongest factors influencing the choice of relativisers in Swabian is the urban/rural divide. Figure 2.3.1 presents frequency counts of relative clauses by community and recording year. Overall, traditional *d*-relatives (in light grey) are favoured at 64% (*n* = 765/1204) over invariant *wo*-relatives (in dark grey) at 36% (*n* = 439/1204) (combined percentages not shown in the figure). While *wo*-relative usage has remained constant in Schwäbisch Gmund over the two recording periods, 41% in 1982 and 39% in 2017, we see a decline in usage in Stuttgart from 41% in 1982 to 24% in 2017. These results partially support two of the hypotheses from Section 2.3.3.6: use of *wo*-relatives is decreasing over time (external social prediction 1), but only in the urban variety of Stuttgart (external social prediction 2), likely a result of the considerable standard language convergence and supralocalisation that has been occurring over the 35-year timeframe of this study.

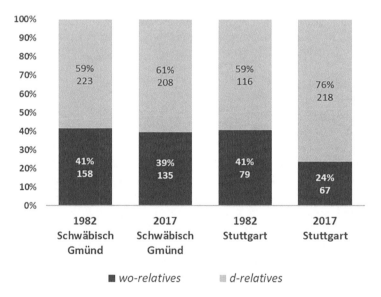

Figure 2.3.1 Frequency of *wo*-relatives and *d*-relatives in Swabian by community and recording year.

2.3.4.3 Relative Marker Case

A second major factor constraining variation in the use of *wo*-relativisers in Swabian is the case of the relative. Figure 2.3.2 shows the distribution of relativisers from the 20 Swabian panel speakers by community, recording year, and case. As expected, use of *d*-relative pronouns follows the Keenan and Comrie (1977:66) *Accessibility Hierarchy* (AH), demonstrating that linguistic constraints on relative clause formation pattern in an implicational hierarchy based on the grammatical function of the relativiser and hence the ease with which noun phrases can be relativised. Specifically, AH predicts that relatives are most common in subject position (nominative), followed by direct object (accusative), indirect object (dative), oblique (dative), genitive, and object of comparison.[6] Figure 2.3.2 confirms that, for both years and both communities, relative clauses in Swabian are most common in the nominative case (60%, *n* = 725/1200), followed by the accusative (19%, *n* = 222/1200) and dative cases (21%, *n* = 253/1200) which show similar frequencies.

However, contrary to our prediction, Figure 2.3.2 clearly reveals that *wo*-relatives are considerably more frequent in the dative case for both communities and in both years (internal linguistic prediction 6). Dative *wo*-relatives increased in Schwäbisch Gmünd from 60% (*n* = 81) in 1982 to 90% (*n* = 78) in 2017, although they decreased somewhat in Stuttgart, from 82% (*n* = 44) to 74% (*n* = 50). As for the nominative case, both communities were fairly similar in 1982: 33% (*n* = 233) in Schwäbisch Gmünd and 28% (*n* = 130) in Stuttgart. However, we see a sharp decline in the use of subject *wo*-relatives in 2017, from 33% (*n* = 233) to 19% (*n* = 170) in Schwäbisch Gmünd and from 28% (*n* = 130) to 7% (*n* = 192) Stuttgart. The implications of these findings will be discussed further in the following sections.

2.3.4.4 Multivariate Analysis

In order to glean the full picture of *wo*-relativiser use in Swabian, we turn to the results of the multivariate analysis. Table 2.3.2 shows the summary results of the best-fit linear mixed-effects regression model (*glmer* function from the R package *lme4*, version 1.1 (Bates et al. 2015; R Core Team 2014)), evaluated with Akaike's Information Criterium (AIC), a standard metric for assessing the quality of a statistical model taking into consideration the trade-off between complexity and goodness of fit. Linear modelling was performed with the full dataset to avoid any type of *post hoc* analysis. Note that positive estimates favour the use of *wo*-relatives, while negative estimates favour *d*-relatives. The predicted values for each of the factors (generated by the *predict* function from the R package *stats*, version 3.5.3, obtained by evaluating the

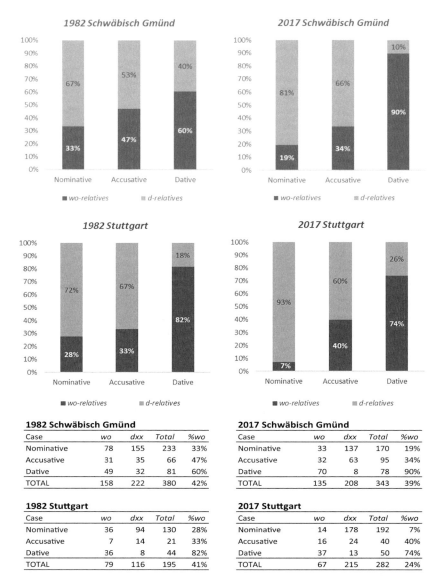

Figure 2.3.2 Frequency of *wo*-relatives and *d*-relatives in Swabian by case, community and recording year.

regression function from Table 2.3.2) are shown in Table 2.3.3, broken down by community.

We look first at the main internal constraints and see that the strongest internal constraints favouring *wo* is an abstract notion of place

Variation in Swabian wo-Relatives   151

Table 2.3.2 Multivariate analysis relative pronoun usage in 20 Swabian panel speakers across two points in time (1982 and 2017)

Predictors	Values	Estimate	Std. Error	z-Value	p-Value	Sig
Model intercept		−0.370	0.476	−7.790	0.436	
Main effects:						
Recording year	2017	0.066	0.383	0.173	0.862	
Community	Stuttgart	0.088	0.720	0.122	0.903	
Education level	university	−1.357	0.356	−3.808	0.000	***
Animacy	animate	−0.302	0.255	−1.185	0.236	
Definiteness	definite	0.593	0.178	3.342	0.001	***
Antecedent distance	less	−0.454	0.124	−3.658	0.000	***
Place	abstract	2.013	0.609	3.306	0.001	***
Relativiser case	dative	2.817	0.386	7.303	0.000	***
Interaction effects:						
Animate + Relative Case	dative	−1.582	0.453	−3.490	0.000	***
2017 + Relative Case	dative	2.170	0.468	4.460	0.000	***
2017 + Place	abstract	−1.954	0.806	−2.424	0.015	*
2017 + Community	Stuttgart	−0.160	0.449	−0.355	0.722	
2017 + Community + Animate	Gmund	−0.308	0.408	−0.754	0.451	
2017 + Community + Animate	Stuttgart	−1.288	0.484	−2.663	0.008	**
Random effects:						
Speaker		2.049				
Summary statistics:						
of relatives (n)	1204					
of speakers	20					
% correctly predicted	83.5%					
baseline %	64.0%					
concordance index	0.899					

Positive estimates (high probabilities) favour and negative estimates (low probabilities) disfavour the use of *wo*-relatives; significance levels: *** 0.001, ** 0.01, * 0.05.

(87.3% in Schwäbisch Gmünd and 93.8% in Stuttgart, Table 2.3.3). As previously mentioned, this likely results through analogy with physical notions of place that exhibit categorical use of *wo* and hence have been eliminated as a knock-out condition. The next strongest predictor favouring the use of *wo*-relativisers is the dative case[7] (74.8% in Schwäbisch Gmünd and 77.7% in Stuttgart, Table 2.3.3). Wo-relatives are also favoured with inanimate antecedents (51.4% in Schwäbisch Gmünd and 49.5% in Stuttgart, Table 2.3.3) and with definite articles (44.7% in Schwäbisch Gmünd and 40.3% in Stuttgart, Table 2.3.3). Greater distance between the antecedent head and the relativiser is also

Table 2.3.3 Summary of predictors influencing the use of *wo*-relatives; obtained with the R *predict* function through the regression function shown in Table 2.3.2, which takes into account random effects by speaker; significance levels: *** 0.001, ** 0.01, * 0.05.

Predictor name	Schwäbisch Gmünd					Stuttgart				
	Estimate	Prob.	% wo	n	Sig	Estimate	Prob.	% wo	n	Sig
Main effects:										
Year: 1982	−0.432	0.394	41.5%	381		−0.467	0.385	40.5%	195	
Year: 2017	−0.729	0.325	39.4%	343		−1.989	0.120	23.5%	285	
Education: no university	−0.322	0.420	43.3%	503		−0.433	0.394	39.3%	305	
Education: university	−1.144	0.242	33.9%	221		−3.004	0.047	14.9%	175	*
Relativiser case: nominative	−1.393	0.199	27.5%	403		−2.283	0.093	15.5%	322	
Relativiser case: accusative	−1.017	0.266	39.1%	161		−1.604	0.167	37.7%	61	.
Relativiser case: dative	1.966	0.877	74.8%	159	***	1.991	0.880	77.7%	94	***
Animacy: animate	−1.182	0.235	31.6%	399		−2.362	0.086	17.7%	288	
Animacy: inanimate	0.175	0.544	51.4%	325	*	0.117	0.529	49.5%	192	***
Definiteness: definite	−0.283	0.430	44.7%	235		−0.571	0.361	40.3%	176	
Definiteness: indefinite	−0.713	0.329	38.4%	489	*	−1.833	0.138	24.7%	304	***
Place: abstract	2.495	0.924	87.3%	63		2.773	0.941	93.8%	32	
Place: no	−0.865	0.296	36.0%	661	***	−1.666	0.159	25.9%	448	***
Antecedent distance: < = 1 word	−0.529	0.371	42.1%	392		−1.374	0.202	28.6%	262	
Antecedent distance: 2–3 words	−0.047	0.488	44.4%	153	***	−0.570	0.167	37.0%	108	.
Antecedent distance: > = 4 words	−1.120	0.246	33.5%	179	***	−2.147	0.105	28.2%	110	***

Variation in Swabian wo-Relatives   153

Predictor name	Schwäbisch Gmünd					Stuttgart				
	Estimate	Prob.	% wo	n	Sig	Estimate	Prob.	% wo	n	Sig
Interaction effects:										
1982 + Nominative case	−1.030	0.263	33.5%	233		−1.086	0.252	27.7%	130	
1982 + Accusative case	−0.419	0.397	47.0%	66		−1.252	0.222	33.3%	21	
1982 + Dative case	1.297	0.785	60.5%	81		1.736	0.850	81.8%	44	
2017 + Nominative case	−1.891	0.131	19.4%	170		−3.093	0.043	7.3%	192	*
2017 + Accusative case	−1.433	0.193	33.7%	95		−1.789	0.143	40.0%	40	
2017 + Dative case	2.660	0.935	89.7%	78		2.216	0.902	74.0%	50	
1982 + Abstract place	3.146	0.959	88.5%	26		3.127	0.958	100.0%	18	
1982 + Non-place	−0.694	0.333	38.0%	355	**	−0.832	0.303	34.5%	177	**
2017 + Abstract place	2.038	0.885	86.5%	37		2.319	0.910	85.7%	14	
2017 + Non-place	−1.064	0.257	33.7%	306	**	−2.211	0.099	20.3%	271	***
1982 + Animate	−0.882	0.293	35.6%	225		−1.086	0.252	28.7%	115	
1982 + Inanimate	0.217	0.554	50.0%	156		0.424	0.604	57.5%	80	
2017 + Animate	−1.571	0.172	26.4%	174		−3.210	0.039	10.4%	173	
2017 + Inanimate	0.137	0.534	52.7%	169		−0.102	0.475	43.8%	112	*
Animate + Nominative case	−1.485	0.185	28.8%	292		−2.558	0.072	14.3%	245	
Animate + Accusative case	−1.301	0.214	25.5%	47		−2.665	0.065	21.1%	19	
Animate + Dative case	0.426	0.605	50.8%	59	**	0.212	0.553	54.5%	22	***
Inanimate + Nominative case	−1.152	0.240	24.3%	111		−1.405	0.197	19.5%	77	
Inanimate + Accusative case	−0.900	0.289	44.7%	114		−1.124	0.245	45.2%	42	
Inanimate + Dative case	2.874	0.947	89.0%	100	***	2.535	0.927	84.7%	72	***

154   *Karen V. Beaman*

a significant constraint disfavouring *wo*; that is, the greater the distance between the antecedent and the relative pronoun, the more likely a traditional *d*-relative will be used. This likely results from psycholinguistic processing demands in that greater distances between the referent and its object could potentially cause processing and communication difficulties, which the *d*-relative with its case, number, and gender markings helps to clarify.

Turning to the main external effects, as expected, a university degree is a significant factor disfavouring the use of *wo*, most notably in Stuttgart (14.9% for those with a university degree versus 39.3% for those without a degree, Table 2.3.3), confirming external linguistic prediction 3. Labov (2001:60) maintains that education is the single best predictor for assessing the social evaluation of a feature, with higher levels of education correlating with features of higher prestige, specifically, those features taught in schools. Not surprisingly, the influence of prescriptivism in the educational system can arrest a change in progress, and, in the case of Swabian, slowing and restricting variation in the use of *wo*-relatives.

We next look at the interaction effects between the different predictors. One of the strongest interaction effects is animacy and case, with *wo* being favoured with inanimate referents in the dative case (89.0% in Schwäbisch Gmünd and 84.7% in Stuttgart, Table 2.3.3), indicating that *d*-relatives, with their case-markings and greater specificity in singling out the object of reference, are the preferred marker for animate antecedents in the nominative and accusative cases. We also see that the use of *wo* with animate referents has declined over the 35 years, somewhat in Schwäbisch Gmünd (35.6% in 1982 to 26.4% in 2017, Table 2.3.3) and substantially in Stuttgart (28.7% in 1982 to 10.4% in 2017, Table 2.3.3), which is likely attributable to greater teacher prescriptivism and standard language convergence in the urban centre of Stuttgart (cf. Duden's comment from above that using *wo* to refer to a person or thing is *landschaftlich salopp* 'country slang' (Duden Online 2018)).

The results of the multivariate analysis also reveal that, over the 35 years, *wo*-relatives in the dative case have significantly increased in Schwäbisch Gmünd (60.5% in 1982 to 89.7% in 2017, Table 2.3.3) and, at the same time, somewhat decreased in Stuttgart (81.8% in 1982 to 74.0% in 2017, Table 2.3.3). At the same time, an abstract notion of place, which categorically favoured *wo* Stuttgart in 1982 (100.0%) has slackened off in 2017 (85.7%). These findings point to the possibility that *wo* may be going through a process of grammaticalisation and semantic bleaching (Matisoff 1991), a topic explored further in the discussion section.

With a concordance index of .899 and a percent correctly predicted of 83.5% (see Table 2.3.2), this model can be considered pretty good at explaining the variability in the use of *wo* versus a *d*-relative in Swabian (Hinrichs, Szmrecsanyi and Bohmann 2015). However, the random effects for speaker are quite high (estimate = 2.049), which can indicate considerable inter-speaker variability, sparsity of data, and/or collinearity between social and linguistic factors. Indeed, there are some speakers who simply use more relatives (such as Manni and Markus) than other speakers (such as Elke and Louise). There are also speakers who predominately use *d*-relatives (such as Helmut and Herbert) and those who mostly use *wo*-relatives (such as Siegfried and Rachael). Such individual variability draws into question whether there are some interactional, stance-taking or other indexicalities at play, a potential topic for future analysis.

2.3.5 Discussion

The preceding analysis has exposed a complex set of interacting factors affecting speakers' choice of relative pronouns in Swabian, involving both internal linguistic constraints – in particular, case, definiteness, animacy, and distance from the antecedent – and external social factors, specifically speech community, level of education, and recording year. The results show considerable change in relative pronoun usage across the 35-year timeframe for these two communities, most notably movement away from nominative *wo* in both communities, most markedly in Stuttgart (from 27.7% in 1982 to 7.3% in 2017, Table 2.3.3), and advancement toward dative *wo*, particularly in Schwäbisch Gmünd (60.5% in 1982 to 89.7% in 2017, Table 2.3.3).

2.3.5.1 The Demise of the Dative

For *wo*-relatives to be favoured in the dative case is not a surprising revelation considering the fact that the dative (like the genitive) has a different structure in German than the nominative and accusative paradigms.[8] Could this distinctive, "more complicated" structure be driving the dative the way of the genitive, which has completely died out in modern spoken German? Could Swabian be moving toward a two-case system as with many of the low German dialects, at least with respect to relative pronouns? One insight can be drawn from Google Books Ngram Viewer (Jean-Baptiste et al. 2011), which shows that use of the dative article and relative pronoun *dem* is in stark decline, from a high of 0.7% in 1860 to 0.6% in 1940 to 0.4% today (see Figure 2.3.3). Whether all dative case markings in German are in decline is clearly beyond the scope of the current analysis; however, it is evident from the current dataset that *wo* is preferred over *dem* and *der* for marking dative relative clauses in Swabian.

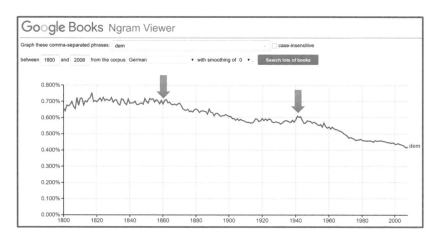

Figure 2.3.3 Google Books Ngram Viewer for German *dem*.

2.3.5.2 *Evidence from the Socio-Historical Context*

In unravelling the use of *wo* as a relative pronoun, it is essential to consider the socio-historical context and its evolution. Use of *wo* as a relativiser in German is not a new phenomenon. Hermann Paul (1897) along with the Grimm Brothers' fairy tales confirm frequent use of *wo* in conditional, temporal, causal, and conjunctive phrases. Some linguists contend that *wo*-relatives evolved from the locative use of *wo*, meaning 'where'. Indeed, the results of the current study show that *wo*-relatives are highly favoured with both physical and abstract notions of place. However, there is some controversy over this interpretation. Brandner and Bräuning (2013) argue quite convincingly that, despite its homophony with the locative adverb *wo*, the *wo*-relative originates from the Middle High German equative particle *so/som*, which was widely used as a complementiser in Early New High German and southern Alemannic dialects. Their claim is supported by the semantics of *wo* and through a historical and comparative analysis based on four arguments:

1. *so*-relatives were widespread in the Early New High German period in the same areas where we see the *wo*-relatives today, precisely the Upper German dialect areas, e.g., Swabian and Bavarian (Paul 1920:238) and Swiss German;
2. *wo*-relatives started appearing in the literature about the same time when the equative particle *als* changed to the *w*-series and became *wie* (Jäger 2010);
3. use of the equative particle *som* to introduce a relative clause is also found in other Germanic languages, specifically various Scandinavian varieties; and,

4. interpreting *wo* as an equative particle provides an explanation for its use in both restrictive and non-restrictive relative clauses and well as for the resumptive or the doubly filled complementiser, *der wo*, which is common in the southern German dialects, Bavarian as well as Swabian (Bayer 1984).

If indeed *wo*-relatives developed from the Early New High German complementiser *so*, this could provide some explanation for the differing levels of usage found in Stuttgart and Schwäbisch Gmünd: *wo*-relatives in the more conservative dialect of Schwäbisch Gmünd may simply be reflecting a more traditional, historical usage.

2.3.5.3 The Effects of Grammaticalisation

As discussed, many linguists have assumed that *wo* has evolved from denoting a physical place and to referring to an abstract notion of place. The results from the multivariate analysis show that an abstract meaning of place has slackened off in 2017. One explanation for the changing role of *wo* may be that it has become "semantically bleached" and hence is losing its traditional meaning of 'where' (Cheshire, personal communication). According to Hopper and Traugott (2003:85), grammaticalistion of relative pronouns through spatiotemporal metaphoric extensions is not uncommon. It appears that Swabian *wo* may be going through a process of grammaticalisation (Brook 2011; Bybee and Pagliuca 1985; Cheshire 2007; Hopper and Traugott 2003), specifically, decategorisation, losing the semantic and syntactic characteristics of an adverbial pronoun and taking on the full properties of a relative pronoun. "[H]uman language users have a natural propensity for making metaphorical extensions that lead to the increased use of certain items" (Bybee and Pagliuca 1985:75). Support for this claim is also found in Bavarian, which uses the doubled-filled complementiser with both a relative pronoun and the complementiser *wo* in forming relative clauses (Bayer 1984).

2.3.5.4 The Widening Urban-Rural Divide

The findings from this study demonstrate that the German urban/rural divide is ever present. The Stuttgart dialect is becoming more standardised – a developing *regiolect* (Auer 2018) – while the dialect of Schwäbisch Gmünd has retained more of its traditional features. The emerging ethnolect in Stuttgart might provide some insights into *wo*-relative usage. Auer (2020) cites Stuttgart as one of the cities with the highest number of foreigners in all of Germany: 46% of the population have at least one parent not from the region, twice as many as in the rest of Germany overall. His research on the developing ethnolect of immigrants in Stuttgart shows exceptionally high use of *wo*-relatives, to the complete exclusion

158   *Karen V. Beaman*

of *d*-relative pronouns with some speakers. *Wo*-relatives' lack of gender, number, and case markings make them an ideal candidate for *koinéisation*, a process by which "new varieties of a language are brought about as a result of contact between speakers of mutually intelligible varieties of that language" (Kerswill 2004:669). Certainly, Stuttgart today comprises a broad amalgam of standard German speakers, Swabian speakers, and multiethnolectal speakers. However, education and prescriptivism play a critical counter-role in language usage. As we have also seen, higher levels of education suppress speakers' choice for *wo* variants. These findings point to the fact that education and intractable teacher prescriptivism can obstruct the natural trajectory of language change.

2.3.5.5 The Role of Prescriptivism

While the constraints on *wo*-relative usage between the two communities appear to be the same, the difference lies in the rate of change. In 2017, *wo*-relatives have become more disfavoured in Stuttgart (40.5% in 1982 to 23.5% in 2017, Table 2.3.3), while their use in Schwäbisch Gmünd has stayed largely the same (41.5% in 1982 to 39.4% in 2017, Table 2.3.3). And, as we have seen, this decrease is particularly strong in Stuttgart for the nominative case (27.7% in 1982 to 7.3% in 2017, Table 2.3.3), with non-place antecedents (from 34.5% in 1982 to 20.3% in 2017), and with inanimate antecedents (from 57.5% in 1982 to 43.8% in 2017). Stuttgart is moving away from *wo*-relatives to standard German *d*-relatives, which are becoming an integral part of the supraregional dialect in south-western Germany. It seems likely that increased dialect contact in Stuttgart, resulting from swelling numbers of non-dialect-speaking, ethnically German migrants, as well the influx of foreign-born immigrants, along with rampant prescriptivism and increasing education ('change from above'), are stemming the use of *wo* as a relative pronoun, certainly among the more educated speakers.

2.3.6 Conclusions

This exploratory investigation of relative markers in 20-panel speakers of Swabian across a 35-year time period has highlighted the intricate interaction between intra- and extra-linguistic factors and the role they play in morphosyntactic change. Returning to the three questions asked at the outset of this chapter, we found that *wo*-relatives are favoured with definite, animate referents in the dative case, influenced by community and education (question 1). We have also seen that the use of *wo* as a relativiser is changing, potentially going through a process of semantic bleaching and decategorisation as a result of metaphoric processes and *koinéisation* (question 2). Yet we also see a counter-force at play in the movement away from *wo*-relatives in Stuttgart, a change that appears

Variation in Swabian wo-Relatives 159

primarily driven by growing regionalisation (i.e., supralocalisation) and persistent prescriptivism (i.e., 'change from above') (question 3). Expanding this panel study investigation to a broader multi-generational trend study may unveil how broadly these changes are spreading or receding in the Swabian system of relativisation.

Notes

1 This research is dedicated to Jenny Cheshire whose ground-breaking academic scholarship and personal and professional munificence have been an inspiration to me and many others. I would like to extend my sincerest thanks to Jenny for encouraging me to look into morphosyntactic variation and to Isabelle Buchstaller for making me aware of the *wo*-relative marker in Swabian. I also wish to thank Jenny, as well as Peter Auer, James Garrett, Gregory Guy, the co-editors of this volume, and two anonymous reviewers for their commentary on earlier versions of this research. Of course, any deficiencies remaining are entirely my own.
2 Duden also describes three other types of relatives: (1) free relatives with *wer/was* 'who/what' (also called 'headless relatives' because they do not appear to have an accompanying noun phrase), (2) relative adverbs such as *als/wie* 'as/how', and (3) *Gradpartikeln* 'correlative conjunctions' *je...desto* 'the...the'; however, since these relatives do not vary with *wo*, they have been excluded from the current analysis.
3 All names used are pseudonyms in order to protect the privacy of the speakers. The four digits after the speakers' name specify the year of the recording: 1982 or 2017.
4 Humanness and collectivities of humans were initially coded separately; however, due to an insufficient number of tokens for analysis, all are combined in the animacy predictor.
5 The education and occupation factors provided similar results, hence to avoid issues of collinearity, the decision was made to keep only education predictor as it more closely represents the prescriptivism effect which appears to have a strong influence on relativiser choice.
6 Subject and direct object equate in German to nominative and accusative, respectively. The indirect object and oblique relations are both encoded by the dative case in German. There were only four genitives in the entire data set and no examples for object of comparison.
7 The precedence of the dative (over nominative and accusative) case was tested via Akaike's Information Criterium (AIC).
8 The paradigms for the nominative and accusative pronouns in standard German are similar (nominative = *der/die/das*; accusative = *den/die/das*) in stark contrast to the paradigms for the dative and genitive paradigms (dative = *dem/der/dem*; genitive = *des/der/dem*), which are more similar to each other, but different from the nominative and accusative paradigms.

References

Auer, Peter. 2018. "Dialect change in Europe – leveling and convergence". In *The Handbook of Dialectology*, C. Boberg, J. Nerbonne and D. Watt (eds.). Oxford: Wiley-Blackwell. 159–176.

Auer, Peter. 2020. "Dialect (non-)acquisition and use by young people of migrant background in Germany". *Journal of Multilingual and Multicultural Development*.

Ball, Catherine N. 1996. "A diachronic study of relative markers in spoken and written English". *Language Variation and Change* 8:227–58.

Bates, Douglas, Martin Mächler, Ben Bolker, and Steve Walker. 2015. "Fitting linear mixed-effects models using *lme4*". *Journal of Statistical Software* 67(1):1–48.

Bayer, Josef. 1984. "Comp in Bavarian Syntax". *Linguistic Review* 3(3):209–274.

Beaman, Karen V. 2018. "Identity and place: The changing role of Swabian in modern Germany". Presented at the *Conference on Language, Place and Periphery*. University of Copenhagen. January 18–19, 2018.

Bidese, Ermenegildo, Andrea Padovan and Alessandra Tomaselli. 2012. "A binary system of complementizers in Cimbrian relative clauses". *Working Papers in Scandinavian Syntax* 90:1–21.

Bohmann, Axel and Patrick Schultz. 2011. "Sacred *that* and wicked *which*: Prescriptivism and change in the use of English relativizers". *Texas Linguistic Forum* 54:88–101.

Brandner, Ellen and Iris Bräuning. 2013. "Relative *Wo* in Alemannic: Only a complementizer?" *Linguistische Berichte* 234:131–70.

Brook, Marisa. 2011. "One of those situations where a relative pronoun becomes a complementizer: A case of grammaticalization in action … again". In *Proceedings of the 2011 Annual Conference of the Canadian Linguistic Association*, L. Armstrong (ed.). Ottawa: University of Ottawa. 1–7.

Bybee, Joan L. and William Pagliuca. 1985. "Cross-linguistic comparison and the development of grammatical meaning". In *Historical Semantics – Historical Word-Formation*, J. Fisiak (ed.). The Hague: Mouton. 59–83.

Cheshire, Jenny. 1987. "Syntactic variation, the linguistic variable and sociolinguistic theory". *Linguistics* 25(2):257–82.

Cheshire, Jenny. 1996. "That jacksprat: An interactional perspective on English 'That.'" *Journal of Pragmatics* 25(3):369–393.

Cheshire, Jenny. 1998. "Taming the vernacular: Some repercussions for the study of syntactic variation and spoken grammar". *Te Reo* 41:6–27.

Cheshire, Jenny. 2003. "Social dimensions of syntactic variation: The case of *when* clauses". In *Social Dialectology: In Honour of Peter Trudgill*, J. Cheshire and D. Britain (eds.). Amsterdam: John Benjamins Publishing Company. 245–261.

Cheshire, Jenny. 2007. "Discourse variation, grammaticalisation and stuff like that". *Journal of Sociolinguistics* 11(2):155–193.

Cheshire, Jenny. 2016. "The future of discourse-pragmatic variation and change research". In *Discourse-Pragmatic Variation and Change in English: New Methods and Insights*, H. Pichler (ed.). Cambridge: Cambridge University Press. 252–266.

Cheshire, Jenny, David Adger and Sue Fox. 2013. "Relative *who* and the actuation problem". *Lingua* 126(1):51–77.

D'Arcy, Alexandra and Sali A. Tagliamonte. 2010. "Prestige, accommodation, and the legacy of relative *who*". *Language in Society* 39(3):383–410.

Duden. 2016. *Die Grammatik: Das Standardwerk Zur Deutschen Sprache. Band 4*, A. Wöllstein (ed.). Berlin: Dudenverlag.

Duden Online. 2018. "*Wo* Relativpronomen: Bedeutungen, Beispiele Und Wendungen". *Bibliographisches Institut GmbH*. Retrieved March 12, 2019 (www. duden.de/rechtschreibung/wo_Fragewort_Relativpronomen#Bedeutung3).

Finegan, Edward and Douglas Biber. 2001. "Register variation and social dialect variation: The register axiom". In *Style and Sociolinguistic Variation. Kindle Edition*, P. Eckert and J. R. Rickford (eds.). Cambridge: Cambridge University Press. 235–267.

Fleischer, Jürg. 2006. "Dative and indirect object in German dialects: Evidence from relative clauses". In *Datives and Other Cases: between Argument Structure and Event Structure. (Studies in Language Companion Series 75)*, D. Hole, A. Meinunger and W. Abraham (eds.). Amsterdam: John Benjamins Publishing Company. 213–238.

Fleischer, Jürg. 2004. "A typology of relative clauses in German dialects". In *Dialectology Meets Typology*, B. Kortmann (ed.). Berlin: Mouton de Gruyter. 211–244.

Fleischer, Jürg. 2005. "Relativsätze in Den Dialekten Des Deutschen: Vergleich Und Typologie". *Linguistik Online* 24(3):171–186.

Günthner, Susanne. 2002. "Zum Kausalen Und Konzessiven Gebrauch Des Konnektors *wo* Im Gegenwärtigen Deutsch". *Interaction and Linguistic Structures (InLiSt)* 31:1–32.

Guy, Gregory R. and Robert Bayley. 1995. "On the choice of relative pronouns in English". *American Speech* 70(2):148–162.

Hendery, Rachel. 2012. *Relative Clauses in Time and Space: A Case Study in the Methods of Diachronic Typology*. Amsterdam: John Benjamins Publishing Company.

Hinrichs, Lars, Benedikt M. Szmrecsanyi and Axel Bohmann. 2015. "*Which*-hunting and the standard English relative clause". *Language* 91(4):0–51.

Hopper, Paul J. and Elizabeth Closs Traugott. 2003. *Grammaticalization (Cambridge Textbooks in Linguistics)* 2nd edition, Kindle Edition. Cambridge: Cambridge University Press.

Jäger, Agnes. 2010. "Der Komparativzyklus und die Position der Vergleichspartikeln". *Linguistische Berichte* 224:467–493.

Jankowski, Bridget Lynn. 2009. "*that* which survives? Relatives in written and formal spoken Canadian English". *New Ways of Analyzing Variation 38*, Ottawa, Canada.

Jankowski, Bridget Lynn. 2013. "A variationist approach to cross-register language variation and change". Ph.D. Thesis. Toronto: University of Toronto.

Jean-Baptiste, Michel, Yuan Kui Shen, Aviva P. Aiden, Adrian Veres, Matthew K. Gray, The Google Books Team, Joseph P. Pickett, Dale Hoiberg, Dan Clancy, Peter Norvig, Jon Orwant, Steven Pinker, Martin A. Nowak and Erez Lieberman Aiden. 2011. "Quantitative analysis of culture using millions of digitized books". *NIH Public Access. Science* 331(6014):176–182.

Katis, Demetra and Kiki Nikiforidou. 2010. "Indeterminacy in grammar and acquisition: An interdisciplinary approach to relative clauses". *Review of Cognitive Linguistics* 8(1):1–18.

Keenan, Edward L. and Bernard Comrie. 1977. "Noun phrase accessibility and universal grammar". *Linguistic Inquiry* 8(1):63–99.

Keenan, Edward L. and Robert D. Hull. 1973. "The logical presuppositions of questions and answers". In *Präsuppositionen in Philosophie und Linguistik*, D. Franck and J. Petöfi (eds.). Frankfurt: Athenäum. 441–466.

Kerswill, Paul. 2004. "Koinéization and accommodation". In *The Handbook of Language Variation and Change*, J. K. Chambers, P. Trudgill, and N. Schilling-Estes (eds.). Oxford: Blackwell Publishing. 669–702.

Krapova, Iliyana. 2010. "Bulgarian relative and factive clauses with an invariant complementizer". *Lingua* 120(5):1240–1272.

Labov, William. 1963. "The social motivation of a sound change". *Word* 19(3):273–309.

Labov, William. 1966. *The Social Stratification of English in New York City*. 2nd edition. Cambridge: Cambridge University Press.

Labov, William. 1972. *Sociolinguistic Patterns*. Philadelphia: University of Pennsylvania.

Labov, William. 1984. "Field methods of the project linguistic change and variation". In *Language in Use: Readings in Sociolinguistics*, J. Baugh and J. Scherzer (eds.). Englewood Cliffs, NJ: Prentice Hall. 28–53.

Labov, William. 1993. "The unobservability of structure and its linguistic consequences". In *New Ways of Analyzing Variation 22*, Ottawa, Canada. University of Ottawa.

Labov, William. 2001. *Principles of Linguistic Change, Volume II, Social Factors*. Malden: Blackwell Publishing.

Labov, William, Sharon Ash, Maya Ravindranath, Tracey Weldon, Maciej Baranowski and Naomi Nagy. 2011. "Properties of the sociolinguistic monitor". *Journal of Sociolinguistics* 15(4):431–463.

Lavandera, Beatriz R. 1978. "Where does the sociolinguistic variable stop?" *Language in Society* 7(2):171–182.

Lehmann, Christian. 1984. *Der Relativesatz: Typologie Seiner Strukturen, Theorie Seiner Funktionen, Kompendium Seiner Grammatik*. Vol. 3. Tübingen: Gunter Narr Verlag.

Levey, Stephen. 2001. "Relative clauses and register expansion in Tok Pisin". *World Englishes* 20(3):251–267.

Levey, Stephen. 2006. "Visiting London relatives". *English World-Wide* 27(1):45–70.

Levey, Stephen. 2014. "A comparative variationist perspective on relative clauses in child and adult speech". In *Linguistic Variation: Confronting Fact and Theory*, R. T. Cacoullos, N. Dion and A. Lapierre (eds.). New York: Routledge. 22–37.

Levon, Erez, Isabelle Buchstaller and Adam Mearns. 2020. "Towards an integrated model of perception: Linguistic architecture and the dynamics of sociolinguistic cognition". In *Advancing Socio-grammatical Variation and Change: Sociolinguistic Research in Honour of Jenny Cheshire*, K. V. Beaman, I. Buchstaller, S. Fox and J. A. Walker (eds.). New York: Routledge.

Lopes Câmara, Aliana. 2018. "El Procesamiento de La Oración Relativa En Español: Interferencias Del Factor «distancia» En El Uso Del Pronombre Reasuntivo". *Forma y Función* 31(2):69–92.

Matisoff, J. 1991. "Areal and universal dimensions of grammaticalization in Lahu". In *Approaches to Grammaticalization, Volume II*, E. C. Traugott and B. Heine (eds.). Amsterdam: Benjamins. 383–454.

Matos, Gabriela and Ana Maria Brito. 2013. "The alternation between improper indirect questions and DPs containing a restrictive relative". In *Information Structure and Agreement*, V. Camacho-Taboada, Á. L. Jiménez-Fernández, J. Martín-González and M. Reyes-Tejedor (eds.). Amsterdam: John Benjamins Publishing Company. 83–116.

Meyerhoff, Miriam, Alexandra Birchfield, Elaine Ballard, Catherine Watson and Helen Charters. 2020. "Restrictions on relative clauses in Auckland, New Zealand". In *Advancing Socio-grammatical Variation and Change: In Honour of Jenny Cheshire*, K. V. Beaman, I. Buchstaller, S. Fox and J. A. Walker (eds.). New York: Routledge.

Milroy, James and Lesley Milroy. 1985. "Linguistic change, social network and speaker innovation". *Journal of Linguistics* 21(2):339–384.

Milroy, Lesley. 1987. *Language and Social Networks*. 2nd edition (first published in 1980). Oxford: Basil-Blackwell.

Moore, Emma and Paul Carter. 2015. "Dialect contact and distinctiveness: The social meaning of language variation in an island community". *Journal of Sociolinguistics* 19(1):3–36.

Nagy, Naomi and Miriam Meyerhoff. 2015. "Extending ELAN into variationist sociolinguistics". *Linguistics Vanguard* 1(1):271–281.

Paul, Hermann. 1897. *Deutsches Wörterbuch. Bedeutungsgeschichte Und Aufbau Unseres Wortschatzes*. 10. Tübingen: Niemeyer.

Paul, Hermann. 1920. *Prinzipien der Sprachgeschichte*. 5th edition. Halle: Max Niemeyer Verlag.

Pittner, Karin. 1995. "The case of German relatives". *Linguistic Review* 12(3):197–231.

Pittner, Karin. 2004. "Wo in Relativsätzen – eine Korpusbasierte Untersuchung". *Zeitschrift Fur Germanistische Linguistik* 32(3):357–375.

Poschmann, Claudia and Michael Wagner. 2016. "Relative clause extraposition and prosody in German". *Natural Language and Linguistic Theory* 34(3):1021–1066.

Pullum, Geoffrey K. 2009. "50 years of stupid grammar advice". *The Chronicle of Higher Education: The Chronicle Review*. https://www.chronicle.com/article/50-Years-of-Stupid-Grammar/25497.

Quirk, Randolph. 1957. "Relative clauses in educated spoken English". *Journal of English Studies* 38(1–6):97–109.

R Core Team. 2014. *R: A Language and Environment for Statistical Computing*. Vienna, Austria: R Foundation for Statistical Computing.

van Riemsdijk, Henk. 1989. "Swiss relatives". *Sentential Complementation. A Festschrift for Wim de Geest* (1975):343–354.

Rohdenburg, Gunter. 1996. "Cognitive complexity and increased grammatical explicitness in English". *Cognitive Linguistics* 7:149–182.

Romaine, Suzanne. 1982. *Socio-Historical Linguistics: Its Status and Methodology*. Cambridge: Cambridge University Press.

Romaine, Suzanne. 1992. *Language, Education and Development*. Oxford: Clarendon Press.

164   Karen V. Beaman

Salzmann, Martin and Guido Seiler. 2010. "Variation as the exception or the rule? Swiss relatives revisited". *Sprachwissenschaft* 35:79–117.

Sankoff, Gillian and Penelope Brown. 1976. "The origins of syntax in discourse: A case study of Tok Pisin relatives". *Language* 52(3):631–666.

Schaffranietz, Brigitte. 1999. "Relativsätze in Aufgabenorientierten Dialogen: Funktionale Aspekte ihrer Prosodie und Pragmatik in Sprachproduktion und Sprachrezeption". Universität Bielefeld.

Scherre, Maria Marta Pereira and Anthony J. Naro. 1992. "The serial effect on internal and external variables". *Language Variation and Change* 4(1):1–13.

Schubö, Fabian, Anna Roth, Viviana Haase and Caroline Féry. 2015. "Experimental investigations on the prosodic realization of restrictive and appositive relative clauses in German". *Lingua* 154:65–86.

Tagliamonte, Sali A. 2002. "Variation and change in the British relative marker system". In *Relativization in the North Sea Littoral*, P. Poussa (ed.). Munich: Lincom Europa. 147–165.

Tagliamonte, Sali A., Jennifer Smith and Helen Lawrence. 2005. "No taming the vernacular! Insights from the relatives in Northern Britain". *Language Variation and Change* 17(1):75–112.

Tottie, Gunnel. 1995. "The man Ø I love: An analysis of factors favouring zero relatives in written British and American English". *Stockholm Studies in English* 85:201–215.

Tottie, Gunnel and Michel Rey. 1997. "Relativization strategies in earlier African American vernacular English". *Language Variation and Change* 9:219–247.

de Vries, Mark. 2002. "The syntax of relativization". Ph.D. Thesis. Amsterdam: Universiteit van Amsterdam".

Walker, James A. 2020. "Modeling socio-grammatical variation: Plural existentials in Toronto English". In *Advancing Socio-grammatical Variation and Change: In Honour of Jenny Cheshire*, K. V. Beaman, I. Buchstaller, S. Fox and J. A. Walker (eds.). New York: Routledge.

Weise, Oskar. 1916. "Die Relativpronomina in den Deutschen Mundarten". *Zeitschrift Für Deutsche Mundarten* 12:64–71.

Wittenburg, Peter, Hennie Brugman, Albert Russel, Alex Klassmann and Han Sloetjes. 2006. "ELAN: A professional framework for multimodality research". In *Proceedings of the Fifth International Conference on Language Resources and Evaluation (LREC)*, Nijmegen: Max Planck Institute for Psycholinguistics, The Language Archive. 1556–1559.

Wright, Sue Ellen Susan and Talmy Givón. 1987. "The pragmatics of indefinite reference: Quantified text-based studies". *Studies in Language* 11(1):1–33.

Zaenen, Annie, Jean Carletta, Gregory Garretson, Joan Bresnan, Andrew Koontz-Garboden, Tatiana Nikitina, Mary Catherine O'Connor and Thomas Wasow. 2004. "Animacy encoding in English: Why and how". In *Proceedings of the 2004 ACL Workshop on Discourse Annotation, Barcelona*, A. Zaenen, J. Carletta, G. Garretson, J. Bresnan, A. Koontz-Garboden, T. Nikitina, M. C. O'Connor and T. Wasow (eds.). East Strouddsburg, PA: Association for Computational Linguistics. 118–125.

2.4 Modelling Socio-grammatical Variation
Plural Existentials in Toronto English

James A. Walker

2.4.1 Introduction[1]

Toronto, Canada's largest and arguably most ethnolinguistically diverse city, provides an ideal site for studying questions about the social stratification of linguistic variables. Several studies have provided evidence of ongoing change in the grammar and phonetics of Toronto English (Clarke et al. 1995; Roeder and Jarmasz 2010; Tagliamonte 2006, 2013). Hoffman and Walker's (2010; Hoffman 2010; Walker 2016) analysis of speakers of different ethnolinguistic backgrounds has revealed statistically significant differences for phonetic variables. However, despite differences in overall rates across groups, the conditioning of the variation by linguistic factors has been found to be largely parallel among younger speakers born and raised in the city. In contrast with the interpretation of ethnically marked ways of speaking ('ethnolects') as indicative of language interference (e.g., Carlock and Wölck 1981; Chambers 2003), these results argue in favour of considering Toronto English as a single linguistic system – at least as far as the phonology is concerned.

But can the same be said for the grammatical system of Toronto English? Unlike phonetic variation, which uncontroversially serves 'socio-symbolic' functions, helping to construct and convey social-group membership (e.g., Eckert 2000; Labov 1972), there is less agreement about the extent to which *grammatical* variation may serve similar functions (e.g., Cheshire 1999; 2003:246, 2005a:479–481; Cheshire et al. 2005:129). Grammatical variation, which tends to be sharply stratified (e.g., Sankoff 1974), is often taken to reflect underlying differences of code (standard versus non-standard/regional, creole versus non-creole) or register (formal versus casual) rather than aspects of social interaction or identity (e.g., Labov 1998).

Such differences in social stratification between phonetic and grammatical variables led Labov (1993) to suggest that syntactic knowledge is too "deep" (i.e., below the level of consciousness) to mark social differences. Phonetic knowledge, which is closer to or above the level of consciousness, lends itself more readily to this purpose (see also Labov 2008a; Labov et al. 2006, 2011; Levon and Buchstaller 2015; Meyerhoff

166   *James A. Walker*

and Walker 2013). Is grammatical variation in Toronto English conditioned similarly to phonetic variation?

An additional difference between grammatical and phonetic variation is methodological. Grammatical variables occur much less frequently in spontaneous speech than phonetic variables (Cheshire 1999), lessening our confidence in interpreting the significance of factors conditioning grammatical variation. To analyse grammatical variation, we may need to look beyond traditional tools of variationist analysis developed to analyse phonetic variation to alternative approaches that take into consideration the relative sparseness of data for grammatical variation (Cheshire 1998, 2003, 2005b, 2013; Cheshire and Williams 2002).

Descriptions of Canadian English are replete with mentions of characteristic phonetic, lexical and discourse features but contain few discussions of characteristic grammatical features (Boberg 2010; Walker 2015). While there is a growing body of research on grammatical change (e.g., Tagliamonte 2013; Tagliamonte et al. 2016), most varieties of Canadian English (with the exception of Newfoundland) are still said to be characterised by a high degree of (grammatical) homogeneity (Chambers 2006).

However, Canadian English does feature notable variation in one area of the grammar, one shared with most other varieties of English (Chambers 2004): existential constructions with plural referents. In such constructions, the verb varies between plural (1a–b) and singular morphology (1c–d), including a variant with contracted *'s* (1e).

(1) a) We had to hang our food because ***there were*** bears. (4/1:05:15)[2]
     b) Obviously ***there are*** no sharks in a swimming pool. (66/1:12:45)
     c) It helps being in the city where ***there is*** other kids around. (70/22:25)
     d) A group of women was upset that ***there was*** prostitutes in the neighbourhood. (24/20:22)
     e) There*'s* black bears, I believe ***there's*** brown bears. (6/4:38)

This paper addresses two questions, one sociolinguistic, the other methodological. First, is grammatical variation in Toronto English socially stratified in the same way as phonetic variation? Specifically, does ethnic background account for patterns of agreement and are the linguistic factors conditioning these patterns shared across ethnic groups? Second, what is the best method for modelling socio-grammatical variation with sparse data?

2.4.2 Variation in Singular Agreement in Toronto English

2.4.2.1 Social Stratification of Singular Agreement

The lack of social stratification in some studies of variable agreement in existentials in other varieties of English led Cheshire (1998:20) to

Plural Existentials in Toronto English   167

speculate that this grammatical variable may not be available "for social evaluation and the consequent marking of social groups". Nevertheless, there is evidence that, at least in some communities, singular agreement is socially stratified similarly to other variables. For example, in line with the general finding that women tend to exhibit more standard language usage (Cheshire 2002; Labov 1990), some studies have found that women tend to use less singular agreement (Britain and Sudbury 2002; Eisikovits 1991; Schreier 2002; Smallwood 1997; Tagliamonte 1998; Woods 1999). The higher use of singular agreement by younger speakers (Britain and Sudbury 2002; Krejci and Hilton 2017; Smallwood 1997; Tagliamonte 1998) may be interpreted as ongoing change toward the loss of plural agreement. Speakers from lower social classes and with lower levels of education tend to use singular agreement more frequently (Britain and Sudbury 2002; Krejci and Hilton 2017; Meechan and Foley 1994; Smallwood 1997; Tagliamonte 1998), and there is some evidence that speakers of different ethnic or racial backgrounds use singular agreement at different rates (Britain and Sudbury 2002). These results suggest that singular agreement holds the *potential* for social stratification, even if it is not stratified along similar lines in all communities. In the case of Toronto, do speakers use singular agreement to mark their ethnolinguistic background?

2.4.2.2 Data and Coding

The data in this study are taken from the "Contact in the City" corpus, assembled as part of an ongoing large-scale project to investigate the ethnolinguistic landscape of English in Toronto (Hoffman and Walker 2010). Making use of their existing social networks, undergraduate research assistants at York University have conducted and recorded sociolinguistic interviews with residents of Toronto, stratified according to ethnic background, generation and sex. The analysis presented in this paper uses a subsample of 78 speakers from this corpus, representing the

Table 2.4.1 Distribution of speakers included in the study by ethnicity, generation and sex

Ethnicity	British/Irish		Chinese		Italian	
Generation/ age-group:	Female	Male	Female	Male	Female	Male
First/older	7	6	4	3	6	3
Second/third/ Younger	6	6	11	11	8	7
Total	13	12	15	14	14	10
Total by ethnicity	25		29		24	
Grand total	78					

168   *James A. Walker*

three largest ethnic groups in the city: the old-line British/Irish-descent population, Chinese-Canadians (who came from or can trace their ancestry to Hong Kong), and Italian-Canadians (who largely come from or can trace their origins to Calabria or Sicily). These speakers are distributed according to ethnic background, sex and generation or age-group as shown in Table 2.4.1.[3]

I began by locating and extracting every existential *there* construction with plural reference in the transcribed sociolinguistic interviews of these speakers.[4] Each of these 1,252 tokens was coded for the individual speaker and their social characteristics and a series of factors that test hypotheses about the language-internal conditioning of the variation.

Verbs in existential constructions with *there* largely consist of *be* and (to a lesser extent) auxiliary *have* (see (2c, 2e) below), with auxiliary *do* and other verbs, such as *seem* and *need*, appearing infrequently. The dependent variable was coded as one of three variants: SINGULAR AGREEMENT, verbs with third-person singular marking (*is*, *was*, *has*), as in example (2a); *there's*, contracted *is* or *has* (2b–c); and PLURAL AGREEMENT, verbs with non-third-person singular agreement (*are*, *were*, *have*) (2d–e).

(2) a) Like, ***there is*** some things that sometimes they come out crooked. (12/14:56)
    b) Actually ***there's*** a lot of other places I want to go. (90/6:56)
    c) Yeah, ***there's*** been a lot of changes in Toronto. (85/15:29)
    d) Like, ***there weren't*** that many houses like at that time, very few, eh. (11/22:55)
    e) ***There have*** been different things going on with the transit systems here. (91/19:12)

Verb tense is an important conditioning factor in most studies, with present tense favouring singular agreement (Britain and Sudbury 2002; Eisikovits 1991; Feagin 1979; Hannay 1985, but cf. Hay and Schreier 2004). As previously noted (Hay and Schreier 2004; Meechan and Foley 1994; Walker 2007), tense overlaps with the form of the verb (contracted or full) since *there's* (which is usually counted with singular agreement) is both present tense and contracted, raising the question of whether tense effects reflect considerations that can be attributed to contraction. Instead of coding tokens for the (morphological) *tense* of the verb, I used clues provided in the discourse context to code the *time* referred to by the verb, distinguishing between present (3a) (or rather, non-past) and past (3b) temporal reference.

(3) a) I feel that if I'm in a Chinese neighbourhood ***there's*** just gonna be far too much gossip, which I don't like. (37/26:09)
    b) We knew that even if ***there's*** anything happen we can still have enough time to run back to the bus. (34/21:50)

Plural Existentials in Toronto English 169

The remaining linguistic factor groups test hypotheses drawn from the literature to account for variable agreement with plural existentials.

Formal syntactic accounts of singular agreement focus on the non-canonical position of the subject NP in existential constructions. Since the verb is typically assumed to seek person-number features from a NP in preverbal subject position, when the NP is post-verbal, the verb either must get person-number features from *there* or surface with a 'default' or unmarked agreement (third-person singular) (e.g., Chomsky 1995; Groat 1995). While the first explanation makes no prediction about the source of variable agreement, the second (what we may call the 'default agreement' hypothesis) predicts that any element separating the verb and subject will increase the likelihood of singular agreement. To test this hypothesis, I coded each token for whether the verb was adjacent to the subject or whether it was separated by intervening material, such as discourse markers (4a), adverbials (4b) or pauses or hesitations (4c) (Britain and Sudbury 2002; Eisikovits 1991; Hay and Schreier 2004; Martinez Insua and Palacios Martinez 2003; Tagliamonte 1998; Walker 2007).

(4) a) *There was* <u>like</u> cans all over the floors. (65/44:36)
   b) *There's* <u>always</u> gonna be people who cut corners. (82/1:22:36)
   c) They don't appreciate that *there's* the <u>uh- uh-</u> poorer people out there. (37/40:43)

Another strategy of formal syntactic accounts of singular agreement is to move it out of the syntax altogether, attributing it to considerations such as online production (e.g., Sobin 1994, 1997). In non-existential contexts, elements within the subject NP that are adjacent to the verb sometimes trigger non-standard agreement (e.g., *the owner of the <u>cats</u> are here*). Although this context is irrelevant here, a similar line of argument proposes that the absence of a plural –s suffix within the NP might make it more likely for the post-verbal subject to be interpreted as singular in production, making singular agreement more likely (cf. Meechan and Foley 1994). To test this 'production' hypothesis, I coded each token for whether plural –s was present in the NP, whether on the head noun (5a) or elsewhere (5b), or absent (5c) (Britain and Sudbury 2002; Hay and Schreier 2004; Meechan and Foley 1994; Walker 2007).

(5) a) There's just a lot of <u>things</u> I want to learn about. (7/1:16:14)
   b) Well it's competitive but then *there are* <u>lots</u> of nice friends too. (37/34:31)
   c) Yes, *there are* a few select <u>people</u> that I wish I could fire. (24/24:28)

As noted above, the most common verb in existential constructions is *be*, generally referred to as the 'copula' (cf. Labov 1969). However, true copula *be* only occurs with non-verbal predicates (NP, AdjP, PP, AdvP);

170 *James A. Walker*

with verbal predicates (progressive and perfective participles), *be* is an auxiliary verb. Current syntactic theory correlates these different grammatical roles with structural positions at different levels of 'visibility' to agreement. For example, Deal (2009: 301) argues that auxiliary *be* is a 'dummy verbalizer' that selects a functional predicate (AspP) requiring different forms of the main verb. Deal's account uses the impenetrability of the functional layer to the features of the lexical verb to block verbs other than *be* (e.g., **There laughed a child* versus *There was a child laughing*). To test the hypothesis that variable agreement stems from the different syntactic configurations in which *be* occurs, I coded for whether the verb was an auxiliary (6a) or a main verb (6b).

(6) a) Um ***there's*** always gonna be homeless people. (85/18:06)
      b) ***There's*** always new people coming and going. (4/25:11)

In an early attempt at operationalising predictions from syntactic theory as factors in variationist analysis, Meechan and Foley (1994) coded the determiner of the head noun based on the hypothesis that definite subject NPs would favour plural agreement more than indefinite NPs (Diesing 1992; Milsark 1977). While definiteness was not statistically significant, a finer-grained division of determiner type correlated with different rates of singular agreement. Subsequent studies attempting to replicate these results have yielded inconsistent results (e.g., Britain and Sudbury 2002; Hay and Schreier 2004; Meechan and Foley 1994), some of which may reflect regional differences in the varieties of English studied, or the different coding systems used, or even the accidental distribution of determiner types within each dataset (e.g., Hay and Schreier 2004: 232). I revisited the 'definiteness hypothesis' using a stricter definition of definiteness. Based on the patterning of variants in initial analyses, I distinguished definite determiners (*the, this, that, these, those*, personal and possessive pronouns) (7a) from indefinite determiners (*a, some, any*) (7b) and coded quantifiers (*more, much, less, few, a lot, a bunch*) (7c) separately.

(7) a) Then ***there's*** like <u>the</u> holidays like Halloween … (2/43:19)
      b) Yeah, ***there were*** <u>some</u> Asian math teachers. (20/4:11)
      c) ***There's*** <u>a bunch</u> of apartments right up on the hill. (32/18:22)

Finally, while negation has been shown to be an important consideration in previous studies (e.g., Britain 2002; Krejci and Hilton 2017; Martínez-Insua and Palacios Martinez 2003, but cf. Britain and Sudbury 2002; Rupp 2005; Tagliamonte 1998), negative determiners are often coded with the type of determiner, making the source of this effect unclear. I coded the polarity of each token (positive or negative)

Plural Existentials in Toronto English 171

separately from the determiner, though for this analysis I will not distinguish between verbal negation (8a) and NP negation (8b).

(8) a) Like, ***there wasn't*** clear distinctive groups. (63/59:16)
    b) ***There were*** <u>no</u> lifts. (83/14:25)

2.4.2.3 Overall Distribution

The overall distribution of the three variants (plural agreement, singular agreement and *there's*) across social factors is shown in Table 2.4.2. The contracted variant *there's* is by far the preferred variant for all groups, except for older speakers of British/Irish descent and first-generation Chinese, who prefer plural agreement. The increase in *there's* between older and younger British/Irish-descent speakers suggests ongoing change (Tagliamonte 1998, 2009). While all younger speakers favour *there's* more than their older cohorts, there are differences across ethnic groups, such that younger speakers of Italian background prefer *there's* more than speakers of Chinese and British/Irish background. The generational differences in the Chinese and Italian groups presumably reflect the non-native status of the first-generation speakers and the potential for interference from their first language and/or aspects of second-language acquisition, as well as the small number of tokens for these groups. Although there is no sex difference for use of *there's*, women tend to prefer plural agreement, and men tend to prefer singular agreement, in line

Table 2.4.2 Overall distribution of variants of *there*-existentials with plural reference in Toronto English by *social* factors

	there's	*Singular agreement*	*Plural agreement*	*Total n*
Ethnicity x generation/age-group				
British/Irish, older	38%	17%	45%	333
British/Irish, younger	52%	18%	29%	277
Chinese, first gen.	38%	18%	43%	120
Chinese, second/ third gen.	57%	12%	31%	298
Italian, first gen.	40%	29%	31%	42
Italian, second/ third gen.	71%	20%	9%	182
Sex				
Female	50%	15%	35%	741
Male	52%	20%	28%	511
Grand total:				1252

172   *James A. Walker*

with other research that shows that women tend to prefer more standard variants, as mentioned above.

The overall distribution of the three variants across linguistic factors is shown in Table 2.4.3. There is a split among variants for temporal reference, with *there's* preferred in the present and singular and plural agreement in the past.[5] There appear to be few differences across determiner type, except for a higher rate of plural agreement with bare nouns. Rates of both *there's* and singular agreement are higher when material intervenes between the verb and subject, lending support to the 'default agreement' hypothesis. For verb status, we see a split between *there's*, which occurs at higher rates with auxiliaries, and singular agreement, which is higher with main verbs. This difference in conditioning, along with the effect of temporal reference, lends support to the view that

Table 2.4.3 Overall distribution of variants of *there*-existentials with plural reference in Toronto English by *linguistic* factors

	there's	*Singular agreement*	*Plural agreement*	*Total n*
Temporal reference				
Past	6%	43%	51%	397
Present	71%	5%	24%	855
Determiner				
Bare	46%	18%	36%	587
Definite	55%	19%	26%	58
Indefinite	55%	16%	29%	399
Quantifier	54%	17%	29%	208
Intervening material				
Absent	50%	16%	34%	974
Present	54%	21%	25%	278
Verb status				
Auxiliary	60%	6%	33%	63
Main	50%	18%	32%	1189
Polarity				
Negative	44%	26%	31%	108
Positive	51%	16%	32%	1144
Plural −s				
Absent	49%	17%	34%	451
Present	52%	17%	31%	801

there's and singular agreement should be considered as separate variants rather than being grouped together (Krejci and Hilton 2017; Walker 2007). For polarity, the only effect is a slightly higher rate of singular agreement in negative contexts. Contrary to the 'production hypothesis', the presence of a plural *-s* in the NP does not exert an effect.

2.4.2.4 Multivariate Analysis

The results in Table 2.4.2 provide some evidence that variable agreement in existentials with plural reference is socially and linguistically stratified in Toronto English. However, since overall rates may vary for a number of reasons, we need to determine whether differences across groups of speakers are statistically meaningful. We also need to investigate whether the conditioning by linguistic factors shown in Table 2.4.3 is consistent across all speakers and groups, or whether differences in linguistic conditioning might reflect aspects of interference from the respective heritage languages of the different groups. Ideally, we need to analyse the contributions of social and linguistic effects simultaneously.

In variationist sociolinguistics, the standard tool for multivariate analysis is (stepwise) logistic regression (Cedergren and Sankoff 1974; Johnson 2009; Sankoff et al. 2015), but there are limitations to this procedure which make its use in analysing grammatical variation less reliable. First, the relative infrequency of the variable yields not only small overall numbers (compared to phonetic variables) but also fewer

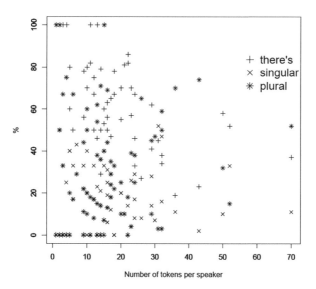

Figure 2.4.1 Overall rates of *there*-existentials per speaker by number of tokens per speaker.

174 *James A. Walker*

tokens per speaker. We can increase our confidence in group effects by using mixed-effects models, in which individual speakers are included as a random effect (Johnson 2009), but these models are problematic if there are outliers in the data (e.g., Roland 2009). In these data, as shown by plotting overall rates of the three variants for each speaker against the number of tokens per speaker (Figure 2.4.1), speaker behaviour becomes more divergent from the group the fewer the tokens (cf. Guy 1980).

Sparseness of data presents a second problem for logistic regression, which assumes that factors operate independently of each other (Baayen 2011; Guy 1988). There are strategies that can be used to overcome this problem, such as creating an interaction factor group or running parallel analyses with different factor combinations (Walker 2010: 41–43), but sub-dividing the data in this way may result in very small numbers per cell, making regression analysis inappropriate.

As a result of these limitations, recent variationist work has adopted an alternative method of multivariate analysis: recursive partitioning (e.g., Tagliamonte and Baayen 2012; Tagliamonte, D'Arcy and Rodriguez Louro 2016). This approach divides tokens into groups on the basis of the factors that produce significant differences in variant distribution. These groups are then sub-divided and sub-divided until no more significant sub-divisions can be made. Successive sub-divisions can be represented graphically, most commonly via a conditional inference tree (CIT): the highest node of a CIT indicates the factor with the most significant grouping, with lower nodes indicating decreasingly significant sub-groupings (Strobl et al. 2008, 2009). While CITs are preferable to other types of recursive partitioning because they do not require tree 'pruning' (i.e., simplifying the model) (Levshina 2015: 292), they produce models that may overfit the data (Baayen et al. 2013; Hothorn et al. 2006a: 652). Since the goal of sampling is to select data that can be generalised to a larger community (Sankoff 1988), overfitting limits generalisation – that is, we do not know whether we would have derived the same model had we sampled different speakers or a different set of their utterances.

The ideal solution to overfitting would be to sample the population more than once, but this solution is impractical or even impossible in sociolinguistic research. Instead, we can create multiple datasets by randomly selecting subsamples of tokens from the existing data (Baayen et al. 2013; Breiman 2001; Strobl et al. 2009), which can be used to generate large numbers (hundreds or thousands) of CITs to compare for consistency of results. In effect, each CIT in a forest of trees 'votes' on the relative importance of factors: if the trees vote consistently, we can be reasonably confident in the explanatory power of the factors that produce the subdivisions. Recursive partitioning and random forests have been recommended for situations in which effect sizes are large but the distribution of data is sparse ("large p, small n") (Strobl et al. 2009), the situation of grammatical variation *par excellence*.[6]

Making use of the ctree() function in R (Hothorn et al. 2006a), I conducted analyses of recursive partitioning and random forests for the distribution of the three variants using the social and linguistic factors discussed in the previous section. Since including all ethnic groups and generations in the analysis resulted in a very complicated tree that was hard to interpret, I separated the analysis by ethnic group for the older speakers in the sample and analysed all the younger speakers together.

The CITs for the older speakers are shown in Figure 2.4.2. For the British/Irish speakers, the most important factor group is temporal reference, with *there's* strongly favoured in the present. The next division is by the speaker sex, with men using more singular agreement and women using no *there's*. Among the women the next division is the

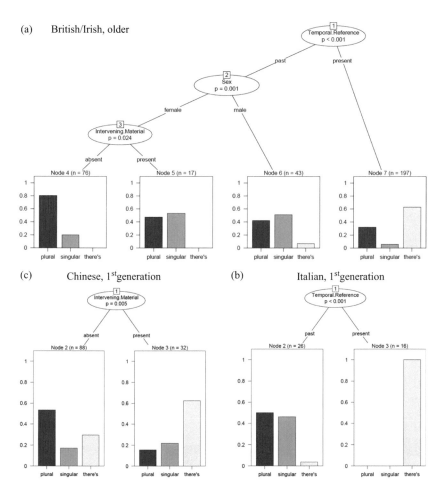

Figure 2.4.2 Conditional inference trees for variants of *there*-existentials with plural reference for older speakers of Toronto English.

presence of intervening material, which favours singular agreement. For the first-generation Chinese speakers, the only significant factor group is intervening material, which favours *there's*. For the first-generation Italian speakers, only temporal reference is significant, with *there's* categorical in the present.

The analysis of the younger speakers (Figure 2.4.3) reveals only two relevant divisions, one linguistic and one social. The most important division is temporal reference, with *there's* preferred more in the present. In the past, there is a division according to ethnic background, with speakers of British/Irish and Italian background favouring the use of singular agreement and speakers of Chinese background favouring plural agreement. There is also an ethnic division in the present, with Italian speakers preferring *there's* over British/Irish and Chinese speakers and the latter preferring plural agreement over the Italians.

To verify whether the grouping decisions shown in Figure 2.4.3 can be generalised to the larger population, I used the cforest() function in R (Hothorn et al. 2006b; Strobl et al. 2007) to generate random forests of trees and the varimp() function (Strobl et al. 2008) to evaluate the relative importance of factors across the forests. The bar graph in Figure 2.4.4 lists the factors in descending order of their variable importance. (The dashed line indicates the limit at which we can interpret the factors to exert a consistently significant effect across the forest.) The variable importance of factors displayed in this graph supports the relative ranking of factors in the CIT shown in Figure 2.4.3, with temporal reference and ethnicity exerting significant effects. Speaker sex and the other

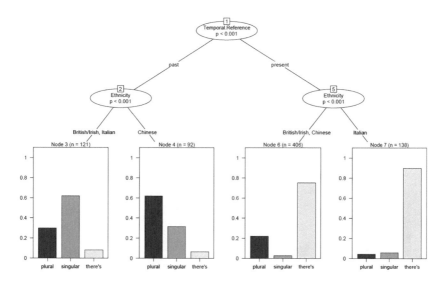

Figure 2.4.3 Conditional inference tree for *there*-existentials with plural reference for younger speakers of Toronto English.

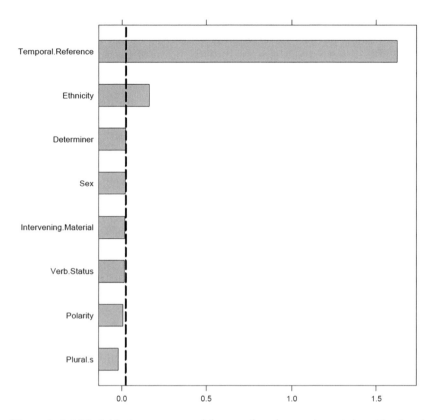

Figure 2.4.4 Variable importance of factors for *there*-existentials with plural reference for younger speakers of Toronto English.

linguistic factor groups exert smaller effects but do not achieve the level of significance reached by the first two.

2.4.3 Discussion

Grammatical variation presents sociolinguistic analysis with methodological and interpretive issues that are not raised by sociophonetic variation. Answering the overriding question addressed by this chapter – whether grammatical variation in Toronto English is socially stratified in the same way that phonetic variants are – is made difficult by the relative infrequency of grammatical variables in speech, and the resultant small number of tokens per speaker, which means that interpreting differences between social groups as reflections of socio-symbolic functions is less reliable.

178   James A. Walker

In this chapter, I have addressed this question through an investigation of variation in verbal agreement in existentials with plural reference in the English of speakers of different generations and ethnic backgrounds in the city of Toronto. The overall distribution of the variants suggests social stratification according to both generation and ethnic background, but this interpretation is vitiated by sparse distribution of data and the existence of outliers. I used recursive partitioning, expressed via conditional inference trees and random forests, to confirm the ranking of factors. This analysis shows that the linguistic and social factors are interwoven in conditioning the variation, but that ethnicity exerts significant effects.

To what can we attribute these social effects? While a common explanation for any differences in language usage on the basis of ethnic background is transfer from the minority language, this explanation does not always bear close scrutiny (Labov 2008b). The heritage languages of these speakers, Cantonese and Italian, use different constructions for existentials. In Cantonese, existentials are expressed by the verb 有 *yáuh* 'have' (negative form 冇 *móuh*), which introduces the referent and which is invariant regardless of number (Matthews and Yip 2011). In Italian,[7] singular referents of existentials are introduced with *c'è* (< *ci è*) 'there is' and plural referents are introduced with *ci sono* 'there are'. Given the use of an invariant verb in Cantonese and a verb that shows agreement in Italian, we would expect higher rates of plural agreement in the Italian speakers and higher rates of singular agreement and/or *there's* with the Chinese speakers, but the analysis revealed the opposite. Therefore, we need to look to explanations of the observed variation other than language transfer.

I believe that we need recourse to different explanations for each generation. For the first generation, I would argue that observed effects are due to differences in second-language learning. While most of the first-generation Chinese speakers studied English formally at different levels and grew up in Hong Kong, where English is a community language, the Italian speakers largely learned English in informal contexts after their arrival in Canada. This interpretation is supported by impressionistic observations that many of the first-generation Italian speakers show evidence of other features, such as zero copula, which are not characteristic of spoken Italian but which have been found in other situations of second-language learning (e.g., Ellis 1994; Preston 1989). These considerations suggest that the higher rates of singular agreement and *there's* observed in the first-generation Italians reflect strategies of second-language learning rather than language transfer.

For the second generation, second-language learning is not an appealing explanation. Regardless of their first language, all second-generation speakers have grown up in neighbourhoods in Toronto, where English is the majority language. In addition, unlike the first-generation speakers, the second-generation speakers show no evidence of other relics of second-language learning, such as zero copula. This interpretation is in line with the results obtained for phonetic variation, which shows superficial differences in overall rates and a shared underlying linguistic system among these younger speakers.

2.4.4 Conclusion

Taken together, the results of this study suggest that the grammatical variation observed in a multilingual and ethnically diverse city like Toronto is the result of a number of factors, some of which have to do with language contact (second-language learning) and some of which have to do with the desire to construct and express ethnic differences in language. Elucidating the role of such variants in the speech community is made more difficult by the methodological challenges presented by modelling socio-grammatical variation. Expanding the toolbox of variationist sociolinguistic analysis beyond traditional statistical methods to employ other methods as additional lines of evidence helps to clarify these issues.

Notes

* The data on which this study is based were taken from the "Contact in the City" project (Hoffman and Walker 2010), funded by the Faculty of Arts at York University and the Social Sciences and Humanities Council of Canada. I thank Rajat Bhardwaj for his help in extracting and coding the data, the audience at New Ways of Analyzing Variation 39 (University of Texas at San Antonio, October 2010), where an early version of this paper was presented. Jason Grafmiller gave advice on plotting random forests and Sali Tagliamonte and several anonymous reviewers provided very helpful critiques and comments. Any remaining errors are my own responsibility.

1 Examples are identified by speaker number in the 'Contact in the City' corpus (Hoffman and Walker 2010) and time index in the recorded sociolinguistic interview.

2 The first-generation Chinese- and Italian-background speakers arrived in Canada after age 18 and have lived there for at least 20 years, while the second/third-generation speakers were born and raised in Toronto or arrived before age five. All British/Irish-background speakers were born and raised in Toronto and are matched to the age-groups of other ethnic backgrounds: younger (18–30) and older (40+). See Hoffman and Walker (2010) for more details about the composition of the corpus.

3 An anonymous reviewer raised the interesting question as to the extent to which *there's* varies with singular agreement in the context of singular and mass nouns. While beyond the scope of this chapter, the topic is being pursued in ongoing research.

4 Recall that this factor tests reference to *time* rather than to morphological *tense*, so these results are not a reflection of the present-tense status of *'s* in *there's*.

5 In fact, Rossi et al. (2005) argue that random forests provide a *more* reliable indication of the relative importance of factors in such a situation than does stepwise regression.

180　*James A. Walker*

6 The Italian speakers in our sample are largely of Sicilian and Calabrian origin, so are not (necessarily) heritage speakers of standard Italian. Nevertheless, I have not been able to find any indication of an invariant copula with existentials in the southern Italo-Romance languages (Ledgeway 2016; Loporcaro 2013).

References

Baayen, R. Harald. 2011. "Corpus linguistics and naive discriminative learning/A linguística de corpus e a aprendizagem discriminativa ingênua". *Revista brasileira de linguística aplicada* 11(2):295–328.

Baayen, R. Harald, Anna Endresen, Laura A. Janda, Anastasia Makarova and Tore Nesset. 2013. "Making choices in Russian: pros and cons of statistical methods for rival forms". *Russian Linguistics* 37:253–291.

Boberg, Charles. 2010. *The English Language in Canada: Status, History and Comparative Analysis*. Cambridge: Cambridge University Press.

Breiman, Leo. 2001. "Random forests". *Machine Learning* 45:5–32.

Britain, David and Andrea Sudbury. 2002. "There's sheep and there's penguins: Convergence, drift and 'slant' in New Zealand and Falkland Island English". In *Language Change: The Interplay of Internal, External and Extra-Linguistic Factors*, M.C. Jones and E. Esch (eds.). Berlin: Mouton de Gruyter. 211–240.

Carlock, Elizabeth and Wolfgang Wölck. 1981. "A method for isolating diagnostic linguistic variables: The Buffalo ethnolects experiment". In *Variation Omnibus*, D. Sankoff and H. Cedergren (eds.). Edmonton: Linguistic Research Inc. 17–24.

Cedergren, Henrietta and David Sankoff. 1974. "Variable rules: Performance as a statistical reflection of competence". *Language* 50:333–355.

Chambers, J.K. 2003. "Sociolinguistics of immigration". In *Social Dialectology: Studies in Honour of Peter Trudgill*, D. Britain and J. Cheshire (eds.). Amsterdam: John Benjamins. 97–114.

Chambers, J.K. 2004. "Dynamic typology and vernacular universals". In *Dialectology Meets Typology: Dialect Grammar from a Cross-Linguistic Perspective*, B. Kortmann (ed.). Berlin/New York: Mouton de Gruyter. 127–145.

Chambers, J.K. 2006. "The development of Canadian English". In *World Englishes: Critical Concepts in Linguistics*, K. Bolton and B.B. Kachru (eds.). London: Routledge. 383–395.

Cheshire, Jenny. 1998. "Taming the vernacular: Some repercussions for the study of syntactic variation and spoken grammar". *Te Reo* 41:6–27.

Cheshire, Jenny. 1999. "Spoken standard English". In *Standard English: The Current Debates*, T. Bex and R.J. Watts (eds.). London: Routledge. 129–148.

Cheshire, Jenny. 2002. "Sex and gender in variationist research". In *The Handbook of Language Variation and Change*, J.K. Chambers, P. Trudgill and N. Schilling-Estes (eds.). Oxford: Blackwell. 423–443.

Cheshire, Jenny. 2003. "Social dimensions of syntactic variation: The case of *when* clauses". In *Social Dialectology*, David Britain and Jenny Cheshire (eds.). Amsterdam: John Benjamins. 245–261.

Cheshire, Jenny. 2005a. "Syntactic variation and beyond: Gender and social class variation in the use of discourse-new markers". *Journal of Sociolinguistics* 9:479–507.

Cheshire, Jenny. 2005b. "Syntactic variation and spoken language". In *Syntax and Variation: Reconciling the Biological and the Social*, L. Cornips and K. Corrigan (eds.). Amsterdam: John Benjamins. 81–106.

Cheshire, Jenny. 2013. "Grammaticalisation in social context: The emergence of a new English pronoun". *Journal of Sociolinguistics* 17:608–633.

Cheshire, Jenny, Paul Kerswill and Anne Williams. 2005. "Phonology, grammar and discourse in dialect convergence". In *Dialect Change: Convergence and Divergence in European Languages*, P. Auer, F. Hinskens and P. Kerswill (eds.). Cambridge: Cambridge University Press. 135–167.

Cheshire, Jenny and Anne Williams. 2002. "Information structure in male and female adolescent talk". *Journal of English Linguistics* 30:217–238.

Chomsky, Noam. 1995. *The Minimalist Program*. Cambridge, MA: MIT Press.

Clarke, Sandra, Ford Elms and Amani Youssef. 1995. "The third dialect of English: Some Canadian evidence". *Language Variation and Change* 7:209–228.

Deal, Amy Rose. 2009. "The origin and content of expletives: Evidence from 'selection'". *Syntax* 12(4):285–323.

Diesing, Molly. 1992. *Indefinites*. Cambridge, MA: MIT Press.

Eckert, Penelope. 2000. *Linguistic Variation as Social Practice*. Oxford: Blackwell.

Eisikovits, Edina. 1991. "Variation in subject-verb agreement in Inner Sydney English". In *English Around the World*, J. Cheshire (ed.). Cambridge: Cambridge University Press. 235–255.

Ellis, Rod. 1994. *The Study of Second Language Acquisition*. Oxford: Oxford University Press.

Groat, Erich M. 1995. "English expletives: A minimalist approach". *Linguistic Inquiry* 26:354–365.

Guy, Gregory R. 1980. "Variation in the group and in the individual". In *Locating Language in Time and Space*, W. Labov (ed.). New York: Academic Press. 1–36.

Guy, Gregory R. 1988. "Advanced Varbrul analysis". In *Linguistic Change and Contact: NWAV-XVI*, K. Ferrara, B. Brown, K. Walters and J. Baugh (eds.). Austin: University of Texas, Department of Linguistics. 124–136.

Hay, Jennifer and Daniel Schreier. 2004. "Reversing the trajectory of language change: Subject-verb agreement with *be* in New Zealand English". *Language Variation and Change* 16:209–235.

Hoffman, Michol F. 2010. "The role of social factors in the Canadian Vowel Shift: Evidence from Toronto". *American Speech* 85(2):121–140.

Hoffman, Michol F. and James A. Walker. 2010. "Ethnolects and the city: Ethnic orientation and linguistic variation in Toronto English". *Language Variation and Change* 21:37–67.

Hothorn, Torsten, Kurt Hornik and Achim Zeileis. 2006a. "Unbiased recursive partitioning: A conditioning inference framework". *Journal of Computational and Graphical Statistics* 15(3):651–674.

Hothorn, Torsten, Peter Buehlmann, Sandrine Dudoit, Annette Molinaro and Mark Van Der Laan. 2006b. "Survival ensembles". *Biostatistics* 7(3):355–373.

Johnson, Daniel E. 2009. "Getting off the GoldVarb standard: Introducing Rbrul for mixed-effects variable rule analysis". *Language and Linguistics Compass* 3:359–383.

182 James A. Walker

Krejci, Bonnie and Katherine Hilton. 2017. "There's three variants: Agreement variation in existential *there* constructions". *Language Variation and Change* 29:187–204.

Labov, William. 1969. "Contraction, deletion, and inherent variability of the English copula". *Language* 45(4):715–762.

Labov, William. 1972. *Sociolinguistic Patterns*. Philadelphia: University of Pennsylvania Press.

Labov, William. 1990. "The intersection of sex and social class in the course of linguistic change". *Language Variation and Change* 2:205–254.

Labov, William. 1993. "The unobservability of structure and its linguistic consequences". In *Paper presented at New Ways of Analyzing Variation 22*, University of Ottawa.

Labov, William. 1998. "Co-existent systems in African-American English". In *African-American English: Structure, History and Use*, S.S. Mufwene, J.R. Rickford, G. Bailey and J. Baugh (eds.). London/New York: Routledge. 110–153.

Labov, William. 2008a. "Cognitive capacities of the sociolinguistic monitor". In *Paper presented at Sociolinguistics Symposium 17*, University of Amsterdam.

Labov, William. 2008b. "Mysteries of the substrate". In *Social Lives in Language: Sociolinguistics and Multilingual Speech Communities*, M. Meyerhoff and N. Nagy (eds.). Amsterdam/Philadelphia: John Benjamins. 315–326.

Labov, William, Sharon Ash, Maciej Baranowski, Naomi Nagy and Maya Ravindranath. 2006. "Listeners' sensitivity to the frequency of sociolinguistic variables". *University of Pennsylvania Working Papers in Linguistics* 12(2):105–129.

Labov, William, Sharon Ash, Maya Ravindranath, Tracey Weldon, Maciej Baranowski and Naomi Nagy. 2011. "Properties of the sociolinguistic monitor". *Journal of Sociolinguistics* 15(4):431–463.

Ledgeway, Adam. 2016. "The dialects of southern Italy". In *The Oxford Guide to the Romance Languages*, A. Ledgeway and M. Maiden (eds.). Oxford: Oxford University Press. 246–269.

Levon, Erez and Isabelle Buchstaller. 2015. "Perception, cognition, and linguistic structure: The effect of linguistic modularity and cognitive style on sociolinguistic processing". *Language Variation and Change* 27:319–348.

Levshina, Natalia. 2015. *How to Do Linguistics with R: Data Exploration and Statistical Analysis*. Amsterdam: John Benjamines.

Loporcaro, Michele. 2013. *Profilo linguistico dei dialetti italiani*. 2nd edition. Rome: Editori Laterza.

Martínez-Insua, Ana E. and Ignacio M. Palacios-Martínez. 2003. "A corpus-based approach to non-concord in present day English existential *there*-constructions". *English Studies* 3:262–283.

Matthews, Stephen and Virginia Yip. 2011. *Cantonese: A Comprehensive Grammar*. 2nd edition. New York and London: Routledge.

Meechan, Marjory and Michele Foley. 1994. "On resolving disagreement: Linguistic theory and variation – there's bridges". *Language Variation and Change* 6:63–85.

Meyerhoff, Miriam and James A. Walker. 2013. "An existential problem: The sociolinguistic monitor and variation in existential constructions on Bequia (St. Vincent and the Grenadines)". *Language in Society* 42:407–428.

Milsark, Gary L. 1977. "Towards an explanation of certain peculiarities of the existential construction in English". *Linguistic Analysis* 3:1–31.

Preston, Dennis R. 1989. *Sociolinguistics and Second Language Acquisition*. Oxford: Blackwell.

Roeder, Rebecca and Lidia-Gabriela Jarmasz. 2010. "The Canadian shift in Toronto". *Canadian Journal of Linguistics* 55:387–404.

Roland, Douglas. 2009. "Relative clauses remodeled: The problem with mixed-effects models". In *Poster presented at the 22nd Annual Meeting of the CUNY Conference on Human Sentence Processing*, University of California, Davis, March 26–28.

Rossi, Alberto, Francesco Amaddeo, Marco Sandri and Michele Tansella. 2005. "Determinants of once-only contact in a community-based psychiatric service". *Social Psychiatry and Psychiatric Epidemiology* 40:50–56.

Rupp, Laura. 2005. Constraints on nonstandard -s in expletive there sentences: A generative-variationist perspective. *English Language and Linguistics* 9:255–288.

Sankoff, David. 1988. Problems of representativeness. In *Sociolinguistics: An International Handbook of the Science of Language and Society*, Ulrich Ammon, Norbert Dittmar and Klaus J. Mattheier (eds.). Berlin: Walter de Gruyter. 899–903.

Sankoff, David, Sali Tagliamonte and Eric Smith. 2015. GoldVarb Yosemite: A Multivariate Analysis Application for Macintosh. (http://individual.utoronto.ca/tagliamonte/goldvarb.html).

Sankoff, Gillian. 1974. "A quantitative paradigm for the study of communicative competence". In *Explorations in the Ethnography of Speaking*, R. Bauman and J. Sherzer (eds.). Cambridge: Cambridge University Press. 18–49.

Schreier, Daniel. 2002. "Past *be* in Tristan da Cunha: The rise and fall of categoricality in language change". *American Speech* 77:70–99.

Smallwood, Carolyn. 1997. "Dis-agreement in Canadian English existentials". In *Proceedings of the 1997 Annual Conference of the Canadian Linguistic Association*, L. Blair, C. Burns and L. Rowsell (eds.). Calgary: Department of Linguistics, University of Calgary. 227–238.

Sobin, Nicholas. 1994. "An acceptable grammatical construction". In *The Reality of Linguistic Rules*, S.D. Lima, R.L. Corrigan and G.K. Iverson (eds.). Amsterdam/Philadelphia: John Benjamins Publishing. 51–65.

Sobin, Nicholas. 1997. "Agreement, default rules, and grammatical viruses". *Linguistic Inquiry* 28:318–343.

Strobl, Carolin, Anne-Laure Boulesteix, Achim Zeileis and Torsten Hothorn. 2007. "Bias in random forest variable importance measures: Illustrations, sources and a solution". *BMC Bioinformatics* 8: 25.

Strobl, Carolin, Anne-Laure Boulesteix, Thomas Kneib, Thomas Augustin and Achim Zeileis. 2008. "Conditional variable importance for random forests". *BMC Bioinformatics* 9:307.

Strobl, Carolin, James Malley and Gerhard Tutz. 2009. "An introduction to recursive partitioning: Rationale, application, and characteristics of classification and regression trees, bagging, and random forests". *Psychological Methods* 14(4):323–348.

Tagliamonte, Sali. 1998. "*Was/were* variation across the generations: View from the city of York". *Language Variation and Change* 10:153–191.

Tagliamonte, Sali. 2006. ""So cool, right?" Canadian English entering the 21st century". *Canadian Journal of Linguistics* 51:309–331.

Tagliamonte, Sali. 2009. "There was universals, then there weren't: A comparative sociolinguistic perspective on 'default singulars'". In *Vernacular Universals and Language Contacts: Evidence from Varieties of English and Beyond*, M. Fillpula, J. Klemola and H. Paulasto (eds.). London/New York: Routledge. 103–129.

Tagliamonte, Sali. 2013. "The verb phrase in contemporary Canadian English". In *The Verb Phrase in English: Investigating Recent Change with Corpora*, B. Aarts, J. Close, G. Leech and S. Wallis (eds.). Cambridge: Cambridge University Press. 133–154.

Tagliamonte, Sali A. and R. Harald Baayen. 2012. "Models, forests, and trees of York English: *Was/were* variation as a case study for statistical practice". *Language Variation and Change* 24:135–178.

Tagliamonte, Sali A., Alexandra D'Arcy and Celeste Rodriguez Louro. 2016. "Outliers, impact, and rationalization in linguistic change". *Language* 92(4):824–849.

Walker, James A. 2007. "'There's bears back there': Plural existentials and vernacular universals in (Quebec) English". *English World-Wide* 28:147–166.

Walker, James A. 2010. *Variation in Linguistic Systems*. New York/London: Routledge.

Walker, James A. 2015. *Canadian English: A Sociolinguistic Perspective*. New York/London: Routledge.

Walker, James A. 2016. "The intersection of sex and ethnicity in language variation and change". In *Paper presented at IGALA9*, City University of Hong Kong, Hong Kong.

Woods, Howard B. 1999. *The Ottawa Survey of Canadian English*. Kingston, ON: Queen's University.

Section 3

Formal Approaches to Syntactic Variation

3.1 A Socio-grammatical Analysis of Linguistic Gaps and Transitional Forms

Sjef Barbiers

3.1.1 Introduction[1]

The question what sociolinguists and generative grammarians can learn from each other, whether they should cooperate and if so, how, has been on the table for quite some time now. It was the central question of the workshop *Syntactic Variation* (ICLaVE 2, Uppsala 2003), with Jenny Cheshire as one of the speakers (see her paper *Syntactic variation and spoken language* and the other papers in Cornips and Corrigan 2005). She took up the question again in a paper at the workshop *Is syntactic variation special?* (ICLaVE 9, Malaga 2017), in which she discussed, among other things, the status quo of syntactic variation research, partly on the basis of the papers delivered at that workshop. She concluded there that syntactic variation research is in a very healthy state and that the future looks bright for an improved understanding of syntactic variation.

However, she also argued that this improvement mainly comes from bringing together the results of the two approaches, not so much from an integration of the respective perspectives, questions, methods and analyses. For this, the goals of sociolinguistics and generative grammar would be too different. Sociolinguistics analyses the impact of the interaction of language, culture and society on language structure and language change, while generative grammar investigates syntactic variation to model syntax as a cognitive property of humans. Sociolinguists and generative linguists do complementary work that contributes to the big picture of syntactic variation, but they do not really need each other. Here Cheshire seems to reach a similar conclusion as Chomsky (2000).

In this chapter I take issue with this conclusion, by showing that integration of sociolinguistic and generative approaches is useful and necessary to explain systematic linguistic gaps and transitional linguistic forms. More specifically, I discuss two case studies to illustrate what the geographic distribution of linguistic forms tells us about language as a cognitive system.

188 Sjef Barbiers

3.1.2 Systematic Linguistic Gaps

This chapter takes systematic linguistic gaps, i.e., cases in which a conceivable linguistic pattern has not been attested, as its starting point. A systematic linguistic gap may be observed at the level of all languages (a macrogap), at the level of languages of one language family (a mesogap), or at the level of a set of closely related language varieties (a microgap), such as the dialects of Dutch in the DynaSAND database (Barbiers et al. 2006). The gap can occur at all levels of the mental grammar, including the Lexicon, Syntax, Logical Form (LF) and Phonological Form (PF). In this chapter I discuss a lexical gap and a word order gap. Since I need more than one level of the mental grammar for the analysis and sociolinguistics to explain these gaps, I use the term sociogrammar rather than sociosyntax. The hypothesis is that these linguistic gaps are not accidental but reveal the limits of possible variation – the "envelope of variation" in the Labovian sense of the term (Labov 1972) – and more broadly tell us something about the abstract building principles underlying natural language.

A good example of a linguistic gap is discussed in Hale and Keyser's seminal 1993 paper. They argue that verbs can be derived from nominals by incorporation of a noun into an abstract verb. For example, in (1a) the complement *calf* is able to incorporate into an abstract counterpart of *have*, yielding (1b). Hale and Keyser claim that derived verbs such as hypothetical *cow* in (1c) do not exist cross-linguistically, hence a macrogap.

(1) a) A cow had a calf.
    b) A cow calved.
    c) *A calf cowed.

They explain this by an independently motivated syntactic principle, the ban on incorporation of an argument from a specifier position, in this case the subject *cow*, as opposed to incorporation of an argument from complement position, here the object *calf* (cf. Baker 1988 for discussion of the properties of incorporation). This ban on incorporation from a specifier position follows in turn from the so-called Empty Category Principle (ECP), by then a commonly accepted syntactic principle regulating the distribution of empty positions in syntactic structures.[2] The structure corresponding to (1b) is given in (Figure 3.1.1.a), and the illegitimate structure corresponding to (1c) is given in (Figure 3.1.1.b). The positions marked with t_i indicate the base positions of the incorporated nouns.[3]

This analysis has the important property that a systematic lexical gap is explained by a syntactic principle, the ECP. In this view, verbs are not lexical atoms but lexico-syntactic treelets that express the structural

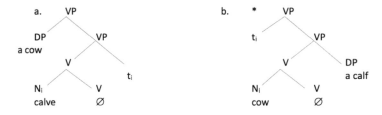

Figure 3.1.1 A lexical gap explained by a syntactic principle.

relations between the arguments and the internal aspect (initiation, process, end point) of the verb. Such lexico-syntactic treelets should obey general syntactic principles such as X-bar structure, the ECP or a modern version of these. Syntax is thus also a condition on lexical structures, not a completely independent module.

3.1.3 Gap 1: Impossible Strong Reflexives

I will now discuss two microgaps in the form of strong reflexives in dialects of Dutch. Parallel to the impossible verbs discussed in the previous section, I show that these microgaps can be explained by a morphosyntactic principle, specifier-head agreement. I then proceed to show that apparent counter-examples to one of these gaps can be explained from the geographic distribution of the forms involved.

3.1.3.1 *The Impossibility of* HIM OWN *and* SIG OWN *as Strong Reflexives*

I define strong reflexives here as reflexive anaphors that typically occur as the internal argument of transitive verbs. Examples for Dutch and English are given in (2) (strong reflexives in bold).

(2) a) Eduard kent **zichzelf** goed.
    b) Eduard knows **himself** well.

We find the following forms of strong reflexives in the dialects of the Dutch language area (taken from Barbiers et al. 2005; Barbiers and Bennis 2004). Given that they were collected under methodologically identical conditions we can safely assume that these forms are semantically and functionally equivalent and true cases of variation (cf. Buchstaller 2009 and references cited there for discussion of these notions of equivalence). The glosses present the parts of the strong reflexives as

190   *Sjef Barbiers*

syntactico-semantic atoms that are quite common in strong reflexives cross-linguistically (cf. Safir 1996).

(3) zich-zelf   SIG-SELF[4]
    hem-zelf   HIM-SELF
    zijn-zelf   HIS-SELF
    zijn-eigen   HIS-OWN
    zijn-eigen-zelf   HIS-OWN-SELF

The geographic distribution of these forms is given in Figure 3.1.2. Some background knowledge of the methodology is necessary for the proper interpretation of the dialect maps in this chapter, as they are an idealisation of linguistic reality. The Dutch dialect data in DynaSAND (Barbiers et al. 2006) were collected between 2000 and 2004 with oral interviews among dialect speakers between 55 and 75 years old that were born and raised in the locations of the interviews, just like their parents. Research into the full linguistic complexity, variation and change in the locations on the map is not possible with these data, as there are no data from people who do not meet these selection criteria, e.g., from younger people, people originating elsewhere, etc. Also, investigation of intra-speaker variation and change is not possible with these data, as they are based on judgement and translation tasks, not on spontaneous conversations. For extensive descriptions of the methodology, see Barbiers and Bennis (2007) and Barbiers, Cornips and Kunst (2007).

We find in Figure 3.1.2 an eastern and north-western (red) area with the standard Dutch form *zich-zelf* SIG-OWN, a north-eastern (blue) area with the (Frisian) form *hem-zelf* HIM-SELF, a central (yellow) area with the form *zijn-eigen* HIS-OWN, and a south-western (brown) area with the (Flemish) form *zijn-zelve* HIS-SELF. There are also some mixed areas, see below for further discussion. A few southern dialects have the complex form *zijn-eigen-zelve* HIS-OWN-SELF (green). This seems to be a secondary form, strengthening *zijn-eigen*, as all of the dialects that have this complex form also have the simpler *zijn-eigen* HIS OWN and the addition of *zelf* SELF as a more general strengthening device. I will not discuss this complex form in this chapter.

The atoms that the strong reflexives in (3) are made of include: the possessive pronoun *zijn* or *z'n* HIS, the personal pronoun *hem* HIM, the reflexive pronoun *zich* SIG, the possessive word *eigen* OWN and the intensifier *zelf* SELF. Since all Dutch dialects have a form for the personal pronoun *hem* HIM and for the possessive word *eigen* OWN, it is striking that there is no dialect of Dutch that has *hem eigen* HIM OWN or *zich eigen* SIG OWN as a strong reflexive. I hypothesise that these are not accidental microgaps but strong reflexive forms that are impossible due to a general syntactic principle. Barbiers and Bennis (2004) and

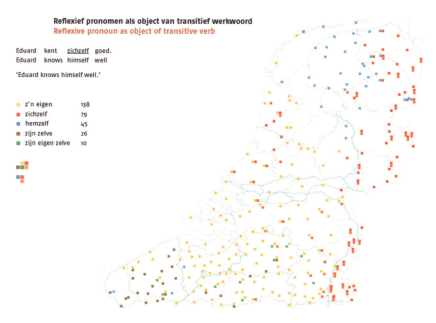

Figure 3.1.2 The geographic distribution of strong reflexive forms in the Dutch language area (from Barbiers et al. 2005).

Barbiers (2009) provide an explanation for these microgaps which I will slightly adapt below.

These explanations are based on work by Helke (1971), Pica (1987), Safir (1996) and Postma (1997), who maintain that strong reflexives cross-linguistically are possessive nominal groups with a pronoun as the possessor and a noun derived from a body part as the nominal head.[5] Postma (1997) proposes that Dutch *zelf* SELF consists of the possessive head *ze* HIS (common in colloquial Dutch as a possessive pronoun) and the body part *lf* (Dutch *lijf* BODY). If we assume that strong reflexives are full nominal groups (DPs), a reasonable assumption given that they have the syntactic distribution of full DPs, their structure would be as in (4).[6]

(4) [$_{DP}$ Spec [$_D$ Possessive Head [$_{NP}$ Body Part Head]]]

a)	hem	ze	lf
	him	his	body
b)	zich	ze	lf
	SIG	his	body
c)	z'n	eigen	Ø[7]
	his	own	

192   Sjef Barbiers

d)	z'n	ze	lf
	his	his	body
e)	*hem	eigen	Ø
	him	own	
f)	*zich	eigen	Ø
	SIG	own	

The claim is now that the impossibility of (4e) is due to the lack of agreement between *hem* HIM and *eigen* OWN. This claim is supported by the observation that there is a general gender and number agreement requirement on non-reflexive possessive DPs in colloquial Dutch, as the examples in (5) show.

(5) a) Jan   ze/*d'r lijf
        Jan   his/her body
        'John's body'
   b) Marie   d'r/*ze lijf
        Marie   her/his body
   c) de man   z'n/*hun lijf
        the man his/their body
   d) de mannen hun/*z'n lijf
        the men   their/his body
   e) hem   ze/*d'r/*hun lijf
        him   his/her/their   body

The feature bundles of the elements involved in (4) are given in (6).

(6) hem   HIM   [3, masculine, singular]
     ze   HIS   [3, masculine, possessive]
     z'n   HIS   [3, masculine, singular, possessive]
     zich   SIG   [3, reflexive]
     eigen OWN   [possessive]

It is clear that *eigen* OWN does not have person, number or gender features itself, as it is compatible with all members of the paradigm (*m'n-eigen* MY OWN, *je-eigen* YOUR OWN, *z'n eigen* HIS OWN *d'r eigen* HER OWN *hun-eigen* THEIR OWN, etc.). The reflexive *zich* SIG only occurs with third-person antecedents, and in this category with masculine, feminszine, singular, and plural ones, and I therefore take it to be underspecified for these features and only have the feature bundle [3, reflexive].

If the specifier-head agreement requirement on possessive DPs is more precisely formulated as *the pronoun in the specifier position SpecDP should agree with the possessive head in D on at least one morphosyntactic feature*, then it is immediately clear why *hem eigen* HIM OWN is an impossible strong reflexive. There is not any feature that these two elements share, as opposed to, for example, *z'n* HIS and *eigen* OWN that share the feature [possessive].[8]

A similar reasoning holds for the other form that is unattested according to Figure 3.1.2, *zich eigen* SIG OWN (4f). The pronoun *zich* SIG has the feature bundle [3, reflexive] and does not share any feature with *eigen* OWN, which only has the feature [possessive]. This analysis is simpler and more elegant than the one provided in Barbiers and Bennis (2004), where we ruled out *zich eigen* SIG OWN by assuming that *-ich* in *zich* and *eigen* are both possessive heads competing for the same D-position. One of the problems with that analysis is that it requires additional assumptions (and structure) to account for the existence of the strong reflexive *zich-zelf* SIG SELF, which contains both possessive heads.

3.1.3.2 Unexpected Cases of Zich Eigen SIG OWN

Van der Feest (2007) observed that the strong reflexive *zich-eigen* SIG OWN occasionally turned up in texts on the internet. She located these hits geographically where possible and then went to the locations identified in this way to check with oral interviews whether these forms were real. The results of this research are given in Figure 3.1.3.[9]

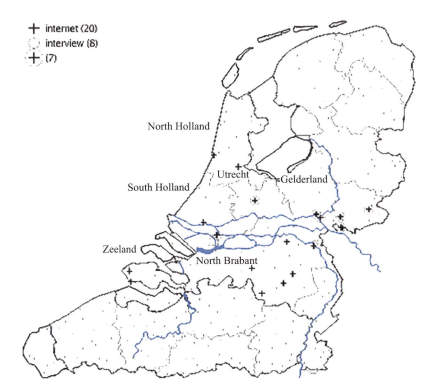

Figure 3.1.3 Attestations of the form *zich eigen* SIG OWN in the Dutch language area (based on van der Feest 2007).

194 *Sjef Barbiers*

If we compare Figures 3.1.2 and 3.1.3, we see that the locations in the east (eastern North Brabant and eastern Gelderland) that have *zich-eigen* SIG OWN are all locations that are close to the border between the eastern *zich-zelf* SIG SELF zone and the central *z'n-eigen* HIS OWN zone. The locations in the west that have *zich-eigen* SIG OWN are in an area with dialects in which both *zich-zelf* SIG SELF and *zijn-eigen* HIS OWN are possible (South Holland) or at the border between the *zijn-eigen* HIS OWN area and the *zich-zelf* SIG SELF area (North Holland and Utrecht). The two dialects of Zeeuws on the peninsula of Walcheren in Zeeland in the south-west seem to be an exception to the observation that dialects with *zich-eigen* are in contact zones.

Putting the two dialects of Zeeuws aside for the moment, this suggests that the form *zich-eigen* SIG OWN is the result of dialect contact, combining the first part of *zich-zelf* and the second part of *z'n-eigen* into the form *zich-eigen*. This fudged form (cf. Chambers and Trudgill 1998) arises in areas with two or more competing grammars (cf. Kroch 1989 and the Introduction in Cornips and Corrigan 2005 for discussion). The fact that it was not found in the fieldwork on which Figure 3.1.2 is based and that it does not have a geographic distribution corresponding to any known dialect area suggests that it is not a stable form, i.e., that it does not belong to the grammatical system of any dialect speaker or group.

That is different for the other logical possibility, the form *z'n-zelf* HIS OWN (4d), which combines the first part of *z'n eigen* HIS OWN and the second part of *zich-zelf* SIG SELF. Figure 3.1.2 shows that this form is typical for West Flanders, a well-established dialect area with many distinctive dialect properties. Put differently, as opposed to *zich-eigen* the form *z'n-zelf* seems to be a grammatically stable option. The explanation for this contrast has already been given above. While *z'n* HIS and the *ze*-part of *zelf* SELF share the features [3, possessive], *zich* SIG and *eigen* OWN do not share any grammatical feature and therefore do not agree with each other.

If this analysis is on the right track, it illustrates how research into syntactic variation requires a socio-grammatical approach, a combination of generative and sociolinguistic methods and perspectives (cf. Adger and Smith 2010 for another illustration). The sociolinguistic (or dialectological) method in this case study is investigating the geographic distribution of the various forms of strong reflexives. The generative method is to analyse the lexico-syntactic forms attested and not-attested as hierarchical structures, DPs, that must meet a specifier-head agreement requirement, and to show that they are different realisations of one abstract form. It is really the interaction between sociolinguistic factors, in this case geographical distribution and ensuing dialect contact, and systematic formal requirements, in this case specifier-head agreement in a hierarchical DP structure representation in the Lexicon, that sheds light on the status of contact forms such as *zich-eigen* SIG OWN and provides a fuller explanation of the properties of the microgaps.

Needless to say, further investigation of the contact dialects and speakers that have *zich-eigen* SIG OWN is necessary to test the correctness of this analysis and to gain further insights. For example, we expect to find in these dialects contact forms for the other members of the reflexive paradigm, as well as beyond the pronominal system. More complex questions for future research about such dialects include: Do these speakers have two distinct dialect systems with occasional contact phenomena, or are the contact phenomena part of a separate, fused dialect system? This question cannot be answered on the basis of the data that are currently available. It requires, among others, a sufficiently large corpus of spontaneous speech to find out whether and how often speakers that use *zich-eigen* also use the strong reflexives from the neighbouring dialects within the same register.

Another question is whether contact forms such as *zich-eigen* SIG OWN can be reanalysed in a later stage of the dialects such that they no longer violate grammatical principles and become stable, and if so, what such a reanalysis would look like? More generally, it is an important question whether there are any constraints on such fudged forms themselves.[10] We can also ask why contact between the *standard* language, which has *zich-zelf* SIG SELF, and dialects that have *zijn-eigen* HIS OWN usually does not seem to lead to the contact forms described above, while contact between dialects does. If contact between the standard language and the dialects would easily yield forms such as *zich-eigen* SIG OWN, we would expect a much larger number of dialects to have it than the ones we find in Figure 3.1.3. The only candidates are the two dialects of Zeeuws mentioned above. Finally, it is an open question whether the West-Flemish form *z'n zelf* HIS SELF is due to contact between dialectal *z'n eigen* and standard *zich-zelf*, or just an independent realisation of one the possible structures.

3.1.4 Gap 2: Impossible Word Orders in Verb Clusters

It has been observed many times (cf. Wurmbrand 2006; Barbiers 2005; Zwart 1996) that there is one word order in three-verb clusters in Dutch and German that seems to be systematically excluded: the so-called 2-1-3 order (7e). The numbers in this notation correspond to the hierarchical positions of the verbs involved: 1. (*moet* 'must' in 7a) for the highest verb in the syntactic tree, that selects 2. (*kunnen* 'can.inf' in 7a), and 3. for the lowest verb in the syntactic tree (*zwemmen* 'swim.inf' in 7a), that is selected by 2. A sequence of the type 2-1-3 thus indicates how the original hierarchical order (1 higher than 2, 2 higher than 3) is linearised. The observation that the linear order 2-1-3 does not exist has been replicated in the large-scale dialect syntax survey *Syntactic Atlas of the Dutch Dialects* (cf. Barbiers et al. 2006). This linguistic gap is illustrated in (7) for a Dutch verb cluster with two modal auxiliaries. The order 2-3-1 in (7f) is excluded as well when the two auxiliaries are modals, but not when the first auxiliary is a perfective auxiliary and the second a modal. I will not discuss this 2-3-1 order any further in this paper (cf. Barbiers et al. 2018; henceforth BBD).

(7) a) Ik vind dat iedereen goed 1-moet 2-kunnen 3-zwemmen.
    I find that everyone well must.INF can.INF swim.INF
    'I think that everyone should be able to swim'.
   b) Ik vind dat iedereen goed 1-moet 3-zwemmen 2-kunnen.
   c) Ik vind dat iedereen goed 3-zwemmen 2-kunnen 1-moet.
   d) Ik vind dat iedereen goed 3-zwemmen 1-moet 2-kunnnen.
   e) *Ik vind dat iedereen goed 2-kunnen 1-moet 3-zwemmen.
   f) *Ik vind dat iedereen goed 2-kunnen 3-zwemmen 1-moet.

Figure 3.1.4 shows the geographic distribution of the attested orders in (7). From north to south roughly three dialect areas can be distinguished: a relatively homogeneous northern (green) area in Frisia and surroundings with dialects that only have the 3-2-1 order, a southern (red) area with only the 1-2-3 order and an area in between where many dialects

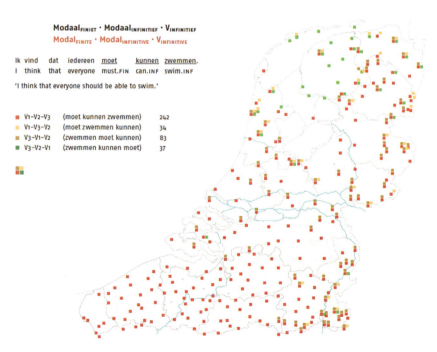

Figure 3.1.4 The geographic distribution of word orders in three-verb clusters containing two modals in the Dutch language area (from Barbiers et al. 2008).

have both the 1-2-3 order and the 3-1-2 order. The distribution of the 1-3-2 order does not correspond to any known dialect area. We see that it occurs particularly along the border with Germany, both in the Low-Saxon area (north-east) and the Franconian area (south-east). In addition, we find this order in the north-western transition zone between the Hollandic dialects and the Frisian dialects, and we find it in the north-eastern transition zone between the Frisian and the Low-Saxon dialect areas. Since 3-2-1 is a possible order in German too, the generalisation seems to be that the order 1-3-2 occurs in transitional areas between dialect areas that have 1-2-3 and dialect areas that have 3-2-1. It is furthermore striking that there is not any dialect in which this 1-3-2 order is the only possible order.

This geographic distribution of the 1-3-2 order is reminiscent of the distribution of the strong reflexive pronoun *zich-eigen* SIG-OWN discussed in the previous section. Like *zich-eigen*, the 1-3-2 order does not occur in any known dialect area, but only in transitional areas where 1-2-3 orders and 3-2-1 orders meet. Like *zich-eigen*, the 1-3-2 order can be seen as a property of fudged varieties in the sense of Chambers and Trudgill (1998) and Britain and Trudgill (2005) as it combines grammatical properties of the two surrounding orders: 1-3-2 is like 1-2-3 in that 1 precedes 2 and 3, and it is like 3-2-1 in that 3 precedes 2. In the words of BBD (2018): dialects of Dutch either have ascending (1-2-3) word order in verb clusters, or they have descending (3-2-1) order. Word orders in transitional dialects are ascending and descending at the same time.

In the case of *zich-eigen* SIG-OWN, I have claimed above that this is an unstable form in current dialects of Dutch, as there is no grammatical agreement between the two parts of the form. Therefore, *zich-eigen* is either bound to show up occasionally in space and time, to be reanalysed or to disappear. The question is now whether 1-3-2 also violates a grammatical principle and is therefore unstable.

According to BBD (2018), the grammar of verb clusters works as follows. In the syntactic module of the mental grammar the hierarchy of all three-verb clusters is identical, regardless of the linear surface word order. This hierarchy looks as in Figure 3.1.5.

The PF-module of the mental grammar is the module where hierarchical structures such as in Figure 3.1.5 get linearised.[11] BBD (2018) claim that there are two linearisation options which are both harmonic: ascending 1-2-3 or descending 3-2-1. All other orders attested in the Dutch language area are exceptional in that they have an additional property that seemingly blurs this harmonic picture. We can therefore clean up maps such as Figure 3.1.4 by removing all orders that are exceptional. Figure 3.1.6 shows the resulting map, for three different types of three-verb clusters, clusters with two modal auxiliaries and a main verb (*moet kunnen zwemmen* 'must.fin can.inf swim.inf'), three-verb clusters with a modal auxiliary, a perfective auxiliary and a main verb (*moet hebben*

198 Sjef Barbiers

Figure 3.1.5 Uniform hierarchical structure of three-verb clusters in Dutch.

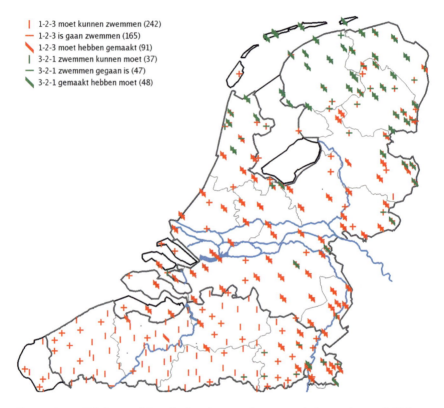

Figure 3.1.6 Dialects of Dutch that have at least one 3-2-1 order and dialects that have at least one 1-2-3 order from BBD (2018).

gemaakt 'must.fin have.inf made.pcp') and verb clusters with a perfective auxiliary, an aspectual auxiliary and a main verb (*is gaan zwemmen* 'is. fin go.inf. swim.inf').

What about the exceptional orders? BBD (2018) provide arguments showing that 3-1-2 orders are not real verb clusters, as 3 should be analysed as an adjective when it is a participle, and as a noun when it is an infinitive. Similarly, 1-3-2 orders are not real verb clusters when 3 is a participle, as in such cases the participle is an adjective as well. This is supported by the fact that the 1-3-2 order with 3 a participle occurs particularly in the Belgian part of the Dutch language area and in this part many dialects allow verb clusters to be interrupted by other types of syntactic constituents as well. Figures 3.1.7 and 3.1.8 illustrate this correlation between verb cluster interruption and 1-3-2 order with 3 = participle.[12]

BBD (2018) explain the possibility of the 2-3-1 order for the cluster type *is gaan zwemmen* 'is.fin go.inf. swim.inf' in a similar way. The impossibility of the order 2-1-3, the systematic linguistic gap, is explained by its disharmonic nature (ascending and descending at the same time) and the fact that this order cannot be derived even if 2 is taken to be adjectival or nominal. Since there is a direct (selectional) dependency between 2 and 3, the verb in position 1 cannot occur in between.

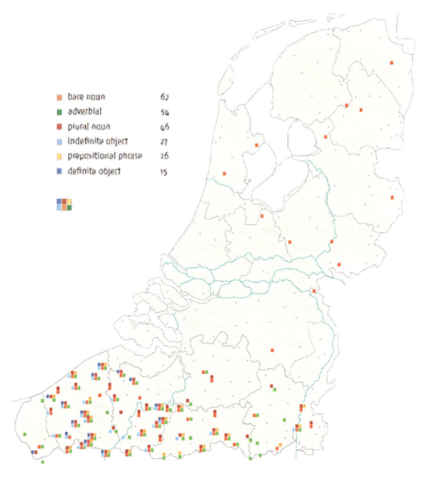

Figure 3.1.7 Geographic distribution of verb cluster interruption (Barbiers et al. 2008).

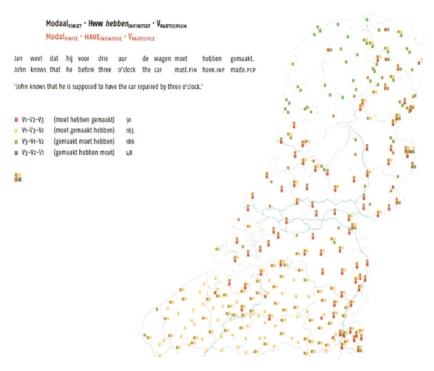

Figure 3.1.8 Geographic distribution of 1-3-2 with 3 = participle (Barbiers et al. 2008).

With this background, we can answer the question of whether the verb cluster order 1-3-2 with 3 an infinitive is an ungrammatical order (cf. BBD 2018 for more extensive discussion). The only possibility to get this order is if 3 can be analysed as a nominalised verb, parallel to the analysis of southern Dutch 1-3-2 orders in which the participle has an adjectival status. However, whereas the latter correlates with other cases of interruption of the verb cluster by non-verbal material, the 34 dialects that have 1-3-2 orders with 3 an infinitive do not allow any of the cluster interruptions that are allowed in southern Dutch (cf. Figure 3.1.7). We conclude, then, that the order 1-3-2 with 3 an infinitive as it occurs in the transitional zone along the border with Germany is an ungrammatical order as it is disharmonic and verb 3 between 1 and 2 cannot be analysed as a nominalisation. Like *zich-eigen* SIG OWN, this order is bound to show up occasionally in space and time, to be reanalysed or to disappear.

An obvious direction of reanalysis would be that 3 is reanalysed as a nominal. As already noted, that would still not make this order a grammatically well-formed order in the eastern transitional dialects, as these do not allow verb cluster interruption. The order is also not expected to get grammaticalised easily in the southern dialects that have verb cluster interruption, as these dialects for some unknown reason resist nominalisation of the main verb in the cluster. This can be seen from another contrast between the southern dialects and the central Dutch dialects. The latter allows the order 3-1-2 with the cluster type *moet kunnen zwemmen* 'must.fin can.inf swim.inf, the former don't. If BBD (2018) are right that 3 is a nominal infinitive in such a case, then the absence of 3-1-2 in the southern Dutch dialects shows that they resist nominalisation of infinitives in verb clusters.

3.1.5 Conclusion

The two case studies in this paper show that explaining the full complexity of linguistic microvariation requires integration of the sociolinguistic and the generative perspectives. The case studies included lexical variation in the expression of reflexive anaphors and word order variation in verb clusters. In both cases the goal was to explain systematic linguistic gaps and the occurrence of exceptional forms. The starting point of each of the case studies was the geographic distribution of the various forms and word orders, a traditional dialectological and sociolinguistic method. This geographic distribution immediately showed that certain logically possible forms and orders are absent, the systematic linguistic gaps. It also showed that there are unexpected lexical forms and word orders that occur in areas that do not correspond to traditional dialect areas.

More specifically, I identified two systematic linguistic gaps, the reflexive anaphors **hem-eigen* SIG OWN and the word order 2-1-3 as in **kunnen moet zwemmen* 'can.inf must swim.inf', and two exceptional forms, i.e. forms that should not exist, the reflexive anaphor *zich-eigen* SIG OWN and the word order 1-3-2, as in *moet zwemmen kunnen* 'must swim.inf can.inf'. The systematic gaps were explained by formal principles from generative grammar: a violation of the specifier-head agreement condition on possessive nominal groups in the case of *hem-eigen* HIM OWN and a violation of harmonic linearisation (ascending or descending) in the case of the 2-1-3 order.

Strictly speaking, the geographic distribution of the various forms and orders would not have been necessary for this explanation of the linguistic gaps, although it certainly helps that we have a dataset at our disposal that covers the entire language area and that was collected systematically with sociolinguistic methods. This makes the chance that the observed gaps are accidental considerably lower.

Taking the geographic distribution into account is crucial, however, for the explanation of forms and orders that are unexpected given the proposed formal explanations of the linguistic gaps. We have seen that the unexpected form *zich-eigen* SIG OWN that violates the specifier-head agreement condition is a fudged form in the sense of Chambers and Trudgill (1998) that shows up occasionally in areas with contact between dialects that have *zich-zelf* SIG SELF and dialects that have *zijn-eigen*

202 *Sjef Barbiers*

HIS OWN. We have also seen that the word order 1-3-2 (*moet zwemmen kunnen* 'must swim.inf can.inf') that violates harmonic linearisation is a fudged word order that shows up in areas with contact between 1-2-3 orders and 3-2-1 orders. These insights could only be gained by integrating the formal analysis that is common in generative grammar and the distributional analysis that is common in dialectology and sociolinguistics.

Notes

1 I would like to thank Isabelle Buchstaller, Karen Beaman and two anonymous reviewers for comments and suggestions that have led to considerable improvement of this chapter.

2 The Empty Category Principle, part of Government and Binding theory (Chomsky 1981), requires that the base position of a moved constituent is properly governed. The idea behind this is that the base position of a moved constituent should be recoverable. The base position of the internal argument is properly governed because the verb V assigns a theta role to it under sisterhood. V does not assign a theta role to the external argument in its base position directly, therefore the external argument is not properly governed by V.

3 These structures abstract away from surface linear order, which is not relevant given the possibility of *It calved a cow* but not *It cowed a calf.*

4 I use SIG to indicate weak reflexive morphemes. One of the contexts in which these occur is inherently reflexive verbs in Dutch, as in *zich herinneren* 'remember'. English does not have a morpheme for SIG, but many other languages do.

5 I will not go into the question here as to why natural language needs these complex forms to express reflexivity. See Barbiers (2000) for a proposal. The core idea there is that identity of arguments of a binary predicate reduces the two arguments to one. To avoid that and retain binarity the two arguments must be formally distinct. This is why the personal pronoun must be embedded in a complex DP.

6 The analysis of the secondary form *z'n eigen zelf* 'his own self' mentioned above as an intensified form of the primary form *z'n eigen* cannot be the same as 4, as *eigen* and the *ze-* part of *zelf* would compete for the same possessive head position. However, it is clear from intensified non-reflexive noun phrases such as *de jongen zelf* 'the boy himself' that *zelf* should be able to occur in other structural positions, possibly adjunct positions, anyway, as in this noun phrase D is already filled by *de* 'the' and N is filled by *jongen* 'boy'.

7 Interestingly, the N head needs to be empty in the dialects of Dutch when the possessive head is filled with *eigen* OWN. It is clear from the analysis of *zelf* SELF in 4 that *zelf* cannot be in N, as it consists of a possessive head and a nominal body part head. It is apparently impossible to use a different body part noun to fill N and to form a strong reflexive. This suggests that reflexive formation is not a productive process. This justifies the assumption that reflexives are represented in the Lexicon as lexico-syntactic units.

8 This implies that in forms such as *me-eigen* MY OWN, *je-eigen* YOUR OWN, *me* and *je* should have a possessive feature to be able to agree with *eigen*. This is correct, given that *me* and *je* can be used as possessive pronouns in noun phrases such as *me boek* 'my boek' and *je boek* 'your book'.

9 The symbol that combines a circle and a cross is assigned to locations where the form was found both on the internet and in the interview.

10 I thank an anonymous reviewer for pointing this out.

11 PF (Phonological Form) is the module of the mental grammar that is the interface between the hierarchical structure built in Syntax and the sensorimotor system that takes care of the externalisation of linguistic structures as sounds or signs. PF maps a hierarchical structure to a linear structure which is read off by the sensorimotor system. Other modules of the mental grammar are the Lexicon and LF (Logical Form). LF is the interface between the hierarchical structure built in Syntax and the conceptual-intentional cognitive system. Cf. Chomsky (2000).

12 Particles, as part of so-called separable compound verbs (e.g., *op-geven* lit. up give 'give up') are deliberately left out of consideration. They can interrupt verb clusters in the entire language area and seem to have a syntactic status that is different from the interrupting categories depicted in Figure 3.1.5.

References

Adger, David and Jennifer Smith. 2010. "Variation in agreement: A lexical feature-based approach". *Lingua* 120(5):1109–1134.

Baker, Mark. 1988. *A Theory of Grammatical Function Changing.* Chicago: University of Chicago Press.

Barbiers, Sjef. 2000. "On the interpretation of movement and agreement: PPs and binding". In *Interface Strategies*, H. Bennis, M. Everaert and E. Reuland (eds.). Amsterdam: Koninklijke Nederlandse Akademie van Wetenschappen (KNAW). 21–36.

Barbiers, Sjef. 2005. "Word order variation in three-verb clusters and the division of labour between generative linguistics and sociolinguistics". In *Syntax and Variation: Reconciling the Biological and the Social*, L. Cornips and K. Corrigan (eds.). Amsterdam: John Benjamins. 233–264.

Barbiers, Sjef. 2009. "Locus and limits of syntactic variation". *Lingua* 119(11):1607–1623.

Barbiers, Sjef and Hans Bennis. 2004. "Reflexives in dialects of Dutch". In *Germania et alia. A Linguistic Webschrift for Hans den Besten*, J. Koster and H. van Riemsdijk (eds.). Electronic Publication, Groningen: University of Groningen. http://odur.let.rug.nl/~koster/DenBesten/contents.htm

Barbiers, Sjef and Hans Bennis. 2007. "The syntactic atlas of the Dutch dialects. A discussion of choices in the SAND-project". *Nordlyd* 34:53–72.

Barbiers, Sjef, Hans Bennis and Lotte Dros-Hendriks. 2018. "Merging verb clusters". *Linguistic Variation* 18(1):144–196.

Barbiers, Sjef, Hans Bennis, Gunter De Vogelaer, Magda Devos and Margreet van der Ham. 2005. *Syntactic Atlas of the Dutch Dialects*, Vol. 1. Amsterdam: Amsterdam University Press.

Barbiers, Sjef, Hans Bennis, Gunther De Vogelaer, Magda Devos and Margreet Van der Ham. 2006. *Dynamische Syntactische Atlas van de Nederlandse Dialecten (DynaSAND).* Amsterdam, Meertens Instituut. www.meertens. knaw.nl/sand/.

Barbiers, Sjef, Johan van der Auwera, Hans Bennis, Eefja Boef, Gunter De Vogelaer and Margreet van der Ham. 2008. *Syntactische Atlas van de Nederlandse Dialecten/Syntactic Atlas of the Dutch Dialects*, Vol. 2. Amsterdam: Amsterdam University Press.

Barbiers, Sjef, Leonie Cornips and Jan Pieter Kunst. 2007. The syntactic atlas of the Dutch dialects: A corpus of elicited speech and text as an on-line dynamic

204   *Sjef Barbiers*

atlas. In *Creating and Digitizing Language Corpora. Volume 1: Synchronic Databases*, J.C. Beal, K.P. Corrigan, and H.L. Moisl (eds.). Hampshire: Palgrave Macmillan. 54–90.

Britain, David and Peter Trudgill. 2005. "New dialect formation and contact-induced reallocation: Three case studies from the English fens". *International Journal of English Studies* 5(1):183–209.

Buchstaller, Isabelle. 2009. "The quantitative analysis of morphosyntactic variation: Constructing and quantifying the denominator". *Language and Linguistics Compass* 3/4:1010–1033.

Chambers, J.K. and Peter Trudgill. 1998. *Dialectology*, 2nd edition. Cambridge: Cambridge University Press.

Cheshire, Jenny. 2003. "Syntactic variation and spoken language". Paper Presented at the Workshop Syntactic Variation, ICLaVE 2, Uppsala.

Cheshire, Jenny. 2005. "Syntactic variation and spoken language". In *Syntax and Variation. Reconciling the Biological and Social*, L. Cornips and K. Corrigan (eds.). Amsterdam/Philadelphia: John Benjamins. 81–106.

Cheshire, Jenny. 2017. "Is syntactic special?" Paper Presented at ICLAVE 7, Malaga 2017.

Chomsky, Noam. 1981. *Lectures on Government and Binding: The Pisa Lectures*. Berlin: Mouton de Gruyter.

Chomsky, Noam. 2000. *New Horizons in the Study of Language and Mind*. Cambridge: Cambridge University Press.

Cornips, Leonie and Karen Corrigan (eds.). 2005. *Syntax and Variation. Reconciling the Biological and Social* [Current Issues in Linguistic Theory 225]. Amsterdam/Philadelphia: John Benjamins.

Feest, J. van der. 2007. *Een ezel stoot zich eigen in 't gemeen niet twee keer aan dezelfde steen*. Unpublished bachelor thesis, Utrecht University.

Hale, Kenneth and Samuel Jay Keyser. 1993. "On argument structure and the lexical expression of syntactic relations". In *The View from Building 20: A Festschrift for Sylvain Bromberger*, H. Hale and S. Keyser (eds.). Cambridge: MIT Press. 53–108.

Helke, Michael. 1971. The grammar of English reflexives, Ph.D. dissertation, MIT.

Kroch, Anthony. 1989. "Reflexes of grammar in patterns of language change". *Language Variation and Change* 1:199–244.

Labov, William. 1972. "Some principles of linguistic methodology." *Language in Society* 1:97–120.

Pica, Pierre. 1987. "On the nature of the reflexivization cycle". In *Proceedings of NELS 17*, J. Mcdonough and B. Plunkett (eds.). Amherst: GLSA. 483–500.

Postma, Gertjan. 1997. "Logical entailment and the possessive nature of reflexive pronouns". In *Atomism and Binding*, H. Bennis, P. Pica and J. Rooryck (eds.). Dordrecht: Foris Publications. 295–322.

Safir, Ken. 1996. "Semantic atoms of anaphora". *Natural Language & Linguistic Theory* 14(3):545–589.

Wurmbrand, Susie. 2006. "Verb clusters, verb raising, and restructuring". In *The Blackwell Companion to Syntax*, Vol. V, M. Everaert and H. van Riemsdijk (eds.). Oxford: Blackwell. 229–343.

Zwart, Jan-Wouter. 1996. "Verb clusters in continental West Germanic dialects". In *Microparametric Syntax and Dialect Variation*, J. Black and V. Motapanyane (eds.). Amsterdam: John Benjamins. 229–258.

3.2 Variation and Change in the Particle Verb Alternation across English Dialects

Bill Haddican, Daniel Ezra Johnson, Joel Wallenberg, and Anders Holmberg

3.2.1 Introduction

In line with Cheshire's (2005a, see also Cheshire, Edwards and Whittle 1989; Cheshire and Milroy 1993) work on the geographical patterns of syntactic variation, this chapter focusses on regional and grammatical effects on the English particle verb alternation.[1] We illustrate this variation in (1), which shows that, with a class of transitive verb + particle combinations, the particle may appear either immediately to the left of the verb or further to the right, following a direct object. We refer to these word orders as the VPO (verb-particle-object) and VOP (verb-object-particle) orders respectively.

(1) a)   She cut open the melon. (VPO order)
     b)   She cut the melon open. (VOP order)

While a considerable body of literature has focussed on different syntactic and processing constraints on the variation in (1) (Dehé 2002; Dikken 1995; Svenonius 1996a, 1996b; Toivonen 2001), relatively little work has discussed regional effects. Graffmiller and Szmrecsanyi (2018) discuss effects on particle placement in a broad sample of world Englishes, based on written corpora. They do not, however, examine regional variation within the UK, nor consider the contrast between UK and US varieties, our principal foci here. In particular, this chapter reports on a controlled judgment experiment and a Twitter corpus study designed to address Hughes et al.'s (2005) claim, based on non-controlled evidence, that the VPO order is favoured in Scotland while the VOP order is favoured in Southern England. We also examine the possibility of regional effects on particle placement variation in North American dialects.

As with Cheshire's work (1996, see also Cheshire and Williams 2002) we also considering information structural effects on this variation. We test for these possible effects with a controlled judgment experiment with 297 native speakers from the British Isles and North America, and a Twitter corpus of tweets from the UK and US. The results from both the acceptability judgment study and the Twitter corpus reveal no

206 *Bill Haddican et al.*

support for a North-South difference across UK dialects, but instead show a trans-Atlantic difference: respondents from the UK and Ireland favoured VOP orders while US participants favoured VPO orders, and Canadians showed an equal preference for both orders. Data from the Brown corpus and the Corpus of Historical American English (COHA) suggest that this cross-Atlantic difference reflects change toward an innovative VOP order that has proceeded more quickly in Old World dialects than in North America.

Our discussion is organised as follows. Section 3.2.2 of this chapter reviews previous literature on social and linguistic effects on particle placement. Section 3.2.3 describes a judgment experiment testing regional and focus effects on particle placement. Section 3.2.4 reports and discusses results from a Twitter corpus providing additional support for the regional analysis in the experimental data. Section 3.2.5 presents data from three sets of historical corpora, which lend further support to the trans-Atlantic difference and suggest that the difference reflects a change toward VOP orders that is proceeding more quickly in Old World dialects. Section 3.2.6 summarises the discussion.

3.2.2 Social and Linguistic Effects on the Particle Verb Alternation

Much of the formal and sentence processing literature on English particle verbs has focussed on two kinds of linguistic constraints on particle placement. One set of studies has discussed the length or prosodic weight of the object as a processing or a phonological phrasing constraint on particle placement. Kroch and Small (1978), Gries (2001) and Lohse et al. (2004) all report evidence from corpus studies showing that "heavy" objects such as those in (2) tend to favour the VPO order.

(2) a) She turned off the fan I bought her for Valentine's Day. (VPO order)
    b) ?She turned the fan I bought her for Valentine's Day off. (VOP order)

Lighter objects, on the other hand, favour the VOP order. Indeed, speakers generally find the VOP order obligatory for unstressed, weak pronouns as in (3).

(3) a) *She turned off it. (VPO order)
    b) She turned it off. (VOP order)

Lohse et al. (2004) explain the object length effect in terms of a more general processing constraint, namely that processing is facilitated by a short distance between members of a syntactic dependency. Lohse et al.

take the relation between the verb and the particle to be a dependency governed by this principle. In the case of VOP orders but not VPO orders, heavy objects as in (2) incur a heavy processing cost because they create a large gap between the two elements in the particle verb dependency. VPO orders are therefore preferred in proportion to increasing object length, not because the VPO orders become easier to process, but because the corresponding VOP orders become harder to process as object weight increases.

A second set of studies has focussed instead on information-structural constraints on particle placement. Bolinger (1971), Svenonius (1996a), Kayne (1998) and Dehé (2002) note that given objects, or topics, favour placement further to the left, as found in the VOP order, while focussed objects favour placement further to the right, as in the VPO order. Svenonius (1996a) notes that, as an answer to the object *wh*-question in (4), the VPO order is more natural than the VOP order for many people.

(4) Q: Who will you pick up?

A: I'll pick (?the girls) up (the girls). (Svenonius 1996a)

In contrast, as an answer to the question in (5), where the object is a previously introduced topic, Svenonius notes that many speakers prefer the VOP order. Svenonius reports that this effect is mild for many speakers and that other speakers report no such effect.

(5) Q: How are Turid and Ingrid going to get here?

A: I'll pick (the girls) up (?the girls). (Svenonius 1996a)

A first goal of the judgment experiment described below is to examine possible focus effects more directly by biasing different kinds of focus interpretation independently of word order.[2] We also include in our design object weight, in an effort to test the possible interaction of object weight and discourse status. We describe these experiments in Sections 3.2.3 and 3.2.4 below.

A second goal of this chapter is to test Hughes et al.'s (2005) claim of a dialectal difference in particle placement preference. Specifically, Hughes et al. (2005: 23) propose that Scottish speakers tend toward VPO orders (1a), while speakers from the south of England tend toward VOP forms (1b). The authors report no supporting evidence for this claim, however, and as far as we are aware, no other published literature has reported evidence to this effect in contemporary UK dialects. Based on limited historical corpus evidence, however, Elenbaas (2007: 273–279) speculates that in the Early Modern English period, VPO orders were favoured in areas most exposed to Scandinavian varieties, that is, the Danelaw in Northern and Eastern parts of England, while VOP orders were favoured elsewhere.

208   Bill Haddican et al.

While no literature to date has discussed geographic correlates of this variation in the US, Hughes et al.'s claim of a Scottish-Southern English difference suggests the possibility of founder effects in North American dialects. That is, if Hughes et al.'s regional difference indeed exists and dates back at least to the time of North American settlement, then we might expect preferences for VPO versus VOP orders to appear in areas settled by Scots/Scotch-Irish migrants and Southern English migrants respectively. In particular, we might expect New England, which was mainly settled by speakers of Southern English dialects, to favour VOP orders, and that Appalachian dialects, which were founded largely by Scotch-Irish settlers, would favour VPO orders. (See Krapp (1925), Kurath (1949) and Montgomery (2006) for discussion of early North American migration and settlement patterns and their possible consequences for the emergence of North American regional dialects.) We assess evidence in favour of possible regional effects in Sections 3.2.3 and 3.2.4 below.

3.2.3 An Acceptability Judgment Study

3.2.3.1 Data and Method

The first data set we report on comes from an online judgment experiment conducted in the spring and summer of 2011. Subjects for the experiment were 297 self-described native speakers of English recruited online through personal contacts of the authors. One hundred forty five of these were from the UK or Ireland and 152 were from the US and Canada. Almost all had BA/BS-level degrees or higher. Subjects ranged in age from 18 to 84 (mean = 30), and 63% were women.

The experiment crossed three within-subjects factors, each with two levels: particle-object order, object length and focus status of the object. The particle-object-order factor had the levels VPO and VOP as illustrated in (1) above. Object length was operationalised as a binary factor: "short" objects were all three-syllable constituents with the definite article and a two-syllable noun, e.g. *the melon*; "long" objects were all seven-syllable DPs with a definite article, two two-syllable adjectives and a noun – for example *the heavy juicy melon*.

We followed Dehé (2002) in operationalising focus as a binary factor by biasing new versus old information interpretations of the object. We did this using a cataphoric pronoun in a preceding clause, bound by either the object of the particle verb in the main clause or the subject of the main clause. In the former case, the object was considered "given" information, in that it was introduced by the pronoun in the preceding clause. In the latter case, only the subject was given, so the VP, including the object was "new" information.[3] Fully crossing these three binary factors yields eight conditions, which we illustrate in (6) and (7).

(6) It$_i$ was about to spoil, so Andrea cut (open) the (heavy juicy) melon$_i$ (open). (old object)

(7) Her$_i$ kids wanted a snack, so Andrea$_i$ cut (open) the (heavy juicy) melon (open). (new object)

Four lexicalisations were created for each of the eight conditions. The particle verbs chosen were all non-aspectual and compositional as described in Lohse et al. (2004). Lexicalisations were blocked by Latin square, such that each block contained a different lexicalisation for each of these eight conditions. These blocks were then grouped into 32 lists, with each list containing four blocks; each subject therefore saw each condition four times. The 32 experimental sentences in each list were pseudo-randomised within blocks with 32 filler sentences, half grammatical and half ungrammatical. Subjects were semi-randomly assigned to lists by the experimental software, using a counter mechanism.

Subjects judged each of these 64 sentences in a self-paced online judgment experiment using Ibex Farm (Drummond 2011). The experiment was anonymous and subjects were neither paid nor did they receive academic credit for participating. Subjects rated each sentence on an 11-point scale by clicking an icon for a value ranging from 0 to 10 in a horizontal array, with endpoints labelled "Bad" and "Good" respectively.

3.2.3.2 Results and Discussion

The data for each subject were first normalised by converting to Z-scores, subtracting the mean and dividing by the standard deviation of the ratings of the 32 filler sentences. Since half of the fillers were ungrammatical, the experimental sentences with particle verbs tended to have positive Z-scores, between +0.5 and +1.0 units on average.

Using the lme4 package in R, we then fit a series of linear mixed effects models, with fixed effects for subject region/country and the above within-subjects factors, and random intercepts and slopes by subject and by item. For example, to test whether subject region significantly affected preference for the VPO or VOP order, two models were fit. Both had a random-effect structure consisting of (region * order | subject) and (region * order | item). The more complex model had a fixed-effect term for the region*order interaction while the simpler model had only main effect terms for region and order. A likelihood-ratio test was used to compare the two models and arrive at a p-value representing the significance of the region*order interaction.

The results support three main findings. First, the regional analysis revealed no support for any regional distinctions within North America (six regions, $p = .65$) or within the British Isles (12 regions, $p = .98$). That is to say, there was no significant region*order interaction on either side of the Atlantic. The analysis did, however, reveal a significant

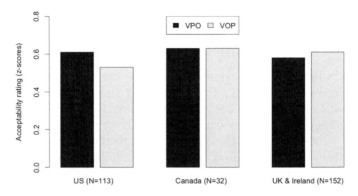

Figure 3.2.1 Mean normalised ratings for VPO and VOP orders by country.

trans-Atlantic difference. When subjects were recoded into a factor with three levels corresponding to the subjects' home country – US (n = 113) versus Canada (n = 32) versus UK/Ireland (n = 152) – the analysis revealed a significant country*order interaction (p = .001), with US subjects preferring VPO orders by .08 units, UK/Ireland subjects preferring VOP orders by .03 units and Canadian subjects showing no preference in either direction (Figure 3.2.1). We return to these results shortly.

The second finding is that there was no significant effect for the focus*order interaction. Figure 3.2.2 shows that VPO orders were in fact favoured somewhat by the new-object condition, in keeping with Dehé's (2002) and Svenonius's (1996a) discussion, but the difference of .04 units between conditions was not significant (p = .12). We speculate that the cataphoric pronoun technique used for biasing given versus new information interpretations of the object may not have been successful with this set of subjects.

Figure 3.2.3 illustrates the third main finding: a significant weight*order interaction (p = .00003). In sentences with light objects, VOP orders are preferred by .05 units, and in sentences with heavy objects, VPO orders are preferred by .07 units. That is, there is a difference of .12 units between the two conditions.

This third result aligns with much previous corpus-based work on placement, which has shown that heavy objects tend to be placed after the particle, while lighter objects and pronouns tend to precede the particle (Gries 2001; Kroch and Small 1978; Lohse et al. 2004). These processing and phonological accounts of the "weight effect" correctly predict that a heavy object is judged worse than a light object in the VOP order, where the object is interposed between the verb and the particle. In our study, this difference was .07 units (p = .0009).

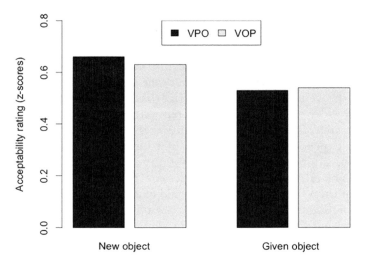

Figure 3.2.2 Mean normalised ratings for VPO and VOP orders by object type.

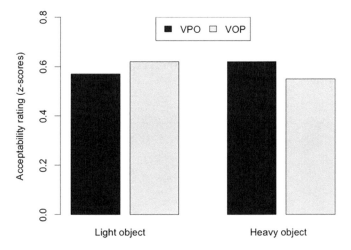

Figure 3.2.3 Mean normalised ratings for VPO and VOP orders by object weight.

In previous experimental studies of this type – and, implicitly, in corpus studies as well – subjects have chosen between two syntactic alternants or distributed a fixed number of rating points between them (Bresnan 2007; Melnick et al. 2011). Such designs make it impossible to independently assess the factors affecting the acceptability of the VPO and VOP orders. The present design, in which each order is evaluated independently, reveals an effect not predicted in the literature: namely that heavy objects are actually judged better than light objects in the VPO order by .05 units (p = .03). Such an effect is unlikely to derive from processing constraints but could be explained if subjects implicitly evaluate sentences exhibiting one structure (e.g. VPO order) with respect to the equivalent sentences with the other structure (e.g. VOP order). That is, the well-motivated weight effect that disfavours heavy objects in the VOP order would lead to a preference for heavy objects in the VPO order, if subjects evaluate the relative acceptability of both orders when they are exposed to either of them, in a kind of perceptual version of competing grammars.

If weight effects in the VPO order are indeed parasitic on weight effects in the VOP order, then we would expect effects in the two word order conditions to correlate across speakers. That is, speakers who show a stronger weight effect in VOP orders should also show a stronger weight effect in VPO orders. Figure 3.2.4 below shows that this is the case, at least on average; for each of the 297 speakers, it plots the (positive) effect of a heavy object on the VPO order against the (negative) effect of a heavy object on the VOP order. We see that the two effects are moderately correlated (r = −.394), and that the range of the VPO effect is smaller, consistent with it being a derivative of the VOP effect. However, we also observe that even those speakers who displayed no weight effect at all in VOP sentences still preferred heavy objects in VPO sentences, implying that there must at least be another, independent motivation for the latter effect.

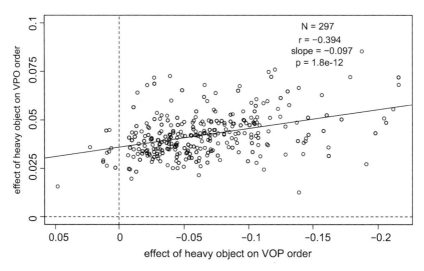

Figure 3.2.4 Correlation between object weight effects for VOP and VPO orders.

Finally, we note that the analysis revealed no significant higher-order interaction between country and focus (country*focus*order, $p = .75$) or country and weight (country*weight*order, $p = .43$), meaning there is no evidence for trans-Atlantic differences in these effects. Nor was there any significant interaction between focus and weight effects (focus*weight*order, $p = .83$).

3.2.4 A Twitter Corpus Study

To test for the possibility of similar regional effects in production, we examined variation between VPO and VOP orders in a bespoke Twitter corpus. The corpus consisted of tweets containing a variation on one of two base strings, *turn on the light* (VPO) and *turn the light on* (VOP). The volume of tweets was augmented by including examples with *turns* and *turned* as well as *turn off* as well as *turn on*, and *lights* as well as *light*. Before analysis, the data were cleaned by hand of song lyrics, quotations, memes, and other examples that did not reflect the production of the user.

The tweets were gathered between February and May of 2011 from Twitter API. The corpus was geocoded to areas within a 150-mile radius of four population centres in the UK and US: Oxford, England; Glasgow, Scotland; Pittsburgh, Pennsylvania; and Concord, New Hampshire. The search on the area centered around Glasgow gathered 236 tweets with

Figure 3.2.5 Twitter corpus catchment for US dialects.

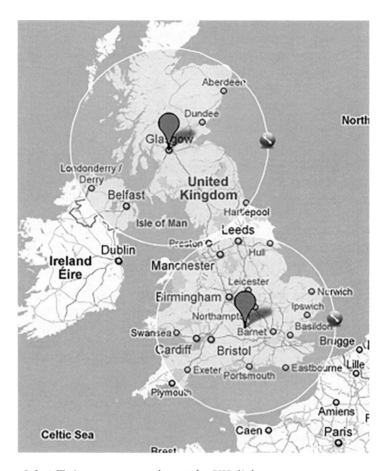

Figure 3.2.6 Twitter corpus catchment for UK dialects.

the relevant strings from Scotland and Northern England. The Oxford-centered search gathered 1472 tweets from an area spanning most of the rest of England (it did not overlap with the Glasgow-centered search). The Concord, New Hampshire-centered search, which yielded 296 tokens, encompassed most of New England, in an effort to target an area founded by Southern English settlers. Finally, the Pittsburgh-centered search gathered 343 tweets and targeted an area of Appalachia and western Pennsylvania, whose founding settlers were largely of Scottish or Scotch-Irish origin (Montgomery 2006). We illustrate the different catchment areas for the US and UK dialect areas in Figures 3.2.5 and 3.2.6, respectively.

The results, again, show no evidence of regional effects within the UK (contra Hughes et al. 2005; Fisher's Exact Test $p = .61$), nor within the

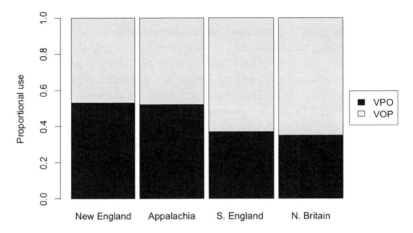

Figure 3.2.7 Proportional use of VPO and VOP orders by region.

US ($p = .87$). But the national results align very well with the acceptability judgment results reported above, in that the US Twitter users tend slightly toward the VPO order (53% VPO), while UK users tend more decidedly toward the VOP order (64% VOP).[4] For this trans-Atlantic difference, $p = 6 \times 10^{-13}$. We illustrate these effects in Figure 3.2.7.

3.2.5 Evidence from Diachronic Corpora

A question that arises in light of the acceptability judgment data and the Twitter corpus data is how to explain the trans-Atlantic difference. We see three main possible explanations: a first possibility is that UK dialects have been innovative in moving toward VOP orders after the period of North American colonisation; a second possibility is that US speakers have been innovative in tending toward the VPO order; a third possibility is that both dialects are changing but doing so at different rates; for example, both UK and US dialects could be moving toward the VOP order, but UK dialects have moved further and/or faster.

For help in adjudicating among these possibilities, we turn first to data from parsed diachronic corpora. We extracted particle verb constructions from four parsed corpora, *The York-Toronto-Helsinki Parsed Corpus of Old English Prose* (Taylor et al. 2003), the Penn-Helsinki *Parsed Corpus of Middle English*, 2nd Ed. (Kroch and Taylor, 2000), the *Penn Parsed Corpus of Early Modern English* (Kroch et al. 2004), the *Penn Parsed Corpus of Modern British English* (Kroch et al. 2010), and the *Parsed Corpus of Early English Correspondence* (Taylor et al. 2006). These corpora, together, cover a span of written British English from 850 to 1910. However, because the earliest period covered in these texts

(850–1430) contained very few unambiguous examples of the relevant verb-particle construction (*n* = 72), data from this period were omitted.

We extracted only sentences with non-quantified, full-DP objects (that is, excluding pronouns and demonstratives, where the VOP order is obligatory). Additionally, we only considered clauses containing an auxiliary, a nonfinite verb, and in which the particle and DP both followed the nonfinite verb. This condition restricts the sample to clauses with head-initial TPs and VPs in earlier stages of English, as the modern verb-particle alternation does not occur in the head-final versions of these structures in Old and Middle English. The resulting sample contained 888 clauses. We plot the proportion of VOP construction use by year in Figure 3.2.8, below. The size of the symbols is proportional to the number of tokens per year: the larger the circle, the greater amount of data for that year. The plot illustrates that the token numbers are unevenly distributed across years, with most years/texts having very few tokens. The plot also shows that, overall, the authors in these texts tend strongly toward VPO orders (91%), a finding likely related to the fact that this is a written corpus and VPO orders are favoured in more formal contexts (Kroch and Small 1978). The grey logistic regression line in Figure 3.2.8 shows a very slight slope (+.001 log-odds/year). A likelihood-ratio test comparing models with and without a term for year does not support the hypothesis of a change toward VOP orders (*p* = .343).

This negative result from the historical written corpora, therefore, provides no help in deciding among the possible diachronic explanations of the cross-Atlantic difference discussed above. A further possibility to consider, however, is that the relevant changes are too recent to be reflected in these corpora. To test this, we use the Brown family of corpora, a set of written US and British English texts from 1961, 1991, and 2006, and a set of UK English texts from 1931 (Hundt et al.

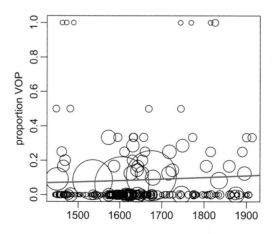

Figure 3.2.8 Proportion of VOP use by year (*Penn/Helsinki/York Corpora*).

Particle Verb Alternation 217

1999a, 1999b; Johansson et al. 1978; Francis and Kučera 1964; Leech and Rayson 2005). The fact that these corpora are (i) matched for genre and style and (ii) span seven decades therefore lets us test the possibility of divergent rates of change in UK and US written English.

We extracted 2568 transitive particle verbs with objects consisting of a single determiner and a one-word noun, e.g. *an umbrella, the boat.* We coded these tokens for two linguistic fixed predictors: object definiteness (with levels *definite* and *indefinite*), and object length (in syllables). Social fixed predictors included year of text (as a continuous variable), country (with levels *UK* and *US*), and category of text (with levels *fiction, general, learned* and *press*). Using *lme4*, we fit a generalised linear model with random intercepts for particle verb and text.

Variables were selected by a step-up procedure similar to that employed in Goldvarb (Sankoff et al., 2005) and Rbrul (Johnson, 2009). Fixed main predictors improving the model significantly (α = .05) were added level-by-level. We then used this same step-up procedure to evaluate those two-way combinations where plotting suggested a possible interaction. Plotting suggested no likely interactions with >2 predictors. Table 3.2.1 summarises the generalised linear mixed model with 1 = VOP. (Level labels for factors appear in brackets to the right of the variable label.)

Table 3.2.1 Coefficients (logits), standard errors, *z*-values and *p*-values for fixed effects in the combined model, with 1 = VOP order. Number of observations = 2568.

AIC	BIC	logLik	Deviance
2110	2168	−1045	2090

Random effects

Groups name	Variance	Std. Dev.
Text (Intercept)	0.73696	0.85846
Particle Verb (Intercept)	3.80080	1.94956

Fixed effects	Estimate	Std. Error	z value	Pr(>|z|)
(Intercept)	−3.411856	0.314954	−10.833	< 2e−16***
Definiteness (Indef.)	−0.472501	0.240199	−1.967	0.04917*
Category (Fiction)	0.613450	0.246381	2.490	0.01278*
Category (General)	0.517391	0.261026	1.982	0.04746*
Category (Learned)	1.164136	0.446426	2.608	0.00912**
Year	0.018322	0.003845	4.765	1.89e−06***
Country (US)	0.692315	0.419829	1.649	0.09914
Year: Country (US)	−0.018462	0.007320	−2.522	0.01167*

Signif. codes: 0 '***' 0.001 '**' 0.01 '*' 0.05 '.' 0.1 ' ' 1.

The intercept is strongly negative (−3.411856 in log-odds units, $p < 2e{-}16$), reflecting the strong tendency in the data toward VPO orders overall in these written data. In addition, indefinites favour VPO orders, as also reported in Gries's (2001) analysis of British National Corpus data. Since indefinite objects are more likely to refer to discourse-new entities, this effect can be linked to the effect of information structure discussed in Section 3.2.2. The text categories *learned*, *general* and *fiction*, all favour VOP orders relative to the reference level (*press*), perhaps reflecting a higher style of writing for *press*-category texts. Note that object length (in syllables) did not emerge as a significant predictor in the modelling, unlike in the experiment described in Section 3.2.3. The absence of length effects may be a consequence of the fact that objects extracted were all two word – article + noun – sequences, that is, this sampling may not have allowed for sufficient variation to make a weight effect detectable. Finally, the model in Table 3.2.1 shows a country*year interaction, which we illustrate in Figure 3.2.9: while in the US data, VPO/VOP variation is stable, in UK dialects, there is a change toward the VOP order. Note also, that the corpus results from 1991 and 2006 also align with the judgement and Twitter corpus findings that UK English speakers tend toward VOP orders more than US speakers. Compared to what we saw in Figure 3.2.7, the Brown family rates of VOP are lower for both countries, reflecting the more formal nature of these texts compared to the Twitter data.

The results from the Brown corpora therefore align with the first of the hypotheses suggested above, namely that this variation is stable in the US, while UK English is diverging in tending toward VOP orders.[5]

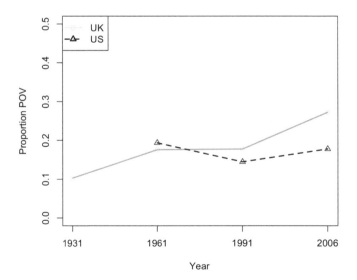

Figure 3.2.9 Proportion of VOP use by year (Brown Corpora).

To examine the possibility of change in American English in greater time depth we turn, finally, to data from the Corpus of Historical American English (COHA). The COHA is a 400-million-word corpus of American texts balanced by genre and style from 1810 to the present. It is not syntactically parsed, making it virtually impossible to extract all particle verb tokens, as we did with the corpora above. Instead, we extracted 685 tokens of five common particle verb strings, shown in the upper left-hand corner of Figure 3.2.10 along with the number of tokens/string. Figure 3.2.10 plots the proportion of discontinuous forms by decade. The results show substantial change toward the discontinuous order during this period. Assuming a constant rate of change, a logistic regression (with a term controlling for the individual string) returns a slope of +0.01 log-odds per year in favour of the discontinuous order ($p = .0003$).

This evidence of change toward the VOP order over time in American English is in keeping with the third possibility suggested above, namely, that both British/Irish and North American Englishes are tending toward VOP orders, but the change began too recently to be reliably observed in the historical corpora.

The evidence of change toward VOP orders presented above suggests the possibility that English is undergoing a syntactic change in progress from an alternating system to a verb-particle system more like that of modern Danish, in which the VOP order is obligatory (Faarlund 1977; Taraldsen 1983, 1991). In fact, given that Norwegian and Icelandic show an alternating system (Svenonius 1996a, 1996b, *inter alia*), and Swedish shows a very limited amount of the VOP order (Toivonen 2003), it is likely that Scandinavian used to uniformly show a verb-particle alternation and that Danish has completed the same change that we have suggested is underway in modern English.

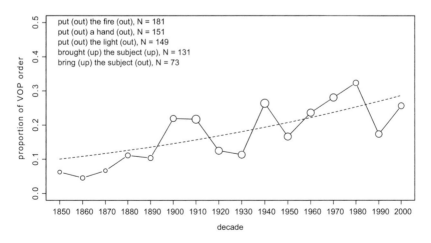

Figure 3.2.10 VOP order in the Corpus of Historical American English 1850–2009.

220   *Bill Haddican et al.*

However, the data are also consistent with another explanation: the apparent change could be due to the loosening of a prescription against the VOP order in written English, with no change in progress at all in spoken English (see Cheshire 1994; Cheshire and Fox 2009 on effects of prescription on morphosyntactic variation, Kroch and Small 1978). If the VOP order has always occurred at a stable frequency but was consistently suppressed in writing until the nineteenth century, that would also explain the COHA and Brown trends and the lack of a change in the Penn corpora of historical English. The kind of data that would be most helpful in deciding between these possibilities would be diachronic corpora containing both spoken and written English from US and UK speakers matched for genre, style, and speaker-related social predictors. Such a data set does not exist as far as we know. Future work might explore these issues further.[6]

3.2.6 On Movement in the Particle Verb Construction

As mentioned in Section 3.2.2, several studies (Gries 2001; Kroch and Small 1978; Lohse et al. 2004) report evidence from corpus studies to the effect that a heavy direct object favours VPO order and disfavours VOP order, and conversely, a light direct object favours VOP and disfavours VPO order. The explanation proposed by Lohse et al. (2004) is that this is the effect of a principle of processing which favours a short distance between the members of a syntactic dependency (Hawkins 2004). The heavier the object is in the VOP order, the longer the distance will be between the verb and its dependent, the particle, and therefore, the more VPO order is preferred over VOP. While this predicts that heavy objects are dispreferred in VOP, it does not straightforwardly predict that light objects are dispreferred in VPO, especially when the structures are evaluated separately by test subjects under experimental conditions, as in our design. A possible explanation is, though, that subjects evaluate the relative acceptability of the two orders even when they are exposed to them separately. Effectively, VPO with a heavy object would be judged good because VOP would be bad with that object, and conversely, VPO with a light object would be judged bad because VOP with that object would be good. As pointed out in Section 3.2.3.2, this, in turn, predicts that subjects who show little or no dispreference for heavy objects in VOP, should correspondingly show little or no dispreference for light objects in VPO. We did, indeed, find such a correlation, but only a moderate one. Moreover, quite a few subjects displayed little or no weight effect in the VOP order, yet they did show a weight effect in the VPO order, dispreferring light objects. This casts doubt on the processing-based explanation: it may explain, or be part of the explanation, why heavy objects are dispreferred in VOP, but does not explain why light objects are dispreferred in VPO. We should, therefore, look for alternative explanations.

The following is a syntactic account of the particle verb alternation that is consistent with our findings. We adopt a version of the theory articulated by Svenonius (1994, 1996a, 1996b) and particularly Ramchand and Svenonius (2002 see also Haddican and Johnson 2012). Following Ramchand's (2002) theory of 'lexical syntax', the maximal expansion of a predicate expresses three subevents, initiation, process, and result, which are syntactically represented as a hierarchy of projections. The predicate of a verb-particle construction has the following structure (R = Result).

(12) $[_{vP}$ Agent v $[_{VP}$ Undergoer V $[_{RP}$ Holder R $[_{PrtP}$ Prt Obj]]]]

vP expresses the Initiation event, with the specifier interpreted as the initiator (Agent) of the event, VP expresses the Process event, the specifier interpreted as undergoer, and RP the Result state, the specifier interpreted as the 'holder of the result'. Notably the same DP can be both undergoer and holder of result by virtue of movement, overt or covert, from specRP to specVP. The particle and the object DP form a constituent below R. Crucially, either the particle or the object must move, the particle by head-movement to R, the object to specRP. Ramchand and Svenonius (2002) suggest that the trigger is a universal requirement to lexicalise the R-projection.[7]

This predicts cross-linguistic and possibly intralinguistic variation, which, of course, is what we find. Idealising the situation somewhat we have (13) (see Svenonius 1996a, 1996b):

(13) Swedish: Prt-movement only → VPO order
      Danish: Object-movement only → VOP order
      English, Icelandic, Norwegian: Prt movement or Object-movement
      → VPO and VOP

We can model this as two grammars, one with Prt-movement (call it Prt-Mvt), one with Object-movement (call it Obj-Mvt). In English, Icelandic, and Norwegian the two grammars are in competition. As we have shown, the choice between the two grammars correlates with heaviness, according to a certain pattern. To account for this, we propose that two connected, universal markedness conditions are at work here governing scrambling or object-shift type movement:

(14) a) Light objects: Movement is unmarked, non-movement is marked.
      b) Heavy objects: Movement is marked, non-movement is unmarked.

222 *Bill Haddican et al.*

It is well known and very well documented in the literature that weakly stressed object pronouns tend to undergo leftwards movement in a variety of languages, including the Germanic languages (Holmberg 1999; Vikner 1994; Wallenberg 2008). This is an effect of (14a). In the Scandinavian languages and earlier stages of English (Wallenberg 2008), this movement is known as Object Shift, shifting an object pronoun across a negation and other constituents in the *Mittelfeld*, provided the verb also moves. In most of the languages Object Shift applies to pronouns only, but in Icelandic also to definite full NPs (Thráinsson 2007). Consider, therefore, the case of Icelandic. (15) exemplifies the fact that movement of a weak object pronoun in Icelandic is obligatory, (16) that movement of a lexical NP is optional, and (17) that the movement is dispreferred if the NP is heavy.[8]

(15) a) *Hún sá   ekki þá. (Icelandic)
            she saw not them
      b) Hún sá þá   ekki.
            she saw them not
(16) a) Hún sá   ekki strákana.
            she saw not   the.boys
      b) Hún sá   strákana ekki.
            she saw the.boys not
            'She didn't see the boys'.
(17) a) Hún sá   ekki strákana frá   Akureyri.
            she saw not the.boys from Akureyri
      b) ??Hún sá   strákana frá   Akureyri ekki.
             she saw the.boys from Akureyri not
             'She didn't see the boys from Akureyri'.

This corresponds exactly to what we see in connection with particle verb alternation in English (as well as Icelandic and Norwegian): With a weak pronominal object, object movement is obligatory, with a lexical NP object the movement is optional, but if the object is heavy, the movement is dispreferred. This is the effect of (14). Note also that no explanation in terms of processing along the lines of Lohse et al. can be appealed to in the case of Object Shift. There is no dependency relation between T (the host of the verb; see Thráinsson 2007) and the negation that would be hampered by a heavy object.

To be more precise, in the case of the verb-particle construction, the impact of (14) is as follows:

- For all speakers, if the object is a weakly stressed pronoun, Obj-Mvt is the only option; it is categorical.
- For a class of speakers, more numerous in the US than in the British Isles or Canada, Prt-Mvt is the preferred option when the object is a

Particle Verb Alternation 223

lexical DP. If the object is heavy, Prt-Mvt is strongly preferred due to the markedness condition (14b).

- For another class of speakers, more numerous in the British Isles than in the US or Canada, Obj-Mvt is the preferred option; heavy as well as light objects can move. However, for heavy objects, markedness condition (14b) enters the picture, favouring Prt-Mvt over Obj-Mvt. The effect is, for these speakers, that VOP is always an option, but VPO is acceptable as well if the object is heavy.

In this perspective, the processing principle favouring short distance between dependents (Lohse et al. 2004) plays at most a supplementary role in the context of particle verb alternation in English. The change that we have found towards VOP order is an effect of increase in the use of Obj-Mvt at the expense of Prt-Mvt. The endpoint of this process is complete loss of the Prt-Mvt option, which is what we see in present-day Danish. The prediction is, however, that as long as Prt-Mvt is employed at all, it will be employed when the object is heavy, due to (14b).

3.2.7 Conclusion

Following Jenny Cheshire's thrust to explore the constraints underpinning syntactic variation, this chapter has focussed on regional and other effects on the particle verb alternation in English. Our main new finding is evidence of a trans-Atlantic difference where British and Irish English speakers prefer the VOP order in both production (in a Twitter corpus) and perception (in a judgment experiment) to a greater extent than Canadian, and especially American, speakers. Analysis of variation in written English from the Brown corpora of UK and US English and from the COHA corpus suggest change toward the VOP order in both US and British Isles dialects but that this change has progressed more quickly in the British Isles.

Our results contribute to a series of recent findings describing changes in probabilities governing word order alternations across English dialects. Bresnan and Ford (2010), for example, report evidence from production and judgment data suggesting that Australian English speakers, more than American English speakers, tend toward prepositional datives (*give the ball to Tanya*) vis-à-vis double object constructions (*give Tanya the ball*). Grimm and Bresnan (2009) report corpus evidence suggesting that both British and American English are changing toward double object constructions, with US dialects leading the change. Similarly, Hinrichs and Szmrecsanyi (2007) present corpus evidence suggesting change in both British and American English (written and oral) toward the synthetic (Saxon) genitive (*the leader's courage*) versus the analytic (Norman) genitive (*the courage of the leader*). One interpretation of the above results sometimes entertained in the literature is "colloquialisation" or

224 *Bill Haddican et al.*

change in the written norms of these dialects toward more colloquial or oral forms (Hinrichs and Szmrecsanyi 2007). Our results suggesting change toward VOP orders which are favoured in spoken English, are in line with these results (Kroch and Small 1978), and highlight the need for a more comprehensive theory of processes of change that appear to affect geographically diffuse dialects concomitantly (D'Arcy et al. 2012).

We also demonstrate the potential benefits of an experimental methodology whereby the members of a syntactic alternation are evaluated independently, rather than by forced-choice or the distribution of rating points. The selection of a syntactic alternant has often been treated as a choice (or the outcome of a competition). Corpus data lends itself naturally to this treatment, which is also in keeping with variationist theory. In this approach, a factor favouring one alternant will necessarily disfavour the other alternant(s) to the same extent. However, by separating the presentation and evaluation of the VPO and VOP orders of the particle verb alternation, our judgment study shows that the situation is not so simple. For example, a heavier direct object makes the VOP order less acceptable (as expected), and it also makes the VPO order more acceptable (expected, perhaps, under a competition analysis). But although those subjects with a greater sensitivity to object weight in the VOP order also tended to show a greater effect in the VPO order, the correlation was only moderate. In addition, quite a few subjects displayed little or no weight effect in the VOP order, where it is motivated by processing considerations, yet, importantly, these same subjects – along with almost every other subject – did show a weight effect in the VPO order, despite the fact that such a weight effect in the VPO order is unmotivated by traditional processing accounts.

Such puzzling and theoretically intriguing findings could not emerge from a corpus study or a forced-choice task. This suggests that judgment studies allowing separate evaluation of the alternants are best equipped to investigate the mechanisms of what surfaces as syntactic "choice", but may be a more complex phenomenon.

Finally, the weight effect we found in VPO order, cutting across other variation, can be understood if the variation is an effect of variation between two grammars, one deriving the particle verb construction by particle movement, which yields VPO; the other by object movement, which yields VOP. In conjunction with a markedness condition which favours movement of light objects and disfavours movement of heavy objects, for movement of the object shift type, the weight effect follows.

Notes

1 We are grateful to Jenny Cheshire for her leadership in the field over the past few decades. We are also grateful to two anonymous reviewers for helpful comments and also to Isabelle Buchstaller, Karen Beaman and to the Spanish Ministerio de Ciencia e Innovación (PGC2018-096380-B-100).

2 See Cheshire (2005a, 2005b) for approaches to variation in focus constructions using corpus data.

3 An alternative way of biasing focus on the object is with wh-questions as the context, e.g. *What did* SUBJECT *do*? (to bias VP-focus readings) and *What happened to* OBJECT? (to bias a given-object reading). A disadvantage of this approach is that it requires repeating the subject and object in the question and answers, which speakers typically find pragmatically odd, particularly for heavy DPs. For this reason we chose the cataphor binding approach explained above.

4 In the judgment experiment, for light objects similar to those in the Twitter study, US subjects preferred the VPO order by .018 units; UK subjects preferred the VOP order by .104 units.

5 Comparing rates of change in US and UK English using the Brown corpora is nevertheless hindered by the fact that we did not have access to 1931-era Brown data for American English, which might indeed have suggested change in American English (Hypothesis 3 above).

6 To the extent that the *category* factor in the Brown modeling can be taken to reflect style differences, "stylistic loosening" explanation, might lead us to expect a country*category*date interaction in these data. No such interaction emerged in the modeling (p = .256).

7 An alternative model, also compatible with our findings, would be that VPO involves no movement, while VOP is derived by object movement.

8 Thanks to Halldór Á. Sigurðsson for data and judgments.

References

Bolinger, Dwight L. 1971. *The Phrasal Verb in English*. Cambridge: Harvard University Press.

Bresnan, Joan. 2007. "Is syntactic knowledge probabilistic? Experiments with the English dative alternation". In *Roots: Linguistics in Search of Its Evidential Base*, S. Featherston and W. Sternefeld (eds.). Berlin: Mouton. 77–96.

Bresnan, Joan and Marilyn Ford. 2010. "Predicting syntax: Processing dative constructions in American and Australian varieties of English". *Language* 86(1):186–213.

Cheshire, Jenny. 1994. "Standardization and the English irregular verbs". In *Towards a Standard English, 1600–1800*, D. Stein and I. Tieken-Boon van Ostade (eds.). Berlin: Walter de Gruyter. 115–133.

Cheshire, Jenny. 1996. "Syntactic variation and the concept of prominence". In *Speech Past and Present: Studies in English Dialectology*, J. Klemola, M. Kyto and M. Rissanen (eds.). Frankfurt: Peter Lang. 1–17.

Cheshire, Jenny. 2005a. "Syntactic variation and beyond: Gender and social class variation in the use of discourse-new markers". *Journal of Sociolinguistics* 9:479–508.

Cheshire, Jenny. 2005b. "Syntactic variation and spoken language". In *Syntax and Variation: Reconciling the Biological and Social*, L. Cornips and K.P. Corrigan (eds.). Amsterdam: John Benjamins. 81–106.

Cheshire, Jenny, Edwards, Viv and Whittle, Pamela. 1989. Urban British dialect grammar: the question of dialect levelling. English World-wide 10 (2):185–225

Cheshire, Jenny and Milroy, James. 1993. Syntactic variation in non-standard dialects: background issues. In J. Milroy, J. and L. Milroy (eds.) Real English:

The Grammar of English Dialects in the British Isles. Harlow: Longman, pp. 3–33.

Cheshire, Jenny and Sue Fox. 2009. "*Was/were* variation: A perspective from London". *Language Variation and Change* 21:1–38.

Cheshire, Jenny and Ann Williams. 2002. "Information structure in male and female adolescent talk". *Journal of English Linguistics* 30:217–238.

D'Arcy, Alexandra, Bill Haddican, Hazel Richards, Sali Tagliamonte and Ann Taylor. 2012. "Asymmetrical trajectories: The past and present of *–body/–one*". *Language Variation and Change* 25(3):278–310.

Dehé, Nicole. 2002. *Particle Verbs in English: Syntax, Information Structure, and Intonation*. Amsterdam: John Benjamins.

Dikken, Marcel den. 1995. *Particles: On the Syntax of Verb–Particle, Triadic and Causative Constructions*. Oxford/New York: Oxford University Press.

Drummond, Alex. 2011. *Ibex Farm*. spellout.net/ibexfarm.

Elenbaas, Marion. 2007. The synchronic and diachronic syntax of the English verb-particle combination. Doctoral dissertation, Radboud University, Nijmegen, Netherlands.

Faarlund, Jan Terje. 1977. "Transformational syntax in dialectology: Scandinavian word order varieties". In *Papers from the Trondheim Syntax Symposium*, T. Fretheim and L. Hellan (eds.). Trondheim: University of Trondheim. 65–83.

Francis, W. Nelson and Henry Kučera. 1964. *The Brown Corpus*. Providence, Rhode Island: Department of Linguistics, Brown University.

Grafmiller, Jason and Benedikt Szmrecsanyi. 2018. "Mapping out particle placement in Englishes around the world. A study in comparative sociolinguistic analysis". *Language Variation and Change* 30:385–412.

Gries, Stefan T. 2001. "A multifactorial analysis of syntactic variation: Particle movement revisited". *Journal of Quantitative Linguistics* 8:33–50.

Grimm, Scott and Joan Bresnan. 2009. "Spatiotemporal variation in the dative alternation: A study of four corpora of British and American English". In *Paper Presented at the Third International Conference Grammar and Corpora*, Mannheim, 22–24 September 2009.

Haddican, Bill and Daniel Ezra Johnson. 2012. "Effects on the particle verb alternation across English dialects". *University of Pennsylvania Working Papers in Linguistics* 18(2), Article 5.

Hinrichs, Lars and Benedikt Szmrecsanyi. 2007. "Recent changes in the function and frequency of Standard English genitive constructions: A multivariate analysis of tagged corpora". *English Language and Linguistics* 11:437–474.

Holmberg, Anders. 1999. "Remarks on Holmberg's generalization". *Studia Linguistica* 53:1–39.

Hughes, Arthur, Peter Trudgill and Dominic Watt. 2005. *English Accents and Dialects*. London: Hodder Arnold.

Hundt, Marianne, Andrea Sand and Rainer Siemund. 1999a. *Manual of Information to Accompany the Freiburg – LOB Corpus of British English ('FLOB')*. Freiburg: Department of English. Albert-Ludwigs-Universität Freiburg.

Hundt, Marianne, Andrea Sand and Paul Skandera. 1999b. *Manual of Information to Accompany The Freiburg – Brown Corpus of American English ('Frown')*. Freiburg: Department of English. Albert-Ludwigs-Universität Freiburg.

Johansson, Stig, Geoffrey Leech and Helen Goodluck. 1978. *Manual of Information to Accompany the Lancaster-Oslo/Bergen Corpus of British English, for Use with Digital Computer*. Oslo: Department of English, University of Oslo.

Johnson, Daniel Ezra, 2009. Getting off the GoldVarb standard: Introducing Rbrul for mixed-effects variable rule analysis. Language and linguistics compass, 3(1), pp. 359–383.

Kayne, Richard S. 1998. "Overt versus covert movement". *Syntax* 1:128–191.

Krapp, George P. 1925. *The English Language in America*. New York: Ungar.

Kroch, Anthony and Cathy Small. 1978. "Grammatical ideology and its effect on speech". In *Linguistic Variation: Models and Methods*, D. Sankoff (ed.). New York: Academic Press. 45–55.

Kroch, Anthony and Ann Taylor. 2000. *The Penn-Helsinki Parsed Corpus of Middle English (PPCME2)*, 2nd edition. Philadelphia: Department of Linguistics, University of Pennsylvania. CD-ROM.

Kroch, Anthony, Beatrice Santorini and Ariel Diertani. 2004. *Penn-Helsinki Parsed Corpus of Early Modern English*. www.ling.upenn.edu/hist-corpora/PPCEME-RELEASE-2/index.html.

Kroch, Anthony, Beatrice Santorini and Ariel Diertani. 2010. *The Penn-Helsinki Parsed Corpus of Modern British English (PPCMBE)*, 1st edition. Department of Linguistics, University of Pennsylvania. CD-ROM.

Kurath, Hans. 1949. *A Word Geography of the Eastern United States*. Ann Arbor: University of Michigan Press.

Leech, Geoffrey and Paul Rayson. 2005. *The BLOB-1931 Corpus*. Lancaster: University of Lancaster.

Lohse, Barbara, John Hawkins and Thomas Wasow. 2004. "Processing domains in English verb-particle constructions". *Language* 80(2):238–261.

Melnick, Robin, T. Florian Jaeger and Thomas Wasow. 2011. "Speakers employ fine-grained probabilistic knowledge". In *Paper Presented at LSA*, Pittsburgh, PA.

Montgomery, Michael. 2006. "How Scotch-Irish Is Your English?" *Journal of East Tennessee History* 77(Supplement):65–91.

Ramchand, Gillian and Peter Svenonius. 2002. "The lexical syntax and lexical semantics of the verb-particle construction". In *Proceedings of WCCFL 21*, L. Mikkelsen and C. Potts (eds.). Somerville, MA: Cascadilla Press. 387–400.

Svenonius, Peter. 1994. Dependent nexus: Subordinate predication structures in English and the Scandinavian languages. Ph.D. thesis, University of California at Santa Cruz.

Svenonius, Peter. 1996a. "The optionality of particle shift". *Working Papers in Scandinavian Syntax* 57:47–75.

Svenonius, Peter. 1996b. "The verb-particle alternation in the Scandinavian languages". *Lingbuzz/000046*.

Taraldsen, Knut Tarald. 1983. Parametric variation in phrase structure: A case study. Ph.D. dissertation, University of Tromsø, Tromsø.

Taraldsen, Knut Tarald. 1991. "A directionality parameter for subject object linking". In *Principles and Parameters in Comparative Grammar*, R. Freidin (ed.). Cambridge, MA: MIT Press. 219–268.

Taylor, Ann, Arja Nurmi, Anthony Warner, Susan Pintzuk and Terttu Nevalainen. 2006. *The York-Helsinki Parsed Corpus of Early English*

228 Bill Haddican et al.

Correspondence (PCEEC), 1st edition. York: Department of Linguistics, University of York. Oxford Text Archive.

Taylor, Ann, Anthony Warner, Susan Pintzuk and Frank Beths. 2003. *The York-Toronto-Helsinki Parsed Corpus of Old English Prose (YCOE)*, 1st edition. York: Department of Linguistics, University of York. Oxford Text Archive.

Thráinsson, Höskuldur. 2007. *The Syntax of Icelandic*. Cambridge: Cambridge University Press.

Toivonen, Ida. 2001. The structure of non-projecting words. Ph.D. dissertation, Stanford University, Stanford, CA.

Toivonen, Ida. 2003. *Non-Projecting Words: A Case Study of Swedish Verbal Particles*. Dordrecht, The Netherlands: Kluwer.

Vikner, Sten. 1994. "Scandinavian object shift and West Germanic scrambling". In *Studies on Scrambling*, N. Corver and H. van Riemsdijk (eds.). Berlin: Mouton de Gruyter. 487–517.

Wallenberg, Joel. 2008. "English weak pronouns and object shift". In *Proceedings of the 26th West Coast Conference on Formal Linguistics*, C. Chang and H. Haynie (eds.). Somerville, MA: Cascadilla Proceedings Project. 489–497.

3.3 Explaining Variability in Negative Concord
A Socio-Syntactic Analysis

David Adger and Jennifer Smith

3.3.1 Introduction

Among the range of variables heard in the Reading playground in Cheshire's (1982) seminal study is robust use of negative concord (1a–d).

(1) a) That's where we go clubbing when there ai*n't nothing* to do. (Jeff)
    b) You can come down here, mate, and talk to me 'cos I wo*n't* have *no-one* to talk to. (Derek)
    c) That bloody stuff do*n't* do *no good* anyway. (Julie)
    d) And I could*n't* get *no sleep*. (Mandy)

Negative concord is the expression of sentential negation involving both a negative clitic (*-n't*) and a negative quantifier (phrase) (*nothing, no-one, no good*). This 'vernacular universal' which "recurs ubiquitously all over the world" (Chambers 1995: 242; e.g. Cheshire 1982; Coupland 1988; Edwards 1993; Howe and Walker 2000; Schneider 1989), is a quintessential linguistic variable: for speakers who have negative concord in their grammar, such as the Reading teenagers, (2a–c) can convey the same meaning.

(2) a) You can know who he is cos he's got one ear bitten by leprosy, but the police do*n't* do *nothing* about it. (Debbie)
    b) You can know who he is cos he's got one ear bitten by leprosy, but the police do*n't* do *anything* about it.
    c) You can know who he is cos he's got one ear bitten by leprosy, but the police do *nothing* about it.

If both the negative clitic and the negative quantifier can express sentential negation on their own (2b–c), the question arises as to why sentential negation can be expressed by both (2a). As Labov (1972:774) notes, the "immediate problem for the linguist [...] is to discover the nature of the rule which produces such an effect." Sociolinguistic research has

230   David Adger and Jennifer Smith

focussed on discovering both social and linguistic constraints on the use of these forms. For example, in Cheshire's Reading playground, the boys use negative concord at higher rates than the girls and there are higher rates of negative concord when the post-verbal negative is a full noun phrase (NP) (3a) as opposed to a pronoun (3b) (Cheshire 1982:65).

(3) a) Oy, Hitler, you're gonna get your head bashed in. *Not* saying *no names*. (Dave)
b) Give us that book, else I won't give you *none*, Alec. (Smithy)

In addition to quantitative differences within and across varieties, categorical differences also exist. In Cheshire's (1982:63) words: "Although negative concord occurs in most non-standard varieties of English, its syntactic distribution often varies." For example, Cheshire states that negative concord in her Reading sample does not occur where there is a subject negative NP (4), but this form is widely attested in other varieties (e.g. Labov 1972:806; Wolfram and Christian 1976:112).

(4) *Nobody* could*n't* handle him. (Appalachian English: Wolfram and Christian 1976:112)

From the perspective of syntactic theory, the challenge is to understand not only how the various negative elements combine to produce meaning, but also to explain the grammatical patterning of negative concord both within and across varieties, and to characterise the syntactic rules underlying both categorical and variable patterns. In a recent evaluation of two syntactic approaches to the syntax of negative concord across a range of UK varieties, Childs (2017) argues for the superiority of an account that appeals to syntactic movement of the negative quantifier. Here we support that position, as well as the broad approach, focussing on variation within a single dialect.

Most previous sociolinguistic research has analysed the variability between negative NPs and adverbials (*no names, nothing, nowhere*) and their non-negative variants (*any names, anything, anywhere*) in the context of sentential negation (the negative marker -*n't* or its non-clitic form *not*). In this chapter, we flip this around and focus on addressing the question of variation in the presence of a sentential negation marker in the context of a negative NP. We argue that, once we take account of sociolinguistic factors, much of the variation can be explained by a range of grammatical factors. The approach we develop also provides a basis for understanding why negative concord is a vernacular universal in English.

3.3.2 Data and Methodology

Buckie is a small fishing town situated on the north-eastern coast of Scotland, 60 miles from Aberdeen. Our data come from a corpus of

Explaining Variability in Negative Concord 231

sociolinguistic interviews with 49 speakers, stratified by age and gender, in conversation with both a community insider and outsider. Here we use the data from the insider interviews only, totalling approximately 400,000 words. We analyse these data quantitatively to motivate a number of generalizations about how the presence of negative concord is influenced by verb-type and we develop a theory to account for these generalisations (cf. Burnett, Koopman and Tagliamonte 2018). In addition to the quantitative data from the corpus, we test novel predictions of the theory that we develop via grammaticality and meaning-form judgments by native speakers of the variety.

3.3.3 Quantitative Analysis

Previous work on negative concord in Buckie (Smith 2001) examined variability in the form of the negative NP: is it realised with a negative determiner *nae* (5a) or a pronominal form (5b)? Or, on the other hand, is it realised as a negative polarity determiner *any* (6a) or a pronominal version (6b)? In addition, what social and linguistic constraints affect this realisation?

(5) a) If it wasna for them there would*na* be *nae shops* in Buckie.
    b) I'm *nae* going to get *nothing* back.

(6) a) I *canna* see *any* tonic, I'm nae drinking gin without tonic.
    b) She *wouldna* let *anybody* call me anything.

Similar to Cheshire's (1982:65) data from Reading, negative pronominals (e.g. *nothing*) in Buckie were found to have higher rates of negative concord than negative NPs (e.g. *nae shops*), an effect that Smith (2001) attributed to frequency arising from the open- versus closed-class status of negative forms, plus accompanying historical factors (cf. Howe 1995).

In the present chapter, in contrast, we concentrate on the variability in the presence of the sentential negation clitic -*n't*, variably realised as *na* in Buckie (5a), or its non-clitic form *not*, variably realised as *nae* (5b), and whether there is a negative NP elsewhere in the sentence. We are particularly interested in explaining the kind of variability illustrated in (7a–b), where both have a sentential negation meaning, but sentential negation itself can be absent.

(7) a) She did*na* have *nothing*.
    b) She had *nothing*.

We first removed tokens of negative subjects from the quantitative analysis, as our observation of the data showed categorical absence of sentential negation when the subject is negative, much as Cheshire (1982:64)

232 *David Adger and Jennifer Smith*

found in Reading. For example, although we have cases like (8a), there are no examples like (8b), and native speakers rejected them. (We return to why this is the case in Section 4.1)

(8) a) *Nobody* left.
    b) *Nobody did*na* leave.

We also removed cases of *or nothing* tags (9), which serve a distinct discourse function and can never be used on their own to express sentential negation, unlike negative NPs.

(9) Apparently you're *nae* allowed phones *or nothing* there.

In the remaining data, three main patterns emerge in the marking of sentential negation. The first is a sentential negation clitic with a negative polarity item (10), which we will call Standard Negation. The second is a sentential negation clitic with a negative NP object (11), which we will call Negative Concord. Finally, there are cases where the negation is expressed solely by a negative NP (i.e. there is no sentential negation clitic present) (12), which we will term NP Negation.

(10) a) I *canna* see *any* tonic, I'm nae drinking gin without tonic.
     b) She *wouldna* let *anybody* call me anything.

(11) a) Stuff like that *wouldna* do you *no harm* anyway.
     b) Fishermen *dona* get *nothing*. Not a penny.

(12) a) I've got *nothing* to worry about.
     b) Then the elevator opened and there was *nobody* there.

Table 3.3.1, which shows the proportion of the three types of sentential negation in Buckie, reveals robust variation: Standard Negation 39% of the time, Negative Concord 34% and NP Negation 27%. However, when we examined the data further, we found that the type of main verb – whether it was existential *be* (13), main verb (possessive) *have* (14) or other lexical verb (15) – has a major impact on the variation.

Table 3.3.1 Distribution of sentential negation in Buckie

Standard negation		Negative concord		NP negation	
n	%	*n*	%	*n*	%
196	39	172	34	139	27

Explaining Variability in Negative Concord   233

Table 3.3.2 Distribution of sentential negation by verb type in Buckie

	Existential be		have main verb		Other lexical verb	
	n	%	n	%	n	%
Standard negation	7	6	0	0	189	51
Negative concord	2	2	3	17	167	45
NP negation	111	93	15	83	13	4

(13) a) *There wasna any* witness.
   b) I was wanting to go to Barcelona but *there wasna nae* places.
   c) *There was really nothing* else I wanted to take fae the list.

(14) a) They *havena any money*.[1]
   b) They've never nae beds and Elgin *havena nae beds*.
   c) I couldna get picked up fae nobody 'cause *they had nae room* in their car.

(15) a) I *dona mind anybody* sticking a needle in.
   b) He didna get much warning, he *didna get nae warning* at all really
   c) I really *ken nothing* about it.

Table 3.3.2, which displays the proportion of verb types across the three negation types, shows that the makeup of Standard Negation and Negative Concord is very similar: nearly all of their occurrences appear with main lexical verbs, with barely any use of existential *be* or main verb *have* with these variants. Looking at existential *be*, from a total of 120 tokens, we find almost all tokens negated via NP Negation (93%). The same is true for possessive *have* (83%), although the total number of tokens here is much smaller ($N = 18$).

As the quantitative analysis shows, the structure of negation differs substantially in Buckie in terms of patterning across verb type. How can such a pattern be explained?

3.3.4 Syntactic Analysis

In this section we provide a syntactic analysis to explain a number of aspects of these patterns of variation. We first outline our assumptions about clause structure and the theory of negation adopted, following Haegeman's (1995) proposal that sentential negation involves syntactically licensing a negative projection in the clause. Section 4.2 then briefly turns to how this approach captures variability in the form of negative objects, and 4.3 addresses the question of the syntax of NP Negation. We take the former to involve variability in morphological form of the negative object (cf. Labov 1972) and argue that the latter involves a licensing of the negative object at a distance from the sentential negation projection. With this in place, in Section 4.4, we show how the Buckie pattern – where negative subjects cannot appear with a sentential negation marker, but negative objects can – follows from the theory. We then look at the quantitative effects discussed above, showing in Section 4.5 why possessive *have* behaves differently from lexical main verbs, and we extend this approach to existential and predicative *be* in Section 4.6.

3.3.4.1 Syntactic Assumptions

We will assume that sentences of English involve a tripartite syntactic structure: a verb phrase (VP) domain, where the verb selects its Subject, Object, and other arguments; a tense phrase (TP) domain, where tense information is specified and where finite auxiliaries appear in English; and a complementiser phrase (CP) domain, which expresses the grammatical force (statement, question, etc.) of the sentence, and is where complementisers in embedded clauses (e.g. *that*, *whether*) appear. We will ignore the CP domain in what follows.

Following much work (see Adger 2003), we represent syntax as a series of hierarchical structures. We use the kinds of structures and terminology associated with Minimalist Syntax, but many other theories adopt broadly similar ideas:

(16) [$_{TP}$ Auxiliaries [$_{VP}$ Subject [Verb Object]]]

We also adopt the idea (again, see Adger 2003) that the Subject is selected by the verb inside the VP, but in many English sentences, it appears in the TP domain, pronounced before finite auxiliaries, as in the following examples, where the emphatic auxiliary *did* and the aspectual auxiliary *have* bear finite tense marking:

(17) The girl DID often see films.
(18) The girl has often seen films.

Here, the Subject (*the girl*) is a selected dependent of the verb (*see*) but appears at some remove from it, in front of the auxiliary, in the TP domain. This means that syntactically, the Subject connects to the verb in terms of meaning (i.e. *the girl* is the semantic agent of the verb *see*) and to the auxiliary in terms of where it is pronounced in the structure. In our structures, we will therefore represent the Subject in both (a) the position

Explaining Variability in Negative Concord   235

that marks a dependency with the verb (not pronounced), and (b) before the auxiliary (pronounced), enclosing the unpronounced Subject token in angle brackets, as in (19).

(19) The girl DID often <the girl> see films.

Minimalist Syntax implements the idea that the Subject bears dependencies to both the TP domain and the VP domain by assuming that the grammatical rules that build up this sentence initially place the Subject inside the VP (local to the verb to which it is Subject) and that further rules displace the Subject to a higher position in the sentence, inside the TP. This displacement operation is tightly constrained: it moves the Subject to the closest position that is grammatically relevant to it. In the current case, this is the position immediately adjacent to the finite auxiliary. In Minimalist Syntax, this position is called the Specifier of the TP (what traditional grammars call the Subject position). Unlike many other languages, English requires that sentences have an NP in this position to be grammatical (Lasnik 2001). This movement operation will become important in our analysis of the variability of negative concord in Buckie.

Negation can be expressed in any domain (Zanuttini 1997), but English sentential negation is expressed in the TP domain via a specialised Negative position, which occurs below the finite auxiliary but above VP modifiers like *often*. The usual expression of English sentential negation is a negative clitic (*-n't* in most varieties, *na* in Buckie) (20).

(20) The girl did*na* often see films.

We can extend our structure for sentences with this negative element as in (21).

(21) [$_{TP}$ Subject [Negation ... [$_{VP}$ <Subject> [Verb Object]]]]

With this in place, the theory we adopt of sentential negation is the following (cf. Haegeman's [1995] Neg-Criterion):

(22) The Negation position must be linked to a pronounced negative element.

The devil will be in the details of what 'linked' can mean. Most commonly, linking is met by simply locating a negative clitic in the Negation position:

(23) [$_{TP}$ *The girl did* [Negation *na* [$_{VP}$ *often see films*]]]

3.3.4.2 Explaining Variability in the Form of Negative Objects

This theory of negation makes it straightforward to handle the variability between Standard Negation and Negative Concord in sentences such as (24)–(25).

(24) I did*na* see *any films*.
(25) I did*na* see *nae films*.

In both cases, all that is happening in Buckie, or in Cheshire's Reading data, is that sentential negation is expressed by *-na/-n't*. Variable expression of the negative determiner (*any* vs *nae*) (what Adger [2006] calls 'Variability in Exponence') follows the line of analysis instigated by Labov (1972), subject to the usual sociolinguistic pressures (Cheshire 1982; Smith 2001).

3.3.4.3 Explaining NP Negation

However, this theory does not yet provide an analysis of cases where there is a negative NP Object but no sentential negation, what we call NP Negation, as in Standard English (26) or in Buckie (27).

(26) I saw no films.
(27) a) There was really *nothing* else I wanted to take fae the list.
  b) I couldna get picked up fae nobody 'cause they had *nae room* in their car.
  c) I really ken *nothing* about it.

So far, the theory we have developed predicts – apparently incorrectly – that NP Negation should not express sentential negation, since the Negation position is outside the VP and has nothing linked to it. However, a closer look at the data shows that the situation is not as straightforward as it first seems.

Looking first at the cases with lexical main verbs in Buckie (27c), it turns out that, in contrast to judgments reported for Standard English (Labov 1972), these examples do not have a simple sentential negation reading. They must involve emphatic focus on the Object, typically expressed by emphatic stress on the Object, as in (28).

(28) I saw *nae films*

In terms of meaning, (28) does not express sentential negation: it does not deny the fact that any films were seen, it is rather a correction of a presupposition that some films were seen (Puskás 2012). We return to the existential and main verb *have* cases below, as these do express sentential negation and remain problematic for the theoretical proposal in (22). The special meaning of a negative NP with a lexical verb is consistent with the low frequency of this combination (4% in Table 3.3.2).

Of course, (22) still leaves open the problem of accounting for varieties like Standard English, where a sentential negation reading of (28) is actually possible.

The solution to this problem turns upon the interpretation of the word 'linked' in our theory of sentential negation. To capture the behaviour of Standard English, we need to say that the link between the Negative position and the negative Object must be 'stretched': that is, the Negative position is linked to *at a distance* by the negative NP Object (whether via movement [Kayne 1998] or c-command [Zeijlstra 2004]). We could represent this as in (29):

(29) [$_{TP}$ *The girl* [Negation [$_{VP}$ *saw no films*]]]

The details of the theory of how this link is made will not concern us here, as our focus is on the Buckie patterns.

Linking at a distance appears to be a highly marked option. Huang (2003) points out that the Buckie pattern, where negative Subjects do not co-occur with a sentential negation marker but negative Objects do, occurs widely cross-linguistically (e.g. Mandarin, Norwegian, Japanese), while the pattern where a negative Object does not occur with a sentential negation marker (as in Standard English), is rarer. We speculate that the Standard English pattern is a solution adopted to conform to prescriptive norms imposed by linguistic ideologies (Cheshire and Milroy 1993). Over the development of Standard English, these ideologies have sought to maintain the idea that a single semantic negation should correlate with a single syntactic expression of negation. However, vernacular Englishes (and languages in general: Haspelmath 2001) appear to work on a much simpler and more direct grammatical rule that imposes no such requirement and therefore allows sentential negation to be directly expressed in the Negation position in clausal structure. This then allows a negative Object to co-occur with a sentential negation marker, giving a negative concord pattern with negative Objects. This is presumably why such negative concord is, as Chambers has pointed out, close to a vernacular universal of English.

3.3.4.4 Negative Subjects

With this basic approach in place, we now turn to the observation we made in Section 3, that when the Subject is a negative NP, we find a categorical absence of the negative clitic to express sentential negation. This is clear from the corpus data, where there are no examples of negative

238   *David Adger and Jennifer Smith*

NP Subjects with the sentential negation clitic *na* or its non-clitic form *nae*, and backed up by grammaticality judgment evidence, where examples like (30b) are rejected by speakers of the variety.

(30)   a)   *Nobody* was any better off than anybody else
     b)   *Nobody was*na* any better off than anybody else

Our syntactic analysis of sentence structure, combined with the theory of negation in (22), leads us to expect this pattern.

To see this, recall that, to express sentential negation, the Negative position must be linked to a pronounced negative element. We have adopted the standard Minimalist view that the Subject, although pronounced once, appears in multiple positions in the syntactic representation: grammatical rules locate the Subject close to the verb that selects it and then move it to a higher grammatically relevant position. In the case of a negative Subject like *naebody*, the NP moves to Negation, which is grammatically relevant for it, before moving to its final position before the finite auxiliary. The first of these movements satisfies the link that needs to be made between Negation and a pronounced negative element, thereby allowing the sentence to express sentential negation. The second places the Subject in the usual surface position for Subjects in English, as shown in (31).

(31)   [TP *Nobody was* [Negation <Nobody> [VP <Nobody> *any better off* ...]]]

In this example, *nobody* satisfies the requirement that Negation be linked with a pronounced expression of negation. This means that this example can express sentential negation. The 'link' here is just the same as the link created when *na* is located in the Negative position. *Nobody* is located in three positions in our example: in the position where it is selected by the verb, in the Negative position, and in the position before the finite auxiliary where it is pronounced. Since *nobody* is located in Negation, *na* is not, capturing the impossibility of *na* in examples like (30b)[2].

Let us now turn to our main quantitative findings: the type of the main verb impacts on the variable realization of the sentential negation clitic.

3.3.4.5 *The Effect of Verb Type: Possessive Have*

We saw that sentential negation appears variably with main verb *have* with a negative Object:

(32)   a)   Elgin *havena nae beds*
     b)   They *had nae room* in their car.

Explaining Variability in Negative Concord 239

Buckie, like many varieties of Scots, allows main verb *have* to appear either inside the verb phrase domain, or in the tense phrase domain. We can see this by looking at adverbs:

(33) a) They've *often* lots to do at the end of the day.
    b) They *often* have lots to do at the end of the day.

Here, *have* appears on either side of the adverb *often*, contracted in (33a). Crucially, in (33a), the adverb separates *have* from its complement *lots to do*, a signature of a verb being displaced out of the VP (Pollock 1989).

This behaviour of *have* in Buckie opens up an explanation for the variability of the expression of sentential negation with a negative NP Object. In cases where *have* appears in the TP domain (the same position where tensed auxiliaries appear), the Object may move to Negation, just as negative Subjects do. This gives us a structure for (32b) in (34).

(34) [$_{TP}$ *They had* [Negation *nae room* [$_{VP}$ <*had*> <*nae room*> *in their car*]]]

In this structure, the position and order inside the VP between *have* and its negative Object are now mimicked higher in the clause (Fox and Pesetsky 2005), with *nae room* linked to Negation, allowing expression of sentential negation. The variant where *na* appears (32a) is legitimate because the Object (*nae beds*) stays in its original position, as shown in (35).

(35) [$_{TP}$ *Elgin have* [Negation *na* [$_{VP}$ <*have*> *nae beds*]]]

There is an important difference between examples like (32a–b) and the situation with negative Subjects. In the latter case, the Subject *must* move higher in the clause to the standard Subject position in English (the highest TP position). As mentioned above, this is a requirement of English sentence grammar. In moving from the VP, the Subject obligatorily passes through Negation, since that position is grammatically relevant. In contrast, there is no independent requirement for a negative Object of *have* to move and thus pass through Negation. This means that the movement of *nae beds* to Negation in (32a) is optional, unlike the movement of a negative Subject. If movement takes place, Negation is linked to the negative Object in accordance with (22). In the case where the option is not taken, Negation is instead linked to *na*. The net effect is that we will find variability in the expression of sentential negation when main verb *have* has a negative Object. Since no such option is available for negative Subjects, *na* is categorically unavailable. Variability in the expression of the sentential negation clitic *na* in sentences with possessive *have* is therefore only possible when *have* raises.

240 *David Adger and Jennifer Smith*

This approach to the syntax of *have* makes a prediction. In Buckie, we can force *have* to remain inside the VP. Only finite *have* can appear in the finite auxiliary position. This means that if we look at sentences where that position is filled by a different finite auxiliary, like a modal, then non-finite *have* must be inside the VP. In that situation, we predict that we must use the negative clitic *na*, since if we do not have *na* and we do not move the negative Object, we cannot express sentential negation. The prediction is correct: when we tested these examples with native speakers, it turned out that (36a) does not have a sentential negation reading, while (36b), as expected, does:

(36) a) *They can have nae bairns.
     b) They canna have nae bairns.

Of course, without saying anything else, if the movement of the negative Object is optional, we also predict (37), which is totally ungrammatical in Buckie, and in all other varieties of English we are aware of (though its analogues are grammatical in older varieties of Norwegian [Christensen 1986]):

(37) *They can nae bairns have.

However, (37) is independently ruled out by what has come to be known as Holmberg's Generalization (Holmberg 1986), which requires that the order of (pronounced) verbs and Objects be maintained both inside and outside the VP (Fox and Pesetsky 2005). In (37), the order of the verb and Object is reversed, violating the generalization. A discussion of the theoretical mechanisms used to explain Holmberg's Generalization will take us too far afield here. We will simply assume that it constitutes an independent reason for why examples like (37) are not found in varieties of English. Holmberg's Generalization will also rule out the movement of a negative Object of a lexical main verb, since such verbs are always inside the VP in English, which means that there is no way to move the Object without reversing the order.

3.3.4.6 *The Effect of Verb Type: Predicative and Existential Be*

We begin this section by discussing predicative uses of *be*, which we show can be explained by the theoretical approach we have developed so far. We then turn to our quantitative findings about existential *be*: we show that although speakers have a strong quantitative preference for NP Negation, their grammars are still variable, as predicted by this approach.

Explaining Variability in Negative Concord   241

In Scots, *none* (often spelled *nane*) may have a more widespread function than in Standard English. *The Dictionary of the Scots Language* describes such use as "*adv.* As an emphatic neg.: not at all, in no way, by no means (n. and m.Sc. 1963). Obs. in Eng. since 17th c" (https://www.dsl.ac.uk/entry/snd/nane, s.v. *nane*). The dictionary provides a number of examples, including (38a–c).

(38) a) Than ours they're *nane* mair fat and fair.
          Edb. 1772: Fergusson Poems (S.T.S.) II. 73
      b) I would hae said he wasna *nane* weel.
          Ags. 1889: Barrie W. in Thrums xxii
      c) He wiz nae *nane* surpriz't to see'r.
          Abd. 1926: Abd. Univ. Review (July) 223

In Buckie, *none* is still used in this function, although it appears to be restricted to a special class of negative psychological adjectives, as shown in (39).[3]

(39) a) She was *none* shy.
      b) He was *none* feart (afraid).

These negative adjectival phrases can appear without *na* expressing sentential negation, as in (39), or with *na*, showing a pattern of variability similar to that observed with main verb *have*, as in (40).

(40) a) She *wasna none* shy.
      b) He *wasna none* feart.

In all varieties of English, the finite forms of the verb *be* appear in the TP domain, not in the VP (Adger 2003), which means we can analyse these two examples on a par with our analysis of main verb *have*, as in (41)=(42).

(41) [$_{TP}$ *She was* [Negation *none shy* [$_{VP}$ <*was*> <*none shy*>]]]
(42) [$_{TP}$ *She was* [Negation *na* [$_{VP}$ <*was*> *none shy*]]]

As we saw with *have*, the negative phrase after the verb can either remain in its original position, in which case sentential negation is expressed by the negative clitic *na* being located in Negation, or by the negative phrase *none shy* itself moving to Negation.

However, there is an interesting difference between main verb *have* with negative quantifiers and main verb *be* with these negative adjectives. Unlike other negative quantifier phrases, *none* in these Scots varieties, as noted by the *Dictionary of the Scots Language*, is emphatic. We saw above that emphatic negatives could remain *in situ*, which leads us

242 *David Adger and Jennifer Smith*

to expect that, when *be* is not finite and has not moved into the TP domain, it should be possible to link Negation to *na*; but it is also possible to leave the emphatic negative adjective phrase *in situ*. This prediction is correct, as shown in (42)–(43).

(42) She will*na* be *none* shy with you.
(43) She'll be *none* shy with you.

Again, Holmberg's Generalization, or rather the syntactic mechanisms underlying it, predicts the impossibility of *She'll none shy be with you.

A similar pattern is observed with finite main verb *be* in cases where a negative NP is inside a prepositional phrase (PP). While adjectives have an emphatic negative degree word, creating negative adjectival phrases, PPs lack any such element. However, it is possible, of course, to have a negative NP inside a PP, as in (44).

(44) He *wasna* in *nae* fights.

In such cases, the negative quantifier is not obligatorily emphatic. Sentential negation in (44) is expressed by *na*, as expected. It is impossible to express sentential negation in such cases without *na*, unless the quantifier is stressed, as in (45).

(45) He was in NAE fights.

Such examples, like the cases with negative Objects of main verbs, only have a corrective reading, and require emphatic stress on *nae*. This can be captured by the approach developed here if we assume that a PP can never be negative (intuitively, the PP is not negative, though the NP inside it is). This means that it will never move to Negation, so the negative clitic *na* will always be required to express sentential negation.[4] Correctional negation can, however, be expressed by stress on the negative.

The final interesting case with main verb *be* is existentials, which our quantitative analysis picked out as having close to categorical absence of the sentential negation marker when a negative quantifier (phrase) appears to the left of the verb. In an existential construction, the Subject is usually assumed to remain inside the VP, with the verb *be* moving to the TP domain. Under this analysis, a sentence like *There were cakes on the table* has the structure in (46) (Adger 2003), with the expletive *there* appearing in the surface Subject position, and the Subject itself appearing lower.

(46) [$_{TP}$ *There were* [$_{VP}$ *cakes <were> on the table*]]

If the VP-internal Subject is a negative NP, we now expect it to (optionally) move to Negation or to remain *in situ*, in which case sentential negation will be expressed by *na*. Adapting the example to Buckie grammatical conventions about agreement in existentials gives us the structures in (47)–(48).[5]

(47) [$_{TP}$ *There was* [Negation *nae cakes* [$_{VP}$ *<nae cakes> <was> on the table*]]

(48) [$_{TP}$ *There was* [Negation *na* [$_{VP}$ *nae cakes <was> on the table*]]

However, as we saw in Table 3.3.2, existentials in the Buckie corpus appear almost without exception without *na*, suggesting a very strong preference for moving the negative Subject to Negation, as in (47).

Interestingly, acceptability judgment tasks with native speakers clearly showed that they allow negative concord with existentials, considering cases like (49) unexceptionable.

(49) There *wasna nae* food for the bairns.

From a perspective where speakers have a surface-oriented representation of the variant, as in Construction Grammar approaches (e.g. Hoffmann and Trousdale 2011), such a judgment is mysterious. Speakers will hear vanishingly few cases such as (49) as they acquire the dialect, so have no basis to posit a negative concord surface variant of the existential construction. However, the theory developed here, where speakers have an abstract grammar of Negation that is responsible for the surface variation, predicts judgments like (49). Speakers must posit an optional movement of a negative NP to Negation to account for optionality of the negative clitic with possessive *have* (more generally, this option is allowed by Universal Grammar, constrained by Holmberg's Generalization). Given this, their grammars will allow that movement in existentials too, even though they have no evidence for it in the input data. This is, we think, an advantage of the perspective we take here, as it provides syntactic underpinning for an understanding of the relationship between the structure of language and its use.

3.3.5 Conclusion

Negative Concord is one of the most widely attested linguistic variables in non-standard varieties of English, with Cheshire's Reading teenagers amply demonstrating this widespread form. In this chapter, we have briefly examined the variable grammar of Negative Concord in Buckie, focussing on variability in the presence of sentential negation markers. We have argued that speakers have an abstract set of grammatical rules that govern the variation and that the complex interactions of categorical and variable phenomena within this domain, noted by Cheshire in her Reading study, can be best explained through an approach that integrates perspectives and ideas from both formal and sociolinguistic theories.

Notes

1 Example (14a) is not found in the current corpus but is grammatical in this variety. The lack of such examples in the data may arise from the very infrequent occurrence of *have* as a main verb more generally, as demonstrated in Table 3.3.2.
2 There are varieties, as we noted earlier, which allow a negative Subject to co-occur with a sentential negation marker (e.g. AAVE, Labov 1972). We take this to be a parametric question of whether the specifier and head can both be filled simultaneously.
3 (39a) and (39b) do not appear in the current corpus but are used in the community.
4 It appears that predicate NPs in Buckie do not allow a negative determiner, which is why sentences like *Sue and Mary arena nae doctors* were judged ungrammatical.
5 A reviewer raises the interesting possibility that just the negative determiner *nae* raises to Negation, leaving the NP stranded in the lower position. Determining the consequences of this alternative would take us too far aside here. We leave this intriguing possibility for future research.

References

Adger, David. 2003. *Core Syntax*. Oxford: Oxford University Press.
Adger, David. 2006. "Combinatorial variability". *Journal of Linguistics* 42:503–530.
Burnett, Heather, Hilda Koopman and Sali Tagliamonte. 2018. "Structural explanations in syntactic variation: The evolution of English negative and polarity indefinites". *Language Variation and Change* 30(1):83–107. doi:10.1017/S0954394517000266
Chambers, J.K. 1995. *Sociolinguistic Theory: Linguistic Variation and Its Social Significance*. Oxford: Blackwell.
Cheshire, Jenny. 1982. *Variation in an English Dialect: A Sociolinguistic Study*. Cambridge: Cambridge University Press.
Cheshire, Jenny and James Milroy. 1993. "Syntactic variation in non-standard dialects: Background issues". In *Real English: The Grammar of English Dialects in the British Isles*, J. Milroy and L. Milroy (eds.). London: Longman. 3–33.
Childs, Claire. 2017. "Integrating syntactic theory and variationist analysis: The structure of negative indefinites in regional dialects of British English". *Glossa: A Journal of General Linguistics* 2(1):1–31.
Christensen, Kirsti. 1986. "Norwegian *ingen*: A case of post-syntactic lexicalization". In *Scandinavian Syntax*, Ö. Dahl and A. Holmberg (eds.). Stockholm: Institute of Linguistics, University of Stockholm. 21–35.
Coupland, Nikolas. 1988. *Dialect in Use*. Cardiff: University of Wales Press.
Edwards, Viv. 1993. "The grammar of southern British English". In *Real English: The Grammar of English Dialects in the British Isles*, J. Milroy and L. Milroy (eds.). New York: Longman. 214–242.
Fox, Danny and David Pesetsky. 2005. "Cyclic linearization of syntactic structure". *Theoretical Linguistics* 31(1–2):1–45.
Haegeman, Liliane. 1995. *The Syntax of Negation*. Cambridge: Cambridge University Press.

Explaining Variability in Negative Concord 245

Haspelmath, Martin. 2001. *Indefinite Pronouns*. Oxford: Oxford University Press.

Hoffmann, Thomas and Graeme Trousdale. 2011. "Variation, change and constructions in English". *Cognitive Linguistics* 22(1):1–23.

Holmberg, Anders. 1986. *Word Order and Syntactic Features in the Scandinavian Languages and English*. Stockholm: Department of General Linguistics, University of Stockholm.

Howe, Darin M. 1995. Negation in Early African American English. Unpublished Master's thesis, University of Ottawa, Ottawa, ON.

Howe, Darin M. and James A. Walker. 2000. "Negation in Early African American English: A creole diagnostic?" In *The English History of African American English*, S. Poplack (ed.). Oxford: Blackwell. 109–140.

Huang, C.-T. James. 2003. "The distribution of negative NPs and some typological correlates". In *Functional Structure(s), Form and Interpretation*, Y. Li and A. Simpson (eds.). New York: Routledge. 264–280.

Kayne, Richard S. 1998. "Overt vs. covert movements". *Syntax* 1(2):128–191.

Labov, William. 1972. "Negative attraction and negative concord in English grammar". *Language* 48:773–818.

Lasnik, Howard. 2001. "A note on the EPP". *Linguistic Inquiry* 32(2):356–362.

Pollock, Jean-Yves. 1989. "Verb movement, universal grammar, and the structure of IP". *Linguistic Inquiry* 20(3):365–424.

Puskás, Genoveva. 2012. "Licensing double negation in NC and non-NC languages". *Natural Language and Linguistic Theory* 30(2):611–649.

Schneider, Edgar W. 1989. *American Earlier Black English: Morphological and Syntactic Variables*. Tuscaloosa: University of Alabama Press.

Smith, Jennifer. 2001. "Negative concord in the Old and New World: Evidence from Scotland". *Language Variation and Change* 13(2):109–134.

Wolfram, Walt and Donna Christian. 1976. *Appalachian Speech*. Arlington, VA: Center for Applied Linguistics.

Zanuttini, Raffaella. 1997. *Negation and Clausal Structure: A Comparative Study of Romance Languages*. Oxford: Oxford University Press.

Zeijlstra, Hedde. 2004. *Sentential Negation and Negative Concord*. Utrecht: Netherlands Graduate School of Linguistics.

Section 4

Language Contact and Multiethnolects

4.1 Tracing the Origins of an Urban Youth Vernacular

Founder Effects, Frequency, and Culture in the Emergence of Multicultural London English

Paul Kerswill and Eivind Torgersen

4.1.1 The London Multiethnolect as a New Dialect

The last 40 years have seen a vibrant line of research focussed on new, urban language varieties in North-West Europe: from Scandinavia to Berlin, via Britain, the Netherlands, and Belgium, high-migration areas of cities are the sites of new varieties of the majority languages, developing alongside, and occasionally supplanting, existing urban dialects (Kotsinas 1988; Quist 2008; Cheshire et al. 2011; Nortier and Svendsen 2015; Wiese forthcoming). Most of these new varieties have become *enregistered* (Agha 2007), in the sense that social, often negative, meaning is attached to them (Kircher and Fox 2019). The external conditions for this emergence have involved the arrival of relatively large numbers of people, in many cases from former colonies in the Global South, a fact which largely determines which languages will form the input to the new varieties. In these multilingual neighbourhoods, the new residents' children are not simply assimilated linguistically to the majority speech community; instead, young people are socialised and acquire language in an environment that is both multilingual and multicultural, which, in turn, has the potential to lead to contact-induced language change. We have argued (Cheshire et al. 2011) that the mechanism for change is via a *feature pool* of available linguistic forms (Mufwene 2001:4–6), from which selections are made.

The above outlines the mechanism behind the linguistic developments leading to what are often referred to as *multiethnolects* (e.g., Quist 2008; Wiese forthcoming), such as Multicultural London English (MLE) (Cheshire et al. 2011). The formation of these varieties has some of the characteristics of koineisation, or new-dialect formation (Trudgill 1986, 2004; Kerswill and Trudgill 2005; Kerswill 2013a), in that a significant element of dialect contact is present, involving not only mutually intelligible dialects, but also, critically and decisively, second-language or learner varieties of the majority language – the key factor distinguishing multiethnolect formation from koineisation (even though second-language and learner varieties may be present in the latter). In particular, we see that language contact leading to language shift is a crucial component because the (mainly adult) L2 speakers of the majority language use features from their first or prior language(s) through the process of interference or *imposition* (Van Coetsem 1988). In this chapter, we pursue the idea that demography is an important part of understanding the products of contact, in a manner consistent with Trudgill's (2004) deterministic model of new-dialect formation.

An important issue, however, is whether or not multiethnolects can be considered as vernaculars, in the sense both of a dialect characteristic of a community and as the psychologically entrenched main variety spoken alongside other less-entrenched varieties, such as the standard (Labov 1972; Sharma 2018). The alternative is to consider multiethnolects as a stylistic resource for speakers (Quist 2008), with no strong implication of entrenchment. However, taking 'vernacular' and 'style' as exclusive categories is never a tenable position, all the more so for multiethnolects, which are more variable in their linguistic features than might be expected for regional varieties in general. Extreme variability means that delimiting MLE linguistically is problematic. However, taking MLE as a salient, *enregistered* (Agha 2007) part of individual repertoires de-emphasises the vernacular/style argument and allows us to see MLE as an entity containing a set of features, with some features 'in' and others 'out'. This may seem essentialistic, but it is intended to tap into people's beliefs and ideologies. Currently there is relatively limited empirical research dealing with the perception of MLE: Cardoso et al. (2019) show that a valid approach is to search for an association between an 'accent density' index and subjective reactions to different degrees of 'broadness' of MLE. Further to this, an important result of Kircher and Fox's (2019) online study of attitudes to MLE is the high degree to which respondents were able to make a direct link from the label 'Multicultural London English' to an entity which they recognised but had perhaps not given a name to (p. 852).

A further issue is to establish how a multiethnolect is distributed across a speaker's lifespan: is it acquired as part of initial language learning, or as a second dialect in childhood or adolescence? Does it become the speaker's dominant variety? When do people stop using it, if indeed they do? The speaker's age on acquisition will affect the types of features acquired (Kerswill 1996). There seems to be agreement that most (but not all) multiethnolects are acquired as second dialects and thus not vernaculars in any strict sense. They invariably build on the phonological, grammatical and lexical structure of the first dialect, which remains the basis of the variety (Wiese 2009:803, footnote 30). In many cases, multiethnolects as second dialects are youth languages, actively deployed to mark a heightened identity, often of an oppositional and exclusionary nature; nevertheless, they may endure into adulthood (Kießling and

Mous 2006; Rampton 2011, 2015). For many speakers MLE is an unmarked choice, acquired in fairly early childhood (by the age of 4–5), thus potentially constituting a vernacular for these speakers (Cheshire et al. 2011:164–165).

Finally, the question arises as to the recency of the individual features which constitute the feature pool. Answering this question is the core concern of this chapter. First, we consider the features that can be said to constitute MLE. In doing so, we evaluate the possible relevance of both Mufwene's (1996) notion of a *founder effect* and Trudgill's (2004) *determinism model* for the formation of this multiethnolect.

4.1.2 Features of MLE

Drawing boundaries between MLE and non-MLE masks the complexity of speakers' observable usage as well as their conceptualisations of their own language use – that is, what they themselves believe they are speaking; the concept of enregisterment is useful here, as we have seen. Nevertheless, we will discuss some of the main features of MLE, comment on their use, and explore the possible origins of the features.

Speakers of a multiethnolect may use features which differentiate it from other relevant varieties on every linguistic level, and MLE is no exception (Cheshire et al. 2011; Kerswill et al. 2008; Torgersen and Szakay 2012; Cheshire et al. 2013b). Individual features may form part of coherent subsystems – especially phonology, morphology, or syntax – as suggested by Wiese and Rehbein (2016). As already noted, many speakers start acquiring the features of the variety at a young age, particularly the phonological features, and may use a sizeable set of features in early adolescence (to say a 'full' set would be misleading) (Kerswill et al. 2013). Our research shows that MLE features are spread via multicultural friendship groups, with the male non-Anglo speakers (descendants of immigrants mainly from the Global South) as the highest users overall. The high-frequency users have been identified as linguistic innovators, and these individuals can have both Anglo and non-Anglo ethnic backgrounds, which demonstrates that MLE is, to some extent, ethnically neutral (Cheshire et al. 2008). The vowel features include near-monophthongal qualities for some diphthongs, notably FACE and GOAT (Kerswill et al. 2008), and an extremely fronted GOOSE vowel (Cheshire et al. 2008). In turn, this has an effect on speech rhythm: the monophthongs (inherently?) have a shorter duration than diphthongal variants used in other varieties, giving rise to a more syllable-timed speech rhythm (Torgersen and Szakay 2012). Both FLEECE and GOOSE lack the characteristic diphthongisation of Cockney with central onsets (Wells 1982:308; and below). Consonantal features include h-reinstatement (i.e. there is little h-dropping in MLE) and k-backing, the backing of /k/ to [q] in stressed position before non-high back vowels (Fox and Torgersen 2018).

252   *Paul Kerswill and Eivind Torgersen*

Morphosyntactic features include loss of indefinite and definite article allomorphy (Gabrielatos et al. 2010; Cheshire et al. 2011), both levelling and innovation for past tense *be* in negative polarity contexts (Cheshire and Fox 2009), use of relative pronoun *who* as a topic-marker (Cheshire et al. 2013a), use of the pronoun *man* (Cheshire 2013), the rise of the quotative *this is + speaker* (Fox 2012), and innovation in the use of pragmatic markers, in particular *you get me* (Torgersen et al. 2011). The use of *you get me* shows age effects, with teenagers being more frequent users than younger speakers and male non-Anglo speakers the highest users overall (Torgersen et al. 2018). A similar age effect is present for the fronting of GOOSE (which shows incrementation; Labov 2007:346), with teenagers having the most fronted qualities (Cheshire et al. 2011). Incrementation is also found for the widespread quotative *be like*, though it is absent for the innovative quotative *this is + speaker* (Cheshire et al. 2011:180). This pattern shows that global English features in MLE, such as GOOSE-fronting and *be like*, follow general trends, while local, innovative features in general do not.

We will argue that understanding the demographic history of post-Second World War London is an initial key to arbitrating between possible geographical and linguistic origins for the features of MLE. Table 4.1.1 provides a summary of potential origins for the key MLE features discussed in this chapter, based on the proportion of immigrants from the respective regions, as well as from London and the South-East of England.

4.1.3 Beginnings, Repertoires, and Boundaries

There are few published accounts of young people's speech in London in the post-Second World War era. The earliest appears to be Hurford (1967), who studied the phonology of members of an East End family in Bethnal Green in London's East End born between 1885 and 1953. The dialect he describes is largely a continuation of that of the four elderly Bethnal Green women studied by Sivertsen (1960). Beaken (1971) studied a sample of four- to nine-year-olds from Bow, also in the East End. While their vowels were similar to those of Hurford's participants, Beaken offers for the first time a comment on ethnicity and language:

> Large-scale immigration into the area [Tower Hamlets in London's traditional East End] had not taken place, either of native English speakers from other parts of London, or of English-speaking but not native-born immigrants. Fordway School had a small minority of children of Asian origin who were not native English speakers. There were also some West Indian children, but those were mainly from families which had been in the area for some time: some of these "West Indians" were in fact English, having been born in the district. *The speech of the older ones was to all intents and purposes indistinguishable from that of the white children. In other words,*

Tracing Origins of Urban Youth Vernacular   253

a slight influx of immigrants into the area had not significantly af-
fected the linguistic homogeneity of the community.
(Beaken 1971:14, quoted in Cheshire et al. 2008:1–2; our emphasis)

We quote Beaken at length because it shows, first, that by the mid-1960s
the traditional East End had not yet become the highly multiethnic area

Table 4.1.1 Possible sources of MLE features

Feature	Possible origins	Comment
Raised, narrow diphthongs or monophthongs for FACE and GOAT Back FOOT Monophthongal FLEECE and GOOSE	Englishes from Caribbean, Africa, Indian Subcontinent; learner varieties	Contrast with FOOT, which is undergoing fronting in South-Eastern varieties
Front GOOSE *speaker + be like*	Global features acquired from local varieties	Age pattern as for other varieties (incrementation)
/d/ for initial /ð/ /t/ for /θ/ in *thing* and indefinite pronouns containing -*thing* and *thief* 'steal'	Caribbean Creoles, African Englishes, learner varieties	/t/ for /θ/ mainly restricted to these items; otherwise fronting to /f/, as in South-East England generally
Uvular /k/ before non-high back vowels	Arabic	Demography of Arabic speakers in London makes this unlikely
Reinstatement of initial /h/	Standard English? Learner varieties? A general feature of South-Eastern varieties	Jamaican Creole and Yoruba English are variably h-dropping. MLE speakers are ahead of other working-class groups in h-reinstatement
Loss of /ə/ ~ /i/ allomorphy in *the*, /ə/ ~ /ən/ allomorphy in *a*	Contact-induced simplification	
Tendency to syllable timing	West African and Subcontinental Englishes, Jamaican English/Creole.	Contact feature? Found in other multiethnolects
Aks for *ask*	Caribbean Creole, West African English	
Relative *who* as topic-marker	Internal change	
Discourse marker *you get me*	Caribbean Creole	
Pronominal *man*	Jamaican Creole; internal changes	Expanded scope and use in MLE
Slang: *blood, man* (as discourse marker), *ends, fam, creps ...*	Jamaican Creole, African American English, local coinage	Salient slang terms from Jamaica, also African American (Green 2014)

254   *Paul Kerswill and Eivind Torgersen*

it would become by the 1980s and, second, that the few non-White British residents had assimilated linguistically with the majority. This observation that the minority ethnic population, specifically the Jamaicans, were not distinguishable from the White British speakers is important, since this did not remain the case, with the emergence of new styles. This increase in the diversity of local varieties of English, to some extent along ethnic lines but still with many shared linguistic features, is part of the development of what we now recognise as MLE. At the same time, it is important to track the rapid demographic development of London's inner city in order to draw conclusions about the linguistic inputs to the area and to interpret changes both in language structure and in speaker repertoires.

The presence of an ethnically neutral, but distinct *youth* variety in London, differing from the local London dialect, was first noted in the academic literature in the 1980s, with Hewitt's study of black youth language (1986, 1990):

> ....in the many urban areas where black and white were born and grew up together, attending the same schools and occupying the same recreational spaces, one linguistic consequence is that both Cockney and Creole have come to have an impact on the speech of black and white alike. Indeed *there has developed in many inner city areas a form of 'community English', or multiracial vernacular which, while containing Creole forms and idioms, is not regarded as charged with any symbolic meanings relating to race and ethnicity and is in no way related to boundary maintaining practices* [our emphasis]. Rather it is, if anything, a site within which ethnicity is deconstructed, dismantled and reassembled into a new ethnically mixed 'community English'. The degree of Creole influence on the specific local vernacular is often higher in the case of young black speakers but the situation is highly fluid and open to much local variation. There is, therefore, a two-way movement ... in which a de-ethnicised, racially mixed local language is creatively being established alongside a strategic, contextually variable use of Creole ... often employed as [a] marker of race in the context of daily anti-racist struggle.
>
> (Hewitt 1990:191–192)

Hewitt notes the rise not of one, but two language varieties. Chronologically the first is London Jamaican (Sebba 1993, 2008; Patrick 2008), which is a variant of Jamaican Creole mixed with British English, characterised by Hewitt as "a strategic, contextually variable use of Creole ... a marker of race", while the second variety is the ethnically neutral "multiracial vernacular". The story of London Jamaican is important for the history of MLE. It was acquired as a second dialect by many

Tracing Origins of Urban Youth Vernacular 255

African Caribbean adolescents as part of a new 'resistance identity' (Castells 1997). This is highlighted by the criminologist John Pitts who, referring to the time when he was a youth worker in South London in 1968–71, states:

> I realised I was witnessing the birth of a resistance identity … when I started working with black kids, in youth work, they all talked like Ian Wright [retired London-born footballer with Jamaican parentage who speaks with a London (Cockney) accent – PK/ENT] and within a few short years they all sounded like Bob Marley [Jamaican reggae artist – PK/ENT].
>
> (Pitts 2012)

Pitts's comments appear to date the beginnings of London Jamaican fairly precisely to the late 1960s/early 1970s, a claim that is at least partly corroborated by Hewitt (1982:217), citing a report by the Community Relations Committee (1976), though it doesn't provide a *terminus ante quem*:

> It is often pointed out to us that sometimes during their early teens at secondary school many West Indian pupils who up till then have used the language of the neighbourhood, begin to use creole dialect … Its use is a deliberate social and psychological protest, and an assertion of identity.

This observation refers to the acquisition of London Jamaican by West Indian children as they enter secondary school – a case of second-dialect acquisition. In their survey of school children's language use in London, Rosen and Burgess (1980) discuss what they call 'London/Jamaican'; this also places the development back to the 1970s at the very latest. They conclude (1980:67): "We can go no further … than to conjecture that … London/Jamaican in all its variety is a relatively independent entity attracting some pupils of Caribbean origin rather than others" – a claim that, although Rosen and Burgess did not collect speech data, suggests that the variety has some social reality and even stability, at least for these commentators.

'Identity' seems central to the emergence of London Jamaican, perhaps linked to London-based Caribbean and other popular music at the time (Sebba 1993:8–9). Its influence on the later, now dominant, grime genre is frequently discussed (Varghese 2017; Beaumont-Thomas 2018), as is grime's pervasive use of MLE with its mainly Jamaican-based lexis and slang (Drummond 2016; Varghese 2017) – a point we return to.

The second new language variety, Hewitt's 'multiracial vernacular', clearly postdates London Jamaican – probably by between five and ten years. From his description, the multiracial vernacular is at its base

London English with a few 'forms and idioms' from Creole. Above all, it 'is not regarded as charged with any symbolic meanings relating to race and ethnicity' but is a "new ethnically mixed 'community English'". Neither he nor Sebba (1993:59–60) provide any specific linguistic information about this variety. Rampton (2011) likewise does not characterise multiracial vernaculars linguistically, rather he emphasises their function in a specific interaction and sees them as having "emerged, [being] sustained and [being] felt to be distinctive in ethnically mixed urban neighbourhoods shaped by immigration and class stratification", while their speakers also use crossing (i.e., the strategic use of features and words from the language of a group other than one's own) as a conversational strategy (Rampton 2011:291).

Some limited indications of the linguistic features of the multiracial vernacular may, however, be deduced from Patrick (2008), who briefly mentions that elements of British Creole are used between whites and blacks, but it is "socially limited and grammatically restricted" (Patrick 2008:255). However, when dealing with the vowel system he lists a full range of realisations covering traditional Cockney, Jamaican Creole, and Jamaican English as well as intermediate forms. Patrick mentions a feature that is very much part of today's MLE (and mentioned in Section 4.1.2 above): the lack of the characteristic London diphthongisation of vowels of the FLEECE and GOOSE classes, which have undergone so-called Diphthong Shift (Kerswill et al. 2008). Table 4.1.2 shows this feature.

Patrick's speculation about this pattern is telling, suggesting by implication a link between London Jamaican and MLE: "One wonders whether BrC [British Creole], like AAVE (Labov 2001), might provide a locus for non-participation in predominant vowel shifts" (2008:260). These monophthongal variants are very much present not only in MLE (Table 4.1.1) but also in the speech of teenage African Caribbean Londoners recorded by Sebba in the early 1980s; these speakers do not otherwise use MLE features or sound Cockney (cf. Kerswill and Sebba 2011). The overall picture, however, is that few of the phonetic and grammatical features of MLE (Section 4.1.2, above) were present in the

Table 4.1.2 Realisation of *fleece* and *goose* vowels in London (Cockney), London Jamaican and multicultural London English

	London (Cockney)	*London Jamaican*	*MLE*
FLEECE	əi	iː	iː
GOOSE	əʉ	uː	ʉː

Adapted from Patrick (2008:260), Kerswill et al. (2008:466–447), Cheshire et al. (2011).

multiracial vernacular. It is London English-based and non-ethnic, but it is not a vernacular in the sense we have defined it here, since it is a second dialect and, to judge from the commentaries, also secondary in the speakers' repertoires. We now consider whether, and in what sense, the multiracial vernacular is a precursor to MLE.

MLE came to the attention of the research community in two sociolinguistic studies of multiethnic inner-city districts in East London between 2004[1] and 2010.[2] The first public mention of the variety is as 'Jafaican', in the *Evening Standard* in April 2006 (Kerswill 2014); 'MLE' was coined by the research group in the same year. Given the commentaries above, its beginnings must postdate the start of Hewitt's multiracial vernacular; the early 1980s is an informed suggestion. Because MLE is so different from London English, particularly in its phonology, and because for some speakers it is a vernacular, it is no longer realistic to claim that it is simply a continuation of the multiracial vernacular, "characterised by both lexis and, perhaps more markedly today, pronunciation" (Cheshire et al. 2008:2) because this account does not capture the transition to vernacular status for many speakers. What MLE does share with the multiracial vernacular is the availability of Jamaican and African American slang (Kerswill 2013b; Green 2014), with some slang being involved in acts of crossing. There is clearly continuity, but the changes seem to have been quite great in both linguistic form and sociolinguistic status.

The stability of form that MLE takes today for many speakers is true particularly of the phonological component: segmental phonology, timing, and prosody are likely to be relatively stable at the individual level. In formal contexts, speakers can produce standard speech maintaining the phonology, while avoiding the morphosyntactic and discourse features. In this respect, MLE is a regional accent indexing a set of social characteristics, in the same way as other regional accents in Britain.

4.1.4 MLE as a Contact Dialect

So far, we have not considered in detail the process by which the features of MLE came into being. Multiethnolects such as MLE are the product of language contact, and in that respect their histories resemble those of creoles: people find themselves in the position of having to acquire new linguistic features in order to integrate linguistically with others. In the creolisation case, there is at first no existing target but rather limited exposure to a language that will become the lexifier. In the multiethnolect case, speakers are exposed to an ambient or majority language for which there are adequate models and some availability, though learning may be constrained by the fact that, initially, the learning is largely performed by adults and without explicit instruction. The first stage of multiethnolect formation, then, is composed of adult language learning and childhood acquisition of the majority language as an L1 or L2. This does not differ

258 *Paul Kerswill and Eivind Torgersen*

from other cases where adults and children migrate. What differs is that MLE speakers do not necessarily integrate into the majority linguistic community because access is restricted, with concomitantly greater contact taking place with other language learners. The first generation of children growing up do not have access to a ready-made community of older adolescent and adult native speakers, either in their own families or in their neighbourhoods and schools. But the formation of MLE is not a once-and-for-all thing. Because immigration rates remain high, the process is presumably being repeated locally. Hence, the durability of the above-mentioned MLE features as a norm remains to be seen; there are already indications of recent sociolinguistic and linguistic change, as well as marked differences between locations and communities (Gates 2018; Ilbury 2019).

Creolisation and dialect formation (including koineisation and, as we shall see by extension, multiethnolect formation) are argued to be points on a continuum and therefore not entirely distinct (Siegel 1997:139; Mufwene 2008; Winford 2017:196). In both cases, the *frequency* of linguistic elements in a situation of language and dialect mixing is seen as crucial (Trudgill 2004; Mufwene 2008:48). At the same time, Mufwene (1996) has argued for a *founder effect*, by which an originating speaker group has an apparently disproportionate effect on the later dialect in relation to their number, due to the fact that they establish a pattern which is then acquired by new arrivals. (See Kerswill 2018:19 on its role in the formation of new dialects in Britain.)

To understand the formation of MLE, we need, then, to look both at the frequency of features and the effect of a founding population, if it can be identified; in other words, we are placing a premium on a demographic argumentation (Trudgill 2004). We have already suggested a special role for African Caribbean varieties – creoles and Englishes – for the post-Second World War development of youth language in London. We must also assume that it is migration in the earlier part of the post-war period that is relevant, up to around 1980. At the same time, we must scrutinise the proportion of London's population that the foreign-born residents constitute at any one time. We now examine what demographic evidence can be adduced.

4.1.4.1 Caribbean Migration

Today's inner-city London is linguistically very diverse; however, it was much less so in the 15 years after the end of the Second World War. Migration to London (Inwood 1998:412; Fox 2015:18–28) has for centuries been a major factor in the city's cultural and economic development, though it is not clear what, if any, linguistic effects there might have been until the post-Second World War period (Kerswill and Torgersen 2016:86). The beginning of post-Second World War immigration is usually said to date from the arrival in London of the *Empire Windrush* in 1948 with 492 "mostly young skilled or semi-skilled workmen from Jamaica" (Inwood 1998:855). This number is minuscule, though it complements around 15,000 people of West Indian birth already present in Britain by 1951, of whom 4,200 were in London (Inwood 1998:856). Immigration from the Caribbean slowly increased in the next two decades, as shown in Table 4.1.3.

Inwood (1998:856) states, "[b]y early 1961, when the census was taken, there were 172,379 people of West Indian birth in the UK, and 98,811 in Greater London. Of the London West Indians, about 55 per cent were Jamaicans [...]". Given that the population of London in 1961 was 8 million (Demographia, n.d.), this indicates that the Caribbean-born population constituted 1.2% of the total – a small proportion.

After a sharp peak in 1960–1961, immigration to the UK from the Caribbean tailed off (see Figure 4.1.1 and Tables 4.1.3–4.1.5), though African Caribbeans continued to be the biggest non-UK-born group until 1981 (Dorling and Thomas 2016:97). The fall in the number of Caribbeans is mirrored by a drop in the number of people who identify ethnically as Caribbean after 1981 (Tables 4.1.4 and 4.1.5). This drop is the consequence of demographic changes which are likely to have had linguistic consequences: Owen (1995:7) states that "[t]he decline in the estimated Caribbean and Cypriot populations is a reflection of the UK-born children of migrants from these ethnic groups leaving the parental home to form their own households". Owen also mentions that there was an increasing number of people of mixed parentage and of people who did not wish to be classified as West Indian (1995:7). This can be taken as an indication of the broadening of West Indian networks to encompass other ethnicities, particularly the majority White British one, and would have been a conduit for the spread of Caribbean linguistic features among the rest of the population at the time.

Table 4.1.3 Total arrivals in the UK from the Caribbean (West Indies), 1948–1961 (home office data)

Year	Arrivals in Britain	Year	Arrivals in Britain
1948	1,200	1955	30,370
1949	1,000	1956	33,400
1950	1,400	1957	27,620
1951	1,000	1958	20,710
1952	2,200	1959	22,390
1953	2,300	1960	57,170
1954	9,200	1961	74,590

Sources: 1948–1951: Inwood (1998:856), 1952–1961: Peach (1967:37).

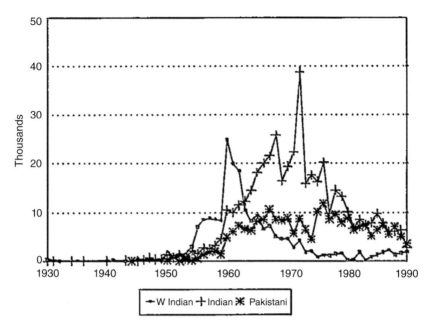

Figure 4.1.1 Dates of entry of West Indian, Indian and Pakistani people to Great Britain (Owen 1995:4, Figure 4).

4.1.4.2 South Asian Immigration: India, Pakistan, and Bangladesh

The post-1961 period continued to see increasing, and much more diverse, immigration. Figure 4.1.1 shows the great increase in immigration from India in the 1960s and 1970s, which reduced before picking up rapidly again in the 1990s and 2000s (Owen 1995; Dorling and Thomas 2016:89), after our period of interest. The vast majority of this large-scale wave of immigration from the Indian subcontinent was from India itself, with a high proportion settling in London. Tables 4.1.4–4.1.6 show the major countries of birth of London residents in the 1971, 1981 and 1991 censuses, with Table 4.1.6 additionally showing the number of people in Great Britain from the corresponding ethnic groups in 1991 (the correspondence with country of birth is necessarily approximate).

The tables show relatively large-scale immigration from the South Asian countries, particularly India and Bangladesh. Immigration from this region had overtaken that from the Caribbean by 1981, though the Caribbeans remained a large group.

4.1.4.3 African Migration

Immigration from Sub-Saharan Africa, principally former British colonies such as Kenya and Nigeria, became significant later than that from

Tracing Origins of Urban Youth Vernacular 261

Table 4.1.4 London: country of birth 1971 (1971 census, via London datastore)

	Count	Percent
Total	7,236,721	100.0
UK	6,331,952	87.5
Africa	74,660	1.0
Caribbean	165,369	2.3
India	104,001	1.4
Pakistan	29,395	0.4

Table 4.1.5 London: country of birth 1981 (1981 census)

	Count	Percent
Total	6,608,598	100.0
UK	5,405,576	81.8
Africa	144,066	2.2
Caribbean	167,407	2.5
India	139,123	2.1
Bangladesh	22,108	0.3
Pakistan	35,625	0.5

Table 4.1.6 London: country of birth and size of New Commonwealth ethnic groups 1991 (1991 census)

	Count	Percent	Ethnic group	Count
Total	6,679,699	100.0		
UK	5,228,658	78.3		
Africa	183,341	2.7	Black African	163,635
Caribbean	150,745	2.3	Caribbean	290,968
India	151,619	2.3	Indian	347,091
Bangladesh	56,657	0.8	Bangladeshi	85,738
Pakistan	44,741	0.7	Pakistani	87,816

South Asia (cf. Tables 1.4.4–1.4.6). The numbers of Londoners born in Africa equalled their Indian-born counterparts in 1981, exceeding them by a comfortable margin by 1991. At the same time, the Caribbean became a less significant source of migrants, while people with a Caribbean background remained roughly on a par numerically with the other two major groups. In 1991, already ten years after our time period, there were still only slightly over half as many Londoners of Black African ancestry as there were African Caribbeans (Table 4.1.6, last two columns). By 2001, the two groups were numerically equal, while only by 2011

262   Paul Kerswill and Eivind Torgersen

did the Africans outnumber the Caribbeans, by a large margin: 573,931 versus 344,597 (London Datastore n.d., Table 31).

4.1.4.4 Conclusion – Migration

After 1948, immigration increased only slowly at first, in numbers that were proportionally small. The question arises as to when incoming varieties began to change the phonology and grammar of inner-city London speech. One possibility is that they never did, that varieties like MLE are always secondary dialects, remaining distinct from the inherited local varieties, and are instead the product of migrants living in communities out of touch with locally descended populations. Most ethnic/linguistic groups in London have not, however, been isolated, with the result that the MLE repertoire is today more or less shared. In Section 4.1.5, we consider the possibility of early post-Second World War contact and change more analytically.

Migration at first mainly involved people from one region: the Caribbean. Notably, roughly half of this group came from Jamaica. Almost all of those who came from the Caribbean spoke an English-lexifier creole and most would have been familiar with English (we consider the consequences of this fact below). Later migrations, at first from South Asia and then Sub-Saharan Africa, were more linguistically diverse – especially the latter. Mitigating this linguistic diversity is the fact that a proportion of these immigrants, being from former British colonies, had at least some knowledge of English. To these must be added a large number of speakers of other languages who came from other regions, such as North Africa, Turkey, and Europe, but whose numbers were initially smaller. Nevertheless, the proportion of residents who were immigrants or the children of immigrants remained small overall in the early years, though, as we argue below, there is evidence of high concentrations at a local level. If there was an influence, we can hypothesise that the order in which the different national groups came had an impact on the outcomes in terms of youth language and, later, local vernaculars.

4.1.5   London Youth Varieties and the *Founder Principle*: Jamaican Advantage?

4.1.5.1 The Demographic Argument

We are now in a position to apply an argument based on demographic change in order to account for the features of the three varieties we have discussed – London Jamaican, the multiracial vernacular, and Multicultural London English. We ask the question of whether Jamaican English and Creole were more likely to leave linguistic traces than other varieties because this group was the first to arrive in numbers in post-war London.

In examining demographic history, we are going beyond the discussion of the origins of MLE features in Cheshire et al. (2011:158–164), where the focus was on the acquisition of MLE by children and adolescents. Mufwene's (2001) *Founder Principle* provides us with a demographic model, albeit focussed on creoles. According to Mufwene, the principle serves "to explain how structural features of creoles have been predetermined to a large extent (though not exclusively!) by characteristics of the vernaculars spoken by the populations that founded the colonies in which they developed" (Mufwene 2001:28–29). By analogy with population dynamics, those linguistic features in the initial mix that are relatively frequent in a new community have a selective advantage. Newly arrived incomers, especially their children, then acquire these features. In subsequent generations, for an incoming population to cause any change to the variety, the proportion of newcomers to the established population needs to be high; Kerswill (2018) estimates that the figure could be as high as 50%. This argumentation is problematic for the claim that the arrival of immigrants in the post-Second World War period in London led to changes in local speech; as we have seen, the proportions of any one ethnic or linguistic group lay between around one and two and a half percent in the period up to 1981, with the UK-born population always in a large majority.

How could the incoming groups have caused change? The first thing to note is that they did not at first. As we have seen, reports from the early period show that the Caribbean migrants' children acquired London dialect (Cockney) features. In his late-1960s study, Beaken (1971:134) observed young West Indians moving away from Caribbean features in their speech as they approached secondary school age, and Labov (2001:507) makes a similar observation in the 1980s that young Jamaicans were using a dialect that was not distinguishable from that of other working-class Londoners. Similarly, in the early 1980s, Sebba found that young Londoners of Jamaican origin were not reliably heard as 'black' and were largely indistinguishable from their Anglo counterparts – though, significantly, some African Caribbean speakers were nonetheless heard as 'black' (Sebba 1993:66–70). But by this decade, the movement was in the opposite direction from that which Beaken describes, with older Caribbean children using *more* Creole features than young children, usage reportedly peaking in the late teens (see discussion in Sebba 1993:38–39). This is entirely consistent with Pitts's comments, mentioned above.

Up to this point, there is no mention of any general change in London's vernacular speech caused by an influx of people speaking languages other than English, nor is there any evidence of a new, relatively stable, pan-ethnic, youthful urban contact vernacular, which is consistent with the idea of a founder effect: London English remained firmly in place; it was certainly changing, but not necessarily in a direction that might be predicted by the presence of extensive language and dialect contact. Instead, there are youth varieties – London Jamaican and the multiracial vernacular – which were very much in-group varieties, used as styles or registers additional to the local vernacular.

It is only with the emergence of MLE that there is any indication that a new contact variety was becoming a central part of some young people's repertoires to the extent that, for some, it became a vernacular in Labov's sense. Thus, it had the potential to influence or even replace the local variety. The formation of MLE, as well as the expansion of its contexts of use, most likely began around the early 1980s, doubtless with local variations. Because of this relatively late timing, we should also examine influences from the other major languages spoken in London, including Punjabi, Bengali, Chinese, Yoruba, and other Asian and African languages as well as Turkish, Greek, and other European languages. London Jamaican is no longer a mainstream youth variety among Caribbean youth, though it continues to be used in social networks dominated by Caribbean-descended people (Christian Ilbury, personal communication; Ilbury 2019). For these speakers, it is likely that London Jamaican features are used on an MLE phonological and grammatical base, not London Cockney, as in earlier decades.

Even in 2001, 20 years after the period we are focussing on, the proportions of people belonging to minority ethnic groups were not in a majority in London, the 'White British' Census classification accounting for 57.8% of the population in that year (and down to 44.9% in 2011). The picture is rather different, however, if we look at African Caribbeans in particular boroughs and parts of boroughs. In 1981, this ethnic group represented 13.6% of the population of Lambeth, where Caribbean migrants first settled, and 15.1% in Hackney. The figure for Greater London as a whole was much smaller, at 4.7% (Richmond 1987:145). Within boroughs, we can look at ward level. Figure 4.1.2 displays the ethnic composition of Hackney as a whole, albeit 20 years later (such information is not easily available for 1981). The data are from the 2001 Census, in which respondents were asked, "What is your ethnicity", with a choice of a closed set of options including 'other' categories. 'Black African', 'Black Caribbean' (equivalent to 'African Caribbean') and 'White Other' were the three largest non-White British groups – each of which is linguistically diverse and each still only accounting for 10%–12% of the total. In this chart, the South Asians are broken down by nationality, obscuring the fact that they form a fourth group of similar size.

How then can we account for what we assume to be the non-London origins of many features of MLE, as suggested by Table 4.1.1? One approach is to use Census data to investigate populations at the ward level, looking out for concentrations of particular groups. The existence of concentrations means that, at a local level, the ethnic group concerned has the chance to dominate linguistically; if, in addition, there is a significant level of contact and integration with other groups, then linguistic

Tracing Origins of Urban Youth Vernacular 265

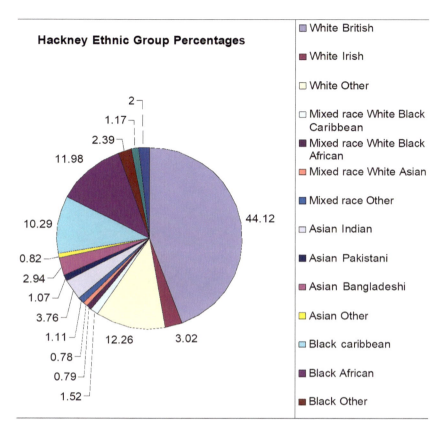

Figure 4.1.2 Ethnic groups in Hackney (percent), 2001.
Source: 2001 Census.

features may be adopted by those groups. Figure 4.1.3 shows that in 2001 there were considerable concentrations of people who were not White British in the east of the borough; it does not show the distributions of African Caribbeans or other groups.

We can go a step further and identify concentrations of particular ethnic groups. Figure 4.1.4 shows the numbers of particular ethnic groups per hectare in smaller sub-areas in 2001. Figure 4.1.4 (top left panel) shows that the White British are the largest single group and that there is variation in their distribution. (Higher relative concentrations are marked in red.) The other panels show three other large groups, Black Caribbeans, Black Africans and Indians. It is noticeable that there are clear concentrations of each group, with Caribbeans more to the east and centre, Africans in the centre and south, and Asians in the north. In several areas, the White British are a clear minority, while for each of the three minority groups there may well be areas where it is close to being an absolute majority.

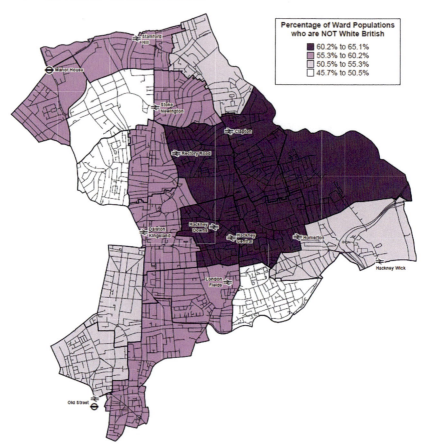

Figure 4.1.3 Percentage of population in Hackney which is not White British, by ward (Census 2001).

Source: Hackney Borough Council (n.d.). Office for National Statistics licensed under the Open Government Licence v.3.0 Contains OS data © Crown copyright and database right 2020.

What these charts do not show is the situation in the past; however, the Census figures we have quoted suggest that similar distributions (high diversity with some ethnic/linguistic concentrations but little segregation) were present then too. Although the immigrant groups together represented, overall, a fairly small minority of London's population in the earlier post-war years, we argue that, on demographic evidence alone, conditions were right for new youth varieties to emerge, certainly as styles which were used for particular kinds of identity work. But this

Tracing Origins of Urban Youth Vernacular 267

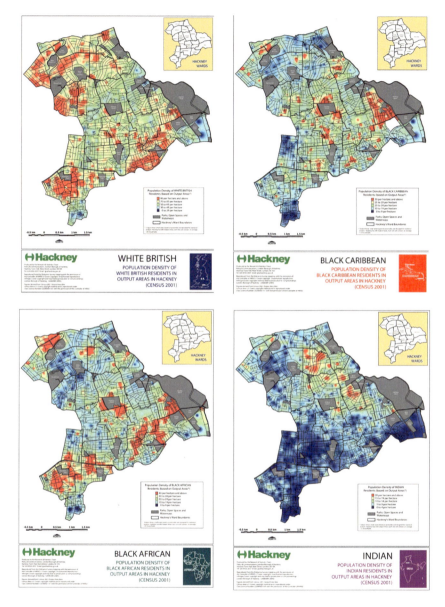

Figure 4.1.4 Population density of four different ethnic groups in Hackney (Census 2001).
Source: Hackney Borough Council (n.d.). Office for National Statistics licensed under the Open Government Licence v.3.0 Contains OS data © Crown copyright and database right 2020.

268   *Paul Kerswill and Eivind Torgersen*

would initially have been restricted to places where the African Caribbeans were present in sufficient numbers: remember that it wasn't until the 1970s that distinctive new varieties emerged (London Jamaican and the specific youth style labelled the 'multiracial vernacular'). Our reasoning is as follows. Because the African Caribbeans were the first to arrive, we assume there were relatively high concentrations of young people of Caribbean origin in places where the White British also lived. This is the context in which London Jamaican emerged, arising from contact between different Caribbean (not White British) groups. Interaction between young people of Caribbean and other linguistic backgrounds facilitated 'crossing' (Rampton 1995) and, later, the appearance of the multiracial vernacular and, after further large-scale immigration, MLE. The fact that African Caribbeans were the first major immigrant group meant that their influence on youth language was significant at the outset, and new immigrant groups would have to relate their own speech to the emerging youth language norms, in many cases choosing to assimilate to them. This is how we see the workings of the *Founder Principle* in post-war London. There is, then, no need to accept the proposition voiced earlier that at least 50% of the population had to be speakers of other language varieties for there to be a linguistic effect on youth styles. Effects on vernacular speech came later, when the proportions of non-speakers of the local London vernacular approached a much higher percentage. One of the results was MLE.

4.1.5.2 *The Cultural Argument*

However, one can claim a *founder effect* for non-linguistic influences too. During this time, up to and incorporating the beginnings of London hip-hop in the late 1980s, Caribbean cultural forms were a fundamental influence on British popular music and London's emerging post-war youth culture (Gidley 2007). A good proportion of the slang in today's grime music is of Caribbean origin, even though several of the most prominent artists, such as Dizzee Rascal, Stormzy, and Big Shaq are of African heritage. A little speculatively, we can say that the most salient and frequent portion of the slang in grime is largely of Jamaican origin (cf. the quantitative methods currently being applied to grime lyrics by Paga 2019). If this is true, it is likely that the popularity of grime has indirectly helped Caribbean language, especially slang, to keep up its currency.

We can assume MLE has a different genesis from its two predecessors, arising in an environment that is much more multilingual and in which African Caribbeans formed just one of a number of groups – albeit large. By the 1970s, as we have seen, the Caribbeans themselves had largely shifted to local forms of English, this switch being facilitated by the dwindling number of new immigrants. This demographic change contrasts strongly with the rapidly growing African, South Asian and other groups.

Yet MLE is sometimes thought of in the media as being a kind of Jamaican Creole and hence 'foreign' (Kerswill 2014; Kircher and Fox 2019), for a time going by the moniker 'Jafaican' in the media. What kinds of evidence is there for this (misleading) assumption? Some of the slang used by young, mainly male MLE speakers is of Jamaican origin, including *bruv* (perhaps an Anglicised version of *brada*), *blood* (both address terms), *ends* 'local area', as well as the plural morpheme *-dem* in *mandem* 'people' and *galdem* 'girls'. *Man* used as a first-person pronoun has possible Jamaican antecedents, but usage has developed locally (Cheshire 2013; Ilbury 2019). Much of the attested slang, however, is not of Jamaican origin. According to Green (2014:70), out of 220 items he collected, 39 were

> from the Caribbean, usually Jamaica ...; 35 from US black slang ...; 41 from US white slang; and 35 from white London slang or Cockney. In addition, 74 home-grown terms ... are used as the core vocabulary of MLE and have evolved independently ...

This result, partial though Green admits, shows that there are still some Jamaican roots but that this part of the linguistic structure is constantly in flux as might be expected in youth language. However, as we noted above, the Jamaican portion of MLE slang may be the most prominent (Kerswill 2014), which maintains the salience of (supposed or real) Jamaican language.

4.1.6 Conclusions

We have presented arguments supporting the apparently disproportionate influence of Jamaican language and culture on youth language in London, culminating in MLE. We return to the linguistic evidence to see how far Jamaican influence is visible in linguistic structure. Clearly Jamaican lexis and music have long permeated London youth language and grassroots music, and this may even be increasing. However, as the summary of MLE features in Section 4.1.2 show, in the morphosyntax there are no identifiable traces of Creole, with the possible exception of the pronoun *man*. This leaves us with the phonology, and here again, the picture is unclear. First, some MLE features are not present in Jamaican Creole, such as uvular [q] for /k/ and a very fronted GOOSE vowel. Unlike Cockney, MLE is an /h/-pronouncing variety, even though Jamaican Creole, like Cockney, is mainly /h/-dropping (Devonish and Harry 2008:272–273) – as is the English of many L1 Yoruba speakers, who also form a significant minority in London (Igboanusi 2006:494). As Table 4.1.1 shows, some of the remaining vowels share some features with Jamaican English, but equally with those of other overseas varieties of English and learner varieties. There is practically no evidence to suggest a direct influence.

This leaves us with a conundrum. The evidence we have of the Caribbean influence on London Jamaican is self-defining, but it is not clear whether any of the distinctive structural (non-lexical, non-discourse) features of MLE can be ascribed to a Creole origin. We end up resorting to argumentation: the deterministic theory of new-dialect formation (Trudgill 2004), which relies solely on demography and frequency of features, has a strong degree of validity for a number of cases such as New Zealand English. The features of MLE are not inconsistent with this theory, as Table 4.1.1 indicates, with Caribbean Creole being the most frequently mentioned origin across the features listed. For a number of reasons, the validity of the deterministic model is hard to prove – though this does not necessarily invalidate it. First, the list in Table 4.1.1 is not exhaustive. Second, and more importantly, MLE is not homogeneous in the same way as a new dialect such as New Zealand English. Third, unlike this variety, MLE is the product of prior language shift, the shift involving many different languages. Fourth, standard varieties of English might have played a stronger role for MLE than, for example, New Zealand English, via teachers and youth workers. And finally, fifth, the social context of MLE is of far greater complexity than that of New Zealand English in that it is used in multilingual and multiethnic contexts, functioning as both a marked style and, for many, as a vernacular, and is always in competition with other varieties of English.

However, among immigrants, their descendants and their White Anglo associates, the African Caribbeans, perhaps for three decades, dominated both linguistically and culturally. It may also be significant that the English-lexifier creoles that most of the original immigrants spoke were accessible to speakers of English in a way that South Asian and West African languages could never be. The Creole speakers had themselves been educated in English and had almost all migrated from countries where English was a dominant part of the linguistic ecology. Both of these factors – linguistic similarity and shared knowledge of English – would have made contacts easier than with immigrants from other linguistic backgrounds.

As for ascribing MLE to a Caribbean origin, we have shown that there is an undoubted continuity from Creole to MLE and have argued that relatively open networks allowed for a good deal of contact. But the characteristic MLE features are found in other input varieties, so we agree with Trudgill (2004) that it is the relative frequency of individual features that count in new-dialect formation. But because of the long time-depth and because different linguistic groups immigrated at different times, many other influences could have made their presence felt along the way, either bolstering the existing Creole features or replacing them. In particular, we must still account for the time-gap between the Caribbean English and Creole speech of the 1950s and 1960s immigrants and the much later emergence of MLE. Added to this is the dynamic nature of language in a multicultural and multilingual city, meaning that other, new processes are at play, mainly related to ongoing language contact and acquisition. The conclusion must be that the story in many respects follows Trudgill's deterministic new-dialect formation model; however this is an imperfect mechanism when applied to a new urban contact dialect; Trudgill (2018) has stated that the model is most suited to the *tabula rasa* situation of new settlements. The situation is, above all, characterised by language shift and group second-language acquisition (Winford 2003:235) with various adult learner varieties forming a significant part of the input. What then is the role of the *Founder Principle*? It is clear that the African Caribbean 'founders' laid the basis for the ensuing varieties – even if, as we have seen, there is little left of the original Creole, except for a vibrant use of Jamaican slang. In a complex situation such as the emergence of multiethnolects, it is only by adding a component of cultural and social interpretation that we can approach an understanding of the outcomes.

Notes

1 October 2004–September 2007 *Linguistic innovators: the English of adolescents in London* (Economic and Social Research Council, ref. RES 000-23-0680). Researchers: Jenny Cheshire, Sue Fox, Paul Kerswill, Eivind Torgersen.
2 October 2007–September 2010 *Multicultural London English: the emergence, acquisition and diffusion of a new variety* (Economic and Social Research Council, ref. RES 062-23-0814). Researchers: Jenny Cheshire, Sue Fox, Paul Kerswill, Arfaan Khan, Eivind Torgersen.

References

Agha, Asif. 2007. *Language and Social Relations*. Cambridge: Cambridge University Press.
Beaken, Michael. 1971. A study of phonological development in a primary school population of East London. Unpublished Ph.D. thesis, University College London.
Beaumont-Thomas, Ben. 2018. 'You can't escape its inspiration': Inside the true history of grime. *The Guardian*, 1 June 2018. www.theguardian.com/music/2018/jun/01/inside-grime-true-history-dan-hancox-dj-target-wiley-dizzee-rascal-stormzy, accessed 06.04.2019.
Cardoso, Amanda, Erez Levon, Devyani Sharma, Dominic Watt and Yang Ye. 2019. "Inter-speaker variation and the evaluation of British English accents in employment contexts". In *Proceedings of the 19th International Congress of Phonetic Sciences*. Melbourne, Australia 5–9th August, 2019, 1615–1619.

Castells, Manuel. 1997. *The Power of Identity*. Malden: Blackwell.

Cheshire, Jenny. 2013. "Grammaticalisation in social context: The emergence of a new English pronoun". *Journal of Sociolinguistics* 17(5):608–633. doi:10.1111/josl.12053

Cheshire, Jenny, Paul Kerswill, Sue Fox and Eivind Torgersen. 2008. "Ethnicity, friendship network and social practices as the motor of dialect change: Linguistic innovation in London". *Sociolinguistica* 22:1–23.

Cheshire, Jenny and Sue Fox. 2009. "Was/were variation: A perspective from London". *Language Variation and Change* 21(1):1–23. doi:10.1017/S0954394509000015

Cheshire, Jenny, Paul Kerswill, Sue Fox and Eivind Torgersen. 2011. "Contact, the feature pool and the speech community: The emergence of multicultural London English". *Journal of Sociolinguistics* 15(2):151–196. doi.org/10.1111/j.1467-9841.2011.00478.x

Cheshire, Jenny, David Adger and Sue Fox. 2013a. "Relative who and the actuation problem". *Lingua*, 126:51–77. doi:10.1016/j.lingua.2012.11.014

Cheshire, Jenny, Sue Fox, Paul Kerswill and Eivind Torgersen. 2013b. "Language contact and language change in the multicultural metropolis". *Revue française de linguistique appliquée* xviii(2):63–76. www.cairn.info/revue-francaise-de-linguistique-appliquee-2013-2-page-63.htm.

Community Relations Committee. 1976. *Select Committee on Race Relations and Immigration Enquiry on the West Indian Community*. London: Community Relations Committee.

Demographia. n.d. Greater London, inner London & outer London population & density history. www.demographia.com/dm-lon31.htm, accessed 15.5.2019.

Devonish, Hubert and Otelemate G. Harry. 2008. "Jamaican Creole and Jamaican English: Phonology". In *Varieties of English 2: The Americas and the Caribbean*, E. W. Schneider (ed.). Berlin: Mouton de Gruyter. 256–289.

Dorling, Danny and Bethan Thomas. 2016. *People and Places: A 21st-Century Atlas of the UK*. Bristol: Policy Press.

Drummond, Rob. 2016. Skepta, grime and urban British youth language: A guide. *The Conversation*, 21 September 2016. https://theconversation.com/skepta-grime-and-urban-british-youth-language-a-guide-65611, accessed 06.04.2019.

Fox, Sue. 2012. "Performed narrative: The pragmatic function of *this is +* *speaker* and other quotatives in London adolescent speech". In *Quotatives: Cross-linguistic and Cross-disciplinary Perspectives*, I. van Alphen and I. Buchstaller (eds.). Amsterdam: Benjamins. 231–257.

Fox, Susan. 2015. *The New Cockney: New Ethnicities and Adolescent Speech in the Traditional East End of London*. Basingstoke: Palgrave Macmillan.

Fox, Susan and Eivind Torgersen. 2018. "Language change and innovation in London: Multicultural London English". In *Sociolinguistics in England*, N. Braber and S. Jansen (eds.). London: Palgrave. 189–213.

Gabrielatos, Costas, Eivind Torgersen, Sebastian Hoffmann and Sue Fox. 2010. "A corpus-based sociolinguistic study of indefinite article forms in London English". *Journal of English Linguistics* 38(4):297–334. doi:10.1177/0075424209352729

Gates, Shivonne. 2018. Language and ethnicity in an East London Secondary School. Unpublished Ph.D. thesis, School of Languages, Linguistics and Film, Queen Mary University of London.

Gidley, Ben. 2007. "Youth culture and ethnicity: Emerging youth interculture in South London". In *Youth Cultures: Scenes, Subcultures and Tribes*, P. Hodkinson and W. Deicke (eds.). London, New York: Routledge. 145–160.

Green, Jonathon. 2014. "Multicultural London English – The new 'youthspeak'". In *Global English Slang: Methodologies and Perspectives*, J. Coleman (ed.). London: Routledge. 62–71.

Hackney Borough Council. n.d. Map Gallery. www.map.hackney.gov.uk/gisMapGallery/, accessed 23.05.2019.

Hewitt, Roger. 1982. "White adolescent creole users and the politics of friendship". *Journal of Multilingual and Multicultural Development* 3(3):217–232. doi:10.1080/01434632.1982.9994086

Hewitt, Roger. 1986. *White Talk, Black Talk*. Cambridge: Cambridge University Press.

Hewitt, Roger. 1990. "Youth, race and language in contemporary Britain: Deconstructing ethnicity?" In *Childhood, Youth and Social Change: A Comparative Perspective*, L. Chisholm, P. Michner, H-H. Kruger and P. Brown (eds.). London: The Falmer Press.185–196.

Hurford, James. 1967. The speech of one family: A phonetic comparison of the speech of three generations in a family in East London. Unpublished Ph.D. thesis, University College London.

Igboanusi, Herbert. 2006. "A comparative study of the phonological features of Igbo English and Yoruba English speakers of Nigeria". *English Studies*, 87:490–497. doi:10.1080/00138380600768221

Ilbury, Christian. 2019. Beyond the offline: Social media and the social meaning of variation in East London. Unpublished Ph.D. thesis, School of Languages, Linguistics and Film, Queen Mary University of London.

Inwood, Stephen. 1998. *A History of London*. London: Macmillan.

Kerswill, Paul. 1996. "Children, adolescents and language change". *Language Variation and Change* 8(2):177–202. doi:10.1017/S0954394500001137

Kerswill, Paul. 2013a. "Koineization". In *Handbook of Language Variation and Change*, J.K. Chambers and N. Schilling (eds.). 2nd edition. Oxford: Wiley-Blackwell. 519–536.

Kerswill, Paul. 2013b. "Identity, ethnicity and place: The construction of youth language in London". In *Space in Language and Linguistics: Geographical, Interactional, and Cognitive Perspectives*, P. Auer, M. Hilpert, A. Stukenbrock and B. Szmrecsanyi (eds.). Berlin: Walter de Gruyter. 128–164.

Kerswill, Paul. 2014. "The objectification of 'Jafaican': The discoursal embedding of multicultural London English in the British media". In *The Media and Sociolinguistic Change*, J. Androutsopoulos (ed.). Berlin: De Gruyter. 428–455.

Kerswill, Paul. 2018. "Dialect formation and dialect change in the Industrial Revolution: British vernacular English in the nineteenth century". In *Southern English Varieties Then and Now*, L. Wright (ed.). Berlin: De Gruyter. 8–38.

Kerswill, Paul and Peter Trudgill. 2005. "The birth of new dialects". In *Dialect Change: Convergence and Divergence in European Languages*, P. Auer, F. Hinskens and P. Kerswill (eds.). Cambridge: Cambridge University Press. 196–220.

Kerswill, Paul, Eivind Torgersen and Sue Fox. 2008. "Reversing 'drift': Innovation and diffusion in the London diphthong system". *Language Variation and Change* 20(3):451–491. doi:10.1017/S0954394508000148

Kerswill, Paul and Mark Sebba. 2011. "From London Jamaican to British youth language: The transformation of a Caribbean post-creole repertoire into a new Multicultural London English". In *Paper Given at the Conference of the Society for Pidgin and Creole Linguistics*, Accra, Ghana, 2–6 August 2011.

Kerswill, Paul, Jenny Cheshire, Sue Fox and Eivind Torgersen. 2013. "English as a contact language: The role of children and adolescents". In *English as a Contact Language*, D. Schreier and M. Hundt (eds.). Cambridge: Cambridge University Press. 258–282.

Kerswill, Paul and Eivind Torgersen. 2016. "London's Cockney in the twentieth century: Stability or cycles of contact-driven change?" In *Listening to the Past – Audio Records of Accents of English*, R. Hickey (ed.). Cambridge: Cambridge University Press. 85–113.

Kießling, Roland and Maarten Mous. 2006. "Vous nous avez donné le francais, mais nous sommes pas obligés de l'utiliser comme vous le voulez" – Youth languages in Africa. In *Trends and Developments in Youth Language Research*, C. Dürscheid and J. Spitzmüller (eds.). Frankfurt am Main: Peter Lang. 385–401.

Kircher, Ruth and Sue Fox. 2019. "Attitudes towards Multicultural London English: Implications for attitude theory and language planning". *Journal of Multilingual and Multicultural Development* 40(10):847–864. doi:10.1080/01434632.2019.1577869

Kotsinas, Ulla-Britt. 1988. "Immigrant children's Swedish – A new variety?" *Journal of Multilingual and Multicultural Development* 9(1–2):129–140. doi:10.1080/01434632.1988.9994324

Labov, William. 1972. *Sociolinguistic Patterns*. Philadelphia: University of Pennsylvania Press.

Labov, William. 2001. *Principles of Linguistic Change, Volume 2: Social Factors*. Oxford: Blackwell.

Labov, William. 2007. "Transmission and diffusion". *Language* 83(2):344–387. doi:10.1353/lan.2007.0082

London Datastore. n.d. *Historical Census Tables*. London: Greater London Authority. https://data.london.gov.uk/dataset/historical-census-tables, accessed 17.05.2019.

Mufwene, Salikoko. 1996. "The founder principle in creole genesis". *Diachronica* 13(1):83–134. doi:10.1075/dia.13.1.05muf

Mufwene, Salikoko S. 2001. *The Ecology of Language Evolution*. Cambridge: Cambridge University Press.

Mufwene, Salikoko. 2008. *Language Evolution: Contact, Competition, and Change*. London: Continuum.

Nortier, Jacomine and Bente Ailin Svendsen (eds.). 2015. *Language, Youth and Identity in the 21st Century. Linguistic Practices across Urban Spaces*. Cambridge: Cambridge University Press.

Owen, David. 1995. "Ethnic minorities in Great Britain: Patterns of population change 1981–91". *1991 Census Statistical Paper* No 10. Coventry: National Ethnic Minority Data Archive, University of Warwick.

Paga, Christian. 2019. "Wagwan, fam?!: Lectal focusing in grime music". In *Poster Presented at the Tenth International Conference on Language Variation in Europe (ICLaVE 10)*. Fryske Akademy, Leeuwarden, 26th–28th June 2019.

Patrick, Peter. 2008. "British Creole: Phonology". In *Varieties of English I: The British Isles*, B. Kortmann and C. Upton (eds.). Berlin: Mouton de Gruyter. 253–268.

Peach, G. C. K. 1967. West Indian Migration to Britain. *International Migration Review* 1(2):34–45.

Pitts, John. 2012. Spinning the Crisis – Riots, Politics and Parenting. Lecture given at the University of Bedfordshire, 5 July 2012. www.youtube.com/watch?v=Gd3SJ6qakyY, accessed 05.04.2019.

Quist, Pia. 2008. "Sociolinguistic approaches to multiethnolect: Language variety and stylistic practice". *International Journal of Bilingualism* 12(1&2): 43–61. doi:10.1177/13670069080120010401

Rampton, Ben. 1995. *Crossing: Language and Ethnicity among Adolescents*. London, New York: Longman.

Rampton, Ben. 2011. "From 'Multiethnic adolescent heteroglossia' to 'Contemporary urban vernaculars'". *Language & Communication* 31(4): 276–294. doi:10.1016/j.langcom.2011.01.001

Rampton, Ben. 2015. "Contemporary urban vernaculars". In *Language, Youth and Identity in the 21st Century: Linguistic Practices across Urban Spaces*, J. Nortier and B. Svendsen (eds.). Cambridge: Cambridge University Press. 24–44. doi:10.1017/CBO9781139061896.003

Richmond, Anthony H. 1987. "Caribbean immigrants in Britain and Canada: Socio-demographic aspects". *Revue européenne des migrations internationales* 3(3):129–150. doi:10.3406/remi.1987.1148

Rosen, Harold and Tony Burgess. 1980. *Languages and Dialects of London School Children: An Investigation*. London: Ward Lock.

Sebba, Mark. 1993. *London Jamaican: Language Systems in Interaction*. London: Longman.

Sebba, Mark. 2008. "British Creole: Morphology and syntax". In *Varieties of English I: The British Isles*, B. Kortmann and C. Upton (eds.). Berlin: Mouton de Gruyter. 463–477.

Sharma, Devyani. 2018. "Style dominance: Attention, audience, and the 'real me'". *Language in Society* 47(1):1–31. doi:10.1017/S0047404517000835

Siegel, Jeff. 1997. "Mixing, leveling and pidgin/creole development". In *The Structure and Status of Pidgins and Creoles*, A. K. Spears and D. Winford (eds.). Amsterdam, The Netherlands: Benjamins. 111–149.

Sivertsen, Eva. 1960. *Cockney Phonology*. Oslo: Oslo University Press.

Torgersen, Eivind and Anita Szakay. 2012. "An investigation of speech rhythm in London English". *Lingua* 122:822–840. doi:10.1016/j.lingua.2012.01.004

Torgersen, Eivind, Costas Gabrielatos, Sebastian Hoffmann and Sue Fox. 2011. "A corpus-based study of pragmatic markers in London English". *Corpus Linguistics and Linguistic Theory* 7(1):93–118. doi:10.1515/CLLT.2011.005

Torgersen, Eivind, Costas Gabrielatos and Sebastian Hoffmann. 2018. "A corpus-based analysis of the pragmatic marker you get me". In *Studies in Corpus-Based Sociolinguistics*, E. Friginal (ed.). Abingdon: Routledge. 176–196.

Trudgill, Peter. 1986. *Dialects in Contact*. Oxford: Blackwell.

Trudgill, Peter. 2004. *New-Dialect Formation: The Inevitability of Colonial Englishes*. Edinburgh: Edinburgh University Press.

Trudgill, Peter. 2018. "Tabula Rasa new-dialect formation: On the occasional irrelevance of language regard". In *Language Regard: Methods, Variation and Change*, B. E. Evans, E. J. Benson and J. N. Stanford (eds.). Cambridge: Cambridge University Press. 266–282.

Van Coetsem, F. 1988. *Loan Phonology and the Two Transfer Types in Language Contact*. Dordrecht: Foris.

Varghese, Sanjana. 2017. Big up MLE – the origins of London's 21st century slang. *New Statesman*, 21 August 2017. www.newstatesman.com/2017/08/big-mle-origins-londons-21st-century-slang, accessed 07.04.2019.

Wells, John C. 1982. *Accents of English*. 3 vols. Cambridge: Cambridge University Press.

Wiese, Heike. 2009. "Grammatical innovation in multiethnic urban Europe: New linguistic practices among adolescents". *Lingua* 119:782–806. doi:10.1016/j.lingua.2008.11.002

Wiese, Heike. Forthcoming. "Urban contact dialects". In *Cambridge Handbook of Language Contact*, S. Mufwene and A. M. Escobar (eds.). Cambridge: Cambridge University Press.

Wiese, Heike and Ines Rehbein. 2016. "Coherence in new urban dialects: A case study". *Lingua* 172/173:45–61. doi:10.1016/j.lingua.2015.10.016

Winford, Donald. 2003. *An Introduction to Contact Linguistics*. Oxford: Blackwell.

Winford, Donald. 2017. "World Englishes and Creoles". In *The Oxford Handbook of World Englishes*, M. Filppula, J. Klemola and D. Sharma (eds.). Oxford/New York: Oxford University Press. 194–210.

4.2 Bare Nouns in Prepositional Phrases in *Cité Duits,* a Moribund Miners' Multiethnolect (and Other Varieties of Dutch and German)[1]

Peter Auer and Leonie Cornips

4.2.1 Introduction

In the thirties and forties of the last century, the children of immigrant coalminers of various ethnic, but usually non-German-L1 backgrounds, developed a new language variety in the coalminers' district of Tuinwijk in the village of Eisden, Belgian Limburg (Auer and Cornips 2018; Pecht 2013). They self-labelled this new variety *Cité Duits*, where *Cité* refers to a miners' housing district and *Duits* is the Dutch word for the German language. According to the memories of these children – who are now elderly men in their late seventies and eighties – they began speaking *Cité Duits* (or rather 'inventing' it) so as to have 'their own language in the streets'. Having become coalminers themselves, they continued to use this variety throughout their lifetime when talking amongst themselves, e.g., while working underground, but also in their private lives.

Cité Duits can be called a multiethnolect in the sense of having emerged as a consequence of the immigration of people from various ethnic and linguistic backgrounds to Eisden but, in contrast to modern European multiethnolects, it is not easily analysed as a variant of one language (such as German or Dutch), despite the speakers' own label for it. Instead, it is characterised by an amalgamation of elements from three different sources: Dutch as one of the national languages in Belgium; Maasland dialect as spoken in the area; and German, which is not indigenous to Eisden (Auer and Cornips 2018). This amalgamation is so intense that it is impossible to argue that *Cité Duits* is 'dominantly' German or Dutch/Maasland dialect. The structure of this amalgam due to language contact also differs from that of the well-known "mixed languages" (cf. e.g., Matras and Bakker 2007), as the three varieties on which it is based are structurally very similar (cf. Pecht 2019). Its multiethnolectal status results from its sociolinguistic function as a marker of the speakers' peripheral social position within mainstream Belgian society, within the isolated mining communities in Belgium at the time, and with respect to the surrounding rural dialect speakers. That German is one of the source languages of *Cité Duits* (despite most of the immigrant workers' L1 being another language) can be explained by the fact that the speakers often came from regions of the pre-1918 Habsburg empire in which German was a relevant L2 and was used in mining, or, alternatively, that their often complex migration history included previous stays in the German mining areas, for instance in the Ruhr area (cf. Auer and Cornips 2018). Quite a few of them will therefore have had a good command of (non-standard) German.

We will focus on a particular type of syntactic variation in a spoken, non-standardised language (Cheshire 2005), which necessarily includes an analysis of its pragmatic functions (Cheshire et al. 2013: 74). Our primary aim is to account for variation in Preposition-Noun Combinations (PNCs), where, in addition to variation in the choice of the preposition itself, the determiner is variable in *Cité Duits*, across speakers and in individuals. Speakers may produce PNCs both without (1a) and with a definite determiner (1b) after the same preposition:

(1) a) dann war wieder ein in haus der **auf pütt** hat gearbeit[2]
'then again someone was in the house who worked **in (the) mine**'

    b) so kommt es dass **auf de Cité** nich überall das Cité-Deutsch datselbe war.
'so it comes that **in the Cité** Cité-Deutsch was not everywhere the same'.

The variable use of the determiner is a syntactic feature which so far has hardly been noticed by variationist sociolinguists who "tend to analyse the same grammatical variables over and over again" (Cheshire 2005: 86), and it is also a relatively new topic in the linguistic literature on the Germanic languages as a whole. The question is whether the omission of the determiner is subject to pragmatic (or other) constraints and/or indicative of a complete loss of the determiner system.

A second aim of this chapter is to address the question as to whether *Cité Duits* differs from or is similar to modern multiethnolects for which omission of both the definite and indefinite determiner within and beyond the PP context has also been reported (Siegel 2018; Wiese 2012; Cheshire et al. 2011; Quist and Svendsen 2010; Cornips 2002/2008).[3] In this context, we will also look at bare nouns in PPs in the speech of coalminers in another substandard variety, i.e., Ruhr German, as it is a possible source for *Cité Duits* (cf. Auer and Cornips 2018).

4.2.2 Bare Nouns in N-based PP Constructions

Within and across the Germanic languages, the use of determiners versus bare nouns in PNCs is highly variable and language-specific (cf. Swart

2015; Kiss and Roch 2014; Pires de Oliveira 2013). For instance, in the *Cité Duits* utterance in (2a), the noun in the PNC *naar kirche* 'church' appears without a determiner. This is exactly what we find in English (2b). Standard German (2c) and standard Dutch (2d), on the other hand (as well as the Maasland dialect of the area), require a definite determiner in this context (CD = *Cité Duits*, E = English, G = German, D = Dutch):

(2) a) CD (die)   geht **naar kirche** in Waterscheid (L: 383.532)

    b) E   the miner   goes **to church**   in Waterscheid

    c) G   (die) geht **in**   <u>die</u>   Kirche in Waterscheid

    d) D   (die) gaat **naar** <u>de</u>   kerk   in Waterscheid

In other cases, PNCs in all source varieties of *Cité Duits* require a bare noun (as does English):

(3) a) CD   da ging wieder eine, hej, ganze zimmer (.) **haus unter wasser**

    b) G   da ging wieder ein ganzes Zimmer, ganzes **Haus unter Wasser**

    c) D   daar ging weer een hele kamer, heel **huis onder water**

      there went again an entire room entire house P water

      'There again an entire room, entire house went under water'

(2a), like (1a), is therefore an innovation of *Cité Duits*, while (3a) is not; the syntactic restrictions on bare nouns in PNCs have been widened in *Cité Duits* compared to its contact varieties.

The reason for this seemingly random variation across closely related Germanic languages is that the historical pragmatic function of the determiner, i.e., to mark definiteness versus indefiniteness, has become irrelevant in many contexts (cf. Flick and Szczepaniak, forthcoming, for diachronic and synchronic details on German). Leiss (2010) argues that the (definite, but also indefinite) determiner is "overdetermined", i.e., its use has become generalised in the course of language history to contexts in which no choice between definite and indefinite determination is possible. Paradoxically then, the diachronic 'success' of the determiner system has simultaneously undermined its *raison d'être* and hence (according to Leiss) will in the long run lead to the collapse of its original function of expressing definiteness. Evidence for the overdetermination of the determiner in German is its recent extension to the context before a (personal) proper name, typical of southern German varieties but spreading throughout the German language area. Given the uniqueness of the referent of a proper name, the determiner is redundant and therefore dysfunctional. Another example of overdetermination is the obligatory use of the definite determiner with proper names for states (such as *die Schweiz* 'Switzerland') or before superlatives (such as *das beste Buch* 'the best book') in German.

While Leiss's theory predicts a wholesale collapse of the determiner system and an increase of bare nouns due to an erosion of their functional basis, other approaches make more precise predictions about the occurrence of bare nouns. One such approach distinguishes between semantic and pragmatic definiteness (Löbner 1985; also see Himmelmann 1997: 39). *Pragmatic definiteness* of an NP presupposes the uniqueness of the referent, i.e., the definite article is linked to a common ground between speaker and hearer in this particular situational context, while the use of an indefinite NP gets an implicature that this is not possible (Tsimpli, Peristeri, and Andreou 2018). In discourse, definite and indefinite NPs mark referents of different degrees of accessibility: definite noun phrases are used to link a referent to previously mentioned referents in discourse, while new referents are marked by the indefinite article (Tsimpli, Peristeri, and Andreou 2018: 332; Doreleijers, van Koppen, and Nortier 2019). In contrast, *semantic definiteness* also presupposes the identification of a unique referent by the hearer, but it does not depend on the situational or discourse context but rather on general world knowledge, as in the case with generic referents, referents that exist only once in a given universe, or proper names. In the case of semantic definiteness, the choice of the article has no pragmatic function. We can therefore predict that bare nouns should be more frequent in this case. The Germanic definite article was first grammaticised in order to mark pragmatic definiteness and only later extended to semantic definiteness (Demske, Forthcoming); bare nouns, in contrast to semantically motivated definite articles, would therefore rewind the grammaticalisation history of the definite article to a previous stage (see Rupp and Tagliamonte 2019 for English).

Closely related is the theory of referential strength (Swart 2015; Broekhuis 2013: 168; Poesio 1994). *Strongly referring* noun phrases identify unique referents (either on pragmatic or semantic grounds); *weakly referring* noun phrases do not. For instance, the definite noun *the church* in (4a) refers to a specific church whereas the bare noun *church* in (4b) does not. Rather, the latter construction has a meaning "enriched" by stereotypical features of church-going (Swart 2015 and references cited). Hence, (4b) means that the subject goes to church regularly, in other words, that he is a churchgoer (Pires de Oliveira 2013: 23).

(4) a) E   The miner goes to the church

    b) E   The miner goes to church.

In English, where alternation between a determiner-noun combination and a bare noun is quite frequent, modification of the noun *church* by an adjective (or other attributes) is excluded with a bare noun but acceptable with a definite noun (Broekhuis 2013), due to the strong referential reading of the modified noun:

(5) a) E *The miner goes **to new church**

   b) E The miner goes **to the new church**

Bare nouns in PNCs are restricted to narrow scope interpretation (Swart 2015). In (6a), the apprentices do not necessarily work in the same office in the sentence without a determiner, as the referent of the noun *kantoor* in Dutch lacks uniqueness or familiarity (weak referentiality), while they work in the same office in the sentence with the determiner (strong referentiality). In (6b), Jan and Marie may go to different offices in the version with a bare noun (weak referentiality), as shown by the ellipsis (Pires de Oliveira 2013: 17), but they go to the same office in the version with a determiner (strong referentiality):[4]

(6) a) Iedere stagiaire werkt **op kantoor/** in de vakantie
                               op het kantoor

   'Every apprentice works **in (the) office** during vacation'

   b) Marie gaat **naar kantoor/** en zo doet Jan
                   naar het kantoor

   'Marie goes **to (the) office** and so does Jan'

As core features of weakly referential nouns, Aguilar-Guevara, Le Bruyn and Zwarts mention incorporation, discourse opacity, number neutrality and stereotypical enrichment (2014: 7).

The theory of weak and strong referentiality predicts that bare nouns should be more frequent when the noun has weak referentiality, and that these nouns should be affected first in language change by a tendency *not* to use the determiner.[5] Definite articles with weakly referring nouns are historically younger than those with strongly referring nouns (see Demske, forthcoming, for German).

4.2.3 Bare Nouns in Preposition-Noun Constructions in *Cité Duits*

4.2.3.1 Data

In this chapter we discuss PNCs in the speech of three former coalminers and one former teacher, who were all born and grew up in the *Cité* and claim to speak *Cité Duits* among each other. The data (approximately

282 Peter Auer and Leonie Cornips

four hours) are extracted from a larger set of interactions recorded in 2012 and 2013 by the second author (see also Auer and Cornips 2018). The recordings took place in the living room of the coalminers' museum in Eisden, Belgium. The material used in this chapter is about 20 minutes of speech by each informant. We will focus on directional and locational PNCs (as in (1)–(6)).

The four speakers investigated were raised in different home languages: Hungarian/ German (dialect),[6] Ukrainian, Austrian-German, and Portuguese/Italian. At the time of the recordings they were in their late seventies. In everyday life their dominant language has always been Dutch, or Maasland dialect, which they also use with their wives and families. Since they have been retired for decades, the opportunities of speaking *Cité Duits* have diminished more and more, although they enjoyed speaking it on the occasion of recording while reminiscing about their working life as coalminers. *Cité Duits* is definitely moribund (Pecht 2019) – coal mining in Eisden ended decades ago.

To exclude the effect of direct language contact, we only consider bare nouns in PNCs in which none of the source varieties (German, Dutch and the Maasland dialect) allows the omission of the determiner. Examples like in (3a) as well as proper names referring to places or people were therefore excluded. Street names were included since they require the definite determiner in Dutch and German. PNCs that occurred in code-switched Dutch utterances were not considered.

An important difference between German and Dutch is that in German, some prepositions and definite determiners case-marked for dative can (and in certain contexts must) be contracted, cf. *im < in dem* 'in the (DAT)' and *am < an dem* (DAT) 'at the' (cf. Nübling 2005). In this case, the determiner is enclitically attached to the preceding preposition:

(7) a) CD der sass da **am küchenfenster** hier, vor Kastanjelaan (J)

    b) G der saß da **am Küchenfenster** hier, vor (vorn an) der Kastanienstraße

    c) D hij zat daar **aan het keukenraam,** hiervoor (aan de) Kastanjelaan
      'he was sitting there **at the kitchen window,** here in front, Chestnut Street' (L: 1383.623)

The number of these contractions in our data is small. Nevertheless, they were included in the analysis in Section 4.2.3.3. We will come back to cliticisation in German in Section 4.2.4. Contractions of a preposition with the accusative singular determiner *das* (as in *an+s, in+s*) are not attested.

If the noun is modified by an attribute, the four *Cité Duits* speakers investigated usually used a definite determiner (as would be predicted from the source varieties, where the same restriction holds):[7]

(8)	CD	in der tonne	**bei**	**de**	**gutter**	**mann**	(L: 1517.513)
	E	In the barrel	**with**	**the**	**good**	**man**	
	D	In de ton	**met**	**de**	**goede**	**man**	
	G	in der Tonne	**bei**	**dem**	**guten**	**Mann**	

Since there is no variation in the data in this case, examples with attributes preceding the noun are not listed in Table 4.2.1 and were not included in the statistics.

4.2.3.2 Results

Table 4.2.1 lists all the PPs containing singular nouns in the data set which would be preceded by the definite article in the source varieties. The first speaker (L) (Portuguese/Italian language background) realised 7 N-based PPs; 3 of the nouns were bare nouns. The second speaker (J) (Austrian-German language background, a former school teacher) produced 11 N-based PPs with 4 bare nouns. The third speaker (Y) (Ukrainian language background) produced 12 N-based PPs, with 6 bare nouns. The fourth speaker (JH) (Hungarian-German language background), read a brief text, in which two N-based PPs introduced by the preposition *nach* 'at' and *von* 'of' occurred (both with a determiner); he additionally gave us a written text[8] with his childhood memories (*Erinnerunge wie ich noch klein war*), which includes 55 PNCs. Of these, 11 included bare nouns. The complete data set is summarised in Table 4.2.1. The four speakers produced a total of 85 PNCs including 24 bare nouns and 61 with a definite determiner in.

The overall percentage of bare nouns in PNCs is 28%. It should be kept in mind that we only included examples in which the bare nouns are not allowed in any of the three source varieties. Hence, one-third of the examples represent true *Cité Duits* innovations, while two-thirds follow the established pattern of (one of) these source languages. Including cases in which at least one source language also allows a bare noun would of course have changed this ratio in favour of the bare nouns.

Although the percentages of bare nouns vary, bare nouns are documented for all four speakers. This supports our claim that the language background of the speakers does not play a role, and that *Cité Duits* is a variety in its own right, not a learners' variety. The four speakers vary between bare nouns and determiner-marked nouns in a similar way, which testifies to the structural sedimentation of *Cité Duits*.

Some prepositions never occur with a bare noun in our data, such as *gege* 'to', *durch* 'through', *vor/für* 'for', *neben* 'next, *hinta* 'behind', *unta* 'beneath, *rond/rund* 'around', *aus* 'out' and *mit* 'with'. The ones that take a bare noun are, in decreasing order, *in* ($n = 9$), *auf* 'on' ($n = 7$), *van/von* 'of' ($n = 4$), *na/nach/naar* 'to' ($n = 3$), *an* 'at' ($n = 1$). But given the small size of the corpus, these numbers must be treated with great

284 Peter Auer and Leonie Cornips

Table 4.2.1 N-based PPs with and without definite determiner in four speakers of Cité Duits

Preposition	Bare noun	Noun	Definite noun	Noun
auf 'on'	7	*Regie* 'administration', *Pütt* 'pit', *Leopoldstrasse* 'Leopoldstreet' (streetname) *Gestaeinjelaan* 'chestnut street' (street name), *Strasse* 'street', *Grund* 'ground' (2x)	14	*Foto* 'picture', *Pen* 'pin', *Berkenlaan* (street name), *Ecke* 'corner' (2x), *Sjtoep* 'pavement', *Kiepe* 'dump', *Sjtoelke* 'small seat' (2x), *Sjtoof* 'stove', *Piene* 'pin',, *Cité (2x)*, *Pek* 'tar', *Strasse* 'street'
in	9	*Kirche* 'church, *Haus* 'house', *Pütt* 'pit', *Garten* 'garden' (2x), *Busch* 'forest', *Put* 'pit' (2x), *Mund* 'mouth'	16	*Boek* 'book', *Schteig* 'walkway', *Busch* 'wood', *Gruppe* 'group', *Brood* 'bread', *Ecke* 'corner' (2x), *Gaarte* 'garden', *Pickelhecke* '(a kind of) hedge', *Luft* 'sky', *Strasse* (3x)'street', *Hecke* 'hedge', *Panne* 'pan', *Haufe* 'heap',
na/nach 'to, after'	3	*Kirche/Kirke* 'church' (2x), *Püüt* 'pit'	1	*Eindstrasse* (street name)
mit 'with'	0		4	*Tote* 'dead person', *Hut* 'cap', *Wasser* 'water', *Knuppel* 'club'
van/von 'of'	4	*Direktor* 'director', *Put* 'pit' (2x), *Kirche* 'church'	3	*Pütt* 'pit', *Kugel* 'bullet', *Piene* 'pin'
an 'at'	1	*Strand* 'beach'	8	*Pütt* 'pit', *Küchenfenster* 'kitchen window, *Sandberge* 'sand dunes', *Kippe* 'dump', *Sassel* 'seat', *Sjtoof* 'stew pan', *Kordel* 'rope', *Piene* 'pin'

caution, as the absence of bare nouns with certain prepositions can be a chance result.

4.2.3.3 Bare Nouns, Semantic Definiteness, and Weak Referentiality

In this section we test the prediction that the tendency to innovate and use bare nouns where all source varieties do not is stronger (a) in weakly referring nouns than in strongly referring nouns, and (b) in pragmatically determined contexts than in semantically determined ones. We categorised all examples of PNCs in the data set while considering the conversational context. Only singular NPs were analysed, as the indefinite plural cannot receive an article in the source varieties.

As the concepts of strong and weak referentiality – and of pragmatic and semantic definiteness – have hardly been used in empirical, corpus-based research so far, it is not easy to operationalise them in such a way that the data in a corpus can be unequivocally and exhaustively assigned to one of the two categories. For semantic versus pragmatic definiteness, where this is particularly relevant, we followed Himmelmann (1997: 39). According to his approach, pragmatic definiteness singles out a referent in its situational or discourse context, while semantic definiteness singles out a referent on the basis of generally shared world knowledge or is determined by the grammatical construction and its meaning. This holds, for instance, for unique referents, for proper names, or for superlatives. The most problematic cases were examples in which the referent of the NP is only accessible via another referent, which Himmelmann categorises as semantically definite. For instance, in the following utterance (9a), the speaker tells about his post-war experiences with ammunition found in the forest, which the children put on the doorstep of their houses:

(9) a) Die hamma na Hause gebracht, **auf dè sjtoep** gelegt, und mit ein dikke Hamma drauf geklopt (JH)

'We brought it home, put it **on the doorstep**, and hit it with a massive hammer'

b) in de Oorloch hamma ein Schutzkella gehat **in Garten** (JH)

'During the war we had a shelter **in (the) garden**'

c) bei uns **in dè Strasse** (JH)

lit. 'with us **in the street**' ('in our street')

In this case of an associative-phoric reference (Hawkins 1978: 123), the referent of *sjtoep* 'doorstep' can only be identified when the referent of the previously mentioned noun *Hause* 'home' is known, of which the 'doorstep' is a part. Hence, *sjtoep* refers back via association to *Hause*. The relation between 'home' and 'doorstep' requires shared cultural knowledge (of the schematic kind: 'houses have doorsteps'), but no situational knowledge. Hence, the example was categorised as semantically definite. In a case like *in Garten* 'in garden' in (9b), presumably an "associative clause" in the sense of Hawkins (1978), reference to the specific garden depends on the identification of the referent of 'we'. Again, schematic (and hence, semantic) world knowledge is needed in order to locate a shelter in the garden of the owner's house. The example was therefore also categorised as semantically definite. Finally, in (9c), the construction *bei X in Y* 'with X in Y' enforces the reading of *dè Strasse* being the street in front or at the back of the speaker's family's house. Here, no schematic world knowledge is required to establish the reference of 'the

286   *Peter Auer and Leonie Cornips*

street' via the reference of 'us'; rather, it is the semantics of the linguistic construction itself which enable this reading. Again, we assumed a semantic basis for definiteness, not a pragmatic one.

Of the 24 examples of non-expanded singular bare nouns, all but two are weak in referentiality and/or semantic definiteness. We give examples in (10):

(10)   *Bare nouns/weak referentiality and/or semantically definite (n = 23)*[9]

Weakly Referential

    a)   Kamerade die schon **in Put** gearbeit habe… (JH)
          'comrades who were already working **in (the) mine**'
    b)   met Pasen, ging_we(r) **naar kirke** (Y)
          'at Easter, we went **to church**'
    c)   maar wenn wir **von kirche** komme… (Y)
          'but when we come back **from church**…' (part of a generic narrative about Easter habits)
    d)   Dè Spitz von dè Kugel is in dè Hecke **von Direktor** reingefloge. (JH)
          'The top of the bullet flew into the hedge **of the director**'
    e)   Wenn dè Pek **in Mund** warm is geworde, dan wa dè zjust goed weich (JH)
          'when the tar got warm **in (the) mouth**, then it was just nice and soft'

Semantically Definite

    f)   oda dè Fatta bracht dat mit **von Put** (JH)
          'or father brought it home **from (the) mine**'
    g)   wie ik (V) arbeiten **naar püüt**,… (Y)
          'when I (unintelligible verb) to work **in (the) mine**…'
    h)   auf Leo'poldstrasse (Y)
          'on Leopold street'
    i)   in de Oorloch hamma ein Schutzkella gehat **in Garten** (JH)
          'During the war we had a shelter **in (the) garden**'

In examples (a)–(c) the highlighted PNCs refer to mining or to church in general, not to a specific place or institution. For instance, (a) is about other men who were already miners, (b) about why one needs a 'Pikeur' in a mine, or (c) refers to the fact that the speaker and his family (regularly) went to church at Easter. In examples (d), the locational descriptions also do not refer to a concrete location: the 'hedge' does not belong to a particular individual but to the house of the director of the mine. Here, no specific referent of the noun *director* is intended; it is irrelevant which individual is the director, and indeed, even whether the mine has

Bare Nouns in Prepositional Phrases   287

a director at all, as long as the building that is shielded off by the hedge can be identified.

There are also examples of bare nouns which refer to specific referents, i.e., they are strongly referring. However, this reference is not established on pragmatic but on semantic grounds. This, we argue, holds for (f)–(i) where the mine referred to (*Put/Pütt*) is the mine in Eisden, but since this mine used to be (and perhaps still is) the overarching frame of the speakers' life-world, it is not an entity referentially selected against a set of alternatives. Rather, it is the mine *tout court,* and the word is therefore treated like a uniquely referring noun in this group of speakers and their milieu. In addition, it is pragmatically enriched, as it refers to a set of activities, rules and institutional structures and their evaluation. (h) is a proper name which by definition refer semantically, not pragmatically. (i)[10] is a case of associative reference, as explained above.

In sum, the bare nouns in *Cité Duits* that do not follow the patterns of the source language but go beyond them and are almost always referentially weak or definite on semantic grounds. There are only two possible exceptions:

(11) *Bare nouns/strong referentiality (n = 2)*

    a) want dan hat mein mutter wä **auf regie** gegange (J)
        'because in this case my mother would have gone **to (the) director's office**'
    b) (wann/wenn) ich hab der foto **in kirch**... (L) (reference to a specific church which is shown in the picture)
        'I have the picture **in (the) church**...'

Regie in (11a) singles out a specific referent. The same applies to (b), where the specific church shown on the photograph is the intended referent.[11]

Of course, this very skewed distribution now needs to be held against the one for nouns produced with a determiner. Note, however, that they simply mirror the situation of the source languages. We only give some examples:

(12) *nouns with determiner/weakly referring and/or semantically definite (n = 30)*

    a) dan het de man **an der Pütt** gemeld (J)
        'then this man reported **to the mine**'
    b) Mein Fatta wa ein Schreinwerka. Die Plankskes hat dè **auf dè Kiepe** geholt (JH)
        'My father was a carpenter. The boards he got **from the dump**'
    c) ein kleine blum(e) steht **im busch** (J)
        'a little flower stands **in-the wood**'

288   *Peter Auer and Leonie Cornips*

> d)   ...un habe ... dè Granate **gegen dè Maua** geschmisse (JH)
> 'and (I) threw the grenade **against the wall**'
> e)   Ich bin gebore **auf dè Berkenlaan numma 3** (JH)
> 'I was born **at the Birch Lane Number 3**'

The examples resemble those in (10) and demonstrate variation between bare nouns and determiner PNCs. They either do not single out a concrete referent (cf. (c)-(d)), establish reference to a referent that is treated as (quasi-)unique on semantic grounds as in (a)-(b), or refer by a proper name (e).

It is worth mentioning at this point that the three examples of contracted preposition-determiner combinations (clitic determiners) all occur in semantically definite PNCs (see (12c), as well as (7a)).

Finally, let us have a look at some examples of strongly referential NPs which establish reference on pragmatic grounds. Mostly these are anadeictic, i.e., the definite noun phrase refers back to a previous mention of the same referent. Some examples are given in (13):

> (13) *nouns with determiner/strongly referring and pragmatically definite* (*n* = 30)
>
> a)   der is ... da auch **in der gruppe** da (Y) (previously mentioned)
> 'he is .... also there **in the group**'
> b)   maar allemaal **mit de(r) tote** (J) (previously mentioned)
> 'but definitely **with the dead (guy)**'
> c)   ... und hat aufgepast wen keine Löchas ware **in dè Pickelhecke.** (JH)
> ... and (he) took care that there were no holes **in the hedge**'
> (previously mentioned)

There is not a single instance of a bare noun used in this way. This means that our speakers deviate from the patterns found in the source varieties of *Cité Duits* when they produce semantically definite and/or weakly referring nouns in 23 out of a total of 53 cases. Strongly referring and pragmatically definite nouns are almost never realised as bare nouns. In our data set, this means that anadeictic references (discourse deixis) are, at the same time, the realm in which the definite determiner in PNCs is unchallenged.

Despite the small numbers, it is instructive to look at the distribution in quantitative terms (see Table 4.2.2). The association of strong versus weak referentiality or pragmatic versus semantic definiteness with the use or non-use of the determiner is highly significant and of medium to high strength (chi square = 11.53, df = 1, p = .0007, Cramer's V = 0.395). This proves that the phenomenon discussed in this chapter, i.e., the presence or absence of the definite determiner, is not a variable

Bare Nouns in Prepositional Phrases 289

Table 4.2.2 PNCs with a bare or definite noun in *Cité Duits,* weak/strong
referentiality, and pragmatic/semantic definiteness[a]

Total n = 85	Weak referentiality/ semantic definiteness	Strong referentiality/ pragmatic definiteness
Bare noun	23	2
Noun with determiner	30	30

a In three cases the context remained unclear and referential strength/type of definiteness could not be analysed.

in the strict Labovian sense, since it is to a certain degree pragmatically and semantically motivated, exactly in line with Cheshire et al.'s (2013) claims. Also, the two variants differ in pragmatic/semantic meaning, which challenges the notion of the linguistic variable in its original definition (confirming Cheshire 2015, 1987). On the other hand, weak referentiality and semantic definiteness are not strong-enough factors to eliminate the variability in the data entirely (see Cornips and Gregersen 2016).

4.2.4 Bare Nouns in Modern Multiethnolects of German and Dutch, and in Ruhr German

Cité Duits is an amalgamation of elements of Dutch, (vernacular) German and the Maasland dialect which has the sociolinguistic function of a multiethnolect for speakers of multiple European migration backgrounds. It emerged in a small work-defined community in Dutch-speaking Belgium 80 years ago. But (non-standard) bare nouns are also a central grammatical feature of modern multiethnolects of various Germanic languages, documented in European cities from the 1980s onward. As in *Cité Duits*, the impact of their speakers' family languages (usually that of their parents) on these multiethnolects is absent, weak or at least disputed (but see below, 4.3). Obviously, these multiethnolects are not hybrid in the same way in which *Cité Duits* is hybrid, as they are varieties of one particular language, such as Dutch or German, while *Cité Duits* combines features of Maasland dialect, Dutch and German in ways that make it impossible to identify a dominant language. Nevertheless, it is of some interest to compare the structural conditions under which bare nouns occur in *Cité Duits* with those in these modern multiethnolects. While the general instability of the determiner systems of the Germanic languages (in the sense of Leiss 2010) can be held responsible for the spread of bare nouns in both cases, if only on a very general level, an exact comparison will enable us to better evaluate the impact of language fusion on *Cité Duits*.

4.2.4.1 German Multiethnolect: Stuttgart

We start with a look at the German multiethnolect.[12] The following analysis is based on a dataset collected in Stuttgart in 2009–2012 among a group of 32 young speakers (analysed in detail in Siegel 2018). Of the group members, 28 were multilingual speakers from immigrant families of various, mainly Turkish and Balkan, backgrounds. They were born and/or brought up from a young age in Germany. Four were monolingual Germans living in close network contacts with the multilingual speakers and using the same variety. All of them had acquired German from childhood and lived in highly multiethnic, low-income neighbourhoods. The data come from informal group conversations, but mostly with an adult ethnographer present. Note that none of the Stuttgart speakers spoke Swabian dialect (Auer, 2020).

Siegel's results (2018, Ch. 4) show that bare nouns occur with considerable frequencies in this multiethnolect in contexts in which standard German – as well as traditional vernaculars or dialects as used by older speakers – would require a definite (19%) or indefinite article (22.4%) (based on $n = 1,857$ tokens). Comparing the occurrence of bare nouns in PNCs with NPs outside of PPs, she found only a small, non-significant difference (19.1% versus 22.6%; Siegel 2018: 60). If the noun is modified by an adjective, the number of bare nouns increases slightly (to 26.7%), resulting in a small but significant difference from simple Det + N sequences (20.4%; Siegel 2018: 71). Note that the theory of referential strength predicts the opposite: bare nouns, according to this theory, show weak referentiality, but nouns preceded by an adjective are referentially strong and therefore should not occur without the determiner (which in fact holds for *Cité Duits*). This suggests that referential strength might not play the same role in the German multiethnolect. On the other hand, Siegel found that bare nouns are more frequent with nouns referring to inanimate referents than with nouns referring to animate referents (23.6 % versus 14.4%, highly significant; cf. Siegel 2018: 77), with the former arguably showing more referential strength on average. The highest rates of bare nouns were found before names of states, streets, regions and other locations, before nouns for documents (such as passport and driving license), educational institutions, social groups (family, gang, etc.), and events (such as war) (all above 30%; Siegel 2018: 80).

In order to compare the Stuttgart data with our *Cité Duits* corpus, we selected all definite, singular PNCs containing no attribute (such as an adjective) and expressing a locational or directional meaning. Of course, only those cases were counted in which the bare noun is not possible in standard German.[13] An important fact to keep in mind here is that the German multiethnolect frequently omits the preposition in this syntactic context (cf. Wiese and Pohle 2016 for the Berlin multiethnolect). Non-use of the preposition always entails the absence of the determiner. It remains an open question whether weak referentiality and/or semantic definiteness are higher in these non-prepositional directional/locational NPs than in PNCs.

A search for all PNCs with the prepositions *auf* 'on', *aus* 'from/out of', *in* 'in', *nach* 'to', *neben* 'next to', 'beside', *von* 'from', *vor* 'in front of, before', *an* 'to, on' satisfying the criteria above resulted in a set of 457 cases, 22% of which were bare nouns (see Figure 4.2.1). This is only a little higher than the percentage which Siegel found for PPs in general (19.1%), i.e., the specific context of locational/directional PPs in the singular without an adjectival attribute does not seem to play a role for the frequency of bare nouns. Note that in *Cité Duits*, determiners in noun phrases outside the PP are not realised as bare nouns.[14]

A third important difference is the huge number of contracted (clitic) forms such as *ins, im, aufs, ans, am,* and *vom* (34%) in the German multiethnolectal data.[15] Although these contain a contracted (definite) determiner (*das > s, dem > m*), Schwarz (2009) argues that cliticisation is associated with lower referential strength. Along the same lines, Nübling (2005: 109) shows that "the domain of the clitic article is semantic definiteness" (instead of pragmatic definiteness; our translation).

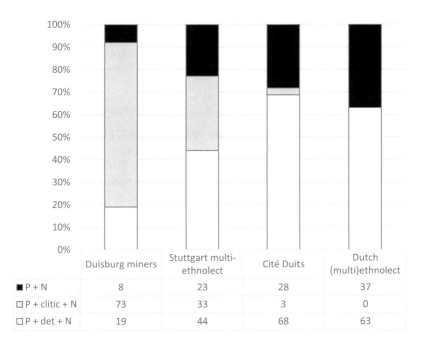

Figure 4.2.1 Percentage of bare nouns, clitic and determiner NPs in *Cité Duits*, the Stuttgart multiethnolect, the Duisburg miners' vernacular of miners and the Dutch (multi)ethnolect.

We therefore counted these two cases separately, as cliticisation seems to be an alternative way of coding semantic definiteness/weak referentiality which may compete with the use of bare nouns.

The results (Table 4.2.3 and Figure 4.2.2) show that, indeed, cliticisation is also strongly associated with referential strength/semantic definiteness. The association between type of PNC and type of reference/definiteness is highly significant and of medium strength (chi square = 21.33, df = 2, p < 0001, Cramer's V = 0.216). Both enclitic realisations of the determiner (Yates chi-square = 11.17, p = 0.0008, Cramer's V = 0.1827) and bare nouns (Yates chi-square = 15.23, p < 0.0001, Cramer's V = 0.2318) are significantly influenced by the pragmatics and semantics of the noun phrase. The effect is slightly stronger for the bare nouns (only 23% of these nouns are referentially strong and pragmatically definite, while this applies to 27% of the contractions), but the difference between the bare nouns and clitic determiners in PNCs is not significant.

Hence, bare nouns in the (Stuttgart) multiethnolect and in *Cité Duits* are similar, but not identical phenomena. In the Stuttgart multiethnolect, the occurrence of bare nouns is not restricted to prepositional phrases, not restricted to definite determiners (indefinite determiners are affected as well), and it is not blocked by NP expansion (attributes), but it is sensitive to referential strength/type of definiteness just as in *Cité Duits*. Another important difference is the role of clitics: Other than in *Cité Duits*, which hardly makes use of this option, the multiethnolect not only employs bare nouns but also preposition/determiner contractions in contexts of weak reference and semantic definiteness.

4.2.4.2 Dutch (Multi)Ethnolect: The Gouda Corpus

For further comparison, let us now have a look at a Dutch (multi)-ethnolect[16] (from Doreleijers, van Koppen, and Nortier, 2019). The data, collected by Khalid Mourigh between November 2014 and June 2015, come from interviews with eight young people of Moroccan background,

Table 4.2.3 PNCs with a bare or definite nouns in the Stuttgart multiethnolect, weak/strong referentiality and semantic/pragmatic definiteness

Total n = 457	Weak referentiality and/or semantic definiteness	Strong referentiality and pragmatic definiteness
Bare noun	77	23
Noun with clitic determiner	110	45
Noun with full determiner	107	95

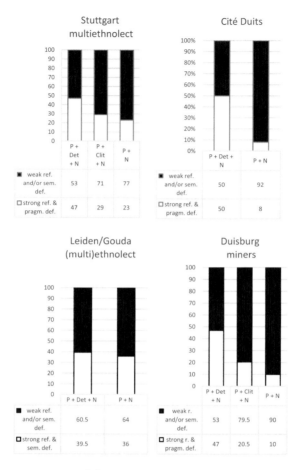

Figure 4.2.2 Percentage of bare nouns, preposition/determiner contraction (cliticisation) and full NPs in PNCs of weak versus strong referentiality in the Stuttgart multiethnolect, *Cité Duits*, the Dutch (multi)ethnolect in Gouda and the Duisburg miners' corpus.

aged 15–21, born in Gouda, the Netherlands. They lived in Gouda and Leiden. Doreleijers's et al. study is based on the first 250 noun phrases that occurred in the data in which a determiner would be expected according to the norms of standard Dutch. In this Dutch ethnolect (as in the Stuttgart multiethnolect), bare nouns are not restricted to the PP context and not restricted to definite noun phrases either (see Table 4.2.4).

The distribution in Table 4.2.4 reveals an interesting and significant positive correlation between the omission of determiner, the type of determiner, and its syntactic position: in object position, the indefinite

294 *Peter Auer and Leonie Cornips*

Table 4.2.4 Frequency distribution and percentages of presence and absence of (definite and indefinite) determiners per syntactic position in a Dutch (multi)ethnolect ($n = 238$) (from Doreleijers, van Koppen and Nortier 2019.)

Syntactic position	With determiner		Bare noun		Total	
	Frequency	%	Frequency	%	Frequency	%
Subject	5	5.0	14	10.1	19	8.0
Direct object	38	38.0	83	60.1	121	50.8
Object after a preposition	53	53.0	36	26.1	89	37.4
Adverbial phrase	4	4.0	5	3.6	9	3.8
Total	100	100.0	138	100.0	238	100.0

determiner is more often omitted than the definite determiner ($\chi 2 = 63.81$; df = 1; $p <. 001$). The direct object position in Dutch yields an indefinite, discourse-new interpretation. Doreleijers et al. therefore argue that new information triggers the non-use of the indefinite determiner linked to the direct object (focus) position. However, their hypothesis that the non-use of the definite determiner would be linked to subject position (topic) is not borne out. Doreleijers et al. assume that this might be due to cross-linguistic interference from Moroccan Arabic.[17] If so, however, the use of 'random' non-use of the definite determiner must be linked to a particular social styling, i.e., to group identification, rather than a learners' variety (see Sharma 2005), since Dutch for most of the Gouda speakers is the dominant language.

We extracted all examples of definite singular NPs in locative/directional PNCs without adjectival modification from the data set (taken from the appendix in Doreleijers, van Koppen, and Nortier 2019) in order to be able to compare the results with *Cité Duits* and the Stuttgart multiethnolect. The young people in the Gouda-corpus produced 60 relevant PNCs of which 37% ($n = 22$) were realised without a determiner. The rate of bare nouns is therefore higher than in *Cité Duits* (27%) and the Stuttgart multiethnolect (23%), cf. Figure 4.2.2. A characteristic feature of this (multi)ethnolect is that the locational preposition *in* always appears with a definite determiner ($n = 18$, 100%), which neither applies to *Cité Duits* nor to the Stuttgart multiethnolect.

Is the choice between bare nouns and determiners in this Dutch (multi)-ethnolect sensitive to referential strength and or semantic versus pragmatic definiteness? Table 4.2.5 summarises the results. There is no relevant association between weak referentiality or semantic definiteness, and bare nouns in this (small) data set (Yates chi-square = 0, df = 1, $p = .0316$, Cramer's $V = 0.0316$).

Bare Nouns in Prepositional Phrases   295

Table 4.2.5 PNCs with a bare or definite noun expressing weak/strong referentiality or semantic definiteness in the Dutch (multi) ethnolect

Total n = 60	Weak referentiality/ semantic definiteness	Strong referentiality and pragmatic definiteness
Bare noun	14	8
Noun with determiner	23	15

The Dutch and the German (multi)ethnolect are to a certain extent similar with regard to the use of bare nouns: both allow them regardless of the structure of the PP, and even outside it. In this sense they differ from *Cité Duits*. The results support the view that present-day (multi) ethnolects show innovations that exploit inherently 'vulnerable' structures of the respective language (in this case German or Dutch) but do so in different ways, which may reflect interferences with the speakers' family languages (Gouda) and/or contact between speakers of different language backgrounds (Stuttgart) combined with identity work.

4.2.4.3 Ruhr German Miners' Variety

While comparison with modern (multi)ethnolects makes it clear that the occurrence of bare nouns in *Cité Duits* PNCs is not a unique phenomenon of this hybrid miners' variety, it also shows that bare nouns can occur in very different grammatical contexts and with different pragmatic/ semantic constraints and functions. As to the first, the restriction of bare nouns to PNCs in *Cité Duits* is well in line with the patterns in the source languages but has no correspondence in the (multi)ethnolects. As to the second, the association between referential strength and the use of the definite determiner in *Cité Duits* is not found at all in the Dutch (multi)ethnolect and is complicated by the third option of using clitics for the same function in the German multiethnolect. How then can the specific patterning of bare nouns in *Cité Duits* be accounted for?

One possible line of reasoning takes us back to the question of historical language contact during the coalminers parents' migration to Eisden. As mentioned before, the first generation of miners that came to Eisden in the pre-war period had already acquired German elsewhere, mostly as a second or third language. As Belgian miners at the time were often recruited from foreign mines, it seems plausible that some of them had worked in the Ruhr area before and acquired German there (see Auer and Cornips 2018). Bare nouns are also a well-known feature of the Ruhr vernacular.[18] But is the choice of bare nouns in Ruhr German conditioned by the factors of referential strength and pragmatic/semantic definiteness, which would support such a contact-based explanation?

296 Peter Auer and Leonie Cornips

Table 4.2.6 PNCs with a bare or definite noun expressing weak/strong referentiality or semantic definiteness in Ruhr German

Total n = 497	Weak referentiality / semantic definiteness	Strong referentiality and pragmatic definiteness
Bare noun	38	4
Noun with clitic determiner	290	75
Noun with full determiner	50	40

In order to answer this question, we investigated a corpus of interviews with nine former miners in Duisburg, a city in the Ruhr area, who were roughly in the same age cohort as our *Cité Duits* speakers (aged 63–70). The corpus was compiled under the direction of Arend Mihm in the 1980s (see Salewski 1998). As children, the miners would have acquired the same Ruhr vernacular that the *Cité Duits* speakers would have been exposed to when their parents had learned German in the Ruhr area as a second language. Using the same criteria as above[19] we extracted 502 PNCs. Table 4.2.6 shows the distribution of contracted, bare and determiner NPs in this data set. With 8%, the number of bare nouns is much lower than in the Stuttgart multiethnolect (23%), in the Gouda/Leiden ethnolect (37%) and in *Cité Duits* (28%). On the other hand, with 73% of all singular, non-expanded NPs, the percentage of cliticised preposition/determiner sequences is much higher than in *Cité Duits* (3%) and even higher than in the Stuttgart multiethnolectal data (34%). (In the Dutch (multi)ethnolect, these contractions are absent).[20] As in *Cité Duits*, bare singular nouns outside the PP are not commonly found in Ruhr German.

Referential strength/type of definiteness is associated with the occurrence of clitics and bare nouns with very high significance (see Table 4.2.5; chi-square = 27.88, df = 2, $p <. 0001$, Cramer's V = 0.2368). Both the difference between full determiner NPs and bare nouns (Yates chi-square = 14.18, p = 0.0002, Cramer's V = 0.345) and the difference between full determiner NPs and clitic determiner NPs (Yates chi-square = 20.58, $p <. 0001$, Cramer's V = 0.219) are highly significant, although the first association is stronger. The difference between bare nouns and clitic determiner NPs is not significant.

4.2.5 Discussion

Figures 4.2.1 and 4.2.2 summarise our findings with respect to the four data sets. In the discussion of these results, it must be kept in mind that the data set is small in the case of *Cité Duits* and the Dutch (multi)

ethnolect and that in-depth studies on a larger basis are needed. These would also need to disentangle the effect of weak referentiality and semantic definiteness, which had to be conflated here due to the small corpora.

First, Figure 4.2.1 shows that in all four varieties, bare nouns in PNCs occur. Their frequency is high in *Cité Duits,* but also in the two modern (multi)ethnolects considered here. Figure 4.2.2 additionally reveals that across all varieties, the occurrence of bare nouns is not random. With the exception of the Dutch (Gouda) (multi)ethnolect, in which interference with Arabic may play a role as a group identification marker, they are favoured by contexts in which the nouns either refer weakly (i.e., do not single out a single referent with the presupposition that the hearer will be able to recognise it) or in which reference is not established on pragmatic, but on semantic grounds (see orange).

The two varieties of German that we have analysed (the Stuttgart multiethnolect and the Duisburg miners' variety of Ruhr German) differ from the Dutch variety (the Gouda (multi-)ethnolect) and from *Cité Duits* in their strong reliance on an alternative strategy to mark nouns of weak referentiality and/or nouns whose referent is identified on a semantic basis. This is the cliticisation of the determiner, which is contracted with the preceding preposition. This tendency is particularly strong in Ruhr German and has been described as one of its grammatical features before (cf., among others, Nübling 1992).

Both the Stuttgart multiethnolect and Ruhr German therefore have two competing grammatical strategies for expressing weak referentiality and/or semantic definiteness, i.e., cliticisation and the non-use of the determiner. Bare nouns are less frequent in the Ruhr miners' vernacular (which uses cliticisation extensively in this function), but when they are used, they almost categorically express weak referentiality or semantic definiteness. This resembles the strong effect of weak referentiality/ semantic definiteness on the use of bare nouns in *Cité Duits.*

At this point, we have to turn to the role of Dutch and the Maasland dialect as source languages for *Cité Duits.* The almost complete absence of cliticisation is an option which *Cité Duits* may have taken from these varieties. In Dutch, only the neuter determiner *het* can proclitically attach to the following noun (*'t*). This type of cliticisation is not attested in *Cité Duits* and in the Gouda/Leiden (multi)ethnolect. Instead, the speakers tend to generalise the determiner *de,* which expresses common grammatical gender in standard Dutch, to all contexts (cf. Auer and Cornips 2018). *De* cannot be cliticised. The option of marking low referential strength by contraction is therefore absent in the (multi)ethnolect and restricted in *Cité Duits* to those cases, in which the German determiner *(dem, den, ...)* is used. Its speakers have to rely on bare nouns instead. Regarding the bare noun in *Cité Duits* and in Ruhr German, we are dealing with a variable in which form and function vary together (see Cheshire 1987). This also means that Leiss's claim (2010) that the Germanic determiner systems have lost their functionality and therefore will collapse is not correct in this strong sense. Rather, although the tendency to eliminate the determiner before the noun is clearly proven by our data for all three varieties, and particularly for the old and new (multi)ethnolects, it is not a random phenomenon, but follows well-defined, functional patterns.

4.2.6 Conclusion

In this chapter we have investigated four varieties: two older miners' varieties, i.e., *Cité Duits* and Ruhr German, and two modern (multi)ethnolects spoken in Gouda (the Netherlands) and Stuttgart (Germany). Bare nouns in preposition-noun combinations (PNCs) occur in all four investigated varieties, and although their occurrence is not random, they emerge in very different grammatical contexts and with different pragmatic/semantic constraints and functions. The modern Stuttgart and Gouda (multi)ethnolects are emergent varieties and still in flux. This is evidenced by the fact that bare nouns function quite differently in the Stuttgart and in the Gouda ethnolect. Both German varieties also use cliticisation of the determiner to mark nouns of weak referentiality and/or nouns whose referent is identified on a semantic basis. The two older miners' varieties are similar in their relative high percentage of bare nouns with weak referentiality and/or semantic definiteness. On the other hand, in contrast to the two older miners' varieties ways of speaking conventionalised either through generational transmission, as in the case of Ruhr German or, in the case of *Cité Duits*, as the result of lifelong sharing of verbal practices in a dense network of speakers who lived their lives in relative social and geographical isolation.

Notes

1 We would like to thank the former coalminers in Eisden for engaging with our research. We also thank FRIAS for awarding a fellowship grant to the second author, and NIAS for awarding fellowship grants to both of us.
2 Boldface is used to highlight passages relevant to the discussion. The Dutch-German mixed orthography is intended very roughly to indicate the amount of fusion in the data. Deviations from Dutch or German orthography are due to our attempt to stick as closely to the spoken form as possible.
3 We use the term multiethnolect here although we are aware of the terminological problems surrounding it, which cannot be discussed here (but see, for instance, Cornips, Jaspers, de Rooij 2015; Jaspers 2017; Cheshire, Nortier and Adger 2015). As the data on which the comparison in Section 4.2.4 is based were collected from young people living in a strongly multi-ethnic neighbourhood and (mostly) in immigrant families, the term seems justified here.

Bare Nouns in Prepositional Phrases 299

4 The set of prepositions that allows such an alternation in Dutch is quite limited (Broekhuis 2013:169), and, not even (near) synonyms behave in the same way (de Swart 2015, and references cited): *in bed/*in couch, at sea/*at ocean.*

5 Kiss and Roch (2014) argue that a unified semantic analysis as proposed by de Swart is doubtful, based on an empirical study of the antonymic prepositions *mit* and *ohne* ('with' and 'without') in written standard German, which differ in the probability of a bare noun following in the PP, although weak referentiality holds in both cases.

6 The speaker's parents belonged to the Hungarian-Swabian language/ ethnic minority in Hungary before 1918 (when the region became part of Romania).

7 The only exception is *Wie hamma auch in Busch hinta dè Kirche, an dè Sandberge viel Kugels gefunte* (JH). 'We also found many bullets in the wood behind the church, in the dunes'. In addition, in three cases, the PNC included a bare noun and a number adjective, always with the noun *diviisi* ('division'). Here, the adjective + noun combination (*erschte diviisi* 'first division' etc.) seems to be treated like a proper noun. These examples were not counted in the statistics below.

8 The text is accompanied by a short grammar of *Cité Duits*. The variable use of the determiner is not mentioned in it.

9 Examples marked JH are taken from the written text by JH, the remaining examples are from the spoken interactions.

10 Alternatively, this example might be interpreted as modelled on the Dutch expression *Ik heb mensen in huis* meaning 'I'm renting rooms' or 'I have guests'. Using the latter interpretation, the example would not be relevant for our analysis, as we excluded cases in which at least one of the contact varieties allows a bare noun.

11 The example is somewhat difficult to understand; presumably, *in kirch* is intended to mean 'of (the) church'.

12 Bare nouns have been reported to occur in multiethnolects spoken in other German cities as well (see, e.g., Wiese 2008, Wiese and Rehbein 2016 for Berlin). It should be stressed that we do not claim that bare nouns do not occur in monolingual German young speakers without a migration background as some features of the multiethnolect are spreading into general German youth language. This de-ethnicisation needs a thorough sociolinguistic study, which is not the aim of our paper. There is, however, general agreement that non-standard features such as the bare nouns studied here have originated in multiethnic youth networks and are still most frequently found in these speakers. It is therefore useful to have a closer look at them.

13 We were as liberal as possible in this categorisation. In particular, this applies to PNCs in which the noun is a nominalised ordinal number referring to a school grade (such as *in fünfte* instead of *in der fünften* 'in fifth grade') or a school type (*ich geh auf Gymmi* 'I to go grammar school'). These bare forms are in general usage among pupils and students and are therefore a sub-standard innovation, but not multiethnolectal.

14 In fact, the speakers even tend to use the determiner in optional contexts such as with proper names.

15 This is of course no innovation of the multiethnolect, but these contractions are found in standard German as well.

16 The brackets around 'multi' are due to the fact that we have no data to ascertain that the structures described here can be generalised to speakers of other language backgrounds.

17 See Sharma (2005) for L1 interference from a similar pattern to mark definiteness by position in Indian languages (particularly Hindi) in Indian English as spoken by first-generation immigrants in Canada. Her article also contains further references regarding *zero* articles in learner varieties and creoles, which we cannot go into here.

18 See e.g., Scholten 1988: 164–172, cf. *mach ma Licht an, mach Tür zu, auf Hörsterstraße, geht nach Bett, in Schule.* Bare nouns are also frequent and even obligatory in the Ruhr miners' professional register, cf. *vor Kohle, auf Schicht, der Stempel steht <u>auf Strebe</u>,* etc. These vernacular bare nouns may in turn be due to Low German substrate influence, cf. Low German *tau Kirke* 'to the church', etc.

19 Additionally, we disregarded the preposition in italics followed by the accusative form of the determiner *den* (*in den*), as the clitic form (*in:*) is extremely hard to distinguish from the bare noun (*in*). Other determiners after the preposition *in* were included (such as *in das/ins, in dem/im*).

20 This is a well-known fact of Ruhr German, where cliticisation is possible in contexts in which Standard German or other vernaculars or dialects would not permit it; cf. forms such as *auf=e zeche* (>*auf der*) 'in the mine', *in=e gewerkschaft* (>*in der*) 'in the union'.

References

Aguilar-Guevara, Ana, Bert Le Bruyn and Joost Zwarts. 2014. "Advances in weak referentiality". In *Weak Referentiality*, A. Aguilar-Guevara, B. le Bruyn and J. Zwarts (eds.). Amsterdam: John Benjamins. 1–15.

Auer, Peter and Leonie Cornips. 2018. "*Cité Duits*: A polyethnic miners' variety". In *The Sociolinguistics of Place and Belonging, Perspectives from the Margins*, L. Cornips and V. de Rooij (eds.). Amsterdam: John Benjamins. 57–90.

Auer, Peter. 2020. "Dialect (non-)acquisition and use by young people of migrant background in Germany". *Journal of Multilingual and Multicultural Development* (special issue on Migration and Dialect Acquisition in Europe edited by P. Auer and U. Røyneland).

Broekhuis, Hans. 2013. *Syntax of Dutch. Adpositions and Adpositional Phrases*. Amsterdam: Amsterdam University Press.

Cheshire, Jenny. 1987. "Syntactic variation, the linguistic variable and sociolinguistic theory". *Linguistics* 25(2):257–282.

Cheshire, Jenny. 2005. "Syntactic variation and spoken language". In *Syntax and Variation: Reconciling the Biological and the Social*, L. Cornips and K.P. Corrigan (eds.). Amsterdam: John Benjamins. 81–108.

Cheshire, Jenny, David Adger and Sue Fox. 2013. "Relative *who* and the actuation problem". *Lingua* 126:51–77.

Cheshire, Jenny, Paul Kerswill, Sue Fox and Eivind Torgersen. 2011. "Contact, the feature pool and the speech community: The emergence of multicultural London English". *Journal of Sociolinguistics* 15(2):151–196.

Cheshire, Jenny, Jacomine Nortier and David Adger. 2015. "Emerging multiethnolects in Europe". *Queen Mary's OPAL* #33.

Cornips, Leonie and Frans Gregersen. 2016. "The impact of Labov's contribution to general linguistic theory". *Journal of Sociolinguistics* 20(4):498–524.

Cornips, Leonie and Jacomine Nortier (eds.). 2008. "The emergence of ethnolects?" Special issue of the *International Journal of Bilingualism* 12(1–2):25–42.

Cornips, Leonie, Jürgen Jaspers and Vincent de Rooij. 2015. "The politics of labelling youth vernaculars in the Netherlands and Belgium". In *Language, Youth and Identity in the 21st Century: Linguistic Practices Across Urban Spaces*, J. Nortier and B. Svendsen (eds.). Cambridge: Cambridge University Press. 45–70.

Demske, Ulrike. 2020. "The grammaticalization of the definite article in German: From demonstratives to weak definites". In *Walking on the Grammaticalization Path of the Definite Article – Functional Main and Side Roads*, J. Flick and R. Szczepaniak (eds.). Amsterdam: Benjamins. 44–73.

Dorelijers, Kristel, Jacomine Nortier and Marjo van Koppen. 2019. Lidwoordomissie in Moroccan Flavored Dutch: Kale nomina in eentalige Nederlandse uitingen. "Article omission in Moroccan Flavored Dutch. Bare nouns in monolingual Dutch expressions". *Nederlandse Taalkunde* 24(3):291–322.

Flick, Johanna and Renata Szczepaniak (eds.). Forthcoming. *Walking on the Grammaticalization Path of the Definite Article – Functional Main and Side Roads*. Amsterdam: Benjamins.

Hawkins, John. 1978. *Definiteness and Indefiniteness: A Study in Reference and Grammaticality Prediction*. London: Croom Helm.

Himmelmann, Nikolaus P. 1997. *Deiktikon, Artikel, Nominalphrase: Zur Emergenz syntaktischer Struktur*. Tübingen: Niemeyer.

Jaspers, Jürgen. 2017. "The colour of Dutch. Some limits and opportunities of identifying Dutch ethnolects". *Dutch Journal of Applied Linguistics* 6(2):231–246.

Kiss, Tibor and Claudia Roch. 2014. "Antonymic prepositions and weak referentiality". In *Weak Referentiality*, A. Aguilar-Guevara, B. le Bruyn and J. Zwarts (eds.). Amsterdam: John Benjamins. 73–100.

Leiss, Elisabeth. 2010. "Koverter Abbau des Artikels im Gegenwartsdeutschen". In *Kodierungstechniken im Wandel. Das Zusammenspiel von Analytik und Synthese im Gegenwartsdeutschen*, D. Bittner and L. Gaeta (eds.). Berlin/New York: de Gruyter. 137–157.

Löbner, Sebastian. 1985. "Definites". *Journal of Semantics* 4:279–326.

Matras, Yaron and Peter Bakker (eds.). 2007. *The Mixed Language Debate*. Berlin, New York: de Gruyter.

Nübling, Damaris. 1992. *Klitika im Deutschen. Schriftsprache, Umgangssprache, alemannische Dialekte*. Tübingen: Narr.

Nübling, Damaris. 2005. "Von *in die* über *in'n* und *ins* bis *im*. Die Klitisierung von Präposition und Artikel als Grammatikalisierungsbaustelle". In *Grammatikalisierung im Deutschen*, T. Leuschner, T. Mortelmans and S. de Groodt (eds.). Berlin/New York: de Gruyter. 105–131.

Pecht, Nantke. 2013. "Siehs' du, du wars (...) besser wie du hast gedacht: Du has' Französisch gesprochen!" *Taal en Tongval* 65(2):149–169.

Pecht, Nantke. 2019. "Grammatical features of a moribund coalminers' language in a Belgian Cité". *International Journal for the Sociology of Language* 258:71–98.

Pires de Oliveira, Roberta. 2013. "Weak (in)definitesness and referentiality". *Revista da Abralin* 12(1):11–37.

Poesio, Massimo (1994). Weak definites, in: Proceedings of SALT IV, 282–299.

Rupp, Laura and Sali Tagliamonte. 2019. "'They used to follow Ø river': The zero article in York English". *Journal of English Linguistics* 47(4):1–22.

302 Peter Auer and Leonie Cornips

Quist, Pia and Svendsen Bente A. (eds.). 2010. *Multilingual Urban Scandinavia. New Linguistic Practices.* Bristol: Multilingual Matters.

Salewski, Kerstin. 1998. *Zur Homogenität des Substandards älterer Bergleute im Ruhrgebiet.* Stuttgart: Steiner.

Scholten, Beate. 1988. *Standard und städtischer Substandard bei Heranwachsenden im Ruhrgebiet.* Tübingen: Niemeyer.

Schwarz, Florian. 2009. Two types of definites in natural language. Ph.D. thesis, University of Massachusetts at Amherst.

Siegel, Vanessa. 2018. *Multiethnolektale Syntax. Artikel, Präpositionen und Pronomen in der Jugendsprache.* Heidelberg: Winter.

Sharma, Devyani. 2005. "Dialect stabilization and speaker awareness in non-native varieties of English". *Journal of Sociolinguistics* 9(2):194–224.

Swart, Henriette, de. 2015. "Constructions with and without articles". In *The Syntax and Semantics of Pseudo-incorporation*, O. Borik and B. Gehrke (eds.). Leiden: Brill. 126–156.

Tsimpli, Ianthi, Eleni Peristerie and Maria Andreou. 2018. "Cross-linguistic influence meets language impairment: Determiners and object clitics in Russian-Greek bilingual children with typical development and with Specific Language Impairment". In *Crosslinguistic Interference in Bilingualism*, E. Blom, L. Cornips and J. Schaeffer (eds.). Amsterdam: John Benjamins. 331–354.

Wiese, Heike. 2008. "Grammatical innovation in multiethnic urban Europe: New linguistic practices among adolescents". *Lingua* 119:782–806.

Wiese, Heike. 2012. *Kiezdeutsch.* München: Beck.

Wiese, Heike and Maria Pohle. 2016. "‚Ich geh Kino' oder ‚...ins Kino'? Gebrauchsrestriktionen nichtkanonischer Lokalangaben". *Zeitschrift für Sprachwissenschaft* 35(2):71–216.

Wiese, Heike and Ines Rehbein. 2016. "Coherence in new urban dialects: A case study". *Lingua* 172–3:45–61.

4.3 When Contact Does Not Matter
The Robust Nature of Vernacular Universals

Daniel Schreier

4.3.1 Introduction

Past *be* regularization (whether pivoted with *was* or *were*) has been widely documented in English varieties around the world (e.g., Hazen 2014; Tagliamonte 1998). This chapter focusses on past *be* regularization under conditions of language contact, restructuring, and 'creoloidization' (contact with a restructured, partially creolized, variety) by providing a first analysis of St Helenian English, the oldest variety of Southern Hemisphere English, which has an intriguingly complex contact history (dialect, language, and restructured second-language varieties; Schreier 2008). The population's founding stock consisted of British settlers (mostly laborers with an agricultural background, but also administration), slaves of various destinations (Africa, Madagascar), speaking African languages, restructured Portuguese and Malagasy, and colonists from various settings throughout Europe (France), all residing in close proximity. Present-day St Helenian English (StHE), the result of dialect contact, language contact, and possible admixture of creolized varieties, has been tentatively classified in a somewhat medial position on Schneider's (1990) 'cline of creoleness' continuum, sharing similarities with mesolectal English-based Creoles spoken elsewhere (notably the Caribbean).

Analyzing past *be* on St Helena offers new insights into this variable's development in an overseas setting and is particularly important for the general question how a variable's internal constraints develop under conditions of extensive contact. A quantitative sociolinguistic analysis of levelled *was* (e.g., *they was there*) in early twentieth-century StHE (in a sample of 16 speakers born between 1916 and 1935) shows internal constraints, levelling frequency and external criteria such as regional origins, gender, and individual variation. These results are discussed with reference to local contact demographics, historical interaction patterns and regional feature pools on the island of St Helena, as well as in terms of their internal constraint patterns in Englishes worldwide.

4.3.2 Past *Be* in Better- and Lesser-Known Englishes

Past *be* levelling, which has been researched for several decades now, is one of the best-studied sociolinguistic variables in World Englishes, not only in major varieties, such as British English (Britain 2002; Cheshire and Fox 2009; Smith and Tagliamonte 1998; Tagliamonte 1998), (White) American English (Feagin 1979; Hazen 2014), New Zealand English (Hay and Schreier 2004), and Australian English (Eisikovits 1991), but also in some dialects of English that are not part of the World English canon, such as Tristan da Cunha (Schreier 2002). These studies indicate quantitative differences between urban and rural varieties in different places around the world (particularly in the US). Past *be* levelling is particularly attractive for variationist research in that it involves alternation of two allomorphs (*was* and *were*) and considerations of person-number concord, which are regularized so that first-/third-person *was* is extended to all grammatical persons in a process that Britain (1997: 141) described as "an increase in grammatical regularity and decrease in formal complexity". Whereas <u>was</u> with all persons is widely attested (e.g., *two dogs **was** in the yard*, *we **was** happier when we **was** young*), a levelling process with *were* as a pivot form is also found, albeit much more regionally restricted (the south of England, including London (Cheshire and Fox 2009) and the English Fens area (Britain 1997)). The most complex pattern of levelling involves the extension of one of the allophones in terms not of grammatical person but of polarity, so that *was* is used with all persons in positive contexts and *weren't* in all negative contexts. This pattern has been reported in the English Fens, where it is far advanced in younger speakers (Britain 2002: 17), and in Ocracoke, North Carolina (Wolfram, Hazen, and Schilling-Estes 1999).

A second point of importance here is that there is a remarkably robust set of constraints on the variation across all varieties. Existential constructions have a particularly strong effect on levelling to *was*, so that *there was* NP_{plural} is by far the most common realization (see discussion in Hay and Schreier 2004), which is even stronger in present *be*, where lexicalization of *there's* has been suggested as an explanatory factor (Walker 2007). The plural persons are levelled as well, although the hierarchy is subject to variation by variety: plural NPs have generally higher rates than personal pronouns, and second-person singulars have higher rates than first- and third-person plurals. An idealized constraint hierarchy of past *be* with pivot form *was* could be modelled as in (1).

(1) EXT there (there was)
>> Plural NP (*the cars was*)
>>> second person singular (*you was*)
>>>> first-/third-person plural (*we/they was*)

It is quite striking that, outside the British Isles, this constraint ranking has been demonstrated mostly in varieties that have well-established British founding populations (the United States, Australia, New Zealand). Whereas it is mentioned in passing elsewhere (e.g., Britain and Sudbury 2002 for Falklands Islands English), most of these varieties are what Kortmann and Lunkenheimer (2013), in their electronic atlas of World Englishes (*eWave*), would classify as "traditional L1 varieties" or as "high-contact L1 varieties". This means that differences in levelling frequency could be interpreted along a continuum of (non-)standardness or explained as a legacy of basilectal working-class dialects that had high percentages of levelled *was* forms (e.g., Schreier 2002).

On the other hand, we know little about past *be* regularization under conditions of language contact, restructuring, and creolization, and there is practically no empirical research on varieties that have undergone heavy language contact ("Indigenized L2 varieties", "English-based Pidgins" or "English-based Creoles" in *eWave*). This paper is an attempt to fill this gap somewhat by reporting on past *be* levelling in St Helenian English (StHE), the oldest variety of Southern Hemisphere English, where other sociolinguistic variables have already been studied (e.g., consonant cluster reduction (CCR) and copula absence; Schreier 2008). As is known, StHE has a complex contact history (involving British English dialects, European, African, and Asian languages, and restructured ESL varieties from Europe; Schreier 2008), so the question is whether there is a similar type of constraint ranking here or whether contact-induced language change would have an alternate trajectory. I begin by detailing the sociolinguistic history of the community.

4.3.3 St Helena and St Helenian English

The volcanic island of St Helena, which lies in the mid-central South Atlantic Ocean, south of the equator and some 1,900 km west of Angola, is home to (geographically speaking) one of the most isolated speech communities in the world. The nearest inhabited islands are Ascension Island (about 1,000 km to the north-west) and Tristan da Cunha (2,300 km to the south). St Helena is a small island (only 122 km^2), shaped by steep, relatively barren and rocky ravines, mostly unsuitable for cultivation, with a rather fertile level in the south-east. Jamestown is the island's capital and only town, but there are smaller settlements, such as Half Tree Hollow, Blue Hill, Sandy Bay, and Longwood (the last served as the final residence of Napoleon Bonaparte, who was exiled to the island from 1815 to his death in 1821).

St Helena is one of the oldest British colonies in the Southern hemisphere (the East India Company established a colony in 1658) and the origins of StHE have been dated to the mid-seventeenth century, making it more than a century older than other major varieties of English (South

Africa, Australia, New Zealand) and pre-dating other lesser-known varieties (Tristan da Cunha, Falkland Islands, Palmerston) by more than 150 years, thus giving mechanisms of contact-induced change more time to operate, favouring focussing und new-dialect formation.

Following a short Dutch Interregnum in the early 1670s, there has been a continuous native-speaker English history on the island ever since, although the population has undergone extensive ethnic mixing (and language contact, as detailed below). The founders of the community came from England, France, West Africa, and Cabo Verde as well as the Indian subcontinent and Madagascar. The evolution and development of StHE involved a complex interplay of dialect and language contact, making it difficult to assess its typological status as a variety of post-colonial English (Schreier 2008 argues that neither criteria for "traditional dialects" nor "high contact L1 varieties" apply, but that full creolization is equally unlikely on sociolinguistic grounds).

The social and sociolinguistic history can be summarized as follows (see Schreier 2008 for a more detailed account). Following its discovery in 1502, the Portuguese charted the island and used it as a refreshment station and sickbay on journeys to and from the East. However, the island was never permanently settled until it was claimed in 1658 by the East India Company (Gosse 1938), which implemented a concerted settlement policy, recruiting soldiers, servants, and planters (employed and contracted by the Company, who held direct control over the island until the 1830s) and supplying slaves on request. The exact origins of the British settlers are not known, but an analysis of the earliest settlers' last names tentatively suggests that most of them came from southern, perhaps south-eastern, England. Moreover, the majority of the planters had working-class origins as many of the soldiers and settlers were recruited from the unemployed in England (Gosse 1938: 72). There are occasional reports of illiteracy[1] but this was of course common for the vast majority of the population in sixteenth century England (cf. Britain 2020).

The origins of the non-white population are somewhat better documented. Slaves were initially imported from the Guinea Coast, the Indian sub-continent and Madagascar, and to a lesser extent from the South African Cape and Larger Table Bay area (Cape Malays), the West Indies, Indonesia, and the Maldives. In 1789, the importation of slaves officially ended, but cheap labour continued to arrive in the form of Chinese indentured workers, who came in the early nineteenth century. However, very few, if any, stayed on permanently and slavery was finally abolished in 1832 (Melliss 1875). The 1815 census, carried out in the eve of Napoleon's arrival, showed that the total population was 3,342, divided by social group as shown in Table 4.3.1 (adapted from Schreier 2008: 110).

The situation changed dramatically in 1834, when the British government assumed administrative responsibilities and St Helena officially

Table 4.3.1 St Helena's socio-demographics in 1815

	Men	Women	Children	Total
White	109	202	383	694
Non-white	342	245	610	1,197
Army personnel (white)		933 (combined)		933
Company slaves (Black)		98 (combined)		98
Free blacks		420 (combined)		420
Total				3,342

became a crown colony. The economic situation became worse, with mass poverty and emigration throughout the nineteenth century. Crucially, this period saw an increase in mobility (primarily geographical, probably less social) and continued ethnic mixing. Governor Charles Elliot remarked in 1868 that "there can be no position on the face of the earth where it would be more difficult to discriminate between the various strains of blood of which the body of the population is composed than here in St Helena" (quoted in Gosse 1938). Other immigrant groups arrived: indentured laborers from China; liberated African slaves who were brought to the island after 1840, when St Helena was used as a temporary residence for slaves from captured slave ships (some of them chose to stay while the majority were sent on to the West Indies or repatriated to the African mainland); and hundreds of Afrikaans-speaking Boer War prisoners, who came in 1902 (as with the Chinese laborers a century earlier, only a handful stayed behind upon their release).

The sociolinguistic status and origins of StHE are by no means clear-cut. There is no doubt that the founding populations were socially and ethnically diverse: settlers, planters, administrative staff, soldiers and slaves (i.e. all those who participated in shaping the local form of English) came to the island from various European, Asian, and African settings, such as (mainly south(-eastern)) England, France, St Iago, Guinea, Nigeria, southern Africa, Madagascar, Maldives, India, Indonesia, China, South Africa, and West Africa (liberated slaves from the 1850s onwards).

Initially, the English founders had particular influence. Henry Gargen's (1665) diary describes the community in detail: Company personnel (administration and soldiers), planters and their families as well as slaves, mostly in the possession of the Company. Although their origins are unknown, we know there were orders that "In case at St. Iago you can procure five or six blacks or Negroes, able men and women, we desire you to buy them, provided they may be had at or under 40 dollars per poll" (*Company Instructions*, quoted in Gosse 1938: 46–47). It is possible that these slaves spoke restructured Portuguese, as half a century later we still find reports of Portuguese being spoken on the island

308   *Daniel Schreier*

(Gosse 1938). A later entry in the *St Helena Consultations* (collected by Janisch 1885) points to Guinea as a place of origin: "There are but twelve out of 42 Guinea Blacks now living yet more dyed from want of care or victuals".

From the 1700s on, the preferred place of origin of slaves was Madagascar, and there were requests to provide slaves exclusively from that island. According to other sources (Brooke 1808; Gosse 1938; Janisch 1885), some of the inhabitants came from France as well (Huguenots who had escaped from prosecution in France). Consequently, the information on the settlers' origins is partly detailed and partly sketchy. The most influential groups, both on historical and socio-demographic grounds, were the English planters and their offspring. Other groups were too small in size and keen to integrate and accommodate (such as the French Huguenots) or they left the island before they could make an impact on the evolution of the local variety (such as the Afrikaner prisoners). The slaves, the majority of whom came from Madagascar, would have been the most influential groups on numerical grounds (Schreier 2008).

In terms of interaction and local contact, it took the community a long time to stabilize. Following the 1672 Dutch Interregnum, there were countless conflicts in the island community, involving soldiers and planters alike. Promises of land grants were broken and the late seventeenth century saw quasi-feudal relationships between the Company directors in London, the local administration and the settlers and their families, who in the reality of every-day life on St Helena were indentured laborers without rights. Most of the planters were dissatisfied with their condition and left the island on the first occasion.

There was heavy fluctuation in army and administrative staff as well. The fort in particular saw revolts and rebellions, which lead to casualties, death penalties and escape attempts. In 1693, for instance, during the infamous 'Jackson Conspiracy', 27 soldiers seized the fort (killing the Governor) and escaped the island on a Company ship. As for the slaves, the St Helena Records (Janisch 1885) mention dozens of escapes, mostly by young male slaves. Several slave uprisings were reported in the 1680s and 1690s, in which slaves were tried and brutally punished, often without proof or on forced confessions. As a result, slaves seized every opportunity to flee the island. The loss of manpower was compensated by the importation of new labour, preferably from Madagascar (which peaked in 1716, when more than 100 slaves arrived from that island).

In the first half of the eighteenth century, illnesses ravaged the community. Thirty planters died in 1718 and there were large numbers of victims in the black population as well. An entry in the *Consultations* (Janisch 1885) from May 26, 1719, reads that "We usually decrease here among the white people five in a hundred per annum – but in each of the two last years not lesser than 10 per 100!!". Census and shipping lists show that there was massive population turnover and that the population only stabilized from the 1740s onwards.

Consequently, we can exclude "founder effects" (Mufwene 2001) for the early period (1670s–1750), simply because many of the founders did not stay on the island long enough to make an impact. Rather, StHE emerged once social conditions turned favourable, when settlers stayed and local children were born in sufficient numbers. As shown in Schreier (2008), ethnic mixing and socio-demographic homogenization throughout the eighteenth century favoured language shift (mostly from Malagasy to English), a process accompanied by dialect levelling and persistent bilingualism (Portuguese-English and Malagasy-English are historically attested). These processes were favoured for three main reasons: that inhabitants lived in close proximity, that there were few slaves per household, and that there were only half a dozen villages 'up country', all of which depended on the capital as a hub for commercial activities such as trade.

In summary, a local (nativized) variety developed in the seventeenth century and the sociolinguistic ecology of StHE involved heavy (language and dialect) contact in a confined topographic setting; with a time depth of about 350 years (roughly 15 generations), making it the oldest variety of English in the Southern Hemisphere. As for its typological status, qualitative and quantitative analyses (Schreier 2008) provided strong evidence that it has undergone morphosyntactic restructuring and simplification. Structurally, it resembles varieties that have creolized (particularly mesolectal English-based Creoles in the Caribbean) while taking a medial position on Schneider's (1990) 'cline of creoleness' continuum.

With regard to the variable studied here, past *be* levelling, the question is whether StHE aligns with traditional L1 varieties or whether its constraint rankings diverge from the common pattern. In particular, how robust is the otherwise consistent Ext Pl > NP PL > Pers. Pron. ranking in high-contact conditions? A quantitative analysis will help us to assess whether the prototypical constraint hierarchy persisted (which would attest to the strength of ancestral varieties from England) or whether it was restructured via contact-induced language change.

4.3.4 Past *Be* on St Helena

The data used for this study come from the *St Helena Language and History project* (SHLH). In 2003, sociolinguistic interviews were conducted with 19 native inhabitants (and residents) of the island (ten women and nine men) born between 1916 and 1940. The corpus consists of 21.5 hours of recorded interviews (about 141,000 words), all of which have been transcribed orthographically and annotated for corpus research. The total number of past tense *BE* tokens (excluding first- and third-person singulars, where *was* is the default) with potential levelling is 315.[2]

The total percentage of past *be* levelling in StHE is comparatively high, at 80% (251/315). Men had an overall levelling rate of 85% (147/174), compared to women at 74% (104/141). As Figure 4.3.1 shows, individual rates of levelling vary considerably, ranging from 23% (FM, female, b. 1916; 10/13) to 100.0% for several speakers (e.g., JJ, male, b. 1920; 0/27). The variation seems to be sociolinguistically robust with no sign of decrease: while all speakers display levelling, it is the oldest who have the lowest rates, whereas all speakers born after 1920 have percentages of 60% or higher (with the exception of GL, a woman born in 1935, but for whom we have very few tokens). To test for language change, we categorized speakers into three groups: those born in or immediately after the First World War (1916–1921); those born between the two world wars (1924–1930), and those born before and during the Second World War (1935–1940). While there may be evidence of language change (increasing levelling), we should bear in mind the shallow time-depth (24 years), the small population sample and the low token numbers for some speakers.

As for grammatical person, existential plurals had the highest levelling rates, at 96% (46/48), followed by NP plurals at 86% (73/85), first-person personal pronouns with 79% (33/42), third-person plurals with 72% (72/100) and second-person singulars with 67% (26/39).[3] The high rate of *was* in third-person plural pronouns is notable in comparison with other varieties (see below). A regression analysis was conducted in GoldVarb Lion (Sankoff, Tagliamonte, and Smith, 2012) with the factors speaker sex, age group, and grammatical person. The step-up/step-down procedure selected all factor groups except sex as significant, as shown in Table 4.3.2.

Finally, we conducted an analysis by speaker origins, as this was shown to have an impact on inter-speaker variation elsewhere (Schreier

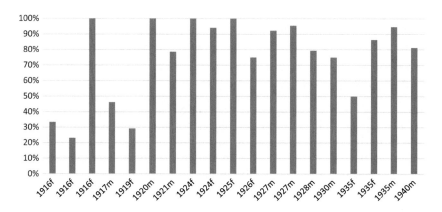

Figure 4.3.1 Past *be* regularisation rates by individual speaker.

Robust Nature of Vernacular Universals 311

Table 4.3.2 GoldVarb analysis of past *be* levelling (age group, internal constraints, speaker sex; default application value: *was*)

	n	%	Factor weight
Age group			
1916–1921	112	65.2	0.287
1924–1930	141	88.7	0.616
1935–1940	61	85.2	0.607
Grammatical person			
Existential plural	48	95.8	0.817
NP plural	85	85.9	0.591
First-person plural	42	78.6	0.419
Third-person plural	100	72	0.357
Second-person singular	39	66.7	0.279
Sex			
Male	174	84.5	[0.573]
Female	140	73.6	[0.427]
Total/Pi	314	79.6	0.846
Log. likelihood: −138.265			

Statistical significance: Age group $p < 0.001$ (1.69e-05); Construction $p < 0.00$ (0.00077): Speaker sex $p = 0.054$ (n.s.). Excluded: 2 pl. ($n = 1$)

2008 reported a rural/urban split in the overall frequency of CCR). However, great care needs to be taken here due to cross-island mobility of individual speakers. Although all speakers were natives of St Helena and had spent most of their lives on the island, they had moved between places (the exception was a couple from Levelwood who had never moved away). Strikingly, mobility mostly involved places 'up country' (e.g., a move from the rural areas to the capital and back was unusual, at least for the islanders interviewed for this study). Table 4.3.3 shows that areas such as Blue Hill and Sapper Way have lower levelling rates, which may be indicative of regional differences (as it was for copula absence, Schreier 2008), although we have to be cautious due to the low speaker numbers for the various regions. While it would be interesting to explore constraints linked to individual speakers and whether they pattern together by place of residence, the speaker sample is too small for such an analysis.

4.3.5 Discussion and Conclusion

Past *be* levelling in StHE is non-standard, strongly favouring *was* as a pivot form, while levelling to *were* (*I **were** happy*) or *weren't* was not found (cf. Cheshire and Fox 2009 for London). This result is not completely unexpected given global levelling trends, as Chambers (2004, 2009) characterized past *be* levelling among vernacular "roots"

312 *Daniel Schreier*

Table 4.3.3 Past *be* levelling in StHE: Regional variation

Residence	Was	Were	%
Thompson's Hill	27	0	100.0% (27/27)
Sandy Bay	44	1	97.8% (44/45)
Pounceys	18	1	94.7% (18/19)
Jamestown	40	3	93.0% (40/43)
Half Tree Hollow	23	4	85.2% (23/27)
Longwood	17	3	85.0% (17/20)
Levelwood	41	13	75.9% (41/54)
Blue Hill	34	22	60.7% (34/56)
Sapper Way	7	17	29.2% (7/24)
Total	**251**	**64**	**79.7% (251/315)**

(Chambers 2004: 128) or "primitives" (Chambers 2009: 242). As Tagliamonte (2009: 104) notes:

> [the] theory of vernacular roots provides an answer by suggesting that the occurrence of default singulars is not the result of diffusion or even simple regularization, but instead represents the more general tendency in all nonstandard varieties of English to gravitate toward more primitive (i.e. not learned) linguistic patterns.

StHE displays this tendency very strongly, as do nearly all other varieties of English around the world. Consequently, the two most important findings of this quantitative study of past *be* levelling are that StHE has a comparatively high rate of levelling (80%) and that the set of internal constraints (grammatical person) does not differ substantially from that reported elsewhere (with the exception of third-person plural levelling rates, which are higher than elsewhere).

To illustrate the relevance of levelling frequency, Table 4.3.4 provides a summary of selected varieties of English (Dominican Republic, Tagliamonte and Poplack 1988; Bermudas, Eberle 2017; Australia, Horvath 1985; England, Tagliamonte 1998; Cheshire and Fox 2009; Scotland, Smith and Tagliamonte 1998; the United States, Feagin 1979; Tristan da Cunha, Schreier 2002). Although we should take care when comparing these results (population samples vary quite a bit), we note considerable differences: adolescents in Sydney have a levelling rate of 13% (Horvath 1985) and York (England) has about 17%, the lowest numbers reported. At the other end of the spectrum, elderly speakers in the Dominican Republic (an enclave of African Americans) have about 90% and speakers of Tristan da Cunha English have 93% (even more remarkable, as this is a sample of the entire speech community; Schreier 2002). StHE aligns more with varieties that have contact histories and strong levelling trends (see discussion below).

Table 4.3.4 Past *be* levelling rates in English varieties around the world in % (adapted from Schreier 2002: 85)

Person	Samaná (Dominican Republic; Elderly)	Bermudian English	Sydney (Australia; Young adults)	English Fens	Anniston (USA)	Appalachian (USA; working class)	Buckie (Scotland; elderly)	York (England)	London (England)	Tristan da Cunha	St Helena (elderly)
Second sg.	58.0	18.2	31.7	71.7	60.4	Pronoun (not	91.0	12.0	69.8	88.9	66.7
First pl.	89.0	9.9	10.5	67.2	47.2	differentiated)	73.0	9.0	60.1	97.7	78.6
Third pl.	92.0	9.7	9.5	47.7	46.6	76.6	0.0	3.0	34.7	90.2	72.0
NP pl.	91.0	20.8	7.4	53.7	45.0	68.5	81.0	7.0	34.7	94.9	85.9
Ext. pl.	(no data)	62.5	44.4	80.7	68.4	92.4	91.0	66.0	78.7	96.3	95.8
Total	**89.0**	**20.1**	**12.9**	**62.8**	**50.3**	**76.9**	**58.0**	**17.0**	**51.2**	**93.8**	**79.1**

314   *Daniel Schreier*

There are several possible interpretations for this observation. Historically, for instance, the working-class origins of the majority of the settlers and planters might provide a worthwhile explanation. Although their regional and social origins remain unclear, most of the founders would have come from the lower strata of English society (Wright 2004). These founder populations (Mufwene 2001) could have brought high levels of past *be* levelling to the island, as a result of which *was* would have been adopted as a default past *be* form when the local variety developed and focussed in the second half on the eighteenth century (levelled paradigms would have an advantage in high-contact scenarios; cf. Schreier 2002 for Tristan da Cunha English). Regularization was arguably driven forward by the minimal education on St Helena at the time the consultants were of school age (1920s – early 1940s). There were country schools, but most of the speakers interviewed obtained minimal education before entering the local workforce as fishermen, foremen, agricultural workers, bakers, and so on.

The sociolinguistic ecology of the population would have provided favourable conditions for such developments: first of all, there was a division between Jamestown (the capital), where the government and administration were located, and 'up country' with all the farms and plantations. Whereas middle-class speakers would have been likely to take up residence in Jamestown, members of the working class (first indentured workers, later laborers, and planters) would have settled in the island's center and along the southern coast. Moreover, non-English speaking settlers and non-Anglophone slaves would have arrived at the same time, and the whites' local vernaculars would have been their target as they learned English and participated in language shift (the overall length of which is not clear, yet we have reports of Malagasy-speaking slaves into the 1780s). The restricted impact of Standard English, coupled by with the lack of schooling and the absence of norm-enforcing authorities, would have favoured a levelled past *be* paradigm, particularly if it was prominent in the input varieties (which seems likely, although it cannot be verified in the absence of reliable historical sources).

While overall rates are not as indicative as persistent internal conditions that govern variation, we note that the StHE constraint ranking is extraordinarily consistent with patterns found elsewhere: Ext Pl. > Pl. NPs > Pers. Pron. (first pers. pl. > third pers. pl. > second pers. sg.). This fact was already noted by Tagliamonte (1998: 158), who found that *was* levelling was subject to a grammatical constraint hierarchy that is "surprisingly consistent across varieties", namely NP existential > *you* > NP plural > *we/they* (Chambers [2004, 2009] made the same observation, except that first-person plural was more frequent than third-person plural, as found on St Helena). In other words, StHE displays the same internal constraints as all other varieties. This finding is remarkable, as the varieties differ in time depth, contact history and sociolinguistic development. The conditioning factors of preceding environments are nearly identical in New Zealand English, York/England English, and Alabama English, and on St Helena, varieties that have no sociohistorical connections whatsoever. In other words, this similarity would suggest that processes of language contact, restructuring and shift toward English may all occur without any impact on the parameters constraining this vernacular feature.

Present-day StHE, which is the result of dialect contact, language contact and possible admixture of creolized (Portuguese) varieties, has tentatively been classified (Schreier 2008) at a somewhat medial position on Schneider's (1990) 'cline of creoleness' continuum, such that it shares similarities with mesolectal English-based Creoles spoken elsewhere (notably the Caribbean). The quantitative analysis reported here shows that past *be* levelling is extraordinarily persistent and the PL Ext > NP Pl > Personal pronoun hierarchy was not modified through language contact and/or creolization. Accordingly, I would advance the (admittedly somewhat bold) hypothesis that vernacular roots in their most robust form (internal constraints) are the most likely features to survive the new-dialect formation process and remain intact when *koinés* (or other contact-derived varieties) stabilize and emerge. Of course, this claim needs to be tested against different types of English (pidgins, creoles, creoloids, perhaps also second-language varieties) but for the time being, StHE provides some tantalizing first evidence.

Finally, this analysis also goes some way toward contributing to a better understanding of the genesis of other forms of South Atlantic English. In a quantitative study of past *be* on Tristan da Cunha, I reported (Schreier 2002: 95) that

> regularization has advanced to the stage that *were* forms are nonexistent in the speech of the oldest members of the Tristan da Cunha community; in a sense, then, it is justified to claim that TdCE has completed the regularization process of past *be*

and suggested that StHE, being a prime input variety to the emerging local dialect, may have had high frequency of levelling to *was*. We can now confirm that StHE does have frequent past *be* regularization, not only because of the high overall levelling rate but also due to the fact that several of our consultants born in the 1920 and 1930s had categorical levelling rates (as did the speakers of Tristan da Cunha English born in the same period). This parallel would suggest that high rates of levelled past *be* were brought to Tristan da Cunha via the St Helenians who arrived in the 1820s, which would have favoured the rather unusual process of categorical levelling that was triggered when TdCE formed (see also Schreier 2016).

316   *Daniel Schreier*

With a focus on the present study, we conclude that StHE aligns itself with other varieties of English around the world in that it displays a strong tendency to past *be* levelling (with the pivot form *was*). It thus strongly resembles non-standard or working-class varieties of British or American English, both in overall levelling frequencies and internal constraints, which invites the inference that past *be* levelling is a robust feature even under contact conditions (or at least the ones we encounter on St Helena). Of course, these conclusions need to be verified against other varieties with extensive language contact and restructuring, a desideratum for future research.

Notes

1 One example is an entry in the *St Helena Consultations* (quoted in Brooke 1808) on February 2nd, 1774: "On 31st Jan. six soldiers deserted in the night taking two Boats ... The deserters were illiterate men of bad character and only a few days provisions and must inevitably perish at sea".
2 The number of tokens per speaker ranged from 3 to 34. With the exception of four speakers (1916f, $N = 3$; 1925f, $N = 5$; 1926f, $N = 8$; 1935f, $N = 4$), the minimum of tokens per speaker was 13.
3 Note that one levelled token for 2nd person plural was excluded from analysis.

References

Britain, David. 1997. "Dialect contact, focusing and phonological rule complexity: The koineisation of Fenland English". In *A Selection of Papers from NWAVE 25. Special Issue of University of Pennsylvania Working Papers in Linguistics*, C. Boberg, M. Meyerhoff and S. Strassel (eds.) 4:141–170.

Britain, David. 2002. "Diffusion, levelling, simplification and reallocation in past tense BE in the English Fens". *Journal of Sociolinguistics* 6:16–43.

Britain, David (2020). A sociolinguistic ecology of colonial Britain. In: Schreier, Daniel; Hundt, Marianne; Schneider, Edgar W. (eds.) The Cambridge Handbook of World Englishes. Cambridge Handbooks in Language and Linguistics (pp. 145–159). Cambridge: Cambridge University Press

Britain, David and Andrea Sudbury. 2002. "There's sheep and there's penguins: 'Drift', 'slant" and singular verb forms following existentials in New Zealand and Falkland Island English". In *Language Change: The Interplay of Internal, External and Extra-Linguistic Factors*, M. Jones and E. Harding-Esch (eds.). Berlin: Mouton de Gruyter. 209–242.

Brooke, Thomas H. 1808. *A History of the Island of St Helena from Its Discovery by the Portuguese to the Year 1806*. London: Black, Parry and Kingsbury.

Chambers, B. Kortmann (ed.), J.K. 2004. "Dynamic typology and vernacular universals". In *Dialectology Meets Typology: Dialect Grammar from a Cross-Linguistic Perspective*. Berlin: De Gruyter Mouton. 127–145.

Chambers, J.K. 2009. *Sociolinguistic Theory: Linguistic Variation and its Social Significance*. Oxford: Wiley-Blackwell.

Cheshire, Jenny and Sue Fox. 2009. "*Was/were* variation: A perspective from London". *Language Variation and Change* 21:1–38.

Robust Nature of Vernacular Universals 317

Eberle, Nicole. 2017. "They're trying to hear English, which they are hearing, but it's Bermudian English": Bermudian English – Origins and Variation." PhD thesis, University of Zurich.

Eisikovits, Edina. 1991. "Variation in subject-verb agreement in inner Sydney English". In *English Around the World: Sociolinguistic Perspectives*, Jenny Cheshire (ed.). Oxford: Oxford University Press. 235–255.

Feagin, Crawford. 1979. *Variation and Change in Alabama English: A Sociolinguistic Study of the White Community*. Washington: Georgetown University Press.

Gargen, Henry. 1665. "A description of the island of St. Helena to whom itt may concerne: by mee Henry Gargen from ye year 1661 to ye yeare of our Lord: 1665". Unpublished manuscript.

Gosse, Philip. 1938. *St Helena, 1502–1938*. London: Cassell.

Hay, Jennifer and Daniel Schreier. 2004. "Reversing the trajectory of language change: Subject-verb agreement with BE in New Zealand English". *Language Variation and Change* 16:209–235.

Hazen, Kirk. 2014. "A new role for an ancient variable in Appalachia: Paradigm leveling and standardization in West Virginia". *Language Variation and Change* 26(1):77–102.

Horvath, Barbara. 1985. *Variation in Australian English*. Cambridge: Cambridge University Press.

Janisch, Hudson Ralph. 1885. *Extracts from the St. Helena Records*. St. Helena: Grant.

Kortmann, Bernd and Kerstin Lunkenheimer (eds.). 2013. *eWAVE*. Leipzig: Max Planck Institute for Evolutionary Anthropology. http://ewave-atlas.org/.

Melliss, John C. 1875. *St. Helena: A Physical, Historical, and Topographical Description of the Island, Including Its Geology, Fauna, Flora, and Meteorology*. London: Reeve and Co.

Mufwene, Salikoko S. 2001. *The Ecology of Language Evolution*. Cambridge: Cambridge University Press.

Sankoff, David, Sali A. Tagliamonte and Eric Smith. 2012. *Goldvarb Lion: A Variable Rule Application for Macintosh*. Department of Linguistics, University of Toronto. (individual.utoronto.ca/tagliamonte/goldvarb.html)

Schneider, Edgar W. 1990. "The cline of creoleness in English-oriented creoles and semi-creoles of the Caribbean". *English World-Wide* 11:79–113.

Schreier, Daniel. 2002. "Past *be* in Tristan da Cunha: The rise and fall of categoricality in language change". *American Speech* 77:70–99.

Schreier, Daniel. 2008. *St Helenian English: Origins, Evolution and Variation* (*Varieties of English Around the World* G37). Amsterdam and Philadelphia: John Benjamins.

Schreier, Daniel. 2016. "Super-leveling, fraying-out, internal restructuring: A century of present be concord in Tristan da Cunha English." *Language Variation and Change* 28.2: 203–24.

Smith, Jennifer and Sali Tagliamonte. 1998. "'We was all thegither, I think we were all thegither.' *Was* regularization in Buckie English". *World Englishes* 17:105–126.

Tagliamonte, Sali. 1998. "*Was/were* variation across the generations. View from the city of York". *Language Variation and Change* 10:153–191.

318   *Daniel Schreier*

Tagliamonte, Sali. 2009. "There was universals, then there weren't: A comparative sociolinguistic perspective on 'default singulars'". In *Vernacular Universals and Language Contacts: Evidence from Varieties of English and Beyond*, M. Filppula, J. Klemola and H. Paulasto (eds.). New York: Routledge. 103–132.

Tagliamonte, Sali and Shana Poplack. 1988. "How Black English past got to the present: Evidence from Samaná". *Language in Society* 17:513–533.

Walker, James A. 2007. "'There's bears back there': Plural existentials and vernacular universals in (Quebec) English". *English World-Wide* 28:147–166.

Wolfram, Walt, Kirk Hazen and Nathalie Schilling-Estes. 1999. *Dialect Maintenance and Change on the Outer Banks*. Tuscaloosa, AL: University of Alabama Press.

Wright, Laura. 2004. "Some data from slave speakers: The island of St Helena, 1695–1711". In *Paper Presented at the Westminster Creolistics Workshop Diachronic Studies and Theories of Creolisation*, London UK, 15–17 April 2004.

4.4 From Killycomain to Melbourne

Historical Contact and the Feature Pool[1]

Karen P. Corrigan

4.4.1 Migration and Multiethnolectal Melbourne

Czaika and de Haas (2015:314) argue that Europe in the nineteenth and early twentieth centuries was a "global source region of emigrants and settlers" while it has now become "a global migration magnet". Moreover, the concentration of population movements in key urban areas of contemporary Europe that has rendered them 'superdiverse' (Vertovec 2007, 2014), as well as the variety of migration categories recorded, has increased the capacity for engendering language contact of novel types. This is on account of the fact that they are grounded in new technologies as well as language practices which scholars have variously labelled 'metrolingualism' (Pennycook and Otsuji 2015), 'plurilingualism' (García 2009), and 'translanguaging' (Blackledge and Creese 2017). Migration in the context of Ireland has induced profound economic, linguistic, and socio-political transformations (Corrigan 2010, 2020; Devlin Trew 2013; Fitzgerald and Lambkin 2008; McDermott 2012).

There are of course similarities as well as differences between historical and contemporary population movements regarding the degree to which they have invoked such changes at the individual and societal levels (see Czaika and de Haas 2015:284). A central aim of this chapter therefore is to further develop the uniformitarian principle by offering a fresh perspective on the "contradictions and paradoxes" (Labov 1994:10) which have arisen when the contribution to Australian English of large-scale emigration from Ireland during the nineteenth century has previously been explored. I will argue that it is very probable that the consequences of such immigratory trends to urban areas like Melbourne historically mirror the outcomes documented for contemporary cities in Western Europe and the United States (Nortier 2008) at least to some degree.

In rapid immigration scenarios, the levels of dialect and language contact have been argued to increase exponentially amongst urban inhabitants (Collins et al. 2009). This process often results in the development of new 'multiethnolects' (Clyne 2000). The latter are thought to arise on account of the fact that such city dwellers have the option to draw from a more diverse 'feature pool' of input dialects and languages (in the sense

320   *Karen P. Corrigan*

of Mufwene 2001:4–6; Cheshire et al. 2011) than would be available in rural communities such as Killycomain that are not generally associated with intense migration.[2] In multilingual and multicultural cities, speakers can choose divergent admixtures of features from the pool that are then often modified to produce novel structures that can come to typify the output variety.

This process is not untrammelled of course and its pathway is likely shaped by a range of internal factors including the regularity and transparency of the features in question as well as others argued for in Cheshire et al. (2011) and Siegel (1997:139) *inter alia*. No doubt the degree to which the languages and dialects in superdiverse cities where multiethnolects are developing are typologically similar will also have a bearing on which features become most prominent within the pool. The more disparate these varieties are from a genetic perspective, the more complex the competition is likely to be. There are external 'language ecology' (Mufwene 2001:20–24) factors to consider too. Hence, Labov (2001:19) contends that "a large part of the problem of explaining the diffusion of linguistic change" is simply the mechanical matter of ascertaining who speakers most regularly interact with (see also Fix 2013:71).

I would argue that the same applies in multilingual as well as multidialectal contact settings and further suggest that gauging the extent of face-to-face contact between individuals has to be measured by addressing issues such as the number of speakers of language X or dialect Y, assessing the status of these varieties and those who speak them as well as untangling the personal social networks they have contracted - which are all likewise bound to play a role in mechanisms of new dialect formation in such contexts (Beal and Corrigan 2009:232; Kerswill 2018:11; Trudgill 2010:300). Key to migratory contexts of course is ascertaining how exactly mobility promulgates language diffusion and subsequent change. Blommaert (2010:21) describes such population movements as "the great challenge: it is the dislocation of language and language events from the fixed position in time and space attributed to them by a more traditional linguistics and sociolinguistics."

This chapter take up this challenge by testing contact models through charting the linguistic input offered by diverse ethnic groups populating nineteenth-century Melbourne. Although the emerging base variety cannot be considered a 'multiethnolect' *sensu stricto* (since it is rather the product of new dialect formation), using the present to explain the past, as articulated in Labov (1994), would suggest that the dialect could, however, likewise have evolved through similar processes of competition and selection from a feature pool. In order to do so, the primary goal will be addressing the following research questions:

i)   What ethnic groups constituted the founder population of Melbourne?
ii) Were Irish migrants sufficiently numerous, and did they have the degree of political and socio-economic clout required for variants

Historical Contact and the Feature Pool 321

of their dialect to make a significant contribution to the feature pool that characterised the early dialects of Australian cities like Melbourne?

iii) What is the nature of the linguistic evidence for putative Irish-English influence in the formation of Australian English, and what are its drawbacks?

4.4.2 Potential Irish English (IE) Variants in Melbourne's Feature Pool

The purported linguistic impact of immigration from places like Killycomain to Melbourne in the nineteenth century on the formation of this and other Australian 'multiethnolects' (in the broad sense which that term is to be understood here) has been contested by scholars. Some, for instance, argue that the contribution of IE dialects to the feature pools of nascent Australian English was negligible (Bernard 1969; Ramson 1966). Researchers such as Cox (2006:4) and Yallop (2003) instead point to the profound influence of "the speech of people from the south-east of England" which they argue to have "dominated in the early colony…[forming] the raw material from which the new dialect evolved". Other studies instead make a case for the important contribution also made to the Australian English feature pool by the so-called Celtic Englishes (including IE) (see Burridge 2010; Burridge and Musgrave 2014; Collins 2014; Fritz 1998, 2007; Horvath 1985; Jones and McDougall 2006; Kallen 2013; Lonergan 2003; Malcolm 2018; Mulder and Penry Williams 2014; Mulder et al. 2009; Newbrook 1992; Troy 1992; Trudgill 1985, 2006). Thus, Trudgill (1985:3–4) goes so far as to claim with respect to the features illustrated in (I) through (VII) below that:

> The evidence that IE played a role in the formation of Australian English, if perhaps a small one, is rather strong – and firm evidence at the grammatical level gives us confidence about some of our more speculative suggestions at the phonological level where apparently…minority varieties have less chance of influencing a mixed dialect.

(I)   Unstressed final [ə] rather than [ɪ]
         As Trudgill (1985:5) notes, Wells (1982:427) argues that Irish-English pronunciations of the vowels underlined in *abbot*, *rabbit* and *grab it* are all rendered with [ə]. There is homophony between *pack it* and *packet* in Australian varieties too while South-Eastern English dialects actually prefer [ɪ] in these contexts.

(II)   Epistemic *must not/mustn't*
         Corrigan (2010:65) and Hickey (2007:191) confirm that epistemic *must* can be negated in northern varieties of IE, particularly. Hence, expressions like *He was born here so he <u>mustn't</u> be Scottish* (Hickey

322 Karen P. Corrigan

2007:191) are commonplace when Standard English speakers would prefer *can't/cannot*. Fritz (1998:15) and Newbrook (1992:4) both ascribe the usage in Australian varieties as originating from contact with IE. Trudgill (1985:5) goes further, contending that the variant provides "especially clear evidence for the role of Irish English in the development of Australian English since an origin in England for this feature is obviously out of the question".

(III)   Punctual *whenever*

Another interesting variant that Trudgill (1985:4) implicates as present in Australia's feature pool and which is often reported as typical of IE (northern dialects) is the use of *whenever* which Montgomery and Kirk (2001) term a 'subordinating conjunction', in a punctual or extended-time sense. In other words, rather than its more conventional application to a situation that is recurring or conditional, this type of *whenever* conjunct is actually used to describe a one-off event. Corrigan (2010:67) cites the following example: *Just whenever my dad came up to Belfast.* This extract is from an interview where the permanent migration of the speaker's father — originally from Omagh, County Tyrone — is described.

(IV)   Sentence-final *so*

Hickey (2007:371) observes that *so* can be "used in sentence-final position to indicate consent or acquiescence" providing the example *I'll have a cup of tea so* in response to an interlocutor's turn which ends *I'm...putting on the kettle.* He argues that while the form is clearly based on English *so* "redeployed for this purpose", he suggests that the interpersonal function of the discourse-pragmatic marker (D-PM) may well be related to an Irish conjunction *más ea* 'if-that-is-so', which also tends to be utterance final and is similar in function (Corrigan 2015:44). By contrast, Trudgill (1985:4) argues that it instead functions as a denial in Australian English and while he contends that this variant is "identical" with the "usage in many parts of Ireland" the argument for cross-dialectal influence would appear from a functional perspective at least to be less strong here.

(V)   *Till* meaning 'in order to'

Trudgill (1985:4) proposes that expressions such as *come here till I kiss you* which is "well-known to many Australians as a non-standard form" cannot have been brought there other than by speakers of IE or Highlands English because it is not "understood in England" and is actually likely to have been "a calque on Gaelic". This IE feature with the same semantics is still current. It also has a long history in the dialect being railed against during the period that Irish migrants were travelling to Australia in significant numbers by the prescriptivist Francis Stoney (1885). He singles out this usage as incorrect in his 1885 manual of Irishisms

Historical Contact and the Feature Pool 323

to be avoided. The Australian example that Trudgill (1985) cites does indeed appear to be a borrowing from the Irish usage illustrated in (1) so it is probably rather more convincing as an exclusively Irish variant that entered the feature pool and got adopted than the sentence-final *so* feature just discussed.

(1)

Tar	anseo	**go dtí**	**go**	bpógfaidh	mé	thú
Come	*here*	*in order*	*for*	*will+kiss*	*me*	*you*

'Come here (un)til I kiss you'

(VI) Second-person plural pronoun *yous*

As Beal and Corrigan (2009:249) remark, several scholars maintain that, for a variety of world Englishes, variability between plural *you* and *yous* was introduced into the local vernacular as a result of contact with IE migrants from the famine period onwards. Harris (1993:139), for instance, states that "in some dialects, particularly those spoken in Ireland, as well as others with Irish connections, we find the vernacular form *youse*", and Hickey (2007:242) claims that it "was transported to Anglophone locations beyond Ireland where it was subsequently picked up and continued". It is no surprise, therefore, that studies of Australian English by Trudgill (1985), Horvath (1985) and Mulder and Penry Williams (2013) mention the variant. The feature is cited as current in contemporary dialects of IE by both Corrigan (2010:53–54) and Kallen (2013:118–120). Dolan (1999:292) implies a substratist explanation for the retention of this singular/plural distinction in IE in the suggestion that it arose originally because "in Irish there is both a singular and a plural second person pronoun, as there used to be in English". P.W. Joyce (1910/1988:88), along with other important chroniclers of nineteenth-century Irish-English like Hayden and Hartog (1909:781), demonstrate that it has a long history in the dialect so that it could indeed have contributed to the early feature pools of Australia's nascent cities.

(VII) Sentence-final *but*

Considerable attention has been paid to the use of *but* as an utterance final D-PM in varieties of English in Ireland (Harris 1993:176; Hickey 2007:375; Kallen 2013:182–185) but also globally where the form is often attributed to the migratory patterns of the Irish diaspora (Clarke 2010:253; Corrigan 2015:47). Thus, Trudgill (2006:19) suggests such a source for the use of the D-PM finally in utterances such as *I don't like it but,* remarking that it is: "well known in colloquial Australian English. It does not occur in England, except in Tyneside, but is common in Ireland and Scotland". His views are echoed in more recent research by Mulder et al. (2009:349) which documents the feature in ICE-Australia in examples like (2):

(2)

> Bridget: We're trying to convince Mum to get a cappuccino maker, but she said, oh. Can you believe it? (H) You'd be at it all the time. (0.9)
>
> Marie: Mmm, that's true. (4.1)
>> *It'd be good to have <u>but</u>. (0.5)*
>> **[ICE-AUS SIA-078:195-9]**

As far as I am aware, with the exception of Corrigan (2015), no previous authors have documented the historical origins of this D-PM. The fact that it is linked to Celtic Englishes or varieties closely connected with them does, however, suggest that it may be like *so* in the respect that it is another English form which, in Hickey's (2007:371) terms has been "redeployed" during the historical contact phase when L1 Irish speakers were adopting English as an L2. It is certainly the case that there are expressions in the former in which the D-PM *ach* 'but' appears to have a similar function and to occur in utterance final position, as (3) indicates from Ó Siadhail (1989:299):

(3)

Tuigtear		dóibh	ná	fuil		aon	diabhal
Think		*to+them*	*Neg.*	*BE*		*any*	*devil*
ní	ag	éinne	le	déanamh	<u>ach</u>		
thing	*at*	*anyone*	*with*	*do*	*but*		

'They think that nobody has any damn thing to do but'

There are two key reasons in my view why the extent of IE influence on Australian varieties remains contentious. First, obtaining suitable linguistic data for the analysis of nineteenth-century 'multi-ethnolects' is not straightforward. Amador-Moreno et al. (2016:30) and Amador-Moreno (2019) argue that emigrant letter corpora are ideal for tracking the potential features that might contribute to the development of new contact vernaculars in the host country since they are generally produced by low literate writers (see also Burridge 2010; Dossena 2012; Fritz 1998, 2007; Kerswill 2018; Troy 1992).

I would propose, however, that the absence in such databases of certain Irish-English morphosyntactic and D-PM features from Trudgill's (1985) list in Fitzpatrick (1995), which is based on such a corpus of historical letters in an Australian context, does not copper fasten the hypothesis against an Irish-English contribution. Instead, it may simply reflect the nature of this genre. In fact, (II-VII) are arguably more explicitly tied to speech than writing while most of the evidence for early Australian English is naturally text based with letters being a key resource. Sentence-final *but,* e.g., is used to indicate the end of a conversational turn or intonation unit, functioning to either deny or mitigate in the context of disagreeing or conveying politeness within a conversation (Corrigan 2015). Its use therefore

Historical Contact and the Feature Pool 325

presupposes that participants are engaged in negotiating meaning by repairing misunderstandings, conveying turn transitional relevance points and so on – all of which is accomplished on the fly in real-time. This is definitely not the function that historical emigrant correspondence serves – not least because it can take many months for exchanges back and forth between the writer and addressee.

In a similar vein, the rarity of *yous* as a second person plural marker in Fitzpatrick's archive mentioned earlier as well as in Fritz's *Corpus of Oz Early English (Oz)* (1998) is to be expected when the dynamics of private letter writing are taken into account. Invariably, authors are addressing a single rather than multiple recipients in their exchanges. Consequently, the following letter penned by William Fife from County Fermanagh and addressed to both his children (Nixon and Fathy) who emigrated from Derry to Sydney via Liverpool in the 1860s is very unusual in this respect.

(4)

> *I followed* **yous** *in imagination every Day of your tedious voyage. I looked at* **yous**
> *Sometimes cast Down and Sorro[f]wul...I imagined I saw* **yous** *Landed in Sydney*
> *Strangers in a Strange Land* (Fitzpatrick 1995:441).

As such, it is small wonder then that attempts to quantify the occurrence of (2–7) in historical datasets drawn from Irish correspondents often prove futile and could lead to misrepresenting the role which this ethnolinguistic group might have played in contributing to the feature pool of Australia's nascent multiethnolects.[3]

Secondly, I would agree with Troy's (1992:460) comment that Irish impact appears to be minimal in cities like Melbourne largely because the type of meticulous analyses of socio-historical statistical resources required is seldom undertaken (see also Mulder and Penry Williams 2014 as well as Newbrook 1992 who use "unacknowledged" and "unrecognised", respectively here). Moreover, accounts embedded within rigorous models of historical language contact and new dialect formation such as those articulated in Beal and Corrigan (2009) or Kerswill (2018) have not generally been applied to assessments of the Irish influence on Australian English. To that end, these frameworks underpin the account in subsequent sections.

4.4.3 Melbourne's European Founder Populations

The nineteenth-century European settlement of Melbourne followed the Port Phillip Association's 'purchase' of Aboriginal lands in 1835 (McCreery 2016; Parsons 1982; Serle 1963; Shaw 1996; Turner 1978). Melbourne's first official census was issued in 1836 and the returns (see

Figure 4.4.1) record a 'founder population' (Mufwene 2001:28–29) of 186 inhabitants, less than a quarter of whom were female.

All of them appear to be exclusively 'Anglo-Celtic' in origin and while the documents make no mention of birthplaces, they do list religious persuasion and surnames which can differentiate between this group to some degree. Thus, there are only 14 Catholics mentioned with surnames such as Carr (an Anglicised form of Gaelic *Ó Carra*) indicating a more likely origin in Ireland as opposed to Scotland or Northern England where it is also common. The denomination 'Protestant' is used for the rest of Melbourne's inhabitants of the time (as no 'Jews' or 'Pagans' are

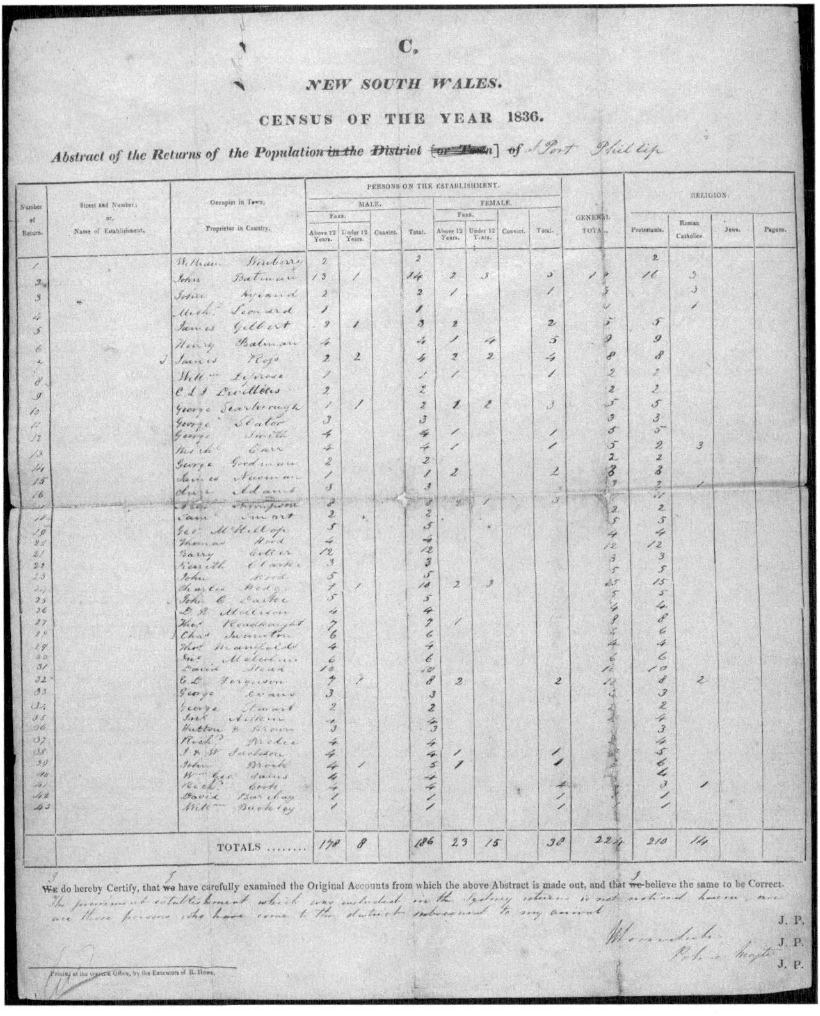

C.

NEW SOUTH WALES.

CENSUS OF THE YEAR 1836.

Abstract of the Returns of the Population ~~in the District~~ [~~or Town~~] of Port Phillip

Number of Return.	Street and Number; or, Name of Establishment.	Occupier in Town, Proprietor in Country.	Male – Free – Above 12 Years.	Male – Free – Under 12 Years.	Male – Convict.	Male – Total.	Female – Free – Above 12 Years.	Female – Free – Under 12 Years.	Female – Convict.	Female – Total.	General Total.	Religion – Protestants.	Religion – Roman Catholics.	Religion – Jews.	Religion – Pagans.
1		William Woodberry	2			2					[illegible]	2			
2		John Batman	13	1		14	2	3		5	19	16	3		
3		[illegible] Wyeand	2			2	1			1	3		3		
4		Mich^l Leonard	1			1					1		1		
5		James Gilbert	2	1		3	2			2	5	5			
6		Henry Batman	4			4	1	4		5	9	9			
7		James Ross	2	2		4	2	2		4	8	8			
8		Willm Diprose	1			1	1			1	2	2			
9		C. S. J. [illegible]	2			2					2	2			
10		George Scarborough	1	1		2	1	2		3	5	5			
11		George Slator	3			3					3	3			
12		George Smith	4			4	1			1	5	5			
13		Mich^l Carr	4			4	1			1	5	2	3		
14		George Goodman	2			2					2	2			
15		James Newman	1			1	2			2	3	3			
16		[illegible] Adams	3			3					[illegible]	2	1		
17		[illegible] Thompson	3			3	2	1		3	[illegible]	[illegible]			
18		Saml Smart	2			2					2	2			
19		Geo. Mc Killop	5			5					5	5			
20		Thomas Hood	4			4					4	4			
21		Barry Cotter	12			12					12	12			
22		Kenneth Clarke	3			3					3	3			
23		John Wood	5			5					5	5			
24		Charles Wedge	9	1		10	2	3			15	15			
25		John C Darke	5			5					5	5			
26		D. R. Mollison	4			4					4	4			
27		Thos Roadknight	7			7	1				8	8			
28		Chas Swanston	6			6					6	6			
29		Thos Manifolds	4			4					4	4			
30		Jno Malcolm	6			6					6	6			
31		David Stead	10			10					10	10			
32		G. L. Ferguson	7	1		8	2			2	10	8	2		
33		George Evans	3			3					3	3			
34		George Stewart	2			2					2	2			
35		Ja^s Aitken	4			4					4	4			
36		Hutton & Brown	3			3					3	3			
37		Richd Wedge	4			4					4	4			
38		J & W Jackson	4			4	1			1	5	5			
39		John Brock	4	1		5	1			1	6	6			
40		Wm Geo. James	4			4					4	4			
41		Richd Cook	4			4					4	3	1		
42		David Barclay	1			1					1	1			
43		Willm Buckley	1			1					1	1			
		TOTALS	178	8		186	23	15		38	224	210	14		

~~We~~ I do hereby Certify, that ~~we~~ I have carefully examined the Original Accounts from which the above Abstract is made out, and that ~~we~~ I believe the same to be Correct.

J. P.

J. P.

J. P.

Printed at the Government Office, by the Executors of R. Howe.

Figure 4.4.1 Digitised copy of the 1836 Census of Port Phillip District (Melbourne).[4]

Historical Contact and the Feature Pool   327

Table 4.4.1 Places of birth and affiliations of the inhabitants of the municipality of Melbourne, according to the 1854 census

Where born	Melbourne municipality
British:	
Born in Victoria	5,588
Born in other Australian Colonies	1,830
Born in other British Colonies and East Indies	941
Born in England	22,304
Born in Wales	531
Born in Scotland	8,460
Born in Ireland	10,786
Foreign:	
Born in France	257
Born in Germany	722
Born in other European Countries	459
Born in the United States	660
Born in other parts of America	62
Born in China	42
Born in other Countries	46
Born at Sea	192
Birth-place not specified	355
Total of inhabitants:	53,235
Allegiance:	
British subjects	51,090
Foreign subjects	2,134
Allegiance unknown	11

recorded). While this is unhelpful in distinguishing English, Scottish and Welsh immigrants (with Scots settlers being more likely to be Presbyterian, for instance), all three ethnic groups do appear to be present since the census lists surnames such as 'Stewart' (Scottish) alongside 'Smith' (English) and Evans (Welsh). The 1854 census, which took place almost a decade after the impact of the Great Famine had reached its peak (Corrigan 2010, 2020; Delaney 2012; Kinealy 1995; Neal 1998), is considerably more useful in this regard, as Table 4.4.1 demonstrates. It distinguishes not only between 'British' ethnic groups but also demarcates the origins of the 'Foreign Born' as well as settlers who declared allegiance to the British Crown and those who did not.[5]

4.4.4 Ethnolinguistic Vitality during the Gold Rush Era

These figures would suggest that the Anglo-Celtic founder population has flourished in Melbourne. Its population has grown in less than two decades by nearly 42,000 on account of Melbourne's changed economic

328　*Karen P. Corrigan*

fortunes brought about primarily by the Victorian Gold Rush (Reeves et al. 2010) and captured in the following letter extract cited in Fitzpatrick (1996:375):[6]

(5)　Killicomane, County Armagh　　　14th May 1844

> Dear Son
> ...we think that Coloney [Melbourne] will Be a poor place in the course of a few years by reason of so much Emigration to it yearly...

Just under a third of these residents were Irish migrants like the recipient of this letter, Joseph Hammond, who had recently emigrated from Killycomain. They were the second-largest Anglo group after those who had migrated from England. Their demographic proportions do not quite meet the 50% threshold conjectured in Kerswill's (2018:20) model in order to accomplish phonological restructuring. However, their numbers are in excess of the 20% figure implied by Llamas (2015:253) and the 31% figure suggested in Beal and Corrigan (2009:238) in connection with the contribution which they argue that Irish migrants made to the formation of Middlesbrough and Newcastle Englishes, respectively.

Leaving such issues aside for future research, the 1854 census indicates quite decisively that the feature pool associated with the original founder population, consisting simply of either Celtic Englishes or British English dialects, has considerably expanded. It now includes a wider range of English varieties, including nascent Australian vernaculars (1,830 inhabitants), British Colonial dialects outwith Australia and indigenised Englishes, such as those spoken in the East Indies since colonial times (941), as well as American vernaculars (722).

Moreover, there is good evidence from research by Clyne (1989) that the autochthonous languages of Britain and Ireland remained a feature of Melbourne's language ecology in domains such as church, education and the media. These Celtic language speakers have been joined too now by Chinese, French and German as well as other European language groups (1,480 inhabitants) which, though not stated explicitly in the census data presented in Table 4.4.1, would have included Albanian, Balto-Slavic, and Dutch as well as Hebrew, Italian, and Scandinavian (Clyne 1989). The multiple-origin, transnationally connected and legally stratified nature of these new immigrants (some of whom arrived as indentured servants, others had been deported from their sending countries and a number belonged to the higher echelons of society) contributed to the super-diversification of Melbourne in this era. Its ecology is thus reminiscent of Vertovec's (2007) concept, although it was originally applied to contemporary migrant communities (such as the Somalis) in the UK.

The Anglo-Celts remained dominant, however, with respect to sheer numbers since 25 times as many 'British' as opposed to 'Foreign Born subjects' feature in Table 4.4.1. In addition, there is also the status of the Anglo-Celtic group to consider and the extent to which they did or did not hold sway over the political and socio-economic fabric of life in Melbourne during this era. An insight into the extent of their influence in this regard is reported by Jackson (1977:122) who argues that the urbanisation patterns that came to typify Australia's largest cities result from the dominant position of such migrant groups (see also Schedvin and McCarty 1978 as well as Statham 1989).

Moreover, Irish input appears to have been especially pronounced in Victoria where the railway track gauge adopted was that conventionally used by Ireland's rather than England's mainline network. The latter was implemented elsewhere but was dispreferred in the environs of 'Australia Felix'[7] due to the influence of Irish engineers such as Francis Webb Wentworth-Sheilds born in County Meath (Jackson 1977: 100). There were other aspects of society in Victoria that were also dominated by migrants who hailed from Ireland (including those from the medical and legal professions and who were often linked to the Anglo-Irish ascendancy class (Forth 1991; Geary 1991; MacDonagh 1971)).

For instance, the meeting of Melbourne's first Legislative Council took place in 1851 in St. Patrick's Hall.[8] The new University of Melbourne was closely associated with Trinity College, Dublin through its first chancellor, Redmond Barry (later knighted) who was a graduate and a member of the first Legislative Council. Other councillors included Sir John O'Shanassy who eventually rose to become premier of Victoria on two occasions as well as the founding chairman of the Colonial Bank of Australasia. He was particularly noted for his promotion of other Irish migrants (particularly Roman Catholics) to positions of socio-political power (O'Brien 2005). Thus, Taylor (2006: 23) records negative comments regarding the practices surrounding his appointments to Melbourne's police force, which also happened to have been structured along identical lines to the Royal Irish Constabulary, i.e.:

> There was compelling evidence of preferential treatment being given…from January 1862, of 30 appointments, 29 were recommended by the Chief Secretary, John O'Shanassy, and 22 were designated as Catholics.

The extent of Anglo-Celtic impact which these and other similar historical reports suggest would lead one to expect there to have been considerable pressure to become bilingual amongst new immigrant groups who spoke Chinese, French, German or other L1s. Their L2 target will have been the English based multiethnolect that will already have begun developing after the 1835 settlements. In this sense, the initial Melbourne contact scenario will have resembled the situation identified by Cheshire et al. (2011) in twenty-first century London's outer-city borough of Havering. Its feature pool shows signs of dialect mixing but the

330   *Karen P. Corrigan*

borough, like the early Melbourne community, experienced relatively little immigration by non-native speakers of English and thus remained "profoundly monolingual" (2011:76).

1850s Melbourne, by contrast, has a language ecology that is closer to that which characterises London's inner-city borough of Hackney. While the sheer number of languages/speakers involved in the historical scenario is fewer of course, there is good evidence that many migrant groups actually maintained their first languages for a period through their establishment of French, Gaelic, German and Welsh schools and churches (Clyne 1989) and thus that the city experienced what Slembrouck (2011:153) terms "heightened multilingualism" to some degree at least. A survey of the linguistic landscape in the form of media outlets in Melbourne during this era also demonstrates that these languages, in particular, retained a foothold in public as well as private life (Clyne 1989). As such, one can conjecture that many settlers remained bilingual with English as their less dominant language just as contemporary immigrants to London's inner city are reported to be (Cheshire et al. 2011). Moreover, both groups are likely to have acquired English outside of formal education through multiethnic personal networks. As a result, these historical immigrants' input to Melbourne's developing multiethnolect will likely also have included interlanguage varieties of one type or another.

Considering the taxonomy articulated in Giles et al. (1977) regarding the factors promoting ethnolinguistic vitality in majority-minority language contact situations, the presence of such 'institutional support' for these autochthonous European languages does indeed bode well for their contribution to a feature pool from which a Multicultural Melbourne English ethnolect could develop. The Giles et al. (1977) model is a tripartite one, though, and there are two other forces that need to be considered which have already been touched upon regarding the dominant position of the Anglo-Celts, i.e., 'status' and 'demography'. The former refers to the different types of prestige (economic, social, socio-historical) which particular ethnic groups and their languages are afforded in inter-group contexts. The latter is concerned with the numbers of ethnic group members relative to one another as well as where they are situated from a territorial perspective.[9]

I would argue that although this model was developed primarily to systematise the factors influencing the ethnolinguistic vitality of minority languages, it can also be readily applied to multiethnolectal contexts in which nascent contact varieties are emerging. This is because prestigious ethnolinguistic groups such as Melbourne's Anglo-Celts, which I have already demonstrated to be numerous, high in status and likely to be in a position to engage in considerable face-to-face contact with others through their extensive cultural, socio-economic and political links, have a greater chance of having their linguistic traits dominate within the feature pool. This will be particularly so if their first languages or dialects have the right internal characteristics of the type identified in Cheshire et al. (2011), Kerswill (2018), Siegel (1997:139), Trudgill (2006, 2010) *inter alia*, noted above.

On the basis of this taxonomy, there are two aspects of nineteenth-century Chinese immigration to Melbourne which suggest that, by comparison to some other ethnolinguistic groups, their ability to influence the feature pool is probably the weakest of all the newcomers. First, as Table 4.4.2 from the 1854 census shows, the Chinese population even at the height of Melbourne's "golden decade" which Reeves et al. (2010) and Turner (1978: 73) date from 1851 have the smallest population of all 'foreign born' residents.[10]

Moreover, the Chinese formed ethnic enclaves in outlying districts of the city such as Sandridge (ten inhabitants) as well as in the municipality of Melbourne proper. Indeed, they formed a Chinatown in Little Bourke Street (which also had ten residents of Chinese extraction in 1854) that persists to the present day (Clyne 1989:70; Kuo 2013). In addition, while Clyne (1989:77–78) finds evidence for a short-lived Chinese newspaper, there appear not to have been any Chinese schools locally and instead there is government paperwork on Public Education dated from 1867 which suggests providing adult evening classes in English for Chinese immigrants. What is more, just as Kuo (2013) argues in connection with the enclave nature of Chinese settlements in Sydney, i.e., that their spatial segregation eventually led to "a rise in anti-Chinese feelings", it is not unlikely that their Melbourne peers also suffered a similar fate. This hypothesis is reinforced by the limits imposed on Chinese immigration to Australia more broadly as well as curtailments of this ethnic group's ability to fully participate in public life, in general, documented in different pieces of legislation pertaining to Victoria and enacted in the years following the 1854 Census. These acts were intended to reduce migration specifically from this region as well as to delimit the influence of this ethnic group within the body politic more broadly which, as we have seen, was indeed dominated by the Anglo-Celts. In that regard, the acts included stipulations such as those in the 'Chinese Immigrants' Statute, No.259 of 1865' which stated that: "no [Chinese]...shall be entitled to vote at the election of members for any mining board" (see Lee 1889).

Clyne (1989:70) argues that — apart from the Chinese in these areas — other ethnolinguistic groups seem to have been dispersed across the city and this will no doubt also have encouraged language shift from their mother tongues by creating greater opportunities for inter-community face-to-face interactions in Melbourne's new English based multiethnolect. Clyne (1989:79–81) argues that like the Chinese, speakers of other European languages (especially German) came under similar pressures to become monolingual partly through education reforms which

Table 4.4.2 Places of birth, affiliations and spatial distributions of the inhabitants of the municipality of Melbourne and its environs, according to the 1854 census

		Inhabitants of											
		Melbourne proper				North Melbourne				East Melbourne (part of Gipps and La Trobe Wards)	Emerald Hill	Sandridge (including scattered population on the banks of the Yarra)	St. Kilda (within the City boundary)	South Yarra (La Trobe Ward, south of the Yarra)
Where born	Total of the Municipality of Melbourne	Bourke Ward (part of)	Gipps Ward (part of)	La Trobe Ward (part of)	Lonedale Ward (part of)	Hotham Ward	Smith Ward	Fitzroy Ward, Collingwood						
British														
Born in Victoria	5,588	907	1,067	598	359	413	255	1,204	72	250	136	237	90
Born in other Australian Colonies	1,830	309	394	200	127	146	138	288	36	64	38	55	35
Born in other British Colonies and East Indies	941	126	168	104	66	74	77	126	28	73	60	9	30
Born in England	22,304	2,737	4,073	2,725	1,586	1,386	1,210	4,393	319	1,698	1,075	529	573
Born in Wales	531	61	99	91	44	31	12	86	5	41	37	7	17
Born in Scotland	8,460	1,561	1,321	864	640	812	588	1,226	111	672	281	142	242
Born in Ireland	10,786	1,750	2,500	1,239	1,042	704	680	1,398	146	596	263	226	242

Foreign

Born in France	257	10	91	63	14	7	11	39	2	10	4	1	5
Born in Germany	722	76	164	194	94	16	9	70	15	22	40	4	18
Born in other European Countries	459	33	154	81	56	14	15	27	5	29	31	3	11
Born in the United States	660	86	118	98	74	17	35	85	14	24	94	9	6
Born in other parts of America	62	8	17	12			8	11	1		4	1	
Born in China	42	10	4	4	4		5	2		1	10		2
Born in other Countries	46	1	3	8	12	2	1	2		8	3	2	4
Born at Sea	192	33	36	25	13	13		35	4	16	10	4	3
Birth-place not specified	355	18	2	32	46	35	16	180			9	13	4
Total of inhabitants	53,235	7,726	10,211	6,338	4,177	3,670	3,060	9,172	758	3,504	2,095	1,242	1,282

Allegiance

British subjects	51,090	7,503	9,672	5,898	3,935	3,626	2,979	8,952	723	3,424	1,914	1,225	1,239
Foreign subjects	2,134	221	536	439	240	44	80	219	35	80	180	17	43
Allegiance unknown	11	2	3	1	2		1	1			1		

334 *Karen P. Corrigan*

promoted English-only policies and also as a result of the rise of what he terms "aggressive nationalism and colonialism" (1989:80). This perspective will also be likely to have curtailed the opportunities of any ethnolinguistic group member who was not Anglo-Celtic in origin to contribute substantially to the feature pool. In Blommaert's terms, these social circumstances promote a system of linguistic inequality whereby access to an Anglo-Celtic repertoire improves your ability to contribute to the body politic which, in turn, promotes the positive indexing of these varieties over others (2010:47).

4.4.5 Conclusion

This chapter on the formation of early multiethnolects in Melbourne has drawn heavily on models articulated in Beal and Corrigan (2009), Giles et al. (1977), Kerswill (2018), and Mufwene (2001) as well as Trudgill (1985, 2006, 2010) and new research in the sociolinguistics of globalisation spearheaded by the arguments in Blommaert (2010) and Slembrouck (2011) *inter alia*. Its orientation is likewise underpinned by the work of Jenny Cheshire and her collaborators that has greatly enhanced our understanding of the dynamics of how multiethnolects emerge in superdiverse cities.

The insights of Cheshire and Fox (2009) as well as Cheshire et al. (2011), in particular, have been used to shed new light on different phases of the language ecology of Melbourne from early inter-group contacts in the 1830s to the population explosion associated with the Gold Rush era of the 1850s. The new findings that this chapter reports regarding the vexed question of whether the dialects of Irish migrants did or did not contribute to the feature pools of Australia's major cities in the nineteenth century indicate that from ush demographic as well as socio-economic and political perspectives, there is good evidence that their input did indeed have greater potential to impact upon the development of Melbourne English than that of other groups such as the Chinese.

The chapter has also shown that while it remains difficult to pin down the precise discourse-pragmatic, morphosyntactic and phonological features which contributed to Melbourne's emerging multiethnolect by Famine immigration from places like Killycomain, this is due more to the limitations of the kinds of historical data currently available than it is to robust proof to the contrary which is yet to appear. The latter will only be possible when researchers start taking cognisance — as I have done here — of what Cheshire and Fox (2009:1) define as "socially realistic models of language change that take account of the social diversity of large multicultural urban cities".

Notes

1 I am grateful to James Walker and La Trobe University, Melbourne for hosting a visit facilitating this research. Thanks also to the AHRC for awarding a grant between 2014 and 2016 to support a project entitled: Múin Béarla do na Leanbháin 'Teach the Chillidren English' (AH/K008285/1) reported on here. Killycomain is a townland in County Armagh, Northern Ireland that was subject to serious decline through migration and mortality during the Great Famine. Fitzpatrick (1995) contains a personal account of Irish emigration to Australia from there in a series of letters composed by local families.
2 This is not always the case, as Corrigan (2020) demonstrates in connection with immigration patterns now typical of rural NI.
3 Fritz (2007), for instance, is led to conclude that sentence-final *but* in contemporary Australian varieties is a later twentieth-century phenomenon on account of its absence in Oz.
4 This document can be viewed at: http://access.prov.vic.gov.au/public/veo-download?objectId=090fe273818842e4&format=pdf&docTitle=FolderNo28183628&encodingId=Revision-2-Document-1-Encoding-1-DocumentData, Last accessed 18.4.19. Digital copy courtesy of the Public Records Office of Victoria (Folder No: 28; 1836/28; VPRS 4; P0000; 1).
5 See: http://hccda.anu.edu.au/pages/VIC-1854-census, accessed on 16.3.19. It is important to bear in mind that historical censuses especially have a number of flaws which there is not space here to rehearse, but see Corrigan (1992) and (2003) for overviews. In this regard, Clyne (1989: 69) notes that the 1857 Census for Victoria "missed a large number of immigrants".
6 A similar dramatic population rise is reported in Llamas (2015) for Middlesbrough. It is recognised as the only noteworthy nineteenth-century new town in Britain. In fact, Middlesbrough has much in common with the Melbourne of this era linguistically and socially as well as with respect to the number of Irish migrants settling there post-1851 (Taylor 2006).
7 Descriptor for Western Victoria (Turner 1978: 63).
8 A photolithograph of the occasion from Canberra's National Portrait Gallery is here: www.portrait.gov.au/portraits/2013.87/opening-of-the-first-legislative-council-of-victoria-by-governor-charles-joseph-latrobe (last accessed 12.4.19). It includes images of prominent Irish migrant members, including: Supreme Court judge Sir Redmond Barry (1813–1880); Sir John O'Shanassy (1818–1883), Premier of Victoria in 1858–1859 and 1861–1863 and Sir William Stawell (1815–1889), who was Victoria's first Attorney-General from 1851 to 1857.
9 This framework has been criticised. However, as Allard and Landry (1996: 7) also note: "despite inherent limitations, the construct has proven to be both viable and productive".
10 See: http://hccda.anu.edu.au/pages/VIC-1854-census, accessed on 19.3.19.

References

Allard, Réal and Rodrigue Landry. 1994. "Subjective ethnolinguistic vitality: A comparison of two measures". *International Journal of the Sociology of Language* 108:117–144.
Amador-Moreno, Carolina P., Karen P. Corrigan, Kevin McCaffery and Emma Moreton. 2016. "Migration databases as impact tools in the education and

336   *Karen P. Corrigan*

heritage sectors". In *Creating and Digitizing Language Corpora Volume 3*, K.P. Corrigan and A. Mearns (eds.). London: Palgrave Macmillan. 25–68.

Amador-Moreno, Carolina P. 2019. *Orality in Written Texts*. Oxford: Routledge.

Beal, Joan C. and Karen P. Corrigan. 2009. "The impact of nineteenth-century Irish-English migrations on contemporary northern Englishes: Tyneside and Sheffield compared". In *Language Contacts Meet English Dialects*, E. Pentillä and H. Paulasto (eds.). Newcastle: Cambridge Scholars Publishing. 231–258.

Bernard, John R. 1969. "On the uniformity of Australian English". *Orbis* 18:62–73.

Blackledge, Adrian and Angela Creese. 2017. "Translanguaging in mobility". In *The Routledge Handbook of Migration and Language*, S. Canagarajah (ed.). Abingdon, Oxon: Routledge. 31–46.

Blommaert, Jan. 2010. *The Sociolinguistics of Globalization*. Cambridge: Cambridge University Press.

Burridge, Kate. 2010. "'A Peculiar Language' — The linguistic evidence for early Australian English". In *Varieties in Writing*, R. Hickey (ed.). Amsterdam: John Benjamins. 295–348.

Burridge, Kate and Simon Musgrave. 2014. "'It's Speaking Australian English We Are': Irish features in nineteenth century Australia". *Australian Journal of Linguistics* 34(1):24–49.

Cheshire, Jenny L. and Susan Fox. 2009. "*Was/Were* variation: A perspective from London". *Language Variation and Change* 21(1):1–38.

Cheshire, Jenny L., Paul Kerswill, Susan Fox and Eivind Torgersen. 2011. "Contact, the feature pool and the speech community: The emergence of multicultural London English". *Journal of Sociolinguistics* 15(2):151–196.

Clarke, Sandra. 2010. *Newfoundland and Labrador English*. Edinburgh: Edinburgh University Press.

Clyne, Michael. 1989. "Multilingual Melbourne nineteenth century style". *Journal of Australian Studies* 9(17):69–81.

Clyne, Michael. 2000. "Lingua Franca and ethnolects in Europe and beyond". *Sociolinguistica* 14:83–89.

Collins, Peter. 2014. "Australian English". In *The Languages and Linguistics of Australia*, H. Koch, and R. Nordlinger (eds.). Berlin: De Gruyter Mouton. 449–484.

Collins, James, Mike Baynham and Stef Slembrouck (eds.). 2009. *Globalization and Language in Contact*. London: Continuum.

Corrigan, Karen P. 1992. "'I gcuntas Dé múin Béarla do na leanbháin": Eisimirce agus an Ghaeilge sa naoú aois deag' ("In the name of God teach the children English": Emigration and the Irish language in the nineteenth century') in *The Irish World Wide Vol. 2, The Irish in the New Communities* P. O' Sullivan (ed.). Leicester: Leicester University Press and New York: St. Martin's Press. 143–161.

Corrigan, Karen P. 2003. "The ideology of nationalism and its impact on accounts of language shift in nineteenth century Ireland". *Arbeiten aus Anglistik und Amerikanistik* 28 (2): 201–230.

Corrigan, Karen P. 2010. *Irish English, Volume 1: Northern Ireland*. Edinburgh: Edinburgh University Press.

Corrigan, Karen P. 2015. "'I Always Think of People Here, You Know, Saying 'Like' after Every Sentence': The dynamics of discourse-pragmatic markers in northern Irish English". In *Pragmatic Markers in Irish English*, C.

Amador-Moreno, K. McCafferty and E. Vaughan E. (eds.). Amsterdam: John Benjamins. 37–64.

Corrigan, Karen P. 2020. *Linguistic Communities and Migratory Processes: Newcomers Acquiring Sociolinguistic Variation in Northern Ireland*. Berlin: Mouton de Gruyter.

Cox, Felicity. 2006. "Australian English pronunciation into the 21st century". *Prospect* 21(1):3–21.

Czaika, Mathias and Hein de Haas. 2015. "The globalization of migration: Has the world become more migratory?" *International Migration Review* 48(2):283–323.

Delaney, Enda 2012. *The Curse of Reason*. Dublin: Gill and Macmillan.

Devlin Trew, Johanne. 2013. *Leaving the North*. Liverpool: Liverpool University Press.

Dolan, Terence P. 1999. *A Dictionary of Hiberno-English*. Dublin: Gill and Macmillan.

Dossena, Marina. 2012. "The study of correspondence". In *Letter Writing in Late Modern Europe*, M. Dossena and C. del Lungo (eds.). Amsterdam: John Benjamins. 13–30.

Fitzgerald, Patrick and Brian Lambkin. 2008. *Migration in Irish History, 1607–2007*. Houndmills, Basingstoke: Palgrave Macmillan.

Fitzpatrick, David. 1995. *Oceans of Consolation*. Ithaca, NY: Cornell University Press.

Fix, Sonya. 2013. Age of Second Dialect Acquisition and Linguistic Practice Across Ethno-Racial Boundaries in the Urban Midwest. University of Pennsylvania Working Papers in Linguistics 19(2):71–80.

Forth, Gordon. 1991. "'No Petty People': The Anglo-Irish identity in Colonial Australia". In *Irish English World Wide, Volume 2*, P. O'Sullivan (ed.). Leicester: Leicester University Press. 100–128.

Fritz, Clemens. 1998. "Letters from Early Australia". *DiG* 6:1–24.

Fritz, Clemens. 2007. *From English in Australia to Australian English 1788–1900*. Frankfurt am Main: Peter Lang.

García, Ofelia. 2009. *Bilingual Education in the Twenty-First Century*. Oxford: Wiley-Blackwell.

Geary, Laurence M. 1991. "Australia *Felix:* Irish doctors in nineteenth century Victoria". In *The Irish World Wide*, Vol. 2, P. O'Sullivan (ed.). Leicester: Leicester University Press. 162–179.

Giles, Howard, Richard Y. Bourhis and Donald. M. Taylor. 1977. "Towards a theory of language in ethnic group relations". In *Language, Ethnicity and Intergroup Relations*, H. Giles (ed.). London: Academic Press. 307–348.

Hayden, Marcus and Mary Hartog. 1909. "The Irish dialect of English". *Fortnightly Review* LXXXV:775–785, 933–947.

Harris, John. 1993. "The grammar of Irish English". In *Real English*, J. Milroy and L. Milroy (eds.). London: Longman. 139–186.

Hickey, Raymond. 2007. *Irish English*. Cambridge: Cambridge University Press.

Horvath, Barbara. 1985. *Variation in Australian English*. Cambridge: Cambridge University Press.

Hymes, Dell. 1974. *Foundations in Sociolinguistics*. Philadelphia: University of Pennsylvania Press.

Jackson Robert, V. 1977. *Australian Economic Development in the Nineteenth Century*. Canberra: Australian National University Press.

Jones Marek J. and Kirsty McDougall. 2006. "A comparative acoustic study of Australian English fricated /t/: Assessing the Irish (English) Link". In *Proceedings of the 11th Australian International Conference on Speech Science & Technology*, P. Warren and C.I. Watson (eds.). 7–12. Retrieved from www.ling.cam.ac.uk/people/kirsty/. (accessed 12.5.2019).

Joyce, Patrick. W. 1910 [1988]. *English As We Speak It in Ireland*. Dublin: Wolfhound Press.

Kallen, Jeffrey L. 2013. *Irish English, Volume 2: The Republic of Ireland*. Berlin: De Gruyter.

Kerswill, Paul. 2018. "Dialect formation and dialect change in the industrial revolution: British vernacular English in the nineteenth century". In *Southern English Varieties Then and Now*, L. Wright (ed.). Berlin: Mouton de Gruyter. 8–38.

Kinealy, Christine. 1995. *The Great Calamity*. London: Gill & Macmillan.

Kuo, Mei-Fen. 2013. *Making Chinese Australia*. Victoria: Monash University Publishing. Retrieved from: http://books.publishing.monash.edu/apps/bookworm/view/Making+Chinese+Australia%3A+Urban+Elites%2C+Newspapers+and+the+Formation+of+Chinese+Australian+Identity%2C+1892%2%E2%80%931912/187/ (accessed 19.3.2019).

Labov, William. 1994. *Principles of Linguistic Change*, Vol. 1. Oxford: Blackwell.

Labov, William. 2001. *Principles of Linguistic Change*, Vol. 2. Oxford: Blackwell.

Lee, Joseph. 1889. "Anti-Chinese legislation in Australasia". *The Quarterly Journal of Economics* 3(2):218–224.

Lonergan Dymphna. 2003. "An Irish-Centric view of Australian English". *Australian Journal of Linguistics* 23(2):151–159.

Llamas, Carmen. 2015. "Middlesbrough". In *Researching Northern English*, R. Hickey (ed.). Amsterdam: Benjamins. 251–270.

MacDonagh, Oliver. 1971. "The Irish in Victoria 1851–91". In *Historical Studies VIII*, D.T. Williams (ed.). Dublin: Gill and Macmillan. 67–92.

Malcolm, Ian G. 2018. *Aboriginal English*. Berlin: De Grutyer.

McCreery, Cindy. 2016. "Two Victorias?: Prince Albert, Queen Victoria and Melbourne". In *Crowns and Colonies*, R. Aldrich and C. McCreery (eds.). Oxford: Oxford University Press. 51–76.

McDermott, Philip. 2012. "Cohesion, sharing and integration? Migrant languages and cultural spaces in Northern Ireland's urban environment". *Current Issues in Language Planning* 13(3):187–205.

Montgomery, Michael B. and John M. Kirk. 2001. "'My Mother Whenever She Passed Away, She Had Pneumonia': The history and functions of *Whenever*". *Journal of English Linguistics* 29(3):234–249.

Mufwene, Salikoko S. 2001. *The Ecology of Language Evolution*. Cambridge: Cambridge University Press.

Mulder, Jean, Sandra A. Thompson and Cara Penry Williams. 2009. "Final *But* in Australian english conversation". In *Comparative Studies in Australian and New Zealand English,* P. Peters, P. Collins and A. Smith (eds.). Amsterdam: John Benjamins. 339–360.

Mulder, Jean and Cara Penry Williams. 2014. "Documenting unacknowledged inheritances in contemporary Australian English". In *Selected Papers from the 44th Conference of the Australian Linguistic Society, 2013*, L. Gawne and

J. Vaughan (eds.). Melbourne: University of Melbourne. 160–177. Retrieved from: http://bit.ly/ALS2013Proceedings (accessed 25.4.2019).

Neal, Frank. 1998. *Black '47*. London: Palgrave Macmillan.

Newbrook, Mark. 1992. "Unrecognized grammatical and semantic features typical of Australian English". *English World Wide* 13:1–3.

Nortier, Jacomine. 2008. "Ethnolects? The emergence of new varieties among adolescents (introduction)". *International Journal of Bilingualism* 12(1–2):1–5.

O'Brien, Antony. 2005. *Shenanigans on the Ovens Goldfields*. Hartwell: Artillery Publishing.

Ó Siadhail, Micheál. 1989. *Modern Irish*. Cambridge: Cambridge University Press.

Parsons, T.G. 1982. "Manufacturing on the banks of the Yarra River, Melbourne". *Journal of Australian Studies* 6(11):21–35.

Pennycook, Alastair and Emi Otsuji. 2015. *Metrolingualism*. Abingdon: Routledge.

Ramson, William S. 1966. *Australian English*. Canberra: Australian National University Press.

Reeves, Keir, Lionel Frost and Charles Fahey. 2010. "Integrating the historiography of the nineteenth-century gold rushes". *Australian Economic History Review* 50:111–128.

Schedvin, Carl Boris and John William McCarty. 1978. *Urbanization in Australia*. Sydney: Sydney University Press.

Serle, Geoffrey. 1963. *The Golden Age*. Melbourne: Melbourne University Press.

Shaw, Alan G.L. 1996. *A History of the Port Phillip District*. Melbourne: Melbourne University Press.

Siegel, Jeff. 1997. "Mixing, leveling and pidgin/creole development". In *The Structure and Status of Pidgins and Creoles*, A.K. Spears and D. Winford (eds.). Amsterdam: Benjamins. 111–149.

Slembrouck, Stef. 2011. "The sociolinguistics of globalization and migration". In *The Sage Handbook of Sociolinguistics*, B. Johnstone, P. Kerswill and R. Wodak (eds.). London: Sage. 153–164.

Statham, Pamela (ed.). 1989. *The Origins of Australia's Capital Cities*. Cambridge: Cambridge University Press.

Stoney, Francis Sadleir, pseud. ['Col. O'Critical'] 1885. *Don't Pat*. Dublin: William McGee.

Taylor, David. 2006. "Melbourne, Middlesbrough and morality". *Social History* 31(1):15–38.

Troy, Jakelin. 1992. "'Der Mary This Is Fine Country Is There In The Wourld': Irish English and Irish in Late Eighteenth and Nineteenth Century Australia". In *The Language Game*, T. Dutton, M. Ross and D. Tryon, Darrell (eds.). Canberra: Research School of Pacific Studies, ANU. 459–477.

Turner, Ian A.H. 1978. "The growth of Melbourne". In *Australian Capital Cities*, J.W. McCarty and C.B. Schedvin (eds.). Sydney: Sydney University Press. 62–81.

Trudgill, Peter. 1985. "The role of Irish English in the formation of Colonial Englishes". In *Perspectives on the English Language in Ireland*, J. Harris, D. Little and D. Singleton (eds.). Dublin: CLCS/TCD. 3–10.

340 *Karen P. Corrigan*

Trudgill, Peter. 2006. *New-Dialect Formation*. Edinburgh: Edinburgh University Press.

Trudgill, Peter. 2010. "Contact and sociolinguistic typology". In *Handbook of Language Contact*, R. Hickey (ed.). Oxford: Blackwell. 299–319.

Vertovec, Steven. 2007. "Super-diversity and its implications". *Ethnic and Racial Studies* 30(6):1024–1054.

Vertovec, Steven. 2014. *Super-Diversity*. London and New York: Routledge.

Wells, John C. 1982. *Accents of English* (3 vols.). Cambridge: Cambridge University Press.

Yallop, Colin. 2003. "A.G. Mitchell and the development of Australian pronunciation". *Australian Journal of Linguistics* 23:129–141.

Section 5

Discourse and Pragmatic Variation

5.1 *That* Beyond Convention[*]
The Interface of Syntax, Social Structure, and Discourse

Sali A. Tagliamonte and Alexandra D'Arcy

5.1.1 Introduction: A Ubiquitous Syntactic Feature

Syntactic variation is generally considered to be among the less frequent types of variation, simply because target structures have fewer opportunities to occur and individual variants may be rare (e.g., Chambers and Trudgill 1991; Milroy 1987). There is, however, one syntactic variable that occurs at sufficient rates in spontaneous speech and has low salience, allowing examination of social, linguistic, stylistic, and—as we argue here—discursive effects on variant probability: the alternation in English complement clauses between an overt complementiser and a null one. Speakers regularly switch between these variants, often in closely related stretches of discourse and even within a single utterance, as illustrated in (1).

(1) a) I began to realise *that* there was much more of the community, and that's when I began to realise Ø there was a Rosedale, there's a Forest Hill, there's a Kensington. (m/1937)[1]
   b) I think *that* we've gone out of control and stuff like that. I think Ø if you're a smoker, first thing you should do is rip that filter off. (m/1941)
   c) I just decided *that* I wanted to learn how to ride properly [...] she kind of decided Ø she didn't want to do it anymore. (f/1965)
   d) I remember Ø we went somewhere [...] I can only remember *that* I stayed home by myself usually. (f/1991)

The ubiquitous and unremarkable nature of this variation makes object complements an appealing test case for investigating a range of linguistic questions, leading to an extensive body of work. Some research is framed within generative syntax, where the concern is theoretical apparatus, implications for structure, and well-formedness conditions (Doherty 2000; Perlmutter 1971; Pesetsky 1982, 1988; Sobin 1987). Some research is functional in orientation, examining discursive effects on reanalysis and related concerns (Aijmer 1997; Thompson 2002; Thompson and Mulac 1991a, 1991b). A host of other work is interested in the effects

344 *Sali A. Tagliamonte and Alexandra D'Arcy*

of frequency, complexity, and processing (Bolinger 1972; Ferreira and Dell 2000; Rohdenburg 1998; Temperley 2003; Underhill 1988; Ungerer 1988; Yaguchi 2001). There is also an extensive variationist literature on complementiser *that*, where the emphasis has been on examining constraints on variation and change (Elsness 1984; Tagliamonte and Smith 2005; Torres Cacoullos and Walker 2009; Warner 1982).

Given this prolific body of literature, the challenge we face in this chapter is this: What can be said about complementiser variation that has not already been said? Can further investigation shed new light on this common syntactic phenomenon? To date, studies have focussed on linguistic aspects of the alternation between *that* and the null variant. What remains less clear is the role of social and discourse-situational factors, and yet the variability is historically entrenched, stylistically constrained, and attested across varieties of English. There is also evidence that the overt form serves an "essential communicative function" (Cheshire 1996:370) in spontaneous interactive discourse, that of conversation regulation. This observation provides the jumping-off point for the current analysis. Essentially, there are good reasons to expect that variation is not strictly determined by language-internal predictors.

5.1.2 A Brief History of *That* (and *Zero*)

Complementiser *that* can be traced to Old English, where it occurred alongside the subordinating particle *þe* (e.g., Mitchell 1985; van Gelderen 2004). The null variant is also attested from this period, but its use in historical texts was exceedingly rare (Kirch 1959; Rissanen 1991), a state of affairs that held through to the Late Middle and Early Modern periods, when the null variant began to increase (Finegan and Biber 1995; Lopez Couso 1996; Rissanen 1991; Warner 1982). However, the trajectory of change was neither monotonic nor an across-the-board increase. The frequency of the null variant rose steadily through the seventeenth century and then rapidly reversed in the eighteenth century (Finegan and Biber 1995; Palander-Collin 1997; Rissanen 1991; Suárez-Gómez 2000). At the same time, formal genres continuously favoured *that*, with the null variant occurring more frequently in informal and more speech-like genres, such as personal letters, fiction, sermons, and trial records (Finegan and Biber 1995; Rissanen 1991).

In current use, the historical stylistic distinction remains entrenched: *that* denotes a more formal register or genre (e.g., Haegeman and Guéron 1999; Huddleston and Pullum 2002), while the null variant is more typical of informal speech (Tagliamonte and Smith 2005; Thompson and Mulac 1991a, 1991b; Torres Cacoullos and Walker 2009). These register-based and stylistic patterns are reinforced by usage-based considerations in which *that* is extolled for its ability to clarify the relationship between clauses in complex structures, what Bolinger (1972:38) summarises as its ability to "preserve the identity of the clause", particularly in cases where other linguistic content intervenes between the matrix clause and the complement clause. With these historical, structural, register, and stylistic factors in mind, we investigate the current sociolinguistic and discursive variation between *that* and the null variant in complement clauses in a variety of Present-Day English, contemporary Canadian English.

5.1.3 Data and Methods

To explore ongoing dimensions of variation between *that* and the null variant, we conducted a quantitative analysis using data from the Toronto English Archive (Tagliamonte 2003–2006), a collection of urban sociolinguistic interviews recorded at the start of the twenty-first century with individuals born in Toronto between the early 1920s and the early 1990s. The sample for the current study, outlined in Table 5.1.1, was designed to probe the effects of four well-known social correlates of linguistic variation: age, sex,[2] education, and occupation.[3]

5.1.3.1 Social Constraints

In western industrialised nations, income, education, occupation, and their related proxies (e.g., neighbourhood, hunger, local safety, local school ratings) are fundamental components of socio-economic status. Following sociolinguistic tradition, we consider education and occupation, which are related but not fully overlapping social vectors.

According to Labov (2001), education provides perhaps the best binary measure of a form's social evaluation: higher levels of education correlate with linguistic features held to have prestige, as forms overtly associated with ideals of standard language. For speakers aged 19 and older, we distinguish between individuals with a post-secondary qualification versus those with none.

Occupation is associated with conceptions of social class: high-status groups tend toward positively valued linguistic features. We categorised speakers according to job type: as professional (professions and 'white

Table 5.1.1 Sample for complementiser variation drawn from *Toronto English Archive* (Tagliamonte 2003–2006)

Age cohort (age at time of recording)	Men	Women	Total
Teens (9–17)	6	6	12
Younger (19–27)	6	5	11
Middle (32–54)	6	5	11
Older (60–87)	8	11	19
Total	26	27	53

346 *Sali A. Tagliamonte and Alexandra D'Arcy*

collar' occupations, such as managers, teachers, consultants, lawyers, and doctors) and non-professional (unemployed, skilled, and unskilled 'blue collar' occupations, such as assembly, shipping-receiving, mechanics, plumbers). We limit this aspect of the analysis to participants who are actively engaged in the workforce and who can therefore be categorised on their own merits (thereby excluding students and younger participants).

5.1.3.2 *Linguistic Constraints*

Multiple linguistic constraints have been reported to operate on *that/Ø*, but we concentrate here on six most commonly reported in the literature: the lexical verb, tense, subject, and argument structure of the matrix clause, adjacency, and the subject of the complement clause.

MATRIX LEXICAL VERB tests individual word-level constraints on variability. Certain verbs are known to highly favour the null variant (e.g., *think, remember, guess*), as in (2a), while others favour *that* (e.g., *know, tell, realise*), as in (2b).

(2) a) I <u>think</u> Ø it was a serious problem but I <u>think</u> Ø it could have been handled differently. (m/1953)
     b) I kind of <u>realised</u> *that* I didn't want to do broadcast. [...] I <u>realised</u> *that* I wasn't really enjoying myself. (f/1976)

Certain combinations of lexical verb and subject have also been found to function pragmatically (i.e., outside the syntax) rather than as matrix clauses. In particular, *I think, I guess, I mean*, and *you know* have been reanalysed as epistemic parenthetical markers, indicating speaker stance toward the proposition (e.g., Huddleston and Pullum 2002; Thompson and Mulac 1991a, 1991b). In such cases, *that* is not possible because these constructions act as adjuncts rather than main clauses. Our initial extraction process included such constructions in initial position (the canonical matrix position) but excluded them in other positions, where they are adverbial (e.g., *That's kind of the more important night, <u>I think</u>* (f/1978)).

These epistemic constructions are relevant here because they implicate two further constraints on the variation. First is the GRAMMATICAL PERSON OF THE MATRIX CLAUSE. Because epistemic parentheticals tend to have first- (and sometimes, second-) person subjects, the null variant is favoured in such contexts, as in (3a, b), whereas *that* is favoured with third-person subjects in the matrix clause, as in (3c). Second is the TENSE OF THE MATRIX CLAUSE. Epistemic parentheticals are typically encoded with simple present tense morphology (cf. (2a), (3a)), whereas *that* tends to co-occur with past tense morphology and other aspectual markers (cf. (2b), (3c)).

That *Beyond Convention* 347

(3) a) <u>I guess</u> Ø it was just repressed emotions. (m/1981)
   b) <u>You didn't figure</u> Ø you were gonna get a car. (m/1941)
   c) <u>They knew</u> *that* there would be a lot of vets coming home. (f/1941)

A further context conditioning the occurrence of *that* is the presence of additional elements in the VP, such as negation, modal auxiliaries, and adverbs, a constraint that we refer to here as MATRIX ARGUMENT STRUCTURE. The null variant is favoured in the simple VP in (4a), while it is inhibited in clauses with more elaborate VPs, as in (4b).

(4) a) I <u>wish</u> Ø they could have the same things I had. (f/1926)
   b) I <u>wouldn't say</u> *that* I don't notice it. (f/1982)

The last two predictors test structural effects on this alternation (i.e., complexity, Rohdenburg 1998; for other complexity considerations see, e.g., Hawkins 2001, 2003; Rohdenburg 1996). The first effect is ADJACENCY: the presence of intervening adverbial or prepositional phrases between the matrix and complement clauses (5b) favours *that*. Where no such intervening material occurs (5a), the null variant is favoured. Also considered a complexity constraint on *that*/Ø variation, the null variant is favoured when the COMPLEMENT SUBJECT is pronominal (5a) and *that* is favoured when it is nominal (5b). In short, less complex syntactic contexts lead to a higher probability of the null variant while more complex contexts lead to a higher probability of *that*.

(5) a) My mother felt Ø [ ] <u>I</u> did. (f/1922)
   b) I want to say *that* sometimes <u>celebrities</u> are dumb. (f/1992)

These constraints have all been discussed at length in the literature, leading to the prediction that the null variant probabilistically coincides with certain verbs (*say* and *think* in particular), with first-person main clause subjects, and with pronominal complement clause subjects. It is also favoured when the main clause carries simple present tense morphology and less complex syntactic structures.

With these points in mind, we now turn to our own data. Following Tagliamonte and Smith (2005:298), we extracted all (apparent) matrix plus complement constructions where *that* or the null variant was possible, i.e., where the target matrix verb occupies its canonical slot. Following Thompson and Mulac (1991a:239–240) and noted above, we excluded all non-initial parentheticals. We then tested the well-known language internal effects on *that*/Ø variation. However, the crux of our analysis is driven by Cheshire's (1996) suggestion that *that* is impacted by interactional constraints in the joint creation of discourse, which may arise through information structure (a topic we touch on briefly) but also through pauses, hesitations, and reformulations, which interrupt the conversational flow and create additional burdens for listeners.

5.1.4 Results

From a diachronic perspective we know that object complementation has changed from virtually categorical use of *that* in Old and Early Middle English texts to high rates of *zero* in contemporary, vernacular spoken usage. The Toronto data are no exception: the overall rate of the null variant is 84.5% (*n* = 4,135). Figure 5.1.1 shows the historical trajectory by combining in one graph the overall frequency of the null variant from the results of several studies and adding to these the results from Toronto.

As noted above, however, certain collocations (*I think*, *I mean*, *I guess*, *you know*) are known to occur at (near) categorical levels with the null variant. These constructions are generally agreed to be adjuncts that function as epistemic markers on the interpersonal plane, to orient the listener toward speaker stance. Table 5.1.2 reports the distribution of the null variant in the Toronto materials in these four constructions.

Table 5.1.2 highlights two things: how frequent these collocations are in vernacular discourse (they account for nearly 57% of the dataset) and their exceptionally high rates of the null variant. In fact, there is no variation at all in *I guess*, and the same is also effectively true for *I mean* and *you know*. *I think* exhibits slightly more variability, yet the rate of the null variant is more than 90%. These findings are consistent with other work on data from contemporary spoken vernacular English (Tagliamonte and Smith 2005; Thompson and Mulac 1991a, 1991b;

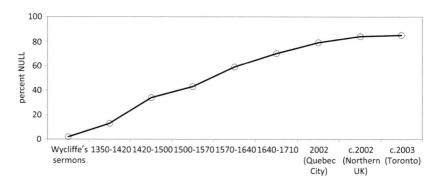

Figure 5.1.1 Frequency of the null complementiser, from Late Middle English and Early Modern English (Rissanen 1991; Warner 1982) to Present-Day English (Tagliamonte and Smith 2005; Torres Cacoullos and Walker 2009).

That *Beyond Convention* 349

Table 5.1.2 Frequency of the null complementiser with *I think*, *I mean*,
I guess and *you know*

Construction	Percent ø	N
I think	91.7	1240
I mean	99.5	368
I guess	100.0	232
you know	98.0	503
Total		2343

Torres Cacoullos and Walker 2009). Given the parallelism with other work and the largely categorical nature of these collocations, we exclude them from further analysis, leaving us with 1,792 tokens. Variability in this subset of the data is more robust, yet the overall distribution of the null variant remains high (70.6%), which means that *that* is the more intriguing variant, in that its occurrence is somewhat exceptional. What predicts the less frequent and at times even somewhat questionable acceptability of this overt form in spontaneous speech?

Because this variable is suited to a statistical model that can take into account the rate of variant use and number of tokens per context without the need for complex interactions or continuous variables, we used Gold-Varb X (Sankoff et al. 2005) for the analysis. The logistic regression procedure in this program assesses factor groups as statistically significant at the .05 level or higher. All other factors are assessed as non-significant as main effects. In the following tables, the results for significant factor groups are provided in detail while, for ease of presentation, non-significant groups are simply listed. Within each factor group selected as significant, the levels (factors) are reported as sum values ordered from highest to lowest so that the patterns within each group can be viewed easily. Importantly, ordered factor weights show the direction of effect of each of the hypotheses being tested. These can be compared with the corresponding proportions in the second column and evaluated along with the number of tokens per cell in the third column. The range offers a non-statistical measure of the relative strength of factor groups in the analysis, with the higher number reflecting a greater contribution of that factor group to the variation within the analysis (see Guy 1988, 1993).[4]

Although we ran a single best-fit model (log-likelihood = –1036.306, p = 0.005), we report the linguistic and social effects separately. Table 5.1.3 reports the results of a fixed effects logistic regression on the probability of *that*, concentrating on language-internal constraints. The results in Table 5.1.3 reveal that all but matrix argument structure and the intervening material complexity constraint have a significant main effect on conditioning the probability that *that* will occur. Moreover, all

350　Sali A. Tagliamonte and Alexandra D'Arcy

Table 5.1.3 Fixed effects logistic regression of linguistic predictors conditioning the use of *that*

Input 0.274	FW	%	n/cell
Matrix verb			
Other verb	.560	32.7	1047
Tell	.546	36.4	77
Know	.474	24.0	225
Say	.380	24.3	296
Think	.338	21.1	147
Range	22		
Matrix subject			
Other pronoun	.559	33.4	934
First person singular pronoun	.426	24.4	739
Range	13		
Matrix tense			
Other tense/aspect	.563	33.1	708
Simple present	.447	26.1	850
Range	11		
Complement subject			
Noun phrase	.572	34.3	341
Pronoun	.481	28.8	1321
Range	9		

Predictors not selected: matrix argument structure, intervening material

factor groups pattern as predicted in the literature, with *that* favoured with verbs other than *think*, *say*, or *know*, with matrix subjects other than first person singular *I*, with tense and aspectual categories other than the simple present, and with nominal subjects in the complement clause. Such results highlight the universality of the constraints on *that*/Ø variability, signalling why (6a) (with first person singular subject and simple present tense in the matrix clause and a pronominal subject in the complement) is perfectly licit but the alternate version in (6b) is somewhat undesirable, even odd-sounding.

(6) a)　I swear Ø I think Ø I have. (f/1984)
　　b)　I swear *that* I think *that* I have.

But what of the social and pragmatic perspectives? Could it be that variation between *that* and the null variant is also conditioned by the dynamics of interaction, and specifically by how these constructions are used in conversation?

That *Beyond Convention*   351

Prescriptivists have long promoted the use of *that* to ensure clarity: they espouse the importance of clausal relationships being signalled overtly. Stylistically, *that* is considered more formal, making it more typical of written language but also lacking personal nuance, being less friendly, non-emotional, even stilted, as perhaps (6b) might seem. These prescriptive and stylistic aspects of complementation suggest that social factors could also be relevant. To explore this possibility, we include the social predictors discussed above (cf. Section 5.1.3.1) in the logistic regression. The results are reported in Table 5.1.4.

Of the traditional social predictors of speaker age, sex, education, and occupation, all but speaker sex (which is not selected as a main effect but which nonetheless patterns as predicted, with women using *that* more than men (31.7% versus 27.1%, respectively)) are selected as significant determinants of complementiser *that*. *That* is favoured among professionals and speakers with a post-secondary education. It also appears, in this aggregate view, to be age-graded, following a curvilinear trajectory. It is favoured among the youngest speakers (pre-adolescent and teenaged), decreases as speakers enter middle-age, and then rises somewhat

Table 5.1.4 Fixed effects logistic regression of social predictors conditioning the use of *that*

Input 0.274	FW	%	n/cell
Age cohort			
Teens (9–17)	.621	34.1	498
Younger (19–27)	.489	32.7	392
Middle (32–54)	.400	23.7	510
Older (60–87)	.486	27.6	392
Range	22		
Education			
Post-secondary	.554	31.1	1214
No post-secondary	.388	25.8	578
Range	16		
Occupation			
Professional	.509	28.7	616
Non-professional	.485	23.4	376
Range[a]	2		

Predictors not selected: speaker sex

a The range for occupation is narrow, yet this predictor is selected as a main effect. As it happens, this result is not unrelated to the failure of speaker sex to emerge overall. There is an interaction between these groups: women use *that* at the same rate, regardless of occupational status. For men, occupation operates as expected.

again. In other words, the factor weights reported here align with the typical pattern of stable, age-graded variants. Cheshire (2005:3) refers to this pattern as reflecting the use of language "considered appropriate to and typical of different stages in the life span". What sets this trajectory apart, however, is that usually what is 'appropriate' to middle age is the more frequent use of standard or prestige variants. Other things being equal, a form that dips in the middle-age cohort is generally associated with speakers who have lower socio-economic indicators (see also Figure 5.1.2).

The well-known stylistic effect corroborates the view that *that* is the more formal complementation strategy. However, there are also prescriptive pressures on the use of *that*. Kroch and Small (1978) have argued that prescriptivism itself should not be disregarded as an object of study because prestige norms can have a powerful influence on speech. In particular, they suggest that standard language norms are believed, ideologically, to be superior to those of the non-standard because they correspond more closely to the logical form of the proposition. In the case of complementation, this is exactly what *that* does: it explicitly encodes the relationship between the matrix verb and the complement clause. In line with their hypothesis, Kroch and Small (1978) find that grammatical ideology is a powerful explanatory factor for patterns of *that* use in speech. On this basis, then, it follows quite naturally that use of *that* should be associated with speakers who are known to adhere to more standard language practices in general: those with higher levels of education and those who hold professional occupations—precisely the effects observed in Table 5.1.4. There is also consistent stratification across the adult portion of the sample with respect to these parameters, as shown in Figure 5.1.2, a cross-tabulation of age cohort and occupation.

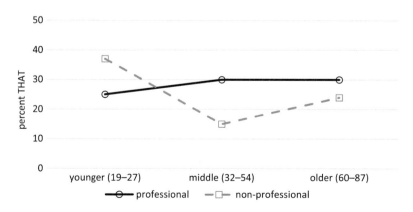

Figure 5.1.2 Cross-tabulation of age and occupation: *that*.

Figure 5.1.2 reveals two further nuances. First, the dip in the middle of the lifespan is not an across-the-board pattern. It is primarily a characteristic of speakers from non-professional economic strata. These groups increase their vernacular usage during middle age. In contrast, professional speakers do not retreat from complementiser *that* during any life stage; instead, its use is quite consistent from one age cohort to the next. Second, and likely related to the first, the younger non-professionals exhibit an exaggerated rate of *that*, surpassing that of the professionals of all age cohorts in the sample. We do not think this is random. Rather, we interpret it as further evidence of the social meaning of *that*. The interviewers for the Toronto English Archive were university students and upcoming professionals. They were age peers with the younger non-professional participants, but they were not social peers. It is therefore possible that the participants heightened their use of *that*, aiming to model more closely the speech of the interviewers (for another effect of social context in these materials, involving subject relative pronoun *who*, see D'Arcy and Tagliamonte 2010).

The evidence thus far leads us to wonder how the social effects fit into the broader picture of object complementation. Figure 5.1.3 presents the significant predictors in descending order, from those exerting the strongest effect on variation to those with the weakest effect.

The constraint rankings show that the effect of matrix verb, a long-recognised powerhouse in the grammar for complementiser *that*/Ø variation, sits at the top of the hierarchy. Other strong predictors are language-external: speaker age and education. These are followed by the other linguistic factors ordered here and, at the bottom, by occupation.

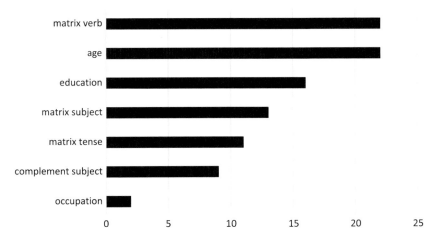

Figure 5.1.3 Constraint ranking of all predictors selected as significant, as reflected by range: *that*.

354   *Sali A. Tagliamonte and Alexandra D'Arcy*

In short, not only are social factors relevant in conditioning the variation between *that* and the null variant but they are also as equally important in constraining variant choices as are the linguistic ones. This result affirms many studies that attest to the intricate interrelationship between internal and external factors in variation.

As noted above, Cheshire (1996) suggested that interactional pressures are also critical factors in constraining variation. Although the nature of the subject of the complement clause has been framed as a complexity condition on the alternation between *that* and Ø in English complement structures, it is also possible to interpret this effect as one of information status. Nominal subjects, which favour *that*, tend to introduce new referents, while pronominal ones, which (weakly) disfavour *that*, tend to have given referents (cf. Table 5.1.3). Under this interpretation, *that* is more likely to arise when interactional considerations require that new information be overtly signalled through additional lexical architecture.

However, we observe an additional quality to the contexts where *that* appears. Consider the examples in (7):

(7) a)   I know Ø my grandmother on my father's side was uh– *that* she came from England as well. (m/1951)
     b)   The worst thing is *that* like, it didn't– it w– it wasn't deadly. (f/1978)
     c)   Nick's happy *that*, you know, he go– he was handed his guitar. (m/1978)
     d)   I think *that* uh– I would definitely– I would definitely say *that* uh– there was never ever ever any pressure on me. (f/1984)

When speakers hesitate, pause, or reformulate, producing what we typically think of as false starts, the rate of *that* is a robust 34.3% (35/102). Such frequency of occurrence parallels that of the overt complementiser in all other contexts in which it is favoured (hovering between 30% and 35%; see Tables 5.1.3 and 5.1.4). While these contexts are relatively rare in the dataset and therefore cannot be included in the statistical models, they suggest that *that* is an important strategy to help navigate disfluencies in discourse.

5.1.5 Discussion and Conclusion: *That* as Linguistic Signpost

We have tested numerous factors influencing variation between *that* and the null variant in English complement clauses in a dataset representing the spoken vernacular of Toronto English at the turn of the twenty-first century. On one hand, our findings confirm what has been reported elsewhere. The same factors are significant and they operate with the same directions of effect (i.e., parallel constraint rankings). On the other hand, we have also documented important social and generational influences on *that/Ø* variation, demonstrating the critical joint contribution of linguistic and social factors in syntactic alternations. Use of *that* is favoured for middle-aged and older speakers with post-secondary education and professional-level jobs. However, hesitations, pauses, and the like also provide an important additional insight into the workings of this variation. When disfluencies occur, the overt complementiser appears at a frequency comparable to its favouring grammatical and social contexts. Why?

We suggest that in addition to prescriptive, register, and stylistic effects, the use of *that* in these contexts serves to reinforce the relationship between two disrupted clauses, one a matrix clause and the other its complement. The link between disfluency and overt complementiser *that* indicates that when syntactic structure is compromised, cognitive constraints exert pressure to signal syntactic structure overtly. In this case, complementiser *that* satisfies that discursive requirement. If *that* were not present in such contexts, communication would be impeded, increasing the decoding burden on speakers and hearers and therefore also increasing the likelihood of a communicative breakdown.

Now let us step back and put this work in broader socio-historical context. The use of overt syntactic markers and their patterning in linguistic and social context has not gone unnoticed. In 1711, Steel personified the relative pronouns *who* and *which* by having them voice a complaint: "Jacksprat *that* supplanted us" (see Bailey 2010:193). In current use, *that* continues to be versatile and frequent in most of its multiple functions, yet it occurs at relatively low levels to mark complement clauses (see Figure 5.1.1). This does not mean that this use of *that*, once a prolific aspect of English complement structures, is falling into obsolescence. It is highly structured linguistically, constrained socially, and it also surfaces in vernacular usage where it is needed to successfully navigate interaction. Cheshire has championed *that*, writing: "the extreme multifunctionality of *that* [...] reflects its importance as an all-purpose linguistic 'signpost' in communication" (Cheshire 1996:390). Like the constraints on argument structure and clausal adjacency, the manifestation of *that* under conditions of hesitation and other disfluencies reveals that structural relationships must be explicit, if not directly from context, then from overt realisation of an underlying syntactic signpost.

In light of this understanding, the results of the logistic regression analysis in Table 5.1.3, which showed that neither argument structure nor clausal adjacency was selected as a significant main effect (though distributionally they patterned as expected), is worth further scrutiny. Both are arguably implicated in syntactic complexity considerations through elaboration of syntactic structure. In contrast, hesitations and reformulations do not necessarily make the syntactic structure more complex. They disrupt it, making the clausal relationships less transparent, but

356 *Sali A. Tagliamonte and Alexandra D'Arcy*

they do not elaborate the grammatical architecture. This suggests, as we have argued above, that the motivation for using *that* in the face of structural discontinuity is not simply motivated by the drive for syntactic clarity but to satisfy interactional pressures as well. On the one hand, the speaker has the need to be understood, a cooperative interpersonal and pragmatic pressure brought on by breaking up the flow of speech. On the other hand, there is grammatical pressure to repair the disjointed phrase structure. Both of these cognitive imperatives combine to increase the likelihood that *that* will be used to mark the complement clause and clarify the syntax under stressed conditions.

To conclude, linguistic constraints, a consistent and robust finding across all studies, are critical for our understanding of *that*/Ø variation. We have argued here that social factors are also involved, pointing to learned patterns relating to ideologies of explicitness and clarity of expression that are valued and conventionalised as symbolic capital among certain sectors of the population. However, interactional pressures are also implicated. Complementiser *that* serves a cooperative function, signalling clausal boundaries in both complex and disjointed structures to help interlocutors navigate discourse (Cheshire 1996:386). We conclude that Cheshire's call for more attention to interactional pressures is critical, with more attention heeded to operationalising cooperation and disfluency in conversation. Indeed, we advocate for a view of variation which recognises the multiple factors that operate on syntactic phenomena in socially embedded data as essential for understanding not only linguistic systems but also how the dynamics of interaction contribute to syntactic and social settings (e.g., Ashby 1988; Barnes 1985; Couper-Kuhlen 2012).

Notes

* We gratefully acknowledge the Social Sciences and Humanities Research Council of Canada, for grants 4102003005 and 410070048 to Tagliamonte, and the Research Assistants at the University of Toronto who helped with the extraction and coding of the data: Sarah Clarke, Derek Denis, Bridget Jankowski, Michael Ritter, and Jenny Seppänen. We extend our heartfelt appreciation to Jenny Cheshire, who has long inspired us with her scholarship and her kindness. Her support has been akin to *that*, surfacing whenever we have needed it.
1 Parenthetical information following examples indicates speaker sex (female, male) and year of birth. See Section 5.1.3 for corpus and sample details.
2 To our knowledge, all the speakers in our sub-sample are cis-gendered.
3 The majority of speakers are of British origin (English, Irish, Scots), but a range of ethnicities is represented in the data (e.g., Chinese, Filipino, Italian, Jamaican, Tamil, Ukrainian, Vietnamese). However, ethnicity has not been found to have a significant effect for any variable that we have examined in these materials.
4 While a group with more than two levels may have an inflated range if the extreme categories have relatively little data in them, we are less concerned with this here, as the matrix verb group is reasonably well populated across all levels, particularly in the 'other verb' category.

References

Aijmer, Karin. 1997. "I think – An English modal particle". In *Modality in Germanic Languages: Historical and Comparative Perspectives*, T. Swan and O.J. Westvick (eds.). Berlin: Mouton de Gruyter. 1–47.

Ashby, William J. 1988. "The syntax, pragmatics, and sociolinguistics of left- and right-dislocations in French". *Lingua* 76(2/3):203–229.

Bailey, Richard. 2010. "Variation and change in eighteenth-century English". In *Eighteenth-Century English: Ideology and Change*, R. Hickey (ed.). Cambridge: Cambridge University Press. 182–199.

Barnes, Betsy K. 1985. *The Pragmatics of Left Detachment in Spoken Standard French*. Amsterdam: John Benjamins.

Bolinger, Dwight. 1972. *Degree Words*. The Hague: Mouton.

Chambers, J.K. and Peter Trudgill. 1991. "Dialect grammar: Data and theory". In *Dialects of English: Studies in Grammatical Variation*, Peter Trudgill and J.K. Chambers (eds.). London: Longman. 182–199.

Cheshire, Jenny. 2005. "Syntactic variation and beyond: Gender and social class variation in the use of discourse-new markers". *Journal of Sociolinguistics* 9(4):479–508.

Cheshire, Jenny. 1996. "That Jacksprat: An interactional perspective on English *that*". *Journal of Pragmatics* 25(3):369–393.

Couper-Kuhlen, Elizabeth. 2012. "Turn continuation and clause combinations". *Discourse Processes* 49(3/4):273–299.

D'Arcy, Alexandra and Sali A. Tagliamonte. 2010. "The prestige legacy of relative *who*". *Language in Society* 39(3):389–410.

Doherty, Cathal. 2000. *Clauses without "That": The Case for Bare Sentential Complementation in English*. New York and London: Garland Publishing.

Elsness, Johan. 1984. "*That* or zero? A look at the choice of object clause connective in a corpus of American English". *English Studies* 65(6):519–533.

Ferreira, Victor S. and Gary S. Dell. 2000. "Effect of ambiguity and lexical availability on syntactic and lexical production". *Cognitive Psychology* 40(4):296–340.

Finegan, Edward and Douglas Biber. 1995. "*That* and zero complementisers in late Modern English". In *The Verb in Contemporary English*, B. Arts and C. Meyer (eds.). Cambridge: Cambridge University Press. 241–257.

Guy, Gregory R. 1988. "Advanced Varbrul analysis". In *Linguistic Change and Contact*, K. Ferrara, B. Brown, K. Walters and J. Baugh (eds.). Austin: Department of Linguistics, University of Texas at Austin. 124–136.

Guy, Gregory R. 1993. "The quantitative analysis of linguistic variation". In *American Dialect Research*, D. Preston (ed.). Amsterdam and Philadelphia: John Benjamins. 223–249.

Haegeman, Liliane and Jacqueline Guéron. 1999. *English Grammar: A Generative Perspective*. Oxford: Blackwell.

Hawkins, John A. 2003. "Why are zero-marked phrases closer to their heads?" In *Determinants of Grammatical Variation in English*, G. Rohdenburg and B. Mondorf (eds.). Berlin ad New York: Mouton de Gruyter. 175–204.

Hawkins, John A. 2001. "Why are categories adjacent?" *Journal of Linguistics* 31(1):1–34.

Huddleston, Rodney and K. Geoffrey Pullum. 2002. *The Cambridge Grammar of the English Language*. Cambridge: Cambridge University Press.

358 *Sali A. Tagliamonte and Alexandra D'Arcy*

Kirch, Max S. 1959. "Scandanavian influence on English syntax". *Proceedings of the Modern Language Association* 74(5):503–510.

Kroch, Anthony S. and C. Small. 1978. "Grammatical ideology and its effect on speech". In *Linguistic Variation: Models and Methods*, David Sankoff (ed.). New York: Academic Press. 45–55.

Labov, William. 2001. *Principles of Linguistic Change, Volume 2: Social Factors*. Malden and Oxford: Blackwell Publishers.

Lopez Couso, María José. 1996. "A look at *that*/zero variation in Restoration English". In *English Historical Linguistics 1994: Papers from the 8th International Conference on English Historical Linguistics*, Derek Britton (ed.). Amsterdam: John Benjamins. 271–286.

Milroy, Lesley. 1987. *Observing and Analysing Natural Language*. Oxford: Blackwell Publishers.

Mitchell, Bruce. 1985. *Old English Syntax*. Oxford: Clarendon Press.

Palander-Collin, Minna. 1997. "A medieval case of grammaticalization, *methinks*". In *Grammaticalization at Work: Studies of Long-Term Developments in English*, M. Rissanen, M. Kytö and K. Heikkonen (eds.). Berlin and New York: Mouton de Gruyter. 371–403.

Perlmutter, David. 1971. *Deep and Surface Structure Constraints in Syntax*. New York: Holt, Rinehart and Winston.

Pesetsky, David. 1982. "Complementizer-trace phenomena and the nominative island constraint". *The Linguistic Review* 1(3):297–343.

Pesetsky, David. 1988. "Some optimality principles of sentence pronunciation". In *Is the Best Good Enough? Optimality and Competition in Syntax*, P. Barbosa, D. Fox, P. Hagstrom, M. McGinnis and D. Pesetsky (eds.). Cambridge, MA: MIT Press. 337–383.

Rissanen, Matti. 1991. "On the history of *that*/zero as object clause links in English". In *English Corpus Linguistics: Studies in Honour of Jan Svartvik*, K. Aijmer and B. Altenberg (eds.). London and New York: Longman. 272–289.

Rohdenburg, Günter. 1996. "Cognitive complexity and increased grammatical explicitness in English". *Cognitive Linguistics* 7(2):149–182.

Rohdenburg, Günter. 1998. "Clausal complementation and cognitive complexity in English". In *Anglistentag Erfurt*, F.-W. Neumann and S. Schülting (eds.). Trier: Wissenschaftlicher Verlag. 101–112.

Sankoff, David, Sali A. Tagliamonte and Eric Smith. 2005. Goldvarb X. http://individual.utoronto.ca/tagliamonte/goldvarb.html (accessed 25.1.2009).

Sobin, Nicholas. 1987. "The variable status of comp-trace phenomena". *Natural Language and Linguistic Theory* 5(1):33–60.

Suárez-Gómez, Cristina. 2000. "*That*/zero variation in private letters and drama (1420–1710): A corpus-based approach". *Miscelánea: A Journal of English and American Studies* 21:179–204.

Tagliamonte, Sali A. 2003–2006. *Linguistic Changes in Canada Entering the 21st Century*. Research Grant. Social Sciences and Humanities Research Council of Canada (SSHRC). #410-2003-0005.

Tagliamonte, Sali A. and Jennifer Smith. 2005. "No momentary fancy! The zero 'complementizer' in English dialects". *English Language and Linguistics* 9(2):1–21.

Temperley, David. 2003. "Ambiguity avoidance in English relative clauses". *Language* 79(3):464–484.

Thompson, Sandra A. 2002. "'Object complements' and conversation: Towards a realistic account". *Studies in Language* 26(1):125–164.

Thompson, Sandra and Anthony Mulac. 1991a. "The discourse conditions for the use of the complementizer *that* in conversational English". *Journal of Pragmatics* 15(3):237–251.

Thompson, Sandra and Anthony Mulac. 1991b. "A quantitative perspective on the grammaticization of epistemic parentheticals in English". In *Approaches to Grammaticalization*, E.C. Traugott and B. Heine (eds.). Amsterdam and Philadelphia: John Benjamins. 313–329.

Torres Cacoullos, Rena and James A. Walker. 2009. "On the persistence of grammar in discourse formulas: A variationist study of *that*". *Linguistics* 47(1):1–43.

Underhill, Robert. 1988. "Like is like, focus". *American Speech* 63(3):234–246.

Ungerer, Friedrich. 1988. *Syntax der englischen Adverbialen*. Tübingen: Niemeyer.

van Gelderen, Elly. 2004. *Grammaticalization as Economy*. Amsterdam and Philadelphia: John Benjamins.

Warner, Anthony. 1982. *Complementation in Middle English and the Methodology of Historical Syntax*. London and Canberra: Croom Helm.

Yaguchi, Michiko. 2001. "The function of the non-deictic 'that' in English". *Journal of Pragmatics* 33(7):1125–1155.

5.2 Sociolinguistic Variation in the Marking of New Information
The Case of Indefinite *this*

Stephen Levey, Carmen Klein, and Yasmine Abou Taha

5.2.1 Introduction

The mismatch between traditional grammatical categories and the facts of usage has been a central theme in Cheshire's many important contributions to research on the syntax of spoken English (e.g., Cheshire 1989, 1999, 2005). As Cheshire (1999:129) observes, "conventional descriptions of English syntax fit written English better than the speech we produce in informal styles". As a result, canonical grammatical accounts may obscure "the structural make-up and structural possibilities of the whole spectrum of variation that makes up a language" (Cheshire and Stein 1997:5).

These remarks provide the point of departure for the investigation described in this chapter. Our focus is on a phenomenon in colloquial English which has received only scant attention in the literature (Rühlemann and O'Donnell 2014:341) and which poses challenges to traditional frameworks of analysis. The feature in question involves variation of the determiner *a(n)* with unstressed *this* to introduce indefinite NPs, as illustrated in (1)–(2) below, taken from a mainstream urban variety of spoken Canadian English.

(1) I was in *a* hostel and there was somebody else in the room and everything. (OEC/003/F/Y/851)[1]
(2) There's *this* insane church and it's absolutely massive. (OEC/002/F/Y/343)

In these examples, both *a* and *this* refer to a newly introduced (i.e., first-mentioned) discourse referent that is specific (i.e., *one particular hostel, a certain church*). The referentially specific interpretation of *this* illustrated in (2) is a necessary condition for its use with indefinite NPs (Prince 1981). By contrast, the determiner *a(n)* is not limited to contexts such as (1), where it has a specific interpretation. Elsewhere, it can also have a non-specific or type-identifiable interpretation (Gundel et al.

1993:276), as in (3), where the speaker refers to a type of film rather than a specific film.

(3) Like we sometimes will have sisters' night. We'll go see *a* cheesy movie. (OEC/025/F/Y/10055)

The existence of pairs such as (1) and (2) initially raises the question of how a demonstrative, typically associated with definiteness in canonical grammatical descriptions (Dik 1989:147), may be used with indefinite reference to introduce discourse-new entities (Ionin 2006). Gundel et al. (1993:277) propose that indefinite *this* may be an extension of its cataphoric use as a proximal demonstrative pronoun referring to a referent or state of affairs in the ensuing discourse (e.g., "*What I wanted to tell you is this. Last night…*"). In this chapter, we build on this foundational insight by investigating constraints that may potentially condition the alternation of *this* and *a(n)* in the expression of referential indefiniteness.

An original component of the research described in this chapter is our attempt to examine the variable expression of referential indefiniteness by drawing parallels with the larger cross-linguistic phenomenon known as *differential argument marking*. The latter is a general and versatile process encompassing a wide range of phenomena understood to involve alternate ways of coding an argument role, depending on factors other than the argument itself (Witzlack-Makarevich and Seržant 2018:3). A classic example concerns the use of the Spanish preposition *a* to explicitly mark a subset of non-prototypical direct objects (i.e., those that are human/animate and specific). Cross-linguistically, differential object marking (DOM), as well as differential subject marking (DSM), are assumed to be manifestations of a general tendency for languages to exhibit asymmetric coding of 'unexpected' or 'non-prototypical' referential properties associated with certain argument roles. Widely recognised constraints on differential marking include animacy, definiteness and specificity (Aissen 2003; Iemmolo 2010), with the range of possible determinants recently extended to information-structural factors such as topicality (Witzlack-Makarevich and Seržant 2018:10). Possible triggers of differential marking are often conceptualised in the form of prominence hierarchies (Aissen 2003), such as the following, reproduced from Iemmolo (2013:379):

- Animacy: human > animate > inanimate
- Definiteness: definite > specific indefinite > non-specific indefinite
- Topicality: topical > non-topical

Exemplifying again with DOM in Spanish, referents ranked higher on the animacy hierarchy are more likely to receive differential or discriminatory marking than those lower down, so that a human referent in

362 *Stephen Levey et al.*

object position would be more susceptible to discriminatory marking than a more prototypical inanimate one. In this chapter, we submit that such hierarchies are also relevant to understanding indefinite *this/a(n)* variation, despite the fact that English (to the best of our knowledge) is not usually cited as a language exhibiting differential argument marking.

As we have noted, indefinite *this* is restricted to (a small subset of) specific indefinites where it competes with *a(n)*, but it is never used with non-specific or type-identifiable indefinites in our data based on vernacular speech recorded in Ottawa. This pattern accords with the predictions of the definiteness hierarchy shown above – that is, specific indefinites are more likely to be the locus of discriminatory marking than non-specific indefinites. Accordingly, we explore whether other hierarchies may potentially impinge on indefinite *this/a(n)* variation, including those relating to animacy and topicality.

Our data come from the *Ottawa English Corpus*, a compendium of vernacular speech recorded in Canada's National Capital Region. Our methodological approach is informed by recent observations that differential marking may operate according to probabilistic rules and is therefore amenable to quantitative analysis (see e.g., Witzlack-Makarevich and Seržant [2018:28] on *fluid differential argument marking*). We incorporate into our investigation a multivariate quantitative assessment of competing motivations for variant choice, enabling us to determine their significance, relative strength, and direction of effect.

The remainder of this chapter is structured as follows: we first provide a brief summary of previous investigations of indefinite *this*, and explore its time-depth in the language as well as the factors reported to condition its alternation with *a(n)*. We then detail our methodological and analytical procedures. After presenting our results, we discuss the implications of our major quantitative findings and conclude with directions for future research.

5.2.2 Background

There is general agreement that the use of indefinite *this* to introduce discourse-new referents is a feature of informal spoken English (Perlman 1969:76, Prince 1981:232). Its impressionistic association with youth speech (Perlman 1969; Wald 1983) raises the issues of stable age-grading or potential change in progress (Wald 1983:94), but the general absence of apparent- or real-time studies of this phenomenon currently makes it difficult to build a solid case for either possibility.

Wald (1983:94) asserts that indefinite *this* experienced "phenomenal geographic expansion in the twentieth century". Whether the rise of indefinite *this* can be correctly characterised as a twentieth-century phenomenon remains unclear. Certainly, its use with the *second* lexical

The Case of Indefinite THIS   363

mention of a previously introduced (and thematically prominent) referent has a lengthy heritage, dating back to Middle English, as shown in (4).

(4) "Ye, certes, lemman", quod Absolon [...] *This* Absolon doun sette hym on his knees [....]
'"Yes, truly, sweetheart", said Absolon [...] *This* Absolon got down upon his knees [...]' (Chaucer, Canterbury Tales A. Mil. 3723)

It has been proposed (e.g., Denison 1999:118; Wald 1983:100) that the Middle English anaphoric use of *this* illustrated in (4) shares important parallels with its capacity in the modern language to denote someone or something not previously mentioned, tentatively suggesting that examples such as (4) may have operated as bridging contexts for the extension of *this* to marking discourse-new or first-mentioned referents.

According to Wald (1983:94), there is no known record of the use of indefinite *this* before the 1930s. Perusal of historical corpora reveals that it surfaces, as in (5), and infrequently in additional American sources several decades earlier, as in (6).

(5) There was *this* cook, a great big guy, and he whipped up the nicest cake you ever sunk your teeth into (ARCHER/*A Sound of Hunting. A Play in Three Acts* by H. Brown, 1946)[2]
(6) He talks no other language than English, but we could not understand half he said: there is *this* marked difference in American and English pronunciation... (ARCHER/*Travel letters from New Zealand, Australia and Africa* by E. W. Howe, 1913)

The earliest example of indefinite *this* introducing a human referent that we have located dates from the late nineteenth century and occurs in a speech-based context in popular fiction hailing from North America.

(7) "Victor", his aunt would cry out,

> I wish – I wish you would consult a physician about this affection of the heart. I am frightened for you – it is not like anything else. There is *this* famous German – do go to see him to please me.
> (CORPUS OF HISTORICAL AMERICAN ENGLISH/*A Terrible Secret* by M. A. Fleming, 1874)

Indefinite *this* occurs intermittently in even earlier historical sources, but not, as far as we can tell, with first-mentioned human referents.[3]

(8) The next morning there was *this* Epitaph posted upon his Tomb. Here restless he doth rest. (EARLY ENGLISH BOOKS ONLINE/ *Aretina; or, The Serious Romance* by G. Mackenzie 1660)[4]

364 *Stephen Levey et al.*

Turning to the functional correlates of the alternation between *a(n)* and *this* to mark specific indefinites, common explanations abstracted from previous research address the capacity of indefinite *this* to indicate "further information forthcoming" (Perlman 1969:78), "something that is going to be talked about" (Prince 1981:235), or something that is flagged for "extended attention" (Wald 1983:97). It is said to introduce discourse-new entities which are: "more pragmatically important" (Cheshire 1989:51); "prone to topic shift" (Chiriacescu 2011:48); and thematically central to the unfolding discourse (Rühlemann and O'Donnell 2014:355). A rough summary of the discourse-structuring potential of indefinite *this* is that it is more likely than *a(n)* to introduce discourse-new entities which will be referentially persistent in the ensuing discourse after their initial introduction (Wright and Givón 1987).

Despite the numerous motivations that have been proposed in the literature to account for indefinite *this/a(n)* variation, few have been simultaneously incorporated into a single analysis or tested on an "exhaustively-sampled body of text" (Wright and Givón 1987:30). In the following sections, we address this issue by drawing on a sizeable body of spoken-language data to operationalise and test a number of possible constraints on indefinite *this/a(n)* variation.

5.2.3 Data

The data described in Table 5.2.1, drawn from the *Ottawa English Corpus* (OEC), are based on the speech of 27 (mostly post-secondary educated) speakers recorded between 2008 and 2010 in the National Capital Region of Canada. Assembled using a quasi-random sampling methodology and incorporating a degree of stratification by speaker age and sex, this corpus was collected by in-group community members using a standard sociolinguistic interview protocol.

We acknowledge that we have less data than we would have liked from older speakers. This is not so much a defect of our sampling methodology as a problem inherent in the data themselves. Indefinite *this*, as we demonstrate below, is infrequent, and out of an additional seven older speakers in the *OEC* that we initially sampled, none produced a single token of indefinite *this*, rendering these speakers inadmissible for inclusion in our investigation. We nonetheless capitalise on whatever

Table 5.2.1 Stratification of informants by sex and age group

	Older (50+)	Younger (20–35)	Total
Male	2	12	14
Female	3	10	13
Total	5	22	27

The Case of Indefinite THIS 365

patterning there is in the discourse of the five older speakers who *do* utilise indefinite *this* in order to elucidate any provisional evidence of age differences in the use of the target variable.

The interviews on which the analysis is based were transcribed in their entirety, amounting to 222,149 words of running text. This procedure enabled us to identify and retrieve all discourse-new (i.e., first-mentioned) referents marked by *this/a(n)* eligible for inclusion in the study.

5.2.4 Method

The variable expression of indefiniteness poses a number of challenges for the delimitation of the variable context. Chief among these is the capacity of the indefinite determiner *a(n)* to introduce non-specific or type-identifiable indefinites which do not permit variation with indefinite *this* (compare *she was looking for a new bicycle, any would do* with ***she was looking for this new bicycle, any would do*). Accordingly, indefinites that are non-specific, as gauged from contextual information, or that are referentially opaque (i.e., licensing a specific *or* a non-specific reading) are excluded from the analysis. Also discounted are instances where indefinite *this/a(n)* occurs in reported speech (i.e.. contexts that might be imitative of another's linguistic usage); fixed expressions and idioms (e.g.. *he took <u>a</u> swing at her*); as well as speech disfluencies and anomalies. On account of their overall infrequency in the data, we also set aside specific indefinites introduced by the numeral *one* or by the quantifier *some* (e.g., *there was <u>one/some</u> guy coming towards me on the street*).

Following exclusions, 629 tokens of specific indefinite NPs introducing discourse-new entities were retained for analysis. Each token was subsequently coded for two speaker-based variables. Age (Older = 50+ versus Younger = 20–35) allows us to tentatively probe any evidence of apparent-time change. Speaker sex, operationalised here as a broad, exploratory variable (Milroy and Milroy 1997:53), enables us to identify any potential sex-based differences in the use of competing options to mark specific indefinites (see e.g., Cheshire [2005:495–6] on different gender-based orientations to the expression of referential meaning).

Turning to the independent linguistic variables incorporated into the analysis, we first coded the syntactic position hosting each specific indefinite NP, distinguishing subject, object and oblique/complement of a preposition, as well as specific indefinite NPs in predicate nominal position (e.g., *there's <u>this TV show</u> on*). Our working hypothesis builds on Comrie's (1989:128) claim that prototypical transitive constructions consist of a transitive subject (AGENT), which is high in animacy and definiteness, and a transitive object (PATIENT) that is lower in animacy and definiteness. We conjecture that any deviation from this prototype should attract differential marking. Subject position, for example, regarded as the most prominent argument position in syntax (Aissen

366   *Stephen Levey et al.*

2003:476), is widely known in English (and many other languages) to be inhospitable to indefinite NPs. The usual explanation for this aversion is that subject position strongly correlates with *given* information, rather than *new* information encoded by indefinite NPs. Accordingly, our expectation is that indefinite NPs in subject position, as deviations from prototypical informational-structural patterns, will be especially likely to attract *this* as a discriminatory marker (see Wald 1983:101; Wright and Givón 1987:20).

We also identified the type of syntactic construction hosting the first mention of each *this/a(n)*-marked specific indefinite. We discriminated a range of syntactic constructions (e.g., *it*-cleft, existential-*there*) that could be conscripted to avoid placing indefinite NPs in subject position. Furthermore, because specific syntactic constructions such as existential-*there* are reported to influence the salience of pragmatically important discourse entities (see e.g., Birch and Garnsey 1995:234; Cheshire 2005:485; Walker, this volume), we reasoned that indefinite *this*, as a putative marker of such entities, would be more inclined to surface in particular construction types.

In coding for humanness of the referent (i.e., human versus non-human), our coding procedure, inspired by Aissen's (2003) prominence hierarchy for animacy, tests the prediction that specific indefinites encoding human referents will be more favourable to discriminatory marking via *this* than those encoding non-human ones.

A number of studies (e.g., Chiriacescu 2011; Wald 1983) suggest that specific indefinites marked by *this* exhibit a propensity to co-occur with post-modifying constructions that serve to immediately provide additional information about the newly introduced referent. We therefore distinguished contexts where a specific indefinite is post-modified (e.g., by a relative clause, prepositional phrase, etc.) from contexts where there was no post-modification of the specific indefinite NP.

Extending the analysis beyond the sentence level, we initially operationalised two measures to assess the discourse structuring potential of competing variants: topic continuity/shift and referential persistence, the latter measuring the likelihood that a *this/a(n)*-marked specific indefinite will recur in the subsequent discourse after its first mention. Preliminary analysis of the data revealed, however, that these two measures are highly correlated (i.e., topics tend to be referentially persistent in discourse), necessitating the creation of an interaction or cross-product factor group – topic persistence – combining both measures in order to enable viable statistical analysis to be carried out (Tagliamonte 2006:234). Before describing how we configured the cross-product factor group for statistical evaluation, we first address what we mean by 'topic'.

Following Lambrecht (1994:127), we understand the topic of a proposition to express the pragmatic relationship of 'aboutness' which obtains

The Case of Indefinite THIS   367

between a referent and a proposition within a particular discourse context. We further understand the topic to be prototypically given information that is identifiable (i.e., a constituent that is definite and specific), although following Reinhart (1981), we also acknowledge that specific indefinites can atypically function as topics (see also Dalrymple and Nikolaeva 2011:53). Topics are strongly correlated with subject NPs, which have unmarked topic status (Lambrecht 1994:168). By way of illustration, consider the example in (9), in which the topic of the first clause is *the people*, which is sustained in the second clause (*they=the people*). The object of the second clause, *this custom home*, is not treated as the topic in traditional frameworks, but as part of the focus domain. This referent does, however, assume topic status (*it=this custom house*) in the following co-ordinate clause.

(9) [...] across the street from us *the people* were completely nuts. *They*'d built *this* custom home, and *it* had to be like a million-dollar house. (OEC/015/Y/F/6146)

Our gradient measure of topic persistence accounts for the subsequent mentions of a *this/(a)n*-marked referent in the following ten clauses after its initial introduction, counting the number of times it occurs as the topic in these clauses.[5] Because a *this/(a)n*-marked indefinite can also recur in the subsequent discourse without being the topic, we include non-topic persistence within the same cross-product factor group. For example, in (10), the topic is *my dad* in the first clause and this topic is sustained in the following two clauses. The newly introduced discourse referent *this air filter system*, by contrast, is not the (primary) topic but is referred to twice in the following two clauses.[6] It has one further mention in the subsequent eight clauses (not shown), resulting in a cumulative persistence value of 3.

(10) and *my dad* just bought *this air filter system* and he's so happy with *it*[1], and he can 't stop talking about *it*[2]

If in the ensuing discourse there are *no* additional mentions of a referent after its initial introduction, then the corresponding persistence value is zero. Following Wright and Givón (1987:23), we interpret persistence values from 0 to 2 as 'low', while values of 3 or more are considered 'high'. Summarising, our coding protocol addresses two interrelated hypotheses: (a) that *this*-marked specific indefinites will be more likely to surface as topics in the following discourse than their *a(n)*-marked counterparts; and (b) that they will be more prone than their *a(n)*-marked equivalents to iterative mentions in the subsequent discourse, as gauged from higher persistence values.

368   *Stephen Levey et al.*

5.2.5 Results

We first observe from Table 5.2.2 that 19% of the 629 tokens retained in the analysis are introduced by indefinite *this*, confirming that it is the non-canonical option in the variable system. Further inspection of the data (not shown in Table 5.2.2) reveals that there is a marginal difference in the overall rate of indefinite *this* according to speaker age: 20% (younger) versus 15% (older). We tentatively interpret the limited quantitative difference between the two age groups as militating against apparent-time change.

In terms of sex-differentiated patterns, the most visible difference resides in the usage rates of younger speakers: females' rate of indefinite *this* (27%) is almost twice that of males' (14%). Why this particular difference should obtain is not immediately clear, especially as there is no parallel effect among the older speakers. Its existence provisionally points to socially conditioned variation in the strategies used by younger speakers to introduce specific indefinite referents, a possibility that may be linked to divergent gender-related orientations to information packaging (see Cheshire 2005).

We next turn to the primary focus of our research: the linguistic conditioning of variant selection. Figure 5.2.1 shows the distribution of specific indefinites according to the syntactic position in which they are first introduced, exhibiting a salient asymmetry between subject and non-subject position.

Only in subject position does the rate of indefinite *this* outstrip that of its competitor, *a(n)* (see also Wald 1983; Wright and Givón 1987). In non-subject position, by contrast, indefinite *this* is very much a minority contender and exhibits almost identical rates in object, oblique and predicate nominal position. To achieve a better understanding of this asymmetry, we turn to a statistical assessment of the data. To determine the relative weight of competing motivations for variant choice, we draw on multivariate analysis using binomial step-wise regression in GoldVarb X (Sankoff et al. 2005).

Table 5.2.2 Overall distribution of indefinite *a(n)* and *this* by speaker sex and age group

	Older (50+)				*Younger (20–35)*				*Total*	
	Male		*Female*		*Male*		*Female*			
	n	%	n	%	n	%	n	%	n	%
a(n)	49	84	38	86	264	86	160	73	511	81
this	9	16	6	14	43	14	60	27	118	19
Total	58		44		307		220		629	

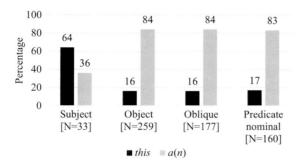

Figure 5.2.1 Distribution of indefinite *this* and *a(n)* in Ottawa English by syntactic position.

Table 5.2.3 below shows the results of a multivariate analysis of social and linguistic factors contributing to the selection of indefinite *this*. Factor weights (or probability values) greater than .5 promote variant selection in the contexts shown in the left-hand side of the table, whereas those below .5 have an inhibiting effect. The *range* provides an indication of the relative strength of significant effects (non-significant effects are in brackets). For interpretative purposes, the major line of evidence can be found in the *direction of effect*, indicated by the ranking of probability values from largest to smallest. The constraint ranking is construed here as a 'window' on the underlying system conditioning the alternation between indefinite *this* and *a(n)* (see Poplack and Tagliamonte 2001:92).

Consideration of social factors confirms that speaker sex is a significant determinant of variant choice, an effect which is entirely attributable, as indicated earlier, to younger speakers, with females showing a preference for indefinite *this*. Statistical evaluation confirms that the modest age-related difference in variant usage rates observed previously is not significant. Further analysis (not shown) revealed no compelling evidence indicating that contextual effects on variant choice pattern differently in the speech of the older group vis-à-vis the younger one. Although this reinforces our belief that there are no compelling indications of apparent-time change in the variable system, to this interpretation we attach the caveat that our analysis is hampered by the paucity of data available from the five older speakers in our sample. Pending further investigation of indefinite *this* in older age groups, along with the availability of appropriate real-time data, we remain agnostic with regard to possibility of change in the variable system.

Turning to linguistic factors, the pre-eminent constraints on variant choice, as gauged from the associated *ranges*, are syntactic position and topic persistence. The association between subject position and indefinite *this* is arguably a product of the non-prototypical status of specific

370 Stephen Levey et al.

Table 5.2.3 Multivariate analysis of the contribution of social and linguistic factors to the probability that indefinite *this* will be selected in subject and non-subject positions

Total N	629		
Log-likelihood	−270.907		
Corrected mean	.162		

SOCIAL FACTORS	*Factor weight*	*%*	*n*
Speaker sex			
Female	.60	25	66/264
Male	.43	14	52/365
Range	*17*		
Age			
Young (20–35)	[.51]	20	103/527
Old (50+)	[.43]	15	15/102
LINGUISTIC FACTORS			
Syntactic position of ref.			
Subject	.79	64	21/33
Non-subject	.48	16	97/596
Range	*31*		
Topic persistence[a]			
Topic persistence (3+)	.64	34	41/120
Topic persistence (0–2)	.64	28	38/137
Non-topic persistence (0–2)	.40	10	37/362
Range	*24*		
Humanness of referent			
Human	.61	34	53/154
Non-human	.46	14	65/475
Range	*15*		
Clausal construction hosting indefinite NP			
Existential	[.60]	25	20/80
Other	[.49]	18	98/549
Post-modification of indefinite NP			
Post-modified	[.51]	19	52/270
Other	[.49]	18	66/359

a A fourth category, non-topic persistence (3+), is excluded from the analysis shown in this table as well as Table 5.2.4.

indefinites as syntactic subjects. That specific indefinites in subject position are highly infrequent and exceptional is clearly demonstrated by the fact that there are 33 such tokens in this position, accounting for only 5.3% of the entire dataset.[7]

The results for topic persistence show that indefinite *this* is strongly correlated with the topicality of the referent in the subsequent discourse, irrespective of whether the topical referent has a high or low persistence value. In keeping with our initial predictions, indefinite *this* is disfavoured with non-topical referents that have low persistence in the following discourse. The strength of topic persistence as the second-ranked constraint confirms that information-structural considerations associated with the wider discourse context play a pivotal role in the selection of indefinite *this*. We infer from this result that *this* functions as a discriminatory marker of pragmatically prominent indefinites (see also Wright and Givón 1987). This finding is in line with the cross-linguistic tendency for topical (or topic-worthy) referents to receive special grammatical marking (Givón 1995:65). It also accords with experimental evidence indicating that indefinite *this* may trigger processing signals that enhance the activation of the referents it marks, improving their accessibility for subsequent reference (Gernsbacher and Jescheniak 1995:29).

Indefinites flagged by *this* as pragmatically important also exhibit a tendency to be human (see Table 5.2.3), corroborating previous reports of its association with human referents (Rühlemann and O'Donnell 2014:351), and also patterning in line with the predictions of the animacy hierarchy outlined earlier.

Neither clausal construction hosting the indefinite NP nor post-modification of the NP return significant effects. The factor weights for post-modification gravitate towards the median indicating the absence of any effect. But in the case of the clausal construction hosting the indefinite NP, the tendency for indefinite *this* to be selected with existential-*there*, as indicated by the constraint ranking, likely reflects the use of a preferred syntactic strategy to avoid placing an indefinite NP in subject position. Moreover, we assume that the association between indefinite *this* and topicality mentioned above increases the likelihood of *this*-marked indefinites occurring in a specific construction that has been identified as a structural device for promoting a new topic (Lambrecht 1994:176).

We have seen that indefinite *this* is strongly correlated with subject NPs (see Table 5.2.3). However, because the majority of indefinite *this* tokens occur in *non-subject* position (see Figure 5.2.1), repeating the analysis for this environment alone allows us to ascertain whether the significant effects uncovered in the aggregated dataset (combining subject and non-subject environments) are also operative when the small number of subject tokens are removed.

Table 5.2.4 depicts the results of such an analysis, omitting the results for social factors, which remain unchanged. The linguistic results are virtually identical with those in Table 5.2.3. Of particular note in Table 5.2.4 is the revelation that the effects of topic persistence and humanness are consistent with their equivalents in Table 5.2.3, despite the fact that non-subject position is known to be less favourable to human referents and is not typically correlated with topicality. This bolsters our

372   Stephen Levey et al.

Table 5.2.4 Multivariate analysis of the contribution of linguistic factors to the probability that indefinite *this* will be selected in non-subject position

Total N	596		
Log-likelihood	−250.654		
Corrected mean	.147		

	Factor weight	%	n
Topic persistence			
Topic persistence (3+)	.64	26	26/99
Topic persistence (0–2)	.65	25	32/126
Non-topic persistence (0–2)	.41	10	37/361
Range	24		
Humanness of referent			
Human	.61	27	34/127
Non-human	.47	13	63/469
Range	14		
Main clause construction			
Existential	[.61]	25	20/80
Other	[.48]	15	77/516
Post-modification			
Yes	[.50]	16	42/257
No	[.50]	16	55/339

conviction that indefinite *this* functions as a marker of pragmatic prominence which enhances the topic-worthiness of referents in the following discourse. Following Dalrymple and Nikolaeva (2011:59), we stress that topic-worthiness is a measure of the likelihood that a *this*-marked referent will be construed as topical in the subsequent discourse, and does not necessarily guarantee that it will be selected as a topic.

5.2.6 Discussion

Inspired by Cheshire (1989:51), we argued that an adequate explanatory account of indefinite *this* could be achieved by viewing it in structural opposition with *a(n)*. These variants constitute a variable system comprising alternative ways of marking specific indefinite (first-mentioned) referents. An important contribution of our methodological approach rests on the demonstration that the choice of *this* or *a(n)* to mark specific indefinites is probabilistically constrained by a combination of predictors (Witzlack-Makarevich and Seržant 2018:12), justifying a multifactorial analysis.

In interpreting our primary findings, we accorded particular importance to situating our results in relation to the larger phenomenon known as differential argument marking. We argued that specific indefinite NPs with referentially, semantically, and pragmatically marked properties attract discriminatory marking in the form of non-canonical *this*. The precise triggers of discriminatory marking may vary according to the syntactic position of a specific indefinite NP. In subject position, the presence of a specific indefinite NP is at odds with the general preference for a discourse-active (i.e., definite and given) referent (see Lambrecht 1994:165). On the other hand, objects (whether direct or the complement of a preposition) are less likely to host a specific indefinite NP encoding a human referent than a more prototypical inanimate one (see e.g., Everett 2009:12). In both cases, deviation from expected patterns attracts *this*. Of central importance is our demonstration that indefinite *this* is preferentially used to mark referents that function as topics in the subsequent discourse. This finding may of course be inextricably linked with the propensity of *this*-marked indefinites to encode human referents, which are inherently more topical and prominent than inanimate referents in discourse.

Summarising, we stress that these results are by no means exceptional and are closely allied with findings reported in relation to the variable expression of referential indefiniteness in other languages (see e.g., Özge et al. 2016 on Turkish) in which differentially marked specific indefinites are claimed to have "forward-looking discourse properties" (von Heusinger and Chiriacescu 2013:16).

We conclude by briefly considering some of the broader ramifications of our findings. Of particular relevance are their diachronic implications. We observed earlier that the origin of indefinite *this* remains unclear. This issue would benefit from a more comprehensive analysis of the diachronic mechanisms implicated in the marking of (specific) indefiniteness in the history of English. Recent research on the evolution of the determiner category suggests that the grammaticalisation of *a(n)* as a generalised indefinite article prompted the emergence of alternative means of expressing the presentative function which was once strongly associated with the specific indefinite markers *a(n)* and *sum* ('some') used in older varieties of English to introduce discourse-new (usually human) referents (Breban 2012:294). There is some evidence suggesting that NPs introduced by *a(n)* are less salient in the global discourse than those introduced by *sum*, mirroring, at least superficially, contemporary patterns of variation between indefinite *a(n)* and *this*. This parallel raises the intriguing possibility that what has remained relatively constant over time are functionally differentiated patterns of marking specific indefinites, but what has changed is the *way* in which they are marked (Trousdale 2012:160). Tracking the evolutionary trajectory of markers of specific indefiniteness and their associated functional repertoires would help to establish more transparent continuities between contemporary patterns of variation and their diachronic antecedents (Cheshire and Stein 1997:5).

374 Stephen Levey et al.

Equally important is the extension of the current investigation to other varieties of contemporary English. If, as current research suggests, the parameters governing differential argument marking vary considerably from one language to another, then we cannot necessarily assume that contextual effects on the selection of indefinite *this/a(n)* will pattern identically across varieties of English. A key issue meriting further investigation relates to the extra-linguistic dimensions of this variation. Does indefinite *this* represent stable age-grading or are there indications of real-time change in the variable system in which it is embedded? These are questions which data limitations did not allow us to sufficiently address in the present study. Likewise, replication in other varieties of the sex effect we uncovered for younger speakers would strengthen the possibility that the variable expression of referential indefiniteness is sensitive to sociolinguistic parameters. An adequate understanding of any such patterns cannot be achieved without a broader investigation of interactive style, narrative construction, as well as preferred strategies for packaging information. Whatever transpires on that front, we submit that an integrated quantitative and discourse-analytical approach of the kind advocated by Cheshire (2005) has the potential to make indispensable contributions to future research on indefinite *this*.

Notes

1 All examples are reproduced verbatim from the digitised recordings. Codes in parentheses identify corpus, individual speaker, age (O = 50+; Y = 20–35), sex and line number in the transcription.
2 Existential-*there* contexts are a key diagnostic for validating the indefinite status of *this* (Prince 1981:233).
3 Los (2015:47) claims that a very early parallel to Modern English indefinite *this* can be found in the use of Old English demonstrative *se* 'that' to signal that a discourse-new referent will play an important role later in the discourse.
4 In (8), *this* may function endophorically by referring to the content of the epitaph in the immediately ensuing text.
5 Where subsequent mention includes realization as nouns or pronouns, as well as null forms, such as the null subject of a second conjunct.
6 Our use of the term 'primary topic' reflects claims in recent research (e.g., Dalrymple and Nikolaeva 2011:55–57) that an utterance can have more than one topic (i.e., a *primary* topic, which is more pragmatically salient than a *secondary* topic).
7 Our inclusion of indefinite subjects in the statistical analysis, though based on a restricted number of tokens, is justified on the grounds that they account for just over 5.3% of the variable context (Guy 1988:131–132).

References

Aissen, Judith. 2003. "Differential object marking: Iconicity vs. economy". *Natural Language and Linguistic Theory* 21(3):435–483.
Birch, Stacy and Susan Garnsey. 1995. "The effect of focus on memory for words in sentences". *Journal of Memory and Language* 34:232–267.

Breban, Tine. 2012. "Functional shifts and the development of English determiners". In *Information Structure and Syntactic Change in the History of English*, A. Meurman-Solin, M.J. López-Couso and B. Los (eds.). Oxford: Oxford University Press. 271–300.

Cheshire, Jenny. 1989. "Addressee-oriented features in spoken discourse". *York Papers in Linguistics* 13:49–63.

Cheshire, Jenny. 1999. "Spoken standard English". In *Standard English: The Widening Debate*, T. Bex and R. Watts (eds.). London: Routledge. 129–148.

Cheshire, Jenny. 2005. "Syntactic variation and beyond: Gender and social class variation in the use of discourse-new markers". *Journal of Sociolinguistics* 9(4):479–509.

Cheshire, Jenny and Dieter Stein. 1997. "The syntax of spoken language". In *Taming the Vernacular: From Dialect to Written Standard Language*, J. Cheshire and D. Stein (eds.). London: Longman. 1–12.

Chiriacescu, Sofiana. 2011. The discourse structuring potential of indefinite noun phrases: Special markers in Romanian, German and English. Unpublished Ph.D. thesis, University of Stuttgart.

Comrie, Bernard. 1989. *Language Universals and Linguistic Typology*. 2nd edition. Chicago: University of Chicago Press.

Dalrymple, Mary and Irina Nikolaeva. 2011. *Objects and Information Structure*. Cambridge: Cambridge University Press.

Denison, David. 1999. "Syntax". In *The Cambridge History of the English Language, Volume 4: 1776–1997*, S. Romaine (ed.). Cambridge: Cambridge University Press. 92–329.

Dik, Simon. 1989. *The Theory of Functional Grammar, Part I: The Structure of the Clause*. Dordrecht: Foris.

Everett, Caleb. 2009. "A reconsideration of the motivations for preferred argument structure". *Studies in Language* 33(1):1–24.

Gernsbacher, Morton A. and Jörg D. Jescheniak. 1995. "Cataphoric devices in spoken discourse". *Cognitive Psychology* 29(1):24–58.

Givón, Talmy. 1995. "Coherence in text vs. coherence in mind". In *Coherence in Spontaneous Text*, M.A. Gernsbacher and T. Givón (eds.). Amsterdam: John Benjamins. 59–115.

Gundel, Jeanette K., Nancy Hedberg and Ron Zacharski. 1993. "Cognitive status and the form of referring expressions in discourse". *Language* 69(2):274–307.

Guy, Gregory. 1988. "Advanced Varbrul analysis". In *Linguistic Change and Contact*, K. Ferrara, B. Brown, K. Walters and J. Baugh (eds.). Austin: University of Texas at Austin. 124–136.

Iemmolo, Giorgio. 2010. "Topicality and differential object marking: Evidence from Romance and beyond". *Studies in Language* 34(2):239–272.

Iemmolo, Giorgio. 2013. "Symmetric and asymmetric alternations in direct object encoding". *STUF-Language Typology and Universals* 66(4):378–403.

Ionin, Tania. 2006. "*This* is definitely specific: Specificity and definiteness in article systems". *Natural Language Semantics* 14:175–234.

Lambrecht, Knut. 1994. *Information Structure and Sentence Form: Topic, Focus, and the Mental Representation of Discourse Referents*. Cambridge: Cambridge University Press.

Los, Bettelou. 2015. *A Historical Syntax of English*. Edinburgh: Edinburgh University Press.

Milroy, James and Lesley Milroy. 1997. "Varieties and variation". In *The Handbook of Sociolinguistics*, F. Coulmas (ed.). Oxford: Blackwell. 47–64.

Özge, Umut, Duygu Özge and Klaus von Heusinger. 2016. "Strong indefinites in Turkish, reference persistence, and salience structure". In *Empirical Perspectives on Anaphora Resolution*, A. Holler and K. Suckow (eds.). Berlin: Mouton de Gruyter. 169–191.

Perlman, Alan. 1969. "'This' as a third article in American English". *American Speech* 44(1):76–80.

Poplack, Shana and Sali Tagliamonte. 2001. *African American English in the Diaspora*. Oxford: Blackwell.

Prince, Ellen. 1981. "On the inferencing of indefinite-*this* NPs". In *Elements of Discourse Understanding*, A. Joshi, B. Wenner and I. Sag (eds.). Cambridge: Cambridge University Press. 231–250.

Reinhart, Tanya. 1981. "Pragmatics and linguistics: An analysis of sentence topics". *Philosophica* 27:53–94.

Rühlemann, Christoph and Matthew B. O' Donnell. 2014. "Deixis". In *Corpus Pragmatics: A Handbook*, K. Aijmer and C. Rühlemann (eds.). Cambridge: Cambridge University Press. 331–359.

Sankoff, David, Sali Tagliamonte and Eric Smith. 2005. *Goldvarb X*. Department of Linguistics, University of Toronto, Canada (individual.utoronto.ca/tagliamonte/Goldvarb/GV_index.htm).

Tagliamonte, Sali. 2006. *Analysing Sociolinguistic Variation*. Cambridge: Cambridge University Press.

Trousdale, Graeme. 2012. "Syntax". In *English Historical Linguistics: An International Handbook*, Vol. 1, A. Bergs and L.J. Brinton (eds.). Berlin: de Gruyter. 148–163.

von Heusinger, Klaus and Sofiana Chiriacescu. 2013. "The discourse structuring potential of differential object marking: The case of indefinite and definite direct objects in Romanian". *Revue Roumaine de Linguistique* 58(4):439–456.

Wald, Benji. 1983. "Referents and topics within and across discourse units: Observations from current vernacular English". In *Discourse Perspectives on Syntax*, F. Klein-Andreu (ed.). New York: Academic Press. 91–116.

Witzlack-Makarevich, Alena and Ilja A. Seržant. 2018. "Differential argument marking: Patterns of variation". In *Diachrony of Differential Argument Marking*, I.A. Seržant and A. Witzlack-Makarevich (eds.). Berlin: Language Science Press. 1–40.

Wright, Susan and Talmy Givón. 1987. "The pragmatics of indefinite reference: Quantified text-based studies". *Studies in Language* 11(1):1–33.

5.3 Tagging Monologic Narratives of Personal Experience

Utterance-Final Tags and the Construction of Adolescent Masculinity[1]

Heike Pichler

5.3.1 Introduction

Jenny Cheshire is consistently breaking new ground with astute insights into the mechanisms underpinning discourse-pragmatic and morpho-syntactic variation. This can be attributed to her firm commitment to analysing linguistic features within their full pragmatic and interactional context. Cheshire explores not just <u>which</u> features individuals or social groups select to use in any particular context but she, unfailingly, also examines <u>how</u> and <u>why</u> individuals or groups choose to use these features in a given context (see, *inter alia*, Cheshire 1981, 1997, 2003, 2005, 2013; Cheshire et al. 2005, 2011, 2013; Cheshire and Williams 2002). In this chapter, I apply Cheshire's methodological approach to investigating patterns of inter- and intra-speaker variation in the use of utterance-final tags (UFTs), a variable whose variants include, among others, canonical tags such as *in't you* and *in I* studied in Cheshire (1981) and the invariant tag *innit* analysed in Cheshire et al. (2005). I will conduct my analysis in a genre that has been at the heart of much of Cheshire's research and in a corpus that she co-compiled: adolescent narratives in the *Linguistic Innovators Corpus* (see Cheshire 2000, 2003; Kerswill et al. 2007). My analysis of UFTs in these data sets out to demonstrate that discourse-pragmatic features are an important resource for the construction of narratives as well as social identities.

Following brief outlines of the study background and the data in Sections 5.3.2 and 5.3.3, I define the variable context in Section 5.3.4. Section 5.3.5 reports the proportion of tagged declaratives and explores the frequency of individual UFT variants; it also describes the fluctuating frequency of the UFT variable across individuals, social groups and narratives. To elucidate these patterns, the following sections analyse UFTs in their full narrative context. Section 5.3.6 describes the distribution of UFTs in the organisation of the adolescent narratives. Section 5.3.7 compares the story worlds and versions of the self that the adolescents create

378 *Heike Pichler*

in their tagged and non-tagged narratives. In the discussion in Section 5.3.8, I propose that male adolescents use UFTs in selected narratives in order to assert their right to audience attention and their desire to claim a certain masculinity. I also briefly explore the social indexicality of the main UFT variants used. I conclude in Section 5.3.9 with a short appraisal of the methodological procedures used and suggestions for areas of further study.

5.3.2 Background and Aims

UFTs are multifunctional discourse-pragmatic features that occur at the end of utterances and broadly function to establish the tagged proposition as common ground between speaker and hearer (Denis and Tagliamonte 2016:87, 90; see further Sections 5.3.4 and 5.3.7). The linguistic features that share both this utterance position <u>and</u> this macrofunction include invariant tags such as *yeah, innit* and *you know* and canonical tags such as *is it* and *din he* (a reduced form of *didn't he*) (see Andersen 2001; Stenström et al. 2002). Both invariant and canonical tags have been widely analysed in terms of their differential distribution across varieties of English (e.g., Cheshire et al. 2005; Childs 2016; Columbus 2010; Hoffmann et al. 2017; Tottie and Hoffmann 2006), their variable frequencies across social groups (e.g., Denis and Tagliamonte 2016; Pichler 2013:Ch. 6; Stenström et al. 2002:Ch. 7; Torgersen et al. 2011), and their functional versatility in casual conversations and sociolinguistic interviews (e.g., Cheshire 1981; Erman 2001; Holmes 1982; Meyerhoff 1992; Stenström et al. 2002:Ch. 7). However, with the notable exception of González's (2004) and Schiffrin's (1987) work on *you know*, little systematic attention has been paid to the use of English UFTs in oral narratives. This is despite indications that many English UFTs regularly occur in this discourse context (see data extracts in Andersen 2001; Cheshire 2000; Moore and Podesva 2009; Pichler under revision; Stenström et al. 2002:Ch. 7), and despite evidence that in other languages, such as Tamil, Portuguese or Mohawk, tags perform important interpersonal and textual functions in narrative discourse (Herring 1991; Gómez González 2014; Mithun 2012).

This chapter investigates the use of UFTs in London adolescent narratives. Adopting Cheshire's methodological practices and Labov and Waletzky's (1967) narrative model, I conduct detailed qualitative analyses of all narrative UFT tokens in context in order to account for their quantitative distribution in the data. My analysis is guided by these questions: which UFT variants do adolescents choose to use for establishing common ground in narratives, and what conditions this choice? Where and how do adolescent narrators employ UFTs? Is there a correlation between certain narrative components and the frequency and functionality of UFTs, as suggested by Schiffrin (1987) for *you know* in American English narratives? Do the adolescents use UFTs mainly to accomplish interactional work, or do they also use UFTs for social meaning making, as suggested by Cheshire (1981) and Moore and Podesva (2009) for canonical tags in British English conversations? My analysis will offer an explanation for the choice, presence and distribution of UFTs in a dataset of London adolescent narratives which is grounded in a detailed understanding of narratives as a structured speech event and as a resource for self-presentation.

5.3.3 Data

The data investigated in this chapter were taken from the *Linguistic Innovators Corpus* (LIC) collected in London in the mid-2000s (Kerswill et al. 2007). From this collection of largely dyadic sociolinguistic interviews, we extracted all monologic narratives of personal experience produced by a sub-set of 27 16–19-year-old adolescents stratified by sex (male, female) and ethnicity (Anglo, non-Anglo); all speakers are from multiethnic boroughs and working-class backgrounds. Following Labov (1972a:360–361) and Blum-Kulka (1993:385), I defined monologic narratives of personal experience as those recountings of speakers' own past experiences which consist of at least two temporally ordered clauses delivered by a single speaker in an extended turn; listener comments or questions, if present, do not affect the telling or the tale (and were not included in the analysis). The narratives were identified and manually extracted by reading through the interview transcripts. This yielded a dataset of 92 monologic narratives of personal experience from approximately 23½ hours of recorded speech. For convenience, I will henceforth refer to these monologic, personal experience narratives as 'narratives'. (The corpus also contains monologic narratives of vicarious experience as well as dialogic and polyphonic narratives which, for considerations of space, are not considered here.)

5.3.4 Variable Context

The optionality and multifunctionality of discourse-pragmatic features present a challenge to their definition as linguistic variables (see, *inter alia*, Cheshire 2016; Pichler 2010; Waters 2016). To ensure an accountable analysis along the parameters of the variationist paradigm (Labov 1972b:71–72), I follow Denis and Tagliamonte (2016) and delimit the variable context in terms of position and function. I thus include in my analysis of narrative UFTs all discourse-pragmatic features that are tagged onto the end of finite declaratives and perform the overarching function of seeking a tacit or non-tacit signal from the hearer that the

380 *Heike Pichler*

tagged proposition has entered common ground. Employing both utterance position and macro-function as criteria for establishing an equivalence relationship between variants makes it possible to close the set of variants that define the UFT variable and to report the frequency of UFTs as a proportion of the total number of finite declaratives. It also makes it possible to include in the variable context the range of invariant tags as well as canonical tags; their overlapping functionality has been established in Andersen's (2001) and Stenström et al.'s (2002:Ch.7) qualitative analyses of the Corpus of London Teenage speech, recorded in the mid-1990s.

Prosodic and syntactic criteria were used to divide all narratives into clauses and determine the clause-final position of target variants. Non-declarative sentence types are excluded from the variable context because they do not allow the same range of variants or affect the functionality of UFTs (see Quirk et al. 1985:810–814; Stenström et al. 2002:175). Also excluded are: truncated declaratives (e.g. *and he put his-* in example (4) below), UFTs in uncertain transcriptions (presented in round brackets) (e.g., *Like I've gotta go home, yeah* in (4)), and UFTs that occur with quoted speech where it is not possible to verify their intended position and scope vis-à-vis the quoted material (e.g., *I was like "I don't like you", yeah* in (4)).

5.3.5 Distribution of UFT Variants and the UFT Variable

5.3.5.1 *Distribution of UFT Variants*

The dataset of 92 adolescent narratives contains 1684 finite declaratives to which a UFT could have been attached. Of these, 6.9% (*n* = 116) occur with a UFT (distributed across 42 narratives).[2] Although the variable has been defined to include a wide range of variants, the UFTs used by the adolescent narrators include only seven variants that are unevenly distributed. Table 5.3.1 shows that *yeah, innit* and *right* account for 94% of all UFTs used in the adolescent narratives. *You know (what I'm saying)*, canonical tags, *no* and *okay* are negligibly instantiated, and the variant *you get me* does not occur at all. This is despite evidence provided by Andersen (2016), Pichler (under revision) and Torgersen et al. (2011) that canonical tags and *you know*-variants are robust in the LIC adolescent data when all discourse contexts are considered, and that *you get*-variants are rapidly gaining ground among London adolescents. Discourse context and/or speaker role, then, affect the choice of UFT variant;[3] Section 5.3.7 shows that these factors also affect UFT functionality. (In contrast to the non-narrative UFTs in LIC (see Pichler, under revision), the narrative UFTs never perform the modal and affective

Utterance-Final Tags and Adolescent Masculinity   381

Table 5.3.1 Distribution of UFT variants in the adolescent narratives

	n	%
Yeah	72	62.0
Innit	26	22.4
Right	11	9.5
You know (what I'm saying)	3	2.6
canonical tags (*din he, is it*)	2	1.7
No	1	0.9
Okay	1	0.9
TOTAL	116	

functions assigned to UFTs by Holmes (1982) and others.) Below, I will propose that the choice of UFT variants may also be constrained by the specific uses to which the male adolescent narrators in LIC put them.

The number of UFTs is too small to establish constraints on the choice of individual variants. The following analysis will, therefore, focus on the distribution of the UFT variable rather than individual UFT variants. Because of the uneven distribution of variants, however, the results and conclusions apply primarily to *yeah, innit* and, to a lesser extent, *right. Yeah* dominates across social groups and narrative segments, but it consistently competes with *innit*, a relative newcomer in the system of narrative UFTs (see Andersen 2001; Pichler under revision).

5.3.5.2 Distribution of UFTs across Individuals, Social Groups and Narratives

The overall frequency of 6.9% UFT use in the adolescent narratives hides a high degree of variability across individuals, social groups and narratives. For each individual and social group listed in columns 1 and 5, Table 5.3.2 gives their total number of narratives, their number of narratives containing one or more UFTs, and their proportion of tagged declaratives (out of all finite declaratives in tagged and non-tagged narratives). As a whole, (non-Anglo) males have a three to four times higher rate of narrative UFTs than (Anglo) females.[4] However, not all individuals contribute narratives to the dataset (see columns 2 and 6), and not all individuals who do so use narrative UFTs (see columns 3 and 7). Moreover, across those individuals who use UFTs in their narratives, the proportion of tagged declaratives varies between 2.5% and 36.1% (see columns 4 and 8). Generally, though, proportions of UFT use are much higher among males than females.

Table 5.3.2 Numbers of (tagged) narratives and proportion of tagged declaratives across individuals and social groups

		ANGLO					
	Female				*Male*		
	n of narratives	n of tagged narratives	% of tagged declaratives		n of narratives	n of tagged narratives	% of tagged declaratives
Katie	0	–	–	Jack	0	–	–
Joanne	0	–	–	Sean	0	–	–
Danielle	3	0	0	Steve	0	–	–
Laura	3	0	0	Andrew	1	0	0
Claire	3	1	6.5	Jake	9	6	2.9
Ellie	1	1	8.0	Freddy	4	2	17.5
				Zack	3	2	18.9
Anglo females	10	2	2.3	**Anglo males**	17	10	7.6

		NON-ANGLO					
	Female				*Male*		
	n of narratives	n of tagged narratives	% of tagged declaratives		n of narratives	n of tagged narratives	% of tagged declaratives
Hadiya	0	–	–	Alan	1	0	0
Kelly	0	–	–	Mark	9	3	4.7
Fatima	1	0	0	Brian	5	2	4.9
Jodie	2	0	0	Alex	19	11	7.5
Nazma	1	0	0	Leon	1	1	11.1
Isabella	3	1	2.5	Talal	1	1	16.7
Tina	15	5	3.1	Rufus	7	6	36.1
Non-Anglo females	22	6	2.7	**Non-Anglo males**	43	24	9.7

Utterance-Final Tags and Adolescent Masculinity 383

What is it, then, that makes some, predominantly male, speakers use narrative UFTs? And how can we account for their use of UFTs in some narratives but not in others? To explore these questions, I turn below to a consideration of the structure of the adolescents' narratives and an analysis of the story worlds and social selves that the adolescents create in tagged and non-tagged narratives. If narrative UFTs index social meanings, as suggested above, consideration of dimensions of UFT use beyond frequency will help us to fully uncover what exactly these social meanings are (see Moore and Podesva 2009:479). I focus below on exploring differences in UFT use between males and females; I leave it to future research of UFTs in a larger dataset to explore any ethnicity effects.

5.3.6 Distribution and Function of UFTs across Narrative Segments

According to Labov and Waletzky's (1967; see also Labov 1972a:Ch. 9) influential model, monologic narratives consist, at a minimum, of two complicating action clauses that recount a series of events in the order in which they occurred in real life. Optionally, narratives also contain any of these components: an abstract which summarises the story to come and suspends turn-taking; an orientation preceding the complicating action to introduce the context and setting of the narrative (participants, time, place, situation); an orientation embedded within the complicating action to give information which story recipients need to interpret adjacent complicating action clauses; an evaluation which comments on narrative events, sometimes from a perspective outside of the narrative; a resolution which releases the tension by stating how the complicating action was resolved; and a coda signalling the end of the narrative and returning listeners to the present.

To establish whether UFTs are associated with particular narrative components, as shown for *you know* by González (2004) and Schiffrin (1987), I applied Labov and Waletzky's model to coding each finite declarative in the 92 adolescent narratives for the structural component to which it belongs. Narratives (1) and (2), two representative examples from the female adolescent dataset, serve as illustrations.[5] Danielle's narrative in (1) begins with an abstract (line a) that claims an extended turn and tells listeners what the story is about: a pet bird attack. (The reference of 'one' is clear from the preceding discourse context.) Danielle then provides a detailed orientation in which she first characterises the cockatoo as a misogynist obsessed with her boyfriend (lines b–e), before describing the domestic setting in which the attack happened (lines f–g). In line (h), Danielle introduces the first complicating action: the cockatoo retreating. She then suspends the complicating

384 *Heike Pichler*

action sequence in lines (i)–(j) to evaluate the cockatoo's behaviour and orient listeners to the narrative peak, i.e., the vicious bird attack in lines (k)–(l). Line (m) provides the resolution: Danielle required vaccination as a result of the attack.

(1) **The cockatoo attack** (Danielle, 18, Anglo)

    a) I took one in my face once. ABSTRACT

    b) Because my boyfriend's mum has a cockatoo. ORIENTATION
    c) And this cockatoo does not like women.
    d) And she didn't tell me that.
       And I was s-
    e) and she loves my boyfriend, this bird.
    f) And I was sitting next to the- next to my boyfriend.
    g) (And) he's putting his (pillow up) to stop her coming to him. *(h)*

    h) And then she walked off, COMPLICATING ACTION

    i) and I thought "alright, then. Fine. Go away." EVALUATION

    j) And the next thing she does, EMBEDDED ORIENTATION

    k) she flew up, COMPLICATING ACTION
    l) and just attacked me all down the side of my face.

    m) I had to have a tetanus done in the side. RESOLUTION

Claire's narrative in (2) also begins with a detailed orientation. Lines (a)–(b) introduce the story location and one of the story participants (the preceding context disambiguates the reference of 'there'), lines (c)–(e) describe the nature of the antagonistic relationship between this participant and the narrator, and lines (f)–(g) introduce the incident that triggers the events reported in the complicating action sequence. In line (h), Claire steps outside of the narrative world to evaluate the information provided in line (g) and distance herself from what had happened. The complicating action sequence in lines (i)–(l) succinctly recounts the verbal and physical confrontation between the girls, which is resolved with a happy ending in line (m). Finally, lines (n)–(r) evaluate the events from outside the narrative frame.

(2) **The friendship fight** (Claire, 18, Anglo)

    a) But erm (..) when I was there, ORIENTATION
    b) there was this girl called {name}. (.)

c)	And (.) she bullied me for three years (.) solid.	
	For I don't know what reason.	
d)	There were so many reasons going around that I meant to have done this and done that.	
e)	But I just tend to keep out of her way.	
f)	And then (.) come to year ten,	
g)	and a sign had been written in the toilets about her.	
h)	I don't know, it was so childish.	EVALUATION
i)	She come up to me,	COMPLICATING ACTION
j)	she was all mouthing off at me,	
k)	and (then) she slapped me.	
l)	Then we got into a fight. (..)	
m)	And (.) after that we become best friends. @	RESOLUTION
n)	It was so weird.	EVALUATION
o)	Like we'd- we'd <u>hated</u> each other for years.	
p)	And then all of a sudden we had a fight,	
q)	and everything was over and done with.	
r)	It was fine then.	

Table 5.3.3 compares the proportion of tagged declaratives across narrative components in the female and male adolescent narratives. UFTs are absent from coda sections and negligible in resolution and evaluation sections. As are the discourse-pragmatic features examined in González's (2004) study of British English young adult narratives (*so, well, then, you know, anyway, you see, okay, now*), UFTs are concentrated in the most frequent and longest narrative components: orientation, embedded orientation and complicating action sections. (Because they are based on low token numbers ($n \leq 36$), results for abstracts are presented in round brackets and not explored further below.) Across narrative components, the frequency of UFTs is markedly higher in male than female adolescent narratives, particularly so in complicating action sequences. To determine the reasons for these differences, I explore below the function of UFTs in the three narrative components in which they occur most regularly and robustly: orientations, embedded orientations and complicating actions.

Extracts (3) and (4) are characteristic examples of the adolescents' UFT use as well as of the story worlds and social selves that the male adolescents tend to construct in their tagged narratives (see Section 5.3.7).[6] The concentration of *yeah* variants reflects its overall frequency

386   Heike Pichler

Table 5.3.3 Proportion of tagged declaratives across narrative components in the female and male adolescent narratives, with an indication of the number of narratives (out of 92) containing each component and the average length (in declaratives) of each component.

	% of declaratives with UFTs		n of narratives with this component	Average length in declaratives
Narrative component	*Female*	*Male*		
Abstract	(8.3)	(13.9)	32	1.9
Orientation	**4.8**	**15.7**	67	3.9
Embedded orientation	**5.6**	**15.2**	53	3.1
Complicating action	**1.1**	**8.0**	92	8.7
Evaluation	1.9	4.4	65	4.0
Resolution	0	1.5	43	2.1
Coda	0	0	12	1.7

Note: Results in round brackets are based on low-token counts ($n \leq 36$) and hence not explored further below.

in the data; space constraints prohibit me from demonstrating that the functions identified for *yeah* in (3) and (4) apply to other UFT variants. In (3), Rufus's inconspicuous sighting of a purse in a public space is followed by a series of goal-directed reactions that culminate in a petty theft. In line (c), *yeah* tags an orientation clause that specifies where the reported incident occurred. The UFT serves to emphasise this information and check whether Rufus's listeners, who – I assume – knew Ilford, can identify and possibly visualise the story location. As such, the UFT helps to establish the tagged information as common ground and stimulate the listeners' involvement in the narrative. The first three complicating action clauses (lines e–g) also occur with UFTs. They report relatively benign events that do not in themselves constitute a petty crime. (Rufus may have pocketed the purse to hand it in to the nearest police station.) Rather, they are the prelude to the theft reported in lines (h)–(j). The UFTs thus occur with complicating actions that heighten narrative tension and form the prelude to the climatic peak. They function to maintain and monitor listeners' continued engagement as well as to mark and demarcate a series of events leading up to the climax. (In the whole dataset, UFTs never occur with narrative peaks.)

Utterance-Final Tags and Adolescent Masculinity   387

(3) **The found purse** (Rufus, 19, non-Anglo)

   a)   But what I've done, though, is I've found a purse *innit*,
       like in a park innit.   ABSTRACT

---

   b)   You know {name of park} in Ilford? (.)   ORIENTATION
   c)   It was just there, *yeah*.
   d)   I was with thingy (?) them boys.

---

   e)   We saw it *yeah*,   COMPLICATING ACTION
   f)   so I just picked it up *yeah*.
   g)   Put in my thingy jacket *yeah*,
   h)   walked away.
   i)   Found about hundred pounds in it.
   j)   Took the money,

---

   k)   and left the purse, *innit*. For the police to find it. (.) RESOLUTION
   l)   Didn't take nothing else.

The next extract demonstrates how the strategic placement of UFTs helps narrators not just to monitor listeners' involvement but also to ensure that information is interpreted in accordance with the narrators' intentions. In (4), a peaceful end of school day routine involving Zack riding his bike is disrupted by a teacher's instruction that Zack dismount his bike; the ensuing verbal confrontation quickly escalates, culminating in a physical confrontation that results in Zack's expulsion. The narrative is replete with features that stimulate listener involvement (see Tannen 1985): detail (lines o–p, x–z), direct speech (lines h–k, v–w, aa–bb), historical present tense (lines h, aa–bb), and the UFT *yeah*. Lines (b) and (l) set out that the recounted events took place at the end of the school day and at a fair distance from the school gates. The UFT *yeah* requests that listeners accept this information as common ground. It thus promotes their interest in the narrative and guides their interpretation of adjacent narrative events: that it was reasonable for Zack to insist on riding his bike, and unreasonable for the teacher to demand otherwise. In line (p), *yeah* occurs with a complicating action clause that details what happened after the teacher had pushed Zack off his bike (see line m). The UFT focuses listeners' attention on what might seem a minor detail in the unfolding story but ultimately serves to negatively portray the teacher: in attempting to exercise his authority over Zack, the teacher used unnecessary force, causing Zack to stumble. The UFT in line (u) occurs in an embedded orientation that suspends the complicating action sequence. *Yeah* emphasises and checks listeners' acceptance of new

388   *Heike Pichler*

information that heightens the narrative tension, namely that the verbal confrontation had at this point escalated into shouting. Finally, in lines (x)–(y), *yeah* requests listeners to note salient actions that constitute the immediate prelude to the climatic peak: Zack takes control of the situation in line (x), and prepares to resolve the dispute through physical aggression in line (y). The strategic tagging of these actions helps Zack make his listeners vicarious participants in the events, at a point where they reach the climax and Zack portrays himself as someone who stands up to authority figures.

(4)   **The bike incident** (Zack, 16, Anglo)

a)	Like it was- like it was the end of school.	ORIENTATION

b)   Yeah, so that school's finished, *yeah.*
c)   And everyone was going home,
d)   I was getting my bike from the bike rack.
e)   And I was going out.
f)   And I was riding my bike,

---

g)	and he stopped my bike.	COMPLICATING ACTION

   And like "yeah?"
h)   And he goes "get off the bike."
i)   (I was like) "why am I getting off the bike? I'm going home now." (Like, I've gotta go home, yeah.)
j)   He was like "no. Get off the bike. Walk the bike outside of school."
k)   I was like "what's the point?"

EMBEDDED ORIENTATION

l)   Yeah. Cos like it's quite far like to get out the school from the entrance like in the school *yeah.*
   And he goes "ah no. Get off the bike," yeah.

COMPLICATING ACTION

m)   So (like) he kind of shoved me off the bike.
n)   So I dropped it,
o)   but I didn't fall over.
p)   Like but I kind of stumbled *yeah,*
   and he put his-
q)   he tried to take my bike up to his office.
r)   Like he was gonna keep my bike there.
s)   I was like "no. No."

EMBEDDED ORIENTATION

t)   (And) this time everyone was gathering round
u)   cos we were shouting at each other *yeah.*

COMPLICATING ACTION

v) He was like "no I'm taking your bike upstairs."
w) I was like "what's the point in that? When I'm just gonna take it back downstairs."
x) So I must have pulled the bike off him *yeah.*
   And I put it- I put it-
y) I leant it up against the wall *yeah.*
z) And I walked over to him.
aa) And this is me "what- what's- what's your problem?"
bb) And he goes "I don't like you."
   I was like "I don't like you," yeah.
cc) So I just swung for him.
dd) And then like- but we had a fight though.

---

ee) And I got kicked out of school.   RESOLUTION
ff) Like I weren't allowed into any school.

---

gg) That's why I came here <u>last</u> year.   CODA

In sum, by requesting non-tacit acknowledgment that tagged orientation, embedded orientation and complicating action clauses have entered common ground, UFTs serve to stimulate listeners' continued involvement in monologic narratives. They focus listeners' attention on information that is important for their understanding of the narrative as a whole, and thus help narrators to guide listeners' interpretation of tagged and adjacent materials in line with their narrative intentions.

5.3.7 Distribution of UFTs across Story Worlds

The importance of narratives for individuals' construction of their identities and selves is widely recognised (Cheshire and Ziebland 2005; Coates 2002; Linde 1993; Schiffrin 1996). Narrators select experiences to report and relay these experiences in ways that highlight <u>their</u> versions of the experience and present <u>their</u> desired versions of their selves (see Schiffrin's [1990] notion of 'selective interpretation'). Table 5.3.4 shows systematic differences between males' and females' tagged and non-tagged narratives in terms of the story worlds and selves created in them.

About two thirds (n = 23/34) of the males' tagged narratives evoke story worlds in which the narrator-protagonist: uses interpersonal violence (e.g., he punches or stabs an opponent); engages in non-physical criminal activity (e.g., he steals money or carries adult fireworks); is guilty of non-violent or non-criminal misbehaviour (e.g., he verbally

390 *Heike Pichler*

Table 5.3.4 Story worlds created in males' and females' tagged and non-tagged narratives

MALE	
Tagged narratives (n = 34)	*Non-tagged narratives (n = 26)*
• Physical conflict stories = narrator using interpersonal violence (**n = 9**) • Criminal offence stories = narrator engaging in non-physical criminal activity (**n = 4**) • Misbehaviour stories = narrator being guilty of non-violent and non-criminal misbehaviour (**n = 6**) • Social contest stories = narrator winning contests through bravery or verbal/ intellectual skills (**n = 4**)	• Physical conflict stories = narrator using interpersonal violence (**n = 1**) • Criminal offence stories = narrator engaging in non-physical criminal activity (**n = 3**) • Misbehaviour stories = narrator being guilty of non-violent and non-criminal misbehaviour (**n = 1**) • Social contest stories = narrator winning contests through bravery or verbal/ intellectual skills (**n = 1**)
• Victim stories = narrator witnessing or (being at risk of) falling victim to a crime or attack (n = 3) • Adulting stories = narrator acting like a socially responsible adult (n = 2) • Interpersonal relationship stories (n = 2)	• Victim stories = narrator witnessing or (being at risk of) falling victim to a crime or attack (n = 5) • Adulting stories = narrator acting like a socially responsible adult (n = 3) • Interpersonal relationship stories (n = 2) • Romantic relationship stories (n = 3)
• Miscellaneous (n = 4)	• Miscellaneous (n = 7)

FEMALE	
Tagged narratives (n = 8)	*Non-tagged narratives (n = 24)*
	• Physical conflict stories = narrator using interpersonal violence (**n = 1**)
• Victim stories = narrator witnessing or (being at risk of) falling victim to a crime or attack (n = 2)	• Victim stories = narrator witnessing or (being at risk of) falling victim to a crime or attack (n = 6) • Adulting stories = narrator acting like a socially responsible adult (n = 2)
• Interpersonal relationship stories (n = 1) • Romantic relationship stories (n = 2) • Miscellaneous (n = 3)	• Interpersonal relationship stories (n = 6) • Romantic relationship stories (n = 2) • Miscellaneous (n = 7)

abuses a teacher or plays truant); and wins contests through bravery or verbal and intellectual skills (e.g., he confronts a thief or outwits a police officer). Less than a quarter of males' non-tagged narratives (n = 6/26) and a negligible number of females' tagged and non-tagged narratives (n = 1/32) construct a story world of this kind. Males' non-tagged narratives are more often about miscellaneous events (e.g., learning horse-riding or winning a raffle), incidents where the narrator-protagonist is the victim rather than perpetrator of a crime or attack (e.g., getting robbed or being held at knifepoint), or actions that portray the narrator-protagonist as a socially responsible young adult (e.g., reporting a crime to the authorities). Females' tagged and non-tagged narratives are also often miscellaneous or victim stories, and a large number are about interpersonal and romantic relationships (e.g., being lied to by a friend or approaching a love interest).

I briefly return to the representative narratives examined in Section 5.3.6 to illustrate key differences between the male adolescent tagged and the female adolescent non-tagged narratives in terms of their creation of specific story worlds and social selves. The uninterrupted succession of complicating action clauses in (3) signals Rufus's purposefulness to violate expected norms of behaviour, i.e., to hand a found purse and all its contents in to the police. Moreover, the lack of an evaluation sequence suggests that Rufus experiences little remorse over committing a petty theft. In (4), Zack portrays himself as someone who will not be bossed around or intimidated by an authority figure; he is someone who stands up for himself and will resort to resolving a confrontation with physical violence, even if this means risking expulsion. (Note how the teacher is portrayed as being unreasonable (lines m, v–w) and his behaviour guided by unprofessional motives (line bb).) Contrast these story worlds and versions of the self with those constructed in the females' non-tagged narratives in (1) and (2). The narrative in (1) portrays Danielle as the innocent victim of a vicious and unprovoked cockatoo attack. It is a narrative of failure in which Danielle is humiliated by a pet animal. Although it involves a verbal and physical confrontation, the narrative in (2) is a story of innocence. Claire portrays herself as a blameless victim of bullying and the recipient (rather than user) of verbal and physical abuse. In contrast to the narrative in (4), the narratives in (1) and (2) have very succinct complicating action sequences. They are outcome- rather than process-focused.

Thus, while different story worlds are not exclusive to one gender or the other or to one type of narrative or the other, a distinct characteristic of the male adolescents' tagged narratives in this dataset is a concern to portray the narrator-protagonist as violent, delinquent, tough, brave or streetwise. This finding echoes earlier research showing that urban working-class male adolescents often use narratives to perform dominant or hegemonic norms of masculinity characterised by fighting,

392   *Heike Pichler*

physical prowess, aggression, toughness and lawbreaking (Bamberg 2004; Coates 2002; Lawson 2015; Wetherell and Edley 1999). The story worlds evoked in the male adolescents' tagged narratives, then, tend to align the narrator-protagonists with dominant norms of urban adolescent masculinity.

5.3.8 Discussion

The preceding analysis started from the observation that, in the present dataset of London adolescent narratives, UFT use is characterised by a high degree of inter- and intra-speaker variability and a strong link with male narrators. Analysis of UFT tokens within their full narrative contexts established that they are concentrated in the (embedded) orientation and complicating action sequences of narratives that serve to create and reinforce a masculinity of violent, delinquent and streetwise behaviour. UFTs are used in these narratives to involve listeners in the created story worlds and to mark information that is key to their understanding and interpretation of the narratives. What do we make of these findings?

Spencer-Oatey (2008) differentiates between the interactional or linguistic management of 'face' and the management of 'sociality rights'. Face refers to the positive face values individuals claim for themselves in interaction (e.g., to be brave); sociality rights refer to the social entitlements that individuals claim in interaction (e.g., to be listened to). Levon (2016) draws on Spencer-Oatey's notion of sociality rights to explain young adult male Londoners' frequent use of High Rising Terminals (HRTs). He argues that male narrators exploit the referential function of HRTs, which is to highlight interesting and brand-new information, in order to assert their sociality rights to interactional and affective involvement. I propose that, in my dataset, UFTs function to manage both narrators' sociality rights <u>and</u> their face sensitivities.

Schiffrin (1987:294) points out that narrators have a stake in making their stories interesting and maintaining their listeners' attention. They otherwise risk losing their floor-holding rights and not getting across the point of their narratives. If the essence of males' tagged narratives is to present a favourable sense of the narrators' selves, i.e., a persona who possesses a certain masculinity, there is status and solidarity to be gained from maintaining listeners' engagement and guiding their interpretation of the narrative. (As far as this is possible to tell from the audio-recordings and transcripts, males' tagged narratives are often directed at their male adolescent co-interviewee rather than the female middle-aged interviewer.) I propose, then, that the male narrators in my dataset use UFTs – and possibly other linguistic resources not examined here (e.g. HRTs) – to: (i) assert and gain their sociality rights to association, i.e., their sense of entitlement to appropriate levels of involvement;

Utterance-Final Tags and Adolescent Masculinity   393

<u>and</u> (ii) to ensure that their face sensitivities are indulged, i.e., that listeners positively evaluate the sense of self that narrators claim in their narratives.

The uses to which the male adolescent narrators put UFTs may explain their narrow choice of UFT variants. As shown in Table 5.3.1 above, the variable context is almost exclusively constituted of _yeah, innit_ and _right_; canonical tags, _you know_-variants and _you get_-variants are negligible. The latter are recognisably reduced interrogative clauses. They are thus ill-suited for use in contexts where narrators do not want to have their version of events or their sense of self questioned or doubted. _Yeah_ has an affirmative meaning; the form _innit_ lacks interrogative transparency; and _right_ signals meanings related to truth and correctness. _Yeah, innit_ and _right_ are therefore far better suited to indexing a narrator's assertive and self-assured stance.

Because of their direct indexicality of assertiveness and self-assuredness in narratives evolving around dominant norms of adolescent masculinity, the UFT variants _yeah, innit_ and, to an extent, _right_ may develop broader social meanings via indirect indexicality (Ochs 1992). Cheshire (1981) and Moore and Podesva (2009) have previously demonstrated the indexical relationship between canonical question tags and their social meanings. Cheshire established that among working-class Reading adolescents, _in't_-tags carry overtones of aggression and hostility, two dominant themes of the adolescents' vernacular culture. Moore and Podesva determined that particular tag designs have assumed social meanings among female adolescent social groups in Greater Manchester. Through their association with narratives of conflict, contest, crime and misbehaviour, _yeah, innit_ and, possibly, _right_ may be(come) indexically linked to the construction of a particular masculinity among working-class male adolescent Londoners (see also Cheshire [2013] on the pronoun _man_). Specifically, these UFT variants may (have) develop(ed) an indirect indexicality of adolescent males who are violent, tough and streetwise.

5.3.9 Conclusion

The results reported in this chapter confirm the value of examining linguistic variation in its full pragmatic and interactional context, thus providing validation – if any were needed – of Jenny Cheshire's methodological legacy. Qualitative analysis of every token of a variable in context is time-consuming and challenging. But as Cheshire has demonstrated, the effort and energy tend to be rewarded by advancements in our understanding of the processes underlying discourse-pragmatic and morpho-syntactic variation. Cheshire has always been careful to acknowledge the limitations of her work and to avoid generalising her findings beyond the data she analysed (e.g., Cheshire 2000, 2013). I wish

394 *Heike Pichler*

to follow her example here. The results presented in this chapter are based on the analysis of a relatively small sample of UFTs in monologic narratives of personal experience. My findings must not be generalised beyond the sample of male and female adolescents and the narrowly circumscribed type of narrative included in my dataset. Future research will benefit from analysing UFTs in a larger dataset, specifically one that allows investigation of their use in monologic, dialogic and polyphonic narratives of both personal and vicarious experience. It will be interesting to see whether the findings uncovered in this study apply more widely.

Notes

1 I am immensely grateful to Jenny Cheshire, Paul Kerswill and their research team for allowing me access to the transcriptions and audio files of the *Linguistic Innovators Corpus*. I thank Joaquín Bueno-Amaro for his help with data extraction and coding and Kaleigh Woolford for literature checks. A version of this paper was presented to the LVC research group at the University of Toronto in March 2019 and at the UKLVC 12 conference at Queen Mary University of London in September 2019. I thank the audience members as well as two anonymous reviewers for their constructive comments and suggestions, even if space restrictions prohibited me from pursuing them all here.

2 The relatively low frequency of tagging in the adolescent data is not unexpected. Discourse-pragmatic features tend to be less frequent in utterance-final than utterance-initial position (Fraser 1999:938; Traugott 2016:27), and their density tends to be lower in narratives than in conversations or general discussions (Coates 1987:122; Maeschler 1998:44). Narrative tagging must not therefore be dismissed as a low-frequency phenomenon not worthy of investigation. Compared with non-tagging, tagging is the marked phenomenon requiring explanation.

3 Future research will explore whether the dearth of *you know*-variants and the absence of *you get*-variants in the narrative dataset is due to the diffusion of discourse-pragmatic innovations from non-narrative to narrative discourse (as suggested for *innit* in Pichler, under review), or due to functional constraints on the use of *you know*- and *you get*-variants.

4 Previous studies of language use in the *Linguistic Innovators Corpus* have identified non-Anglo males as the leaders of linguistic innovations in London (e.g., Cheshire et al. 2008, 2011). The association of narrative UFTs with non-Anglo males noted above, together with the observation that three of the regular UFT users (Alex, Tina, Zack) have previously been identified as linguistic innovators (see Cheshire et al. 2008), suggests that the use of narrative UFTs might be increasing. Apparent- or real-time data are needed to test this hypothesis.

5 In examples (1)–(4), narrators' names are pseudonyms; story characters' names or non-generic place names have been replaced with {name (of park)}. The following transcription conventions are used:

-	false start, truncation	.	final intonation contour
(h)	audible in-breath	,	continuing intonation contour
@	laughter	?	rising intonation contour
underlining	emphatic stress	(text)	uncertain talk
(.), (..)	short, medium pause	(?)	indecipherable talk

6 UFTs included in the variable context and discussed in the text are italicised and bolded, those included in the variable context but not discussed are italicised, and those excluded from the variable context appear in regular font.

References

Andersen, Gisle. 2001. *Pragmatic Markers and Sociolinguistic Variation. A Relevance-Theoretic Approach to the Language of Adolescents.* Amsterdam: John Benjamins.

Andersen, Gisle. 2016. "Using the corpus-driven method to chart discourse-pragmatic change". In *Discourse-Pragmatic Variation in English. New Methods and Insights*, H. Pichler (ed.). Cambridge: Cambridge University Press. 21–40.

Bamberg, Michael. 2004. "Form and function of 'slut bashing' in male identity construction in 15-year-olds". *Human Development* 47:331–353.

Blum-Kulka, Shoshana. 1993. "'You gotta know how to tell a story': Telling, tales, and tellers in American and Israeli narrative events at dinner". *Language in Society* 22:361–402.

Cheshire, Jenny. 1981. "Variation in the use of *ain't* in an urban British English dialect". *Language in Society* 10:365–381.

Cheshire, Jenny. 1997. "Involvement in 'standard' and 'nonstandard' English". In *Taming the Vernacular. From Dialect to Written Standard Language*, J. Cheshire and D. Stein (eds.). Harlow: Longman. 68–82.

Cheshire, Jenny. 2000. "The telling or the tale? Narratives and gender in adolescent friendship networks". *Journal of Sociolinguistics* 4:234–262.

Cheshire, Jenny. 2003. "Social dimensions of syntactic variation: The case of *when* clauses". In *Social Dialectology. In Honour of Peter Trudgill*, D. Britain and J. Cheshire (eds.). Amsterdam: John Benjamins. 245–261.

Cheshire, Jenny. 2005. "Syntactic variation and beyond: Gender and social class variation in the use of discourse-new markers". *Journal of Sociolinguistics* 9:479–508.

Cheshire, Jenny. 2013. "Grammaticalisation in social context: The emergence of a new English pronoun". *Journal of Sociolinguistics* 17:608–633.

Cheshire, Jenny. 2016. "Epilogue: The future of discourse-pragmatic variation and change research". In *Discourse-Pragmatic Variation in English. New Methods and Insights*, H. Pichler (ed.). Cambridge: Cambridge University Press. 252–266.

Cheshire, Jenny and Ann Williams. 2002. "Information structure in male and female adolescent talk". *Journal of English Linguistics* 30:217–238.

Cheshire, Jenny and Sabine Ziebland. 2005. "Narrative as a resource in accounts of the experience of illness". In *The Sociolinguistics of Narrative*, J. Coates and J. Thornborrow (eds.). Amsterdam: John Benjamins. 17–40.

Cheshire, Jenny, Sue Fox, Paul Kerswill and Eivind Torgersen. 2008. "Ethnicity, friendship network and social practices as the motor of dialect change: Linguistic innovation in London". *Sociolinguistica* 22:1–23.

Cheshire, Jenny, Sue Fox, Paul Kerswill and Eivind Torgersen. 2011. "Contact, the feature pool and the speech community: The emergence of Multicultural London English". *Journal of Sociolinguistics* 15:151–196.

Cheshire, Jenny, David Adger and Sue Fox. 2013. "Relative *who* and the actuation problem". *Lingua* 126:51–77.

396 Heike Pichler

Cheshire, Jenny, Paul Kerswill and Ann Williams. 2005. "Phonology, grammar, and discourse in dialect convergence". In *Dialect Change. Convergence and Divergence in European Languages*, P. Auer, F. Hinskens and P. Kerswill (eds.). Cambridge: Cambridge University Press. 135–167.

Childs, Claire. 2016. "Variation and change in English negation: A cross-dialectal perspective". Unpublished Ph.D. thesis, Newcastle University, UK.

Coates, Jennifer. 1987. "Epistemic modality and spoken discourse". *Transactions of the Philological Society* 85(1):110–131.

Coates, Jennifer. 2002. *Men Talk. Stories in the Making of Masculinities*. Oxford: Blackwell.

Columbus, Georgie. 2010. "A comparative analysis of invariant tags in three varieties of English". *English World-Wide* 31:288–310.

Denis, Derek and Sali A. Tagliamonte. 2016. "Innovation, *right*? Change, *you know*? Utterance-final tags in Canadian English". In *Discoures-Pragmatic Variation in English. New Methods and Insights*, H. Pichler (ed.). Cambridge: Cambridge University Press. 86–112.

Erman, Britt. 2001. "Pragmatic markers revisited with a focus on *you know* in adult and adolescent talk". *Journal of Pragmatics* 32:1337–1359.

Fraser, Bruce. 1999. "What are discourse markers?" *Journal of Pragmatics* 14:931–952.

Gómez González, María de los Ángeles. 2014. "Canonical tag questions in English, Spanish and Portuguese: A discourse-functional study". *Languages in Contrast* 14:93–126.

González, Montserrat. 2004. *Pragmatic Markers in Oral Narrative*. Amsterdam: John Benjamins.

Herring, Susan C. 1991. "The grammaticalization of rhetorical questions in Tamil". In *Approaches to Grammaticalization*, Vol. 1, E. Closs Traugott and B. Heine (eds.). Amsterdam: John Benjamins. 253–284.

Hoffmann, Sebastian, Anne-Katrin Blass and Joybrato Mukherjee. 2017. "Canonical tag questions in Asian Englishes: Forms, functions and frequencies in Hong Kong English, Indian English and Singapore English". In *The Oxford Handbook of World Englishes*, M. Filppula, J. Klemola and D. Sharma (eds.). Oxford: Oxford University Press. 674–714.

Holmes, Janet. 1982. "The functions of tag questions". *English Language Research Journal* 4:40–65.

Kerswill, Paul, Jenny Cheshire, Sue Fox and Eivind Torgersen. 2007. "Linguistic innovators: The English of adolescents in London: Full research report". ESRC End of Award Report, RES-000-23-0680. Swindon: ESRC.

Labov, William. 1972a. *Language in the Inner City. Studies in the Black English Vernacular*. Oxford: Blackwell.

Labov, William. 1972b. *Sociolinguistic Patterns*. Oxford: Blackwell.

Labov, William and Joshua Waletzky. 1967. "Narrative analysis: Oral versions of personal experience". In *Essays on the Verbal and Visual Arts*, J. Helm (ed.). Seattle: University of Washington Press. 12–44.

Lawson, Robert. 2015. "Fight narratives, covert prestige, and performances of 'tough' masculinity: Some insights from an urban centre". In *Language and Masculinities. Performances, Intersections, Dislocations*, T.M. Milani (ed.). London: Routledge. 53–76.

Levon, Erez. 2016. "Gender, interaction and intonational variation: The discourse functions of High Rising Terminals in London". *Journal of Sociolinguistics* 20:133–163.

Linde, Charlotte. 1993. *Life Stories. The Creation of Coherence*. Oxford: Oxford University Press.

Maeschler, Yael. 1998. "*Rotsè lishmoa kéta?* 'Wanna hear something weird/ funny?' Segmenting Israeli Hebrew talk-in-interaction". In *Discoures Markers. Descriptions and Theory*, A.H. Jucker and Y. Ziv (eds.). Amsterdam: John Benjamins. 13–59.

Meyerhoff, Miriam. 1992. Sounds pretty ethnic, *eh*? A pragmatic particle in New Zealand English. *Language in Society* 23:367–388.

Mithun, Marianne. 2012. "Tags: Cross-linguistic diversity and commonality". *Journal of Pragmatics* 44:2165–2182.

Moore, Emma and Robert Podesva. 2009. "Style, indexicality, and the social meaning of tag questions". *Language in Society* 38:447–485.

Ochs, Elinor. 1992. "Indexing gender". In *Rethinking Context. Language as an Interactive Phenomenon*, A. Duranti and C. Goodwin (eds.). Cambridge: Cambridge University Press. 335–358.

Pichler, Heike. 2010. "Methods in discourse variation analysis: Reflections on the way forward". *Journal of Sociolinguistics* 14:581–608.

Pichler, Heike. 2013. *The Structure of Discourse-Pragmatic Variation*. Amsterdam: John Benjamins.

Pichler, Heike. under revision. "Exploring the role of grammaticalization and language contact in a discourse-pragmatic change in progress: The spread of *innit* in London English".

Quirk, Randolph, Sidney Greenbaum, Geoffrey Leech and Jan Svartvik. 1985. *A Comprehensive Grammar of the English Language*. London: Longman.

Schiffrin, Deborah. 1987. *Discourse Markers*. Cambridge: Cambridge University Press.

Schiffrin, Deborah. 1990. "The management of a co-operative self during argument: The role of opinions and stories". In *Conflict Talk. Sociolinguistic Investigations of Arguments in Conversations*, A.D. Grimshaw (ed.). Cambridge: Cambridge University Press. 241–259.

Schiffrin, Deborah. 1996. "Narrative as self-portrait: Sociolinguistic constructions of identity". *Language in Society* 25:167–203.

Spencer-Oatey, Helen. 2008. "Face, (im)politeness and rapport". In *Culturally Speaking. Culture, Communication and Politeness Theory*. 2nd edition, H. Spencer-Oatey (ed.). London: Continuum. 11–47.

Stenström, Anna-Brita, Gisle Andersen and Ingrid Kirstine Hasund. 2002. *Trends in Teenage Talk. Corpus Compilation, Analysis and Findings*. Amsterdam: John Benjamins.

Tannen, Deborah. 1985. "Relative focus on involvement in oral and written discourse". In *Literacy, Language, and Learning. The Nature and Consequences of Reading and Writing*, D.R. Olson, N. Torrance and A. Hildyard (eds.). Cambridge: Cambridge University Press. 124–147.

Torgersen, Eivind, Costas Gabrielatos, Sebastian Hoffmann and Sue Fox. 2011. "A corpus-based study of pragmatic markers in London English". *Corpus Linguistics and Linguistic Theory* 7:93–118.

398 Heike Pichler

Tottie, Gunnel and Sebastian Hoffmann. 2006. "Tag questions in British and American English". *Journal of English Linguistics* 34:283–311.

Traugott, Elizabeth Closs. 2016. "On the rise of types of clause-final pragmatic markers in English". *Journal of Historical Pragmatics* 17:26–54.

Waters, Cathleen. 2016. "Practical strategies for elucidating discourse-pragmatic variation". In *Discourse-Pragmatic Variation in English. New Methods and Insights*, H. Pichler (ed.). Cambridge: Cambridge University Press. 41–55.

Wetherell, Margaret and Nigel Edley. 1999. "Negotiating hegemonic masculinity: Imaginary positions and psycho-discursive practices". *Feminism and Psychology* 9:335–356.

Index

a allomorphy 56, 59–60, 64–66, 69, 252–253; *see also* indefinites
the allomorphy 56, 59, 65, 66, 68, 69, 252–253; *see also* definites
Abou Taha, Yasmine 8, 360–376
abstract *see* narrative *or* **relativisers (German)**
accent 70, 250
accessibility 280
  degree of 280
  hierarchy 120–121, 143, 149
acquisition *see* language acquisition
Acton, Eric 73, 74
Adger, David 2, 7, 98, 134–135, 194, 229–246
adjacency (factor)
  complementisers 346, 347, 355
  existentials 169
  relativisers (German) (*see* antecedent distance)
  subject-verb agreement 22
adjectival phrase, negative 241–242
adolescents 5, 8, 23, 75, 393
  discourse 22
  story worlds 377, 383
  working class, Reading xxiii
adverbs 87
  syntactic position 239
  clauses 23
  (factor), **complementisers** 347
age 107–108, 125, 369
  (factor) 124, 167, 179
    complementisers 345, 351–353, 355
    ethnicity 68
    existentials 23, 167–168, 171, 175, 178
    indefinite *this* 364–365, 368, 370
    negative concord 231
    phonetic/phonological variation 165, 179

  GOOSE vowel 252
  quotative 68, 252
  relativisers 103–109, 124 (*see also* **relativisers** (German))
  right dislocation 74
  was/were variation 61, 310, 311
age-grading 362, 374
  complementisers 351–352
age-group *see* age
agreement 19, 63
  gender and number 192
  plural/singular 166–179
  specifier-head 15, 19, 21, 24, 27, 87, 189, 192, 194, 197, 201, 304
  subject-verb 15, 21, 23–24, 27, 87
Aguilar-Guevara, Ana 281
Aissen, Judith 366
Albanian (language) 328
allomorphy *see a* allomorphy, *the* allomorphy
Amador-Moreno, Carolina 324
anadeictic reference 288
Andersen, Gisle 380
animacy 144, 158, 361–362, 365, 373
  (factor), **relativisers** (English) 95, 116, 120, 124–125, 135 (*see also* **relativisers**)
  hierarchy 361, 366, 371
antecedent
  abstract (factor) (*see* **relativisers** (German))
  case (factor) (*see* **relativisers** (German))
  definiteness (factor), **relativisers** (English) 124, 126, 128–129 (*see also* **relativisers**)
  distance (factor) (*see* **relativisers** (German))
  (factor) (*see* relatives, **relativisers**)
  grammatical category (factor) (*see* **relativisers** (German))

400 *Index*

length (factor) (*see* **relativisers** (German))
number agreement (factor) 192
object (factor), **relativisers** (English) 120, 126–127
subject (factor), **relativisers** (English) 120, 126–127
semantics of (English) 125–128
apparent-time *see* language change, apparent-time
Arabic (language) 253, 294, 297
arguments (syntactic) 116, 120, 188–189, 202, 361
  marking 8
    differential 361–362, 373–374
    structure (factor), **complementisers** 347, 349, 350, 355
articles xxvi, 4, 59, 60, 64–69, 144, 151, 155, 208, 252, 280–281, 283, 290, 373
allomorphy *see a* allomorphy *or the* allomorphy omission 69
aspect 26, 346, 350
attitudes *see* language attitudes
attrition, dialect *see* dialects, attrition
Auckland Voices (corpus) 122–123, 125, 128, 130
audience attention 378
Auer, Anja 17
Auer, Peter 7, 157, 159, 277–302
auxiliary
  aspectual 198
  be 168
  perfective (Dutch) 196–197

Ball, Catherine 48, 126, 130, 135
Ballard, Elaine 6, 115–133
Balto-Slavic languages 328
Barbiers, Sjef 7, 187–204
Bayley, Robert 135
be (main verb) 234, 240–242, 252; *see also* copula
be like (quotative) *see* quotatives
Beaken, Michael 252–253, 263
Beal, Joan 16, 18, 21–22, 25–26, 34, 48, 99, 320, 323, 325, 328, 334
Beaman, Karen V. 1–12, 134–164, 202, 224
Beltrama, Andrea 73, 74
Bender, Emily 75, 85
Bennis, Hans 193
Bewick, Thomas (naturalist) 18, 22, 25
bidialectalism 58
bilingualism 309, 329–330

Birchfield, Alexandra 6, 115–133
Blommaert, Jan 320, 334
Bohmann, Axel 136
Bolinger, Dwight 207, 344
Bonfiglio, Thomas P. 24
boomerang effect 66, 70
Braber, Natalie 99
Bresnan, Joan 223
Britain, David 6, 25, 93–114, 197, 304
British (language) *see* English, British
British (people)
  African-Caribbean 63, 256
  Anglo (White) 35, 63, 123, 251, 254, 259, 263–266, 268, 270
  Asian (South Asian) 57, 59–60, 63, 65, 69
    Bangladeshi 63, 65
    British-born 57
    lower middle class 56, 62
    Punjabi 56
  Jamaican 254
  non-Anglo 251–252
  Somali 328
British National Corpus 120, 218
British Nationality Act 57
Brown corpus 206, 216, 220, 223, 225
Buchstaller, Isabelle 1–12, 32–54, 60, 67, 134, 159, 165, 189, 202, 224
Burgess, Tony 255
but, sentence-final 323–324

Campbell-Kibler, Kathryn 32, 33
Canadians
  British/Irish descent 168, 171, 175, 179
  Chinese descent 168, 171, 176, 178–179
  Italian descent 168, 171, 176, 178, 179, 180
Cantonese (language), existentials 178
Cardoso, Amanda 250
Caribbeans, African 7, 255, 263, 264, 265, 268, 271
case (factor) *see* **relativisers** (German)
case matching (factor) *see* **relativisers** (German)
cataphora 8, 208, 210, 225, 361
cforest() function (R) 176
Chambers, J.K. 58, 63, 197, 237, 311, 314
change *see* language change
change-point analysis 36–39, 41, 48–49

Index 401

changepoint package (R) 36
channel (factor), **relativisers** 135; *see also* relatives, **relativisers**
Charters, Helen 6, 115–133
Cheshire, Jenny 1–9, 15, 19–20, 22–24, 27, 33, 47, 51, 55–56, 59–61, 63, 70–71, 73, 86–87, 93, 95, 98, 100, 103, 110–111, 116, 118–120, 123, 129–130, 134–135, 140, 142–144, 157, 159, 165–167, 187, 205, 220, 223–225, 229–231, 236–237, 243, 249, 251–253, 256–257, 263, 269, 271, 278, 289, 298, 304, 311–312, 320, 329–331, 334, 344, 347, 352, 354–356, 360, 364, 365–366, 368, 372–374, 377–379, 389, 393–394
Childs, Claire 34, 230, 378
Chinese (Mandarin) (language), negation 237
Chomsky, Noam 2, 117, 169, 187, 202–203
Cité Duits 7, 277–300
Clark, Lynn 34, 36–37, 49, 51
class (factor) *see* social class
clefts 366
climactic peak 388
clitics
  determiners (German) 288, 292, 295–296
  negative 229–232, 235, 237–243
    -n't 229–231, 235–236
    na 231, 235–236, 238–243
cliticisation (German) 282, 291–293, 297–298, 300
  coding semantic definiteness 292
Clyne, Michael 319, 328, 330–331, 335
co-occurrence of features 32–33
Cockney *see* English, British, London
coda *see* narrative, coda
code-switching, Dutch/German 282
codification 47, 87
cognition, sociolinguistic 51
collinearity, of social and linguistic factors 155
collocation, subject-verb 346, 348–349
colonialism 334
communicative goals 85
community (factor) *see* **relativisers** (German)
community of practice 5, 75, 78–84
competence, second-language 69

complement 188, 239, 343–356, 365, 373; *see also* **complementisers**
complementation 348, 351–353; *see also* **complementisers**
complementiser phrase (CP)
  as relativiser 117
  CP domain 234
  complexity 135
    (factor), **complementisers** 344, 347, 349
    principle 145
    syntactic 355
complementisers 234, 343, 345
  double 142, 144
  der wo (German) 157
  as linguistic sign-post 8
  socio-historical context 355
  that 6, 8, 106–107, 128–129, 344, 346–349, 352–356
    cognitive constraints 355
    complement subject (factor) 346, 347, 350, 353, 354
    cooperative function of 356
    linguistic signpost 135, 354
    pragmatic meaning 123
    prescriptivism 351
    as relativiser 123 (*see also* **relatives**)
  wo (German) (*see* relatives, **relativisers** (German))
  zero 344–345, 348
  þe (Old English) 344
    as relativiser 121
complicating action *see* narrative, complicating action
Comrie, Bernard 365
conditional inference tree 174, 176, 178
constraint ranking 305, 309, 314, 353–354, 369
Construction Grammar 243
contact *see* language contact
contact dialects 195
Contact in the City corpus 167, 179
contraction 239
  clitic forms 291
  (factor), **existentials** 168 (*see also* **existentials**)
  preposition-determiner (German) 282, 288
convergence, standard language 148, 154
cooperative activity 135
copula 169; *see also* auxiliary *be*, *be* (main verb)
  zero 178–179, 305, 311

402 Index

Cornips, Leonie 7, 194, 277–302
Corpus of Historical American English 206, 219, 220, 223
Corpus of London Teenage speech 380
Corpus of Oz Early English 325
Corrigan, Karen 8, 99, 194, 319–340
count, structural (factor) *see* **relativisers** (German)
counterurbanisation 6, 94, 111
Cox, Felicity 321
creoles 257, 263
  Caribbean 270
  cline of creoleness 303, 309, 315
  creolisation 258, 305, 306, 315
  creoloidisation 303
  English-based 256, 262, 270–271, 303, 305, 309, 315
    Atlantic 116
    Jamaican 254, 269
crossing 257, 268
ctree() function (R) 175
cultural forms, Caribbean 268
Czaika, Mathias 319

D'Arcy, Alexandra 8, 118, 135, 343–359
Dalrymple, Mary 372
Danish (language), **particle-verb alternation** 219, 223
data mining 49
dative case (German), decline 155
Deal, Amy Rose 170
decategorisation 157, 158
declaratives 379–382, 385–386
definiteness 144, 158, 279, 361, 365, 367
  (factor) (*see* **relativisers** (German))
  (factor), **existentials** 170 (*see also* **existentials**)
  (factor), **particle-verb alternation** 217, 218
  hierarchy 362
  pragmatic 280, 285–288, 292, 294
  semantic 280, 285–288, 292, 294–295, 297
definites
  article allomorphy 67
  determiners 278–279
  noun phrases, function 280–281, 288
Dehé, Nicole 207, 208, 210
deictic *that* 129

Dekeyser, Xavier 119
demographic churn 94, 100
demonstratives 74
  definite 361
  pronoun, as relativiser 121
  semantics 73
  that 129
  them 26
  themuns 26
  theseuns 20, 21
Demske, Ulrike 281
Denis, Derek 379
Denison, David 17
dependency, syntactic 206–207, 220
determiners
  a(n) 360
  case-marked 282
  collapse 280
  definite (*see* definites)
  evolution of 373
  negative 236
    nae 231, 244
    polarity, *any* 231
  pragmatic function 279
  them 21
  these 20
  type (factor), **existentials** 170–172
determinism *see* new-dialect formation
dialects
  area 194
  attrition 93–94
  change, rapidity of 93
  contact 6, 7, 25–26, 93, 194, 303, 306, 315, 319–320
    mobility 94
    social class 111
    zones 194
      transitional 197, 200
  formation 258
  vs. languages 20
  levelling (*see* levelling, dialects)
  shift 56
diffusion, language 320
discontinuity, structural 356
discourse
  constraints 343
  context (factor), utterance-final tag 380
  factors 344
  features 8
  marker 322
  opacity 281

reference, new 8, 362–365, 373
referent 360
structure 364
  indefinite *this* 366
variation (*see* variation,
  discourse-pragmatic)
discriminatory markers 362, 366,
  371, 373
disfluency 354–355
dislocation, right 4, 5, 73–90
syntactic function 74
  intersubjective functions 84
  pragmatic function 84
distance (factor) *see* **relativisers**
  (German)
Docherty, Gerry 93
Dolan, Terence 323
Dovaston, John 22
Duden (German language reference)
  137, 159
dummy verbaliser 170
Durham, Mercedes 74
Dutch (language) 7, 188–193, 195,
  199–201, 277, 279, 289, 299, 328
Belgian 199, 277
dialects 194 (*see also Syntactic Atlas
  of the Dutch Dialects*)
Limburg 7
Maasland dialect 277, 279, 282,
  289, 297
(multi-)ethnolect 292–297
DynaSAND database 188, 190

ecology
language 320, 334
sociolinguistic 314
education 73, 158
(attribute) 70, 122
dialect contact 111
dialect shift 94
(factor) 3, 5, 25, 78 (*see* **relativisers**
  (German))
  complementisers 345, 351,
    353, 355
  perception 51
  verbal *-s*, historical 19
policy 2
system 154
ELAN 37, 124, 140
*Electronic Atlas of World
  Englishes* 305
Elenbaas, Marion 207
Elizabeth I, Queen of England, use of
  verbal inflection 18

Ellis, Alexander 95–97, 99
emigrant letter corpora 324
Empty Category Principle 188, 202
enclisis 282
English, African American 21, 312
negation 244
English, American 73, 363, 379
historical 219
Massachusetts, phonetic/
  phonological variation 1
New York City 24, 25
  phonetic/phonological variation 1
Ocracoke, North Carolina 304
Southern 25
standard 67
was/were variation 304
English, Australian 8, 319, 322–325
Irish English input 321
Melbourne 8, 321, 334
Sydney, *was/were* variation 312
vernacular 328
was/were variation 304
English, British 120, 379, 385; *see also*
  English, England; English, Scotland;
  Scots
Anglo (White) 59
Asian (South Asian) 5, 55–56,
  58–59, 61–64, 66, 67, 70
colloquial 74
dialects 116
northern 22, 119–120
Southern Standard 55, 56, 58–65,
  67–68
urban 60
was/were variation 304
white working class 59
English, Canadian 8, 345, 360
Ottawa 119, 369
Toronto 6, 8, 119, 125, 165–167,
  169, 171–173, 175–179, 181,
  183, 348, 353–354
English, Caribbean 271
English, Celtic 321, 324, 328
English, contact varieties 116, 314,
  319–340
dialects 7
diaspora varieties 120
English, Dominican Republic, *was/
  were* variation 312
English, Early Modern 119, 344, 348
particle-verb alternation 207
English, English 120; *see also* English,
  British
central 20

404 *Index*

dialects (*see also Survey of English Dialects*)
- boundary 111
- East Anglia 6, 94, 99–100, 102, 104, 108–112
- English Fens, *was/were* **variation** 304
- London 25, 59–60, 69, 100–101, 110–112, 119, 123, 136, 256–257, 378–379, 392
  - Cockney 55–56, 58, 60–61, 64–65, 67–68, 71, 251, 254–256, 263–264, 269
  - influences from other languages 264
  - inner-city speech 67, 257–258, 262
  - Jamaican 254–256, 262, 264, 268
    - Caribbean influence on 270
  - Multicultural London English xxvi 7, 55–56, 58–61, 63–71, 249–276
    - origins 257
    - possible sources of features 253
  - pre-adolescents 98
  - regional differences 98
  - vernacular 61, 263
  - *was/were* **variation** 252, 304
- Manchester 393
- Milton Keynes 23
- Middlesbrough 328
- nonstandard dialect xxiv
- northern 20, 74, 99
  - north-east 33, 35, 39, 48–49, 51
  - north-west 5, 35, 51, 75
- Newcastle 5, 26, 33, 35, 328
- Northumberland 24–25
- Norwich 24–25
  - **verbal** *-s* 17
- Reading 1, 95, 98, 119, 229–232, 236, 243, 393
- regional dialects 96–100
- Scilly, Isles of 34
- southern 5, 20
  - south-eastern 321
- Tyneside 16, 21, 25, 99
- York, *was/were* **variation** 312
English, Falklands Islands 305
English, Indian 5, 55–71
- educated 66, 69
English, Irish 8, 25, 321, 322, 323
- influence on Australian English 321, 325
- Northern Ireland 24–25, 120

Belfast 5, 16, 19–22, 25–26
English, Middle 344, 348, 363
- **particle-verb alternation** 216
English, New Zealand 120, 124–125, 128, 130, 270
- Auckland 6, 115, 119, 124–125, 128–129
- *was/were* **variation** 304
English, Old 344, 348, 374
- **particle-verb alternation** 216
English, Saint Helenian 7, 303, 305, 306, 309
English, Scottish 24–25, 35, 120; *see also* English, British; Scots
- Buckie 7, 21, 230–231, 234–236, 239–241, 243, 244
- Edinburgh 25
- Glasgow 20, 25
- Highlands 322
English, second language 60–61, 63–64, 250, 315
- indigenised 305, 328
English, South Asian 60
English, Standard 322
- negation 237
English, Tristan da Cunha 315
- *was/were* **variation** 304
English, vernacular 348
- negation 237
enregisterment 249–251
enrichment, stereotypical 281
envelope of variation 23–24, 188; *see also* variable context
epistemics
- *must* 321
- parentheticals 346, 348
equative particles
- *als* (German) 156
- *so/som* (German) 156
- *wo* (German) 157 (*see also* **relatives, relativisers** (German))
equivalence
- functional 3, 189
- semantic 140, 189
ethnicity 6, 57, 63, 123, 251–252, 254, 256, 264–265, 356
- Belfast 25
- de-ethnicisation 299
- ethnic mixing 306–307, 309
- (factor) 167, 171, 176, 178
  - **existentials** 168, 171, 175, 178
  - phonetic/phonological variation 165
  - **utterance-final tags** 379, 383

multiethnicity 136
re-ethnicisation 70
ethnography 75, 290
ethnolect *see* (multi)ethnolect
ethnolinguistic vitality 330
evaluation 32
  function 85
    of tags 81
  listener 39, 41, 48
  perceptual 49, 51
  real-time 36, 39
  speaker 33
evaluation (narrative) *see* narrative,
  evaluation
excitability (attribute) 73
existentials 6, 23–24, 60–63, 166,
  168–169, 173, 177–178, 232–234,
  237, 240, 242–243, 304, 366,
  371–372, 374
  Cantonese 178
  clauses 67
  (factor), **indefinite *this*** 370
  (factor), ***was/were* variation**
    310, 311
  regional differences 170
  there's 168, 171–173, 175–176,
    178, 304
  with auxiliary *do* 168
  with auxiliary *have* 168
exonormativity 27
Experigen (software) 36
exponence, variability in 236
extraposition 141

FACE vowel *see* phonetic/phonological
  variation, vowels
face
  threat to 81, 84
  value of 392–393
factor weights 126, 311, 349, 352,
  369, 370–372; *see also* GoldVarb
  and Rbrul
feature pool 8, 26, 55, 70, 93, 249,
  251, 303, 319–322, 330–331, 334
Fitzpatrick, David 324, 335
Fix, Sonya 320
FLEECE vowel *see* phonetic/
  phonological variation, vowels
focus (factor), **particle-verb
  alternation** 207–208, 210, 213
focussing 306
Foley, Michele 170
FOOT vowel *see* phonetic/phonological
  variation, vowels

Forby, Robert 99
force, grammatical 234
Ford, Marilyn 223
form-function relationship 16
formality 48, 129
  (factor), **complementisers** 344
  (factor), **relativisers** 119
Foulkes, Paul 93
founders
  effect 7, 208, 251, 258, 268,
    309, 314
  population 271, 326
    Melbourne 325, 327–328
  Principle 263, 268
Fox, Sue 1–12, 32, 34, 41, 47, 55–56,
  59–61, 63–65, 93, 98, 111, 134–
  135, 220, 239–240, 249–252, 258,
  269, 271, 304, 311–312, 334
Freiburg English Dialect corpus 97
French (language) 328
  existentials 23
  ne 16
  Norman 122
  schools and churches in
    Melbourne 330
frequency (factor) 3, 5, 32, 55–56,
  66, 69, 251, 258, 270, 303, 305,
  312, 315
  bare nouns 291, 294, 297
  complementisers 344, 348–349,
    354, 355
  negative concord 231, 237
  right dislocation 78–80, 84
  utterance final tags 377–378,
    380–385, 394
  wh-forms 116, 119–120, 130 (*see
    also* relativisers, *wh*-forms)
  wo-relatives (German) 146–150
    (*see also* **relativisers** (German),
    wo-relatives)
friendliness (attribute) 73
Fritz, Clemens 322, 325, 335
fudged form 194, 202

Gaelic (language) 322
  schools and churches in
    Melbourne 330
gap
  lexical 188–189
  linguistic 187–188, 199
    macrogap 188
    mesogap 188
    microgap 189–191, 194
  word order 188

406   *Index*

Gargen, Henry 307
gender *see* agreement *or* sex/gender
gender-related orientations 368
generalised additive models 49
generation *see* age
genitive
  analytic (English) 223
  case (German), decline 155
  synthetic (English) 223
genre (factor) 136
  complementisers 344, 351
  particle-verb alternation 217–220
  relativisers 119, 135
geographic diffusion
  contagion diffusion model 94
  gravity model 102
  urban hierarchical model 94, 110
geographic distribution 199–200
  ethnic groups in Hackney 266–267
  (factor), **particle-verb alternation**
    206, 208–210, 213–215,
    223, 225
  (factor), **strong reflexives** 191
  (factor), syntactic variation 205
  (factor), verb cluster interruption
    (Dutch) 199
  (factor), word order (Dutch) 196,
    198, 200
German (language) 7, 136–137, 195,
  197, 277–280, 282, 289, 328, 331
  Alemannic 138, 156
  Austrian 282, 283
  dialects 134, 138, 155, 156, 157
  Duisburg 291, 293, 296–297
  equative *so/som* 156
  existentials 23
  Low 155, 300
  multiethnolect 290–295
  non-standard 7, 278
  Ruhr 278, 289, 293, 295–298, 300
  Schwäbisch Gmünd 138–141, 145,
    148–155, 157–158
  southern 134, 136, 138, 157, 279
  standard 134, 136–137, 158–159,
    278–279, 290, 299
  Stuttgart 138–141, 145, 148–155,
    157–158, 290–298
  Swabian 6, 134–159
  Swiss 137, 156
  youth language 299
Germanic
  determiner system 278–280, 298
  languages 156, 222, 278, 289
Giles, Howard 330, 334
Gisborne, Nikolas 116–117, 119–122

Givón, Talmy 367
Glass, Leia 74
glmer() function (R) 149
GOAT vowel *see* phonetic/phonological
  variation, vowels
GoldVarb 217, 310–311, 349, 368;
  see also Rbrul
González, Montserrat 378, 383, 385
Google Books Ngram Viewer
  155–156
GOOSE vowel *see* phonetic/
  phonological variation, vowels
Graffmiller, Jason 205
grammatical
  competition 7
  formulation 73
  norms 3
  person (factor)
    complementisers 346
    was/were variation 311
  variables, infrequency 3, 6, 15, 17,
    118, 166, 173–174, 178, 343
grammaticalisation 3, 154, 157, 373
  of definite article 280
  of relativisers 157
  principle of persistence 116, 129
  principle of semantic bleaching 3,
    129, 154, 157–158
Green, Jonathan 269
Gricean principles 85
Gries, Stefan 206
Grimm, Scott 223
Gunn, Brendan 25
Günthner, Susanne 137
Guy, Gregory R. 5, 135, 145, 159,
  174, 349, 374

de Haas, Hein 319
Haddican, Bill 7, 205–228
Haegeman, Liliane 233
Hale, Kenneth 188
Hallam, Thomas 96
Halliday, Michael 75
Harris, John 16, 21, 25–26, 323
have (main verb) 34, 232–234,
  237–241, 243–244
Hawkins, John 285
Healy, Alice 67
Hebrew (language) 328
*Helsinki Corpus of Early English
  Correspondence* 17–19, 22
Henry, Alison 20
Herrmann, Tanja 97
Hewitt, Roger 254–255, 257
Hickey, Raymond 321–324

High Rising Terminals *see* phonetic/
phonological variation
Himmelmann, Nikolaus 285
Hinrichs, Lars 118, 135–136,
143–145, 155, 223–224
historical sociolinguistics *see*
sociolinguistics, historical
Hoffman, Michol F. 58, 165, 167, 179
Holmberg, Anders 7, 205–228, 240
Holmberg's Generalisation 240,
242–243
Hopper, Paul 129, 157
Horvath, Barbara 312, 321, 323
Huang, James C.-T. 237
Huddleston, Rodney 76
Hudson, Rachel 23
Hughes, Arthur 207, 208
humanness 363, 373
(factor), **indefinite *this*** 366,
370–372
Hungarian (language) 282, 299
Hurford, James 252
hypercorrection 48

Ibex Farm (software) 209
Icelandic (language)
object shift 222
particle-verb alternation 219, 222
identification, postponed 74, 76; *see
also* **dislocation, right**
identity 64, 70, 84–85, 138, 165, 250,
255, 377, 389
Asian 69
British Asian 66
Swabian 147
ideology 5, 70, 237, 250, 352, 356
social 70
standard language 15–27, 48,
135, 136
idiom 365
Ilbury, Christian 264
imposition 250; *see also* language
interference
incorporation 188, 281
incrementation 252–253
indefiniteness, referential 361, 374
indefinites 370–371
antecedent 128
article 280, 373
allomorphy 60 (*see also a*
allomorphy)
markers 373
noun phrase 8, 128, 360, 365, 366,
371, 373
pronoun 125–129

referents 368
specifics, as topics 367
this 8, 361–374
diachronic implications 373
independence of linguistic constraints
and social constraints 67
indexicality 34, 47, 49, 51, 70, 73, 85,
118, 128, 147, 155, 165, 257, 334,
378, 393
Asian 66
context 32
education 122
meaning 33
prestige 122
second language 56
target 65
working class 56, 74
zero subject relativiser 48
individual speaker effects 120, 155,
174, 278, 392
was/were **variation** 310
inequality, linguistic 334
inflectional case (factor) *see*
relativisers (German)
information structure 7, 81, 208, 210,
347, 361, 371, 374
complementation 354
given information 366
indefinite noun phrases 366
new information 392
right dislocation 76
information structure (factor),
particle-verb alternation 207, 211
initiation event 22; *see also* verb, **verb-
particle alternation**
innovation 27, 55, 123, 215, 252
endogenous 122
linguistic 2
innovators, linguistic 251, 394
insularity, social 63
integration, social 70
intensifier 69, 73–74
zelf 190
interaction 8, 155
complementiser 350, 354
constraints 347
context 377
(factor) 3
pressure 356
risk 85
social 87
speaker 5
work 379
interactive style 374
interference 165, 173

408 *Index*

Arabic 297
first language 300
interlanguage varieties 330
interpersonal function 322
interpretation, selective 389
interrogative 393
 functions 16
 source of relativiser 134
 wo (German) 136
intervening material (factor)
 complementisers 345, 349
 existentials 176
 particle-verb alternation 211
Inwood, Stephen 259
Irish diaspora 323
isolation, social 63, 298
Italian (language) 73, 282, 328
 existentials 178, 180

Jackson, Robert 329
'Jafaican' 257, 269
Jakobson, Roman 122
Jankowski, Bridget 136
Japanese (language), negation 237
Johnson, Daniel Ezra 7, 205–228

Kallen, Jeffrey 323
Kayne, Richard 207
Kerswill, Paul 7, 93, 249–276, 325, 328, 331, 334, 394
Keyser, Samuel Jay 188
King, Ruth 122
Kirkham, Sam 75
Kiss, Tibor 299
Klein, Carmen 8, 360–376
koinéisation 6, 111, 158, 249, 258
koinés 315
Kökeritz, Helge 99
Kortmann, Bernd 116, 305
Krapp, George 208
Kroch, Anthony 206, 352
Kurath, Hans 208

Labov, William xxiv–xxv, 1, 3–4, 16–17, 19, 24–26, 41, 47, 129, 229, 236, 252, 263–264, 289, 320, 345, 378–379, 383
Lambrecht, Knud 366
lame xxiv
language acquisition
 adult 257
 childhood 257
 context 63

language attitudes 26, 250
language change 2, 158, 166, 187, 281, 310, 334, 368–369
 apparent-time 103–110, 124, 362, 365, 368–369
 contact-induced 122, 249, 305–306, 309
 diachronic 2, 117, 129, 215–220, 279, 348, 373
 from above 123, 135–136, 142, 145–146, 154, 158–159, 220
 from below 19, 123
 internal 122
 lifespan 250, 352–353
 morphosyntactic 56, 158
 phonetic/phonological 56
 in progress 3, 124, 154, 167, 219, 362
 real-time 16, 33–34, 36–39, 48–51, 138–139, 325, 362, 369, 374
 real-time (factor), **particle-verb alternation** 216
 synchronic 115, 119, 123, 129, 279
language contact 7, 59–60, 129, 179, 250, 257, 277, 303, 305–306, 315–316, 319, 325
 French and English 121–122
 majority-minority 330
Lawrence, Helen 99, 135
Le Bruyn, Bert 281
Leiss, Elisabeth 279–280, 298
levelling
 count-mass 69
 dialect 25, 26, 93–95, 321
 existentials 63
 negation 63
 past *be* (*see was/were* variation)
 relativisers 100, 103, 108, 111, 124, 127
Levey, Stephen 8, 98, 119, 135, 143–144, 360–376
Levin, Beth 75
Levon, Erez 5, 32–54, 250, 392
lexical 23, 69, 74, 135, 201, 250, 354, 362
 density 136
 gap 188–189
 syntax, theory of 221
 verb 170, 222–223, 232–234, 237, 240
 verb (factor), **complementisers** 346
lexicalisation 74, 209, 221, 304
likelihood (statistical)

log 349
maximum 36
ratio test 209
linearisation 195, 197, 201–202
Linguistic Innovators Corpus 377, 379, 394
linking
of negative clitic 235
of negative object 237–239, 242
literacy 63, 65–66
Llamas, Carmen 328
lme4 package (R) 149, 209, 217
locative *wo* (German) *see* **relatives, relativisers** (German)
logical form 203
complementation 352
Lohse, Barbara 206, 209, 220, 222
London
history
northern migrants to 19
southern English dialect 19
London Innovators Corpus 380
Londoners
African Caribbean 256
British South Asian 70
British-born 66
Los, Bettelou 374
Lunkenheimer, Kerstin 116, 305

Maegaard, Marie 33
Malagasy (language) 314
man (pronominal) *see* pronouns, *man*
markedness condition 223, 224
marker
relative (*see* relatives, relativisers)
syntactic, of dialect division 100
verbal (*see* verbs)
masculinity (attribute) 8, 378, 391–392
matrix clause
argument structure (factor), **complementisers** 346–347
subject (factor), **complementisers** 350
tense (factor), **complementisers** 350
verb (factor), **complementisers** 350, 353
meaning
social 4–5, 47, 49, 73–75, 85–87, 134, 249, 379, 383, 393
of *that* 353
theory of 3
Mearns, Adam 5, 32–54

Meechan, Marjory 170
Meier, Hans Heinrich 122
Melbourne
ethnic groups 320
founder population 320
Mencken, H.L. 24
methods
acceptability judgment 205
controlled judgment experiment 205
corpus data 224
experimental 224
forced-choice task 224
grammaticality judgment 238, 243
judgment experiment 207, 208, 223, 225
matched-guise experiment 49
translation task 96
metrolingualism 319
Meyerhoff, Miriam 3, 4, 6, 60, 66, 115–135, 140–141, 144, 147, 165, 378
middle class 3, 25, 55–56, 62, 65, 69, 86, 94, 111, 135, 314; *see also* social class
migration
to America
Scottish 21
Ulster 21
to Australia 8
British/Irish 326–327
Chinese 328, 331, 334
Irish 319, 321
to Melbourne 328–333
Irish 328, 334
to Victoria, Irish 329
to Belgium 277–278
to Britain
African 260, 262
Bangladeshi 260
Caribbean 259
Indian 260
South Asian 262
Pakistani 260
West Indian 260
from Europe, historical 319
to Europe 319
to Germany 295
global 7
internal 94
to London 252, 258, 261
African 57, 269
Caribbean 263–264, 268

410 *Index*

English, 258
as a factor in Multicultural
London English 258
Indian 57
Jamaican 259
South Asian 57, 269
to New Zealand 123
Asian 123
Pacific Island 123
to North America, British/Irish 208
to Saint Helena 307–308
Mihm, Arend 296
Milroy, James 16, 19, 21, 26, 140, 365
Milroy, Lesley 5, 15–31, 24–26,
34–35, 95, 139–140, 206, 343, 365
mixed effects *see* regression analysis
mixed language 277
Multicultural London English *see*
English, British, England, London
mobility 311
and dialect contact 93, 94, 111
modals 74, 196
auxiliary (factor),
complementisers 347
auxiliary (Dutch) 197
Mohawk, utterance-final tag 378
monitor, sociolinguistic 4, 32, 41,
47, 134
Montgomery, Chris 34
Montgomery, Michael 22, 208
Moore, Emma 5, 34, 73–90, 379, 393
movement
head 221
leftward 222
Mufwene, Salikoko S. 7, 249, 251,
258, 263, 309, 314, 320, 326, 334
Mulac, Anthony 347
Mulder, Jean 323
multicultural
enclaves 130
friendship groups 251
multiethnic
contact 7, 55, 124, 158, 250, 271,
290, 298, 379
contexts 270
(multi)ethnolects 2, 7, 249–251, 257,
277, 289–290, 298, 319–321,
324–325
acquisition 250
Melbourne 8, 320–321, 329–331,
334
Stuttgart 157, 293–294, 296–297
multilingualism 179, 320
Melbourne 330
multilingualism, urban 7

neighbourhoods 249
multiple negation 15, 19, 23, 26–27;
see also negative concord
multivariate analysis *see* regression
analysis
Murray, James 21–22

narratives 378–394
abstract 384–387
adjacent events 387
adolescent 377
coda 383, 385–386, 389
components 378, 385–386
construction 374
complicating action 383–389, 392
evaluation 383–386
model 378
narrator-protagonist 391
orientation 383–388, 392
embedded 384, 386–388
peaks 386
resolution 383–387, 389
tension 388
nativisation 64, 70, 309
negation
adverbial 230
(factor) 67
complementisers 347
existentials 170, 171
was/were variation 63
noun phrase 232, 234, 236, 240
sentential 229
clitic *-n't* 231, 236
clitic *-na* 236, 239 (*see also*
English, Buckie)
nae 231 (*see also* English, Buckie)
not 231
negative
concord 7, 87, 229–233, 236, 243
(*see also* multiple negation)
determiner 170
(factor), existentials 173
non-standard 15
not/-n't 230
noun phrase 237, 242
object, licensing of 234
polarity item 232
Neg-Criterion 235; *see also* negation
networks
adolescent 2
friendship 63, 136
social 62–63, 136, 139, 167, 264,
270, 290, 298, 320, 330
role in language contact 320
West Indian 259

working class 56, 57, 70
  youth 299
orientation, social (factor) *see*
  relativisers (German)
origin of speaker (factor), ***was/were***
  variation 310
Nevalainen, Terttu 17–19, 27
New Zealanders
  Asian 123
  Polynesian 123
Newbrook, Mark 322
new-dialect formation 249, 270, 306,
  315, 320, 325
  deterministic model 7, 250–251,
    270–271
Nikolaeva, Irina 372
nominalisation of infinitives
  200–201, 299
Non-Mobile Old Rural Females *see*
  NORFs
Non-Mobile Old Rural Men *see*
  NORMs
non-standardness (attribute) 24
NORFs 99
normalisation (*vs.* standardisation) 26
NORMs 96–99
Northern Subject Rule 21, 22, 27
Norwegian (language)
  negation 237, 240
  particle-verb alternation 219, 222
Norwich, language contact in 16th
  century 17
number
  approximation 69
  neutrality 281

object
  length (factor), **particle-verb**
    alternation 206–207
  marking, differential 361
  shift 221–222, 224
  weight (factor), **particle-verb**
    alternation 208, 210–212,
    220, 223
Observer's Paradox xxiv
occupation (factor) 78; *see also*
  relatives, relativisers (German)
  complementisers 345–346,
    351–353, 355
Ochs, Elinor 85
Ojanen, Timo 99
orientation *see* narrative, orientation
Orton, Harold 95
otherness (attribute) 25
Ottawa English Corpus 362, 364

outlier, statistical 174, 178
Owen, David 259
Özge, Umut 373

Palmer, Frank xxiii
panel study 138–139, 148–149, 151,
  158–159
parallelism 144, 349
parentheticals 346–347
Parsed Corpus of Early English
  Correspondence 215
particle-verb alternation 7, 205–225
  corpus studies 206, 215
past *be* levelling *see* tense, **past *be***
  ***was/were* variation**
past tense *see* tense
past tense *be* *see* tense, **past, *be***
Patrick, Peter 256
Patterson, David 16
Paul, Hermann 156
peer group
  norms 58–59
  ties 63
Peitsara, Kirsti 99
Penn Parsed Corpus of Early Modern
  English 215–216, 220
Penn Parsed Corpus of Modern British
  English 215–216, 220
Penn-Helsinki Parsed Corpus of
  Middle English 215–216, 220
Penry Williams, Cara 323
perception 250
  real-time 48–49, 51
  speech 32, 33, 49
  theory of 33, 36
performance, linguistic 2
persistence
  principle of (*see* grammaticalisation)
  structural (factor) (*see* **relativisers**
    (German))
  topic (*see* topic)
persona 69, 85, 86, 392
Petyt, K.M. 99
Pharao, Nicolai 32–33
phonetic/phonological variation 5, 32,
  49, 56, 66, 73, 93, 95, 165–166,
  179, 253
  consonant cluster reduction 305
  h-dropping 251
  High Rising Terminals 392
  (ing) 34–35, 39–41, 45–46, 48, 51,
    69
  /k/-backing 251
  palatal glide deletion 94
  retroflex /t/ 58

412 *Index*

rhoticity 24
t-glottalisation 35, 48, 52, 58, 66, 70
/v/~/w/ 70
vowels
(a) 16, 25–26
FACE 34–46, 51, 251, 253
FLEECE 251, 253, 256
GOAT 35, 251, 253
GOOSE 35, 251–253, 256, 269
unstressed 321
Phonological Form 203
phonological phrase 206
phonological restructuring 328
Pichler, Heike 8, 377, 398
Pittner, Karin 136–137
Pitts, John 255, 263
place (factor) *see* **relativisers** (German)
plural agreement *see* agreement
plural -*s* (factor), **existentials** 173, 169
plurilingualism 319
Podesva, Robert 379, 393
polarity 172; *see also* negatives
Policansky, Linda 20
Portuguese (language) 282
utterance-final tags 378
Poschmann, Claudia 141
poshness (attribute) 66
position, syntactic (factor)
indefinite *this* 369–370, 373
relativisers 135
positionality 5
possessives 193
determiner phrase (DP) 192
eigen (Dutch) 190
nominal groups 191
non-reflexive 192
pronoun 191
zijn (Dutch) 190
post-modification (factor), **indefinite *this*** 366, 370–372
Potts, Christopher 73, 74
Poussa, Patricia 99, 100, 110, 111
pragmatic
factors 3
function 73, 87, 278
affective 76
determiner 279
evaluative 76
expressive 76
information 118
pressure 356
Pratt, Lynda 17
predication
non-verbal 169

verbal 170
predict() function (R) 149, 152
preposition-noun combinations (*Cité Duits*) 278–299
directional 282
locational 282
prescriptivism 3, 6, 15, 23–24, 27, 47–49, 129, 135–136, 145–146, 154, 158–159, 237, 352, 355
complementisers 351
particle-verb alternation 220
prestige 5, 19, 24, 47, 55, 56, 58, 66, 125, 128–129, 154, 330, 345
complementisers 352
overt 69
relativisers 122
Preston, Dennis 26
priming 144
Process event 221
processing 51, 154, 344, 371
cognitive 144
utterance 76
production, language 169, 173; *see also* processing
professional (attribute) 35–36, 39, 47–48, 51–52
progressive *–ing* 69
prominence hierarchy 361
pronominalisation 140
pronouns
(factor), **particle-verb alternation** 206
(factor), **right dislocation** 80, 82, 84
hem 190
indefinite (*see* indefinites)
man 252–253, 269, 393
possessive (*see* possessives)
relative (*see* relativisers)
resumptive (*see* resumptives)
them 21, 26
these 20
themuns 26
theseuns 20–21
youse (second person plural) 325
proper names 282, 285
prosodic weight (factor), **particle-verb alternation** 206
Proto-Indo-European 120
Pruned Exact Linear Time algorithm 36
Pullum, Geoffrey K. 76
punctual *whenever* 322
purposive *till* 322

Index 413

quantifier 365
  negative 229–230, 242
Quirk, Randolph 76, 135
quotatives 56, 59–60, 67, 69
  be like 67, 252–253
  pragmatic load 67
  this is + speaker 252

R (software) 36, 141, 149, 152, 175, 176, 209
Ramchand, Gillian 221
Rampton, Ben 256
random effects *see* regression analysis
range (GoldVarb) 349, 369
Raumolin-Brunberg, Helena 18
Rbrul 126, 217; *see also* GoldVarb
reaction 34, 36–37, 41, 47
  evaluative 47
real time *see* language change *or* evaluation
reallocation 58, 70
Received Pronunciation 24–26
recording year (factor) *see* **relativiser** (German)
recursive partitioning 174–175, 178
reduplication 69
reference
  associative 287
  associative-phoric 285
  meaning 365
  strength 280
referentiality 134, 281, 287, 295, 299, 360
  (factor), **preposition noun combinations** 284–286, 289–294, 296–297
reflexives 202
  anaphors 201
  pronoun *zich* (Dutch) 190
  strong 190–194
region (factor)
  particle-verb alternation 214–215
  was/were **variation** 311–315
regionalisation 159
register (factor), **complementiser** 344, 355
regression analysis 126, 136, 146–147, 149, 151–154, 157, 173–174, 219, 310, 349–351, 355, 362, 368–372
  mixed-effects models 149, 151, 174, 209, 217
  random effects 126, 151–152, 155, 174–176, 178–179, 209, 217
  random intercepts 209, 217
regularisation 312, 314–315

Reinhart, Tanya 367
relative specifier *see* relatives, **relativisers**
relatives
  formation 120
  free 121, 159
  gapping 49
  identifying information (German) 140
  non-restrictive 112, 115–116
    (German) 141–143, 147, 157
  restrictive 95, 103, 112, 115–116, 121, 124
  wh-form relativiser 121
    (German) 141–143, 147, 157
  subject, of matrix clause 47, 48, 50, 95, 104, 109, 120, 126
  unmarked 110, 111, 141
relative clauses 93–114, 115–133, 134–164
relativisation 129, 159
  typology (English) 100
  typology (German) 136
relativisers (English) 6, 52, 94, 96, 99–100, 103–104, 111, 118–119, 122, 124–126, 129
  agreement (factor) 21
  as 95–100, 105–108, 111
  history 117
  levelling 100, 103, 111
  linguistic sign-post 135
  Middle Scots 17
  non-restrictive, non-standard 95
  non-standard 98, 105
  non-subject 103–105, 108, 110, 116, 125–127
  subject 103–104, 108, 110, 121, 125, 126–127
  synchronic pattern 119
  that 95, 99–100, 103–104, 106–110, 115–117, 125–127, 129
  topic-marker 6, 110, 136, 252, 259
  wh-forms 100, 103–104, 109, 115–122, 125–129, 135
    historical emergence 119
    interrogatives 121
    prestige 122
    subject role 120
  what 95–100, 103, 105–108, 110–111, 119
  which 95, 106–108, 110, 119, 355
    origin 121

414 *Index*

who 95, 99, 106–108, 110–111,
119, 125, 127, 136, 355
origin 121
subject 353
topic-marking 6, 10, 252–253
whom 95
zero 17, 34–35, 47–48, 50, 67,
94–99, 103–111, 115–119,
122, 125–129, 135, 136
relativisers (French)
dont 122
qu-forms 122
relativisers (German) 6, 134,
137, 143
age/generation (factor) 138, 139,
140, 146
antecedent
abstract (factor) 143, 150–157
animacy (factor) 135, 144, 147,
151–152, 154–155, 158
case (factor) 143, 147,
149–152, 154–155
definiteness (factor) 147,
151–152, 155
distance (factor) 145, 147,
151–152, 154, 155
grammatical category (factor)
143, 147
length (factor) 144–145, 147
place/locative reference (factor)
143, 151–152, 154
temporal reference (factor) 143
topic persistence (factor) 144
case matching (factor) 137, 143
community (factor) 145,
147–148, 150, 151, 155
distance (factor) 151
education (factor) 6, 135,
138–140, 145, 147–148,
151–152, 154–155, 158, 159
inflected *w*-pronouns 136
non-inflected pronoun 136
occupation (factor) 138,
145–147, 159
recording year (factor) 145,
147–148, 150, 152, 155
resumptive 137, 142, 144,
147, 157
sex/gender (factor) 138–140,
146–147
so/som relatives 156
social orientation (factor)
146–147
structural count (factor) 144
structural persistence (factor) 144

wo-relatives 134–164
reported speech 365
resolution (narrative) *see* narrative,
resolution
restructuring 303, 305, 309, 315–316
Result
holder 221
Phrase 221
state 221
resumptives 69, 137, 142
rhythm, speech 251
right dislocation *see* **dislocation, right**
Robinson, Jonnie 99
Roch, Claudia 299
role, syntactic (factor)
indefinite *this* 365
relativisers 103
Romaine, Suzanne xxiii, 16, 117–118,
120, 135
Rosen, Harold 255

Saint Helena Language and History
project 309
Sakalauskaitė, Julija 121–122
salience 33, 66, 147
of complementiser 343
of indefinite noun phrase 373
narrative 388
of non-standard form 15
perceptual 41
pragmatic 366
of syntactic role 368
Salzmann, Martin 137
Scandinavian languages 328
Schiffrin, Deborah 378–379, 383,
389, 392
Schilling-Estes, Natalie 23
Schneider, Edgar 309, 315
Scholten, Beate 300
Schreier, Daniel 7, 306–318
Scots 241
Buckie (*see* English, Scotland)
Middle 21, 130
relativiser 17
Sebba, Mark 256, 263
second dialect acquisition 250, 257;
see also acquisition
second language acquisition 70, 171,
178–179, 271; *see also* acquisition
Seiler, Guido 137
self-effacement (attribute) 85
sex/gender 125, 127, 175
the allomorphy 65, 66
complementisers 345, 351
existentials 23, 167–168, 171, 176

(factor) 5
indefinite *this* 364, 365, 368, 369, 370, 374
negative concord 230–231
perception 35
relativisers 123–124 (*see also* relativiser (German))
right dislocation 74
utterance-final tags 8, 379, 381–383, 385–386, 389–391
verbal *-s*, historical 18–19
was/were variation 62, 310–311
shared parallel innovation 120
Sharma, Devyani 5, 55–72, 250, 300
Sherrod, Nancy 67
shibboleth 47
shift, language 250, 270, 315
Siegel, Vanessa 290
Siegel, Jeff 331
Sigley, Robert J. 116
signpost, linguistic 8, 135, 354–355; *see also* complementisers
Silverstein, Michael 85
singular agreement *see* agreement
Sivertsen, Eva 252
Skeggs, Beverley 94
slang 253, 268–269, 271
African American 257
Jamaican 257
Slembrouck, Stef 330, 334
Small, Cathy 206, 352
Smith, Jennifer 7, 99, 135, 229–246, 347
Snell, Julia 74, 86
so, sentence-final 322
social class 3, 55, 69–70, 73, 86, 125; *see also* middle-class, working-class
(attribute) 8
(factor) 25, 47, 75, 76, 167
a allomorphy 65
complementisers 352
dialect contact 111
existentials 23
negative concord 19
perception 51
relativisers 135
right dislocation 74, 78
verbal *-s*, historical 18
was/were variation 62, 314
social selves 383, 391
social styling 294
sociality, rights 392
socio-grammar 188
sociolinguistic monitor *see* monitor, sociolinguistic

sociolinguistics
historical 15, 17, 22, 27
variationist, third wave 87
sociophonetics 2
primacy of 5
socio-pragmatics 73–74, 78
space, sociolinguistic 70
Spanish (language), object marking 361
specificity 361, 365, 367
Spencer-Oatey, Helen 392
stance 5, 85, 155, 346, 348, 393
evaluative 74–78, 81–84
standard language 15, 24, 136, 137, 195, 345, 352
convergence 145, 148, 154, 167
ideology (*see* ideology, standard language)
as reference point 24
standard variant, complementisers 352
standard, written 73
standardisation 4–5, 26, 47, 145
stats package (R) 149
status 26
Staum Casasanto, Laura 73–74
Stenström, Anna-Brita 380
stereotype 142
stigmatisation 26, 59, 62, 66–69, 87, 142, 249
story worlds 377, 383–385, 390–392
stratification, social 24, 26, 47, 73, 134, 165, 167, 173
existentials 23
stress 67
style 250
(factor) 3, 5, 25
complementisers 351–352, 355
particle-verb alternation 217, 219–220, 225
relativisers 135–136
resource 73
vernacular 66
subject
marking, differential 361
negative 243–244
type
complement clause (factor), complementisers 346
(factor), agreement 20, 22
(factor), complementisers 346, 347, 350, 354
(factor), negative concord 230
(factor), right dislocation 74–75, 84

416 *Index*

(factor), *was/were* variation 62, 63, 304, 305, 310
and topic 367
subordinate clauses 22, 116, 117, 128, 138; *see also* complementisers, relatives
superdiversity 319, 320, 328
superlatives 280, 285
supralocalisation 6, 25, 36, 34, 51, 145, 148, 159
Survey of English Dialects 95–98, 105
Svenonius, Peter 207, 210, 221
Swabian *see* German, Swabian
Swedish (language), **particle-verb alternation** 219
syllable timing *see* speech rhythm
synchronic *see* language change, synchronic
Syntactic Atlas of the Dutch Dialects 195
syntax, formal 2, 6–7, 16, 243, 343
generative 187, 194, 201–202
Government and Binding 202
Minimalist Program 7, 234–235, 238
Principles and Parameters theory 20
micro-variation 87
person-number features 169
syntax, functional 343
Szmrecsanyi, Benedikt 118, 135, 136, 143, 144, 145, 155, 205, 223, 224

Tagliamonte, Sali 8, 21, 23, 99–100, 118, 120, 135, 312, 343–359, 379
tags
canonical 380
declarative 377
invariant 378, 380
innit 377
non-finite verb phrase/clause 76, 79–81
noun phrase 76, 79–81
pronoun 76, 79–81, 84, 86
demonstrative 79–81
utterance final 8, 377–395
Mohawk 378
Portuguese 378
Tamil 378
tails *see* **dislocation, right** 74
Tamil (language), utterance-final tag 378
temporal reference (factor)
existentials 168, 172, 175–176 (*see also* **relativisers** (German))

temporal *wo* (German) 137, 141
tense 26, 346, 350
(factor), **complementisers** 346, 350
phrase (TP) domain 234–235, 239, 241–242
morphological 179, 346, 347
past *be* 7, 303–305, 309–316
past forms 26, 252, 309, 346
present 17, 34, 94, 168, 346, 350, 387
verb 168
there's see **existentials**
theta criterion 117
theta role 202
this is + speaker (quotative) *see* quotatives
Thompson, Sandra 347
topic 361, 366–367, 370, 373
(factor), **indefinite *this*** 370
(factor) (*see* **relativisers** (German))
marking (*see* **relativisers, topic-marker**)
persistence 144, 366–367, 369, 371–372
shift 364, 366
Torgersen, Eivind 7, 93, 249–276, 380
Toronto English Archive 345
Tottie, Gunnel 135
transfer, language 58, 178 (*see also* interference)
transition, linguistic 187
transitivity 189, 365
translanguaging 319
Traugott, Elisabeth 157
treelets, lexico-syntactic 188, 189
trend study 159; *see also* language change
Troy, Jakelin 325
Trudgill, Peter xxv, 7, 17, 24–25, 94, 112, 197, 250–251, 270–271, 321–322, 323–324, 331, 334
Truswell, Robert 116–117, 119–122
Turkish (language) 264, 373
turn-taking 383
Twitter corpus 205, 206, 213–218, 223, 225
typology
relativisation (*see* **relatives**)
verbs 75

Ukrainian (language) 282, 283, 356
uniformitarian principle 17, 319
Universal Grammar 243
universals 7, 221, 303
constraints 7, 63, 135
markedness conditions 221

negation 7, 63
vernacular 59, 229, 230, 237
urban (attribute) 8
urban/rural divide 6, 94, 100, 139, 148, 157, 304, 311
urbanisation 123, 249, 329

Van den Eynden Morpeth, Nadine 99
variable
covert 135
(socio)linguistic, defining 1, 73, 140, 289
variable context
definition of 380
delimitation of 365
relativiser 140
variable importance 176–177
variant, non-standard 5, 15, 35, 87
variation
discourse-pragmatic 2, 378–379
intralinguistic 221
intra-speaker 190
morphological 15, 19, 94
pragmatic 2
synchronic 129
syntactic 2, 7, 187, 223–224, 278, 343
micro-, 87, 201
varimp() function (R) 176
verb
clusters 198–199
derived 188
light (v), Phrase (vP) 221
main (factor), **negative concord** 232, 234
markers
-*eth*, historical 18–19
-*s*
historical 18, 19, 27
hyper -*s* 34–35, 39–43, 48
zero, third person singular present tense 94
processes 74, 82–85
status (factor), **existentials** 170, 172
tense (factor), **existentials** 168
type (factor), **negative concord** 231, 233
typology 75
verb-object-particle (VOP) 205–228
verb-particle-object (VPO) 205–228
verb phrase (VP)
domain 234–235, 239–241
semantics 75
vernacular 47, 49, 69, 250, 251, 264
affiliation 70

continuum 5, 16, 27
culture 393
features 39
multiracial 254–257, 264, 268
as precursor to MLE 257
non-standard 62
roots 312
universals 59, 229–230
usage 353
Vertovec, Steven 328
Voeste, Anja 17

Wagner, Michael 141
Waletzky, Joshua 378, 383
Walker, James A. 1–12, 23, 47, 58, 60, 134, 165–184, 335, 344, 348, 349, 366
Wallenberg, Joel 7, 205–228
was, non-standard 21; *see also was/ were* variation
was/were variation 7
levelling 56, 59–63, 66–69, 252, 303–305, 309–316
negative clauses 60–61, 63, 68
stigmatisation 62
Watson, Catherine 6, 115–133
Watson, Kevin 34, 36
Watt, Dominic 25, 35, 250
well-formedness conditions 343
Wells, John C. 321
Welsh (language) 330
what see relatives, relativisers
wh- interrogatives *see* relativiser
who see relatives, relativisers
whom see relatives, relativisers
wh-specifiers *see* relativiser
Wolfram, Walt 22–23
working class 8, 25, 55–56, 59, 62–63, 65, 70, 74, 86, 253, 263, 305–306, 313–314, 316, 379, 391, 393; *see also* social class
Wright, Susan 367

X-bar structure 189

Yallop, Colin 321
Ye, Yang 250
York-Toronto-Helsinki Parsed Corpus of Old English Prose 215
you get me (discourse marker) 252, 253
youth language 7, 250, 254, 258, 262, 268, 269, 299
youth vernacular 249–271

Zwarts, Joost 281